Tolley's VAT Business by Business 1998–99

PricewaterhouseCoopers

*Edited
by*
Penny Hamilton, LLB FTII Barrister,
PricewaterhouseCoopers
and
Alan Dolton MA (Oxon)

Tolley Publishing Company Limited

A member of the Reed Elsevier plc group

Whilst every care has been taken to ensure the accuracy of the contents of this work, no responsibility for loss occasioned to any person acting or refraining from action as a result of any statement in it can be accepted by any of the writers or the publishers.

Published by
Tolley Publishing Company Ltd
Tolley House
2 Addiscombe Road
Croydon CR9 5AF England
0181-686 9141

Typeset in Great Britain
by
Tradespools Ltd, Frome, Somerset

Printed in Great Britain
by
Redwood Books,
Trowbridge, Wiltshire

© Tolley Publishing Company Ltd 1998

ISBN 1 86012 597-2

Preface

VAT is now twenty-five years old. As it matures, this 'simple' tax is becoming increasingly complex. It is essentially a European tax, based on sometimes unfamiliar concepts of European law, and it is impossible to avoid this dimension. As if that were not enough, VAT legislation is overlaid by a wealth of tribunal and court decisions, Customs and Excise guidance and concessions, many of which are specific to particular businesses. The result is a technical minefield through which taxpayers and their advisers have to tread a wary path.

This book provides a map through that minefield. It is a practical, hands-on guide to VAT as it applies to individual businesses, and the particular way in which they operate. It is not intended to be an in-depth consideration of general VAT issues but, to ensure that these are taken into account, it is cross-referenced to other standard Tolley publications such as *Tolley's VAT* and *Tolley's VAT Cases*.

The authors are all practitioners who are advising their clients on a day to day basis, and therefore have up-to-the-minute practical experience of the issues being discussed. This also means that they are busy people who have had to find time to write this book between client commitments and I thank them for their efforts.

I should also like to thank Margaret O'Donohoe, ably assisted by her then secretary, Michael Dickson, for project-managing and helping me to edit the work, and all other colleagues who have given their time and support.

Penny Hamilton
PricewaterhouseCoopers
July 1998

Contents

	Page
Preface	iii
Table of Cases	xxv
Table of Statutes	xxxiii
Table of Statutory Instruments	xxxix
Table of EC Legislation	xlii

	Paragraph
1. Accountants	
MD Glaser, CA(SA), ATII	
Introduction	1.1
Liability of accountant's supplies	1.2
Main services	1.2
Supplies of goods	1.3
The treatment of disbursements	1.4
Time of supply	1.5
'One-off' supplies	1.6
Continuous supplies	1.7
When payment is received	1.8
Place of supply	1.9
Services that are supplied where received	1.9
Who receives a supply?	1.10
Other services that are supplied where received	1.11
Services relating to land	1.12
Training, presentations, seminars and similar services	1.13
Overseas VAT or indirect taxes	1.14
Value of supplies	1.15
Insurance and other commissions offset against fees	1.16
General issues	1.17
Employee-related expenditure	1.18
Partial exemption	1.22
Accounting and records	1.24
Invoices in respect of supplies made by an accountant	1.24
Input tax evidence	1.27
Practical points	1.28
Use of special schemes for small businesses	1.28

Contents

Dealing with disbursements	1.29
Partners holding offices	1.30
Accounting for commissions	1.31

2. Auctioneers
Dorothy Ramsey

Introduction	2.1
Operation of the second-hand goods margin scheme	2.2
Eligible goods	2.2
Ineligible goods	2.3
Requirements for use of the margin scheme	2.4
Acquisitions and dispatches within the EC	2.6
Imports and exports outside the EC	2.7
Bulk purchases	2.9
Purchases of repossessed goods from insurance companies or finance houses	2.10
Calculation of the margin	2.11
Auctioneers' margin scheme (AMS)	2.12
Goods which are eligible for the scheme	2.13
Requirements for use of the scheme	2.14
Margin scheme calculation	2.15
Charges which should be included in the AMS calculation	2.16
Time of supply	2.17
Global accounting scheme	2.18
Eligible goods	2.19
Conditions for using the scheme	2.20
Bulk purchases and collections	2.21
Accounting and records	2.22
General requirements	2.22
Invoicing requirements under the second-hand margin scheme	2.23
Invoicing requirements specific to the auctioneers' margin scheme	2.25
Completion of the VAT return	2.29
Records and accounts for the global accounting scheme	2.30
Transactions with overseas persons	2.40
Acquisitions by UK dealers from dealers in other Member States	2.40
Acquisitions by UK dealers from private individuals in other Member States	2.41
Imports by UK dealers from outside the EC	2.42
Sales by UK dealers to dealers/private individuals in other Member States	2.43
Exports by UK dealers outside the EC	2.44
Miscellaneous supplies	2.45
Auction catalogues	2.45
Gifts	2.46
Mechanical breakdown insurance ('MBI') & warranties	2.47
Other insurance products	2.48
Private sales	2.49

3. Banking and Securities
Cathy Hargreaves

Introduction	3.1
VAT exemption	3.2
Overview of VAT liability	3.4
Valuation of supply	3.9
Time of supply	3.10
Specific liability of particular transactions	3.11
Dealing in money	3.12
Foreign exchange	3.14
'Securities for money'	3.19
Broking or arranging dealings in money, foreign exchange or securities for money	3.22
Account operations	3.24
Deposits, loans and overdrafts	3.25
Hire purchase and leasing	3.29
Securities	3.37
Stockbroking or acting as intermediary for securities transactions	3.41
Safe custody services	3.45
Corporate finance and mergers/acquisitions	3.46
Investment management	3.52
Foreign currency options	3.56
Interest rate swaps, forward rate agreements, caps, collars and floors	3.58
LIFFE	3.62
Non-exempt activities	3.65
Advice and research	3.67
Partial Exemption	3.71
Income which is taxable	3.73
Income which is exempt	3.75
Direct attribution	3.76
Methods of calculation	3.78
Specific issues	3.94
Accounting and records	3.100
Input tax identification	3.100
EU/non-EU information	3.102
Cost allocations	3.104
Partial exemption calculations	3.105
Reverse charges	3.106
Practical issues	3.110
Registration	3.110
Industry agreements	3.112
Public notices	3.114
EU legislation	3.115
Representative offices	3.116
Appendix 1	
Appendix 2	

Contents

4. Barristers
Deborah Sharp

Introduction	4.1
Liability	4.2
Legal advice	4.2
Judicial office	4.3
Other supplies	4.4
VAT recovery	4.5
Chambers expenses	4.6
Supplies to and by the Head of Chambers	4.7
Proportional attribution of input tax	4.8
A combination of the above	4.9
Devilling fees	4.10
Travel costs	4.11
Personal expenses	4.12
Reverse charge services	4.13
Accounting for VAT	4.14
Special rules for barristers	4.14
Death or cessation of practice	4.15
Record-keeping	4.16
Practical points	4.17
Receipts	4.17
Registration	4.18

5. Bloodstock
Richard Read

Introduction	5.1
Owner-breeders	5.4
Pure owners	5.7
Company owners	5.9
Trainers and dealers	5.11
Liability	5.13
Owners and owner-breeders	5.15
Sale of foals, yearlings and horses in training	5.15
Stallion shares and nominations	5.19
Mare visiting from Third Countries (or acquired for covering and export)	5.23
Mare visiting from EU	5.24
Related transport	5.26
Keep of mares, stallions and progeny	5.28
Stallion syndications	5.32
Income from racing	5.33
Agents and dealers	5.35
Transactions as agent	5.37
Transactions as principal	5.41
Valuations	5.43
Auctioneers	5.45
Racecourses	5.48

Trainers	5.52
Jockeys	5.57
VAT Recovery	5.64
Joint or multi-ownerships	5.66
Overseas VAT	5.69
UK VAT	5.72
Accounting and records	5.73
Owners and breeders	5.74
Owners scheme requirements	5.77
Flat rate farmers	5.78
The second-hand scheme for horses and ponies	5.82
Practical points	5.84
The temporary movement trap	5.85
The goods or services trap	5.88
VAT registration options	5.92
Registration in other EU Member States	5.94
Temporary importations	5.100
Flat rate farming	5.103
Appendix I	
Appendix II	
Appendix III	

6. Books and Publications
Daphne Hemingway, BA Hons, ATII

Introduction	6.1
The law	6.5
Definitions	6.6
Books and booklets	6.9
Brochures and pamphlets	6.10
Leaflets	6.11
Newspapers, journals and periodicals	6.17
Children's books	6.19
Music scores	6.22
Maps, charts and topographical plans	6.23
Printed matter supplied with other goods or services	6.24
Training and educational courses	6.29
Children's activity packs	6.31
Brochures, pamphlets and leaflets with areas for completion	6.32
Printed matter supplied as a package	6.34
Clubs, associations and organisations	6.36
Book clubs	6.39
Incidental reports	6.40
Binders and loose-leaf works	6.41
Advertising	6.44
Charitable advertising	6.46
Promotional items	6.48
Competitions	6.55
Fantasy football league	6.56

Contents

Premium rate telephone lines	6.58
Vouchers and discount booklets	6.59
Book tokens	6.62
Distance selling	6.63
Authors	6.66
Accounting and records	6.67
Library books	6.68
Importation of printed matter	6.69
Appendix I	
Appendix II	
Appendix III	

7. Charities
Nigel Dismore

Introduction	7.1
European Community Law	7.2
Liability	7.3
Meaning of 'business'	7.4
Economic activity	7.5
Non-business income	7.6
Donations	7.7
Donations: sponsorship	7.8
Donations: fund-raising events	7.9
Donations in kind	7.10
Donations: charity auctions	7.11
Grants	7.12
Investment income/transactions in securities	7.13
Non-business advertising	7.14
Non-business welfare supplies	7.15
Membership subscriptions	7.16
Affinity cards	7.17
Exports	7.18
Business income	7.19
Exemptions (VATA 1994, 9 Sch)	7.20
Education	7.21
Welfare	7.24
Fund-raising events	7.28
Cultural services	7.35
Zero-rating (VATA 1994, 8 Sch)	7.36
VAT recovery	7.39
Attribution of VAT costs	7.40
Non-business attribution	7.41
Changing an apportionment method	7.42
Partial exemption	7.43
De minimis	7.44
VAT on the purchase of assets	7.45
VAT reliefs on purchases	7.46
Zero-rating reliefs	7.47

Reduced rate	7.62
Importations by charities	7.63
Administration	7.64
Registration	7.64
Cost-sharing	7.65
Trading subsidiaries	7.66
Conclusion	7.67

8. Clubs and Associations
AJ Dawbarn, ATII

Introduction	8.1
Business for VAT purposes	8.5
Non-profit-making bodies	8.15
Liability	8.21
Subscription income	8.22
Income other than subscriptions	8.42
General fund-raising activities	8.67
VAT recovery	8.88
General	8.88
Non-deductible input tax	8.89
Non-business activities	8.94
Partial exemption	8.100
Accounting and records	8.105
General	8.105
Preservation of records	8.111
Records of output tax	8.113
Record of input tax	8.114
Annual accounting	8.117
Practical points	8.118
Voluntary registration	8.118
Payment to 'umbrella' organisations	8.121
Netting-off and barter arrangements	8.123
Sports exemption	8.129
Apportionment of subscription income	8.132
Partial exemption	8.137
Business/non-business apportionment	8.139
General VAT planning	8.140
Land and property transactions	8.148
Sports club—whether a 'non-profit-making body'	8.154

9. Construction Industry
Steve Botham, MAAT, AIIT, ATII

Introduction	9.1
Liability	9.2
Zero-rating	9.3
In the course of construction	9.4
What is meant by 'New'?	9.5
New dwellings	9.6

Contents

New dwellings—evidence required to support the zero-rating	9.7
Relevant residential purposes	9.8
What is a 'relevant residential purpose'?	9.9
In the course of construction—relevant residential	9.10
Relevant residential—evidence required to support the zero-rating	9.11
Incorrect certificates	9.12
Mixed use buildings	9.13
Sub-contractors	9.14
Relevant charitable building	9.15
What is 'a building intended for use solely for a relevant 'charitable purpose'?	9.16
Business use	9.17
Relevant charitable purpose—evidence required to support zero-rating	9.18
Mixed use	9.19
Building materials	9.20
Approved alterations	9.21
What is a 'protected building'?	9.22
What is an 'approved alteration'?	9.23
Alteration for VAT purposes	9.24
What services are covered?	9.25
Approved alterations—evidence required to support zero-rating	9.26
Mixed use	9.27
Conversions of a non-residential building	9.28
What is a 'registered housing association'?	9.29
What is a 'non-residential' building?	9.30
Conversions—evidence required to support the zero-rating	9.31
Civil engineering services	9.32
Records	9.33
Input tax recovery	9.34
Posting of purchase invoices	9.35
Cash accounting scheme	9.36
Tax points	9.37
Applications for payment	9.38
Self-billing	9.39
Authenticated tax receipts	9.40
Tax invoices	9.41
Agreed price variations	9.42
Liquidated damages	9.43
Non-VAT-registered customers	9.44

10. Doctors and Dentists
Richard Smith and Harinder Kaur

Introduction	10.1
VAT liability	10.6
Supplies by doctors	10.8
Supplies by dentists	10.23

Accounting records	10.27
VAT registration	10.27
Records	10.29
Practical Points	10.33
Expense-sharing agreements	10.34
Partnerships	10.39
Employer/employee relationships	10.40
Associate agreements	10.41

11. Education
Carl Neilsen

Introduction	11.1
Business activities	11.3
Liability	11.4
Definition of education	11.5
Definition of research	11.6
Definition of vocational training	11.7
Definition of private tuition	11.8
'Closely related' supplies	11.10
Eligible bodies	11.11
The Concordat	11.13
Universities and other higher education providers	11.17
Income	11.19
Research	11.20
Consultancy	11.24
Vocational training	11.25
Closely-related supplies	11.26
Catering	11.27
Accommodation	11.29
Sales of goods	11.30
Conferences, etc.	11.31
Sporting activities	11.33
Car parking	11.34
Advertising	11.35
Further education colleges	11.36
Education provided by local authorities	11.47
Independent schools	11.49
Charities	11.51
Providers of teaching English as a foreign language	11.52
Examination and inspectorate services	11.55
Youth clubs	11.57
Input tax recovery	11.64
VAT recovery in the higher education sector	11.64
Removal of the Concordat	11.66
Alternative partial exemption methods	11.67
VAT recovery in the further education sector	11.71
VAT recovery for schools	11.74
Practical points	11.77

Contents

Customs & Excise	11.77
Property planning	11.78
Student accommodation	11.79
Self-supply rules	11.81
Catering concession	11.82
Trading companies and VAT grouping	11.83

12. Employment Businesses
Jane Stacey

Introduction	12.1
Principal contracts	12.3
Agency contracts	12.5
VAT liability	12.11
Nursing agencies	12.15
Time of supply	12.20
Value of supply	12.21
VAT recovery	12.23
Accounting and records	12.24
Practical points	12.26
Employment law	12.31
Pay As You Earn (PAYE) and National Insurance Contributions (NIC)	12.35
Dual status	12.39
Training	12.40
Holiday and sick pay	12.41
Indemnities	12.42
Commercial aspects	12.44
Conclusion	12.47

13. Farming and Agriculture
Julie Moss

Introduction	13.1
Background	13.1
Contract farming and share farming	13.2
Landfill tax	13.5
VAT liability	13.6
Principal activities	13.6
Ancillary activities	13.10
Agricultural land and property	13.20
Sporting rights	13.28
Shooting activities	13.29
Grazing rights and animal keep	13.30
Livery services	13.31
Milk quota	13.32
Landlords and tenants	13.33
VAT Recovery	13.40
Partial exemption	13.41
Election to waive exemption ('Option to tax')	13.43

Contents

Repairs to farmhouses	13.44
Retrospective claims	13.45
Farming companies	13.46
Work on tenanted properties	13.47
Tied accommodation	13.48
Assured shorthold tenancies	13.49
Private use	13.50
Business entertainment	13.51
Motor vehicles	13.52
Grants and subsidies	13.55
Accounting and records	13.56
Flat-rate farmers' scheme	13.56
Accounting records	13.62
Accounting systems	13.65
Correction of errors	13.68
Three-year cap	13.69
Cash accounting	13.70
Annual accounting scheme	13.71
EU transactions	13.72
Practical points	13.75
Part exchange	13.75
Returnable containers	13.76
Legal entities	13.77
Common errors	13.82
Appendix	

14. Hospitals and Nursing Homes
James Selby, ACCA, ATII

Introduction	14.1
Liability of supplies	14.2
Provision of care or medical or surgical treatment	14.2
Accommodation	14.3
Blood, organs and tissue	14.4
Home care services	14.5
Status of NHS trusts	14.6
Dispensing of drugs	14.7
Welfare	14.8
Supplies of aids for the 'handicapped'	14.9
Goods catering for special needs	14.10
Facilitation of access	14.11
Supplies to charities and other eligible bodies	14.12
Zero-rating certificates	14.13

15. Hotels and Holiday Accommodation
Louise Croft

Introduction	15.1
Liability	15.2
Hotels, inns, boarding houses and similar establishments	15.2

Contents

Service charges	15.3
Booking fees, deposits and cancellation charges	15.4
Disbursements	15.7
Reduced value rules—stays of over four weeks	15.8
Rooms supplied for the purpose of catering	15.10
Supplies to staff	15.11
Holiday accommodation	15.12
Caravans	15.20
Supply of a caravan	15.26
Camping	15.27
VAT recovery	15.28
Input tax recovery	15.28
Hotel disbursements	15.29
Accounting and records	15.30
Calculating the reduced value hotel accommodation exceeding four weeks	
Registration threshold	15.31
Calculating VAT on the removable contents of caravans	15.32

16. Housing Associations
David Dormer, ATII

Introduction	16.1
Terminology	16.2
Liability	16.3
Core activity	16.3
Service charges to tenants	16.4
Other services to tenants	16.5
Disposals of property	16.6
Right to buy	16.7
Shared ownership	16.8
BES Assured Tenancy Arrangements	16.9
Services supplied to other organisations	16.10
Design and build contracts	16.11
Management contacts	16.12
Large Scale Voluntary Transfers	16.13
Consortium agreements	16.14
Provision of care	16.15
Emergency alarm systems	16.16
Nomination rights	16.17
Guest accommodation	16.18
Other standard-rated supplies	16.19
Outside the scope supplies	16.20
Recovery of input tax	16.21
New buildings	16.22
Land	16.23
Converting non-residential buildings	16.24
Demolition	16.25
Charitable reliefs	16.26

Expenditure on protected buildings	16.27
Partial exemption	16.28
Practical points	16.29
Professional fees on new building	16.29
Relevant residential	16.30
Capital expenditure	16.31
Parallel charities	16.32
Joint contracts of employment	16.33
Charity advertising	16.34
Consortium agreements	16.35
Demolition works	16.36
Accounting records	16.37

17. Insurance
Keith Moore

Introduction	17.1
Liability	17.5
Supplies made by insurers and reinsurers	17.7
Supplies made by insurance intermediaries	17.23
Miscellaneous points affecting certain supplies	17.44
Input tax recovery	17.67
Partial exemption	17.67
Input tax incurred on claims	17.71
Accounting and records	17.81
Tax points	17.82
Reverse charge	17.86
Disclosure requirements	17.90
Practical issues	17.91
Industry agreements	17.91
VAT notices	17.92
Overseas businesses	17.93
Appendix A	
Appendix B	
Appendix C	

18. Leasing and hire-purchase
Kevin J Thorogood, ATII

Introduction	18.1
Scope of this chapter	18.3
Terminology used	18.5
Liability	18.6
Nature of supply as it affects the lessor	18.7
Nature of supply as it affects the lessee	18.12
Time of supply	18.13
VAT liability of supplies—Lessor	18.21
VAT documentation—Lessor	18.25
Effect of VAT on lessors	18.27
VAT Recovery	18.28

Contents

Lessors and Input Tax Recovery	18.28
Partial exemption methods	18.31
The effect of a change in VAT rate	18.36
Practical points	18.39
Lease termination payments	18.39
Part-exchange transactions	18.43
Documentation fees	18.46
Disposal of leased assets/Rebates of rentals	18.48
Repossession of goods	18.52
Sale of repossessed goods	18.54
Transfers of agreements	18.55
Specific leasing activities	18.57
Cars	18.57
Cross-border leasing	18.65
Arrears of rentals/Bad debts	18.81
Appendix 1	

19. Local Authorities
Wendy Andrews, BA (Hons), ATII

Introduction	19.1
Special position of local authorites	19.1
Refund mechanism	19.2
Definition—what is a local authority?	19.3
Unregistered authorities—obtaining a refund	19.4
Customs guidance	19.5
Vires—is s 33 legal?	19.6
Registration	19.7
Obligation to register	19.7
'Section 102 committees'—shared registration	19.8
Other bodies	19.9
Practical steps	19.10
Liability	19.11
Ability to recover all input tax	19.11
Goods and services generally	19.12
Correct coding	19.13
Problem areas	19.14
Local government review	19.17
Transfer of assets	19.18
Registration	19.19
Debt and errors	19.20
Options to tax	19.21
Awareness	19.22
VAT recovery	19.23
Taxable, exempt and non-business supplies—implications for VAT recovery	19.24
Tax invoices—need for the supply to be made to the authority	19.25
Requirements of a tax invoice—practical problems/agreements with Customs	19.26

Business entertaining—special rules for local authorities	19.27
Self-billing	19.28
Estimation	19.29
Relocation expenses	19.30
Insurance-related payments	19.31
Imports and acquisitions	19.32
Agency payments	19.33
Local authority pension funds	19.34
Identification and attribution of exempt input tax	19.35
Partial exemption methods	19.36
Accounting records	19.38
Coding of income and expenditure	19.38
Computer systems—approval by Customs & Excise	19.39
Devolved accounting	19.40
Volume of transactions	19.41
Error adjustments	19.42
Practical points	19.43
Agreements with Customs & Excise	19.43
Changes in activities	19.44
Appendix	

20. Motor Dealers
Steve Kettle, FCCA

Introduction	20.1
Liability	20.2
Qualifying cars	20.3
Non-qualifying cars	20.4
Second-hand cars	20.5
Transactions outside the scope of VAT	20.6
Road fund licences	20.7
Delivery and pre-delivery inspection ('PDI') charges	20.8
Accessories	20.9
Extended warranties	20.10
International supplies of new means of transport	20.11
Self-supply	20.12
VAT recovery	20.13
Demonstration and courtesy cars	20.14
Accounting and records	20.15
New cars and other qualifying cars	20.15
Second-hand car scheme	20.16
Practical points	20.17
Part-exchange transactions	20.17
Definition of a motor car	20.18
Sale or return transactions	20.19
VAT group registrations	20.20
'Premium and nearly new' and 'personal import' cars	20.21

Contents

21. Property Development
Hugh GM Love, ATII

Introduction	21.1
VAT liability	21.13
Exemption	21.13
Zero-rated transactions in land and property	21.27
The 'option to tax'—standard-rating by choice	21.32
VAT recovery	21.46
Input tax on new dwellings	21.69
Capital goods scheme (CGS)	21.70
Accounting records	21.74
Practical points	21.78
The transfer of a business as a going concern ('TOGC')	21.78
Covenants	21.84
Variations to leases	21.86
Statutory payments	21.87
Compulsory purchase	21.88
Dilapidations	21.89
Inducements	21.90
Surrenders	21.94
Reverse surrenders	21.95
Co-ownership	21.100
Beneficial interest and trustees	21.103
Service charges	21.107

22. Public Houses
Tom Perkins, BA, ATII

Introduction	22.1
Managed houses	22.2
Tenanted houses	22.3
Leased houses	22.4
Free houses	22.5
Liability of supplies	22.6
General principles	22.6
Catering	22.7
Accommodation and functions	22.8
Gaming and amusement machines	22.9
Vending machines	22.10
Payphones	22.11
VAT recovery	22.12
Accounting and record-keeping	22.13
Purchases	22.13
Sales	22.14
Practical points	22.15
Business splitting	22.15
Wastage	22.16
Prices and price reductions	22.24
Pilferage by employees	22.25

Own consumption		22.26
Free food and drinks		22.27
Conclusion		22.29

23. Retailers
Mary Cook

Introduction	23.1
VAT Liability	23.2
Standard Schemes and Bespoke Schemes	23.3
Daily Gross takings ('DGT')	23.6
Definition of gross takings from 1 March 1997	23.7
Choosing a retail scheme	23.11
General principles	23.11
The Point of Sale scheme	23.12
The Apportionment schemes	23.13
The Direct Calculation schemes	23.16
Bespoke Retail Schemes	23.19
Ceasing to use a Scheme	23.20
Point of Sale Scheme	23.21
Apportionment Scheme 1	23.22
Apportionment Scheme 2	23.23
Direct Calculation Scheme 1	23.24
Direct Calculation Scheme 2	23.25
Specific retail businesses	23.26
Cinemas and theatres	23.26
Garages and filling stations	23.27
Catering and take-away food suppliers	23.28
Pharmacists	23.29
Retail florists	23.33
Sub-post offices	23.37
Vending and amusement machine operators	23.38
VAT Recovery	23.39
Accounting Records	23.40
Daily gross takings record	23.41
Purchase invoices	23.42
VAT account	23.43
Computer records	23.44
Practical points	23.45
Provision of VAT invoices by retailers	23.45
Shops within shops	23.46
Disposals of a business	23.47
Deregistration	23.48
Cash accounting and annual accounting	23.49

24. Small Businesses
MD Glaser, CA(SA), ATII

Introduction	24.1
VAT registration limits	24.2

Contents

Liability to register	24.2
Monitoring turnover	24.3
Choosing to remain unregistered	24.4
Voluntary registration	24.6
Backdating registration	24.7
Cash accounting	24.8
Introduction	24.8
Benefits of using the scheme	24.9
Potential disadvantages	24.10
Eligibility to use the scheme	24.11
Exclusions from use of the scheme	24.12
Operating the scheme	24.13
Date payment is received	24.14
Leaving the scheme	24.15
Annual accounting	24.16
Introduction	24.16
Conditions for admission to the scheme	24.17
The scheme conditions	24.18
Deciding whether to use the scheme	24.19
Leaving the scheme	24.20
Partial exemption 'de minimis' limits	24.21
Introduction	24.21
VAT incurred before registration	24.22
'Toothbrush' schemes	24.23

25. Solicitors
Maryann McLaughlin, MA (Hons)

Introduction	25.1
Liability of a solicitor's supply	25.2
Place of supply	25.3
Services relating to land	25.9
Commission	25.11
Disbursements	25.16
Oath fees	25.24
Other activities	25.27
Recovery of VAT	25.28
Accounting and Records	25.30
Time of supply	25.30
Accounting for commission	25.35
VAT treatment of counsel's fees	25.36
Credit notes	25.43
Reverse charge services	25.45
Practical points	25.47
Third party costs	25.47

26. Tour Operators
Peter Coombs, MSc

Introduction	26.1

Liability	26.4
Definition of a TOMS supply	26.4
Tour Operator	26.5
'Direct benefit of a traveller'	26.7
Material alteration or further processing	26.10
Special exclusion	26.12
Single supply of TOMS services	26.13
Place of supply of TOMS services	26.15
Value of supply	26.17
Zero-rating	26.18
Travel agents' commission	26.19
VAT recovery	26.23
Accounting and records	26.27
Annual accounting	26.28
Tax points	26.30
Bad debt relief	26.31
The simplified calculation	26.32
The full TOMS calculation	26.34
The provisional output ratio calculation	26.37
Practical points	26.38
VAT registration	26.38
Single supply of transport services	26.39
Avoiding the TOMS on bought-in passenger transport	26.40
Mathematical effects of the TOMS	26.44
Maximising TOMS costs	26.45

27. Transport and Freight
Dominique Morcom-Harneis and Alison Isaac

Introduction	27.1
Liability	27.2
Zero-rating applied to certain means of transport	27.2
Passenger transport	27.18
Freight transport	27.22
VAT recovery	27.26
Recovery of VAT incurred on the purchase of a car	27.26
Accounting and records	27.27
Practical points	27.28

	Page
Index	559

Table of Cases

References in the right-hand column are to paragraph numbers.

Abbotsley Golf & Squash Club Ltd (15042)	8.149
Adland Group Co Ltd (10397)	6.13
Allied Dancing Association Ltd (10777)	8.29
Allied Medicare Nursing Services Ltd (5485)	12.2, 12.30
All Saints Church (Tilsworth) Parochial Church Council [1993] VATTR 315 (10490)	9.24
American Real Estate (Scotland) Ltd [1980] VATTR 80 (947)	15.18
Amministrazione delle Finanze dello Stato v Simmenthal SpA [1978] 3 CMLR 263, CJEC	7.2
Apple and Pear Development Council v C&E Comrs [1988] STC 221, CJEC	7.4
Arbib (M) v C&E Comrs [1995] STC 490, QB	9.24
ARO Lease BV v Inspecteur der Belastingdienst Grote Ondernemingen [1997] STC 1272, CJEC	18.71
Arts Council of Great Britain [1994] VATTR 313 (10034)	7.5
Ashworth (Mrs BA) [1994] VATTR 275 (12924)	15.15, 15.21
Astor (The Hon Sir JJ) [1981] VATTR 174 (1030)	5.21
Automobile Association, The v C&E Comrs [1994] STC 192, QB	6.38
Ayuntamiento de Sevilla v Recaudadores de Tributos de las Zonas Primera y Segunda [1993] STC 659, CJEC	14.6
Baltic Leasing Ltd [1986] VATTR 98 (2088)	18.55
Banstead Manor Stud Ltd [1979] VATTR 154 (816)	5.25
Barclays Bank plc [1993] VATTR 466 (6469)	17.25
Barkworth (JR) v C&E Comrs [1988] STC 77, QB	10.9
Bass plc v C&E Comrs [1993] STC 42, QB	15.6
Batty (KM) (2199)	13.54
Beheersmaatschappii Van Ginkel Waddinxveen BV and Others v Inspecteur der Omzetbelasting Utrecht [1996] STC 825, CJEC	26.7
Bell Concord Educational Trust Ltd v C&E Comrs [1989] STC 264, CA	7.22, 7.25, 8.18
Bennachie Leisure Centre Association (14276)	7.52
Bennett (JA) (865)	10.26
Benton (G) [1975] VATTR 138 (185)	22.25
Beresford (B) (9673)	13.8
Binder Hamlyn v C&E Comrs [1983] VATTR 171 (1439)	1.9

Table of Cases

Blaydon Rugby Football Club (13901)	7.29
BNR Company Services Ltd (13783)	6.15
Boardmans (J) Ltd (2025)	5.10
Bookmakers Protection Association (Southern Area) Ltd v C&E Comrs [1979] VATTR 215 (849)	8.29
British Airways plc v C&E Comrs [1990] STC 643, CA	27.28
British Airways Authority (No 1) [1977] STC 36, CA	21.17
British Nursing Co-operation Ltd (8816)	12.12
British Telecommunications plc [1988] STC 544, CA	20.8
British United Provident Association ('BUPA') v C&E Comrs [1995] STC 628, QB	10.13
Brooks (LVJ) (1722)	7.41
Bulthuis-Griffioen v Inspecteur der Omzetbelasting [1995] STC 954, CJEC	14.2
BUPA Nursing Services Ltd (10010)	12.2
Butler & Tanner Ltd [1974] VATTR 72 (68)	6.42
C&E Comrs v Arbib (M) [1995] STC 490, QB	9.24
C&E Comrs v Automobile Association, The [1974] STC 192, QB	6.38
C&E Comrs v Bass plc [1993] STC 42, QB	15.6
C&E Comrs v Bell Concord Educational Trust Ltd [1989] STC 264, CA	7.22, 7.25, 8.18
C&E Comrs v British United Provident Association ('BUPA') [1995] STC 628, QB	10.13
C&E Comrs v JH Corbitt (Numismatists) Ltd [1980] STC 231, HL	2.29
C&E Comrs v Colour Offset Ltd [1995] STC 85, QB	6.9
C&E Comrs v DFDS A/S [1997] STC 384, CJEC	26.16
C&E Comrs v David Lewis Centre [1995] STC 485, QB	7.54, 7.56
C&E Comrs v Help the Aged [1997] STC 406, QB	7.56, 7.57, 7.59, 14.9
C&E Comrs v Jeynes (t/a Midland International (Hire) Caterers) [1984] STC 30, QB	20.18
C&E Comrs v Link Housing Association Ltd [1992] STC 718, CS	16.7
C&E Comrs v Lord Fisher [1981] STC 238, QB	7.4, 8.7, 13.29
C&E Comrs v McLean Homes Midland Ltd [1993] STC 335, QB	9.20
C&E Comrs v Redrow Group plc [1997] STC 1053, CA	1.19
C&E Comrs v Reed Personnel Services Ltd [1995] STC 588, CA	12.2, 12.6
C&E Comrs v Richmond Theatre Management Ltd [1995] STC 257, QB	1.7
C&E Comrs v St Mary's Roman Catholic High School [1996] STC 1091, QB	9.4
C&E Comrs v Trinity Factoring Services Ltd [1994] STC 504, CS	16.3
C&E Comrs v Tron Theatre Ltd [1994] STC 177, CS	7.8, 8.78
C&E Comrs v Trustee for R & R Pension Fund [1996] STC 889, QB	21.57
C&E Comrs v Viva Gas Appliances [1983] STC 819, HL	9.24
C&E Comrs v Woolford Motor Co Ltd [1983] STC 715, QB	1.6
Cameron (Dr A) [1973] VATTR 177 (41)	14.4
Cantor Fitzgerald International (15070)	21.91

Table of Cases

Carlton Lodge Club v C&E Comrs [1974] STC 507, QB	8.59
Celtic Football & Athletic Club Ltd v C&E Comrs [1983] STC 470, CS	8.92
Central Capital Corporation Ltd (13319)	21.99
Centurions (9015)	9.13
Cheltenham Countryside Race Day, The (12460)	7.11
Chobham Golf Club (14867)	8.19
City Cabs (Edinburgh) Ltd (928)	8.29
Clinical Computing Ltd [1983] VATTR 121 (1915)	7.56
Comune di Carpaneto Piacentino and Others v Ufficio Provinciale Imposta sul valore Aggiunto di Piacenta [1990] 3 CMLR 153, CJEC	14.6, 19.14
Cooper & Chapman (Builders) Limited v C&E Comrs [1993] STC 1, QB	15.12
Corbitt (JH) (Numismatists) Ltd v C&E Comrs [1980] STC 231, HL	2.29
Colour Offset Ltd v C&E Comrs [1995] STC 85, QB	6.9
Countryside Insurance Marketing Ltd v C&E Comrs [1993] VATTR 277 (11443)	17.25
Crothall & Co Ltd [1973] VATTR 20 (6)	14.4
Croydon Hotel & Leisure Co Ltd (14920)	18.40
Curtis Edington & Say (11699)	17.25
Davenport Brickwork Ltd (10692)	9.24
David Lewis Centre v C&E Comrs [1995] STC 485, QB	7.54, 7.56
Dean and Chapter of Hereford Cathedral (11737)	7.41
Dean and Chapter of the Cathedral Church of St Peter (3591)	7.43
Deutsche Ruck UK Reinsurance Co Ltd [1995] STC 495, QB	17.75
DFDS A/S v C&E Comrs [1997] STC 384, CJEC	26.16
Dodson Bros (Thatchers) Ltd [1995] VATTR 514 (13734)	9.24
Dunn, Bryant, Lee & Franklin (14788)	10.28
Durham Aged Mineworkers' Homes Association v C&E Comrs [1994] STC 553, QB	7.63
Easyway Productions Ltd (14938)	10.10
EC Commission v Netherlands [1987] ECR 1471, CJEC	14.6
EC Commission v United Kingdom [1988] STC 456, CJEC	7.47, 7.52
Eddery (Patrick) Ltd [1986] VATTR 30 (2009)	5.60
Elder Home Care Ltd (11185)	10.11
Ellicot (Mrs V) (11472)	11.9
Emily Patrick (12354)	7.11
English-Speaking Union of the Commonwealth [1980] VATTR 184 (1023)	8.24
Ernst & Young (15100)	1.19
European Publishing Consultants Ltd (13841)	6.18
Evans (Dr AR) [1976] VATTR 175 (285)	10.10
Evans (CN) (4415)	9.24
Exeter Golf & Country Club Ltd v C&E Comrs [1981] STC 211, CA	8.46

Table of Cases

Fencing Supplies Ltd v C&E Comrs [1993] VATTR 302 (10451)   21.49
Fidelity International Management Holdings Ltd (7323)   3.89
Financial and General Print Ltd (13795)   18.39, 18.40, 18.42
First National Bank of Chigago [1995] VATDR 306 (13556)   3.14, 3.95
Flipcards Ltd (13916)   6.16
Foley (CN) (13496)   9.24
Foster (Betty) (Fashion Sewing) Ltd [1976] VATTR 229 (299)   6.30
Freight Transport Leasing Ltd [1991] VATTR 142 (5578)   18.23

Glasgow Miles Better Mid-Summer Fifth Anniversary Ball (4460)   7.9
Graham Leisure Ltd (1304)   6.60
Geddes (HB and DD) v C&E Comrs (3378)   9.13
Goodfellow (RW & MJ) v C&E Comrs [1986] VATTR 119 (2107)   15.11

Hardy (NF) [1994] VATTR 302 (12776)   9.24
Hastings & Rother YMCA (2329)   11.61
Help the Aged v C&E Comrs [1997] STC 406, QB   7.56, 7.57, 7.59, 14.9
Hinckley Golf Club Ltd v C&E Comrs (9527)   8.47
Holiday Inns (UK) Ltd v C&E Comrs [1993] VATTR 321 (10609)   18.39, 18.40
Holy Trinity Church (Heath Town Wolverhampton) Porochial Church Council (13652)   9.24
Howletts (Autocare) Ltd (14467)   20.17

Independent Coach Travel (Wholesaling) Ltd [1993] VATTR 357 (11037)   26.8
Institute of Chartered Accountants in England and Wales v C&E Comrs [1997] STC 1155, CA   8.64
Intercraft UK Romania (13707)   13.54
Interleisure Club Ltd (7458)   6.61
International Bible Students Association v C&E Comrs [1988] STC 412, QB   7.26
International Gymnastic School Ltd (6550)   11.63
International Master Publishers Ltd (8807)   6.43

Jeynes (t/a Midland International (Hire) Caterers) v C&E Comrs [1984] STC 30, QB   20.18
Joseph Rowntree Foundation (12913)   11.6
Jubilee Hall Recreation Centre Ltd v C&E Comrs [1997] STC 414, QB   7.52, 9.16

Kaul (t/a Alpha Care Services) (14028)   14.2
King (JA) [1980] VATTR 60 (933)   13.30
KPMG Peat Marwick McLintock [1993] VATTR 118 (10135)   1.18

Laidlaw (James A) (Edinburgh) Ltd; Laidlaw (James A) (Dunfermline) Ltd (1376)   20.17

Table of Cases

Lancaster Insurance Services Ltd (5455)	17.66
Lea (J&E) (2018)	25.22
League of Friends of Kingston Hospital (12764)	7.51
Lean & Rose [1974] VATTR 7 (54)	25.27
Leighton Park School (9392)	9.16
Lennartz v Finanzamt Munchen [1995] STC 514, CJEC	7.45
Link Housing Association Ltd v C&E Comrs [1992] STC 718, CS	16.7
Liverpool Commercial Vehicles, Re [1984] BCLC 587, Ch D	18.54
Llandudno Cabinlift Co Ltd [1973] VATTR 1 (1)	27.19
London Borough of Haringey [1995] STC 830, QB	19.35
London Cyrenians Housing (14426)	6.10
Lord Fisher v C&E Comrs [1981] STC 238, QB	7.4, 8.7, 13.29
Lubbock Fine & Co v C&E Comrs [1994] STC 101, CJEC	13.34, 21.91
Madgett (TP) & Baldwin (RM) [1996] STC 167, QB	26.5
Mallalieu v Drummond [1983] STC 665, HL	4.12
Mannesmann Demag Hamilton Ltd [1983] VATTR 156 (1437)	18.52
Manor Forstal Residents Society Limited [1976] VATTR 63 (245)	8.10
Marbourne Ltd (12670)	21.98
Marchday Holdings Ltd [1997] STC 272, CA	9.5
Marks & Spencer plc (15476)	13.69
McDonald's Restaurants Ltd (3884)	6.51
McLean Homes Midland Ltd v C&E Comrs [1993] STC 335, QB	9.20
McMeechan v Employment Secretary [1997] IRLR 353	12.32, 12.33
Meanwell Construction Co Ltd (10726)	9.24
Metropolitan Borough of Wirral [1995] STC 597, QB	19.33
Mid-Derbyshire Cheshire Home (4512)	7.54
Mohr v Finanzamt Bad Segeberg [1996] STC 238, CJEC	13.55
Mowbray Properties Ltd (6033)	5.2
Multiform Printing Ltd (13931)	6.14
National Council of YMCAs Inc [1990] VATTR 68 (5160)	11.62
National Society for the Prevention of Cruelty to Children [1992] VATTR 417 (9325)	7.13
Newcourt Property Fund (5825)	21.50
New Ash Green Village Association [1976] VATTR 63 (245)	8.11
Newsvendors Benevolent Institution (14343)	7.29
Newtownbutler Playgroup Ltd (13741)	7.51
Norman Allen Group Travel Ltd (14158)	26.9
Northern Ireland Council for Voluntary Action [1991] VATTR 32 (5451)	7.31
North Anderson Cars Ltd (15415)	20.7
Norwich Camera Centre Ltd (11629)	7.56
Notts Fire Service Messing Club [1977] VATTR 1 (348)	8.12
Nuffield Nursing Home Trust v C&E Comrs [1989] VATTR 62 (3227)	14.4, 16.18

Table of Cases

Oathplan Ltd [1982] VATTR 195 (1299)	15.18
Odhams Leisure Group Ltd [1992] STC 332	6.13
Ormiston Charitable Trust (13187)	7.52
Panini Publishing Ltd (3876)	6.12
Payne (WH) & Co [1995] VATDR 490 (13668)	1.8
Peninsular & Oriental Steam Navigation Co Ltd v C&E Comrs [1996] STC 698, QB	26.39, 27.28
Pertemps Group plc v Nixon ('Metal Box' case) (1 July 1993, unreported)	12.34
Poole Borough Council [1992] VATTR 88 (7180)	13.11
Poole General Hospital League of Friends (10621)	14.4
Powell (RG) (t/a Anwick Agricultural Engineers) (14520)	9.24
Princess Louise Scottish Hospital [1983] VATTR 191 (1412)	7.54
Rapid Results College Ltd, The [1973] VATTR 197 (48)	6.29
Rayner & Keeler Ltd v C&E Comrs [1994] STC 724, QB	9.20
Reading Cricket & Hockey Club (13656)	7.29, 8.70
Redrow Group plc v C&E Comrs [1997] STC 1053, CA	1.19
Reed Personnel Services Ltd v C&E Comrs [1995] STC 588, CA	12.2, 12.6
Rhodes (NF) (14533)	9.24
Rice (BJ) & Associates v C&E Comrs [1996] STC 581, CA	24.3
Richmond Theatre Management Ltd v C&E Comrs [1995] STC 257, QB	1.7
Roberts (AW) (353)	10.36
Rothley Park Golf Club (2074)	8.46
Rowe & Maw v C&E Comrs [1975] STC 340, QB	25.21
Royal Photographic Society of Great Britain [1978] VATTR 191 (647)	8.30
Royal Society for Prevention of Cruelty to Animals [1991] VATTR 407 (6218)	7.4
Royal Society for the Encouragement of Arts, Manufacture and Commerce [1997] STC 437, QB	7.58
Royscot Leasing Ltd, Allied Lyons plc and TC Harrison Group Ltd (Case 305/97), CJEC	18.57, 18.61, 18.63
Rynkeld Thoroughbred Co Ltd (6894)	5.2
Schemepanel Trading Ltd [1996] STC 871, QB	24.5
Sheppard (RW & B) v C&E Comrs [1977] VATTR 272 (481)	15.12
Shuttleworth & Co (12805)	25.22
Sinclair Collis Ltd (14950)	21.17
Snushall, Geoffrey E [1982] STC 537, QB	6.45
Sunningdale Golf Club (14899)	8.131
South Church Workmen's Club & Institute Ltd (613)	8.25
St Annes-on-Sea Lawn Tennis Club Ltd v C&E Comrs [1977] VATTR 229 (434)	8.50
St Dunstan's Educational Foundation (14901)	9.16

St Mary's Roman Catholic High School v C&E Comrs
    [1996] STC 1091, QB   9.4
Sussex County Association of Change Ringers (14116)   7.58

Thorn EMI plc; Granada plc v C&E Comrs [1993] VATTR 94
    (9782)   9.13, 17.62
Triangle Thoroughbreds Ltd (5404)   5.2
Trident Housing Association Ltd (10642)   9.5
Trinity Factoring Services Ltd V C&E Comrs [1994] STC 504, CS   16.3
Tron Theatre Ltd v C&E Comrs [1994] STC 177, CS   7.8, 8.78
Trustee for R&R Pension Fund v C&E Comrs [1996] STC 889,
    QB   21.57
Trustees of the Victoria and Albert Museum (13552)   7.42
Tynewydd Labour Working Men's Club and Institute Ltd
    [1979] STC 570   9.13

Ufficio Distrettuale delle Imposte Dirette di Fiorenzuola d'Arda v
    Comune di Carpaneto Piacentino [1991] STC 205, CJEC   14.6
Ufficio Provincale Imposta sul Valore Aggiunto di Piacenza v
    Comune di Riverago and Others [1991] STC 205, CJEC   14.6
Union of Students of the University of Warwick [1995] VATDR
    219 (13821)   7.54
University of Bath (14235)   9.9
University of Edinburgh (6569)   11.67
University of Hull (180)   9.4
University of Wales College Newport; Allt-Yr-Yn & Caerleon
    Enterprises & Services Ltd (15280)   7.37
Urdd Gobaith Cymru (14881)   9.9, 16.3
Ursula Becker v Finanzamt Munster-Innenstadt [1982] 1 CLMR
    499, CJEC   7.2

Viewpoint Housing Association Ltd v C&E Comrs (13148)
                                                     7.26, 14.4, 16.5
Virgin Atlantic Airways Ltd [1993] VATTR 136 (11096)   26.5
Virgin Atlantic Airways Ltd v C&E Comrs [1995] STC 341, QB   27.28
Viva Gas Appliances v C&E Comrs [1983] STC 819, HL   9.24

Wade (SH) (13164)   9.20
Walshingham College (Yorkshire Properties) Ltd [1995] VATDR
    141 (13223)   9.24
Watters (J) (13337)   21.44
Wellcome Trust Ltd, The (12206)   7.5, 7.13
Wellington Private Hospital Ltd v C&E Comrs [1997] STC 445,
    CA   14.7, 14.8
Westbury (BL) (1168)   25.22
Whitechapel Art Gallery v C&E Comrs [1986] STC 156, QB   7.39, 8.97
Wimpey Group Services v C&E Comrs [1988] STC 625, CA   9.5
Wolverhampton & Dudley Breweries plc v C&E Comrs
    [1990] VATTR 131 (5351)   21.17

Table of Cases

Woolford Motor Co Ltd v C&E Comrs [1983] STC 715, QB   1.6
World Association of Girl Guides and Girl Scouts
    [1984] VATTR 28 (1611)   11.60
Wright (Mrs AE) (10408)   11.8

Yeardley (Brian) Continental Ltd (2035)   5.10
Yoga for Health Foundation v C&E Comrs [1984] STC 630, QB   7.24

Table of Statutes

1894 **Merchant Shipping Act**
Pt XI　　Ch 19, Appendix

1897 **Public Health (Scotland) Act**
Pt X　　Ch 19, Appendix

1938 **Nursing Homes Registration (Scotland) Act**　　14.2

1947 **Fire Services Act**
s 6　　Ch 19, Appendix

1948 **National Assistance Act**
　　14.8

1950 **Employment and Training (Northern Ireland) Act 1973**
s 1A　　11.7

1954 **Landlord and Tenant Act**　　13.36, 21.87

1960 **Professions Supplementary to Medicine Act**　　10.8

1965 **Industrial & Provident Societies Act**
　　16.1, 16.2, 16.10

1967 **Abortion Act**　　14.2

1968 **Firearms Act**　　2.4

1967 **General Rate Act**
s 56　　16.20

1968 **Gaming Act**
Pt II (ss 9–25)　　8.87

1968 **New Towns (Scotland) Act**
　　Ch 19, Appendix

1968 **Transport Act**
Pt II　　Ch 19, Appendix

1970 **Local Authorities (Goods & Services) Act**
s 1(1)　　19.14

1971 **Historic Monuments (Northern Ireland) Act**
　　9.22, 9.23
s 10　　9.23

1972 **Finance Act**
4 Sch
　　Group 16
　　　　item 3　　7.56

1972 **Local Government Act**
s 102
　　(1)　　19.8
　　(4)　　19.9
s 246(4)　　Ch 19, Appendix

1972 **Town and Country Planning (Scotland) Act**
　　9.22, 13.25, 16.27
Pt IV　　9.23

1973 **Employment and Training Act**
s 2　　11.7

1973 **Local Government (Scotland) Act**　　19.3
s 135　　Ch 19, Appendix

1973 **Powers of Criminal Courts Act**
s 47(1)　　Ch 19, Appendix
3 Sch
　　para 2　　Ch 19, Appendix

Table of Statutes

1977 Health Service Act   14.8

1979 Ancient Monuments and Archaeological Areas Act   9.22
Pt I   9.23

1979 Justices of the Peace Act
s 19   Ch 19, Appendix

1980 Education (Scotland) Act
s 135(1)   11.12

1980 Water (Scotland) Act
s 109   Ch 19, Appendix

1981 New Towns Act
   Ch 19, Appendix

1982 Civil Aviation Act
s 105(1)   27.10

1982 Insurance Companies Act   17.8
s 2   15.6, 17.8
s 3   17.8
s 4   17.8
1 Sch   17.8
2 Sch   17.8

1983 Medical Act
s 18(3)   10.12

1983 Value Added Tax Act
s 21   7.51
1 Sch   Ch 5, App 1, para 7.3

1984 Mental Health (Scotland) Act   14.2, 14.8

1984 Public Health (Control of Disease) Act
   Ch 19, Appendix

1984 Registered Homes Act   14.2

1985 Housing Act   16.2, 16.6, 16.7

1985 Housing Associations Act   9.29

1985 Local Government Act
s 10   Ch 19, Appendix

1986 Agricultural Holdings Act   13.35, 13.36

1986 Housing Act   16.2

1987 Landlord And Tenant Act   16.4

1988 Housing Act   16.2
s 54   16.1

1988 Housing (Scotland) Act   16.2

1988 Income and Corporation Taxes Act
s 134   12.35, 12.36
s 505(1)(e)   7.67
s 839   9.13, 9.20, 21.41, 27.20

1989 Local Government and Housing Act   19.8

1989 Self-Governing Schools (Scotland) Act   11.12

1990 Broadcasting Act
s 31(3)   Ch 19, Appendix

1990 New Towns (Scotland) Act
s 2   11.7

1990 Planning (Listed Buildings and Conservation Areas) Act 1990
   9.22, 13.25, 16.27
Pt I   9.23
s 60   9.23

1992 Further and Higher Education Act   11.46, 11.48
s 91
   (3)(a),(b)   11.12
   (5)(b)   11.12

1992 Further and Higher Education (Scotland) Act
s 36(1)   11.12
s 44(2)   11.12

Table of Statutes

1993 Education Act
s 22	11.12
s 182(3)	11.12

1994 Value Added Tax Act
s 6	1.6, 18.13
(3)	1.6
(4)	1.6
(5)	1.6
s 7	
(10)	25.4
(11)	25.4
s 9	1.8, 5.18, 25.4
(2)	3.6
(5)	26.16
s 24	
(3)	13.46
(5)	13.50
s 25	20.13
s 26	
(2)(c)	3.71, 25.15
(3)	11.70
s 30	
(1)	14.1
(5)	7.18
(6)	27.5
s 33	14.8, 16.10, 19.2, 19.6, 19.8–19.11, 19.14, 19.25, 19.27, 19.34, Ch 19, Appendix
s 35	7.51
s 36(1)(b)	18.83
s 41	
(2)	14.6
(3)	14.6
s 42	19.7
s 47	
(1)	5.42
(2)	5.42
(2A)	5.42
s 50A	2.12
s 51A	21.102
s 53	26.2
(3)	26.5
s 56	13.53
s 62	
(1)	9.12
(2)	9.12
(3)	9.12
s 89(1)	18.36
s 94	7.4, 7.16
(1)	8.6
(2)(a)	8.8, 8.10, 8.11
(3)	8.8, 8.22, 8.24, 8.25, 8.69
(4)	4.3, 4.4
s 95	27.17
s 96	
(1)	27.3
(4)	19.3
A1 Sch	7.19, 7.60
1 Sch	
para 1	4.1, 24.2
(1)(a)	24.2
para 2	24.2
(1)–(5)	13.78
para 3	24.2
para 5	
(1)	24.2
(2)	24.2
para 10	3.116
para 14	3.110, 24.4
4 Sch	
para 1	18.7
(1)	5.17
(2)	18.7
para 5	
(1)	13.22
(4)	7.45
5 Sch	3.106, 4.13, 8.41, 25.45
Group 3	4.2, 4.3
para 1–8	25.5
para 1	1.10
para 3	1.8
para 5	3.45
para 6	1.10
6 Sch	
para 1	9.20
para 6(2)	13.22
para 9	15.8
para 10(2)	15.11
8 Sch	7.19, 7.47, 21.18, 21.29, 21.18
Group 1	13.6
items 1–5	13.15
Group 2	8.38

Table of Statutes

Group 3	6.5	note (6)	13.26
Group 4	7.48	Group 7	
Group 5	7.49, 13.6, 21.14, 21.28	item 1	5.25, 14.7
		Group 8	17.59, 26.14, 27.2
item 1	16.8	item 1	27.8, 27.9, 27.11, 27.12
item 2	7.67		
(a)	9.6, 9.8, 9.15	item 2	27.4, 27.8, 27.9, 27.11, 27.12
(b)	9.32		
item 3	9.28	item 2A	27.7
item 4	9.20, 13.26, 16.22	item 3	7.53, 27.16
note (2)	9.6, 16.3	item 4	7.53, 27.19
note (3)	9.6		
note (4)	9.9, 16.3	item 6(a)	27.13
		item 6A	27.10
note (5)	9.10, 16.3	item 7	27.15
		item 8	27.15
note (6)	7.50, 7.51, 16.3	item 9	27.14
		item 10	26.19
(a)	7.52	item 11(b)	27.10, 27.14
(b)	7.53		
note (7)	9.30	item 12	26.18
note (8)	9.30	note (A1)(b)	27.4
note (9)	9.30	note (1)	27.12
note (11)	9.13, 9.28	notes (2)–(4)	27.16
note (12)	9.11, 9.18	note (2)	27.7, 27.11
(b)	7.59		
note (16)	9.5, 9.16	note (2A)	27.7
		note (4A)	27.20
note (17)	9.5, 9.16	note (4B)	27.20
		note (6A)	27.10
note (18)	9.5	note (7)	27.10, 27.14
note (22)	9.20, 13.26, 16.22	Group 9	
note (23)	16.22	item 1	15.20
Group 6	7.49, 9.23, 13.6, 21.14, 21.28	item 3	15.20
		Group 12	7.54, 10.13, 16.3, 16.26, 23.29–23.31
item 1	13.27	item 1	14.10
item 2	9.21, 13.26	item 1A	10.14, 14.10
item 3	13.26	item 2	7.56, 14.10
note (1)	9.22		
note (4)	13.27	(g)	7.54

item 4	14.10	(e)		13.11, 15.12, 15.18, 15.20, 15.27
items 11, 12	7.54	(f)		13.12, 15.21
item 20	16.16	(g)		15.27
note (1)	10.15	(h)		13.12, 16.3
note (3)	16.16	(l)		5.49
note (5)	10.15	(n)		15.13
note (5A)	14.7	note (1)		21.94, 21.99
note (9)	16.16	note (1A)		21.99
note (19)	16.16	note (8)		13.28
Group 15	7.36, 7.55	note (9)		15.2
item 1	7.11, 7.37, 7.55	note (13)		15.12
item 2	7.37, 7.55	note (14)		15.21
item 3	7.38, 7.55	note (16)		8.51, 11.33
items 4–7	7.55	Group 2		17.5, 17.23, 25.11
item 8	6.46, 7.58	item 1		17.7, 17.54
(b)	7.58	item 2		17.7
(c)	7.58	item 3		17.9
item 9, 10	7.55, 14.10	item 4		17.23
note (3)	7.55	Group 5		3.2, 3.4, 3.58, 8.65, 17.10, 17.53
(a)	7.56, 7.57	item 1		3.56, 3.57
(e)	7.56	item 2		3.25
(g)	7.56	item 3		18.22
note (4)(f)	7.55, 7.57	item 4		3.26
note (4A),(4B)	7.57, 14.9	item 5		7.17
note (5A),(5B)	7.57	item 6		3.38, 18.46
note (6)	14.10	item 7		3.41, 3.43, 3.46, 3.53, 25.14
note (7)	14.10	item 8		3.24
note (10)	7.55	item 9		3.52
9 Sch	7.19, 7.20, 8.38	item 10		3.52
Group 1	13.7, 21.13–21.15, 21.25, 21.38	note (5)		25.14
item 1		Group 6		7.12, 11.4, 11.8, 11.9, 26.14
(a)–(n)	21.14, 21.18	item 1		11.4, 11.4, 11.10
(a)(ii)	21.21	(b)		11.6
(c)	13.28	item 2		11.4
(d)	13.11, 15.2, 15.10			

Table of Statutes

item 4	7.23, 11.55		Group 13	7.35, 8.73, 8.76
item 5	11.7		item 1	7.35
item 6	11.57, 11.63		item 2	7.35, 8.69
(a)	11.57		10 Sch	16.3
(b)	11.57		para 2	16.23, 21.14
note (1)	7.22, 11.12		(1)	8.53, 8.144
(e)	7.22, 7.23		(2)	
note (3)	11.7		(a)	21.41
note (4)	11.55		(b)	21.41
note (5)	11.7		(c)	21.41
Group 7	10.2, 10.9, 10.26, 12.16, 17.54		(d)	21.41
			(3)	
item 1	10.36, 12.23, 14.5		(a)	16.23, 21.41
(a)	10.7, 10.8, 10.10		(b)	21.41
(b)	10.7, 10.8, 10.10		(3A)	21.41
item 2	10.7, 10.24, 10.43		(3AA)	21.41
		para 3		21.67
item 4	14.2		(3)	21.62, 21.66
items 6–8	14.4		(6)	21.49
item 9	7.24, 7.25, 14.8, 16.15		(9)	21.52, 21.54
		para 4		21.67
item 10	7.24, 7.25, 7.26		para 8	13.80, 21.104
		11 Sch		
note (2)	10.10		para 2 (4)	27.17
note (4)	10.12		(5)	27.17
note (6)	7.25		para 6(3)	4.16
Group 9	8.26		**1995 Agriculture Tenancies**	
item 1	8.33		Act	13.35, 21.87
Group 10	8.16, 8.35, 8.129		**1995 Environment Act**	
		s 63		Ch 19, Appendix
item 1	8.49		**1995 Finance Act**	
item 2	8.49		s 23	5.42
item 3	8.156, 8.157		**1996 Finance Act**	13.5
Group 12	7.35		**1996 Housing Act**	16.1
item 1	7.28		**1997 Finance Act**	14.7, 24.2
item 2	8.68, 8.83		s 31	13.78
note (1)	7.28, 7.29		**1997 Finance (No 2) Act**	
		s 6		7.60
note (2)	7.28		s 34	14.9

Table of Statutory Instruments

1973/173	VAT Terminal Markets Order	3.64
1978/1689	Categorisation of Earners Regulations	12.37
1984/746	VAT (Imported Goods) Relief Order	
	Ch 6, App III	7.61
1985/1204	Betting, Gaming & Lotteries & Amusements (Northern Ireland) Order	
	Chapter III	8.87
1986/594	Education and Libraries (Northern Ireland) Order	11.12
	art 66(2)	11.12
1987/1806	VAT (Tour Operators) Order	26.2, 26.3, 26.7
	art 3	
	(3)	26.26
	(4)	26.12
	art 10	26.14
1989/2406	Education Reform (Northern Ireland) Order	11.12
	art 65	11.12
1991/1220	Planning (Northern Ireland) Order	9.22, 13.25, 16.27
	Pt V	9.23
1992/662	NHS (Pharmaceutical Services) Regulations	
	reg 20	10.14
1992/2123	VAT (Input Tax) (Specified Supplies) Order	3.42
1992/3120	VAT (Imported Goods) (Relief) (Amendment) Order	7.61
1992/3121	VAT (Place of Supply of Services) Order	1.8, 1.11, 17.6, 17.11, 17.15, 17.37, 17.38
	art 5	25.9
	art 6	27.18, 27.22
	art 8	27.18
	art 9	27.24
	art 10	27.23
	art 13	5.38

	art 14	5.38, 27.23
	art 15	5.58
	(a)	1.13
	art 16	1.8, 25.4, 25.5, 25.7, 25.15
1992/3122	**VAT (Cars) Order**	13.54
	art 2	20.1
	art 4	18.54
	art 5	20.12
	art 8	2.4, 2.5, 2.7, 2.29
1992/3123	**VAT (Input Tax) (Specified Supplies) Order**	3.71, 17.6, 17.11, 17.38
	art 3(a)	3.76
1992/3220	**VAT (Flat-rate Scheme for Farmers) (Designated Activities)**	13.58
1992/3222	**VAT (Input Tax) Order**	20.13
	art 5	8.92
	(1)	13.51
	para 7	4.11
1994/2969	**VAT (Education) (No 2) Order**	11.53
1995/416	**NHS (General Medical Services) (Scotland) Regulations**	
	reg 34	10.14
1995/280	**VAT (Construction of Buildings) Order**	9.6, 16.22
1995/283	**VAT (Protected Buildings) Order**	13.26
1995/652	**VAT (Supply of Pharmaceutical Goods) Order**	10.14
1995/1268	**VAT (Special Provisions) Order**	2.18
	art 2	2.2
	art 4	17.60, 18.54
	art 5	
	(1)	21.78
	(2)	21.78, 21.80
	(3)	21.78
	(4)	18.55
	art 12	2.5, 2.29
	(3)	2.4
	(4)	2.4
	art 13	2.19, 2.20, 2.35
	(1)	2.30
	art 129	2.8
	art 130	2.8
1995/1269	**VAT (Cars) (Amendment) Order**	2.5, 2.29

Table of Statutory Instruments

1995/2518	**VAT Regulations**	
	reg 13	
	(3)	9.39
	(4)	9.40
	reg 22(6)	27.17
	reg 29	
	(1A)	24.5
	(3)	19.29
	reg 67	23.28
	reg 68	23.19
	reg 89	9.37
	reg 90	1.5, 1.7, 12.20
	(1)	18.18
	(2)	18.17
	(3)	18.37
	reg 91	1.6
	reg 92	4.14, 24.10
	(c)	4.15
	reg 93	9.37
	reg 101	
	(2)	3.76
	reg 102	3.78
	reg 105	18.30
	(1)	18.30
	reg 106	3.93, 25.28
	reg 111	24.5, 24.22
	reg 148	27.17
	reg 155	27.17
	reg 204	13.58
1996/1256	**VAT (Cultural Services) Order**	7.35
1996/1661	**Value Added Tax (Anti-Avoidance) (Heating) Order**	7.60
1997/1614	**Value Added Tax (Amendment) (No 3) Regulations**	
	paras 10-13	21.71
1997/2744	**VAT (Drugs, Medicines and Aids for the Handicapped) Order**	14.7, 14.10

Table of EC Legislation

EC Second Directive
    Art 17 — 7.46, 7.52

EC Sixth Directive — 14.1
    Art 4 — 7.5
        (5) — 14.6, 19.1
    Art 5 — 18.67
        (1) — 18.67
        (4)(b) — 18.67
    Art 6(1) — 18.67
    Art 9 — 18.71
        (1) — 18.71
        (2)
            (e) — 18.72, 25.5
        (3) — 18.74
            (a) — 18.73
            (b) — 18.72
    Art 11A
        (3)(c) — 25.18
    Art 13A — 7.20, 11.4
        (1)
            (b) — 14.1, 14.2
            (c) — 10.6
            (g) — 7.24, 7.26, 14.1
            (m) — 8.129
            (n) — 7.35
            (o) — 7.28
        (2) — 7.22
    Art 13B
        (a) — 17.25
    Art 15
        (4) — 27.3
        (5) — 27.2, 27.4
        (6) — 27.2
        (10) — 11.23
    Art 19(1) — 7.43
    Art 26 — 26.1, 26.2, 26.4, 26.5, 26.8, 26.9

Art 28(2)	7.46
Annex H	14.1
EC Eighth Directive	17.94, 18.69, 26.23
EC Thirteenth Directive	17.94

Chapter 1

Accountants

Introduction

1.1 Most accountants provide a range of services, many of which would not immediately be associated with the mainstream services offered by an accountant such as audit and accountancy services. This diversity makes it necessary for an accountant to take particular care in deciding whether, when and how to account for VAT.

The number of cases concerning the place of supply of an accountant's services are testimony to the problems faced in this area. Other issues that regularly arise are questions of the time when VAT must be accounted for on his services and the value of his services.

While most of an accountant's mainstream services will be fully taxable, there are some activities, regularly undertaken by accountants, which are exempt. Thus, while it would be unusual for an accountant to have significant problems with the recovery of VAT incurred, the issue should not be overlooked.

Liability of accountant's supplies

Main services

1.2 The main supplies made by an accountant, e.g. accounting, audit, bookkeeping, insolvency, secretarial and taxation services, are services which, when provided in the UK, are subject to VAT at the standard rate. For consideration of whether or not the services of accountants are supplied within the UK, see paragraphs 1.9 to 1.13 below.

Most other services of accountants will also be standard-rated when supplied within the UK including—

- Seminars, training and other presentations by the accountant;
- Certain services relating to land (note that general advisory services and services relating to the accounting for receipts and payments in respect of land are *not* services relating to land);

1.3 VAT Business by Business

- Certain of the services of acting as a trustee since these services generally go beyond simple accounting and advisory services.

The distinction between the services normally supplied by accountants and the other services is mainly of relevance when considering the place of supply (see paragraphs 1.9 to 1.13 below).

While most services will therefore be standard-rated in the UK, there are a number of exceptions which are exempt e.g.—

- *Certain 'corporate finance' services.* The services of making arrangements for the issue, transfer, receipt or dealing in securities are exempt. Customs & Excise guidance is set out in *Notice 701/44/94, para 11.* The range of corporate finance services which is exempt is narrow and does not include services such as general advice on flotations or sales of shares, nor does it include due diligence work. The making of arrangements for the sale of a business, rather than the shares of the company owning the business, is not exempt;

- *Making arrangements for insurance.* For commentary on the making of arrangements for insurance, see *Tolley's VAT 1998/99, para 37.9*;

- *Making arrangements for credit or investments*, e.g. placing funds for a client with a financial institution.

Supplies of goods

1.3 The supply of goods as part of a service, e.g. copies of an auditor's report or lecture notes, is generally speaking subsumed into the service and therefore, whether or not there is a separate charge for the goods, must be treated as part of the overall service provided by the accountant. Sales of goods by accountants will therefore usually be limited to transactions such as the sale of their publications or, where the accountant performs bookkeeping or secretarial services, the purchase of stationery on behalf of the client.

The treatment of disbursements

1.4 Although expenses incurred by an accountant may be separately stated on his invoices, in most cases, the amount of expenses recovered does not represent any separate supply and their liability or otherwise to VAT depends on the nature of the actual service supplied. For detailed consideration of what conditions must be met in order that an expense may be regarded as a disbursement, see *Tolley's VAT 1998/99, para 4.7* and paragraph 1.24 below.

Time of supply

1.5 VAT is due in the VAT accounting period in which the *tax point* falls. The tax point of a particular service will depend on the nature of the agreement between the accountant and his client for the services to be performed. Most services are likely to be *continuous services* and the tax point will be determined in accordance with *VAT Regulations 1995 (SI 1995 No 2518), reg 90*. However, the accountant is also likely to perform a number of *one-off services* to which different rules apply.

'One-off' supplies

1.6 A one-off supply is one where the work is of a non-recurring nature. One-off services are subject to the usual tax point rules in respect of services, i.e. the basic tax point is the date of completion of the service [*VATA 1994, s 6(3)*] but the earlier issue of a tax invoice or the receipt of a payment on account prior to completion will be treated as a supply to the extent of the invoice amount or payment made [*VATA 1994, s 6(4)*]. The issue of a tax invoice within fourteen days of the date of completion or such longer period allowed by Customs & Excise will delay the tax point until the date of the issue of the invoice [*VATA 1994, s 6(5)*].

In many cases, an accountant may not be able to issue his bill on completion. For example, it may be necessary to wait for the receipt of an invoice for services provided by an overseas associate before the value of the service can be ascertained. The tax point where this situation applies should probably be determined by *VAT Regulations 1995 (SI 1995 No 2518), reg 91*. This provides that the tax point is the earlier of the date that an invoice is issued for the accountant's services or the date a payment is made.

A provision in an engagement letter that a payment on account must be made does not convert a one-off supply into a continuous supply, nor does the payment for a one-off service in instalments bring the service within the continuous supply rules.

Continuous supplies

1.7 Customs & Excise accept that certain work which might otherwise appear to be a one-off supply can be regarded as a continuous supply. Thus, although an accountant is usually appointed as auditor of a company for one year, the relationship tends to be a continuous one because of the likelihood of reappointment and the fact that the services themselves tend to be rendered over the period for which the accountant is appointed. Services, which are rendered as part of the audit relationship, are also likely to be regarded as part of a continuous supply, e.g. accounting services such as assistance in preparing annual accounts, and some taxation and advisory services. The

1.8 VAT Business by Business

accountant's engagement letter may make it clear that a series of continuous services is envisaged.

An accountant will be providing continuous supplies where he agrees to provide services over a period of time and the agreement provides for bills to be rendered from time to time, rather than on completion of the services. In general terms, audit and accountancy, tax compliance and insolvency services should be regarded as continuous services. Consulting and other services provided on similar terms will also fall within this category.

The tax point for continuous supplies of services is the earlier of—

- the date on which an invoice is issued for the service; and

- the date when a payment is received by the accountant for his services. [*VAT Regulations 1995 (SI 1995 No 2518), reg 90*]

The date of issue of an invoice is not necessarily the date upon which it is raised—it is the date that the accountant actually makes the invoice available to the client e.g. by despatching it [see *C & E Commrs v Woolford Motor Co Ltd, QB [1983] STC 715* and *C & E Notice 700, para 5.1*]. However, in the absence of evidence to the contrary, Customs & Excise are likely to take the view that the date of an invoice is the date of issue. It is therefore good practice to ensure that the date on the invoice is the actual date that it is issued to the client.

The issue of a document which is not a tax invoice does not create a tax point. Therefore, subject to any commercial considerations, the accountant will effectively be able to account for VAT on most of his supplies of services when the cash is received if, instead of issuing a tax invoice, he issues a request for payment and only issues a tax invoice when payment for the services is made. It is important to ensure that any request for payment cannot be regarded as a tax invoice. This may be achieved by not showing the VAT separately or by omitting the accountant's VAT number. In either event, the document should always make it clear that it is a request for payment and not a tax invoice by being appropriately titled and having the words 'THIS IS NOT A TAX INVOICE' endorsed on it.

When payment is received

1.8 In most cases, the date of payment will be fairly straightforward, i.e. the receipt of a client's cheque or other means of payment will, subject to its being met by the client's bank, be the date of payment.

Problems can occur with payments received by an accountant on behalf of a client, either directly from the client or from a third party. Unless such funds are clearly distinguished from the accountant's own funds, Customs & Excise are likely to take the view that they should be treated as payments on account of services to be rendered by the accountant. To avoid any argument that the funds are not held in trust for the client, the accountant should ensure that the funds are kept in a separately designated client account and that there is specific agreement with the client that the funds will, unless they are dealt with in accordance with instructions of the client, be refunded to the client when requested. [See *C & E Commrs v Richmond Theatre Management Ltd, QB [1995] STC 257.*]

Place of supply

Services that are supplied where received

1.9 The nature of the services that an accountant performs determines whether the service is regarded as performed within the UK or performed elsewhere. The main supplies made by an accountant, e.g. accounting, audit, bookkeeping, insolvency, secretarial and taxation services, are regarded as supplied where received by virtue of the *VAT (Place of Supply of Services) Order 1992 (SI 1992 No 3121), article 16* and *VATA 1994, 5 Sch 3*.

The determination of where a service is received is a regular problem for the accountant. In UK law, the place where the services of an accountant are received is determined by reference to the place where the recipient of the services 'belongs' [*VATA 1994, s 9*]. The place where a person belongs is in turn determined by reference to where the person has a business establishment or, where he has a fixed establishment in more than one country, the establishment most directly connected with the supply. It has been held that a company can only have one place where it has established its business [*WH Payne & Co, [1995] VATDR 490 (13668)*], i.e. its head office or 'seat of business', although it can have more than one fixed establishment to which a supply is made. In the absence of any establishment, the place where the person receiving the services resides or, in the case of a company, where it is incorporated, determines the place of supply.

Who receives a supply?

1.10 Problems can arise where a person has a fixed establishment in more than one country and it is necessary to determine which establishment receives the supply. The following steps should assist in determining the matter—

- If the person who authorises the work, normally the person signing the engagement letter, is also the person to whom any report or service is delivered, it is the place where that person is based that determines the place of supply;

- A company's registered office is regarded as a fixed establishment capable of receiving supplies [*Binder Hamlyn, [1983] VATTR 171*

1.10 VAT Business by Business

(1439)]. In general, certain supplies are normally regarded as being received at a company's registered office including—

- the performance of any obligation under Company Law which is required to be done at the company's registered office;

- a statutory audit [because the report is to shareholders and communications with shareholders are formally via the registered office];

- The fact that instructions are issued via a third party on behalf of a client does not affect the place of supply unless the third party acts as principal in issuing the instructions, e.g. a local solicitor might be asked to instruct an accountant to prepare a report for an overseas client. If it is clear that the report is to the client and not to the instructing solicitor, the service is performed outside the UK. Similarly, where an accountant acts on the instructions of another firm of accountants based overseas to perform work in respect of a UK company, the fact that the company is based in the UK is irrelevant—it is the place where the instructing accountants belong that determines the place of supply.

Particular problems are sometimes encountered in respect of tax services. It frequently happens that an accountant may be instructed to perform services in respect of UK tax returns for a client. Here the fact that the return is to the UK revenue authorities is irrelevant. The service of preparing the return is not supplied to them. It is the client that is responsible for the return. The normal rules therefore apply, i.e. the accountant must look to see where the service is received. In the case of a company with a UK establishment, it may well be that the preparation of a UK VAT return is supplied within the UK. However, the preparation of a UK Corporation Tax return would be supplied outside the UK if the accountant prepared the return and submitted it to the company's overseas Tax and Treasury Department for final approval. Personal tax returns will almost always be supplied wherever the individual is resident when the service is performed.

A further problem that arises is who is the recipient of a service where a company instructs an accountant to prepare the tax return of one of its staff. It is possible in these circumstances that the service is supplied to the employee with payment being made by the employer, or indeed that a service is supplied to both the employer and the employee to the extent that each makes a payment in respect of the service. One circumstance in which the employer may pay for an employee's tax return to be prepared will be where the employee is an expatriate whose guaranteed remuneration package is to be determined on a basis which takes into account the fact that his working overseas will have different tax consequences from those that would have pertained had he remained in his own country. In such circumstances, although the individual may obtain a benefit because his tax return is prepared for him, it is the employer who has both requested and received the supply and it is the place where the employer is established which determines the place of supply of the service. The fact that the employee is based in the UK and the return is to the UK tax authorities is irrelevant.

Where the employer has fixed establishments in both the UK and elsewhere, it is the establishment to whom the accountant is required to report and which uses the information, e.g. the overseas personnel department which determines his remuneration, which receives the supply.

Other services that are supplied where received

1.11 Apart from accounting services, the accountant may supply other services falling within *VATA 1994, Sch 5*. The treatment of these services will be the same as for other accounting services. Other *Sch 5* services often supplied by accountants include—

- services to a publisher such as writing a book or article for which a royalty is received [*para 1*];

- the secondment of staff to a client [*para 6*].

Services relating to land

1.12 The place of supply of services relating to land is the place where the land is situated. [*VAT (Place of Supply of Services) Order 1992 (SI 1992 No 3121), article 5*]. However, the fact that a service has some vague connection with land does not mean that it is a service relating to land. In general, the term 'services relating to land' covers services such as those of an estate agent, construction or repair services relating to land, property management services or legal fees in connection with the conveyance of land. Taxation advisory services, even when related to a specific piece of land and accounting services, e.g. keeping the accounting records of a property, are not services relating to land.

Training, presentations, seminars and similar services

1.13 The place of supply of cultural, artistic, sporting, educational and entertainment services as well as exhibitions, conferences and meetings and services ancillary to them is the place where the services are performed [*VAT (Place of Supply of Services) Order 1992 (SI 1992 No 3121), art 15(a)*]. A training course or seminar presented by an accountant falls within this provision. It does not matter that he spends the vast majority of his time in the UK preparing material and incurs other costs such as slide making and printing of lecture notes there. The fact that the persons charged for the services are established solely in the UK will also be irrelevant.

1.14 *VAT Business by Business*

Overseas VAT or indirect taxes

1.14 Where a service is not supplied within the UK, it will not be subject to VAT in the UK. However, it may be necessary to consider whether or not there are VAT implications in the country where the services are actually performed and this should normally be done before the terms of any engagement are finalised. A discussion of overseas VAT is beyond the scope of this book. However, in general terms, the accountant will wish to ensure that he does not incur any liability for overseas indirect taxes or, if he does, the taxes can be taken into account in setting his fees. Although the basis upon which VAT is charged in other EU Member States is the same as the UK, there are differences, e.g. VAT may be withheld from any payment for services. In countries outside the EU, the scope for variation is even greater and it will be appropriate to consider the incidence of overseas indirect taxes in all but insignificant engagements.

Value of supplies

1.15 In most cases, the value of an accountant's services will be straightforward. The consideration will simply be the total amount charged including disbursements (see paragraph 1.4 above).

Insurance and other commissions offset against fees

1.16 One problem that is likely to affect most accountants is the question of the set-off of insurance and other commissions against the fees of an accountant. Under current rules of professional conduct [*ICAEW Members Handbook, para 1.314*], an accountant, who acts as an intermediary between his client and someone who supplies financial services, e.g. a permitted insurer, must disclose to his client the fact that he will receive any commission for so acting. In addition, unless he has agreed with the client that he can retain the commission received, he must account for such commission to the client. If no agreement exists to the contrary, the strict position is that the accountant earns the commission (which will be exempt from, or outside the scope of, VAT). The reduction of the amount payable occasioned by accounting for the fee to his client does not reduce the value of the supply for VAT, which would be due on the gross fee before set-off.

However, an accountant may agree in advance with a client that he will retain such commission and that the amount of the commission will be taken into account in setting the level of his fees for services to the client. Customs & Excise accept that in those circumstances, the value of the supply of the accountant's services is the net amount and not the gross. [See paragraphs 1.24 to 1.27 below for accounting issues].

Recovery of VAT

General issues

1.17 Except where an accountant also carries on other non-accountancy businesses, he should normally be able to recover all of his VAT except for the following—

- VAT relating to business entertainment, the private use of motor vehicles and any non-business expenditure;

- VAT relating to the few exempt supplies that are commonly made by accountants, mainly commissions and other income for the making of arrangements for financial services and possibly some property income; and

- VAT relating to exempt corporate finance services.

Employee-related expenditure

1.18 VAT on employee-related expenditure is intrinsically deductible but there are exceptions. The proprietor or partners of a firm of accountants are not employees and the VAT incurred on certain types of expenditure will be disallowed where it relates to them even though the VAT on similar expenditure relating to an employee would be allowed.

Subsistence and business entertainment

1.19 In general terms, VAT on expenditure by staff, charged to client codes, is likely to be deductible. This includes VAT on accommodation and subsistence expenditure and travel.

VAT on business entertainment is not deductible. Where an employee incurs expenditure on subsistence while away from the office and at the same time entertains a client, an apportionment of the VAT should be made.

Staff entertainment is not business entertainment and the VAT on staff entertainment is deductible. Until November 1997, Customs & Excise took the view that only 50% of the VAT on staff entertainment was deductible even where only staff were involved in a function. [See *C & E Notice 700, Appendix D* and *Tolley's VAT 1998/99, para 9.3*]. There did not appear to be any justification for such a view, although where a sole practitioner or partner of a firm is involved in the staff entertainment, it is arguable that, to the extent that VAT is incurred in respect of the partner, it is not deductible. In the case of *Ernst & Young (15100)*, the tribunal specifically disapproved the Commissioners' practice, laid down in *Leaflet 700/55/93*, of allowing only 50% of input tax attributable to entertainment of employees. Following this

1.20 VAT Business by Business

decision, Customs issued Business Brief 25/97, stating that 'Customs & Excise now accepts that where a business provides entertainment to its employees in order to maintain and improve staff relations it does so for wholly business purposes and any VAT incurred is input tax and recoverable, subject to the normal rules. However where the expenditure has no discernible business purpose, and no connection with the business activities, any VAT incurred is not input tax.'

The question of whether or not input tax could be deducted in respect of guests of staff attending a function given by a firm of accountants has been considered in two cases. In *KPMG Peat Marwick McLintock [1993] VATTR 118 (10135)*, the Tribunal found that the VAT attributable to the guests was deductible. In the later decision of *KPMG (a firm) (No 2) (14962)*, another Tribunal found that although the guests of staff attended only by virtue of their relationship with the member of staff, they nevertheless received a separate supply of hospitality from the appellant. Since they were not staff members, the VAT on that entertainment was not deductible. In the earlier decision, both parties had taken the view that either all the VAT was recoverable or none of it was. (It would appear that Customs & Excise departed from their practice of only allowing 50% of the VAT on the staff proportion of the function costs in the second case, since the assessment raised was to recover only 45% of the VAT deducted by the appellant. If they had disallowed all of the cost of the non-staff entertainment and 50% of the cost of the staff entertainment, the percentage disallowed might have been expected to be greater.)

Staff relocation

1.20 Larger firms of accountants will frequently relocate staff to other offices. The VAT on staff relocation expenses will be recoverable subject to the usual rules provided that it is the firm which contracts with the supplier for the services to be provided and that the expenditure does not relate to the making of any exempt supply by the firm. In the author's view, the recent decision in *C & E Commrs v Redrow Group plc, CA [1997] STC 1053* should not affect the deductibility of staff costs incurred by an employer. There is clearly a nexus between the employer's business and the expenses incurred by the employer in respect of his employees.

Expenditure of partners or sole proprietors

1.21 Although the directors, or anyone engaged in the management, of a company are specifically included within the definition of 'employees' of the company for the purposes of the business entertainment rules, there is no such extension to the proprietor or partners of a firm. Nevertheless, there are no specific provisions disallowing the VAT on their expenditure. The proper position would appear to be that where the expenditure relates to client or staff affairs, it is expenditure for business purposes and therefore deductible. In other cases, Customs & Excise are likely to seek to disallow VAT on proprietors' expenditure on the basis that it is not for business purposes, e.g. VAT on meals is usually disallowed unless the proprietor or partner is away from his office on business. In some cases, it is possible that an apportionment may be appropriate. VAT on a partner's or proprietor's accommodation is also treated by Customs & Excise as disallowable.

Partial exemption

Expenditure directly attributable to exempt supplies

1.22 Most accountants are unlikely to have very much expenditure directly attributable to exempt supplies. Possible exceptions include VAT on exempt supplies of property, if any, and VAT incurred in staff expenses relating to an exempt client service, e.g. a corporate finance engagement. Since accountants' client cost systems are usually geared to charging client accounts with the expenditure net of any VAT, it may be necessary to make special provision for expenditure relating to exempt supplies, e.g. by setting up a separate client code for an assignment which will produce exempt supplies, and charging expenditure including VAT to that code.

Where only minimal exempt supplies are made, the position may be more complex with the need to retain a record of exempt input tax not recovered in order to give consideration to whether or not the *de minimis* rules apply [see *Tolley's VAT 1998/99, para 49.4*] so that VAT initially disallowed is recovered.

Expenditure attributable to both taxable and exempt supplies

1.23 In most cases, it will be inappropriate for accountants to use the standard method of determining the deductible proportion of input tax that is referable to both taxable and exempt supplies. In general terms, the expenditure referable to exempt supplies is unlikely to bear any direct relationship to the exempt turnover.

While it will be for each accountant to decide what method is most appropriate, two possible methods which are simple and appropriate are—

- The disallowance of a fixed amount of input tax referable to overheads each VAT accounting period, the amount being negotiated with the firm's VAT Officer;

- Where it is possible to identify the actual directly attributable exempt input tax, the disallowance of a fixed percentage of the exempt input tax.

The standard method may nevertheless prove attractive where there is little exempt input tax in any event under that method so the whole of the exempt input tax is recoverable under the *de minimis* limits.

1.24 *VAT Business by Business*

Accounting and records

Invoices in respect of supplies made by an accountant

Client expenses

1.24 Where an accountant acts as agent in incurring expenses on behalf of clients, he may adopt one of two methods, i.e.—

(i) Provided that the supplier's invoice is made out in his name, he can recover the VAT. He must then charge VAT on the whole amount of his invoice including the net disbursement.

(ii) Alternatively, he should require the supplier to make the invoice out to his client, show the gross amount of the disbursement on his own invoice and not add VAT to the disbursement. A special concessionary treatment applies in respect of Counsel's fees even where Counsel's invoice is made out to the accountant.

Where the accountant's own service is exempt, e.g. certain corporate finance services, care will be needed since the disbursement will be subject to VAT but the actual service supplied by the accountant will not. [See *Tolley's VAT 1998/99, para 4.7(i) and (ii)*].

The above treatment applies only to expenses incurred as client's agent and not to expenses, the recovery of which is part of the consideration for the accountant's service.

Self-billed supplies

1.25 It is common for some clients of an accountant to insist on using the provisions for self-billing. [See *Tolley's VAT 1998/99, para 40.2*]. For example, publishers and seminar providers may require accountants to agree to self-billing. One of the conditions to which the accountant must agree is that he will not issue a tax invoice to his client. A tax invoice is not issued unless it is actually sent or given to the client (see paragraph 1.7 above). Accountants, whose accounting systems require the raising of an invoice in order to capture the VAT payable, will therefore need to ensure that the system-generated VAT invoice is kept and not sent to the client, to comply with the self-billing rules.

Services which are outside the scope of VAT and zero-rated supplies

1.26 Where an accountant's supplies are not subject to VAT, he must indicate on the invoice for his supplies the reason why no VAT is charged. In general terms, where a customer in the EU claims that a service should be treated as outside the scope of UK VAT, he should be asked to provide his registration number in another Member State. However, Customs & Excise are prepared to accept other evidence that the recipient of a supply of an accountant's services is in business and therefore entitled to receive the service VAT-free (see *C & E Notice 741, para 9.4*).

Input tax evidence

Staff expenses

1.27 As already indicated, staff expenses are usually expenses of the business and not a disbursement on behalf of a client. It follows that VAT should be recovered on any expenses that are billed to a client account unless the expense relates to a service which will be exempt from VAT, such as certain corporate finance work. The normal rules regarding evidence of input tax will apply, i.e. expenses should be charged to the firm and not the individual unless it is one of those expenses where Customs & Excise are prepared to accept an invoice billed to the member of staff, e.g. accommodation and meals.

Similarly, Customs & Excise are prepared to agree that a proportion of any mileage allowance paid to a member of staff represents VAT on the petrol element and allow such amount to be recovered. Staff expense claim forms should therefore be drawn up to ensure that the appropriate details are identified.

Practical points

Use of special schemes for small businesses

1.28 Smaller firms of accountants may be eligible to use the special schemes available for small businesses. The cash accounting scheme (see *Tolley's VAT 1998/99, paras 63.2 to 63.8*) allows persons whose total taxable supplies are less than £350,000 per annum to account for VAT when payments are received or paid. However, where the accountant's supplies are mainly of a continuous nature (see paragraph 1.5 above), the accountant may be able to use other means to defer payment until cash is received without delaying the right to recover VAT until payment is made for the supplies on which it is incurred.

The annual accounting scheme is directed mainly at relieving taxable persons whose turnover does not exceed £300,000 per annum from the need to make quarterly returns. This benefit should not normally be of considerable importance to accountants. There can however be cash flow advantages, particularly for persons whose turnover is less than £100,000, and it may therefore be worthwhile considering these options.

1.29 *VAT Business by Business*

Dealing with disbursements

1.29 The accountant will frequently incur expenses in the course of the provision of any services to a client. The treatment of any amount recovered in respect of services depends on the nature of the disbursement. Where the accountant merely acts as paymaster in discharging an expense which is the liability of the client, e.g. stamp duty on the transfer of shares, the amount paid is not part of the consideration for a supply by the accountant and is not therefore subject to VAT where the main supply is standard-rated. However, expenses incurred by the accountant or his staff are part of the consideration for the services supplied even though the exact amount of the expense is recovered. Amounts received as expenses, which will generally be part of the consideration for the supply, include—

- Travel and subsistence expenses of partners and staff;

- Office expenses such as postage and telephone calls if recharged.

The issue of whether or not expenses charged to a client are part of the consideration for his services or not has implications on the right to recover any VAT incurred on those expenses.

Partners holding offices

1.30 Partners of firms of accountants may be appointed to an office, e.g. as secretary of a company. If the office is held by virtue of his being a partner of the firm, any remuneration received is likely to be regarded as consideration for a supply of services by the partnership. For the avoidance of doubt, it is necessary to ensure that it is clear from the terms of any appointment that it is held either personally or as a member of the firm. If the appointment is not personal, it is important that provision is made in any contract for the charging of VAT on the remuneration. [See *Tolley's VAT 1998/99, para 50.6*].

Accounting for commissions

1.31 Where an accountant reduces his fee because he has received a commission from an insurer or other institution, he may wish to record the fact that the reduction has been made for the benefit of the client. In these circumstances, there is no objection to indicating on the face of the tax invoice that the fee has been reduced. He should not however make it appear that what he is doing is setting off the commissions received against the gross fee. An alternate method of disclosing the commission would be to bill the net fee and refer to the amount of the reduction made in the letter accompanying the fee note.

Chapter 2

Auctioneers

Introduction

2.1 Auctioneers may account for VAT in one of three ways. Firstly, they may use the general margin scheme for second-hand goods (see paragraph 2.2 below). Alternatively, they can use the Auctioneers' Margin Scheme (see paragraph 2.12 below) which is a scheme specifically for the use of auctioneers. Auctioneers who trade in large quantities of low value second-hand goods may find the rules for using a margin scheme too onerous and may wish to use the 'Global Accounting Scheme' (see paragraph 2.18 below). Where goods are ineligible for inclusion in either of the margin schemes or global accounting, or there are services related to the sale of goods by the auctioneer, the normal VAT rules for agents will apply (see *Tolley's VAT 1998/99, para 4.4*).

Operation of the second-hand goods margin scheme

Eligible goods

2.2 The following goods are eligible for inclusion in the margin scheme, from 1 January 1995.

(a) second-hand goods such as tangible moveable property which is suitable for further use as it is or after repair, *other than* works of art, collectors' items or antiques, precious metals and precious stones.

(b) works of art, which are defined in Customs & Excise Notice 718 as:

  (i) pictures, collages and similar decorative plaques; paintings and drawings executed by hand by the artist, other than plans and drawings for architectural engineering, industrial, commercial, topographical or similar purposes; hand-decorated manufactured articles; theatrical scenery, studio back cloths or similar painted canvas;

  (ii) original engravings, prints and lithographs, being impressions produced in unlimited numbers directly in black and white or in colour of one or of several plates executed entirely by hand by the artist, irrespective of the process or of the material employed by

2.3 VAT Business by Business

him, but not including any mechanical or photomechanical process;

(iii) original sculptures and statuary in any material, provided that they are executed entirely by the artist; sculpture casts which are limited in production to eight copies and are supervised by the artist or his successors in title (in exceptional circumstances the limit of eight copies may be exceeded for statuary casts produced before 1 January 1989);

(iv) tapestries and wall textiles made by hand from original designs provided by the artists, provided that there are no more than eight copies of each;

(v) individual pieces of ceramics executed entirely by the artist and signed by him. Enamels on copper, executed entirely by hand, limited to eight hundred copies bearing the signature of the artist or the studio, excluding articles of jewellery and goldsmiths' and silversmiths' wares;

(vi) photographs taken by the artist, printed by him or under his supervision, signed and numbered and limited to 30 copies, all sizes and mounts included.

(c) collector's items, which are defined as:

(i) postage or revenue stamps, postmarks, first day covers, pre-stamped stationery and the like, which are franked. If unfranked they may not be legal tender and must not be intended for use as legal tender;

(ii) collections and collectors' pieces of zoological, botanical, mineralogical, anatomical, historical, archaeological, palaeological, ethnographic or numismatic interest.

(d) antiques, which are defined as objects which are over 100 years old and do not qualify as works of art or collectors' items.

[*VAT (Special Provisions) Order 1995 (SI 1995 No 1268), Article 2; Customs & Excise Notice 718*].

Ineligible goods

2.3 Customs & Excise Notice 718, Annex 1, also provides details of goods for which the margin scheme *cannot be used* and VAT must be accounted for on the full selling price under the normal VAT rules for agents (see *Tolley's VAT 1998/99, para 4.7* for an explanation of the rules of agency). These include:

Precious metals

(a) Goods consisting of precious metals or any supply of goods containing precious metals, where the consideration for the supply (excluding any VAT) is, or is equivalent to, an amount which does not exceed the open market value of the metal contained in the goods. (Goods in this case includes coins.) Where gold and coins are sold at or below the open market value (i.e. the daily 'fix' price) the special accounting and payment system for gold transactions applies (see *Customs & Excise Notice 701/21 Gold*).

Precious stones

(b) Precious stones of any age which are not mounted, set or strung are ineligible for the margin scheme.

Prior to 1 January 1995, only motor cars; works of art as defined in paragraph 2.2(b)(i)–(iii) above; collectors' items as described in 2.2(c)(ii) but excluding items of numismatic interest; antiques within 2.2(d) above; motor cycles, caravans and motor caravans; boats and outboard motors; aircraft; electronic organs; firearms and horses and ponies were eligible for the margin scheme.

Transitional provisions at 1 January 1995

Goods which had been purchased prior to 1 January 1995, and which were not eligible for the margin scheme when purchased, can be sold under the margin scheme if they qualify as eligible goods at the time of sale, the conditions for use of the margin scheme are met, and evidence of the purchase price is held.

Requirements for use of the margin scheme

2.4 A taxable person must meet the following conditions to use the margin scheme:

(a) he took possession of the goods either:
- (i) on a supply on which no VAT was chargeable;
- (ii) on a supply on which VAT was chargeable on the profit margin under the UK margin scheme or under the corresponding provisions in the Isle of Man or another Member State;
- (iii) under a transaction treated as neither a supply of goods nor a supply of services;
- (iv) if the goods are a work of art, after 31 May 1995, on a supply, or acquisition from another Member State, from the creator or his

2.4 VAT Business by Business

successor in title (whether or not the purchase invoice shows VAT separately);

    (v) by importing the goods himself if the goods are works of art, collectors' items or antiques; or

    (vi) on a supply of a motor car, on which VAT was charged on the margin because of an earlier input tax restriction.

(b) the supply by the taxable person is not a letting on hire;

(c) on selling the goods, the taxable person does not use a VAT invoice or similar document showing an amount as VAT or as being attributable to VAT;

(d) if the supply is of an airgun, the taxable person is registered for the purposes of the *Firearms Act 1968*;

(e) if the supply by the taxable person is the sale of repossessed assets, the supply satisfies the conditions for treatment as outside the scope of VAT;

(f) if the supply by the taxable person is a motor car which he produced himself, the car has previously been supplied by him in the course or furtherance of his business or treated as self-supplied;

(g) before 1 August 1995, in the case of a motor car, the car was not supplied to, or acquired or imported by, the taxable person for the primary purpose of being:

    (i) provided by him for hire with the services of a driver for the purposes of carrying passengers;

    (ii) provided by him for self-drive hire;

    (iii) used as a vehicle in which driving instruction is given by him; or

    (iv) let on hire to a person who is not a taxable person on condition that he uses the car primarily for one purpose within (i)–(iii) above, unless the car had previously been treated as self-supplied to the taxable person because of use for some other purpose or use by the person to whom it is let on hire in breach of the condition.

(h) the taxable person keeps such records and accounts as Customs & Excise specify.

[*VAT (Special Provisions) Order 1995 (SI 1995 No 1268), Article 12(3)–(4); VAT (Cars) Order 1992 (SI 1992 No 3122), Article 8*].

Works of art etc.

2.5 Where a taxable person opts to use the margin scheme for eligible goods supplied or acquired under paragraph 2.4(a)(iv) above, he must also exercise the option for any eligible goods imported under 2.4(a)(v), and vice versa. Where an option is exercised, it must be made in writing to Customs & Excise. The effective date is the date of notification, or a later date if specified in the notice. From the date of notification, the option will apply to all supplies of such goods made by the taxable person in the period ending two years after the effective date or until the date on which written revocation is given to Customs & Excise, whichever is later. The taxable person can still account for VAT on the full value of supplies, but input tax on the supply, acquisition or importation cannot be recovered until the period in which VAT is accounted for on the sale.

[*VAT (Cars) Order 1992 (SI 1992 No 3122), Article 8; VAT (Special Provisions) Order 1995 (SI 1995 No 1268), Article 12; VAT (Cars) (Amendment) Order 1995 (SI 1995 No 1269)*].

Acquisitions and dispatches within the EC

2.6 The margin scheme is available throughout the EC Member States from 1 January 1995.

Purchases

The treatment of eligible goods purchased from other Member States depends on the taxable status of the supplier:

(a) *Goods bought from a private individual in another Member State.* No VAT will be due on the acquisition in the UK and the margin scheme (or global accounting) can be used on the sale of the goods, provided that the auctioneer meets all the conditions of the scheme;

(b) *Goods bought from a registered business in another Member State on a VAT invoice.* The goods will be liable to VAT on acquisition. The acquisition VAT can be reclaimed subject to the normal rules, but the margin scheme cannot be used for the sale of the goods.

(c) *Goods bought from a registered business in another Member State under the margin scheme or global accounting.* Goods will not be liable to acquisition VAT and the margin scheme (or global accounting scheme) can be used for the sale of the goods as VAT will not be shown as a separate item on the invoice.

2.7 VAT Business by Business

Sales

From 1 January 1995, eligible goods sold under the margin scheme in any Member State are taxable in the Member State of origin and are not subject to the distance selling rules:

(a) *Sales to a registered business in another Member State.* From 1 January 1995, sales made under the margin scheme (or global accounting scheme) are treated the same way as sales within the UK. The scheme changes the place of supply to the country of origin, not destination. These sales cannot be zero-rated if they are made under the margin scheme (or global accounting scheme) and tax will be due on the margin. No further tax will be due from the purchaser when the goods are dispatched to the other Member State. If the sale is made outside of the margin scheme the sale can be zero-rated under the normal EC supply rules. The purchaser must then account for VAT in his own country and cannot sell the goods under the margin scheme.

(b) *Sales to a private individual in another Member State.* These sales will be taxable in the UK on the margin. (This also applied prior to 1 January 1995.)

Imports and exports outside the EC

Imports

2.7 Second-hand goods which are imported are normally subject to import VAT and the margin scheme (or global accounting scheme) cannot be used to sell the goods. If the goods are subsequently sold, the VAT paid at importation can be deducted, subject to the normal rules. The following are exceptions to this rule:

(a) Prior to 1 June 1995, certain works of art, antiques, collections and collectors' pieces were relieved from import VAT. From 1 June 1995, they are entitled to a reduced valuation at importation. Where any of the works of art etc. shown at paragraph 2.2(b) above are imported, the purchaser may use either the margin scheme or global accounting scheme, or may import and resell the goods under the normal VAT rules.

(b) Imported second-hand cars on which input tax is irrecoverable may be sold under the margin scheme.

[*Customs & Excise Notice 700/64/96, para 10; VAT (Cars) Order 1992 (SI 1992 No 3122), Article 8*].

Exports

2.8 Where eligible goods are sold for direct export, the sale is zero-rated provided that the appropriate evidence of export is held (see *Tolley's VAT 1998/99, para 25.24*). Where a trader is registered for the retail export scheme, it is possible to zero-rate sales to overseas visitors provided that the relevant requirements are met (see *Tolley's VAT 1998/99, para 25.11*).

[*Customs & Excise Notice 703; VAT (Special Provisions) Order 1995 (SI 1995 No 2518), Articles 129, 130*].

Bulk purchases

2.9 When a number of eligible goods are bought at an inclusive price with the intention of reselling them separately, the price must be apportioned. There is no set way of doing this but the method must be 'fair and reasonable' and must be as accurate as possible. The separate figures must be shown in the stock book (see paragraph 2.22 below).

Purchases of repossessed goods from insurance companies or finance houses

2.10 Sales by insurance companies of eligible goods which have been acquired as a result of an insurance claim, or sales by a finance house which has repossessed goods, are outside the scope of VAT if certain conditions are met (see *Tolley's VAT 1998/99, para 27.22*). The goods can be purchased for onward sale under the margin scheme if they qualify as eligible goods under paragraph 2.2 above.

Calculation of the margin

2.11 As supplies of goods through auctioneers are treated as supplies both to them and by them, auctioneers will have both a purchase and selling price for the margin scheme. VAT is due on the amount by which the selling price exceeds the purchase price (the gross margin). The profit margin is regarded as VAT-inclusive.

(a) *Purchase price* is the gross amount which the auctioneer passes on to the seller of the goods.

(b) *Selling price* is the total price for the goods including any incidental expenses and commission charged to the buyer. (Optional charges which are not directly linked to the goods, e.g. insurance, packaging, etc. are outside the margin scheme and the normal VAT rules apply.)

(c) *Margin* is the difference between the purchase and selling price.

(d) *Output tax* is calculated as VAT-inclusive margin $\times$ VAT fraction (currently 7/47).

2.12 *VAT Business by Business*

The profit margin cannot be reduced by deducting expenses such as repairs, spare parts, etc.

Auctioneers' margin scheme (AMS)

2.12 For the purposes of the AMS, an auctioneer is defined as a person who sells or offers for sale goods at any public sale where persons become purchasers by competition, i.e. sales to the highest bidders. If an auctioneer invoices in his own name for goods sold at auction on behalf of a third party vendor, the goods are treated for VAT purposes as supplies both to and by the auctioneer. The AMS was developed to allow auctioneers to account for VAT only on the margin, rather than deducting input tax and charging output tax when selling 'eligible goods' on behalf of a third party (*VATA 1994, s 50A*). The auctioneers' scheme is optional and the auctioneer and his client may decide not to use the scheme. Auctioneers can use the margin scheme for some sales and the general rules for agents for others. The auctioneers' scheme differs from the general scheme in that for the basic margin scheme any commission or other charges made to the seller do not affect the margin. Auctioneers, however, can take into account the value of their services in calculating the profit margin.

Goods which are eligible for the scheme

2.13 See paragraph 2.2 above for goods which are eligible for inclusion in the AMS.

Requirements for use of the scheme

2.14 Once it has been established that the goods being sold are eligible for inclusion in the margin scheme, it must be determined whether the third party on whose behalf the auctioneer is selling the goods meets the requirements to use the scheme. The margin scheme can be used when the third party meets the following criteria, the goods are eligible for inclusion in the scheme and the auctioneer meets the record-keeping requirements set out at paragraph 2.29 below. The seller of the goods (the third party) must be:

(a) not registered for VAT; or

(b) a VAT-registered person supplying goods under the margin scheme or global accounting (see paragraph 2.18 below); or

(c) an insurance company selling eligible margin scheme goods which it has acquired as a result of an insurance claim, provided that they are sold at auction in the same state (i.e. no repairs are made to them); or

(d) a finance house selling eligible goods which it has repossessed, provided that they are sold at auction in the same state.

Auctioneers **2.16**

Margin scheme calculation

2.15 Whenever an auctioneer sells goods under the AMS, he will be liable to account for output tax calculated on the basis of the margin between the selling and the purchase price. No input tax is deductible in respect of the supply of goods that the auctioneer receives, because the supplier will have charged no VAT.

The *purchase price* is calculated as the *hammer price* less:

(a) commission, and

(b) any other charges which are made to the seller for services connected with the sale of the goods.

(If the seller of the goods is operating the margin scheme or Global Accounting, this amount will be his selling price.)

The *selling price* is the hammer price plus:

(a) the buyer's premium, or

(b) any other commission (including any incidental expenses) which the auctioneer has incurred in relation to the sale which he then recharges to the buyer. Other items which are optional charges must be charged separately from the scheme.

Example A

An auctioneer sells goods at auction for a hammer price of £100. A seller's commission of 10% is deducted (net of VAT) and a buyer's premium of 50% is also charged (net of VAT):

	£
Commission = (£100 × 10%) + 17.5%	11.75
Purchase Price = £100 − £11.75	88.25
Buyer's Premium = (£100 × 50%) + 17.5%	58.75
Selling Price = £100 + £58.75	158.75
Margin = £158.75 − £88.25	70.50
Output tax due is therefore £70.50 × 7/47	**10.50**

Charges which should be included in the AMS calculation

2.16 Charges for supplies of services by the auctioneer to the seller, or to the buyer, are taken into account when calculating the margin on the supply of goods and are not separately charged for VAT purposes. Any commissions or other charges the auctioneer makes to the vendor or buyers which are dependent on the sale of goods must be included in the auctioneers' scheme calculation, for which see paragraph 2.15 above. This includes any incidental

2.17 VAT Business by Business

expenses which the auctioneer has incurred and then recharged to their client. The treatment of other charges is as follows:

(a) *Disbursements for VAT purposes.* If the auctioneer passes on costs to the client and they meet all the conditions regarding VAT disbursements (see *Tolley's VAT 1998/99, para 4.7*), they may be excluded from the auctioneers' scheme calculation;

(b) *Exempt supplies.* If the auctioneer supplies services to either the buyer or the seller which are exempt from VAT (e.g. if the auctioneer makes arrangements for the provisions of insurance by a permitted insurer), the supplies should be excluded from the scheme calculation;

(c) *Services to an overseas seller.* Certain services, where the seller is overseas and the place of supply is outside the UK, are outside the scope of UK VAT and should not be included in the scheme calculations (see *Tolley's VAT 1998/99, paras 64.7 to 64.15* for the rules relating to the place of supply of services). However, if the place of supply is the UK, even though the services are supplied to an overseas client, these must be included in the auctioneers' scheme calculation;

(d) *Other charges.* Charges made by the auctioneer for supplies which are optional and not directly related to the hammer price, e.g. transporting goods after sale, must be excluded from the auctioneers' scheme and accounted for under the normal VAT rules.

Time of supply

2.17 As described at paragraph 2.12 above, under the AMS the goods are treated as supplied both to and by the auctioneer. There is a common tax point for both these supplies and this is determined by reference to the actual sale of the goods at auction. The tax point for both supplies will normally be the earlier of:

(a) the handing over of the goods by the auctioneer to the buyer; or

(b) the receipt of payment by the auctioneer.

Global accounting scheme

2.18 The global accounting scheme was introduced with effect from 1 January 1995 (although *VAT (Special Provisions) Order 1995 (SI 1995 No 1268)*, giving effect to the scheme, did not come into force until 1 June 1995). It was recognised that, due to the volume of low value goods handled by some second-hand dealers, they may find it impractical to keep the detailed records of purchases and sales necessary for the operation of the normal margin scheme. An optional, simplified system of accounting for VAT on low value, bulk volume, margin scheme goods was therefore introduced.

Under the global accounting scheme, dealers (including auctioneers) account for VAT on the difference between the total purchases and total sales of eligible goods in each prescribed accounting period (rather than on an item by item basis). One advantage of the scheme is that, unlike the basic margin scheme, it allows the offsetting of a loss on one transaction against the profit made on others.

Eligible goods

2.19 The global accounting scheme may be used for all second-hand goods, works of art, antiques and collectors' items which are eligible for the margin scheme apart from those listed below:

(a) boats and outboard motors;

(b) aircraft;

(c) motor vehicles including motor cycles;

(d) caravans and motor caravans;

(e) horses and ponies.

[*VAT (Special Provisions) Order 1995 (SI 1995 No 1268), Article 13*].

This is because it is more practical for dealers in these goods to keep records on an item by item basis and they are therefore able to use the normal margin scheme of accounting.

Conditions for using the scheme

2.20 To qualify to use the scheme, a VAT-registered person must satisfy the following requirements:

(a) The price of every item covered by the scheme must not exceed £500. See paragraph 2.11 above for the calculation of the price. See paragraph 2.21 below for bulk purchases and collections;

(b) The goods must not be purchased on an invoice on which VAT is separately identified;

(c) The goods must not be sold on a VAT invoice or comparable document showing a VAT amount or an amount attributable to VAT;

(d) All records and accounts are maintained as specified by Customs & Excise.

[*VAT (Special Provisions) Order 1995 (SI 1995 No 1268), Article 13*].

2.21 *VAT Business by Business*

Bulk purchases and collections

2.21 The scheme may be used for bulk purchases with a combined value in excess of £500, but individual items with a purchase value over £500 should be deducted from the total purchase value and excluded from the scheme. Items costing over £500 may be sold under the margin scheme (if they qualify as eligible goods), or under the normal VAT rules with VAT charged on the full selling price.

Collections of items purchased, for example stamp collections, may be split and sold separately or formed into other collections for sale under the scheme. Two or more items purchased separately may also be combined to produce only one item for resale (for example by using one item as a spare part for another).

Accounting and records

General requirements

2.22 In addition to the general record-keeping requirements (see *Tolley's VAT 1998/99, para 57.1*), a person using the margin scheme is required to meet the following requirements:

(a) the purchase invoice and copy sales invoice must be kept together with a stock book (see paragraph 2.22 above);

(b) all records must be kept for six years.

[*VAT (Cars) Order 1992 (SI 1992 No 3122), Article 8; VAT (Special Provisions) Order 1995 (SI 1995 No 1268), Article 12; VAT (Cars) (Amendment) Order 1995 (SI 1995 No 1269)*]

Failure to comply with these requirements could result in the taxable person becoming liable for VAT on the full value of his sales (*C & E v JH Corbitt (Numismatists) Ltd, HL [1980] STC 231*). The seller is not required to verify the identity of the purchaser under these provisions.

Where an auctioneer elects to use any of the margin schemes when selling second-hand goods, he must keep a detailed stock book or similar record. The following details must be set out in the stock book or record:

(a) *Purchase details:*

  (i) stock number in numerical sequence;

  (ii) date of purchase;

  (iii) purchase invoice number;

  (iv) name of seller;

(v) any unique identification number (e.g. car registration);

(vi) description of the goods (e.g. make or model).

(b) *Sales details:*

(i) date of sale;

(ii) sales invoice number;

(iii) name of buyer.

(c) *Accounting details:*

(i) purchase price;

(ii) selling price or method of disposal;

(iii) margin on sale;

(iv) VAT due.

Other entries may be made in the stock book for the auctioneer's own accounting purposes but the above details must be included in the stock record and the record must be kept up to date.

[*Customs & Excise Notice 718, Part II, para 13*].

Invoicing requirements under the second-hand margin scheme

Purchases

2.23 When an auctioneer makes purchases which he intends to include in the margin scheme, he must first check that the goods are eligible for inclusion in the margin scheme (see paragraph 2.2 above) and then, when purchasing from a private individual, he must make out a purchase invoice showing:

(a) seller's name and address;

(b) his own name and address;

(c) stock book number (in numerical order) and day book number or similar reference to the accounting records (see paragraph 2.22 above);

(d) invoice number;

(e) date of transaction;

(f) description of the goods including any unique identification number (e.g. registration number, hallmark etc.);

(g) total price.

2.24 VAT Business by Business

The buyer must get the seller to sign and date the invoice, certifying that he is the seller of the goods and that the goods have been sold at the stated price. The certification can be made on a separate letter, provided that it is cross-referenced to the invoice. Details of the purchase must be entered in the stock book (see paragraph 2.22 above).

When purchasing from another dealer, the same procedures above apply, but the invoice will be made out by the other dealer who must additionally certify that 'Input tax deduction has not been and will not be claimed in respect of the goods on this invoice'.

Sales

2.24 When an auctioneer sells eligible goods and intends to include the sale in the margin scheme, he must first check that the rules for purchase of goods were applied. If they were not applied, the scheme cannot be used. If the rules were followed correctly, then a sales invoice must be issued showing:

(a) own name, address and VAT registration number;

(b) buyer's name and address;

(c) stock book number and day book number or similar reference number;

(d) invoice number;

(e) date of sale;

(f) particulars of the goods including any unique reference number (e.g. registration number, hallmark etc.);

(g) the total price including VAT. When more than one item is sold on an invoice, a separate price must be shown for each (the invoice must not show VAT as a separate item).

The customer must sign and date the invoice making a declaration that he is the buyer of the goods at the price shown and additionally state that 'Input tax deduction has not been and will not be claimed by me in respect of goods sold on the invoice'.

The seller must then enter the details of the sale in the stock book (see paragraph 2.22 above) and keep a copy of the sales invoice.

(*Customs & Excise Notice 718, Part II*)

Invoicing requirements specific to the auctioneers' margin scheme

2.25 Special invoicing requirements are required for the AMS. Although these are not contained in the VAT legislation, Customs & Excise Notice 718 details the requirements in Part II, which carries the force of law.

Purchase invoices

2.26 The auctioneer must issue the third party vendor with a statement, or other document which meets the requirements set out in paragraph 2.23 above, showing:

(a) the hammer price of the goods;

(b) the amount of commission due from the vendor; and

(c) the net amount due to the vendor.

This acts as an invoice from the vendor to the auctioneer.

Sales invoices

2.27 The auctioneer will also issue the buyer of the goods with an invoice or similar document showing:

(a) the hammer price of the goods;

(b) any other charges made; and

(c) the amount due from the buyer.

A less detailed invoice can be issued omitting a full description of the goods if it is cross-referenced to another document which fully describes the goods, for example the lot number can be shown on the invoice and cross-referenced to the auction catalogue.

If both scheme and non-scheme supplies are made to a customer, they can be shown on the same invoice provided that the two types of supply are clearly distinguished. In the case of sales invoices, the amount of the selling price, which will form the purchase price for the buyers' margin scheme calculations or global accounting records, must be clearly shown.

Reinvoicing

2.28 If, once the goods have been sold, the buyer decides that he wished to treat the transaction outside the scheme, i.e. paying VAT separately on the hammer price and any additional charges, the auctioneer may reinvoice for the transaction under the normal VAT rules provided that:

(a) the auctioneer can comply with all the relevant VAT regulations relating to the substitute transaction, e.g. issue of a valid VAT invoice;

(b) at the time of the amendment, the auctioneer and buyer hold all the original evidence relating to the transaction;

(c) the auctioneer cancels his first entry in his records and cross-refers to the amended transaction;

2.29 VAT Business by Business

(d) any substitute document (e.g. a VAT invoice) issued to the buyer refers to the original transaction and states that it is cancelled and that the buyer should cancel the original entry in his records.

Completion of the VAT return

2.29 There are special rules for completion of the VAT return where the margin scheme has been used:

Box 1 Output tax on all eligible goods sold in the return period.

Box 6 The full selling price of all eligible goods sold during the period, less any VAT.

Box 7 The purchase price (inclusive of VAT) of eligible goods purchased in the return period.

Records and accounts for the global accounting scheme

2.30 Global accounting records do not have to be kept in any set format, but must be complete, up-to-date and clearly distinguishable from any other records. Records must be kept of purchases and sales as described below and of copies of any workings used to calculate the VAT due. As with the AMS, the record-keeping requirements are not detailed in the law but the relevant section of the public notice carries the force of law. All scheme records must be held for six years. Failure to comply with any of the requirements regarding records renders the taxable person liable for VAT on the full value of his sales.

[*VAT (Special Provisions) Order 1995 (SI 1995 No 1268), Article 13(1); Customs & Excise Notice 718, Part III*].

Purchase records

2.31 When purchasing from a private person, a dealer must verify that the goods are eligible for the global accounting scheme and, if so, issue a purchase invoice setting out:

(a) own name and address;

(b) invoice number;

(c) date of transaction;

(d) description of goods;

(e) total price;

(f) an endorsement stating 'global accounting scheme'.

Details of the purchase should be entered in the global accounting purchase records or summary.

[*Customs & Excise Notice 718, Part III*].

2.32 When purchasing from another dealer, the same procedure applies as that above except that the invoice will be issued by the other dealer, who will certify that it is not a tax invoice. The VAT included in the total price must not be separately identified.

Sales

2.33 When selling eligible goods, the dealer must verify that the purchase conditions above were complied with.

When selling to another dealer, a dealer must issue (and retain a copy of) a sales invoice setting out:

(a) own name and address and VAT registration number;

(b) invoice number;

(c) date of sale;

(d) description of the goods;

(e) total price, including VAT;

(f) an endorsement stating 'global accounting scheme'.

The VAT included in the total price must not be separately identified.

All other sales should be recorded in the usual way (e.g. by using a cash register). Details of the daily gross takings and/or totals of copy invoices should be entered in the global accounting sales records or summary. It is important to be able to distinguish between sales made under the global accounting scheme and other types of transactions at the point of sale.

[*Customs & Excise Notice 718, Part III*].

Purchase and sales summaries

2.34 Summary records must be kept of purchases and sales for each accounting period. These do not have to be kept in any set way but should include the following details from any invoices issued:

(a) invoice number;

(b) date of sale;

(c) description of goods;

2.35 VAT Business by Business

(d) total price.

At the end of each VAT period, the total sales and purchases for that period should be added up and the totals used to calculate the VAT due on global accounting sales, using the method set out below.

Calculation of VAT due

2.35 VAT is chargeable on the 'total profit margin' on goods supplied during a prescribed accounting period. 'Total profit margin' is the amount (if any) by which the total sales exceed total purchases in the VAT period and is regarded as inclusive of VAT.

If total purchases exceed total sales, then there will be a negative margin. No VAT is due and the negative margin may be carried forward and offset against the global accounting margin of the following prescribed accounting period. A negative margin cannot be set off against other VAT due in the same VAT period on transactions outside the global accounting scheme.

If total sales exceed total purchases, then there will be a positive margin. If a positive margin is produced (which is expected in most cases) then VAT is due. This is calculated by multiplying the margin by the VAT fraction (currently 7/47) and should be included within Box 1 of the VAT return.

Copies of all calculations must be kept as part of the global accounting records for six years.

[*VAT (Special Provisions) Order 1995 (SI 1995 No 1268), Article 13*].

Adjustments

2.36 Where purchases are initially included in the global accounting scheme purchase records, but it is later decided to sell the goods outside the scheme (e.g. because they are zero-rated on sale for export outside the Member States), the scheme records should be adjusted accordingly. In the period in which the goods are removed from the scheme, total purchases should be reduced by an amount equal to the purchase value of the excluded goods. There is no set way to apportion values to individual items but it must be fair and reasonable and it must be possible to demonstrate to Customs & Excise how the value was determined.

Any evidence and calculations in relation to the above must be retained with the global accounting scheme records for six years.

[*Customs & Excise Notice 718, Part III, para 35*].

Auctioneers **2.40**

Goods lost or destroyed

2.37 Any loss of goods by breakage, theft or destruction must be adjusted by the deduction of their purchase price in the global accounting scheme purchase records.

[*Customs & Excise Notice 718, Part III, para 40*].

Stock on hand when starting to use the global accounting scheme

2.38 Eligible stock may be treated in either of the following ways:

(a) *incorporated into the scheme and included in the calculations for the first accounting period.* A stock-take or valuation will be required to be undertaken for this purpose. Where possible, eligible stock on hand should be identified separately and its purchase value taken from purchase invoices. Where stock on hand cannot be attributed to original purchase documents, its value should be determined in another way. There is no set way of doing this but Customs & Excise must be satisfied that the method used is fair and reasonable. Evidence of the method used should be retained with other global accounting records for six years.

(b) *not incorporated into the scheme.* If the goods are then sold under the global accounting scheme, there is no 'purchase credit' to set against the sale and VAT will need to be accounted for on the full selling price rather than the profit margin.

[*Customs & Excise Notice 713, Part III, para 37*].

Eligible goods included in the stock records of a previous margin scheme

2.39 Eligible goods already included in the stock records under a previous margin scheme may either be sold under the margin scheme or transferred to the global accounting scheme. In the latter case, the stock must be deleted from the existing margin scheme stock book and cross-referred to and included in the global accounting scheme records.

[*Customs & Excise Notice 713, Part II, para 38*].

Transactions with overseas persons

Acquisitions by UK dealers from dealers in other Member States

2.40 Eligible goods are subject to VAT in other Member States with no liability to acquisition VAT on entry into the UK. The invoice will not show

2.41 VAT Business by Business

VAT as a separate item if the goods are under the global accounting scheme. Therefore, the goods are eligible for onward sale under global accounting.

If the goods are bought from a dealer in another Member State and global accounting is not applied to the purchase, the onward sale cannot be included in the global accounting scheme. The goods will be liable to acquisition VAT on entry to the UK. Provided the other dealer has issued a valid VAT invoice, the VAT can be recovered under the normal VAT rules.

Acquisitions by UK dealers from private individuals in other Member States

2.41 No VAT is due when the goods are brought into the UK and the goods can therefore be sold under the scheme.

Imports by UK dealers from outside the EC

2.42 VAT is due on importation of the goods in the normal way and the global accounting scheme cannot be used to sell imported goods. VAT must be charged on such goods at the full selling price. The VAT paid at importation is deductible subject to the normal rules.

Sales by UK dealers to dealers/private individuals in other Member States

2.43 Such sales are taxable in the UK and there is no liability to pay VAT when they are removed to another Member State. Eligible goods can be included under the scheme.

Exports by UK dealers outside the EC

2.44 Where eligible goods are sold for export, the sale is zero-rated provided that appropriate evidence of exportation is held. Such sales should therefore be dealt with outside the scheme.

Taxable dealers may elect to use the margin scheme or global accounting for the onward sale of goods bought at auction, provided that the goods are eligible for inclusion and the accounting requirements are fulfilled.

Miscellaneous supplies

Auction catalogues

2.45 Where catalogues are provided at auction, it may be possible to zero-rate these sales provided that they meet the relevant requirements (see *Tolley's VAT 1998/99, para 54.17*).

Gifts

2.46 Where an item is received as a gift, it is not eligible for inclusion in any second-hand goods margin scheme and VAT must be accounted for on the full selling price.

If you give an item away for free which could have been sold under the scheme, no VAT is due.

Mechanical breakdown insurance ('MBI') & warranties

2.47 Where MBIs or warranties are provided free of charge, the price of the vehicle shown on the invoice to the customer must be the same as that entered in the auctioneer's stock book. If the MBI or warranty is shown on the invoice, it must be clear that no separate charge has been made.

The VAT liability of any sales of MBIs or warranties will depend on who provides the MBI or warranty and whether any risk covered relates to the auctioneer or the customer. Recent changes to the VAT legislation have changed the treatment of MBI and warranties in certain cases. This is covered in detail in Chapter 17—Insurance.

Other insurance products

2.48 If an auctioneer sells an insurance product, he should also disclose the full price of this on the invoice, plus any fees charged on the product over and above the premium stated on the insurance contract.

Private sales

2.49 The private sale of goods which are not business assets will normally be outside the scope of UK VAT. However, where a sole proprietor transfers an eligible item from his private holdings to his business and he subsequently sells the item through his business, the VAT can be accounted for through the margin scheme.

Chapter 3

Banking and Securities

Introduction

3.1 VAT can represent a considerable burden to businesses in the banking and securities sector, whether through the amount of irrecoverable VAT incurred, or as a result of the necessary compliance. Businesses in this sector will often have to balance compliance with the amount of VAT recovery such compliance would secure. This balancing act is not an absolute science, and will vary from business to business depending upon the profile of activities, and the ability of the systems to provide the necessary information.

VAT exemption

3.2 Under *VATA 1994, 9 Sch, Group 5*, banking and securities transactions are exempted from VAT. Consequently, no VAT is chargeable on these services, but no VAT can be recovered on related expenditure. The complexity created by VAT for the banking and securities sector largely results from determining whether it is possible to secure VAT recovery in respect of any activities. Some activities are subject to VAT at the standard rate (and thus allowing recovery), whilst trading with non-EU counterparts can secure recovery on transactions which otherwise would not give recovery (see 3.71 below). It can also be important to establish the value of the supply for VAT purposes so that the correct figures are put into the calculations for determining the level of VAT recovery (partial exemption calculations). The VAT treatment of activities can also be dictated by the status of the supply i.e. whether the services have been supplied as an agent or a principal. Thus, it is possible to detail the decisions of businesses in the banking and securities sector as follows:

- do the services being supplied fall within the exemption schedule?

- where does the recipient of the service belong for VAT purposes?

- are these services being supplied as agent or a principal?

- what is the value of the supply?

3.3 VAT Business by Business

- will I be able to recover VAT on expenditure in relation to this supply?

3.3 The aim of VAT accounting in the banking and securities sector is thus to identify, to the maximum extent possible, the transactions which enable VAT recovery. The answer will dictate whether it is cost effective to secure the potential VAT recovery and the method used to secure that recovery.

Overview of VAT liability

3.4 The following activities are exempted under *VATA 1994, 9 Sch, Group 5*:

(1) The issue, transfer or receipt of, or any dealing with, money, any security for money or any note or order for the payment of money.

(2) The making of any advance or the granting of any credit.

(3) The provision of the facility of instalment credit finance in a hire-purchase, conditional sale or credit sale agreement for which facility a separate charge is made and disclosed to the recipient of the supply of goods.

(4) The provision of administrative arrangements and documentation and the transfer of title to the goods in connection with the supply described in item 3 if the total consideration therefore is specified in the agreement and does not exceed £10.

(5) The making of arrangements for any transaction comprised in item 1, 2, 3 or 4 or the underwriting of an issue within item 1.

(6) The issue, transfer or receipt, or any dealing with, any security or secondary security being:

    (a) shares, stocks, bonds, notes (other than promissory notes), debentures, debenture stock or shares in an oil royalty; or

    (b) any document relating to money, in any currency, which has been deposited with the issuer or some other person, being a document which recognises an obligation to pay a stated amount to bearer or to order, with or without interest, and being a document by the delivery of which, with or without endorsement, the right to receive that stated amount, with or without interest, is transferable; or

    (c) any bill, note or other obligation of the Treasury or of a Government in any part of the world, being a document by the delivery of which, with or without endorsement, title is transferable, and not being an obligation which is or has been legal tender in any part of the world; or

Banking and Securities 3.5

(d) any letter of allotment or rights, any warrant conferring an option to acquire a security included in this item, any renounceable or scrip certificates, rights coupons, coupons representing dividends or interest on such a security, bond mandates or other documents conferring or containing evidence of title to or rights in respect of such a security; or

(e) units or other documents conferring rights under any trust established for the purpose, or having the effect of providing, for persons having funds available for investment, facilities for the participation by them as beneficiaries under the trust, in any profits or income arising from the acquisition, holding, management or disposal of any property whatsoever.

(7) The making of arrangements for, or the underwriting of, any transaction within item 6.

(8) The operation of any current, deposit or savings account.

(9) The management of an authorised unit trust scheme or of a trust-based scheme by the operator of the scheme.

Notes

(1) Item 1 does not include anything included in item 6.

(2) This Group does not include the supply of a coin or a banknote as a collectors' piece or as an investment article.

(3) Item 2 includes the supply of credit by a person, in connection with a supply of goods or services by him, for which a separate charge is made and disclosed to the recipient of the supply of goods or services.

(4) This Group includes any supply by a person carrying on a credit card, charge card or similar payment card operation made in connection with that operation to a person who accepts the card used in the operation when presented to him in payment for goods or services.

(5) Item 7 includes the introduction to a person effecting transactions in securities or secondary securities within item 6 of a person seeking to acquire or dispose of such securities.

(6) In item 9—

(a) 'authorised unit trust scheme' and 'operator' have the same meanings as in section 207(1) of the Financial Services Act 1986;

(b) 'trust based scheme' has the same meaning as in regulation 2(1)(b) of the Financial Services Act 1986 (Single Property Schemes)(Exemption) Regulations 1989.

3.5 Supplies which do not fall within the finance exemption schedule will be subject to VAT at the standard rate (or, of course, the zero rate).

3.6 VAT Business by Business

However, the activities exempted by *Group 5* are subject to further categorisation depending upon the place of belonging of the recipient of the supply (see paragraph 3.6 below). This categorisation is important as it will determine whether recovery of related VAT is possible. In general terms, where the recipient of the supply is within the UK, the supply will be exempt from VAT. Where the recipient of the supply is a taxable person who belongs within the European Union ('EU'), the supply will be outside the scope of UK VAT ('OS'), but usually with no recovery of related VAT. However, supplies to a person belonging outside the EU, will be outside the scope of UK VAT, but with recovery of related VAT ('OSR'). In order to secure maximum tax recovery, it will be necessary at all times to identify the place of belonging of the recipient of the service in order to maximise this OSR income.

3.6 Under *VATA 1994, s 9(2)* a person belongs where:

- he (the supplier) has his business establishment, or some other fixed establishment from which the service is supplied;

- if there is more than one business establishment, the business establishment most closely associated with the service being supplied; or

- if there is no business or fixed establishment, the usual place of residence.

For VAT purposes, the territory of the UK includes the Isle of Man. The Channel Islands are not in the EU.

3.7 These rules are often quite difficult to implement for businesses in the banking and securities sector. Firstly, even if the identity of the recipient is known, the computer systems may not store the required information to easily record whether this is an OSR supply, especially where there are large numbers of transactions involved. Also, in some cases because of the way particular markets operate, the counterparty may not be identified or indeed identifiable. For this purpose, by concession, Customs have allowed 'easement rules' to be used when determining the place of supply of securities transactions. In these circumstances, the counterparty is deemed to 'belong':

- where the market is, upon which the sale is transacted;

- if the above is not known, where the security is listed;

- finally, if neither of the above are known, the place where the final broker belongs.

3.8 It is important that these rules are only used where the place of belonging of the recipient is not known, and they must be used in strict descending order.

Valuation of the supply

3.9 Whilst output VAT need not be declared on any of the transactions, their value is still important as it may be used in partial exemption calculations, and is also needed for completion of statistical boxes within the VAT return. It is also important to note, that whilst in some cases, such as commission, the value will be obvious, in other cases the value will not necessarily correspond with the value put into the balance sheet or profit and loss account and thus separate systems may be necessary for tracking the values.

Time of supply

3.10 The normal tax point rules will apply to standard-rated income *(see Tolley's VAT 1998/99, paragraphs 64.25 and 64.26)*. However, as no tax is due on the exempt, OS or OSR supplies, there is no tax point as such, although it remains necessary to identify the time of supply for including the income within the partial exemption calculations. Thus, the basic rule of performance or receipt of cash will apply. In the case of continuous supplies of services, as no tax invoice can be raised, the time of supply will be when the cash is received. For imported services (see 3.106 to 3.109 below), the time at which the reverse charge should be calculated is when payment is made or, if the charges are between connected parties, the time of supply will be when the books of account are posted with an amount due under an intercompany account, with an offsetting entry by the other party to the transaction.

Specific liability of particular transactions

3.11 The intention of this section is to consider specific transactions undertaken in the banking and securities world. Each activity covered will include details of VAT liability, and where necessary the value for VAT purposes. This information is also given in chart form at Appendix 1.

Dealing in money

3.12 The simple activity of exchanging cash is not a supply for VAT purposes unless the money is exchanged above face value. In normal circumstances, the cash is simply exchanged for another amount of cash and, thus, there would only be a supply if a fee was charged for the transaction or if the money were exchanged at a price over and above the relevant values of the money. If this is the case, the value will only be the difference between

3.13 VAT Business by Business

face value and the amount charged whether this is reflected in a fee or a profit or turn.

3.13 Where there is a value above the face value, and therefore a supply, the VAT liability will be exempt from VAT where the recipient belongs in the UK or where the recipient is a private individual within the EU. The supply will be outside the scope where a business recipient belongs within the EU and OSR where the recipient belongs outside the EU.

Foreign exchange

3.14 As for cash, the simple swapping of one currency for another has not been regarded by Customs & Excise as a supply for VAT purposes, and at the time of writing this is still, in practical terms, the case. However, there have been various challenges to this, the latest being the case of *First National Bank of Chicago, [1995] VATDR 306 (13556)*.

3.15 Under the current rules, if one currency is simply swapped for another at market rate, there is no supply for VAT purposes. Hence, foreign exchange is outside the scope of VAT wherever the recipient of the services belongs. Consequently, VAT relating to foreign exchange is, in principle, not recoverable in any circumstances (but see 3.18 below). However, Customs have allowed businesses to treat foreign exchange activities which are support functions (e.g. for hedging purposes where a currency exposure exists) as, at least in part, allowing some recovery. See paragraphs 3.94 and 3.95 below which detail how foreign exchange transactions are treated within partial exemption calculations.

3.16 If a supply has resulted because the currency is being exchanged at above market value, or if indeed foreign exchange is confirmed as a supply following the *First National Bank of Chicago* tribunal case, the supply to a person belonging within the UK will be exempt from VAT as it will to a private individual elsewhere in the EU. The supply to a business person belonging within the EU is OS and a supply to a person belonging outside the EU is OSR.

3.17 However, if foreign exchange does become a supply, new rules will have to be determined for valuation. At the time of writing, this point was still under consideration and indeed the Tribunal Chairman in the *First National Bank of Chicago* case, having ruled that foreign exchange is a supply, directed the parties to give consideration as to what the quantum of that supply might be. However, an appeal has been made to the High Court and a reference has been made to the European Court of Justice, so an early resolution of the matter is unlikely.

3.18 Pending the outcome of the *First National Bank of Chicago* case, some businesses have submitted claims on the basis of this tribunal case commensurate with the level of their non-EU business in foreign exchange.

Thus, it may well be appropriate for businesses which have not already submitted claims to do so, especially in view of the introduction of the three-year rule for input tax recovery. In the meantime, however, businesses should agree a method of recovery either on the old basis (supportive—see paragraph 3.15 above) with a view to making eventual claims for the input tax unclaimed pending the outcome of the case, or on the new basis (a supply) with the realisation that, in the latter case, this VAT may have to be paid back to Customs & Excise should they be successful.

'Securities for money'

3.19 These instruments are referred to by Customs & Excise as securities for money, and for VAT purposes their treatment was distinct from securities such as stocks, bonds etc. (see paragraphs 3.37 to 3.40 below). Historically, there was only a supply if the instrument was traded for more than face value. As this was rarely the case, these instruments usually being traded below par, there was no supply for VAT purposes. Customs have accepted since 1995 (see Business Brief 25/95, dated 20 November 1995) that the value for VAT purposes is the price paid by the drawer and also by any subsequent purchaser (except for redemption). The issue of a security for money is an exempt supply when issued, for a consideration, as surety, guarantee or indemnity provided that it is secondary to a primary contract (not warranties or repair/servicing contracts). Specifically, this applies to contracts of security issued by guarantors and sureties obliging the guarantor to indemnify a party to the primary contract for loss arising from failure or default of the other party to fulfil obligations.

3.20 Many businesses have submitted claims for past years in relation to the amount of non-EU sales of securities, which had previously been regarded as securities for money, and hence non-EU sales had not secured recovery. Any businesses which have not made claims should still do so if appropriate, but the level of any such claim may be affected by the three-year restriction imposed by Customs.

3.21 Securities for money include bills of exchange, trading coupons, eurocurrency paper, some euronotes, local authority bills, certain promissory notes and paper negotiable for cash.

Broking or arranging dealings in money, foreign exchange or securities for money

3.22 Where a broker arranges any of the above transactions, the liability of the commission will depend upon the place of belonging of the broker's client. Consequently, if the client belongs within the UK or is a private individual in the EU, the commission will be exempt from VAT. If the client is a business client belonging in the EU, the commission will be OS and if the client belongs outside the EU, the commission will be OSR.

3.23 VAT Business by Business

3.23 If the underlying principal transaction is a supply under the valuation rules, then the rule at paragraph 3.22 above will still apply, but there are also other reliefs which allow recovery of VAT relating to commission earned on a principal supply which is itself OSR even though the commission is earned from someone belonging within the UK or EU. These rules will not be detailed here, but see paragraphs 3.41 to 3.42 below which detail the VAT treatment of commission for dealing in securities such as shares, bonds etc. Where there is an underlying value for dealing with money, for foreign exchange transactions or bills of exchange, promissory notes etc., the chart at Appendix 1 will apply to broker's commission. If there is no underlying supply, e.g. foreign exchange, only the main rule explained at paragraph 3.22 can be used to decide the liability of the commission.

Account operations

3.24 Any charges for operating bank accounts are exempted by *VATA 1994, 9 Sch, Group 5, Item 8*. Charges will be exempt when made to a person belonging within the UK and to a private individual in the EU, OS to other EU clients and OSR to non-EU clients.

Deposits, loans and overdrafts

3.25 Deposits, loans and overdrafts are exempt from VAT under *VATA 1994, 9 Sch, Group 5, Item 2* when supplied to a customer within the UK, OS to a customer within the EU and OSR to a person belonging outside the EU, the value of the supply being the interest.

3.26 Fees for arranging a loan, deposit etc., will be exempt from VAT under *VATA 1994, 9 Sch, Group 5, Item 4* when supplied to a person within the UK and a private individual in the EU, OS when supplied to a business person belonging within the EU and OSR to a person belonging outside the EU. It is important to note that for valuation purposes any expenses of the lender which are recharged, e.g. solicitor's fees, will be regarded as part of the consideration for VAT purposes.

3.27 Where syndicated loans are put in place, the VAT liability of the interest received or fees charged by the participating banks will depend on the contractual relationship with the leading bank or the client.

3.28 If the contractual relationship for a participating bank is with the lead bank, the VAT liability will depend upon the place of belonging of the lead bank, e.g. interest received by the participating bank will be exempt if the lead bank is in the UK. If, however, the contractual relationship is directly with the client, the VAT liability will depend upon the place of belonging of the client. As usual, the liability decision will be UK and EU private—exempt, EU business—OS and non-EU—OSR. The value will be the interest, fees and costs received.

Hire purchase and leasing

3.29 Where possession of the goods passes, or there is an option for the goods to be purchased, the supply, whether by hire purchase or by conditional or credit sale, is one of goods for VAT purposes and taxed at the standard rate (if supplied in the UK). VAT is due when the goods are removed, i.e. at the outset of the contract (the normal tax point rules for supplies of goods will apply). If no finance house is involved in the transaction, any credit charge separately disclosed to the customer is exempt. If no separate credit charge is made, there is a single, standard-rated supply of goods.

3.30 Where a finance house is interposed between the supplier of the goods and the customer, the supplier sells the goods to the finance house and the finance house sells them on to the customer. Both legs of this transaction will be subject to VAT. If the finance house discloses the credit charge, it will be exempt from VAT as detailed in paragraph 3.29 above.

3.31 The time of supply for a separately disclosed credit charge is each time a payment is received. It is possible to agree with Customs & Excise that the time of the exempt supply is the same as for the goods, i.e. at the outset of the contract. Such an agreement has to be made in writing.

3.32 If the purchaser of the goods is outside the UK, the movement of the goods will be an export, or despatch, from the UK and thus zero-rated (provided the necessary evidence is obtained). The credit charge will be OS to a business in the EU, and OSR to a person outside the EU.

3.33 The hire of goods, where no transfer of possession of any goods is contemplated, is a supply of services, whether an operational or finance lease is entered into. VAT on all related costs is recoverable, including that on cars from 1 August 1995.

3.34 The place of supply rules for leasing are complex and will depend on the nature of the item being leased. For items other than means of transport, the place of supply will be where the recipient of the supply belongs. Thus, a French business lessee will not have to pay UK VAT, but will have to operate the reverse charge. To summarise, if the lessee is in the UK or is a private individual in the EU, UK VAT will be due on each lease instalment. If the lessee belongs outside the EU, or is a business in the EU, the leasing charges will be OSR.

3.35 If the lease concerns the means of transport, e.g. a car, further advice should be taken as the above rules do not necessarily apply.

3.36 The rules detailed here for hire purchase and leasing apply only in the UK. Other Member States in the EU may apply VAT differently as a result of different interpretation of the nature of the supplies being made. Therefore, if cross-border transactions are being undertaken it is important to take advice on the VAT treatment in the other country.

3.37   VAT Business by Business

Securities

3.37   It is particularly important, when considering the VAT treatment of securities transactions, to be sure whether one is acting as principal or agent. This may be clear in many circumstances, but it can be important to look at the facts of a particular transaction to determine whether it is a principal or agency transaction. For example, are the securities taken onto the books; is any risk taken; what regulatory authorisation is necessary for undertaking the deal?

3.38   Where one is acting as principal, the issue, transfer or any dealing in securities is exempt from VAT under *VATA 1994, 9 Sch, Group 5, Item 6*. Included within this item are all stocks, shares, units, bonds, warrants, commercial paper, certificates of deposit, treasury bills, etc. (see paragraph 3.4 above for the full listing).

3.39   The sale or issue of a security to a person belonging within the UK, or to a private individual in the EU, is exempt from VAT. The sale to a business person belonging within the EU is OS and the sale to a person belonging outside the EU is OSR.

3.40   In principal transactions, the value for VAT is the full selling price. Where an intermediary acts as a principal (e.g. where error deals result in the securities being acquired and then sold by the intermediary), the selling price will include commission as part of the overall value.

Stockbroking or acting as intermediary for securities transactions

3.41   The service of broking, or acting as intermediary (making arrangements) for a principal transaction to take place in securities, is exempted by *VATA 1994, 9 Sch, Group 5, Item 7*.

3.42   The liability decisions for broking are particularly complex as more than one set of rules is applicable. The basic rule is the usual rule, i.e. where the client belongs. Thus, if the broker's client belongs in the UK or is a private individual within the EU, the commission is exempt. If a business client belongs within the EU the commission is OS, and outside the EU the commission will be OSR. However, it is also possible under the *Value Added Tax (Input Tax) (Specified Supplies) Order 1992 (SI 1992 No 2123)* to treat commissions as exempt with the right of recovery where the underlying principal transaction involves a sale of securities to a person belonging outside the EU. Consequently, it is necessary to be able to track the principal transaction, even if the client belongs within the UK or EU, as the underlying principal transaction may give recovery of VAT relating to the commission earned. Please see the chart at Appendix 1 which details this liability.

Underwriting

3.43 The service of underwriting a new issue of securities is exempted by *VATA 1994, 9 Sch, Group 5, Item 7*. Underwriting fees will be exempt if received from an issuer within the UK, OS when received from an issuer within the EU, and OSR from an issuer belonging outside the EU.

3.44 Where an underwriter guarantees the issue by subscribing, there is a purchase of securities with an onward sale. In these circumstances, this is regarded as a principal transaction and no separate fee needs to be accounted for, i.e. any fee element is rolled up in the eventual selling price. The VAT treatment will, thus, be as for securities dealing (see paragraphs 3.37 to 3.40 above). Of course, if there is a mixture of subscription and underwriting, the separate underwriting fee will not be rolled up in the sale of the securities.

Safe custody services

3.45 It is important to be aware of the exact service being supplied as exemption may not always apply. Safe custody services, i.e. purely physical services of safe-keeping, will always be standard-rated regardless of where the recipient belongs (*VATA 1994, 5 Sch 5*). However, where the service of safe-keeping amounts to more than just physical safe-keeping, the exemption may well apply. If a global service is supplied which includes dividend collection, dealing with scrip and bonus issues, settlement etc., the exemption will apply. In these circumstances, any incidental physical safe-keeping will also be exempt. The global custody service will be OS to a business client within the EU, and OSR to a client belonging outside the EU.

Corporate finance and mergers/acquisitions

3.46 When involved in a corporate finance deal, it is important to be clear as to the type of service being provided and whether it is an advisory service or whether it falls within the finance exemption as making arrangements for a share transaction (*VATA 1994, 9 Sch, Group 5, Item 7*). For example, a merchant bank which co-ordinates and negotiates the flotation of a company will be regarded as having arranged the flotation, i.e. an issue of shares, and its fee for so doing will be exempt. If, however, the bank simply advises on the most appropriate method of raising capital, but does not actually get involved in raising that capital, the supply will be taxable for VAT purposes.

3.47 A corporate finance deal will only fall within the exemption if the business can be said to be bringing parties to the share transactions together, i.e. acting as a middleman. This includes:

- co-ordinating negotiations;

- co-ordinating and providing a central point or other advisers or services necessary to the deal;

3.48 VAT Business by Business

- dealing with any regulatory authorities.

3.48 The fee structure must also be considered, as different fees charged to the same client may have different VAT liabilities. A success fee, paid only when a deal is successfully negotiated or transacted, will fall within the exemption, as will a stage or periodic fee for acting in a negotiation/co-ordination capacity if there is a clear objective under the agreement to issue, sell or buy securities. However, if a client initially asks for advice on the best course of action and has not given a clear mandate for some form of share transaction from the outset and a fee is charged for that work, the supply will be taxable.

3.49 Where fees are paid for transactions which are aborted, the VAT liability will depend upon the liability of the fee had the transaction been finalised. For example, where the activity clearly involved negotiation and co-ordination, exemption is likely to apply. If, however, it was mainly advisory work for which a separate fee would always have been contemplated under the agreements, it is likely to be taxable.

3.50 It is important to remember that it is only the middleman who arranges the transaction in shares who can exempt his fees. Legal advisers, reporting accountants, printers, etc. will not be arranging the transaction and will not be able to exempt the services. However, the corporate finance activities provided by accountants may increasingly extend to acting as middlemen and they may, therefore, have a mixture of exempt 'making arrangements' and taxable advice.

3.51 Where corporate finance services are supplied to overseas clients, the VAT liability will again depend on whether advisory or arrangement fees are being supplied. Advisory services will remain standard-rated when supplied to a private individual in the EU and OSR when supplied to a business person in the EU and to a person belonging outside the EU, and VAT on related costs will be fully recoverable. In contrast, arrangement services will either be exempt or OS when supplied within the EU and, therefore, will not allow recovery of related input tax. If supplied outside the EU, the related input tax will be recoverable.

Investment management

3.52 Investment management services are not exempted except to the extent that the management is of an authorised unit trust or a single property trust scheme (*VATA 1994, 9 Sch, Group 5, Item 9*). From 24 March 1997 management of an open-ended investment company ('OEIC') by the authorised corporate director is also exempt under *VATA 1994, 9 Sch, Group 5, Item 10*. Consequently, any other investment management fees relating to any other form of investment will be standard-rated when received from a person within the UK, or from a private individual within the EU. If the client is a business within the EU, the services will be OSR, as will investment management provided to a person belonging outside the EU (whether private or business).

3.53 Fees linked to the funds under management will be standard-rated, but if transaction fees are charged, e.g. if a broking fee is charged each time an investment is bought or sold, the exemption detailed at paragraph 3.38 above may apply. Where broking charges are passed on as disbursements or where additional fees are charged which are specific to a transaction, exemption can apply under *VATA 1994, 9 Sch, Group 5, Item 7*, as the 'making of arrangements'. However, the documentation must support this interpretation and it is recommended that if this fee structure is to be put in place, it is agreed with the local VAT officer in advance to avoid questions and difficulties in the future.

3.54 As mentioned above, investment management of authorised unit trusts and single property trusts is exempt from VAT. In practice, it is only possible to receive exempt fees in relation to these activities as only UK unit trusts, single property trusts and authorised corporate directors for UK OEICs are authorised.

3.55 PEP management can involve exemption and standard-rating of fees. Initial charges will be exempt where the PEP is 'self select'. However, the periodic charges are more akin to portfolio management and will be subject to VAT. There is an agreement on the VAT liability of PEP-related charges between Customs & Excise and AUTIF, for details of which see paragraph 3.112 below.

Foreign currency options

3.56 These options are similar to LIFFE options (see paragraph 3.62 below), although they are not as uniform. The premium for a currency option is exempt under *VATA 1994, 9 Sch, Group 5, Item 1*, although the exercise of the option itself is outside the scope of VAT.

3.57 Fees for forward foreign exchange contracts are also exempt under *VATA 1994, 9 Sch, Item 1*. In both cases the options are OSR when the purchaser belongs outside the EU.

Interest rate swaps, forward rate agreements, caps, collars and floors

3.58 Interest rate swaps are regarded by Customs as an exempt supply within the provisions of *VATA 1994, 9 Sch, Group 5*, but OS when supplied to a business person belonging within the EU, and OSR to a person belonging outside the EU. A supply only crystallises, however, to the extent that any money changes hands. Settlement of such a hedging mechanism will normally be by setting off the notional fixed and floating rates of interest and the net payment made from one party to the other will be the value for VAT purposes (provided the agreement contemplates netting-off).

3.59 VAT Business by Business

3.59 Where differential stage payments of interest arise, e.g. six-monthly against yearly payments, gross payments will arise and each payment will be a supply, i.e. the recipient of the payment, whichever party that may be, will have made a supply for VAT purposes, the liability of which will be determined by the place of belonging of the payer—exempt to recipients in the UK and to private EU individuals, OS to businesses elsewhere in the EU and OSR outside the EU.

3.60 Within a tripartite supply, significant exempt, OS or OSR supplies may be generated for a party such as an investment bank which is the intermediary for two other bodies as a result of the various payments made.

3.61 Forward rate agreements are treated on the same basis as interest rate swaps, i.e. the value of the supply is the money changing hands. For caps, collars and floors, the premium or guarantee charge is the income for VAT purposes.

LIFFE

3.62 LIFFE contracts are exempt from VAT and the value for VAT purposes is the 'turn' or 'commission' charged by the LIFFE member to his client. There is no supply by the client to the member in a closed-out transaction. When short-term contracts run to maturity, there is no further supply. However, if a long-term contract, in a gilt or bond transaction, runs to maturity, there is a further supply valued at the price agreed when the contract was entered into.

3.63 LIFFE options are also exempt and, in the case of equity options, there will be a further supply of a security when the option is exercised. There are also rules applying to 'locals' and further advice should be taken on this or, indeed, if there is an intention to become greatly involved in dealing on the LIFFE market.

3.64 It is important to note that LIFFE is *not* covered by the *Value Added Tax Terminal Markets Order (SI 1973 No 173)*. Zero-rating is *not* available from this legislation for LIFFE trading, which is largely exempt.

Non-exempt activities

3.65 Most activities of businesses in the banking and securities sector will be exempt from VAT, or at least will not be subject to VAT at the standard rate. However, some activities are not exempted and are subject to the VAT at the standard rate, and these must be identified in order to ensure that VAT is accounted for wherever appropriate. For the banking and securities sector the taxable activities are likely to include:

- advisory and research services (see paragraphs 3.67 to 3.70 below);

- fund management services (excluding unit trust management);
- management and administrative services;
- sale of assets such as furniture, plant and equipment;
- equipment leasing;
- certain staff benefits;
- freehold sales of most new or partly-completed commercial buildings, or income from properties on which the option to tax has been exercised;
- sales of goods under hire purchase;
- condition of sale or credit sale agreements;
- supplies of staff;
- transactions involving commodities, unless covered by the Terminal Markets Order;
- safe custody services.

3.66 VAT must be added to the supply of these goods or services, but of course related VAT will be recoverable. However, often these are only a small element of the total business and are often confined to one identifiable profit centre. Such income will, therefore, often not increase VAT recovery to any significant degree.

Advice and research

3.67 Advisory services will always be standard-rated, but see paragraph 3.46 above on corporate finance, as it is important to be aware of when advisory services become the making of arrangements for a financial transaction.

3.68 Advice supplied to a person belonging within the UK and to a private individual within the EU is standard-rated. Advice to a business belonging within the EU or to a person belonging outside the EU is OSR.

3.69 If a charge is made for research services, the supply will be standard-rated and the same liability decisions will apply as for advice at paragraph 3.68 above.

3.70 VAT Business by Business

3.70 Zero-rated supplies may also arise where any goods are exported or, for example, where the supplies are of means of transport (including in specified cases, the leasing or chartering of commercial ships or aircraft), for supplies of gold between central banks or between a central bank and a member of the London Gold Market, and also for the issue of bank notes. Also included are transactions involving commodities which are dealt with on specific UK terminal markets. Many of these supplies can be zero-rated, but it is not intended to consider commodity dealing in any more detail in this chapter.

Partial exemption

3.71 Businesses are only able to recover VAT on expenditure which relates to specified income. Such income is often referred to as 'taxable income' and for partial exemption purposes this should be analysed as:

- standard-rated income;

- reduced rate income (currently 5%);

- zero-rated income; and

- income which is outside the scope of VAT, but in relation to which there is a specific right of recovery under *VATA 1994, s 26(2)(c)*. (Specifically, these are services specified under the *Value Added Tax (Input Tax) (Specified Supplies) Order 1992 (SI 1992 No 3123)*. This right of recovery is given under the *EC Sixth Directive, Article 17(3)(b)(c)*.)

3.72 Where any reference is made to 'taxable' income in this chapter, it will include all of the above categories of income except where specifically defined. It is imperative that a business analyses, as far as is administratively feasible, all income which gives rise to a right of deduction.

Income which is taxable

3.73 In practice, the core activities of any bank or securities house will not be subject to VAT at the standard rate and nor, indeed, be zero-rated. Consequently, the right to deduction will centre around exempt services which are specified as giving a right of deduction, i.e. services which are supplied to a person belonging outside the EU or which involve arranging a supply which takes place outside the EU.

3.74 The analysis and assessment of the extent of this income will dictate the possible level of recovery and as a result the amount of administrative effort which is put into the related recovery achieved. It could be the case that a more complicated method may produce more input tax recovery, but the amount of this extra recovery may not justify the administrative procedures required. Consequently, this balancing act is something which must be considered in the early stages of devising the partial exemption method.

Income which is exempt

3.75 Income which is exempt from VAT, or which is outside the scope of VAT, will not generally carry a right of recovery of related input VAT. In this chapter such income will be referred to collectively as 'exempt' income.

Direct attribution

3.76 Every method of partial exemption must involve the initial steps of direct attribution. These steps are dictated by the *VAT Regulations 1995 (SI 1995 No 2518), reg 101(2)*. In essence, any VAT which is incurred on a specific item of expenditure or on an importation of goods, and which can be related to a particular supply, must be attributed to that supply and recovered according to the VAT liability of that supply. If the supply in question does not carry a right of recovery, for example because it is exempt or because it does not carry a specified right of recovery, then VAT on the item of expenditure will not be recoverable at all. If, however, the supply is one which is taxable for VAT purposes, the VAT on that item of expenditure will be fully recoverable. To give examples, if a legal fee is incurred which relates to the granting of a loan to a private individual in the UK, the VAT on that legal fee will relate to an exempt supply which carries no right of deduction and the VAT will not be recoverable. Conversely, if the same loan was made to a private individual outside the EU, for example in Jersey, the supply would carry a right of deduction under the *VAT (Input Tax) (Specified Supplies) Order 1992 (SI 1992 No 3123), Article 3(a)*. No partial exemption method can, or will, be authorised by Customs & Excise which does not involve these steps of direct attribution and the extent to which businesses have to directly attribute will depend upon whether their business involves mainly overhead expenditure rather than expenditure in relation to specific supplies.

3.77 A business which has directly attributed its VAT to the fullest extent possible will have a rump or residual amount of VAT remaining which will consist of those costs which relate to both 'taxable' and 'exempt' income, i.e. which does not relate to any specific supply made by the business. Consequently, a method has to be devised for calculating how much of this rump, pot or pool of VAT can be recovered. This is where judgment needs to be exercised upon the complexity or otherwise of a method. Any method of calculating how much of the pot is recoverable must be fair and reasonable, but it must reflect the use to which the input tax is put, i.e. input tax is only recoverable to the extent that it is used in making taxable supplies. This is the core philosophy behind partial exemption methods and it should be borne in mind at all times when devising a method so that any steps taken, or calculations used, can be justified on the basis that they do reflect the use to which the input tax is put.

3.78 VAT Business by Business

Methods of calculation

3.78 A standard method of calculation exists within the regulations which a business can use without prior approval from Customs & Excise. However, Customs & Excise rarely accept that the standard method is appropriate for businesses within the financial services sector and will insist upon a different method being used. This is usually done through negotiation, but Customs also have the power to direct the use of a different method under *VAT Regulations 1995 (SI 1995 No 2518), reg 102*. This regulation also allows businesses to apply for a special method.

3.79 The standard method is a global pro rata method which, once direct attribution has been carried out, will arrive at a percentage recovery of input tax based on the value of taxable supplies (in this case, standard, reduced or zero-rated) as a proportion of all supplies made. When using a values pro rata calculation of this nature, various items of income should be left out of the calculations as they are regarded as incidental or distortive. These include:

- income from sales of capital assets;

- incidental land transactions, whether exempt, zero-rated or standard-rated, and incidental financial services;

- the value of any reverse-charged items (see paragraph 3.106 below).

3.80 In addition, Customs & Excise consider that the standard method does not contemplate the inclusion of income which gives a right to deduction, but which is not standard, reduced or zero-rated for VAT purposes, within the numerator of the calculations. Thus, this method would not be fair for businesses which have considerable OSR income. It is possible to agree a global pro rata calculation which includes OSR income which carries a right to deduction. However, such a method would be regarded as a special method and would need to be agreed in writing with Customs in advance of being used. It is worth noting that Customs are unwilling to accept that a global pro rata calculation based on value of income is appropriate for any business in the banking and securities sector. See, however, the decision in *Liverpool School of Performing Arts, [1998] STC 274*.

3.81 Notwithstanding the position of Customs & Excise, the operation of this method is not suited to businesses which have different activities all of which bear different values of income which may distort the results. For example, a business which acts as principal and agent in dealing and securities will find that agency commissions will be swamped by the value of the sales of securities as principal. However, the amount of effort put into the transactions may be identical and, thus, using income values would be unlikely to give a fair result. Consequently, one would not seek to use a method which did not cater for distortions in value.

3.82 Further, if a business is sectored into profit or cost centres for management information purposes, Customs are extremely unlikely to agree to a global pro rata calculation being used. Consequently, it would be necessary to consider the use of an alternative method. Again, it is worth reiterating that a special method is anything other than the standard method, and must reflect the use of the input tax.

3.83 Anything other than a single, simple pro rata calculation will involve the allocation of VAT to different sectors within the business. The number of sectors will normally be dictated by the structure of the business itself and could be cost centres, profit centres, legal entities, individual business lines within profit centres or activity centres. The method used to allocate VAT to these different sectors is for the business to decide and should reflect the use these different sectors make of the input tax. If a business already allocates costs on a management accounting basis, or indeed on any other basis, the VAT can often follow that basis. However, if this does not reflect the use of the input tax, for example because other issues dictate the allocation of costs within a business, it is possible to agree a different basis of allocation. Some methods of allocation will involve allocating the VAT by, for example, the management accounts, the number of staff within the different sectors, the square footage occupied by the activity, or indeed the number of transactions generated by that activity. In fact, any method of allocation can be used or devised by the business which is capable of valuation by Customs & Excise and which can be fairly said to represent the use of the input tax by those different activities. An example of different allocations is given below:

(1) VAT on global/head office costs = £1,500,000

(2) This must be allocated across three profit centres (i.e. fund management, corporate finance and equities trading).

(3) This could be allocated on the basis of floor space, head count or the number of transactions.

(4) The chart below calculates the percentage of VAT which would be allocated to each profit centre using the three different bases of allocation.

	Floor Space	%	Head Count	%	Transaction Count	%
Fund Management	1,636	17.5	220	25.6	4,210	1
Corporate Finance	3,560	38	310	36.2	7,254	1.8
Equities	4,150	44.5	327	38.2	384,210	97.2
Total	9,346		857		395,674	

3.84 VAT Business by Business

(5) The chart below illustrates how much of the £1.5 million VAT would be allocated to each profit centre by using each of the bases of allocation.

	Floor Space %	VAT allocated	Head Count %	VAT allocated	Transaction Count %	VAT allocated
Fund Management	17.5	262,500	25.6	384,000	1	15,000
Corporate Finance	38	570,000	36.2	543,000	1.8	27,000
Equities	44.5	667,500	38.2	573,000	97.2	1,458,000
		1,500,000		1,500,000		1,500,000

3.84 Once VAT has been allocated to different sectors, legal entities or activities etc., it is necessary to determine what method is used to calculate how much of this allocated VAT can be recovered. Again, the method used should reflect the use to which the input tax is put, but it is possible to use different methods of calculation within each sector. For example, one sector may find that an income values pro rata calculation is appropriate, whilst another sector may use the number of transactions. Yet another may use a headcount method if specific individuals are involved in specific activities which give a right of deduction or otherwise, or if it is possible to accurately measure time spent on taxable activities.

3.85 Devising such a method can be complicated and also may be difficult if sufficient information is not available to test whether the method used is, in fact, the optimum method. Often, a method is devised on 'gut feel' and experience, rather than mathematical certainty.

3.86 Using the example given above for equity trading, it is necessary to determine a figure for input VAT used by the profit centre. If we assume that it has already directly incurred VAT of £2,000,000 and that the basis of allocation which is most appropriate for the business is head count, there is an additional figure of £573,000 from the global head office allocation, giving a total of £2,573,000 VAT which has to be pro-rated as it does not relate to one specific supply (i.e. it is all residual VAT).

3.87 Assuming the different methods of calculation available for equities trading are:

(a) value of transactions (assuming distortions do not arise);

(b) volume of transactions;

(c) head count (it is possible to identify the time spent by individuals on OSR activities).

	Value	Volume	Head Count
Exempt/OS	21,498,260	121,810	198
OSR	11,185,090	262,400	129
Total	32,683,350	384,210	327
Percentage Recovery (OSR Total × 100)	34.22	68.29	39.45
VAT Recovered from £2,573,000	880,480	1,757,101	1,015,048

3.88 Mathematically, the best result is the transaction count. However, it is necessary to determine whether the result is distorted in any way, whether the information used is valid, whether it fairly reflects use of the input tax, and indeed whether future changes are likely to impact unfavourably on the result.

3.89 Once a business has determined the method that it wishes to use, it should write to Customs & Excise outlining the method. Customs & Excise may wish to visit to discuss the proposals in more detail, but they will eventually respond in writing giving full details of the method to be used and their requirements surrounding that method. This will be by way of a formal letter which has to be signed and returned to Customs for their records. This method, once agreed, is regarded as a contract and should be adhered to by both parties until such time as it is renegotiated. Any business changes, e.g. a new line of business being added, must be notified to Customs & Excise so that the method can be amended. As businesses change frequently and also very rapidly, methods are now often drafted in such a way as to allow elements to be changed and updated without altering the method overall. However, it is worth reiterating that the method, once agreed and signed by both parties, is a contract and must be adhered to. In the case of *Fidelity International Management Holdings Ltd (7323)*, Customs & Excise had agreed a method which actually gave favourable recovery to Fidelity. However, as Customs & Excise were bound by the terms of the method, they had to allow the recovery and could only change the method prospectively.

3.90 A method need not be used for any specific period of time before it can be changed, but Customs & Excise are unlikely to agree to a method being changed on a quarterly basis unless, of course, the underlying business is changing at this pace. Even so, Customs would expect the core method to remain the same with only variations for changes in business.

3.91 VAT Business by Business

3.91 When using a special method, any pro rata calculations undertaken should be to two decimal places.

3.92 As already mentioned at paragraph 3.79 above, distortive and incidental income should be left out of any values pro rata calculations. In the case of banking and securities, it is often impossible to gain Customs' acceptance that financial transactions are incidental or distortive, but in the case of some treasury transactions, such as sales of certificates of deposit which have been held for liquidity purposes, this may, in fact, be the case and such income should still be left out of the calculations if a values method is used.

3.93 Regulations exist for allowing businesses which are, in the main, fully taxable, but which have a minor exempt activity, to be treated as fully taxable by ignoring this income, or alternatively, where the exempt input tax identified within a partial exemption calculation is below certain de minimis limits, to allow for recovery. These rules will not, in general, apply to the banking and securities sectors because the core activities are exempt. However, in exceptional circumstances, the de minimis rules under the *VAT Regulations 1995 (SI 1995 No 2518), reg 106* may apply. These rules are that where input tax calculated is less than £625 per month on average and less than 50% of all input tax incurred, the business is able to recover all its VAT. This may arise in the case of some representative offices (see paragraphs 3.116 to 3.119 below) where it is only possible to identify a small amount of input tax which relates to supplies which would carry no right of deduction if carried on in the UK. Otherwise, businesses in the banking and securities sectors must resign themselves to the fact that they will be partially exempt, and, if they wish to recover VAT on expenditure, must involve themselves in the necessary compliance.

Specific issues

Foreign exchange

3.94 The VAT treatment of foreign exchange has already been discussed at paragraphs 3.14 to 3.18 above. The general rule has been that VAT is not recoverable in respect of foreign exchange transactions where these are outside the scope of VAT (i.e. there is no consideration for the transaction and thus it is not a supply). Consequently, banks which have large foreign exchange dealing rooms have found that the loss of input tax is a considerable burden. However, it has been possible to negotiate some recovery in respect of foreign exchange in partial exemption methods, although only to the extent that foreign exchange transactions are undertaken to hedge other transactions. Normally, a proportion of foreign exchange transactions is agreed with Customs & Excise as being supportive of other activities of the bank and a corresponding proportion of VAT on expenditure allocated to foreign exchange can then be put back into the calculations to be recovered in the appropriate proportion, i.e. the proportion for the sector which the foreign exchange transaction is hedging. The VAT relating to the remaining foreign exchange transactions will not be recoverable at all.

3.95 The position for the treatment of foreign exchange transactions will no doubt change once the *First National Bank of Chicago, [1995] VATDR 306 (13556)* case has been decided by the European Court of Justice. (The Advocate-General delivered his Opinion in October 1997, indicating that such transactions should be treated as supplies for consideration, and that the amounts paid by the customers should be divided between consideration for the foreign currency and consideration for the service of foreign exchange. See De Voil Indirect Tax Intelligence, November 1997. At the time of writing, the CJEC has not yet passed judgment in this case.) Where foreign exchange deals are supplies, this will need to be recognised in the partial exemption method.

Securities

3.96 A business which deals in securities, as part of its business activities, will have to include these within the partial exemption calculations. The method should be calculated to avoid distortions arising from the values of any securities transactions. It is extremely difficult to argue that securities of transactions undertaken for the purposes of the treasury or liquidity of the business should be left out of any partial exemption method (see paragraph 3.92 above). Thus, it is advised that any calculation which includes these transactions should minimise any impact of their value by using a transaction count.

Interest income

3.97 Similarly to securities, it is not possible for a business in the banking and securities sector to ignore interest income. Consequently, any method should seek to isolate the impact of exempt interest to the greatest degree. It is possible, if a method is used which is based on transaction count for the number of interest payments received, to swamp the partial exemption calculations so that the method ceases to reflect how input tax is used. One should, therefore, seek to minimise the effect of this by sectoring interest earned and allocating relevant costs to that cost centre and recovering as appropriate. This is often the most fair result as usually very little administrative time is spent in earning the interest income and thus this income should not be allowed to distort the partial exemption calculations.

Industry agreements

3.98 Various trade bodies have agreed standard partial exemption methods for their specific sectors. The agreements which are in existence are listed at paragraphs 3.112 to 3.113 below.

3.99 VAT Business by Business

3.99 It is not generally necessary to gain advance approval from Customs & Excise to use one of these methods, but it is also not necessary to use the method if it is not appropriate for the business. It is also possible to use the prescribed method as an element of a wider method. For example, a bank may have a leasing and hire purchase profit centre. This sector of the business could use the method agreed by the Finance Houses Association, whilst the remaining business of the bank uses a tailor-made special method.

Accounting and records

Input tax identification

3.100 A business seeking to recover VAT on its costs must initially identify the VAT element of its costs. Quite often systems will record the VAT figure on each item of expenditure and will produce reports which can then be used for input tax recovery. Where systems do not report VAT separately because costs are input to the system gross, it is necessary to agree a method with Customs & Excise for extracting the VAT figure. This will often be done by identifying those costs which must be VAT-bearing and calculating the VAT element of the total cost for that expense.

3.101 Depending on how complex the partial exemption method is, the input tax will need to be reported in a format which enables a ready identification of the figures for the calculations. It is important that the input tax system has an audit trail so that Customs can be sure that the input tax figures being used can be traced back to the source documents.

EU/non-EU information

3.102 It is also important to obtain information of all the income which allows VAT recovery. Often this will include ensuring that customer information is sufficiently detailed to allow recognition of those non-EU clients from the EU clients as, if this split is not available, it is difficult to determine how much VAT may be recoverable.

3.103 Once the EU/non-EU information is available, it will be necessary to determine whether the information on the system lends itself to the performance of the partial exemption calculations. Often, the availability of information from the system will dictate how the method is put together. If income values or the number of transactions are available, it will be possible to test the potential benefits of the different methods. In fact, the more information the business has available, the more permutations and possibilities it has for recovering VAT.

Cost allocations

3.104 Whilst it is important to be able to analyse income into its different categories for VAT purposes, it is also necessary to determine how costs are allocated within the business and at what level the partial exemption calculation should be undertaken. As already mentioned at paragraph 3.80 above, Customs are unwilling to accept global pro-rata calculations, and if costs are allocated around the business by way of management accounts or activity-based costings, or indeed by any other method, Customs will often expect partial exemption methods to calculate at the different cost allocation levels. However, one should note that simply because the business decides to allocate costs on the basis of management accounts, this does not mean that this is the best method for allocating costs for VAT purposes. The partial exemption method should reflect use of the input tax in making taxable supplies, and if the management accounts do not actually allocate VAT to those sectors which 'use' the input tax, a different allocation should be used. A business is able to use any method of allocation it wishes, but for ease of administration, following the business's method of allocating costs may be the most appropriate. If the system simply allocates costs and not the VAT, it is important to determine how to allocate the VAT. For example, it can be allocated on the basis of the amount of the costs allocated to particular sectors. If this does not make sense then allocating VAT by way of floor space, or headcount, or indeed any other method, can be as logical as using the management accounts.

Partial exemption calculations

3.105 Partial exemption calculations will generally have to be carried out for each VAT return. All the calculations should be retained with the return for checking by Customs & Excise. Of course, the usual six-year rule which applies to retaining records will also apply to partial exemption calculations. At the end of each VAT year, an annual adjustment will have to be carried out. All the calculations for the year will have to be amalgamated and one calculation undertaken for the full year. Any adjustment either way will have to be made on the following VAT return. Annual adjustment working papers should also be retained for the partial exemption calculations.

Reverse charges

3.106 A major concern for the banking and securities sector is the reverse charge on services received from overseas. Those services affected are those listed in *VATA 1994, 5 Sch* (see Appendix 2), but not services which would be exempt or zero-rated if supplied in the UK (e.g. dealing in shares).

3.107 The reverse charge procedure was introduced to ensure that overseas businesses could not unfairly compete with domestic businesses by not charging VAT. UK persons receiving the services from outside the UK must account for VAT as if *they* had supplied them in the UK. The VAT is also the

3.108 *VAT Business by Business*

UK person's input tax. A fully taxable person will be unaffected (reverse charge VAT equals input tax) but a partly exempt person will lose some reverse charge VAT under the partial exemption rules. Thus, if a legal service is received from a law firm in the United States, output VAT will have to be accounted for on the sterling value. A corresponding amount can be treated as input tax and recovered, as appropriate, in the partial exemption calculations. If the legal fees have been incurred in relation to a specific transaction, the VAT will be directly attributable and either recovered in full if that transaction is taxable or not recovered at all if that transaction is exempt. If the fees are general in nature, the reverse charge VAT will be recovered within the residual partial exemption calculation.

3.108 It is important that all these services are recognised and the correct accounting treatment accorded to them to avoid possible assessment from Customs & Excise.

3.109 Since 1 April 1987, the value of imported reverse charge services has had to be included in taxable turnover for the purpose of monitoring the VAT registration limits. This means that a company which makes only exempt supplies may need to register due to the value of services received from abroad.

Practical issues

Registration

3.110 Many businesses in the banking and securities world may have no actual liability to register because they have no taxable income which exceeds the VAT registration limit and no reverse charge items which exceed the VAT registration limit (if reverse charge items are received from overseas in excess of the VAT registration limits, a liability to register for VAT will arise). If there is no actual liability to register, it may not be worthwhile registering if the level of VAT recovery which the business might achieve is below that which justifies the necessary administration and compliance of being VAT-registered. In these circumstances a business can ask for exemption from registration under *VATA 1994, 1 Sch 14*. Exemption from registration will necessitate monitoring the position to ensure that, should a liability to register arise, the business can take the necessary action promptly. Also, before taking the decision to become exempt from registration, it is worthwhile testing out the different methods or calculations which could be undertaken to give VAT recovery to determine finally that it is not worthwhile.

3.111 If a business is registered, but there is no output tax and indeed very little input tax to claim in a particular period, it is possible to submit a nil return and not go to the effort of calculating how much VAT is actually recoverable. However, a word of warning is appropriate! It is not advisable to delay recovering VAT as one may find, on subsequently claiming it, that the claim is in fact out of time. Rules were introduced in 1996 to prevent recovery of VAT three years after the VAT period in which it was incurred.

Industry agreements

3.112 Customs have entered into industry agreements, mainly in the field of partial exemption methods. The agreements which are in existence are as follows:

(1) *Supplies of bullion: Agreement with the London Bullion Market Association.* The agreement concerns the application of zero-rating to transactions involving bullion and also rules concerning safe carriage, safe custody and storage and refining.

(2) *Partial exemption: Agreement with the Association of British Factors & Discounters.* This method involves sectoring activity between invoice discounting and mainline factoring. It also specifies what transactions should be used in the pro-rata calculation. Its use should be agreed with Customs & Excise in advance.

(3) *Partial exemption: Agreement with the Finance Houses Association.* The agreement specifies that 15% of the input VAT related to hire purchase credit can be recovered as relating to the sale of the goods. There is also guidance on identifying recoverable VAT where hire purchase is mixed up with leasing and lending.

(4) *Partial exemption & unit trusts: Agreement with the Association of Unit Trust & Investment Managers.* This method gives details of the position on VAT recovery for certain costs, and of the pro-rata calculation to be used.

(5) *Personal equity plans: Agreement with AUTIF* concerning the VAT liability of various charges.

(6) *Electronic banking/cash management: Agreement with the British Bankers Association.* This gives details of the VAT liability of these transactions.

(7) *Partial exemption: Agreement with the Association of Investment Trust Companies.* This deals with input tax relating to sales of investments.

3.113 Where Customs & Excise have entered into industry agreements, it is important to note that, in the case of the partial exemption methods, whilst these give guidance and a framework for calculations to be undertaken, it is not essential to use these methods. If there are reasons why a particular business would not find them appropriate or indeed acceptable, a different method should be negotiated with Customs & Excise.

3.114 VAT Business by Business

Public notices

3.114 Customs & Excise have published various notices which are useful to businesses within the Financial Services Sector. These are as follows:

Notice No 701/29/92	Finance
Notice No 701/44/94	Securities
Notice No 701/43/93	Financial futures and options
Notice No 706	Partial exemption
Notice No 741	Place of supply of services
Notice No 701/9/95	Terminal markets/Commodities

EU legislation

3.115 The legislation relevant to banking and securities within the EU is contained in the *EC Sixth Directive*. Particularly relevant articles within the Directive are *Article 13B(d)* and *Article 15(14)* which provide for exemption of financial services. *Article 9* details the place of supply of services and *Articles 17-20* govern the right to recovery of VAT on expenditure and partial exemption calculations.

Representative offices

3.116 Overseas businesses setting up in the UK will often firstly form a representative office which does not actually trade in the UK. A representative office is able to register for VAT under *VATA 1994, 1 Sch 10* and recover VAT on expenditure subject to the following rules:

(1) The representative office is not actually making supplies in the UK; and

(2) the business worldwide makes supplies which would allow recovery of VAT if those activities were undertaken in the UK.

3.117 For example, a representative office of a computer supplier could register for VAT here. As the sale of computers would be a supply in the UK which would be subject to VAT at the standard rate, and would thus allow input tax recovery, the representative office, whilst not actually selling any computers itself, would be able to recover all the VAT on its costs. However, for the banking and securities industry the position is rather more problematic. As the business, worldwide, would be making supplies which may not carry a full right of recovery within the UK (for example, the customer base may include clients within the EU), the representative office may be forced into considering a partial exemption method and thus only obtaining partial recovery of the VAT on its costs. As set-up costs can be quite significant, and as representative offices have tended, in the writer's experience, to be non-EU based businesses, quite a significant recoverable proportion can be established and in some circumstances the de minimis rules can apply, for which see paragraph 3.93 above.

3.118 Often, the activities of representative offices vary widely in their scope. A representative office may have dealers who look for UK clients and who are able to agree deals up to certain parameters, but the contractual relationship with the client is between the head office, e.g. in the United States, and the UK client. The deal is executed in the States and settled in the States, with the UK representative office receiving reimbursement of costs or a percentage of the business. In strict terms these are still treated as representative offices because the UK office is not the part of the business which is making the supply to the UK client. However, it is important to note that VAT recovery will often have to be considered on the basis of the particular supplies which the representative office is helping to promote and whether or not recovery will be achieved will depend upon whether that transaction would allow VAT recovery in the UK if it was undertaken in the UK.

3.119 The position for representative offices is indeed quite complicated, as is the position for a representative office ceasing to act in that capacity and becoming a trading branch. Whilst there is no need to change the VAT registration in any way, it is important to realise that it can be necessary to adjust any VAT which has been recovered in full, but which may relate to future exempt supplies by the branch. This is a complicated area and should be carefully considered and advice taken.

3.App 1 VAT Business by Business

Appendix 1

VAT liability of financial instruments

(E = Exempt, S = Standard Rated, O/S = Outside the Scope, O/S(R) = Outside the Scope with Input Tax Recovery)

CUSTOMERS BELONGING IN

INSTRUMENT	UK & IOM	EU (BUSINESS)	EU (PRIVATE)	NON-EU	VALUE FOR VAT PURPOSES
STERLING COMMERCIAL PAPER	E	O/S	E	O/S(R)	FULL PRICE PAID
BILLS OF EXCHANGE	E	O/S	E	O/S(R)	FULL PRICE PAID
PROMISSORY NOTES	E	O/S	E	O/S(R)	FULL PRICE PAID
LOCAL AUTHORITY BILLS	E	O/S	E	O/S(R)	FULL PRICE PAID
COMMERCIAL BILLS	E	O/S	E	O/S(R)	FULL PRICE PAID
EUROBONDS	E	O/S	E	O/S(R)	FULL PRICE PAID
EURONOTES	E	O/S	E	O/S(R)	FULL PRICE PAID
DEEP DISCOUNT BONDS	E	O/S	E	O/S(R)	FULL PRICE PAID
FLOATING RATE NOTES	E	O/S	E	O/S(R)	FULL PRICE PAID
EQUITIES	E	O/S	E	O/S(R)	FULL PRICE PAID
GILTS	E	O/S	E	O/S(R)	FULL PRICE PAID
TREASURY BILLS	E	O/S	E	O/S(R)	FULL PRICE PAID
INTEREST & CURRENCY SWAPS	E	O/S	—	O/S(R)	NET AMOUNT OF MONEY PASSING

Banking and Securities **3.App 1**

FOREIGN CURRENCY & INTEREST RATE OPTIONS	E	O/S	—	O/S(R)	PREMIUM PAID
FORWARD RATE AGREEMENTS	E	O/S	—	O/S(R)	AMOUNT PAID
ADVISORY FEES (INCLUDING MERGERS & ACQUISITIONS)	S	O/S(R)	S	O/S(R)	FEE PAID
MANAGING & UNDERWRITING ISSUE OF SECURITIES	E	O/S	—	O/S(R)	FEE PAID

It should be noted that the treatment of Forex transactions is likely to change as a result of the *First National Bank of Chicago* VAT Tribunal case (*[1995] VATDR 306*), for which see paragraph 3.14 above. Such transactions may have to be recognised in their own right as exempt when with counterparties belonging within the EU, and as O/S(R) for transactions with non-EU counterparties.

3.App 1 *Banking and Securities*

The VAT liability of broking/arrangement services

PRINCIPAL SUPPLY			VAT LIABILITY OF BROKERAGE SERVICE	
FROM	TO	VAT LIABILITY OF PRINCIPAL SUPPLY	TO SELLER	TO BUYER
UK/IOM or EU private	UK/IOM or EU private	E	E	E
UK/IOM or EU private	EU business	E	E	E
UK/IOM or EU private	Non EU	OS(R)	E(R)	OS(R)
EU business	UK/IOM or EU private	E	OS	E
EU business	EU business	OS	OS	OS
EU business	Non-EU	OS(R)	OS(R)	OS(R)
Non-EU	UK or EU private	E	OS(R)	E
Non-EU	EU business	E	OS(R)	OS
Non-EU	Non-EU	OS(R)	OS(R)	OS(R)

Notes

E = exempt

E(R) = exempt, but with refund of related input tax

OS = outside the scope with no refund of related input tax

OS(R) = outside the scope with refund of related input tax

NB. This chart applies only where the principal transaction is a supply for VAT purposes.

Appendix 2

VATA 1994, Schedule 5

'Reverse charge' services

(1) Transfers and assignments of copyright, patents licences, trademarks and similar rights.

(2) Advertising services.

(3) Services of consultants, engineers, consultancy bureaux, lawyers, accountants and other similar services; data processing and provision of information (but excluding from this head any services relating to land).

(4) Acceptance of any obligation to refrain from pursuing or exercising, in whole or part, any business activity or any such rights as are referred to in paragraph 1 above.

(5) Banking, financial and insurance services (including reinsurance, but not including the provision of safe deposit facilities).

(6) The supply of staff.

(6A) The letting on hire of goods other than means of transport.

(7) The services rendered by one person to another in procuring for the other any of the services mentioned in paragraphs 1 to 6A above.

(8) Services

    (a) of the transportation of goods which begins in one Member State and ends in a different Member State;

    (b) of loading, unloading, handling and similar activities carried out in connection with services of the description specified in sub-paragraph (a) above;

    (c) consisting of the making of arrangements for, or of any other activity intended to facilitate, the making by or to another person of:

        (i) a supply of a description specified in sub-paragraph (a) or (b) above; or

        (ii) any supply not falling within (i) above, except a supply of any services of a description specified in paragraphs 1 to 7 of this Schedule.

which are treated as supplied in the United Kingdom by virtue of the recipient's having made use of his registration number for the purpose of the supply; and section 7(1) of this Act shall have effect in relation to the services

3.App 2 VAT Business by Business

described in sub-paragraphs (a) to (c) above as if the recipient belongs in the United Kingdom if, and only if, he is a taxable person.

Chapter 4

Barristers

Introduction

4.1 Barristers, in common with all businesses, are only liable to register for VAT when their turnover exceeds, or is likely to exceed, the registration threshold. The threshold is currently £50,000 (see *VATA 1994, 1 Sch 1*). This means that barristers, at the start of their career, are unlikely to have to register for VAT. There are sometimes advantages in registering for VAT at an early stage, and these are discussed at paragraph 4.18 below.

Special rules apply to barristers in respect of two areas of VAT. These special rules are designed to correct anomalies and prevent unfairness which would otherwise arise out of the way in which barristers practise. The first relates to the recovery of VAT on chambers expenses (see paragraph 4.5 below) and the other relates to the cessation of practice (see paragraph 4.15 below). In all other respects barristers are taxed according to general principles.

Liability

Legal advice

4.2 The principal supply made by a member of the Bar is that of legal advice. This is a supply of services, and where it is supplied to anyone in the UK, the supply is standard-rated. Where, however, legal advice is supplied to a client belonging outside the UK, the liability of the supply depends on the status of the recipient. This is because the status of the recipient determines whether the supply is treated as being supplied in the UK and therefore standard-rated, or supplied where it is received, and thus outside the scope with the right of recovery of related input tax.

Where the non-UK recipient is resident in the EC, the supply is treated as being supplied where it is received (*VATA 1994, 5 Sch, Group 3*) if the recipient is registered for VAT in the Member State in which it belongs and uses the supply for the purposes of its business. If, however, a barrister advises a private citizen of another EC Member State in his personal capacity, the supply would be treated as being made in the UK and therefore would have to be standard-rated. Where the recipient belongs outside the EC,

4.3 VAT Business by Business

then the supply is outside the scope with the right of recovery of related input tax, whether or not the recipient is in business.

The above rules do not apply to the supply of legal advice in connection with land in the UK. Supplies of legal advice in connection with land in the UK are standard-rated wherever the recipient is based (*VAT (Place of Supply of Services) Order 1992 (SI 1992 No 3121), article 5*).

Judicial office

4.3 Other supplies made by a barrister which are related to his profession as barrister are treated as business activities and are taxed accordingly. The same is normally true of offices obtained from or as a result of the barrister's profession. *VATA 1994, s 94(4)* states that:

> 'Where a person, in the course or furtherance of a trade, profession or vocation, accepts any office, services supplied by him as the holder of that office are treated as supplied in the course or furtherance of the trade, profession or vocation'.

This means that the consideration received by a barrister in respect of any office is taxable at the appropriate rate. There is, however, one major exception to this rule. Where a barrister accepts a part-time judicial appointment, by concession Customs & Excise accept that payment for the appointment is outside the scope of VAT. In practical terms this means that the barrister need not charge or account for VAT on a part-time judicial appointment. The appointments to which the concession applies are:

- Deputy High Court Judge
- Recorder
- Assistant Recorder
- Deputy Circuit Judge
- Deputy Metropolitan Magistrate
- Deputy Provincial Stipendiary Magistrate
- Deputy County Court and District Registrar
- Deputy Master/Registrar of the Supreme Court
- Coroner
- Deputy and Assistant Coroner

Barristers **4.6**

- Chancellor of a Diocese of the Church of England
- Dean of the Court of Arches
- Auditor of the Province of York (Church of England)
- Assistant Local Government Boundary Commissioner

Payments in respect of other offices, which are judicial in nature, but not in the list above, do attract VAT. Thus if, for example, a barrister sits on an Industrial or similar Tribunal he must charge and account for VAT on the fees paid by the Tribunal for his services.

Other supplies

4.4 As a result of *VATA 1994, s 94(4)*, any supplies made by a barrister in which he acts in the same legal capacity, and which are carried out as a business, are taxable. Activities commonly include teaching, writing or anything else done for a consideration. One area often overlooked is the fact that the sale of goods used in a barrister's practice, which were standard-rated when purchased by him, are also taxable supplies when sold by him. For example, if a barrister sells a computer, furniture, his wig, or any other item, he must account for VAT on the sale. A barrister selling his library of books and periodicals will not have to account for VAT on their sale as the items are zero-rated.

VAT recovery

4.5 As explained above, the principal services supplied by barristers are standard-rated or zero-rated. This, prima facie, gives rise to an entitlement to recover all the input tax incurred in the making of these supplies. (For a general commentary on the recovery of input tax, see *Tolley's VAT 1998/99, chapter 35*.) There are, however, several exceptions to the general position. These arise out of the way in which barristers practise as sole practitioners, but share some expenses, and also because of the need to differentiate between personal and professional expenditure. The exceptions are dealt with individually below.

Chambers expenses

4.6 The first point to be made is that this section only refers to 'chambers expenses', and not those expenses which an individual member of a set of chambers incurs solely for his or her own practice. The normal rule for the recovery of input tax is that only the person who *receives* both the supply and the tax invoice may recover the VAT. Clearly, where expenses are incurred for chambers as a whole, there must be a method of charging and

4.7 VAT Business by Business

apportioning chambers' expenditure. By concession Customs & Excise accept three methods. These are:

(a) supplies to and by the Head of Chambers;

(b) proportional apportionment of input tax, and

(c) a combination of the two.

Supplies to and by the Head of Chambers

4.7 Here the Head of Chambers receives all the supplies, and pays for them. VAT invoices are made out to him, and he recovers all the input tax thereon as his input tax. He then supplies the goods and services to the other members of chambers. As these are supplies made by him in the course of his professional activities, these recharges themselves attract VAT. Thus he must issue VAT invoices to all members of chambers, whether they are VAT-registered or not. The VAT-registered members of chambers may, of course, recover this VAT as their own input tax.

Under this scheme the tax has a 'wash-through' effect for the VAT-registered barrister. Notwithstanding the tax neutrality of the position, it can still impose a significant administrative burden where the chambers are large or the clerking facilities are overburdened. Thus Customs & Excise have agreed that the Head of Chambers does not need to issue tax invoices for chambers' expenses. In theory this could mean that the unregistered members of chambers may benefit by receiving services and goods net of VAT where they would have no right to recover the VAT if the goods or services were supplied to them directly.

Proportional attribution of input tax

4.8 In this method members of chambers pay into a common fund. These payments do not attract VAT. Invoices for chambers' expenses, for example, are made out to the chambers or the Head of Chambers. These invoices are paid from the common fund. It is important to note that the Head of Chambers will not issue VAT invoices to members of chambers under this method. The individual members of chambers then reclaim the VAT element on their share of the chambers expenses directly from Customs & Excise.

This is a major deviation from the normal rules governing the recovery of input tax. The deviation is that the individual members of chambers are claiming input tax in respect of invoices not made out to them, and not for the full amount of the invoice. Normally Customs & Excise verify the right to recover input tax, initially at least, by checking that the supply has been made to the person who is recovering the input tax. It also means that unregistered members of chambers will receive a gross invoice with no entitlement to recover the VAT. One of the features of this method of recovering VAT on chambers expenses is that accurate records will need to be kept of the proportions paid by each member of chambers.

A combination of the above

4.9 This method is only available where every member of chambers is VAT-registered. It works on the common fund basis. Again no VAT is charged on contributions to the common fund. The difference is that only one person, usually the Head of Chambers, pays the bills. The tax invoices are made out to him, and he recovers the VAT in full. He does not issue tax invoices to his fellow members of chambers, but he pays the amount of the VAT recovered from Customs & Excise into the common fund. The result is that each individual member only pays the net amount of chambers expenses. Again, an accurate record is essential if Customs & Excise are to be satisfied that the chambers may use this method.

Devilling fees

4.10 Where a barrister pays devilling fees to a VAT-registered barrister, he should receive a VAT invoice, and may recover the VAT thereon.

Travel costs

4.11 If a barrister incurs expenses in travelling to and from a case, or staying in a hotel, he may recover his expenses. It is worth pointing out that public transport, such as rail, air and bus travel, is zero-rated, and therefore if the barrister travels by this method no VAT has been incurred and, obviously, none may be recovered.

VAT on subsistence costs, i.e. meals for the barrister, may be recovered. If, however, the barrister takes his lay and/or professional client out for dinner during a case, only the VAT relating to the barrister's own meal may be recovered as the remainder constitutes 'business entertainment' on which VAT is not recoverable (see *Tolley's VAT 1998/99, chapter 9*).

Where a barrister uses his own car to travel to and from cases, he may recover the VAT on a proportion of the running costs of the car. He may recover VAT on all the petrol he purchases, but then must apply the fuel scale charge. This enables the barrister to recover VAT on his fuel purchases, but he must then account for output tax on the deemed personal use of the fuel. This rate is set by statute and is determined by engine size and type. The current rates vary from £29.19 to £58.97 per quarter. If the benefit of reclaiming VAT on fuel is outweighed by the fuel scale charge (because the individual does very low mileage) he may choose not to recover any input tax on fuel and therefore will not have to pay the fuel scale charge. The current legislation (*VAT (Input Tax) Order (SI 1992 No 3222), para 7*) does not permit the recovery of input tax on the purchase of a vehicle which is to be used partly for business and

4.12 VAT Business by Business

partly for domestic purposes (for more details see *Tolley's VAT 1998/99, chapter 45*) and so unless a barrister is able to show that the car is wholly and exclusively for business purposes, he cannot recover input tax on its purchase.

Personal expenses

4.12 Where a barrister incurs expenses wholly for the purposes of his business, he may recover the VAT incurred thereon in full. For example, if a barrister redecorates his room in chambers, buys a new desk or computer, or purchases his wig and gown, he may claim the input tax on this expenditure in the period in which it is incurred, provided he has the relevant invoices in support of his claim. Where, however, the goods or services are for a mixed purpose, the barrister must apportion the VAT element between his business use and his personal use. A good example of this is a barrister having a mobile phone which he uses both for work and socially. Both the call costs and the line rental must be apportioned. Similarly, a barrister working from home in the evenings will be entitled to recover the VAT on some of his domestic running expenses. On the issue of dark suits for court wear, Customs & Excise are prepared to accept that two such suits are purchased for the purpose of the barrister's business each year, and will allow the input tax on these suits. Customs & Excise's view is not consistent with the Inland Revenue's. The House of Lords held in *Mallalieu v Drummond [1983] STC 665* that clothes for court wear were not wholly and exclusively for business purposes, and so denied a tax deduction.

Reverse charge services

4.13 There may be occasions where the barrister obtains legal advice or similar services from a person in another EC Member State. These services attract VAT under the reverse charge procedure. Accordingly the barrister must remember both to account for output tax on the supply and recover input tax. Where the barrister is fully taxable, this will be entirely neutral. For the full list of supplies attracting the reverse charge see *VATA 1994, Sch 5*.

Accounting for VAT

Special rules for barristers

4.14 The tax point of a barrister's supply is determined by *VAT Regulations 1995, reg 92* which provided that the time of supply for the services of an advocate shall be the earliest of the following:

(a) when the fee in respect of those services is received by the barrister or advocate,

(b) when the barrister or advocate issues a VAT invoice in respect of them, or

(c) the day when the barrister or advocate ceases to practise as such.

Barristers normally, therefore, do not issue a valid tax invoice until they have been paid by their clients. Instead they issue a request for payment, or a fee note which does not contain a VAT number and contains wording to the effect that it is 'valid only when receipted'. By following this method of invoicing, a barrister need not suffer the expense of accounting for VAT on fees upon which he has not yet been paid.

Death or cessation of practice

4.15 *VAT Regulations 1995, reg 92(c)* automatically crystallises the tax point of a barrister's supply when he ceases to practise or on his death. Strictly, all the VAT due on unpaid fee notes, and completed work, becomes payable when the barrister dies or ceases to practice.

Customs & Excise recognise the difficulty this could cause and have agreed that, where the barrister or his personal representative so elects, he can pay the VAT due on post-cessation receipts when he is paid. In essence this is an extension of the position when the barrister was practising, but it requires a specific election on the part of the barrister. As a matter of practice, Customs & Excise now send out a leaflet explaining the rules relating to post-cessation receipts when they are advised of the death or retirement of a barrister.

Record-keeping

4.16 A barrister has exactly the same obligations to keep records as every other VAT-registered trader. He must still keep all records in support of both his outputs and claims for input tax for a period of six years (*VATA 1994, 11 Sch 6(3)*) notwithstanding that, in the absence of fraud, Customs & Excise may not normally raise an assessment for a VAT accounting period more than three years from the end of the period.

Practical points

Receipts

4.17 Customs & Excise tend to look very carefully at claims for input tax where there is a possibility that the goods or services in question could be used for both a business and private purpose. It is therefore prudent to keep good receipts for meals, etc.

4.18 *VAT Business by Business*

Registration

4.18 Although registration is compulsory where the registration threshold is exceeded (see paragraph 4.1 above), a person may register for VAT at any time when he is or intends to make taxable supplies, whether or not the registration threshold has been reached. This is known as voluntary registration. A barrister may wish to be voluntarily registered for VAT for any of the following reasons:

(a) His clients are likely to be VAT-registered and therefore VAT is not a real cost to the client;

(b) It enables the barrister to recover VAT on his expenses and on the purchase of capital items such as computers;

(c) Where a barrister is unregistered, he announces that his fee income is less than £50,000 per annum, and he may prefer to let it appear that this is not the case.

Chapter 5

Bloodstock

Introduction

5.1 The bloodstock industry was, at one time, subject to one of the most complex sets of VAT rules imaginable. Ownership of racehorses was regarded by Customs as a non-business activity, thus mirroring the position of the Inland Revenue for direct tax purposes. For example, a typical 'owner-breeder' business would have to pay output VAT calculated under a complicated formula on every transfer of a horse into training because the horse was being put from a 'business' to a 'non-business' use.

5.2 The 'non-business view' resulted in many important VAT cases such as *Triangle Thoroughbreds Ltd (5404); Mowbray Properties Ltd (6033)* and *Rynkeld Thoroughbred Co Ltd (6894)*. These cases are worth studying for an insight into both Customs' and the Tribunals' views as to what constitutes business activity and, in that context, are still relevant today.

5.3 However, from the standpoint of the bloodstock industry, the cases reflect a position which no longer exists. Today, matters are more straightforward, although still not without complications. Under a Memorandum of Understanding between Customs and bloodstock industry representatives, effective from 16 March 1993, owners and breeders of racehorses are divided into four basic groups, each with its own set of rules governing the payment and recovery of VAT. The full Memorandum is reproduced as Appendix 1.

The relevant provisions were amended from 1 January 1998. See paragraph 5.8 below for a summary of the key changes.

Owner-breeders

5.4 These are typically mixed breeding and racing operations with their own stud premises housing a number of broodmares and their progeny, possibly also 'standing' one or two stallions. In addition, the business will own a number of horses in training.

5.5 VAT Business by Business

5.5 The description covers a huge range, from those with half a dozen mares and even fewer racehorses to multi-national 'players' (such as the well-known Shadwell, Godolphin and Juddmonte Farms operations).

5.6 Customs accepts that this category should be regarded in the same light as any other VAT-registered person with wholly business activities, i.e. that the breeding and racing aspects are part of an integrated single business. Output VAT and input VAT are payable and recoverable according to the normal rules.

Pure owners

5.7 This category covers owners of racehorses who have no other bloodstock interest, such as breeding from their own mares or ownership of stallion shares. Ownership could be as an individual, or via partnerships and/or syndicates.

5.8 This group is not regarded as being automatically in business but has the opportunity to register for VAT under the so-called Owners' Scheme. Currently, registration under the Scheme requires the owner to give an undertaking to generate taxable supplies from appearance money, prize money and sponsorship arrangements. Once registered, an owner is able to fully recover VAT on normal racing costs (e.g. training fees) subject to the normal rules. Following a review of the Scheme it was announced that, from 1 January 1998, owners may only register *once sponsorship has actually been obtained*. In addition, sole proprietors who are joint owners are only able to apply the Scheme to those racehorses in which they have at least a 50% share. However, those owners having less than a 50% interest will continue to be able to register as part of a partnership. See Customs Notice 700/67/97.

Company owners

5.9 Many companies whose main business activity is otherwise unrelated to horse racing will own a number of horses in training; often because the owner of the business is also a racing enthusiast.

5.10 Such 'company owners' can sometimes be regarded as pursuing their racing activity as an integral part of the overall business, e.g. where there is a clear advertising intention. This is a matter of negotiation and agreement with Customs, and there have been several notable VAT Tribunal cases on the issue, for example *J Boardmans Ltd (2025)* and *Brian Yeardley Continental Ltd (2035)*. In other cases, it should be possible for the owner to register individually under the Scheme with the company providing sponsorship.

Trainers and dealers

5.11 These are professionals within the industry who train or buy and sell horses for a living. Customs accepts that their racing activities may be seen as a part of their general business operations subject to the numbers not being disproportionate and, in the case of dealers, that the horses are held as trading stock.

5.12 Trainers and dealers who race horses on their own account may, alternatively, qualify for registration under the Owners' Scheme. In addition to the groups defined above, the wider bloodstock industry includes jockeys, racecourses and auctioneers such as the world-famous 'Tattersalls' situated in Newmarket.

Liability

5.13 The bloodstock industry is a truly international one. Many 'players' have establishments in all of the key racing countries, i.e. the UK, France, Ireland and the USA. Transactions often, therefore, involve movements of horses both between EU Member States and to or from so-called third countries. Deciding the liability of any particular supply will often involve first establishing the place of that supply.

5.14 For ease of reference, the types of supply are categorised under the industry grouping most likely to be involved with that activity. However, it should be noted that certain supplies are not exclusive to particular groups, e.g. sales of nominations to stallions could be made by owners, trainers, jockeys or dealers.

Owners and owner-breeders

Sales of foals, yearlings and horses in training

5.15 Where the horse is physically located in the UK at the time of the sale, that will be the place of supply and VAT will be due at the standard rate unless:

(i) the sale is for export to a destination outside the EU in which case it will be zero-rated; or

(ii) the sale is to a person VAT registered in the EU and the horse is despatched to that person's Member State in which case it may be zero-rated with the buyer accounting for 'acquisition' VAT under the rules for intra-EU supplies.

5.16 Where the horse is physically located in another EU Member State at the time of the sale, VAT will, in principle, be due on a supply in that Member State subject to the rules for VAT registration in that country. It

5.17 *VAT Business by Business*

should be noted that both France and Ireland have special VAT rates for sales of thoroughbred horses, of 5.5% and 2.5% respectively. In addition, the actual VAT position will in practice depend on whether the sale is by a VAT-registered business or, alternatively, by a racing operation which may not be regarded as a business registrable for VAT in the particular Member State.

5.17 The above rules apply to sales of whole horses, which are supplies of goods. It is very common for part ownership in a horse to be sold, in which case the supply will be one of services not goods (*VATA 1994 4 Sch 1(1)*). If the seller 'belongs' in the UK (see *Tolley's VAT 1998/99, para 64.8*), the supply of a part interest will always be subject to UK VAT irrespective of the whereabouts of the buyer. If the seller belongs in another EU Member State, there will be a supply in that country and the same considerations should be applied as for sales of whole horses. This could also be the case for sales in third countries with VAT or similar systems.

5.18 A supplier is defined as 'belonging' either:

(i) at the place where the supplier has established his business or has a fixed establishment from which the service is supplied; or

(ii) in the absence of such a place, at the place where the supplier has a permanent address or usually resides.

The detailed rules for determining 'belonging' in relation to any supply of services are set down at *VATA 1994, section 9*.

Stallion shares and nominations

5.19 A stallion share is a part interest in the ownership of the horse (usually one-fortieth), whereas a nomination is the right to have a broodmare covered by a stallion. Both are supplies of services and it is very common for owners to assume that the VAT liability position is the same for both, often resulting in significant VAT errors.

5.20 The place of supply of a share is always the place where the owner belongs (see the definition at paragraph 5.18 above). Thus a share sold by a UK taxable person is subject to VAT at the standard rate. However, if the sale is by a person belonging in another EU Member State it will be outside the scope of UK VAT (but subject to VAT in the Member State of belonging). There might also be a VAT liability if the person belongs in a third country with a VAT system.

5.21 In the very important case of *The Hon Sir JJ Astor, [1981] VATTR 174 (1030)* Customs argued that the sale of a one-fortieth share in a stallion was a supply of services, subject to UK VAT. However, the tribunal found that because the whole of the stallion had been sold to a single (Japanese) buyer there was a supply of goods not subject to VAT. Customs have since then accepted that in these precise circumstances the supply of services in the

UK can be 'looked through' and no VAT accounted for. They also accept this principle as applying to sales of horses other than stallions, both for export to a third country and for transfer to another EU Member State.

5.22 The place of supply of a nomination is the place where the covering takes place. Therefore, a nomination to a stallion standing in the UK will, in principle, always be subject to UK VAT at the standard rate. The exceptions to this rule are coverings of mares owned by persons established outside the EU or in other EU Member States.

Mare visiting from Third Countries (or acquired for covering and export)

5.23 Where the mare is either acquired in, or temporarily imported into, the UK for the purposes of covering and is subsequently exported, the supply is zero-rated, provided that proper evidence of export is held.

Mare visiting from EU

5.24 Where the mare is sent from another EU Member State (and the owner is registered for VAT in that Member State), the responsibility for VAT accounting shifts to the owner in that Member State provided that the mare is despatched from the UK following the covering. There is no precise time limit for the despatch but Customs expect this to take place within a 'reasonable time' following the covering. In practice, this would normally be by the end of the relevant covering season.

5.25 Owners taking advantage of the above reliefs should ensure that all of the relevant conditions can be satisfied, otherwise UK VAT will be due. These reliefs are available under the 'work on goods' provisions for EU and Third Country goods (*VATA 1994, 8 Sch, Group 7, Item 1*). As such, the reliefs extend to other services supplied in connection with the covering such as keep charges, groom's fees and veterinary fees. This principle was established by the case of *Banstead Manor Stud Ltd, [1979] VATTR 154 (816)*. However, items not associated with the covering are not included and are subject to VAT at the standard rate. The table at Appendix III sets down the position for all non-UK mares and, where appropriate, their foals.

Related transport

5.26 The transport of a mare between destinations within the UK is standard rated for VAT purposes. However, if the supply is initially made to the UK stud at which the mare is boarding, it can recover the VAT and include the transport cost in its onward VAT-free supply to the owner.

5.27 The transport of a mare travelling either way between the UK and another EU Member State is outside the scope of UK VAT if it is supplied to

5.28 VAT Business by Business

an EU VAT-registered business. It is zero-rated in the UK for a mare travelling either way between the UK and a non-EU Member State.

Keep of mares, stallions and progeny

5.28 Bloodstock studs will offer various keep services. Some will provide livery for mares, yearlings and foals whilst others will operate as 'stallion studs' specialising in the keep and management of thoroughbred stallions and mares visiting to be covered.

5.29 The services offered by these studs are generally subject to VAT at the standard rate, following the 'belonging' principle for supplies of services. Where, exceptionally, a field is let for grazing only (no other care or management service being supplied) the supply is zero-rated as it is deemed to be one of animal feeding stuffs.

5.30 See also paragraphs 5.23 and 5.24 above (mares visiting from EU and non-EU countries) for circumstances where keep and other charges may be zero-rated.

5.31 Stallion studs will often receive so-called 'free nominations' as part of the remuneration package for the keep and management of stallions. These nominations form part of the consideration for the supply to the stallion owner(s) and, as such, must be valued and output tax accounted for. There is a Memorandum of Agreement between the Industry and Customs which sets down the precise rules by which this VAT should be calculated. This is reproduced as Appendix II.

Stallion syndications

5.32 When a racing colt is first syndicated as a stallion, the owner will usually retain a number of shares and sell the balance to other breeders. Each sale of a part share in the horse is a supply of services subject to VAT according to the place of belonging of the owner. Thus, a UK VAT-registered owner syndicating a stallion will charge VAT at the standard rate on each sale of a share irrespective of the belonging of the buyer.

Income from racing

5.33 Owners will derive various types of income from their racing activities. In practice, the VAT position will be largely dealt with by Weatherbys who will issue tax invoices on behalf of owners. The following income is subject to VAT at the standard rate:

- Added prize money;

- Appearance money;

- Income from sales of horses via 'selling' races.

5.34 In addition, owners may arrange their own sponsorship deals. Any such income is taxable at the standard rate.

Agents and dealers

5.35 In the bloodstock world, the term 'agent' usually covers a range of activities which includes the sale and procurement of horses, shares and nominations either on behalf of a third person (the principal) or by the agent acting as a principal himself. In other words, the term 'dealer' is not generally used as a title but a bloodstock agent will to all intents and purposes be a dealer.

5.36 It is vitally important for an agent to decide in respect of each transaction whether he is acting for VAT purposes as an agent or a principal. It can also be the case that whilst legally he may be an agent, for VAT purposes he will be seen as a principal.

Transactions as agent

5.37 Where an agent simply acts as an intermediary between two other parties, he is not required to account for VAT on the main goods or services in the transaction. For example, where a horse is purchased at auction on behalf of an owner, the auctioneer will usually invoice the purchaser (owner) directly and the agent need not be concerned with VAT on the horse itself.

5.38 Any commission charged by the agent relating to a supply of goods is subject to VAT in the country where the intermediary service is supplied, which is usually the same as the place of supply of the goods (*VAT (Place of Supply of Services) Order 1992 (SI 1992 No 3121), article 13*). However, for transactions wholly within the EU, if the customer is located in a different EU Member State to the seller *and* is VAT-registered, the intermediary supply will be in the Member State of the customer. For example, if an agent arranges a purchase of a horse in Ireland on behalf of a UK VAT-registered owner, the agent's commission will be subject to UK VAT. If the owner is not VAT-registered in the UK then the commission will be subject to VAT in Ireland. *Article 14* of *SI 1992 No 3121* refers.

5.39 Where the agent's commission relates to a supply of services, the general rule is that the intermediary supply is made in the same country as the main supply of services. However, if the customer belongs in another EU Member State *and* is VAT-registered, the intermediary supply is made where the customer belongs. For example, if a UK agent arranges the sale of a stallion share to a buyer in France who is registered for TVA, the agent's commission will be subject to TVA. If the customer is not registered for TVA, the agent's commission will be subject to UK VAT.

5.40 *VAT Business by Business*

5.40 In both the above examples it is possible for the VAT (or TVA) registered customer to account for VAT (or TVA) on the agent's commission using the so-called reverse charge procedure, thus obviating the need for the agent to register for VAT (or TVA) in the Member State of the customer. If the agent is already so registered then VAT or TVA should be charged in the normal way.

Transactions as principal

5.41 Agents will sometimes purchase horses or shares speculatively in the hope of placing them with owners. In these cases, the agent acts as a principal. An agent is also deemed to act as a principal where he arranges a supply of goods (not services) in his own name, even though legally he may be strictly an agent. For example, if an agent issues a sales invoice in his own name, he would normally be deemed to be acting as a principal for VAT.

5.42 In the above circumstances, the agent must account for the transaction as both a purchase and a sale (*VATA 1994, s 47(1)(2)(2A); FA 1995, s 23*). VAT should be accounted for on the sale according to the principles laid down elsewhere in this chapter. In cases of doubt it would be sensible to consult with a professional adviser or clear the treatment with Customs.

Valuations

5.43 Agents will frequently carry out professional valuations of bloodstock. The place of supply of a valuation is the place where the services are physically carried out. This would normally be the place where the horse itself is actually located.

5.44 It can be seen from the above that agents will often have difficulty in deciding the proper place of supply for their services, especially as the bloodstock business is increasingly an international one. The position is not made any more simple by the fact that the tax authorities in other Member States of the EU do not always take the same position as the UK Customs. For example, in Ireland sales of stallion shares and nominations are regarded as supplies of goods, not services. Bloodstock agents, therefore, should be especially mindful of the possibility that they could be registrable for VAT in a number of Member States where they would not necessarily think of themselves as 'trading'.

Auctioneers

5.45 Bloodstock auctioneers will usually act in their own name for VAT purposes even though they will strictly be agents from a legal standpoint. As such, where they sell horses, they are required to account for VAT as if they are both the buyer and seller of the horse (see paragraphs 5.41 and 5.42

Bloodstock **5.52**

above). The main impact of this is that even though the legal owner of the horse may not be VAT-registered, the sale by the auctioneer will nevertheless be subject to VAT, because the auctioneer will inevitably be registered for VAT.

5.46 An auctioneer selling services, e.g. stallion nominations, or selling goods but not acting in his own name, has a practical choice of accounting for VAT as either an agent or a principal. In most cases the auctioneer will prefer to adopt a consistent approach for all trading.

5.47 Auctioneers will often offer horses for sale on behalf of overseas vendors. In these situations, the vendor will need to carefully consider his position under UK VAT legislation. These issues are covered in more detail in paragraphs 5.94 to 5.99 below.

Racecourses

5.48 UK racecourses are generally in a more straightforward VAT position now than before the introduction of the 1993 Memorandum of Understanding. Race entry fees paid by owners used to be regarded as *exempt* income in the hands of the race course. The new position is that the payment of an entry fee by an owner is not regarded as consideration for any supply by the racecourse.

5.49 The principal sources of income for racecourses are gate money, annual memberships and receipts from the sale of rights to occupy private boxes. These are all subject to VAT at the standard rate, the latter under *VATA 1994, 9 Sch, Group 1 Item 1(l)*.

5.50 Other income chiefly derives from the granting of rights to occupy parts of the racecourse and is exempt unless the election to waive exemption is exercised (see Chapter 21—Property Developers). Possible sources of exempt income are:

(i) payments by bookmakers for 'pitches';

(ii) receipts from the granting of catering concessions;

(iii) receipts from the Tote for the right to occupy buildings and/or kiosks.

5.51 Racecourses will need to consider whether to elect to waive exemption on all or specified parts of the racecourse in order to remain fully taxable.

Trainers

5.52 A racecourse trainer's principal source of income is from fees charged to owners.

5.53 VAT Business by Business

5.53 For a UK-based trainer these are always subject to VAT at the standard rate, irrespective of the 'belonging' of the owner, because the place of supply is where the training services are physically performed.

5.54 Trainers often also derive income from dealing activities and from the ownership and exploitation of stallion shares. The rules for establishing the VAT liability of supplies of horses, nominations and shares are the same as set down at paragraphs 5.15 to 5.25 above.

5.55 Trainers often receive from their owners what are described as 'gifts'. These may take the form of cash payments, shares in racehorses or stallions or possibly stallion nomination rights. In all such cases it is vital to establish whether the value received by the trainer forms part of the consideration for their supply of training services. Where it does, VAT must be accounted for on the additional consideration received. The most critical factor in establishing the proper position is whether the 'gift' is given pursuant to a prior agreement between the parties such that the trainer has a contractual right to receive it. If so, Customs will take the view that it does represent additional consideration.

5.56 Where, on the other hand, it can be demonstrated that the owner has merely chosen to make a gift of whatever type to the trainer (perhaps to show his delight at winning a big race), Customs will accept that there is no additional consideration for the training services supplied. In view of the often high value of shares and nominations, care should be taken to ensure that the VAT position is fully considered in all situations where a trainer receives such payments.

Jockeys

5.57 A jockey's usual sources of income are riding fees payable under the rules of racing, and retainer payments or similar received under specific agreements with owners or trainers.

5.58 In order to determine whether income from these sources is subject to UK VAT, it is necessary to decide where the jockey's services are performed. The riding service itself is of a physical performance nature and, as such, is supplied where actually performed (*VAT (Place of Supply of Services) Order 1992 (SI 1992 No 3121), article 15*). It follows that many jockeys are, in principle, liable to register and account for VAT not only in the UK but also in other EU Member States where they regularly ride e.g. France, Italy, Germany.

5.59 The actual requirement to register will depend on the precise rules in the Member State concerned. For example, Ireland has no registration threshold for overseas entrepreneurs; therefore a jockey riding in Ireland and receiving payment for his riding services should register for Irish VAT.

Bloodstock 5.66

5.60 Payments received under retainer or other similar agreements can take many forms. There will usually be an agreed annual fee for services to be performed. Following the decision in the VAT Tribunal case of *Patrick Eddery Ltd, [1986] VATTR 30 (2009)*, concerning an agreement between the jockey Patrick Eddery and the Irish trainer Vincent O'Brien, it is accepted that such a payment is made in return for actual riding services (rather than the right to receive those services). As such, the VAT liability position is the same as for riding fees, i.e. the place of supply for VAT is where the riding services are actually carried out.

5.61 Particular agreements will often also specify other types of remuneration, e.g. additional cash payments in certain circumstances, shares in stallions and/or nomination rights where a horse usually ridden by the jockey is ultimately syndicated as a stallion. It is necessary to look at each such payment separately and take a view on the VAT liability according to the circumstances under which it is made. As a general rule it is often possible to tie such payments to specific performances and thus fix the place of supply. Where this is not possible, an apportionment based on the number of rides and/or horses in different countries may be possible. It should be noted that this is a potentially complex question and it is advised that, where appropriate, agreement is reached with Customs before accounting for VAT.

5.62 As with riding fees, particular riding agreements may give rise to a liability to register for VAT in a number of EU Member States.

5.63 The more famous jockeys will also often receive payment for personal performances at events or on TV and radio. Again, the place of supply for such services is where the performance takes place and the VAT liability should be decided using the same principles as for riding fees.

VAT recovery

5.64 Since the introduction of the 1993 Memorandum of Understanding, recovery of VAT has not presented too many serious problems for those in the industry. Owners and breeders are now able to register and recover VAT on purchases of racehorses and can also recover VAT on training fees. Other categories of bloodstock business are either fully taxable or can readily make themselves so by electing to waive exemption, e.g. racecourses.

5.65 However, there are a number of specific areas which can give rise to difficulties in recovering VAT and this section will look at each of those.

Joint or multi-ownerships

5.66 It is very common for owners to join together in the ownership of racehorses. Joint ownership vehicles range from multi-member syndicates to , typically, two, three or four individuals or businesses each owning one or two

5.67 VAT Business by Business

'legs' of a horse. In the latter case problems often arise because the person recovering VAT does not hold a tax invoice in the correct name. Simply, the invoice must be made out to the entity which wishes to recover any VAT as input tax.

5.67 For example, in the case of a horse purchased four ways, either the seller could invoice each part-owner separately or, alternatively, invoice one of the four who would then re-invoice the other three. It is not acceptable to photocopy the original and distribute to the other co-owners as they will not then hold an invoice made out to them and will be at risk of assessment by Customs for any VAT recovered.

5.68 In the above example, where the horse is purchased overseas, particular care should be taken. A horse being imported from a third country will be subject to VAT on entry to the UK. Only one person may be declared as the importer, so the invoice will need to be addressed to one of the co-owners who should recover all of the import VAT and then invoice the others, including VAT. In practice it is probably best for a purchase from an EU vendor to be dealt with in a similar manner (with one party providing a VAT number and accounting for acquisition VAT). Otherwise, depending on the rules in the Member State concerned, the vendor might have to charge VAT on a number of separate supplies of *services* in his own Member State (see paragraphs 5.17 and 5.18 above regarding shares in horses). Each co-owner would then have to consider how to recover VAT charged in another jurisdiction.

Overseas VAT

5.69 There are many examples of bloodstock businesses incurring VAT in other EU Member States. Typically, a UK agent attending bloodstock sales in, for example, France or Ireland would be in this position regarding subsistence costs. Such VAT may be recoverable in one of two ways.

5.70 If the person incurring the VAT charge is also making taxable supplies in the Member State concerned, he should consider whether it is necessary to register for VAT in that country. It should be noted in this context that most other countries have either very low registration thresholds or none at all. Registration in another Member State will enable the person to recover input VAT subject to the normal rules in that country.

5.71 Alternatively, the VAT might be recoverable through either the Eighth or Thirteenth Directive Refund Schemes for EU and non-EU persons respectively. Details of these schemes are published in Customs Notice 723 or, alternatively in the Coopers & Lybrand publication *VAT Refunds to Foreign Businesses by EU Countries,* which also gives extensive practical tips on how to get the best out of the schemes in other Member States. The general rule when considering whether VAT should be recoverable via the refund scheme is 'would the VAT be recoverable under the normal rules in my own country?'. However, in addition, most Member States have imposed specific restrictions in respect of all claims.

UK VAT

5.72 Overseas persons suffering UK VAT should consider whether they are registrable in the UK or, alternatively, could use the Eighth or Thirteenth Directive schemes. It should be noted in this context that, under an administrative agreement with Customs, an overseas owner of horses in training in the UK will *not* be allowed to recover VAT on purchases, training fees etc. via the refund schemes but instead must register under the Owners Scheme.

Accounting and records

5.73 This section deals with specific accounting or record-keeping requirements for particular groups within the industry.

Owners and breeders

5.74 It is very important for this group to maintain full and accurate records of the movement, particularly within the EU, of horses. It is advised that a 'bloodstock movements register' should be set up as a means of being able to demonstrate the following:

(i) the whereabouts and dates of movements of any given horse;

(ii) whether the animal is in free circulation or in the EU as a Temporary Import;

(iii) whether a movement from one EU Member State to another is permanent or temporary and whether acquisition VAT has been accounted for;

(iv) the date of disposal of each horse and the relevant VAT treatment.

5.75 Maintaining such a record will enable the taxpayer to demonstrate to Customs that VAT accounting requirements have been properly dealt with, prevent unnecessary and time-wasting inquiries and also assist considerably in the avoidance of some of the VAT traps discussed in paragraphs 5.85 to 5.102 below.

5.76 As discussed earlier, the industry is an international one. As such, owners and breeders need to be constantly aware of the VAT position, not just in the UK but in the wider EU and also third countries, many of which now have their own VAT systems. Failure to do so will almost certainly result in some additional VAT costs arising. Movements within the EU are no longer subject to overt Customs controls, and thus the onus falls on those

5.77 VAT Business by Business

within the industry to maintain adequate records to protect themselves from costly VAT assessments.

Owners scheme requirements

5.77 It is a precondition of registration under the Scheme that an owner will seek to generate taxable income through sponsorship. Clearly, the setting up of actual sponsorship deals is desirable. However, the specific undertaking is to attempt to attract sponsorship. It is, therefore, very important that every owner registered under the Scheme keeps a file containing details of all such attempts, e.g. lists of approaches made to possible sponsors, responses, etc.

Flat rate farmers

5.78 Bloodstock breeders are able, if they so choose, to opt to be treated as 'Flat Rate Farmers'. This term describes a person who carries on an agricultural activity of the type listed in the Annex to VAT Leaflet 700/46/92, and who has applied to Customs for a certificate under the Agricultural Flat Rate Scheme.

5.79 It should be noted that trainers and persons whose principal activity comprises the buying and selling of horses (e.g. bloodstock agents) are not eligible to be Flat Rate Farmers. The scheme is effectively only open, therefore, to the traditional breeder or owner-breeder and might suit those whose businesses are labour-intensive with relatively low levels of VAT on purchases and expenses (see also paragraphs 5.103 to 5.107 below).

5.80 The scheme exists as an alternative to VAT registration under the normal rules and is, essentially, a simplification measure requiring less detailed bookkeeping and reporting. Under the scheme, farmers may charge a 'Flat Rate Addition' on certain goods and services supplied to their VAT-registered customers. This acts as a compensation for not recovering Input VAT in the normal way. At the time of writing, the addition is set at 4%.

5.81 Breeders choosing to be Flat Rate Farmers should note that they will still be required to keep normal business records and copies of all invoices on which the Flat Rate Addition is charged.

The second-hand scheme for horses and ponies

5.82 This scheme exists as an alternative to normal VAT accounting for horses which are usually owned by persons who are not VAT-registered but which are often traded via VAT-registered dealers. For this reason, it is not widely used for thoroughbred horses but is more likely to be used for eventers, showjumpers and similar animals.

5.83 Those using the scheme are required to keep particular records, details of which are set down in Customs Notice 726.

Practical points

5.84 The bloodstock industry, by its very nature, is one that contains many 'VAT traps' to ensnare the unwary. Some of these have been touched upon earlier in this chapter. It also offers ways of mitigating VAT costs by structuring transactions appropriately. This section sets down some practical points, explains a number of traps and, where appropriate, gives guidance on how best to avoid them.

The temporary movement trap

5.85 It is very common for owners to send horses abroad to race and often this will be for an extended period. Movements between EU Member States may be treated as temporary provided that there is an intention to return the horse to the originating Member State within two years. The obvious advantage of such treatment is that there is no supply or acquisition under the rules for intra-EU movements of goods.

5.86 However, a problem arises if the horse stays longer than two years or is sold within the two-year period without a further movement taking place, e.g. a horse sent from UK to France is then sold in France after 12 months. In either case, the original temporary movement is altered to a permanent one and there is a supply for VAT purposes. If the owner is registered in both Member States this need not be a problem as, taking the above example, there will be a zero-rated supply in the UK and an acquisition in France. However, if there was no French registration, a UK VAT liability would be triggered and the owner would have to regard 7/47ths of the sale proceeds as VAT to be paid across to the UK Customs. This is a potentially expensive mistake!

5.87 This potential trap illustrates the importance of maintaining an up to date and comprehensive movements register so that the status of every animal is known at any given time. A commercial decision can then be made in every case as to whether to incur a VAT liability, or alternatively, as to the transport cost of moving the horse prior to sale.

The goods or services trap

5.88 The distinction between goods and services is one which is vital to understand if expensive mistakes are to be avoided. Briefly, whole horses are goods whereas part shares in horses are services. Nominations to stallions are also generally treated as supplies of services, although in Ireland they are goods. Problems often arise in this area because the type of supply (i.e. goods or services) also determines the place of supply.

5.89 VAT Business by Business

5.89 The VAT trap can be illustrated by the following example. A UK owner has 30 shares in a stallion, the other 10 being held by another UK owner. The other owner sells his 10 shares to an Australian stud. Six months later, the first owner sells his 30 shares to the same stud, which then exports the horse to Australia. Both UK owners have made supplies of services, subject to UK VAT, but it would be very easy for the first owner to mistreat his supply as a zero-rated export of goods. With a high-value transaction of this nature, that could be very costly. If both owners had sold their shares simultaneously, then, following the principle established in the *Astor* case (see paragraph 5.21 above), both could, in fact, have treated their supplies as goods for export and, therefore, zero-rated!

5.90 If the stallion had been in Australia before any of the shares were sold, the outcome for VAT would have been precisely the same. Each party would have been making a supply of services in the UK, subject to VAT. The whereabouts of the stallion would be irrelevant in this case because the place of supply is where the seller belongs. However, if the stallion had been in another Member State of the EU, another outcome would have been possible had the shares all been sold at the same time to a single buyer. UK Customs have exceptionally said that in such cases they will, by extension of the *Astor* principle, 'look through' the UK supplies of services provided that VAT is charged in another Member State on the supply of the whole horse. This avoids the same transaction being subject to VAT in two Member States and is more likely to be the case in practice when a horse is sold at auction in Ireland because all such sales are automatically subject to Irish VAT.

5.91 The above examples show that it is often possible to structure transactions so as to create the best possible VAT outcome. However, this cannot be done after the event. It is, therefore, vital with high-value bloodstock transactions to consider in advance the VAT implications and any possible planning opportunities.

VAT registration options

5.92 Since the introduction of the Owners Scheme, there are two possible ways to register for VAT, i.e. under the Owners Scheme or as an ordinary business. Owner-breeders are regarded under the Memorandum of Understanding as ordinary businesses, whereas those persons who merely own racehorses and have no other business activity are not, and can only register under the Owners Scheme.

5.93 The practical point is that it should now be the case that most racehorses, however owned, can be covered by a VAT registration. For example, if a company director wishes to be involved with racing, he now has a practical choice of owning the horses in his own name and being registered under the Owners Scheme, or alternatively letting the company own the horses. In the latter case, Customs would have to agree that there was sufficient advertising and promotional benefit deriving to the company for the associated VAT to be properly recoverable.

Registration in other EU Member States

5.94 Many in the industry will find themselves liable to register for VAT in more than one country. This is often perceived as something to be avoided whereas, in fact, it can often have a very positive side.

5.95 In principle, any person making taxable supplies in a particular country is liable to register and account for VAT on those supplies. Generally speaking, most Member States have either very low registration thresholds or none at all. For example, Ireland has thresholds for persons established in Ireland but not for overseas entrepreneurs.

5.96 It follows that a person who, for instance, regularly sells bloodstock at overseas sales should be registered for VAT in the countries concerned. The exception would be where horses are sold out of training where the Member State does not recognise the racing activity as being a business for VAT purposes. It should be noted in this context that Tattersalls in the UK operates the 'Docket System' whereby it acts as importer for horses entering the UK from third countries and, therefore, takes responsibility for any VAT due on importation. This system also obviates the need for the overseas seller to register for UK VAT (unless he is registrable for other reasons), as the horse is sold under Tattersalls' own VAT number.

5.97 As mentioned earlier, many jockeys regularly ride in other EU Member States. The place of supply of such services is the Member State in which they are physically provided. Thus, registration for VAT will often be necessary.

5.98 Bloodstock agents increasingly do business on an international scale. A UK agent might buy horses at Tattersalls for, say, an Irish client. UK VAT will be payable on the purchase and the client may not be registered for Irish VAT and will not, therefore, be able to recover the UK VAT via the Eighth Directive scheme. In this case the UK agent could register for Irish VAT and thus sell the horse in Ireland at the lower Irish VAT rate of 2.5%, saving the client the difference between the UK and Irish rates.

5.99 It should also be noted that holding VAT registrations in other Member States can often be preferable to making Eighth Directive refund claims for any VAT suffered in those territories. Member States have six months in which to repay satisfactory Eighth Directive claims, whereas VAT claimed via a normal return under a country's VAT system should be repayable in a much shorter time.

5.100   VAT Business by Business

Temporary importations

5.100   Horses entering the UK or other EU Member State from third countries will often qualify for temporary importation (TI) treatment, thus avoiding payment of VAT on entry. Horses temporarily imported for dressage, training, breeding or grazing all qualify for TI relief. The relief is for up to 24 months and controlled by payment of a bond or deposit or the setting up of a bank guarantee. Breach of TI conditions, e.g. any sale of the horse in the EU, causes VAT to become payable on the value at the date of diversion from TI, not the date of original entry.

5.101   TI relief may also be transferred between persons either in the same Member State or in different Member States, but this does not have any impact on the time limit for re-exportation. In some circumstances, UK Customs will allow a six-month extension of the normal 24-month limit. This must be agreed in advance with Customs in all cases.

5.102   It should be noted that a TI horse is not subject to VAT on its sale in any Member State but purely on its value when diverted. Consequently, when selling privately, vendors should be aware that the price agreed will effectively be inclusive of VAT at the appropriate rate and negotiate accordingly.

Flat rate farming

5.103   The UK Flat Rate Farming Scheme was introduced as a means of preventing the major bloodstock auctioneers from leaving the UK prior to the completion of the EU Single Market on 1 January 1993. In this regard it has been superseded by the Owners Scheme but remains as an alternative for all farmers and bloodstock breeders.

5.104   However, particular types of bloodstock business may still find the scheme attractive, particularly because of the advantages of selling VAT-free to customers. Businesses with a lot of unregistered customers such as, for instance National Hunt stallions owners or livery stables could well find a balance of advantage in joining the scheme.

5.105   Anyone contemplating becoming a Flat Rate Farmer should consider the timing of the application very carefully. For example, a bloodstock breeder may well find it advantageous to remain registered until shortly before selling the bulk of his progeny in the Autumn sales. Exceptionally, those becoming deregistered from VAT in order to become Flat Rate Farmers do not have to account for VAT on closing stocks and assets. It can be seen that this provision allows for maximum flexibility on the timing of such a change.

5.106   It should be noted that there is a restriction placed on those wishing to make the switch. If Customs consider that the total of Flat Rate Additions

Bloodstock **5.107**

will exceed the total of input VAT suffered by more than £3,000, they may refuse Flat Rate status. However, it is possible to remain in the scheme by choosing not to charge the addition in every case, thus managing the position under the '£3,000 Rule'.

5.107 Anyone considering a change to Flat Rate Farming status should read Customs Leaflet 700/46/92 very carefully before doing so.

5.App 1 VAT Business by Business

Appendix I

VAT and bloodstock: memorandum of understanding

1. Introduction

1.1 This memorandum records the agreement reached between the Thoroughbred Horseracing and Breeding Industry and HM Customs and Excise on the VAT position of persons involved in the breeding, training and dealing in horses used for racing. It also sets out the Customs' response to the proposals of the industry on the VAT registration of racehorse owners and maps out a way forward on this issue which has been endorsed by the industry.

1.2 VAT registration has always been required for persons dealing in horses and for breeders and trainers where their taxable supplies exceed the registration threshold. However, as racing has been regarded as a non-business activity, restrictions have been placed on the amount of tax reclaimable by those businesses which also engage in racing, either by denying input tax itself when incurred for racing purposes and/or through an agreement with the Industry for output tax payment when horses are put to racing.

2. New arrangements

2.1 As a result of representations from all sections of the Thoroughbred Horseracing and Breeding Industry to Ministers and officials, and in response to the new proposals put by the Jockey Club on behalf of the Industry, Customs and the Industry are now prepared to move forward together in a number of important areas. In essence, Customs are prepared to respond positively to the Industry's initiative on sponsorship and appearance money, by recognising that persons racing horses with a view to income from sponsorship, appearance money and prize money are intending to make taxable supplies and are subject to VAT registration under the normal rules. There are also changes in the Customs' treatment of racing by breeders, trainers and dealers currently registered for VAT which will provide greater opportunity to reclaim VAT incurred by the business.

2.2 The new arrangements are:-

(a) The Rules of Racing will be amended as necessary to create a framework whereby owners can exploit opportunities for increased income through sponsorship and appearance money to a more commercial level.

(b) Owners whose taxable activities exceed the turnover threshold will be liable for registration, but Customs will also accept applications from owners seeking voluntary VAT registration in respect of their racing activities so long as they have a business intention and they make a declaration to that effect.

(c) Customs will accept that racing of horses by breeders, trainers and dealers can have a genuine purpose and value in promoting the business activities and will no longer regard racing as non-business by definition.

3. Breeders

3.1 Customs will continue to require or allow VAT registration where a business of breeding horses for sale exists. Customs are now prepared to accept that, where breeders engage in racing activities with the intention of enhancing the value of their stock and/or the general standing of the business, those activities will be regarded as being by way of business. For these purposes stock means both colts and fillies but not geldings. With regard to colts, Customs would expect the breeder to demonstrate that he is involved or intends to become involved in the production and/or ownership of stallions or stallion shares.

3.2 Breeders who meet these conditions will be able to reclaim all input tax in accordance with the normal rules. No liability to output tax will arise on the transfer of stock to training. Output tax will become due, subject to the normal rules, on the full amount realised on the sale of all stock.

3.3 Breeders who own horses on their own account for racing purposes may not enjoy deduction of input tax under the above but in future they may qualify to do so under the arrangements for owners outlined in this memorandum in section 7 below.

4. Trainers

4.1 Customs will continue to require or allow VAT registration where a business exists of providing training services to owners. Customs take the view that, where horses are owned by the trainer and trained by him, providing that the number of such horses is not disproportionate to the main activity, the related costs will be regarded as being business expenditure for VAT purposes.

4.2 Trainers who own horses on their own account for racing purposes may not enjoy deduction of input tax under the above but in future they may qualify to do so under the arrangements for owners outlined in this memorandum in section 7 below.

5. Dealers

5.1 Persons engaged in the purchase and sale of horses commercially will continue to be regarded by Customs as liable or eligible for VAT

5.App 1 VAT Business by Business

registration. The racing, for business purposes, of horses held as trading stock by a VAT-registered dealer will be accepted by Customs as part of the main business activity, whilst that trading stock remains available for sale.

5.2 Dealers who purchase horses on their own account for racing purposes may not enjoy deduction of input tax under the above but in future they may qualify to do so under the arrangements for owners outlined in this memorandum in section 7 below.

6. Company owners

6.1 At present, Customs examine the claims of company owners that horses have been purchased for advertising their own products or services against a number of criteria. If they are satisfied that there is business use, input tax may be deducted under the normal VAT rules. These arrangements will of course continue and, if changes to racing do materialise, such companies may have greater scope for deduction of input tax relating to racehorses. Company owners which are racing companies set up specifically to acquire racehorses would now fall to be considered for VAT registration under the arrangements outlined for owners in section 7 below.

7. Owners

7.1 This covers persons who own horses for racing, and breeders, trainers or dealers whose ownership of horses is not regarded as a business activity under the arrangements set out elsewhere in this document.

7.2 It is recognised that initiatives being proposed by the Industry to encourage income opportunities from sponsorship and appearance money now provide scope for owners to qualify for registration provided they intend to exploit the opportunities available in a businesslike manner.

7.3 Appearance money and sponsorship of racehorses are new to racing; both Customs and the Industry agree that it will take some years for these opportunities to be nurtured and to flourish. Consequently, this could prove a source of difficulty for owners and for Customs' staff in dealing with applications for VAT registration, and adherence to normal rules might stifle these initiatives. On the basis that owners who intend to pursue their racing activities in a businesslike way are intending trading and are therefore liable to or eligible for VAT registration under the VAT Act 1983 Schedule 1, Customs will introduce a special scheme (The Scheme) which will offer across the board registration to all owners who accept the conditions of the Scheme.

The scheme conditions

7.4 Owners will have to complete a declaration confirming their intention to seek sponsorship, appearance money and prize money and accepting the conditions laid down as part of The Scheme. The declaration will have to be certified by an approved body nominated by the racing industry to confirm that the application is registered with the Jockey Club as an owner. On receipt of the declaration and VAT registration application form (VAT 1) Customs will register the owner subject only to normal checks on status and completeness.

7.5 Owners whose application for registration has been accepted, and those whose racing activities are to be included within an existing registration, will be subject to the normal rules applying to new registrations. Given that the ownership of racehorses has not hitherto been treated as a business activity, input VAT will not be deductible on supplies received before the introduction of The Scheme. This means that input VAT cannot be reclaimed on stocks and assets on hand at the commencement of The Scheme but equally no output VAT need be accounted for on disposal of stock and assets on which input VAT deduction has been denied.

7.6 Otherwise owners will be eligible to deduct input VAT on their business activities, subject to the normal rules. Output tax will, of course, have to be accounted for on income, e.g. sponsorship, appearance money, prize money (excluding the sweepstake/race entry fee element), proceeds of sale. Tax will also fall due on horses diverted to non-business use when the tax will be calculated on the lower of cost and current market value.

7.7 Owners registered pursuant to The Scheme will be subject to normal periodic visits for VAT control purposes and will have to show that income is still being actively pursued. If, at any time, this is not the case, repayment of input tax claimed may be required, and action taken to cancel the registration. Owners will be able to appeal any such decision to the independent VAT Tribunal.

Scheme review

7.8 Customs will review the operation of the Scheme in consultation with the trade bodies concerned during its fourth year to assess whether the levels of income available to the industry as a whole warrant The Scheme's continuing operation. If it becomes clear that the climate in the industry has not in fact changed to enable owners generally to exploit the opportunities for income to a business level, The Scheme will be withdrawn and all registrations accepted under its terms will be cancelled from a date no earlier than three months thereafter. Customs, however, will not require refund of input tax reclaimed unless, in the case of particular owners, it is clear that reasonable efforts were not made to seek income, nor will the Commissioners require output tax to be accounted for on stock and assets

5.App 1 *VAT Business by Business*

held at the date of deregistration. Individual owners who believe that they have in fact carried on their activities in a business-like way may ask to have their registration retained.

7.9 In the event of The Scheme being discontinued the normal rules would require each application for registration to be decided on its own merits with owners having to demonstrate individually that they have a business intention.

Appendix II

Memorandum of agreement

Keep stallions at stud

Calculation of open market value

Value added tax is chargeable on the value of the taxable supplies made by a VAT-registered person. If a registered person makes supplies for a consideration which is less than the market value of those supplies, and there is also a non-monetary consideration, VAT is chargeable on the open market value.

It is common practice for a stallion stud to keep a stallion either for no cash charge but for a number of nominations to the stallion, or for a reduced cash charge plus one or more nominations. HM Customs and Excise, being apprised of such arrangements in the course of control visits to stallion studs, are concerned to establish the market value of the supply of keeping a stallion on a stud.

Discussions have taken place with a view to establishing guidelines within which stallion studs and HM Customs and Excise can work in order to establish for each stud and each stallion the relevant figures upon which VAT will have to be calculated.

The following Memorandum of Practice has been agreed:

(1) Where there is a charge for keeping a stallion, to the stallion syndicate or stallion owner, expressed only in cash terms and 'free' nominations are not involved, no negotiations will be necessary so long as Customs and Excise are satisfied that the cash charge represents the true open market value of the supply and there is no other form of non-monetary consideration.

(2) Where there is no charge for keeping a stallion, expressed as payable in cash, and only 'free' nominations are involved, or where there is a combination of cash plus 'free' nominations, a value will have to be established for the keep of the stallions. This will take into account:

    (a) The values of the free nominations as shown by their sales by the stallion stud, or, if no sales have taken place (e.g. where used for own mares), by reference to average reported sale values.

    (b) The varying types of contracts for nominations. These may be used by applying the following formula to arrive at the value of VAT which will be the total of the amount charged plus the value of the nominations:

5.App 2 VAT Business by Business

Straight nomination 100% of the figure from 2(a)

1 October Pregnancy 70% of the figure from 2(a)
Nomination

Split Payment Nominations 100% of the first payment from 2(a)

70% of the second payment from 2(a)

Live Foal Nomination 60% of the figure from 2(a)

The VAT on the calculated value of the service supplied by the stud should be accounted for quarterly i.e., having established the value of the service for a year, 25% of that value and the relevant VAT will be brought to account in the normal quarterly returns.

(c) A maximum figure to be agreed annually by the TBA and Customs and Excise. This maximum will operate when the value of the nominations (or cash plus the nominations) arrived at as in 2(a) and 2(b) above exceed the agreed figure. The maximum has been set at £30,000 for the 1984 breeding season.

This agreement should make it possible for stallion studs to assess the proper value of the service in keeping the stallion(s) and to account for VAT accordingly. The local VAT office should be consulted in the event of any problems arising from the implementation of these arrangements.

Appendix III

Supplies of relevant services to mares (and their foals) visiting UK stallions from 1 January 1996

Mares

(1) Where mare leaves the UK

(a) Owner/Breeder registered for VAT in EU (not UK). Outside the scope of UK VAT

(b) Non-EU Owner/Breeder, providing mare imported into/acquired within EU for covering and exported from EU Zero-rated

Foals

(2) Where foal leaves the UK

(a) Owner/Breeder registered for VAT in EU (not UK) Outside the scope of UK VAT

(b) Non-EU Owner/Breeder and foal exported outside EU Zero-rated

Chapter 6

Books and Publications

Introduction

6.1 Currently in the UK, zero-rating is available for a wide range of printed matter. As with any zero-rated supply, the supplier benefits from the ability to recover input tax on his own related expenditure without the necessity of charging VAT on the sale price. This in turn benefits the consumer either by increasing cashflow or, if the business is unable to recover the VAT charged, by saving what would otherwise have been an additional cost. In some circumstances, there are opportunities for suppliers and consumers to save significant costs by ensuring that zero-rating is applied to publications where available.

6.2 The present legislation governing zero-rating for books, newspapers and publications is relatively simple and has not materially changed since the introduction of VAT in 1973. Nevertheless, a disproportionate number of cases have been heard at the VAT tribunal and higher courts to determine the correct VAT liability of publications. Included in this chapter is a detailed synopsis of a wide range of printed items together with specific examples arising from decisions of the UK courts.

6.3 The issues which are likely to affect the VAT treatment of the sale and production of books, newspapers and publications are many and varied. The majority of VAT liability mistakes arise because each item must be considered in isolation. Zero-rating usually depends on the size or shape of an item but it is also essential to consider the nature of the whole supply, for example, where the printed article is only a part of a larger supply. There are several instances where a publication may be eligible for zero-rating but becomes standard-rated due to the circumstances in which it is supplied.

6.4 In addition to determining the VAT liability of the supply, there are a number of further factors which need to be addressed in order to maximise zero-rating relief. The extent of the use of publications within a business is extremely wide and concerns most business sectors in addition to publishers. Businesses which produce marketing brochures, leaflets or newsletters will not only need to be aware of the zero-rating of publications but also the VAT treatment of any advertising, vouchers, application forms or competitions displayed therein.

6.5 VAT Business by Business

The law

6.5 The VAT legislation is set out in *VATA 1994, 8 Sch, Group 3*, which zero-rates the following categories:

- Books, booklets, brochures, pamphlets and leaflets;
- Newspapers, journals and periodicals;
- Children's picture books and painting books;
- Music scores;
- Maps, charts and topographical plans.

Examples of items which Customs & Excise accept are zero-rated, and of non-qualifying standard-rated items, are set out in Appendices I and II.

Definitions

6.6 The law does not provide any definitions or the criteria for zero-rating and, therefore, the VAT treatment of each particular item has to be considered separately. As a rule, the question of eligibility of an item tends to be based on its physical characteristics rather than merely its function.

6.7 Zero-rating is not restricted to printed products. Typed, hand-written or photocopied documents are also accepted. However, text itself is not specifically relieved from VAT if it appears in some other format, such as e-mail or computer disk. An identical product, such as a textbook, available from the same supplier via the Internet, on a CD-ROM or computer diskette would be standard-rated. Unfortunately, the UK has no authority to apply for an extension of the zero-rating provisions to include information obtained by more modern media.

6.8 The VAT tribunal and higher courts have considered various publications over the years and, in nearly all cases, have reached their decision by considering the 'ordinary and everyday' meaning of the words in the statute. The following descriptions have been based on the various decisions of the courts.

Books and booklets

6.9 'Books and booklets' normally consist of text or illustrations bound in a stiffer cover than the pages. However, books which contain a significant number of blank pages intended for completion are excluded from zero-rating. Generally, but not exclusively, zero-rating is based on the ability of an item to disseminate information. For example, the VAT liability of a blank

Books and Publications **6.13**

diary or address book was considered by the High Court in *Colour Offset Ltd, QB [1995] STC 85*. In that case, the Court found that the diary or address book was not an article to be read and looked at and, accordingly, was not zero-rated. In other cases, a publication may contain a mixture of text and blank pages. For further details of the VAT treatment of brochures, pamphlets and leaflets with areas for completion, see paragraphs 6.32 and 6.33 below.

Brochures and pamphlets

6.10 'Brochures and pamphlets' normally consist of several sheets of reading matter fastened or folded together and not necessarily bound in covers. In the same way as books and booklets, brochures and pamphlets can consist of text or illustrations. However, in some cases, the physical characteristics of the article are quite different from the expected format. For example, in *London Cyrenians Housing (14426)*, the VAT tribunal considered whether a charity's annual report constituted a booklet or brochure when the format was changed to that of a calendar made of stiff card, with a flap intended to allow the whole to stand upright on a desk. The tribunal held that, although a calendar would have been standard-rated, the new format of the annual report did not exclude it from the zero-rated category of a booklet or brochure.

Leaflets

6.11 'Leaflets' normally consist of a single sheet of paper which may contain a significant proportion of text and are designed to be held in the hand for reading.

6.12 Whether or not a particular article qualifies as a leaflet is a matter of fact and impression. In some instances, the size of the article gives a good indication. However, Customs & Excise introduced a 'limpness' test following the VAT tribunal's decision in *Panini Publishing Ltd (3876)*. In that case, the VAT tribunal held that stickers were not 'leaflets' even though the reverse side of each sticker contained information about the photograph of the character or personality on the cover. The stickers were sold separately, but formed part of a series, and were designed for insertion in an album. The VAT tribunal held that the fact that the stickers were designed to be read was not conclusive, and ruled that a leaflet must be limp and printed on unlaminated paper.

6.13 A similar decision was reached in *Adland Group Co Ltd (10397)*, where the VAT tribunal considered whether inserts for 'Yellow Pages' telephone directories were eligible for zero-rating as leaflets. The tribunal decided that, as the inserts were printed on shiny paper which was substantially heavier than the directory sheets, they did not qualify as leaflets.

6.14 VAT Business by Business

6.14 However, in a later decision, *Multiform Printing Ltd (13931)*, the VAT tribunal considered whether card inserts with a tear-off reply slip advertising a publication qualified for zero-rating as a leaflet. Customs & Excise argued that the thickness of the paper disqualified the card, relying on the limpness test introduced following the VAT tribunal's decision in *Panini Publishing Ltd*, but the tribunal rejected this argument and held that the flimsiness of the item or the thickness of the paper was not an absolute test of whether an item was a leaflet. Customs & Excise subsequently issued an amendment to VAT Leaflet 701/10/85 'Printed and similar matter' regarding the thickness of paper, recommending that written guidance should be obtained in respect of the VAT treatment of items where the paper used has a grammage exceeding 180gsm.

6.15 In *BNR Company Services Ltd (13783)*, the VAT tribunal rejected an appeal on the question of whether a registered business name certificate, for display on the client's premises, qualified for zero-rating as a leaflet.

6.16 In *Flipcards Ltd (13916)*, the VAT tribunal rejected an appeal on the question of whether a pack of Highway Code revision cards qualified as leaflets.

Newspapers, journals and periodicals

6.17 'Newspapers' normally consist of several large sheets of printed matter, folded rather than bound together, and containing information about current events of national and international interest and are issued daily or once a week under the same title and usually dated.

6.18 'Journals and periodicals' are magazines issued in a series or in regular intervals more frequently than once a year. They may contain information of a specialised nature, such as legal, sporting, gardening or fashion articles. Although posters are excluded from zero-rating, the VAT tribunal considered whether a fortnightly poster magazine qualified for zero-rating as a periodical in *European Publishing Consultants Ltd (13841)*. In that case, the tribunal decided that the magazine was not merely a collection of posters but included significant text and smaller photographs which were intended to be of real interest to the intended readers of the publication. The tribunal relied on the dictionary definition of a 'periodical', which was 'a publication issued at regular intervals'.

Children's books

6.19 'Children's picture books' are normally printed on paper or textiles and consist wholly or mainly of pictures. However, books which are essentially toys, such as 'pop-up' books and cut-out 'assembly' books, may not always qualify for zero-rating.

6.20 'Children's painting books' are zero-rated if they consist of bound pages with sample pictures for copying or outlines of pictures for colouring, painting or drawing. However, colouring books, sketch books and painting books intended primarily for adults are standard-rated.

6.21 If the printed articles are supplied together with other non-qualifying children's items in a single pack, the VAT treatment is particularly complex and depends on whether the whole is a composite or multiple supply. The VAT liability of children's activity packs is considered separately in paragraph 6.31 below.

Music scores

6.22 'Music' is normally printed or in manuscript, bound or on loose sheets for instrumental or vocal purposes. Blank music manuscript designed for composing is excluded from zero-rating.

Maps, charts and topographical plans

6.23 'Maps, charts and topographical plans' are zero-rated whether printed on paper or other material, such as cloth. Publications which are designed for hanging up or for general display purposes and posters are not eligible for zero-rating. Industrial, architectural or engineering plans or drawings used for commercial purposes are excluded from zero-rating relief. Other standard-rated items include framed maps, posters, pictorial wall charts, aerial photographs and decorative maps printed on textile articles, such as scarves, tea towels or rugs.

Printed matter supplied with other goods or services

6.24 Occasionally, books and manuals are supplied together with other goods or services and it is necessary for VAT purposes to determine whether the transaction constitutes a 'composite' or 'multiple' supply. For example, a standard-rated article may be supplied with zero-rated printed matter, such as a children's colouring book issued with a crayon. A child can use the crayon on any paper but it is sold with the colouring book as a marketing device.

6.25 Given that there are a number of different ways in which publications can be supplied with associated goods or services, the VAT treatment is not always straightforward. Depending on how the supply is structured, the payment received by the supplier can be treated as either;

(i) wholly zero-rated;

(ii) wholly standard-rated;

(iii) wholly exempt; or

6.26 VAT Business by Business

(iv) apportioned between the separate elements.

6.26 As a rule, if a number of articles are sold together for an inclusive price and the majority are zero-rated, the whole should be zero-rated. In these circumstances, the supply would be a composite supply. However, if no article is dominant or the main purpose of the supply, then the VAT liability of the inclusive price should be apportioned between each of the separate elements. In these circumstances, the supply would be multiple.

6.27 A multiple supply is a number of separate supplies charged at a single inclusive price. If there is a mixture of a standard-rated article or exempt service supplied with zero-rated printed matter, the tax value of each supply must be determined and an equitable apportionment made. Alternatively, a composite supply may be wholly zero-rated, wholly standard-rated or wholly exempt depending on the VAT liability of the main supply. Not surprisingly, there have been a number of cases which have considered the VAT liability of products where printed matter is supplied together with other goods or services.

6.28 In order to determine whether a supply is a single composite supply or a series of multiple supplies, it is necessary to consider whether the constituent elements are either:

- 'physically and economically dissociable' from each other, i.e. separate and therefore, multiple, or;

- 'incidental' or 'integral' to the main supply, i.e. one whole and therefore, composite.

Training and educational courses

6.29 A typical area where printed publications are supplied with other services is in respect of educational or training supplies. In *The Rapid Results College Ltd, [1973] VATTR 197 (48)*, the VAT tribunal held that the fees for correspondence and residential courses were multiple supplies and should be apportioned between the zero-rated supply of course literature and the standard-rated tuition.

6.30 In another case, *Betty Foster (Fashion Sewing) Ltd, [1976] VATTR 229 (299)*, the VAT tribunal went one stage further and held that a course in dress designing and pattern construction packaged in a stiff paper folder containing an instruction booklet, a fabric planner and miniature patterns was a single composite supply of a 'brochure' and, accordingly, zero-rated.

Children's activity packs

6.31 Children's activity packs are particularly complex. In *Odhams Leisure Group Ltd, QB [1992] STC 332*, the High Court decided that a

Postman Pat pack containing a series of children's illustrated story sheets and dictionary cards designed for pre-school children was not a composite supply of leaflets, because the pack also contained a play mat and jigsaw puzzle, which were accepted as standard-rated if separately supplied. The High Court ruled that the polythene envelope package constituted a composite supply but, as the majority of the items were standard-rated, the whole was standard-rated.

Brochures, pamphlets and leaflets with areas for completion

6.32 Publications which have a considerable number of blank pages intended for writing in are not zero-rated (see paragraph 6.9 above). However, some brochures, pamphlets and leaflets have areas for completion, such as a tear-off portion to be detached and returned. Customs & Excise have issued guidance that, if an otherwise zero-rated publication contains more than a 25% area which is blank and available for completion, the whole item becomes standard-rated. However, this guidance is merely Customs & Excise's policy and has no basis in statute.

6.33 Advertising agencies, graphic designers and marketing businesses with responsibility for the creation and format of publications will need to be aware of the possible VAT implications to avoid incurring unnecessary and potentially irrecoverable VAT charges for their customers. This is particularly relevant to exempt businesses which are unable to recover any or only a small proportion of the VAT charged, for example, banks, educational colleges and universities, insurance companies and other financial institutions. VAT incurred on publications which are used in connection with exempt supplies is not recoverable. By changing the design to ensure that any tear-off portion or blank pages are less than 25% of the whole, the publication satisfies the zero-rating criterion and saves the customer a potential VAT cost.

Printed matter supplied as a package

6.34 Alternatively, the printed matter can be supplied as a package. Customs & Excise accept that a package containing printed articles including a mixture of standard-rated items and zero-rated items may be zero-rated in its entirety as a 'composite' supply if the number of standard-rated items is less than 25% of the total package. Consequently, as a VAT planning measure, printers and other producers of publications should consider the VAT recovery status of their intended customer to maximise zero-rating relief, where appropriate.

6.35 For example, a financial institution, such as a bank, would not be able to recover the VAT on mortgage application forms as they are more than likely to be attributable to the exempt supply of the mortgage, in which case, the VAT would become an additional cost. However, if the application forms

6.36 *VAT Business by Business*

were supplied within a package, for example, a folder containing other relevant zero-rated items, such as marketing leaflets and general information regarding the types of mortgages available, the whole supply could be zero-rated and could thus save the bank a potentially large irrecoverable VAT cost.

Clubs, associations and organisations

6.36 The majority of clubs, associations and other similar bodies are not exempt from VAT registration. Generally, if an organisation provides tangible benefits to its members, it is treated like a commercial business for VAT purposes.

6.37 Frequently, a club or association's membership subscription covers the receipt of a regular newsletter or magazine. In most cases, it is possible to agree with Customs & Excise that the supply of the publication is a separate supply to the standard-rated or exempt subscription and an apportionment may be made to relieve the value of the zero-rated publication. In circumstances where the membership subscription is exempt, for example a charity or qualifying professional body, the separation of the zero-rated publication is the only means whereby recovery of any VAT on related costs may be made. This issue is considered in further detail in Chapter 8 'Clubs and Associations'.

6.38 One such case was *The Automobile Association, QB [1974] STC 192*, where the High Court ruled that the supply of the Automobile Association manual was a separate zero-rated supply from the exempt motor recovery insurance and the annual subscription should be apportioned accordingly.

Book clubs

6.39 However, in *The Leisure Circle Ltd (1362)*, the VAT tribunal ruled that the supply of books by a mail order company was a single 'composite' supply of books and not, as Customs & Excise contended, two separate supplies, one being a nominal club subscription fee and postage and packing chargeable at the standard rate.

Incidental reports

6.40 Notwithstanding the above, if the supply is essentially one of services but the resultant product is a report or booklet, the supply could be wholly standard-rated. Printed matter is a convenient means of communication, and frequently documents are produced to evidence the outcome of a supply of services. An example is a supply of professional services, where a written translation or an auditors' report are an incidental product of translation or accountancy services and, in either case, the supply is a single composite standard-rated supply of services.

Books and Publications **6.45**

Binders and loose-leaf works

6.41 The supply of a ring binder, dust cover, clasp or presentation folder can be regarded as zero-rated provided that the items are sold together with the paper inserts. The separate supply of binders and files used to store magazines or menu cards is standard-rated. However, Customs & Excise allow the supply of a separate binder to qualify for zero-rating if it is clearly designed to hold a particular loose-leaf book, provided that the exact title of the book is printed on the outside.

6.42 Parts of books, manuals or journals, such as unbound pages or separate illustrations, can be standard-rated. Occasionally, a printer or bookbinder may supply component parts of a book, including the cover, the endpapers, the unfolded and uncut printed sheets of the pages. As the component parts themselves are not assembled and do not constitute a self-contained work, none of them are eligible for zero-rating. See *Butler & Tanner Ltd, [1974] VATTR 72 (68)*.

6.43 However, a larger work, such as a reference book published in instalments, can be zero-rated. Customs & Excise issued an extra-statutory concession following the VAT tribunal's decision in *International Master Publishers Ltd (8807)*, allowing components of a loose-leaf book to qualify for zero-rating even though the individual articles purchased over a period, such as wildlife cards intended to be held in a ring binder, would not themselves qualify for zero-rating.

Advertising

6.44 The supply of advertising space in newspapers, journals and periodicals is always standard-rated. Nevertheless, the extent of the advertising within a publication will determine the VAT treatment of the publication itself. For example, the VAT liability of a football programme advertising various sponsors will remain zero-rated provided that there is significant other information contained therein.

6.45 However, the nature of advertising products is extremely diverse and each supply must be considered separately. For example, a marketing brochure, the main purpose of which was to promote a business's products or services, was considered by the High Court in *Geoffrey E Snushall, QB [1982] STC 537*. In that case, the Court found that an estate agent's property guide sold to other estate agents which consisted almost entirely of advertisements for houses was not regarded as a 'newspaper, journal or periodical'. The Court considered that an item is not within the ordinary meaning of a 'periodical' unless it is made available to the public.

6.46 *VAT Business by Business*

Charitable advertising

6.46 Charities are specifically relieved from VAT on certain qualifying advertisements under *VATA 1994, 8 Sch, Group 15, Item 8*. The relief applies where a charity displays an advertisement for the purpose of raising money or making known the objects or reasons for the charity. Additionally, where a brochure, annual report or programme contains a significant element of non-commercial advertisements, such as private individuals' acknowledgements, the whole is eligible for zero-rating.

6.47 The VAT tribunal has considered the scope of 'advertising services' which can qualify for relief and has held that a promotion should involve the conveyance of a message to inform consumers of the existence and objects of the charity. This issue is considered in further detail in Chapter 7 'Charities'.

Promotional items

6.48 Frequently, newspapers and periodicals will offer additional goods or services as part of a promotion to increase publication sales. For VAT purposes, there may be a separate supply of the promotional item. Generally, if the customer provides non-monetary consideration for receiving the item, VAT will be due on the value of the promotional goods or services by the publisher.

6.49 Typically, magazines will include a cover-mounted item as a 'free gift', such as a sachet of shampoo or a computer diskette. Unless the supplier is able to prove that the article is genuinely freely given, the sale proceeds would need to be apportioned between the value of the zero-rated publication and the separate standard-rated article. Customs & Excise accept that, provided that the magazine is sold at the same cover price as other issues, there is no separate VAT liability for the standard-rated cover item. VAT charged to the publisher on the purchase of the cover item is recoverable as a business expense provided that the cost is not more than £15.00, in accordance with the business gift rules.

6.50 Customs & Excise have issued an extra-statutory concession that, provided that the cost of the cover-mounted item does not exceed 20% of the total cost of the composite magazine or £1 (excluding VAT), the supplier does not need to make an apportionment for VAT purposes.

6.51 In *McDonald's Restaurants Ltd (3884)*, a tabloid newspaper ran a promotional scheme whereby the newspaper's readers had to cut out a number of vouchers in separate editions of the newspaper and present them in return for a McDonald's hamburger. Although no payment passed between the newspaper and McDonald's, the VAT tribunal ruled that the production of the vouchers was consideration for the supply of the hamburger and, consequently, VAT was due from McDonald's on the reciprocal supply. The tribunal rejected McDonald's argument that the hamburgers were given away freely as gifts.

6.52 It is not clear whether the newspaper was also assessed for a reciprocal supply of general promotional services received from McDonald's which potentially resulted in increased newspaper sales from readers collecting the vouchers who may not have otherwise purchased the newspaper. Customs & Excise could have sought additional VAT from the newspaper, which highlights the importance of reviewing the full VAT implications of running any promotion considered by a publisher.

6.53 However, Customs & Excise have subsequently revised their policy and clarified the uncertainty regarding joint promotions with newspaper publishers in VAT leaflet 700/7/94 'Business promotion schemes', which now includes a paragraph regarding the VAT implications of a promotion whereby vouchers are printed for collection in return for a third party's goods.

6.54 The rules governing the VAT treatment of business promotions have always been complex, and the number of court decisions have only served to complicate this area further. All businesses contemplating promotional activities need to pay careful attention to the VAT consequences, as failure to do so could result in a substantial VAT cost. In cases of doubt, it would be prudent to seek professional advice.

Competitions

6.55 Generally, competitions run by newspapers and magazines are organised in conjunction with a third party who provides the prize.

Fantasy football league

6.56 A number of newspapers run fantasy sports and financial leagues to promote newspaper sales. Customs & Excise originally released a Business Brief dated 12 September 1994, which warned that newspapers and magazines had a potential liability to pool betting duty at 37.5% of the gross receipts in respect of these competitions, which they considered could constitute betting. Customs & Excise sought to attack any competition published in a newspaper whereby the winner would receive money from a pool for the most accurate forecasting of the result of various imaginary sporting events.

6.57 The High Court has recently ruled in *C & E Commrs v News International Newspapers Ltd* that entry fees, registration fees or dealing charges payable for participation in the fantasy football league and other similar competitions are subject to pool betting duty. The Court of Appeal upheld this decision on 30 March 1998. However, most of these types of

6.58 VAT Business by Business

competitions are played by using a premium rate telephone line, and the income derived from British Telecom is not treated as a stake for betting purposes and, therefore, is not subject to pool betting duty.

Premium rate telephone lines

6.58 Some competitions run by newspapers involve a reader telephoning a premium rate telephone number to participate in the competition. In such cases, the profit earned on the premium rate line is split between the newspaper and British Telecom. Payments paid by British Telecom to operators of competition lines is standard-rated income. Consequently, newspapers and magazines deriving income from British Telecom should account for VAT to Customs & Excise on the tax-inclusive amount.

Vouchers and discount booklets

6.59 A common form of business promotion is the issue of vouchers, either printed separately or forming part of a booklet, such as a restaurant guide. The vouchers generally represent a standard-rated right to a discount but a booklet or leaflet containing vouchers could qualify for zero-rating if the entire article itself qualifies as a publication.

6.60 In *Graham Leisure Ltd (1304)*, a 'booklet' contained vouchers for admission to certain entertainment within a holiday complex. The booklets contained a number of vouchers and information concerning the entertainment outlets. The VAT tribunal held that the relevant supply amounted to a supply of services and must be regarded as standard-rated.

6.61 In *Interleisure Club Ltd (7458)*, the VAT tribunal decided that a 'leisure guide', containing vouchers which enabled the purchaser to obtain discounts at hotels and restaurants, was not eligible for zero-rating as the real value of the booklet was in the vouchers, which represented standard-rated services. In reaching its decision, the tribunal put emphasis on the fact that the guide was marketed and priced to promote the discount aspect of the publication.

Book tokens

6.62 The publication of book tokens is standard-rated, but if book tokens are sold to the general public there is no supply.

Distance selling

6.63 Frequently, publishers undertake the circulation of newspapers and magazines outside the UK either to other European distributors or to individual subscription-holders. Even if a book, newspaper or magazine publisher has no business establishment in any country other than the UK, the fact that printed articles are sent and distributed overseas will have European VAT implications. The other European Union Member States do not have an equivalent zero-rate for books and publications and, in some cases, foreign VAT should be charged and accounted for to the relevant overseas tax authorities.

6.64 As with any business operating in a European Union Member State, there are local VAT registration thresholds which, once exceeded, would necessitate a local VAT registration or the appointment of a VAT representative in order to satisfy local compliance requirements.

6.65 Distance selling occurs when the supplier is responsible for the delivery of goods to a non-registered person in another European Union Member State. Each Member State has set distance selling thresholds of either 35,000 ECU (approximately £24,000) or 100,000 ECU (approximately £70,000). Once the threshold has been exceeded, the UK supplier is automatically liable to register for local VAT registration and the goods are taxed at the applicable local VAT rate.

Authors

6.66 Although the supply of books is zero-rated, the basic contents of a work which will later become an article of printed matter do not meet the criteria for zero-rating. Manuscript or articles supplied by an author for publication, and pieces of music supplied by a composer, are standard-rated supplies. Similarly, royalties from book sales are subject to VAT.

Accounting and records

6.67 Where a newspaper or magazine receives regular articles or photographs from freelance journalists or photographers, there is a means by which the newspaper can self-bill and recover VAT which would be recoverable from an invoice. The main benefit for a newspaper or magazine publisher is the certainty that input tax is recovered in a timely manner without the necessity for chasing individual VAT-registered contributors. Application simply requires a request to Customs & Excise, provided that adequate records of suppliers' VAT registration numbers are maintained.

Library books

6.68 The hire or loan of any publication which is eligible for zero-rating, or the transfer of part ownership in any publication is zero-rated. Therefore, public libraries, university and college libraries may zero-rate the hire of all qualifying books.

6.69 *VAT Business by Business*

Importation of printed matter

6.69 See Appendix III.

Appendix I

Customs & Excise examples of standard-rated items

Acceptance cards
Account books
Albums
Amendment slips
Announcement cards
Appointment cards
Autograph books (blank)
Badges
Ballot papers
Bingo cards
Biorhythm charts
Book tokens
Bookmakers' tickets
Business cards
Calendars
Cassette inlay cards
Certificates
Cheque books
Cigarette cards
Cloakroom tickets
Colour cards
Compliment slips
Cookery cards
Copy books
Coupons
Credit cards
Delivery notes
Dividend warrants
Draft forms
Dressmaking patterns
Engineers' plans

Envelopes
Exercise books
Fashion drawings
Folders
Forms
Football pool coupons
Games
Greetings cards
Index cards
Invitation cards
Invoices
Knitting patterns (single sheets)
Labels
Letter headings
Log books
Lottery tickets
Manuscript paper
Medical records
Memo pads
Menu cards
Microfiche
Microfilm
Note books
Order books
Photograph albums
Playing cards
Postcards
Printed pictures
Questionnaires
Receipt books
Record books and labels

6.App 2 VAT Business by Business

Registers
Rent books
Reply-paid coupons
Scrap books (blank)
Seals
Stickers
Tags

Tickets
Transcripts
Visiting cards
Vouchers
Wastepaper
Wills

Appendix II

Customs & Excise examples of zero-rated items

Accounts (fully printed)
Advertising leaflets
Agendas (fully printed)
Almanacs
Amendments (loose leaf)
Annuals
Antique books and maps
Articles of Association
Astronomical charts
Atlases
Autograph books (completed)
Bibliographies
Bulletins
Catalogues
Circulars
Company reports
Comics

Crossword books
Football programmes
Handbills
Holiday and tourist guides
Knitting pattern books
Mail order catalogues
Manuals
Memorandum of Association
Monographs
Programmes
Recipe books
Road maps
Scrap books (completed)
Staff journals
Timetables
Travel brochures

Appendix III

Importation of printed matter

The *VAT (Imported Goods) Relief Order 1984* allows the following items to be imported from a country outside the European Community free from VAT:

- Documents sent free of charge to public services in the European Community.

- Publications of foreign governments or official international organisations for free distribution.

- Ballot papers for elections organised by bodies outside the European Community.

- Specimen signatures and circulars concerning signatures forming part of exchanges of information between banks and public services.

- Official printed matter sent to a Central Bank in the European Community.

- Documents from a company incorporated outside the European Community to shareholders and subscribers.

- Files and other documents for use at international conferences and reports of those conferences.

- Plans, technical drawings and other documents sent by any person participating in a competition in the European Community or to obtain or fulfil an order executed outside the European Community.

- Documents to be used in examinations held in the European Community on behalf of institutions established outside the European Community.

- Printed forms to be used as official documents in international trade.

- Printed forms, labels, tickets and other similar documents sent to travel agents in the European Community by transport or tourist agencies outside the European Community.

- Used commercial documents.

6.App 3 VAT Business by Business

- Official printed forms from national or international authorities.

- Printed matter sent from associations outside the European Community for distribution by corresponding associations within the European Community.

- Documents for free distribution to encourage persons to visit countries outside the European Community in particular to attend cultural, tourist, sporting, religious, trade or professional meetings or events (provided the goods do not contain more than 25% private or commercial advertising).

- Hotel lists and yearbooks published for free distribution by official tourist agencies outside the European Community and timetables for transport services in those countries (provided the goods do not contain more than 25% private or commercial advertising).

- Yearbooks, lists of telephone and telex numbers, hotel lists, catalogues for fairs, specimen craft items of negligible value and literature on museums and universities supplied as reference material to accredited representatives appointed by official national tourist agencies and not intended for distribution.

- Official publications issued under the authority of the country of exportation, international institutions, regional or local authorities and bodies governed by public law established in the country of exportation (provided that VAT or similar tax has been paid on the publication in the country of exportation).

- Printed matter distributed by foreign political organisations on the occasion of elections to the European Parliament or national elections in the country in which the publication originates (provided that VAT or similar tax has been paid on the publication in the country of exportation).

- Photographs and slides sent to press agencies, newspapers and magazines.

Chapter 7

Charities

Introduction

7.1 Charities are not offered any general relief from VAT; however, the nature of their activities does mean that a considerable number of charities avoid having to charge VAT on at least part of their income. To that extent, and contrary to popular belief, the VAT regime is not that different from the direct tax treatment of charities, which does not exempt the sector *per se*, but rather exempts specific sources of income. Charities involved in trading activities which do not fall within their primary purpose are liable to corporation tax in the same way as any other business. The problem with VAT for charities is not so much the liability of their income, it is the cost of financing irrecoverable VAT on expenditure.

The term 'charity' is not defined in the VAT legislation and Customs recognise any organisation with charitable objects as having charitable status. Charitable objects are established by case law and fall under one of four heads: the relief of poverty; the advancement of education; the advancement of religion and a general head covering other activities beneficial to the community. If an organisation is registered with the charity commissioners or is recognised as having charitable status by the Inland Revenue, Customs will have no difficulty recognising it as a charity for VAT purposes. Organisations without this recognition will have to demonstrate to Customs that they have charitable status.

European Community Law

7.2 It is a general principle of European Community Law that the law of the European Economic Community prevails over any contrary provision in national law (*Amministrazione delle Finanze dello Stato v Simmenthal SpA, CJEC [1978] 3 CMLR 263*) and 'wherever the provisions of a Directive appear, as far as their subject matter is concerned, to be unconditional and sufficiently precise, their provisions may... be relied upon as against any national provision which is incompatible with the Directive or in so far as the provisions define rights which individuals are able to assert against the state' (*Ursula Becker v Finanzamt Münster-Innenstadt, CJEC [1982] 1 CMLR 499*).

7.3 VAT Business by Business

This principle gives EC legislation direct effect in the UK when UK legislation is found to be defective, ambiguous or inconsistent with EC law. As will become evident throughout this chapter, this principle has been (and is increasingly being) used by the charity sector in an effort to protect and enhance its position within the UK VAT legislative framework.

Liability

7.3 This section examines the VAT liability of charities' activities where the liability is determined by their status or the nature of their income.

The majority of charities in this country have levels of income which would put them on a par with 'small businesses'. However, unlike many small businesses, a charity's funds can come from a diverse range of income streams. The position is further complicated because the level of income from each stream may not be consistent or regular, and so a single receipt may trigger a liability to register for VAT or, if the incorrect liability is applied, exposure to a penalty or interest charges. Income may be taxable (at any of the three rates), exempt or outside the scope. To identify the liability of a particular source of income, a charity needs to be disciplined into asking two basic questions based on fundamental VAT principles:

- Is the income generated in the course or furtherance of a business?

- If it is, what is the VAT liability of that income?

Meaning of 'business'

7.4 The term 'business', as defined in the VAT legislation, 'includes any trade, profession or vocation'. It also specifically includes the provision of membership benefits by clubs, associations and similar bodies in return for a subscription or other consideration and admission to premises for a charge (*VATA 1994, s 94*).

The definition is intended to have a wide meaning to capture as many business activities as possible. Hence the deliberate use of the word 'includes'. Recognising whether or not an activity or income stream is in the course or furtherance of a business is critical for a charity: if it is, then the charity could have a potential VAT liability; if it is not, then it falls outside the scope of the tax.

As the legislation is drafted to encompass a wide range of activities, the meaning and extent of the term has been determined by case law. The case of *C & E Commrs v Lord Fisher, QB [1981] STC 238* (for a summary of the case, see *Tolley's VAT Cases 1998, para 7.5*) listed the following criteria as a guide to what would constitute a 'business activity':

- the activity is a serious undertaking earnestly pursued;
- there is continuity;
- the activity has substance measured by the value of taxable supplies;
- the activity is conducted on sound and recognisable business principles;
- the activity is predominantly concerned with making taxable supplies for a consideration;
- the taxable supplies are of a kind which are commonly made by those who seek to profit by them.

It is not essential that the activity is carried on with a view to making a profit. If all or sufficient numbers of the criteria are satisfied and there are no contra-indications to suggest otherwise, the activity must be held to be a business. However, the criteria are not conclusive and a common sense approach should be taken when deciding whether or not an activity is 'business'.

The criteria were expanded following the case of the *Apple and Pear Development Council v C & E Commrs, CJEC [1988] STC 221* (for a summary of the case, see *Tolley's VAT Cases 1998, para 21.75*) which established that, for a supply to be for a consideration, and therefore, potentially, a business supply, there had to be a direct link between the payment received and the supply made.

The case of the *Royal Society for Prevention of Cruelty to Animals [1991] VATTR 407 (6218)* is an excellent example of how these criteria work in practice in the context of a charity. Customs contended that the RSPCA was not in business and could not claim input tax relating to its veterinary activities because its clients were not obliged to pay for their animals' treatment. However, the tribunal found that the RSPCA was in business: it carried on a taxable activity and, where payment was made, there was a direct link between the service supplied and those payments. It was irrelevant that the RSPCA did not trade with a view to a profit and that the cost of providing the service was not met fully by its clients.

Economic activity

7.5 The principle giving EC legislation direct effect in the UK, referred to at paragraph 7.2 above, has been used recently by charities and other similar bodies in an attempt to bring their activities within the scope of VAT by arguing that, although they may not be in 'business' within the meaning used in the UK legislation, they do undertake an 'economic activity' as defined in the equivalent EC Directive (*EC Sixth Directive, Article 4*).

In *Article 4*, economic activity is defined as comprising 'all activities of producers, traders and persons supplying services including mining and agricultural activities and activities of professions'. It also includes the

7.6 VAT Business by Business

exploitation of tangible and intangible property for the purposes of obtaining income on a continuing basis.

This definition is far wider than the UK definition of business and should therefore bring more activities into the scope of VAT (should it be desirable to do so). However, to date, charities and similar organisations have not been successful in arguing that activities which are not 'business' qualify as 'economic activities', (see *The Arts Council of Great Britain, [1994] VATTR 313 (10034)—Tolley's VAT Cases 1998, para 7.89*—and *The Wellcome Trust*, discussed further at paragraph 7.13 below).

Non-business income

7.6 It is impossible to provide a definitive list of business activities. However, Customs do offer a list of activities and sources of income which they consider are 'non-business' (VAT Notice 701/1/95). These include:

- donations/legacies/voluntary contributions;
- grants;
- voluntary services;
- some advertising;
- some welfare services;
- investment income;
- transactions in securities;
- some membership subscriptions;
- part payment from Affinity cards.

The list presupposes an understanding of the terminology used and does not always cater for the complications which may arise from a charity's fund-raising efforts. This may result in income which a charity considered to be non-business being treated by Customs as 'business income' potentially liable to VAT. The two most common areas of misunderstanding are donations and grants. There is also considerable confusion surrounding the nature of income received from investments and share dealing. These areas are explored below.

Donations

7.7 Donations which are freely given with no obligations placed on the charity by the donor are clearly 'non-business'. This includes cases where the donor receives an emblem or other token to acknowledge the donation. However, if the receipt of the token is conditional on a minimum payment, that income could fall within the scope of the tax.

Charities 7.8

Donations: sponsorship

7.8 Sponsorship is gaining popularity as a means of raising funds for charities. It has the obvious attraction to sponsors in that they receive a tangible benefit for their money. Charities are becoming increasingly aware of the potential difficulties sponsorship can cause for them in terms of the potential exposure to direct taxation and threat to their charitable status (generating income from sponsorship cannot be a charitable object) and therefore they place the activity in a trading subsidiary (see 7.66 below). However, protecting sponsorship income in this way depends on recognising it as such in the first place.

The point at which a donation becomes sponsorship or payment for a tangible benefit is not always clear-cut. If a charity receives a donation from a sponsor and merely provides an acknowledgement of that donation, the income is outside the scope. However, additional benefits offered to sponsors will bring the income generated from the sponsorship into the scope of the tax at the standard rate even when the payments far outweigh the value of those benefits.

The case of *Tron Theatre Ltd, CS 1993, [1994] STC 177* highlighted this problem and the VAT consequences that can follow from misunderstanding the liability issue.

Tron Theatre Ltd ('Tron') ran a charitable trust promoting modern drama in Glasgow. As part of its fund-raising activities to finance the refurbishment of the Theatre, it offered patrons who donated £150 a range of benefits. These benefits were: public acknowledgements of the donation, i.e. a personalised brass plaque displayed on a Theatre seat and an acknowledgement in the Theatre foyer, a commemorative limited addition print and priority booking for two gala evenings. Customs ruled that the £150 was a payment for the benefits received and was therefore subject to VAT at the standard rate. Tron appealed to a VAT tribunal against that ruling. The tribunal held that, although there had been a supply of services by Tron, the payment made by patrons also included a large element of donation.

However, following an appeal by Customs against the tribunal's decision, the Court of Session held that, in determining the value of the supply of goods or services, one should not be concerned with the motives of either the supplier of the services or the recipient of those services. In this case, the consideration for the supply of the benefits was the amount of money which had to be paid in order to receive them which was £150. The fact that the consideration paid far outweighed the value of the benefits was immaterial. Therefore, the value of the supply which was subject to tax was £150.

In the current economic climate and with the threat of the National Lottery, charities are having to find more imaginative ways of raising funds for their causes. This often involves imaginative schemes like Tron's where limited benefits are offered to attract prospective patrons. However, it would clearly

7.9 VAT Business by Business

be self-defeating if the value of those benefits equalled the payment made by the patron. In the Tron case, patrons giving evidence at the tribunal admitted that they considered that the benefits they had received had only nominal value and that their motive in making the payment was to support the charity. Unfortunately, as the Court of Session has pointed out, VAT law does not recognise motive or intent in this situation. If a supply is made and that supply is taxable, any payment made relating to it is subject to tax.

Following Tron, if charities are to avoid the risk of VAT being charged on certain donations by sponsors, they may have to abandon the idea of offering tangible benefits unless they can place a value on them, set a basic minimum contribution that they are prepared to accept for those benefits, and then request that patrons offer a further minimum donation. This approach would limit any VAT charge to that basic minimum contribution. However, charities adopting this course do need to be aware that they cannot insist on the minimum donation being given nor deny the benefits offered to anyone paying the minimum contribution (see also 7.9 below).

Donations: fund-raising events

7.9 Fund-raising events may be exempt from VAT (see 7.28 below), but exemption may not be available, either because the charity, its trading subsidiary or the event itself does not meet the criteria for exemption, or because the event is run by a non-qualifying body. When an event is likely to be taxed at the standard rate, its promotion needs to be structured carefully if a full VAT charge on any income generated is to be avoided.

In the case of *Glasgow's Miles Better Mid-Summer 5th Anniversary Ball (4460)*, an association organised a fund-raising ball. It printed application forms showing a ticket price of £50. In small print at the foot of the form it was stated that: 'for VAT purposes the entrance fee is £20. The balance of £30 represents a minimum voluntary donation in aid of hospice funds'. The association accounted for VAT on the £20 only. Customs assessed for VAT on the full £50 and the tribunal upheld the assessment as the request for the 'minimum donation' indicated an element of compulsion. Admission was only allowed if the full £50 was paid.

Organisers following the route of a fixed charge (subject to VAT) and a minimum (outside the scope) voluntary donation need to be aware of Customs' views on the matter if they are to avoid the problems encountered in the above case.

Customs advise that, when a fund-raising event does not qualify for exempt treatment, and the organisers set a basic minimum charge which will be standard-rated and invite those attending the event to supplement this with a voluntary donation, the extra contributions will be outside the scope of VAT if all the following conditions are met:

Charities **7.11**

- it is clearly stated on all publicity material, including tickets, that anyone paying only the minimum charge will be admitted without further payment;
- the extra payment does not give any particular benefit (e.g. better seats);
- the extent of further contributions is ultimately left to ticket holders to decide, even if the organiser indicates a desired level of donation;
- for film or theatre performances, concerts, sporting fixtures, etc., the minimum charge is not less than the usual price of the particular seats at a normal commercial event of the same type; and
- for dances, dinners and similar functions, the minimum total sum upon which the organisers will be liable to account for VAT will not be less than their total costs incurred in arranging the event.

If any publicity material suggests that those paying an extra amount are more likely to be admitted than those who do not, the extra amount becomes taxable.

Donations in kind

7.10 Charities often receive donations in kind, e.g. gifts of equipment, materials, services etc. Where these donations do not involve any benefit for the donor, there are no VAT consequences for the charity. However, if the donor receives a tangible benefit, the gift must be treated as 'consideration' and VAT accounted for on its value.

Donations: charity auctions

7.11 Charity auctions are popular fund-raising events. However, there can be difficulties in organising a charity auction without creating a VAT cost, particularly when third parties are involved. In the tribunal case of *Emily Patrick (12354)* a painting by the appellant was sold at a charity auction. Although title to the painting did not pass to the charity on whose behalf the auction was being run, it was made quite clear that the proceeds from the sale of the painting would be divided equally between the charity and the artist. Following the sale, the appellant accounted for VAT on her share of the sale price, i.e. 50% of the proceeds. However, Customs ruled that she was liable for VAT on the full sale price as she had been the seller of the painting with the charity acting as her agent at the auction. In Customs' view, the fact that the sale proceeds were subsequently divided equally between the artist and the charity did not affect the nature of the supply.

The tribunal acknowledged that the supply of the painting had been from the artist to the bidder with the charity acting as agent. However, it considered that the fact that the auction bidding slip made it clear that the appellant had limited her entitlement to only one half of the sale proceeds demonstrated that the consideration received by Emily Patrick was, and could only have been, a

7.12 VAT Business by Business

half share of the proceeds. The balance belonged to the charity, being partly consideration for its services in promoting and organising the auction, and partly a donation by the buyer.

In the case of *The Cheltenham Countryside Race Day (12460)*, the appellant was a committee which organised an auction for the benefit of a range of charities. The auctioned items were provided free by individuals. Customs assessed the committee for VAT on the proceeds of the auction. The committee appealed against the assessment on the grounds that it never acquired title to the goods sold but arranged the auction as an agent on behalf of the donors who donated the proceeds of the sale to the committee. It contended that the supply was by the donors with the committee providing its services as auctioneer free of charge, and that no VAT should be payable on income received from the auction. Unfortunately for the committee, the auction catalogue indicated that the goods had already been donated to the committee. The tribunal was not satisfied that there had been an agency relationship between the committee and the donors, and the appeal was dismissed.

These two cases illustrate some of the difficulties facing organisers of charity auctions seeking to minimise the impact of VAT. Organisers of auctions need to pay careful attention to detail. In particular, care should be taken to ensure that any documentation associated with the event is not ambiguous and that it does not contradict the desired tax position.

If there is to be a charity auction, the ideal position from a VAT viewpoint is for goods to be donated for sale and for the vendor, be it a charity or an organisation or individual who has covenanted all profits from the event to a charity, to sell those goods as principal. The sale of the goods would then qualify for zero-rating relief under *VATA 1994, 8 Sch, Group 15, Item 1* (see 7.37 below) and therefore any VAT incurred on expenditure relating to the event could be recovered.

Where it is not practical to donate the goods directly for sale, for example because proceeds are to be shared between the vendor and the charity as in the case of Emily Patrick, then it would be prudent to set out in the auction brochure how the proceeds are to be allocated.

Grants

7.12 Grants which are not payment for services rendered can be treated as non-business income. However, it is common practice in the charity sector to call payments, particularly from local authorities, 'grants' merely because they are being paid to a charity. Recent changes in local authority funding have resulted in grants being converted into contract payments, particularly in the welfare sector (see 7.27 below). It is therefore essential to examine any conditions placed on the grant or obligations placed on the grantee which benefit the grantor, to establish whether or not a service is to be rendered by the charity.

Investment income/transactions in securities

7.13 Dealing in shares or any other form of security by a charity is not a business activity. This view was challenged unsuccessfully in the cases of the *National Society for the Prevention of Cruelty to Children [1992] VATTR 417 (9325)* (for a summary of the case, see *Tolley's VAT Cases 1998, para 11.21*).

It was challenged again in the case of *The Wellcome Trust Ltd (12206)* where the tribunal recognised that the Trust's investment powers were far more extensive than the activities of a normal investor and are similar to those of a large institutional investor. The tribunal was undecided as to whether this constituted an 'economic activity' within the scope of VAT (see 7.5 above) and referred the matter to the CJEC. In a decision released on 20 June 1996 (*[1996] STC 945*), the CJEC concluded that the purchase and sale of shares and other securities by a trustee in the course of the management of the assets of a charitable trust is not an 'economic activity'.

Interest from bank accounts is treated as (VAT-exempt) business income by Customs, but it can be ignored when deciding if the charity is in business if that is the only business income it receives.

Non-business advertising

7.14 Charities can treat, by concession, advertising revenue from advertisements placed in their own brochures, annual reports, programmes, etc. as donations outside the scope of VAT provided that no less than 50% of the total number of advertisements in each publication are from private individuals. A qualifying advert must not mention the advertiser's business. The selling of advertising space to commercial organisations is regarded as a business activity even if the advertisement makes no specific reference to trading activities. If the 50% test is not met, then all advertising revenue from the publication is standard-rated unless other reliefs apply (see 7.34 and 7.58 below).

Non-business welfare supplies

7.15 The definition of 'welfare services' capable of relief from VAT is examined at paragraphs 7.24 and 7.25 below. Welfare services and related goods supplied by charities are non-business when made consistently below cost to distressed people for the relief of their distress.

'Below cost' means that the cost of the welfare service is subsidised by at least 15% from the charity's own funds.

7.16 VAT Business by Business

Membership subscriptions

7.16 Although membership subscriptions are specifically included as a business activity in VATA 1994, s 94, if the subscription paid to the charity only entitles the members to no more than the right to receive copies of financial accounts and other reports and the right to vote at general meetings, the income will fall outside the scope of VAT. If other benefits are offered, the subscription may be taxable (see Chapter 8—'Clubs and Associations'). The Court of Appeal decision in *C & E Commrs v British Field Sports Society, CA [1998] STC 315* suggests that many 'campaigning' or 'active' charities which limit membership benefits to lobbying on behalf of members or their causes may now be 'in business'. Cases such as this and the changing demands of members mean that charities need to review constantly the benefits offered if they wish to maintain the non-business treatment of subscription income. Depending on the level of VAT incurred on related costs and the liability of other benefits supplied (e.g. zero-rated publications), charities should also consider whether or not there is an overall cash advantage in having taxable subscriptions.

Affinity cards

7.17 Affinity card arrangements with banks and financial institutions are also proving popular with charities as a means of fund-raising. The financial institution pays the charity for the right to use its name to promote a credit card or similar and the charity provides an address list of its supporters. The charity's income usually comprises a fixed payment and an agreed percentage of retail spending made using the card.

Provided that the contract between the charity and the institution allows a clear separation between the payment for promotional and other services and contributions for which the charity is not obliged to do anything in return, only part of the initial payment (one-fifth) is taxable: the remainder, and any other contributions, will be outside the scope.

Affinity card payments are also exempt from corporation tax provided that the charity does not become actively involved in marketing the card. If it does become involved in marketing, the charity may protect its income by routing the business through a trading subsidiary which would then shed its profits, tax-effectively, back to the charity. However, the VAT treatment outlined above only applies if the charity is undertaking the arrangement. If a trading subsidiary enters into an affinity card contract, its income may be taxable unless it is exempt on the grounds that the subsidiary is 'making arrangements' for credit (*VATA 1994, 9 Sch, Group 5, Item 5*). As the financial institution is unlikely to be able to recover any VAT charged, the VAT treatment of any arrangement involving a subsidiary needs careful consideration.

Exports

7.18 With effect from 1 May 1995 (and before that by extra-statutory concession ESC A7), any goods exported by a charity may be treated as if they were a supply in the UK in the course of a business carried on by the charity (*VATA 1994, s 30(5)*). This enables a VAT-registered charity to treat the VAT charged on these goods at the time of purchase as input tax even if they are given away overseas as part of a non-business activity such as relief aid.

Business income

7.19 If it is established that the income is 'business income', the second question posited in 7.3 above was: 'what is the VAT liability of that income?'

In answering that question, general VAT principles apply: if the income is from a supply made in the course or furtherance of business then it is within the scope of VAT and will either be taxable or exempt. If the supply is not included in Schedule 9 (exemptions), Schedule 8 (zero-rating) or Schedule A1 (reduced rates), then, by default, it will be standard-rated. Fortunately, as noted in the introduction to this chapter, many of the supplies made by charities fall within these schedules and so are relieved from the standard rate. However, the reliefs do have stringent conditions attached and it is essential that charities ensure that all the conditions stipulated in respect of their supply can be met.

Exemptions (VATA 1994, 9 Sch)

7.20 The source of the UK VAT legislation which provides the majority of the VAT exemptions utilised by charities bodies is *EC Sixth Directive, Article 13A*, 'Exemptions for certain activities in the public interest'. As noted at paragraph 7.2 above, it is becoming common practice to resort to EC law if the UK legislation appears flawed. *Article 13A* has been quoted in the tribunals and the courts to clarify the scope for exemption, particularly in the education and welfare sectors and has resulted in the introduction of new exemptions for sport and cultural services.

In paragraphs 7.21 to 7.35 below, references to 'Groups' mean Groups falling within *VATA 1994, 9 Sch* unless otherwise stated.

Education

7.21 The reliefs for the supply of education and training are set out in *Group 6*. Chapter 11—Education deals with this exemption in depth. However, it is worth reviewing the exemption in this section in so far as it relates to charities other than universities, colleges, schools and other public bodies.

7.22 VAT Business by Business

'Otherwise than for profit'

7.22 The legislation exempting the supply of education was revised with effect from 1 August 1994. Prior to that date, non-profit making bodies which were not schools, universities or other similar institutions could only exempt their supplies of education and training if they were provided 'otherwise than for profit'. The meaning of this term was explored in depth in the case of *Bell Concord Educational Trust Ltd, CA [1989] STC 264*.

In that case, the company, which was an educational charity, fixed its course fees such that it made a surplus to re-invest in expanding its service. Customs registered the company for VAT on the grounds that it was trading with a view to making a profit and therefore its activities were outside the scope of the exemption. The case reached the Court of Appeal where, after deciding that the term 'otherwise than for profit' was ambiguous and required reference to the relevant European Law (*EC Sixth Directive, Article 13A2*), the Court held that: '"otherwise than for profit" referred to the objects for which an organisation is established and not to the budgeting policy being pursued for the time being by the organisation in question'.

Customs accepted this decision, but limited it to cases where any surplus is ploughed back into the activity which generated it, i.e. if the surplus came from education, then it could only be used to further education. Difficulties arise when a charity has more than one activity and the surplus is used to maintain that other activity or fund overheads. In such cases, it is Customs' view that the activity generating the surplus could not qualify for exemption.

Customs' interpretation of the judgement and *Article 13A2* is questionable, but the revisions to the exemption for education confirmed this view by re-defining the exemption criteria for non-profit making bodies which are not schools, colleges, universities or other 'eligible bodies' as defined in *Group 6, Note (1)* The term 'otherwise than for profit' has been dropped and to qualify a body must be 'precluded from distributing and does not distribute any profits it makes; and applies any profits made from supplies within this Group to the continuance or improvement of such supplies' (*Group 6, Note (1)(e)*). If a charity meets these criteria, then all its supplies of education and vocational training will be exempt.

Educational conferences

7.23 For charities which are broadly non-educational but which hold conferences or seminars with an educational content, there is scope to exempt both the supply of the conference itself and the services supplied to the charity in delivering the conference.

For a charity to be in a position to exempt conference income, it needs to satisfy *Note 1(e)* above. Assuming it has other activities which are non-educational, it would have to satisfy Customs that its conference had educational content and either that it made no surplus from its conference; or, if a surplus was made, that that surplus was used exclusively to further education or support future educational conferences. For example, the charity would not be eligible for exemption if it used any surplus for its general administration.

If a charity's conference does qualify for exemption and the event is held at the premises of another 'eligible body', e.g. a university campus, then the supply of accommodation, catering and other related services to the charity running the conference may also qualify for exemption in so far as they relate to supplies used by the delegates receiving education (*Group 6, Item 4*). Supplies to staff, conference administrators and lecturers (unless they also attend as delegates) would be standard-rated.

Welfare

7.24 The exemption for welfare services provided by charities is enacted in *Group 7, Items 9 and 10*.

Item 9 exempts 'the supply, otherwise than for profit, by a charity or public body of welfare services and of goods supplied in connection therewith.'

Item 10 exempts 'the supply, otherwise than for profit, of goods and services incidental to the provision of spiritual welfare by a religious community to a resident member of that community in return for a subscription or other consideration paid as a condition of membership.'

These exemptions were introduced in 1986 following the case of *Yoga for Health Foundation v C & E Commrs, QB [1984] STC 630* (see paragraph 11.29 of *Tolley's VAT Cases 1998*) where it was held that the UK had not enacted *EC Sixth Directive Article 13A1(g)* which exempts:

'the supply of services and goods closely linked to welfare and social security work, including those supplied by old people's homes, by bodies governed by public law or by other organisations recognised as charitable by the Member State concerned.'

Meaning of 'welfare services'

7.25 In common with other reliefs, these exemptions are qualified by Notes to the Group and case law. The meaning of 'otherwise than for profit' is that given to it in the case of *Bell Concord Educational Trust Ltd, CA [1989] STC 264* (see paragraph 7.22 above). ' Welfare services' are defined in *Group 7, Note (6)* as:

'services which are closely connected with—

7.26 VAT Business by Business

(a) the provision of care, treatment of instruction designed to promote the physical or mental welfare of elderly, sick, distressed or disabled persons;

(b) the protection of children and young persons; or

(c) the provision of spiritual welfare by a religious institution as part of a course of instruction or a retreat, not being a course or a retreat designed primarily to provide recreation or a holiday.'

Customs offer the following examples of 'welfare services' qualifying under items 9 and 10:

- residential care for elderly and disabled people;

- the provision of accommodation in hostels for the homeless and in children's homes;

- meals, etc. in day care centres; and

- children taken into care.

Customs define 'care' to mean some form of continuing personal contact in looking after, helping or supervising people (VAT Notice 710/1/95).

The supply of accommodation and catering

7.26 Group 7, Note 7 excludes from the exemption, the supply of accommodation or catering except where it is ancillary to the provision of care, treatment or instruction. The meaning of 'ancillary' was considered in the case of *Viewpoint Housing Association (13148)* where the provision of sheltered accommodation to the elderly included meals in a restaurant facility. Customs ruled that the supply of catering was taxable, being separate from the supply of care: the association claimed exemption under *Group 7, Item 9* and *Article 13A1(g)*. The tribunal found that the association had contracted to provide catering as part of the care package available to those unable to cater for themselves and was therefore eligible for exemption.

In the case of *International Bible Students Association v C & E Commissioners, QB [1988] STC 412*, the Association organised conventions to promote the teachings of the Jehovah's Witnesses. Although admission to the conventions was free, the Association made profits from catering at the events. Customs sought to tax these receipts; however, the QB held that the provision of catering services at religious conventions were closely linked to the spiritual welfare work of the convention and accordingly were exempt under *Article 13A1(g)*.

Local authority contracts

7.27 At paragraph 7.12 above, reference was made to the change in the nature of local authority funding for the provision of care services. Where, previously, charities engaged in the provision of care were funded by grants from the local authorities, funding is now by way of a contractual arrangement between the charity and the local authority. When this change was first introduced by local authorities, there was concern that, as charities were now making supplies of care services to the local authorities under a contractual obligation, this would have the effect of changing the supply of exempt health care by the charity into a taxable supply of subcontracted services. However, Customs have recognised this problem and accept that where a charity is, in a physical sense, actually providing care to the persons who need it, but in contractual terms the supply is made to, and paid for by, the local authority, the supply falls within the exemption as being 'directly connected with' the provision of care.

However, other services not covered by the exemption would be taxable and charities negotiating contracts with local authorities need to ensure that provision is made to charge VAT where appropriate.

Fund-raising events

7.28 *Group 12, Item 1* exempts: 'the supply of goods and services by a charity in connection with a fund-raising event organised for charitable purposes by a charity or jointly by more than one charity.'

Exemption for fund-raising events is permitted under *EC Sixth Directive Article 13A1(o)* which exempts the supply of services and goods by (certain) organisations in connection with fund-raising events organised exclusively for their own benefit provided that exemption is not likely to cause distortion of competition. Member States may introduce any necessary restrictions, in particular, as regards the number of events or the amount of receipts which give entitlement to exemption.

To comply with the requirement that exemption does not distort competition, the relief is heavily qualified. In the Notes to the Group, a 'fund-raising event' is defined as meaning 'a fete, ball, bazaar, gala show, performance or similar event which is separate from and not forming any part of a series or regular run of like or similar events' (*Note 1*). The interpretation of this Note by the VAT tribunal is examined in paragraphs 7.29 to 7.31 below.

The legislation does recognise that many events are run by subsidiary companies of charities for direct tax reasons. Consequently, the definition of 'charity' for the purposes of this relief has been extended to include: 'a body corporate which is wholly owned by a charity and whose profits (from

7.29 VAT Business by Business

whatever source) are payable to a charity by virtue of a deed of covenant or trust or otherwise' (*Note 2*).

Meaning of 'fund-raising event'

7.29 The meaning of 'fund-raising event' was addressed in *Blaydon Rugby Football Club (13901)*. Although the tribunal rejected Customs' contention that a fund-raising event must be one intended to raise capital, it considered that the main purpose of the event had to be to raise funds. Therefore, if fund-raising is only incidental to the purpose of the event, it would not qualify. In this case, the tribunal decided that the main purpose of the events was 'social' (they were barbecues, stag nights, dinners etc.) rather than 'fund-raising'. The tribunal also stated that the burden of proof as to the main purpose of the event rested with the club and not with Customs.

The tribunal in *Newsvendors Benevolent Institution (14343)* took a more moderate view, holding that, as long as fund-raising was at least a subsidiary purpose of the event, it qualified for relief.

Prior to the Blaydon case and *Reading Cricket & Hockey Club (13656)*, Customs had viewed the purpose of the list in *Note 1* as being illustrative of the fact that the exemption covered events of a short duration. Therefore, other events not specifically listed could potentially qualify for exemption. However, in the Reading and Blaydon cases, the tribunals considered that the types of event must fall specifically into one of the categories listed. This was reinforced in the NBI case. Customs are using this interpretation to exclude certain active events like sponsored walks, bike rides, marathons, etc. from the scope of the exemption on the basis that they are participatory, rather than a performance or similar event to those listed in *Note 1*.

Meaning of 'series'

7.30 The 'series' or regularity test has caused difficulties for charities seeking to exploit this relief. Customs, in paragraph 27 of VAT Notice 701/1/95, refer to the exemption as being for 'one-off' fund-raising events. However, this is to some extent misleading. Charities can hold a number of the same types of event in the year and, provided that they are reasonably spaced apart, they can all benefit from the exemption. Similarly, the same type of event held in different locations can also qualify.

In the Blaydon case, the tribunal defined a 'series' of events as having taken place if 'there is some quality in those events which removes them from the category of separate events and unites them under the head of a series'. In this case, the tribunal identified the common quality as being that they were all 'social events'. In the NBI case, the tribunal supported this view, commenting that the quality which removes events from the category of separate events and unites them under the head of a series must be a quality inherent in the nature of the events themselves.

Customs allow a certain latitude in the case of national fund-raising campaigns. They allow exemption for similar events organised in different parts of the country by a national charity, even when events take place in the same week, follow the same theme and may be publicised in a single brochure, provided that they are held in venues which are reasonably far apart.

Events lasting more than a day

7.31 The scope for exemption becomes more complicated when looking at events lasting more than one day. Customs accept that a two or three day event, for which there is a single admission charge, does come within the terms of the exemption, but a weekend event where a separate admission charge is payable for each day is not eligible for exemption. Nor does the relief extend to a programme of events for which patrons can buy, for example, a season ticket for a series of concerts, or a ticket whereby they pay a lesser amount or are excused payment altogether on second subsequent events.

Repeat performances of a film or play do not qualify either. In the case of *Northern Ireland Council for Voluntary Action [1991] VATTR 32 (5451)*, a registered charity arranged seven performances of a play, and the pre-released screening of a film. The charity appealed against a decision by Customs that the performances fell outside the scope of the exemption. The tribunal dismissed the appeal, holding that the performances constituted a 'series' and this excluded them from exemption.

However, the Reading case produced a different result. The club runs an annual event known as the Reading Real Ale and Jazz Festival which takes place on three successive days, starting on Thursday and ending on Saturday. Patrons may buy tickets for more than one day, but this is not a requirement of entry. The tone and character of the Festival changes over the three days. Although jazz and real ale are available throughout the Festival, on the first day the emphasis is on the jazz music; on the second, the emphasis moves to the real ale 'testing' with the third day being a more relaxed combination of the two.

The club contended that the Festival was planned this way to create a single coherent whole to attract the maximum number of patrons. However, Customs interpreted the event as three evenings of separate entertainment for which a separate admission fee was charged and therefore it could only be viewed as a series or regular run of like or similar events which could not qualify for exemption.

The tribunal rejected parallels with the NICVA case, and decided that the manner in which the Festival was planned and advertised, and the differing character of each day, meant that the event should be viewed as a 'single organic whole' and therefore exemption should apply.

7.32 VAT Business by Business

Joint fund-raising

7.32 If two charities enter into a partnership to organise an event, and that partnership is a separate legal entity from the charities when they act individually, they will not be able to benefit directly from the exemption unless the partnership is itself a charity. However, if the arrangement falls short of a formal partnership, each party to the joint venture can qualify in its own right for the exemption.

Agents

7.33 Where a company or club organises a qualifying event as agent for the charity the income passed to the charity is covered by the exemption. However, if the agent keeps any of the receipts to cover expenses, that element will be considered to be payment for its services and will be subject to VAT.

Income covered by exemption

7.34 Where exemption does apply, all income from the event is covered, including admission charges, the sale of commemorative brochures, the sale of advertising space in those brochures and other items sold by the charity at the event, for example, T-shirts, auction goods, etc. It also includes any sponsorship payments directly connected with the qualifying event.

Cultural services

7.35 Exemption for 'cultural services' was introduced in the UK in response to the legal obligation to implement *EC Sixth Directive, Article 13A1(n)* which exempts 'certain cultural services and goods closely linked thereto supplied by bodies governed by public law or by other cultural bodies recognised by the Member State concerned.'

A consultation exercise prior to the implementation of this exemption raised a number of concerns about its financial effects, especially on capital projects. Other concerns listed included increased administration costs and distortion of competition. Most of the respondents in favour of exemption wanted it to be restricted in some way. Consequently, the government decided that the scope of the exemption would be kept to the minimum possible to comply with the EC Directive.

A Treasury Order, *The Value Added Tax (Cultural Services) Order 1996 (SI 1996 No 1256)*, came into effect from 1 June 1996 creating a new Group (*Group 13—Cultural Services, etc.*) which exempted the supply of admission to:

(a) a museum, gallery, art exhibition or zoo; or

Charities **7.37**

(b) a theatrical, musical or choreographic performance of a cultural nature,

by: (*under Item 1*) a 'public body' or (under *Item 2*) an 'eligible body'.

A 'public body' (local authority, government department, etc.) must demonstrate that exemption does not distort competition. An 'eligible body' is restricted to 'non-profit-making bodies applying profits from exempt cultural services to the continuance or improvement of such supplies and which are managed and administered on a voluntary basis by persons who have no direct or indirect financial interest in its activities'. In the case of *Glastonbury Abbey (14579)*, the tribunal took the view that the 'management' condition was too restrictive. *EC Sixth Directive, Article 13A2(a)* only allowed the UK to disqualify non-profit-making bodies which are not managed on an 'essentially voluntary basis' and so the employment of a limited number of management staff does not necessarily exclude a body from the exemption.

The Order also extended exemption for fund-raising events (*Group 12*) to include eligible bodies falling within the new exemption.

Zero-rating—VATA 1994, 8 Sch

7.36 This section covers zero-rating reliefs for supplies by charities under *VATA 1994, 8 Sch, Group 15*. Additional reliefs are available for supplies made either to or for charities or by charities to other charities. These are covered in paragraphs 7.47 to 7.60 below.

Donated goods

7.37 *Group 15, Items 1 and 2* zero-rate the supply to, and the supply by, a charity of goods donated for sale.

Item 1 zero-rates: 'The supply by a charity of any goods which have been donated for sale or the supply of such goods by a taxable person who has covenanted by deed to give all the profits of that supply to a charity.'

To counter perceived avoidance, *Note 1* restricts this relief to goods made available to the public for purchase (e.g. through a shop) and excludes any sales arising from agreements entered into before the goods were put on general sale. However, by extra-statutory concession, Customs will allow donated goods which are unsuitable for sale to the general public by reason of their poor quality to qualify for relief when sold to scrap businesses, rag merchants and the like.

This relief brings VAT into line with direct tax treatment, which also allows donated goods to be sold 'tax-free'. Charities primarily involved with the sale of donated goods should consider the benefits of VAT registration (see 7.64 below).

7.38 VAT Business by Business

Item 2 zero-rates: 'The donation of any goods for sale or export by a charity described in *Item 1* or by a taxable person described in that item.'

This Item allows VAT-registered businesses to recover VAT on goods donated to charities for resale or export.

Both reliefs extend to trading companies which may, for direct tax reasons, run a shop on behalf of a charity. Charities may hive off shops to subsidiary trading companies because they sell goods other than those which have been donated. Although profits from the sale of donated goods are free from direct tax, profits from bought-in goods are not. Similarly, any goods sold which have not been donated (e.g. Christmas cards and stationery) are subject to the normal VAT liability rules, unless sold as part of a one-off fund-raising event (see 7.28 above).

It is important to note that zero-rating relief for donated goods sold by non-charities is conditional on there being a deed of covenant in place. It is not sufficient to pass the profits back to a charity through dividends of gift aid.

An avoidance scheme, intended to take advantage of the provisions of *Group 15*, was held to be ineffective in *University of Wales College Newport; Allt-Yr-Yn & Caerleon Enterprises & Services Ltd (15280)*. For the Commissioners' practice following this decision, see Business Brief 6/98, issued on 11 February 1998.

Customs also take the view that buildings and land are not covered by these relieving provisions because they are not 'goods which have been donated for sale'. C & E Business Brief 12/92 states that: 'in most cases, where dwellings or land is bequeathed to a charity, the property in question would not have been a business asset of the deceased person or the charity. Any supply of the property would normally be outside the scope of VAT and the charity would not be able to claim input tax deduction on expenses in connection with the sale'.

Exports of goods by a charity

7.38 *Group 15, Item 3* zero-rates the exports of any goods by a charity to a place outside the Member States (see also 7.18 above).

VAT recovery

7.39 Most charities make a mixture of taxable and exempt supplies and receive income which falls outside the scope of VAT. Where income is derived from business and non-business activities, only VAT attributable to the business activity may be recovered (see *Whitechapel Art Gallery v C & E Commrs, QB [1986] STC 156*, summarised at *Tolley's VAT Cases 1998, para 11.19*). VAT attributable to a business activity may have to be further restricted if that activity is an exempt supply. Consequently, charities are unlikely to be able to recover all the VAT incurred on expenditure and some method of attributing VAT costs to a particular income stream may be required.

However, charities should not assume that, just because they receive non-business income, they have to restrict VAT recovery. If that non-business income subsidises a taxable activity, then VAT may be fully recoverable. For example, a theatre may receive grant funding to reduce seat prices but the only supplies it makes are taxable supplies of admission to the theatre and therefore all its input tax can be attributed to that taxable supply and recovered in full.

Attribution of VAT costs

7.40 Charities need to identify VAT on expenditure and attribute it wherever possible to the supply or the source of income to which it relates. In accordance with VAT general principles, only VAT attributable to taxable supplies is recoverable.

VAT on overheads, etc. which cannot be directly attributed to a supply will need to be apportioned between business and non-business activities or income to identify business-related input tax. Business-related input tax will need to be further apportioned between taxable and exempt supplies in accordance with a partial exemption method.

Non-business attribution

7.41 In Appendix F of VAT Guide 700, Customs offer an example of a method to apportion VAT on overheads between business and non-business use. The example offered is based on the ratio of business income to total income (for a worked example of this method, see *Tolley's VAT 1998/99, para 35.9*).

Customs acknowledge that there is no standard or special method for apportioning VAT costs between business and non-business activities: the only conditions placed on the choice of method is that it is 'fair and justifiable'.

In fact, most charities would be ill-served by a method based on income, as this approach does not usually reflect the use of VAT-bearing resources. For example, receipt and processing of donations may represent a substantial element of a charity's income but require minimal use of VAT-bearing expenditure compared to a business activity which may require substantial input from such expenditure but produce a small proportion of the charity's income.

7.42 VAT Business by Business

Clearly, when choosing a method, the object of the taxpayer is to maximise the VAT recoverable. The commercial sector has been very successful in devising and securing beneficial VAT recovery methods. However, the charity sector has, until relatively recently, been rather unsophisticated in its choices. For many charities, this has resulted in less recovery than might otherwise have been possible.

A wide variety of methods are available including: staff time, actual use of an asset (e.g. a computer or telephone system), number of transactions, areas occupied by staff employed on transactions, actual or budgeted costs or combinations of these.

In the case of *Dean and Chapter of Hereford Cathedral (11737)*, the cathedral incurred VAT on the refurbishment of two dwellings situated within its cloister. The vergers occupying the dwellings were required to reside there to facilitate and enhance the performance of their duties which included the raising of funds by secular activities. The tribunal agreed that the dwellings were used for both business and non-business activities and, in deciding the proportional use of these assets between business and non-business, the tribunal considered that there would be no business without the cathedral nor any cathedral without the funds generated from the business to maintain it. It therefore directed a 50/50 apportionment.

The reasoning behind the tribunal's decision to opt for a 50/50 apportionment is worth reviewing. The tribunal considered a variety of methods for reaching a fair and reasonable apportionment including 'time and use' and an income-based method. However, it ultimately opted for the method used in the appeal of *LVJ Brooks (1722)* in which the tribunal chairman had said:

> 'it seems to me that if a subjective test is to be applied in determining the question of "purpose", where there is a duality of purpose, an apportionment should be made by considering the relative importance of each separate purpose in the mind or minds of the business or person carrying on the business concerned.'

The tribunal in the *Hereford Cathedral* case took the view that as the cathedral's business activities and non-business activities complemented each other, the only fair apportionment was an equal apportionment.

Changing an apportionment method

7.42 If the current method used offers lower recovery than an alternative, it is possible to change it with effect from a current date, but not retrospectively.

In the case of the *Trustees of the Victoria and Albert Museum (13552)*, the Board had negotiated with Customs a change from its income-based method to one which offered improved recovery. However, the Board felt justified in applying the newly-agreed method retrospectively on the grounds that its original choice of method was an error because a different method would produce a more favourable result. Customs rejected this approach and the tribunal agreed with them in deciding that the choice of a less favourable method was not an error.

This case demonstrates the importance of choosing the best method from the start and ensuring that, where circumstances change or a method offering better recovery becomes apparent, any change to the method is promptly acted upon.

It is worth noting that, had the Board not had a method in place at all, it would have been justified in making a retrospective claim because it would be a new claim for unrecovered VAT rather than an adjustment to VAT already recovered. The problem arose because the Board had already implemented a method and was seeking to substitute an alternative retrospectively.

It is also worth noting that Customs agreed to a method (albeit for future use) which gave improved recovery without a material change in the Board's circumstances. Customs are generally prepared to allow new methods which improve recovery as long as they are fair and reasonable.

Partial exemption

7.43 It is beyond the scope of this chapter to cover the mechanics of partial exemption (see *Tolley's VAT 1998/99, chapter 49*). However, certain matters relevant to the choice of partial exemption method by charities are worth addressing.

Some charities choose to simplify their VAT accounting by having a global VAT recovery method incorporating both the non-business and partial exemption calculation. Invariably, this is income-based and VAT recoverable on non-attributable expenditure is calculated on the ratio of taxable to total (i.e. non-business, taxable and exempt) income.

In *The Dean and Chapter of the Cathedral Church of St Peter (3591)* this approach was found not to be contrary to the *EC Sixth Directive. Article 19(1)* allows Member States to include 'subsidies' in the denominator of an income-based partial exemption calculation. 'Subsidy' is not defined, but the tribunal felt that the term was capable of including grants, collections and donations.

However, as apportioning business and non-business VAT costs on the basis of income is seldom beneficial (see 7.41 above), this approach is not recommended unless the VAT at stake is minimal. In the *Cathedral Church of St Peter* case, the Dean and Chapter were trying to extricate themselves from that method (see *Tolley's VAT Cases 1998, para 40.53*).

7.44 VAT Business by Business

This is not to say that an income-based partial exemption method is disadvantageous: frequently it is the only viable method. However, it is possible to have a completely different basis for non-business attribution method to that adopted for partial exemption.

Once a special method has been agreed with Customs, it is impossible to change the method retrospectively (see the cases reported in *Tolley's VAT Cases 1998, paras 40.55 to 40.61*). Therefore, it is essential that the most beneficial method (acceptable to Customs) is identified and implemented from the start, and that any changes to the charity's activities which may reduce those benefits and call for a change in method are reacted to as soon as possible to maintain maximum VAT recovery.

De minimis

7.44 Only the input tax relating to taxable supplies may be recovered. However, if the charity's exempt input tax qualifies as being 'de minimis' (see *Tolley's VAT 1998/99, para 49.4*), it can recover it in full. However, there is no de minimis limit for non-business VAT costs.

VAT on the purchase of assets

7.45 It is common practice for charities to apportion the VAT incurred on the purchase of assets using the method agreed for apportioning VAT on overheads (see paragraph 7.41 above). However, following the case of *Lennartz v Finanzamt München, CJEC 1991, [1995] STC 514*, VAT recovery on the purchase of assets may be treated in another way. The Lennartz case concerned a German taxpayer who used a car partly for business and partly for private use. In Germany, there is no VAT restriction on the purchase of cars provided that they are used for business. Although Lennartz used the car principally for private use, the business use increased significantly and he tried to make an input tax claim. The German tax authorities rejected this and an appeal was made to the European Court.

The European Court ruled that, where goods are acquired solely for a private (or non-business) purpose, the tax incurred is not recoverable even if the goods are put to a deductible business use at a later stage. The right to deduct tax arises, and is exercisable, at the time when the tax is incurred.

If, however, a taxable person acquires goods and uses them partly for the purpose of his taxable supplies and partly for private (or non-business) purposes, he has a right to total and immediate input tax deduction. Under European law, the element of private or non-business use is treated as a taxable supply for a consideration, on which output tax is due.

Following on from that judgment, Customs accept that a taxable person acquiring an asset which is used for both business and non-business purposes may recover the VAT incurred on the purchase of that asset in full. However, the taxable person must account for output tax on the private or non-business use. Customs do not accept that this ruling extends to the purchase of services.

Charities therefore have the option either to recover VAT in full on assets used for both business and non-business purposes and charge themselves output tax in accordance with *VATA 1994, 4 Sch 5(4)* (based on the full cost of the asset) in each accounting period according to non-business use, or to apportion the VAT on the asset when it is acquired.

Full recovery with a non-business use charge can offer a cash flow benefit. If the charity anticipates that business use is likely to increase over the lifetime of the asset, then it also offers an actual VAT saving as the non-business use will diminish, thereby reducing the amount on which output tax has to be accounted for. Conversely, if business use is likely to decrease, the cash flow benefit is likely to be outweighed by the extra output tax chargeable for non-business use, and therefore apportionment at the time of purchase will usually give the better result.

VAT reliefs on purchases

7.46 Charities are offered a range of VAT reliefs on goods and services they may purchase (or supply to other charities). As in the case of the rules on the liability of supplies made by charities, Customs limit the application of these reliefs by construing the legislation as narrowly as possible.

Zero-rating reliefs

7.47 Zero-rating relief is permitted under *EC Sixth Directive, Article 28(2)* under certain conditions. In particular, any relief must satisfy the condition laid down in the last indent of *EC Second Directive, Article 17* which states that provisions for reduced rates may only be taken for clearly defined social reasons and for the benefit of the final consumer.

7.48 In the case of *EC Commission v United Kingdom, CJEC [1988] STC 456*, the UK government was successfully challenged on its decision to zero-rate the supply of construction and fuel and power to businesses. The CJEC defined a final consumer as anyone who acquires goods or services for personal use, as opposed to a taxable person who acquires goods or services for use in an economic activity: a final consumer is always a person who can not obtain a deduction for VAT charged to him but has to bear the burden of the tax.

However, the CJEC also decided that: 'the provision of goods or services at a stage higher in the production chain which is nevertheless sufficiently close to the consumer to be of advantage to him must also be considered to be for the benefit of the final consumer as so defined.'

7.49 VAT Business by Business

Thus, charities can obtain relief on a wide range of goods and services, including fuel and power and certain construction services for non-business use, because the relief is to the advantage of the 'final consumer', i.e. the beneficiaries of the charity.

Reference to Groups in paragraphs 7.49 to 7.60 below means Groups in *VATA 1994, 8 Sch*, unless stated otherwise.

Talking books

7.49 *Group 4* zero-rates the supply of talking books for the blind and handicapped, and wireless sets for the blind, where the supply is to the Royal National Institute for the Blind, the National Listening Library or other similar charities.

Construction of buildings

7.50 *Group 5* and *Group 6* zero-rate the construction of certain buildings and the alteration and/or reconstruction of listed buildings respectively. To secure zero-rating under these reliefs, the building must either be designed as a dwelling, used solely for a relevant residential use, or solely for a relevant charitable purpose. The VAT aspects of property and construction are considered in depth in Chapter 9—Construction Industry and Chapter 21—Property Development. Therefore, this section concentrates on the implications of *Group 5, Note 6*, which sets out the meaning of 'relevant charitable purpose'.

Note 6

7.51 *Note 6* states that: 'Use for a relevant charitable purpose means use by a charity in either or both of the following ways, namely—

(a) otherwise than in the course or furtherance of a business;

(b) as a village hall or similarly in providing social or recreational facilities for a local community.'

Note 6(a): otherwise than in the course or furtherance of a business

7.52 It is important to stress that, to obtain relief under *Note 6(a)*, it is not sufficient for the building to be used by a charity: it must also be used otherwise than in the course or furtherance of the business. This is consistent with the European law set out in paragraph 7.48 above.

Thus, premises used to make exempt or taxable supplies would not be eligible for relief. However, by concession, where there is incidental or minor business use of a building, e.g. by letting the building from time to time, such use can usually be ignored if it accounts for less than 10% of the time the building is to be normally available for use.

If only part of a new building is going to be used by a charity for non-business use, it is possible to obtain zero-rating relief for the part which is to be used for non-business purposes, with the costs of the work being apportioned between a zero-rated and a standard-rated supply.

Customs can take a hard line when applying *Note 6(a)* if the building is used to generate income. In the case of *Newtownbutler Playgroup Ltd (13741)*, Customs refused to allow a refund of VAT under the DIY scheme (*VATA 1983, s 21*: now *VATA 1994, s 35*). The playgroup, an incorporated charity run by the parents of children attending it, had constructed a new building to accommodate the increasing demand for its facilities. To qualify for a refund of VAT on the basis that the building was used for a relevant charitable purpose, it had to satisfy the 'non-business' test.

The playgroup did receive income from parents of children attending the centre; however, this was to defray the cost of refreshments, was in the region of only £2.00 per parent per week, and was waived where family circumstances prevented a contribution being made. Income for the year averaged £3,000. Customs contended that the fact that income was received for use of the facility meant that the building was used in the course or furtherance of a business (i.e. the provision of playgroup facilities) and therefore it did not qualify.

The tribunal considered that there was no single test applicable to determining whether or not a building is being used for business; however, it felt that two matters strongly militated against Customs' contention in this case. One was the level of income: although the supply of playgroup facilities is a business activity, the tribunal felt that it was proper to investigate the question of substance as compared to activities of an unarguable business nature. The second was that the basis for charging parents was such that, in fact, there was no supply for a consideration. On those grounds, the tribunal found for the playgroup.

Customs will also refuse relief if the ultimate user of the building is not a charity, even if the person constructing it was a charity which allowed the user free occupation. In the case of the *League of Friends of Kingston Hospital (12764)*, a charity allowed an NHS Trust to use a new building paid for by donated funds 'rent-free'. Customs refused relief on the cost of the construction because the user was not a charity.

Applying the narrow construction to this relief, as required by European law, the tribunal took the view that 'use' has, in this context, a functional meaning. Consequently it was necessary to first of all identify the use to which the building was put and then ask whether that use was by a charity otherwise than in the course or furtherance of a business. In this case it was used by a hospital which was not a charity and therefore it could not use the building

7.53 *VAT Business by Business*

for a relevant charitable purpose. The Friends did not 'use' the building in the relevant sense; they made it available free of charge to the hospital. Therefore the tribunal was unable to accept that the building qualified for zero-rating relief, and rejected the appeal.

Note 6(b)

7.53 There is no formal definition of a village hall. In Customs' view, a village hall is a communal building situated in a small community and controlled by an elected committee. It provides a facility for the whole community to enable various groups to carry out a range of local activities. The word 'similarly' in *Note 6(b)* should be taken to mean '... of the same nature as a village hall' and the phrase 'local community' as a general alternative for 'village', and as such as having a fairly narrow geographical range. Sports pavilions may fall within the scope of the relief provided that they are used similarly to a village hall. A hall qualifying under this Note should not be used for 'business', although short-term lettings to user groups would not compromise eligibility for the relief.

Zero-rating relief for the construction of a village hall which undertakes 'business activities' (no matter how limited) may appear at odds with the EC Directive which only permits such relief when the supply is 'for the benefit of the final consumer' (see para 7.48 above). If the village hall is supplied to others by way of letting, it can hardly be described as the 'final consumer'. However, the UK government and the EC Commission agreed that a community-run hall was 'sufficiently close to the final consumer' to qualify.

As the National Lottery releases more funds for sporting and recreational projects, there has been an increase in the development of sports and recreation facilities by charitable trusts. Many of these trusts attempt to secure zero-rating for their recreational or sports centre under *Note 6(b)*. This has led to a series of tribunal cases and one High Court judgment examining the meaning of the Note.

In the cases of *Ormiston Charitable Trust (13187)* and *Jubilee Hall Recreation Centre Ltd (14209)* (heard by the same tribunal chairman), the decisions supported Customs' view that, to qualify for relief as a 'village hall' a building had to be 'owned, organised and administered by the community for the benefit of the local community'. The tribunals decided that halls which only served a section of the community were not operated in the same manner as a village hall and were excluded from relief, although use solely for sporting or recreational activities did not automatically disqualify them.

In the *Jubilee Hall* case, the tribunal referred to *EC Second Directive, Article 17* and *EC Commission v United Kingdom, CJEC [1988] STC 456* (see 7.48 above) as authority for the view that, to qualify, halls should not be concerned with economic activity other than occasional lettings.

However, in *Bennachie Leisure Centre Association (14276)*, the tribunal disagreed with the tests put forward in the *Ormiston* case that, to qualify, the building had to be 'owned, organised and administered by the community', observing that the whole purpose of zero-rating is to deal with something which is not owned by the community, but by a charity. Nor was the tribunal comfortable with the concept of a building which was required to provide facilities used by the entire community, since a building can only be used by those who wish or have a need to use it. The tribunal expressed the view that each case must be decided on its merits. For example, what qualifies as a local community in an urban setting may be very different from what would qualify as such in a rural setting, and what the appropriate provision of facilities for that community would be may differ on the facts of each case.

Jubilee Hall appealed against the tribunal decision to the High Court (*Jubilee Hall Recreation Centre Limited v C & E Commrs, QB [1997] STC 414*). The Court adopted the approach in *Bennachie Leisure*, concluding that the 'similarly' test meant that the building had to be made available to the local community for social and recreational activity and not that it had to be 'owned, organised and administered by the community'. Moreover, to be a member of the local community, one did not have to live in the area: other forms of connection which meant some attachment to the locality, e.g. through the workplace, would suffice.

The widening of this relief continued in the case of *St. Dunston's Educational Foundation (14901)* where the construction of a sports hall used principally by a local school (but also made available to the local community) was found to qualify for relief.

Transport

7.54 Relief for the supply of lifeboats, launching equipment (including tractors), and the construction and maintenance of slipways is available for sea rescue charities under *Group 8, Item 3*.

The supply of transport in vehicles capable of taking twelve or more passengers is zero-rated under *Group 8, Item 4*. Transport in vehicles with less carrying capacity is standard-rated; however, by concession (*ESC A24*), where the carrying capacity of a vehicle has been reduced below this number because it has been equipped with facilities for persons in wheelchairs, the supply can be zero-rated even if the users are not disabled.

Aids for the handicapped

7.55 *Group 12* offers zero-rating relief on a wide range of goods and services supplied to charities for use by the 'handicapped', defined in the legislation as 'the chronically sick or disabled'. These include:

– certain appliances and equipment;

7.55 VAT Business by Business

- adapting goods for use by the disabled;
- certain construction work including facilitating access and providing bathrooms, lavatories and washrooms for the disabled;
- emergency alarm systems;
- repair, maintenance and/or installation of most of the above.

Full details of these reliefs can be found in *Tolley's VAT 1998/99, para 32.17*. These reliefs can only be exploited if all the conditions attached to them are met. Customs apply these conditions strictly and it should not be assumed that, just because something is being supplied to a disabled person or a charity supporting the disabled, it qualifies for relief.

For example, where a condition of relief is that the goods have to be designed solely for use by the disabled, (e.g. *Item 2(g)*) that condition is applied strictly. In *The Princess Louise Scottish Hospital [1983] VATTR 191 (1412)*, overbed tables which were used by the disabled were found not to qualify because they were not designed solely for use by the disabled.

However, in *The David Lewis Centre (10860)*, when considering whether or not a special heating system installed in a centre for epileptics qualified under *Item 2(g)*, the tribunal considered that the correct test was to examine the purpose for which the goods supplied were designed. In this case, the tribunal considered that the heating system was designed specifically for the needs of the centre's patients and so qualified. The fact that other able-bodied people, e.g. the staff, could benefit from the heating system did not detract from its eligibility for relief. (For another issue in this case, taken to the High Court, see paragraph 7.58 below.)

The supply to any charity of a service of providing, extending or adapting a washroom or lavatory facilities in a building used for 'charitable purposes' (e.g. a church hall, day centre or village hall), and similarly with regard to bathrooms where the building is a residential home, is zero-rated. However, in the case of *Mid-Derbyshire Cheshire Home (4512)*, the tribunal found that the installation of washbasins and showers in bedrooms of a residential home did not qualify for relief as the rooms' primary purpose was not for washing but to provide sleeping accommodation.

Lifts installed by charities in a residential home or day centre to facilitate movement by the disabled may also qualify (*Items 11* and *12*). 'Day centre' is not defined in the legislation. However, in *Union of Students of the University of Warwick, [1995] VATDR 219 (13821)*, the tribunal turned down an appeal and held that a lift installed in a students union building to facilitate movement by disabled students did not qualify for relief. To qualify as a 'day centre', the building must be provided *for* the disabled specifically and not for groups in general of which the disabled may form part: simple use of the premises by the disabled is not enough to qualify.

Other zero-rating reliefs for charities

7.56 *Group 15* offers a wide range of miscellaneous reliefs for charities. Reliefs on donated goods (*Items 1* and *2*) and exports (*Item 3*) have already been discussed in paragraphs 7.37 and 7.38 above respectively. The remaining Items in this Group are discussed in paragraphs 7.57 to 7.61 below.

Relevant goods for eligible bodies

7.57 When this relief was introduced on 23 August 1974 as *FA 1972, 4 Sch, Group 16, Item 3*, it was limited to: 'the supply for donation to a designated hospital or research institution, of medical or scientific equipment solely for use in medical research, diagnosis or treatment where such equipment is purchased with funds provided by charity or from voluntary contributions'.

Since then, the scope of the relief has expanded in terms of the bodies which can exploit it, the classes of goods available, and the uses to which those goods can be put.

Relief is currently available under *Item 4* for the supply (by sale or hire) of any 'relevant goods' for donation to a nominated 'eligible body' provided that the goods are purchased with funds provided by a charity or from voluntary contributions. If the donee is not a charity in its own right, it must not contribute funds towards the financing of the purchase of the donated goods.

Item 5 zero-rates the supply (by sale or hire) of 'any relevant goods' to an 'eligible body' which pays for them with funds provided by a charity from voluntary contributions or to an eligible body which is a charitable institution providing care or medical or surgical treatment for handicapped persons. A charitable eligible body can use its own funds to finance the supply wholly or in part. *Item 5* does include the provision of computer software, but relief is only available if it is used solely for medical research, diagnosis or treatment (*Note 10*).

Items 9 and *10* are also concerned with zero-rating supplies used for charitable medical or veterinary research. *Item 9* zero-rates medicinal products used solely for such research (or for care or treatment). *Item 10* zero-rates substances used for testing or synthesis in the course of such research.

'Relevant goods' is defined in *Note 3* of the Group and means:

'(a) medical, scientific, computer, video, sterilising, laboratory or refrigeration equipment used in medical or veterinary research, training, diagnosis or treatment;

(b) ambulances;

7.58 VAT Business by Business

(c) parts or accessories for the use in or with goods described in paragraph (a) or (b) above;

(d) goods of the kind described in item 2 of Group 12 of this schedule;

(e) motor vehicles (other than vehicles with more than 50 seats) designed or substantially and permanently adapted for the safe carriage of the handicapped person in a wheelchair;

(f) motor vehicles for use by an eligible body providing care for blind, deaf, mentally handicapped or terminally sick persons mainly to transport such persons;

(g) telecommunication, oral, visual, light enhancing or heat detecting equipment (not being equipment ordinarily supplied for private or recreational use) solely for use for the purpose of rescue or first aid services undertaken by a charitable institution providing such services.'

Note 4 defines eligible body as meaning Health Authorities, non-profit making hospitals, research institutions and, at *Note 4(f)*, other charitable institutions providing care or medical or surgical treatment for handicapped persons.

Item 6 relieves the repair and maintenance of relevant goods owned by an eligible body and *Item 7* relieves goods supplied in connection with *Item 6*.

Meaning of 'relevant goods'

7.58 Although the classes of relevant goods have expanded, if a supply does not fit into a listed class, it will not be eligible for zero-rating. This is evident in all the cases heard on the subject.

In the case of *Clinical Computing Ltd, [1983] VATTR 121(1915)*, which was heard when the relief for relevant goods used for medical research was restricted to medical and scientific equipment, the tribunal decided that, to qualify as 'medical goods', equipment should have specialised features identifying and limiting its use to the medical field. This excluded computers used for medical research (the subject of the appeal) because 'the man in the street' would not consider a computer to be medical or scientific equipment.

Following this decision, the definition of 'relevant goods' was expanded to include computer equipment. However, computer equipment is strictly defined. In the case of *The Dyslexia Institute Ltd (12654)*, the tribunal decided that electronic 'spell-checking equipment' for use in teaching and spelling was not 'computer equipment' and therefore did not qualify for relief.

In *C & E Commrs v David Lewis Centre, QB [1995] STC 485*, the High Court ruled that a charity which provided care for epilepsy sufferers could not claim zero-rating relief on the installation of observation windows, on the grounds that they could not fall into any of the classes of 'relevant goods'. Quoting the tribunal in *Clinical Computing Ltd, [1983] VATTR 121 (1915)* (see above), the High Court held that, even though it accepted that the windows were used in medical diagnosis and treatment, to qualify as medical goods, they must be capable of being described and recognised by the 'man in the street' as such and this was plainly not the case here. As the observation windows could not fit into any other category within *Note 3(a)* (i.e. scientific, computer, video, sterilising or refrigeration), they could not be described as relevant goods and therefore could not qualify for relief.

Although the supply of parts and accessories for qualifying goods can be zero-rated under *Note 3(c)*, this does not extend to consumable materials needed to operate qualifying goods. In the case of *Norwich Camera Centre Ltd (11629)*, the tribunal dismissed an appeal by a company which claimed that chemicals and paper supplied to a charity for X-ray work qualified for relief as 'parts and accessories'. The tribunal held that materials worked on by 'relevant goods' could not constitute a part or accessory.

Prior to 1 May 1990, relevant goods supplied under *Note 3(a)* could only be zero-rated if they were used *solely* for medical research etc: since that date, partial qualifying use is sufficient to qualify. The 'sole use' criterion now only applies to *Note 3(g)*.

This does not stop Customs trying to apply restrictive criteria to the use of relevant goods. For example, Customs insist that the principal reason for acquiring the goods must be for a qualifying use and, in the case of *Note 3(a)*, they apply a strict definition to 'medical research' (see Chapter 11— Education). However, in *Help The Aged (14180)*, Customs' attempt to exclude adapted vehicles from relief under *Note 3(e)* on the grounds that they may be used by able-bodied people was not supported by the tribunal. The tribunal found that 'provided adaptations allowing safe carriage of handicapped persons were permanent, it was not a requirement of *Note 3(e)* that the adaptations had to be made solely and exclusively to enable the vehicle to be used for such carriage'. The tribunal's decision was upheld by the High Court (*C & E Commrs v Help the Aged [1997] STC 406*).

Eligible bodies

7.59 Although the list of eligible bodies is, in the main, clear-cut, the scope of *Note 4(f)* was addressed in the *Help The Aged* case referred to at 7.58 above. Help The Aged was supplying adapted vehicles to a range of charities on the basis that they were eligible bodies under this Note. Sample charities examined by the tribunal included a residential care home for the elderly; a charity offering transport for people with restricted mobility, and a day care centre.

Customs contended that only user charities which provide care for the chronically sick or disabled as *a specialised function* could be eligible bodies,

7.60 *VAT Business by Business*

and that merely providing transport to 'handicapped persons' as part of a wider charitable function was not sufficient to qualify.

The tribunal preferred to define 'care' in a wider context to mean having the charge or protection of someone or something. In the context of *Note 4(f)*, care needs to be provided for a class of people (i.e. the handicapped) where the facility provided involves the charge or protection of those people in the sense of directly affecting them and involving a direct contact with them. It can cover for example, the provision of suitable accommodation, providing for daily needs, safe transportation and a secure environment. Using this approach, the tribunal decided that all three sample charities qualified as 'providing care'.

The tribunal also observed that *Note 4(f)* did not require that the care is provided for the handicapped to the exclusion of all others, or even mainly for the handicapped. The tribunal preferred the view that the charity should be one whose objects include the provision of care for the handicapped and which actually does provide such care. All three sample charities satisfied this criterion.

As a consequence of this case, the law was amended with effect from 26 November 1996, to limit the eligibility of charitable institutions to exploit this relief. To qualify, an institution must now:

(a) either provide day centre care or be registered under the relevant social legislation to provide residential care or medical or surgical treatment;

(b) use the 'relevant goods' within those establishments;

(c) ensure that the majority of people receiving their care or treatment are disabled (*Notes 4A, 4B,* and *5A*).

An extra-statutory concession extends the relief for mini-buses to charities which, although not operating their own institutions or day centres, do provide care services exclusively to the handicapped and use their vehicles solely for that purpose.

However, all care providers are able to purchase medical equipment listed in *Note 3(a)* at the zero rate if they provide domiciliary medical care for handicapped people in their own homes and use the goods in connection with the provision of that care (*Note 5B*).

Advertising

7.60   One of the most popular zero-rating reliefs available to charities is the one for advertising, fund-raising or making known the objects of the charity.

Group 15, Item 8 zero-rates:

Charities **7.60**

'the supply to a charity, for the purposes of raising money for, or making known the objects or reasons for the objects of, the charity, of—

(a) the broadcast on television or radio or screening in a cinema of an advertisement; or

(b) the publication of an advertisement in any newspaper, journal, poster, programme, annual, leaflet, brochure, pamphlet, periodical or similar publication; or

(c) any goods or services in connection with the preparation of an advertisement within (b) above.'

Customs interpretation of this legislation, as set out on pages 19 to 21 of VAT Notice 700/1/95, was substantially revised following the case of *The Royal Society for the Encouragement of Arts, Manufacture and Commerce (14007)*. In that case, the tribunal held that Parliament's intention when drafting *Item 8* was to relieve a charity of the liability to pay VAT when seeking publicity to raise funds or to make known its charitable objectives. However, it observed that Customs' views as expressed in VAT Notice 701/1/95, paragraph 16 did not have force of law and commented that Customs' suggested 'minimum wording' for a qualifying advert in paragraph 16(a)—i.e. that, to qualify, an advert needs more than a charity's name: examples offered of minimum acceptable wording for suitable slogans were: 'please support X' and 'X exists to prevent cruelty to children'—was not laid down by statute. In the tribunal's view, so long as the wording actually conveyed the objects of the charity in question, it did not matter how long or short that wording may be. (The case concerned the self-supply of posters advertising a special awards scheme, which were designed and prepared outside the relevant VAT group but printed within the group. The charity treated the self-supply of the posters as zero-rated. The Commissioners issued an assessment on the basis that the supply did not qualify for zero-rating and the charity appealed. The tribunal allowed the appeal but the High Court reversed this decision and restored the assessment (*QB 1996, [1997] STC 437*). Scott-Baker J held that the purpose of *VATA 1994, 8 Sch, Group 15, Item 8* was to help charities obtain supplies of advertising services from third party suppliers. The legislation was not intended to promote 'in-house' advertising, which did not need such assistance. *Item 8(c)* zero-rated goods or services supplied in connection with the publication of a qualifying advertisement within *Item 8(b)*, but did not apply where the goods or services were merely supplied in connection with the preparation of an advertisement which was not within *Item 8(b)*. The self-supply of the posters was therefore not within *Item 8(c)* and thus was standard-rated.)

Paragraph 16(a) of VAT Notice 701/1/95 also states that adverts which are not primarily fund-raising in nature but indirectly benefit a charity (e.g. schools advertising for pupils) can also qualify if they include a qualifying advert (i.e. an appropriate slogan). However, the tribunal could not accept that the addition of a qualifying slogan of the type suggested by Customs in that paragraph 16(a) converted what would otherwise be a non-qualifying

7.61 *VAT Business by Business*

advert into a qualifying one. The tribunal held that, to obtain relief, the qualifying purpose of the advert must be the principal (but not necessarily the only) purpose. The tribunal stated that an advert which is, in the words of *Item 8*, 'for the purpose of... making known the objects of' a charity 'is not an expression apt to describe an advertisement which is primarily, or perhaps entirely, for some purpose outwith *Item 8* but has a footnote which is intended to epitomise the objects of the charity'.

This view was reinforced in *Sussex County Association Of Change Ringers (14116)*. The tribunal confirmed the view that, to qualify for relief, an advert's principal objective had to be either the raising of funds or making known the objects of the charity; however, it does not have to do both. Whether or not a particular advertisement meets the requirement is a matter of fact.

The tribunal applied four principles in making its decision with regard to the advertisements under appeal in this case: (1) an advert for the purpose of making known the objects of the charity does not necessarily have to contain some indication of the objects for which the charity exists and it certainly is not a requirement for a fund-raising advert; (2) a minimum form of words stating the objects of a charity was not a legal requirement; (3) it was not necessary to make known information to the general public if it could be understood by the target audience; (4) a fund-raising advert does not have to specifically state that that is its purpose, nor does it have to solicit donations or carry a slogan.

Following the RSA case, Customs reviewed their views on charity advertising and they no longer accept that recruitment adverts qualify (unless for volunteers). However, those for university courses, school open days held in order to attract potential pupils, conferences connected with the furtherance of the charity's objectives, church services, fund-raising events and requests for aid goods will continue to qualify for relief (Business Brief 9/96).

Business Brief 18/96 further restricted relief by excluding stickers, draw tickets, notepaper and general use envelopes. Items used directly in fund-raising campaigns, pre-printed paper or card collecting boxes, pre-printed collecting envelopes, and pre-printed letters appealing solely for money for the charity, continue to qualify, as do envelopes used in conjunction with appeal letters and for forwarding donations provided that they are overprinted with an appeal request related to that contained in the letter. Customs also announced that Paragraphs 16(a) and 16(b) of Notice 701/1/95 are cancelled.

Zero-rating certificates

7.61 Most supplies which are zero-rated to charities because of their charitable status require a declaration in the form of a Certificate to be made to the supplier confirming the use and the user of the supply.

Charities 7.62

Certificates are required for supplies of:

- recording and playback equipment for the blind;
- lifeboats, slipways and launching and recovery equipment;
- aids for the disabled;
- charity advertising;
- medicinal products used in medical or veterinary research;
- zero-rated property.

Certificates to zero-rate the grant of an interest in property must be issued to the grantor before the grant is made, in order to be valid (*VATA 1994, 8 Sch, Group 5, Note 12(b)*). Other certificates should be placed at the time of the order.

Although the intention of issuing a Certificate is to take the onus for determining the liability of a supply off the supplier and place it on the customer, the supplier should still take reasonable steps to satisfy himself that the Certificate has been correctly issued. *ESC A16* states:

> '*Incorrect customer declarations.* Where a customer provides an incorrect declaration claiming eligibility for zero-rating under Group(s) of the zero-rating Schedule and the supplier, despite having taken all reasonable steps to check the validity of the declaration, nonetheless fails to identify the inaccuracy and, in good faith, makes the supply at zero rate, Customs and Excise will not seek to recover the tax due from the supplier.'

In the *Help The Aged* case referred to in paragraphs 7.58 and 7.59 above, Customs argued that Help The Aged had not taken 'reasonable steps' to check the validity of Certificates. The issue was decided in Help The Aged's favour based on the facts of the case, but Customs' attitude does serve as a warning to those suppliers who consider that, by merely accepting a Certificate, they are free to zero-rate a supply.

Reduced rate

7.62 The supply of fuel and power for a 'qualifying use' is charged at a reduced rate, 8% from 1 April 1994 to 31 August 1997 and 5% thereafter (*VATA 1994, A1 Sch; F(No 2) A 1997, s 6*). Qualifying use includes use by a charity otherwise than in the course or furtherance of a business (*paragraph 2(b)*).

Where a supply is used partly for qualifying use and partly not, an apportionment should be made to determine the extent to which the suppliers use for a qualifying use. However, if at least 60% of the goods are supplied for qualifying use, the whole supply qualifies for the reduced rate.

7.63 *VAT Business by Business*

The reduced rate covers the supply of coal, coke, other solid fuels, various forms of gas, oils, or electricity, heat or air conditioning. It does not extend to the supply of heated water (i.e. water which has been heated so that it is supplied at a temperature higher than that at which it was before it was heated) which is standard-rated with effect from 26 June 1996, following the *Value Added Tax (Anti-Avoidance (Heating)) Order 1996 (SI 1996 No 1661)*.

Importations by charities

7.63 The *Value Added Tax (Imported Goods) Relief Order 1984 (SI 1984 No 746)*, as amended by *SI 1992 No 3120*, relieves from VAT a wide range of goods imported by charities from outside the Member States (*Group 6*). For the full list, see *Tolley's VAT 1998/99, para 12.11*.

Administration

Registration

7.64 The registration limits applicable to charities are the same as those for other businesses (for details of registration limits, etc. see *Tolley's VAT 1998/99, chapter 59*). Charities making taxable supplies do not have to register until they exceed those limits; however, as many charities (or their subsidiaries) make significant zero-rated supplies, it may be in their interest to register voluntarily even if their taxable supplies do not exceed the registration limit, e.g. where they would be in a net VAT repayment position (i.e. VAT recovered exceeds VAT payable). Each case should be assessed on its merits, paying particular attention to the compliance costs associated with a VAT registration compared to the VAT recoverable.

Where a charity operates a branch network which is centrally controlled, Customs will expect the taxable income of all branches to be taken into consideration when determining taxable turnover. However, if branches are autonomous, each branch must assess its liability individually and registration of one branch or the main charity does not necessarily mean that all branches must register.

Charities which are not registered should not be complacent: the liability of many of the supplies typically made by the sector is complex and ever-changing, and it is easy for a charity to become liable to register without knowing it. It is essential that activities and income are monitored and registration is effected at the right time to avoid unexpected liabilities and penalties.

Cost-sharing

7.65 It is common practice for charities to share office, staff and other administrative costs. As most charities are unable to recover all their VAT,

Charities **7.66**

and 'management charges' are ordinarily standard-rated, it is essential to structure these sorts of arrangements correctly to avoid the risk of irrecoverable VAT being charged.

In the case of *Durham Aged Mineworkers' Homes Association v C & E Commrs, QB [1994] STC 553*, the High Court held that the recharge of shared accommodation and staff costs by Durham Aged Mineworkers' Homes Association (Aged) to another association, Durham Mineworkers' Homes Association (Mineworkers) were outside the scope of VAT. In the absence of a written agreement, the decision was based on the implied contractual relationship between the Associations to share accommodation and administrative expenses, to the effect that Aged would pay for them as principal in respect of its own agreed share, and as agent for Mineworkers in respect of that association's share. It followed that there was no separate supply from Aged to Mineworkers.

Informal arrangements such as this are common between organisations which, although legally separate entities, work together so closely as to be viewed almost as having the same identity. As a consequence of this closeness, informal agreements over payments and reimbursements often arise. It is advisable that organisations in similar circumstances set out each party's responsibilities in writing.

Following this case, Customs are generally prepared to accept that, under certain conditions, where staff and other overheads are shared by charities, the supply can be treated as a non-business activity.

Those conditions are that:

(a) the supplies between the charities concerned are similar in all respects to the *Durham Aged Mineworkers' Homes Association* case;

(b) all the conditions relating to disbursements in VAT Notice 700 are met;

(c) some evidence exists of an agency agreement;

(d) the supplies are separately quantified, i.e. the supply is not just an annual 'management charge'.

Trading subsidiaries

7.66 The use of trading subsidiaries by charities to protect profits from direct taxation is becoming increasingly popular as charities exploit their resources in trades outside their primary purpose.

The use of trading subsidiaries has been discussed in paragraphs 7.8, 7.17, 7.28 and 7.37 above. Trading subsidiaries are also widely used to provide consultancy services, certain types of training and advertising services.

7.66 VAT Business by Business

The key point to note is that VAT reliefs available to charities rarely extend to trading subsidiaries (one-off fund-raising events are the exception). This means that supplies which could be relieved from VAT if undertaken by a charity will almost certainly be subject to VAT at the standard rate if carried on by a trading subsidiary.

It is unlikely that a charity would routinely place activities which qualify for VAT exemption in a trading subsidiary to avoid direct taxation. Such activities, by their very nature, would usually be exempt from direct taxation, being 'primary purpose' trading, relieved under *ICTA 1988, s 505(1)(e)*. However, trading subsidiaries can be used to mitigate the impact of VAT on the charity by moving certain activities, which would be exempt from VAT, into a trading subsidiary (thereby making them taxable) if, for example, the charity's client is entitled to full VAT recovery on any services supplied. The subsidiary would be able to recover input tax attributable to the supply, and the addition of VAT would not add to the client's costs.

Trading subsidiaries may also be used to mop up those hidden VAT costs in zero-rated building projects like the construction of residential homes or village halls. Although construction costs may be zero-rated, professional fees of architects, surveyors etc. are specifically excluded from zero-rating (*VATA 1994, 8 Sch, Group 5, Item 2*).

The VAT charged on these services may be avoided if the building contract is one of 'design and build', which wraps up the professional costs in the main build contract. Customs accept that a supply of professional services supplied as part of a design and build contract follow the liability of the main supply (VAT Notice 708, para 10.1). However, if the charity does not want to enter into a design and build contract with a third party, it can achieve the same effect by inserting a subsidiary between the institution and the contractors to act as the design and build company. The subsidiary would buy in all the services and goods required including professional services. The subsidiary would incur VAT on the professional costs, but it would be able to recover that VAT in full: its onward supply of these 'bundled' costs to the institution would be zero-rated.

The same principle can be used to bundle other standard-rated goods and services which can be used to produce zero-rated goods. For example, if a charity produced books or literature itself for free (i.e. non-business) distribution, it would suffer VAT costs on the paper, typesetting, printing etc. However, if a subsidiary took over the production and supplied the finished books on to the charity, its supply would be zero-rated, so there would be no VAT cost to the charity and it could recover all the VAT on the production costs.

Because trading subsidiaries are usually set up to shelter profits from direct taxation, they tend to be 'shell' companies with no assets which buy in resources like staff and administration from the parent charity. Any supplies of goods and services made by the charity must be charged for (to avoid exposure to direct taxation). These charges are usually subject to VAT. Provided that the charity is aware of this, these taxable supplies can improve the charity's own VAT recovery position; however, it is important that these VAT charges are not overlooked.

VAT on supplies between a charity and a trading subsidiary can be avoided if they register as a VAT group (subject to satisfying the relevant criteria). There is a school of thought that, as group registration creates a joint and several liability for VAT debts incurred by a group member, a charity should not enter into such a registration, as charities cannot guarantee to fund the debts of their subsidiaries. Therefore, the decision to form a VAT group needs to be based on sound professional advice that it would be in the financial interests of the charity to do so.

Conclusion

7.67 The exemptions and other reliefs available for charities do place them in an advantageous position when compared to other commercial businesses. Most would agree that this is right and proper. However, over the past few years, the scope for relief has withered, not because the legislation has necessarily changed, but rather because the interpretation of that legislation has drifted towards a narrow and stricter construction. Charities have long clamoured for a refund mechanism to reimburse their VAT costs: a more immediate problem is to protect the reliefs that they already have. This can only be achieved through lobbying, recourse to the courts and sound VAT planning.

Chapter 8

Clubs and Associations

Introduction

8.1 This chapter examines the VAT issues affecting clubs and associations of all types, from commercial enterprises to members' sports clubs through to trade unions and professional bodies. As we will see, such bodies are often faced with very complex VAT issues, which can be many and varied. This is largely due to the fact that they often receive income which traverses all possible VAT treatments—exempt, outside the scope, standard-rated, zero-rated and even lower-rated. Whilst this is true of most clubs and associations, it is necessary at the outset to draw a distinction between those organisations which are run on a 'commercial' basis and those which are not. This is because the VAT issues facing each type are markedly different.

8.2 On one hand, there are those clubs which are run for commercial purposes, the primary purpose of which is to make a profit. Whilst their administrators may not agree, it is probably true to say that such clubs are more straightforward from a VAT perspective.

8.3 Then there are those which are non profit-making members' clubs or associations. Members' clubs will often be run by enthusiasts for others like them, perhaps on a fairly informal basis, and nearly always for 'the love of the game'. On similar lines, there are trade or professional associations which are not run for commercial gain but exist to support a particular cause. Financially, these types of organisation will not normally be run with a view to making a profit. Their aim in generating income will be to break even and cover the running costs incurred. Any surplus which does arise will be ploughed back into the club, often under the terms of its constitution (further consideration of this point, as well as a definition of 'non-profit-making bodies' for VAT purposes is set out at paragraphs 8.15 to 8.20 below).

8.4 As mentioned above, there is a marked difference in the VAT issues facing a commercial club or association compared to those which are 'owned' and run by the membership and which are not profit-driven. This has been accentuated in recent years by the introduction of an exemption from VAT for sporting and leisure pursuits and for cultural activities. Both exemptions apply specifically to non profit-making bodies, clubs and associations being a case in point. In each case, the introduction of the

8.5 *VAT Business by Business*

exemptions was heralded as advantageous to those affected. Whilst this is true to some extent, the exemptions can lead, and indeed have led, to increased costs to clubs and associations, for reasons which are explored later in this chapter. Furthermore, they have also led to a significant increase in the administrative burden faced by some clubs and associations which should not be underestimated, particularly when these are often run by part-time, unpaid members or committees which can ill afford such added pressures. As a result, clubs and associations must now tackle the more complex areas of the tax, such as partial exemption, and many may not have the resources to cope adequately with such issues, which are considered in detail later in this chapter.

Business for VAT purposes

8.5 From a VAT perspective, the first and most basic matter which must be addressed by a club or association is whether or not it is in 'business'. Clearly such a question does not arise in the case of a club or association which is run as a commercial enterprise. Such clubs will often be privately owned, either by a single proprietor or by any number of stakeholders. Many clubs are owned and run by public limited companies and will exist in order to pay a dividend to the investors. Whichever way such clubs are owned, it is clear that they are run to generate a 'profit', a return on the owners' investment, and are therefore very much in business, in the ordinary meaning of the word.

8.6 When a group of individuals gets together and forms a club or association it is often not at all clear, however, whether it is in business. It is very important from a VAT viewpoint that this is established early on. This is because the question of whether the activities of a club or association constitute business is critical in determining whether those activities fall within the scope of VAT. *Chapter 8* of *Tolley's VAT 1998/99* provides a detailed discussion on what constitutes business. For the purposes of this chapter, it is sufficient to say that the term 'business' has a very general definition in the legislation and includes any trade, profession or vocation (*VATA 1994, s 94(1)*). Conversely, non-business activities are defined as those activities which are not concerned predominantly with the making of supplies for a consideration. They may include free admission to a club's premises for non-members, spreading political beliefs, lobbying for a cause or providing free literature to non-members.

8.7 In the absence of a specific definition, the question of what constitutes a business activity is one which has been tested in front of the VAT tribunals and courts on several occasions. One of the leading cases in this context is *C&E Commrs v Lord Fisher, QB [1981] STC 238; [1981] 2 All ER 147*. In this case, it was held that Lord Fisher, who formed a club and held pheasant shoots for friends, relatives and selected invitees, each of whom were asked for a contribution towards costs, was not, by so doing, carrying on a business. The tribunal found that the shoots were for pleasure and enjoyment and not predominantly concerned with the making of taxable supplies for a consideration.

8.8 In general terms, however, the provision by a club or association of facilities or benefits available to its members for a subscription (or any other consideration, whether monetary or otherwise) is deemed to be a 'business' activity *(VATA 1994, s 94(2)(a))*. There is one notable exception to this and this is where subscriptions are paid to a body whose objects are in the public domain and are of a 'political, religious, philanthropic, philosophical or patriotic nature'. Such a body is not treated as carrying on a business solely because its members subscribe to it, provided that the subscription paid obtains no advantages or benefits for the subscriber other than the right to participate in its management or receive reports on its activities *(VATA 1994, s 94(3))*.

8.9 By and large, however, the provision of tangible benefits to members for a subscription constitutes business. The following VAT tribunal decisions bear testament to this although, as always seems to be the case with VAT, nothing is ever entirely straightforward.

8.10 In *Manor Forstal Residents Society Limited, [1976] VATTR 63 (245)*, the provisions of *VATA 1994, s 94(2)(a)* were held to be applicable. In this case, which concerned an association of local residents, it was held that a society established for the upkeep of the appearance of the local area of the residents, to which its members paid a subscription, was carrying on a business.

8.11 The above provisions were not, however, held to be applicable in *New Ash Green Village Association, [1976] VATTR 63 (245)*. This case similarly concerned an association which had been established for the upkeep of communal land in the area, whose income was derived from payments from all the householders in the locality. However, under the terms of its constitution, the homeowners were not the members of the association; membership was by appointment from societies established for each sub-divided parcel of the land, known as 'neighbourhood areas'. As a result, the tribunal found that the provisions of *VATA 1994, s 94(2)(a)* did not apply and that the association was not carrying on a business.

8.12 This was also the view of the tribunal in *Notts Fire Service Messing Club, [1977] VATTR 1 (348)* which concerned the running of a canteen at a fire station. Here, a very informal arrangement existed whereby an officer of the fire station received £1 per week to act as 'mess manager'. In this case, the canteen club was not held to be in business.

8.13 The above examples serve to demonstrate the difficulties which can arise in determining whether the activities of a club or association constitute 'business'. If it is decided that a club or association is not in business then, by definition, those activities are outside the scope of VAT. Such a body need not therefore be concerned with any requirement to register for VAT and the

8.14 *VAT Business by Business*

administrative burden which this entails. Conversely, if it is decided that the activities of a club or association are being carried on by way of business, it is necessary to consider whether those activities fall within the scope of VAT. In cases of doubt, it is strongly recommended that professional advice is sought.

8.14 As has already been established, if a subscription or similar is charged, then subject to the exception described in paragraph 8.8 above, the VAT legislation deems that the activities of a club constitute business. As such, the club or association must consider whether it is required to be registered for VAT. If its taxable business income exceeds the registration threshold (currently £50,000 per annum), then it is required to be registered and account for VAT on some or all of its income (see paragraph 8.21 below for further details).

Non-profit-making bodies

8.15 Paragraph 8.4 above has already touched on the important question of the status of a particular club or association and whether or not it is run with a view to making a profit. Having decided on the question of being in business, a further consideration for clubs and associations is whether or not they are a 'non-profit-making body'. This is particularly important if the club is concerned with sporting and leisure pursuits or with cultural activities.

8.16 It is necessary to make this distinction because, in relation to sports clubs, certain types of income, for example, the subscriptions paid by members, can qualify for exemption from VAT where the club is a 'non-profit-making body' (*VATA 1994, Sch 9, Group 10*). Whilst *Note 3* to this Group provides some clarification of the term, this is only by reference to what is not considered to be such a body. A local authority, for example, is not considered to be a non-profit-making body for the purposes of this exemption. As the legislation does not provide a clear definition, the term non-profit-making is given its natural meaning.

8.17 One important indicator in deciding if a club is non-profit-making is whether its constitution, rules or articles of association preclude any distribution of profits or surpluses of income over expenditure to members, shareholders or any other person. Whilst Customs & Excise have indicated that they do not consider the absence of such a clause to be the sole deciding factor in making such a determination (see C&E Leaflet 701/45/94, paragraphs 6-8), it clearly provides a strong indication of the status, motivation and culture of the organisation. Nevertheless, provided that it can be shown, for example from the club's annual accounts, that in practice it has not distributed any profits, Customs & Excise should accept that a club is non-profit-making (C&E Leaflet 701/33/97).

8.18 The approach of Customs & Excise is to apply the principles arising from the Court of Appeal judgment in *C&E Commrs v Bell Concord*

Educational Trust Ltd, CA [1989] STC 264; [1989] 2 All ER 217; [1989] 1 CMLR 845. This case concerned a charity whose income exceeded its expenditure by a substantial margin, the surplus being retained with a view to subsequent expansion. The important principle which the case established was that the words 'otherwise than for profit' can relate to the objects for which an organisation is established and not to the budgeting policy being pursued for the time being by the organisation in question. In the context of a sports club or association, the provision of sporting services should not be excluded from exemption simply because a club makes profits on its bar and catering activities and uses them to subsidise subscriptions.

8.19 Another important tribunal case in this area is *Chobham Golf Club (14867)*. This case concerned the question of whether a sports club was non-profit-making and therefore eligible to treat certain of its supplies as exempt (see paragraph 8.21 *et seq.* below for details of which of the club's supplies qualify for exemption). In this case, the club had been founded as one which was privately owned. The original owners had, however, sold it and it was now managed as a members' club.

8.20 The tribunal allowed the club's appeal, holding that the facts that the club paid significant sums in rent to the company which owned its course, and paid management fees to a management company, did not necessarily take it outside the definition of a 'non-profit-making body', since 'income is not profit'. On the evidence, the tribunal was satisfied that any surplus which remained after paying the club's overheads (which included rent and management fees) would be 'used in the improvement of the club's facilities'. Accordingly, the club was within the definition of a 'non-profit-making body', and its supplies to its members qualified for exemption. Customs have, however, announced that they have appealed to the High Court against this decision (Business Brief 18/97, issued on 22 August 1997).

Liability

8.21 The following paragraphs provide some details of the different VAT liability of the types of income generally received by clubs and associations. As outlined above, such bodies often receive income which traverses all the different VAT treatments—standard-rated, zero-rated, lower-rated, exempt and outside the scope of VAT. For this reason, clubs and associations can be faced with very complex VAT issues.

Subscription income

8.22 The most common form of income received by clubs and associations is undoubtedly subscriptions from their members. Subscription income is normally liable to VAT at the standard rate. However, as described at paragraph 8.8 above, subscriptions to certain organisations are deemed to be 'non-business'. This applies where a body has objects which are in the

8.23 VAT Business by Business

public domain and are of a 'political, religious, philanthropic, philosophical or patriotic nature'. Such a body is not to be treated as carrying on a business only because its members subscribe to it, provided that a subscription obtains no advantages or benefits for the subscriber other than the right to participate in its management or receive reports on its activities (*VATA 1994, s 94(3)*). The subscription income of such associations is regarded as non-business and outside the scope of VAT.

8.23 In this context, 'membership benefits' also includes any items for which a separate additional charge is made, provided that such advantages are restricted to members or can be obtained more cheaply than by a non-member.

8.24 In the case of the *English-Speaking Union of the Commonwealth, [1980] VATTR 184 (1023)*, it was held that other facilities available to members in addition to the right to participate in management or receive reports on its activities could not be ignored on 'de minimis' grounds. The only benefits available to members over non-members were a journal published every few months issued free and the ability to obtain contacts and introductions to other members. The journal was free to members but carried a charge to non-members (15 pence at the time of the decision) and this was held to be important in this case. The tribunal found that the benefits received by the members exceeded those described in *VATA 1994, s 94(3)* and held that the English-Speaking Union was therefore in business, following the principles set out at paragraph 8.22 above.

8.25 Where a club or association supplies any additional benefits or advantages to members other than those described in *VATA 1994, s 94(3)*, its subscriptions are within the scope of VAT. Such benefits can include free advice, free publications or information regarding the organisation of social events or similar. For example, the VAT tribunal held in the case of *South Church Workmen's Club & Institute Ltd (613)* that the subscriptions received were in the course of business and therefore within the scope of VAT because the club allowed the membership the use of the club's facilities and other advantages.

Trade unions and professional bodies

8.26 As seen above, the provision of facilities and advantages to members of clubs, associations and other such organisations is normally standard-rated. The provision of such services by certain professional, learned or representational associations can, however, qualify for exemption under the provisions of *VATA 1994, 9 Sch, Group 9*.

8.27 In order to be eligible to apply this exemption, associations must be non-profit-making bodies, as defined in paragraphs 8.15 to 8.20 above, and be either:

(a) a trade union or similar body;

(b) a professional association, membership of which is wholly or mainly restricted to individuals who have or are seeking a qualification appropriate to the practice of the profession concerned;

(c) an association, the primary purpose of which is the advancement of a particular branch of knowledge or the fostering of professional expertise;

(d) an association, the primary purpose of which is to make representations to the Government on legislation and other public matters which affect the business or professional interests of its members; or,

(e) an organisation or association, the membership of which consists wholly or mainly of constituent or affiliated associations which as individual associations would be within (a) to (d) above.

8.28 In relation to (a) above, a trade union is defined as an organisation which consists wholly or mainly of workers whose main objective is to negotiate the terms and conditions of employment of its members.

8.29 In relation to the professional associations in (b) above, 'profession' is not defined but appears to be restricted to those occupations which would be regarded as professions, giving that word its ordinary meaning. This has been held by the VAT tribunal to include the teaching of dance (*Allied Dancing Association Ltd (10777)*) but not bookmaking (*The Bookmakers' Protection Association (Southern Area) Ltd, [1979] VATTR 215 (849)*) or driving a taxi-cab (*City Cabs (Edinburgh) Ltd (928)*). Customs & Excise consider that membership of such associations should be obligatory, or at least customary, for those pursuing a career in that profession (C&E Leaflet 701/33/97).

8.30 Membership of associations in (c) above must be restricted wholly or mainly to individuals whose present or previous professions or employment are directly connected with the purposes of the association. In the VAT tribunal case of *Royal Photographic Society, [1978] VATTR 191 (647)*, it was held that the Society did not qualify for exemption as there was no restriction on membership.

8.31 Membership of associations in (d) above must be restricted to individuals or corporate bodies whose business or professional interests are directly connected with its aims.

8.32 Supplies of services, and related goods, by organisations listed at (a) to (e) above to their members are exempt from VAT provided that they are made available without payment (other than a membership subscription) and provided that they relate to the aims of the organisation.

8.33 Exemption does not apply to supplies that do not relate to the body's aims as set out in its rules or constitution, or to the supply of any right of

8.34 VAT Business by Business

admission to any premises, event or performance, to which non-members are admitted for a consideration. Similarly, exemption does not extend to any supplies which are not provided automatically as a result of membership and for which an additional sum is charged, or to supplies to non-members (*VATA 1994, 9 Sch, Group 9, Item 1*).

8.34 The value of the exempt supply is normally the full amount of the subscriptions. Where, however, subscriptions also cover taxable supplies (including zero-rated supplies) the subscriptions must be apportioned. See C&E Leaflet 701/33/97, and paragraph 8.38 below for further details on this subject.

Sports clubs

8.35 From 1 April 1994, subscription income paid to members' clubs, which are non-profit-making bodies providing sport and physical education services, has been treated as exempt from VAT (*VATA 1994, 9 Sch, Group 10*). The treatment of income in this way was introduced in 1 April 1994 with backdated effect to 1 January 1990 and this led to substantial back claims of overpaid VAT by such clubs (see paragraph 8.130 below for further details on this subject).

8.36 Under the terms of the exemption, a non-profit-making body operating a membership scheme has to account for VAT on all services supplied to non-members. However any club or association, which is not operating a membership scheme, can exempt sporting and physical education services supplied to all individual participants, for example, where usage is entirely on a pay and play basis.

8.37 Customs & Excise have issued a definitive list of sports which can be included within the scope of the exemption. The full list of these sports can be found in Customs & Excise Notice 701/45/94, which is reproduced in *Tolley's VAT 1998/99* at para 58.11. It is perhaps worth noting that such diverse activities as baton twirling and dragon boat racing are included within Customs & Excise's definition of 'sport'. It has been held by the VAT tribunal, however, that pigeon racing, for example, does not qualify for exemption.

Apportionment of subscription income

8.38 Subscription income received by a club or association which is not sports related could also qualify for exemption for VAT, albeit under one of the other headings for VAT exemption which can be found in *VATA 1994, 9 Sch*. Indeed, we have already explored this area in relation to trade unions and professional bodies. Alternatively, it is possible that some of the subscription income could be zero-rated. For example, when part of the subscription income paid relates to the provision of a publication, a magazine or book perhaps, then it can be argued that part of the payment relates to a supply which is zero-rated by virtue of *VATA 1994, 8 Sch, Group 2.*

8.39 Where some of the benefits of membership to an organisation are identifiable supplies of zero-rated or exempt goods and services, subscriptions may be apportioned so that the part which relates to such supplies is relieved from VAT. Joining fees as well as life membership fees can also be treated in this way, unless special additional benefits are received by such members which are not available to ordinary members. See 8.132 below for details of the practical points to be borne in mind when an apportionment of the subscription income received by a club or association is being contemplated.

Overseas members

8.40 Subscriptions paid by overseas members of a UK organisation normally have the same VAT liability as subscriptions paid by members who belong in the UK.

8.41 If, however, the services provided to overseas members consist almost entirely of the provision of information or consultancy, then these services may be zero-rated under *VATA 1994, 5 Sch.* Clubs and associations may be able to justify such subscriptions being outside the scope of UK VAT where the recipients either belong in another EU Member State and use the supply for business purposes, or the recipient belongs outside the Member States.

Income other than subscriptions

8.42 Clubs and associations often receive other forms of income than simply subscriptions. Some of the more common types of receipt are set out below, together with details of the VAT liability of each source of income.

Joining fees

8.43 Where an initial fee is charged in addition to the annual subscription this will have the same liability as the subscription income (see 8.22 above).

Levies & loans from members

8.44 Where a levy payment is made and the member has no right to a return of his money, this must be treated as additional subscription for the year in which the levy is received. This means that the payments follow the same liability as the subscription income.

8.45 In the case of compulsory loans from members, where these are levied, VAT must also be accounted for at the beginning of each subscription

8.46 VAT Business by Business

year on the value of the loans to the club. This applies only where the subscription income is also standard-rated. The value of the loans will not be the amount of the entire loan made available to the club, as is commonly thought, but will be the amount of the notional interest the club might have incurred if it had resorted to external borrowing. For the purposes of calculating this value, it is usual to use the clearing banks' base lending rate in force at the beginning of the month in which subscriptions are due to be paid.

8.46 If subscriptions are reduced or waived for members who agree to make a loan of a minimum amount, the loans are optional and not compulsory. VAT on such loans must be accounted for at the beginning of the subscription year on the appropriate normal rate of subscription (the amount payable by a member who has not agreed to make a voluntary loan). See *Exeter Golf & Country Club Ltd v C&E Commrs, CA [1981] STC 211*. The tribunal case of *Rothley Park Golf Club (2074)* also involved similar circumstances to those described above.

Shares and debentures

8.47 Payment for a share or debenture in a club is regarded as being an additional payment for the advantages of membership and the amount paid, including any premium payable, should be treated as a compulsory interest-free loan (see 8.45 above). In the case of *Hinckley Golf Club Ltd (9527)*, the VAT tribunal held that the primary objective of the persons subscribing for shares was to make an investment with a view to a profit. The offer of free membership to certain shareholders was simply an inducement to invest and the only supply to those shareholders was an exempt supply of shares in consideration for the purchase price of those shares.

8.48 This is another complex area of the tax and it is strongly recommended that clubs seek professional advice when considering a share or debenture type fund-raising venture.

Entry fees

8.49 Competition entry fees are standard-rated unless they fall within the specific exemptions set out in this paragraph. They are exempt from VAT when paid by members of a non-profit-making members' club. Where such a body does not operate a membership scheme, such fees also qualify for exemption when they are charged to individuals. Competition entry fees are exempt from VAT if the entry fee is allocated wholly towards the provision of prizes awarded in that competition (*VATA 1994, 9 Sch, Group 10, Item 1*). Entry fees are also exempt from VAT when the right to participate in the competition is granted by a non-profit-making body established for the purposes of sport or recreation (*VATA 1994, 9 Sch, Group 10, Item 2*). (Prior to 1 April 1994, where the entry fee consisted wholly or partly of a charge which the body ordinarily made for the use of its facilities or the admission to its premises, it was standard-rated. However, it was exempt if the body running the competition at the ground belonged to another organisation which ordinarily made a charge for facilities.)

Court fees

8.50 Fees for the hire of, for example, a squash or tennis court, and green fees for golf courses, are exempt from VAT where these are paid by members of a non profit-making members' club. Where such a body does not operate a membership scheme, such fees also qualify for exemption when they are charged to individuals. Otherwise, they are standard-rated. When payments are linked to the operation of lighting, for example, squash courts or snooker tables, the full amount payable follows the above liabilities as the charge is for the right to use the facilities. The charge, or a proportion thereof, does not relate to the supply of electricity, which would be subject to VAT at the lower rate of 5%. It is considered that the supply of electricity is incidental to the supply of the playing facilities. This issue was tested in the case of *St Anne's on Sea Lawn Tennis Club Ltd, [1977] VATTR 229 (434)*.

Hire of pitches

8.51 The hire of pitches for the playing of sport (football, hockey and rugby being three common examples) is normally standard-rated. It is, however, exempt from VAT where supplied to the members of a non profit-making club. If a club or association does not operate a membership scheme, such fees also qualify for exemption when they are charged to individuals. Income received by members' clubs from the hire of pitches to non-members can also qualify for exemption from VAT where certain conditions are met. These are quite complex and full details can be found in *VATA 1994, 9 Sch, Note 16*. However, in summary, if the letting or hiring of a pitch is for a period in excess of 24 hours or there is a series of lettings to the same person over a period of time which meets certain specified conditions, such income could be exempt from VAT.

8.52 This so-called 'block bookings exemption' also applies where:

- each period is in respect of the same activity carried on at the same place;
- the interval between each period is not less than one day and no more than 14 days;
- consideration is payable by reference to the whole series and is evidenced by written agreement; and
- the person making the block booking has exclusive use of the facilities.

8.53 VAT Business by Business

8.53 If a club or association has elected to waive exemption (commonly referred to as the 'option to tax'), then the above exemption will not apply and any income received will be taxable to the standard rate (*VATA 1994, 10 Sch, para 2(1)*). Further details on this subject can be found in paragraph 8.142 below.

Match and training fee income

8.54 Such income is normally taxable at the standard rate. However, when received from a non profit-making club's own membership, it is exempt from VAT. Where such a body does not operate a membership scheme, this type of income also qualifies for exemption when received from individuals. Where such income is taxable, it is important that VAT is accounted for on the full gross receipts before any deduction for expenditure, such as payments to match referees or in respect of catering, is made.

Prizes

8.55 If prizes are given in cash, or challenge cups and other perpetual trophies remaining the property of the club are awarded, then this is outside the scope of VAT. Prizes of goods are regarded as gifts and VAT must be accounted for on the full value if the cost exceeds £15. Otherwise, no VAT is due.

Fixture cards

8.56 The sale of fixture cards will generate income which is zero-rated. However, clubs should note that Customs & Excise take the view that the sale of fixture cards is standard-rated if any portion for completion by the member occupies more than 25% of the total area.

Other types of participation fee

8.57 As has been seen above, in general terms, where participation fees are received from a non-profit-making club's own membership, these are exempt from VAT. Where a club or association does not operate a membership scheme, this type of income also qualifies for exemption when received from individuals. Otherwise, it is taxable at the standard rate. There are one or two exceptions to this rule. For example, a fee charged by some very popular clubs to prospective members simply to remain on the waiting list is always taxable, as are parking and mooring fees. Customs & Excise have produced a very useful matrix showing the VAT liability of all the above charges (C&E Leaflet 701/45/94, paragraph 18). This also provides further details on the VAT treatment of some of the more obscure charges.

Bar sales, catering and teas

8.58 The provision of food and drink, where supplied by way of catering, is always standard-rated. This includes hot food and drink wherever it is consumed (i.e. even if it is 'taken away' to be eaten) as well as all food and drink which is consumed on the premises.

8.59 The concept of 'mutual trading', which applies for direct tax purposes, does *not* apply to VAT. The High Court has held that, where a club's members purchase drinks from the club bar, this is a supply for VAT purposes (*Carlton Lodge Club v C&E Commrs, QB [1974] STC 507*). It is therefore necessary to account for VAT on the sale of such items, whether to members or guests alike.

Amusement machines and games of skill

8.60 The income received from amusement machines, juke boxes and games of skill, for example, pool tables, is standard-rated.

Gaming machine takings

8.61 VAT is due on the total amount put into the machine by players, less amounts returned as winnings.

Telephones

8.62 Clubs will often rent a pay phone from a telecommunications supplier. Where this occurs, the person renting the machine makes the supplies to the users and VAT is due on these supplies. Output tax must therefore be calculated by applying the VAT fraction (7/47) to the money removed from the call box.

Registration fees

8.63 In relation to professional associations and similar bodies, there are certain professions, in which persons cannot practice unless they are registered with a statutory body and have paid fees which are prescribed by law. Such registration fees are normally outside the scope of VAT because, in carrying out these statutory functions, the organisation is not supplying a service in the course of its business. Where, however, in return for these fees, the organisation supplies clearly identifiable services over and above registration, or where registration procedures have no statutory backing, the registration fees should be treated in the same way as subscription income.

8.64 This issue was examined in the case of *Institute of Chartered Accountants in England and Wales v C&E Commrs, CA [1997] STC 1155*,

8.65 *VAT Business by Business*

where Customs issued a ruling that the services supplied by the Institute in the course of its licensing activities were not supplied in the course or furtherance of a business. The tribunal held that the relevant supplies were not 'of a kind which...are commonly made by those who seek to make profit from them', nor were the relevant activities 'predominantly concerned with the making of taxable supplies for a consideration'. The licensing activities were predominantly concerned with 'the implementation of the statutory policy of protecting the public interest through self-regulation of the relevant practitioners', and 'charging fees for investigative and monitoring services is not the predominant concern or characteristic of the activities'. The Court of Appeal upheld this decision, although the case has now been referred to the House of Lords.

Collection charges for trade union subscriptions

8.65 Charges raised by employers for deducting trade union subscriptions from employees' pay are exempt under *VATA 1994, 9 Sch, Group 5*.

Bank interest

8.66 The interest received from banks is normally exempt from VAT. However, it is likely that most clubs and associations will be able to ignore the receipt of such income for the purposes of their partial exemption calculation. This is because such income is considered to be incidental to the main activities of the club.

General fund-raising activities

8.67 In addition to the above types of income which clubs may receive as part of their day to day activities, many clubs seek to supplement their income by raising funds in various ways. Some of the more common types of fund-raising activities are set out below, together with details of the VAT liability of each source of income.

One-off fund-raising events

8.68 Where certain fund-raising events are held by non profit-making bodies, income received can qualify for exemption from VAT, provided that certain conditions are met (*VATA 1994, 9 Sch, Group 12, Item 2*).

8.69 In order to qualify, events must be 'one-offs'; in other words, they must not form part of a series or regular run of like or similar events. This does not mean, however, that such events must be 'once only'. For example, Customs & Excise do not consider that annual events are precluded from qualifying for exemption—see *Tolley's VAT 1998/99, para 12.9*. Events must also be held exclusively for the benefit of the club or association in question. Perhaps most importantly, the club or association must be a 'non profit-making body whose objects are in the public domain and are of a political, religious, philanthropic, philosophical or patriotic nature (*VATA 1994, s 94(3)*); a trade union, professional association or similar body; a members' sports club, or a club involved in cultural activities (*VATA 1994, 9 Sch, Group 13, Item 2*).

8.70 The exemption is aimed at events such as fetes, balls, bazaars, gala shows and similar, and has been held by the VAT tribunal to include three-day festivals where tickets were sold separately for each day (*Reading Cricket and Hockey Club (13656)*). The restriction to 'one-off' events is designed to prevent clubs and associations gaining an unfair advantage over the activities of commercial organisations. A club can hold a number of similar events in a year and, provided they are reasonably spread apart, they can all benefit from exemption. Customs & Excise are prepared to accept that low key events, jumble sales, for example, can be held on the same premises and at any frequency and still come within the exemption because the risk of distortion of competition is less (Chapter 7—*Charities* provides more details on this topic).

Admission charges

8.71 Many clubs and associations will hold a variety of events, for example, fetes and shows, which for whatever reason will not qualify for the above exemption. More often than not, the event will be held for the purposes of fund-raising and one way of generating extra funds is to charge an admission fee. Normally admission charges are standard-rated. This includes admissions to swimming pools, funfairs, dances, sports events, museums and galleries, zoos, safari parks and air shows, but see paragraph 8.73 below.

8.72 Where admission is by programme only, this will not qualify for zero-rating if Customs & Excise consider that this is no more than an elaborate ticket which has been bought to get into the event. Payment for such a programme is the consideration for admission and standard-rated even if the payment cannot be legally enforced. A programme may however qualify for zero-rating where it contains a substantial amount of reading matter or information. Where it does so qualify, an apportionment can be made between the standard-rated element of payment for admission and the zero-rated element for the programme. The zero-rated element can be based on the unit cost of the programme plus a reasonable mark-up, although other methods are available.

8.73 Where clubs and associations are involved with cultural activities, admission charges to certain events, premises and performances may be eligible for exemption, provided certain conditions are fulfilled (*VATA 1994, 9 Sch, Group 13*).

8.74 The admission charge must relate to:

8.75 VAT Business by Business

(i) a 'museum, gallery, art exhibition or zoo', or

(ii) a theatrical, musical or choreographic performance of a cultural nature.

8.75 In order to qualify for exemption, the club or association making the charge for admission must be an 'eligible body'. In essence, this means that it must fulfil the non-profit-making criteria outlined at paragraphs 8.15 to 8.20 above. However, in order to qualify as an eligible body for the purposes of this exemption, there is an added stipulation that the organisation must be managed and administered on a voluntary basis by persons who have no direct or indirect financial interest in its activities. If the club or association makes any payment for managerial or administration services, it is not eligible for exemption.

8.76 Certain payments such as the reimbursement of expenses, honoraria and payments of a similar nature will not necessarily disqualify a club or association from exemption. Customs & Excise also consider that the employment of staff or payments for zoo keepers, guides, producers or choreographers etc. does not preclude a club or association from qualifying for exemption provided such persons are not involved in the management or administration of the organisation (*VATA 1994, 9 Sch, Group 13*).

8.77 Customs & Excise also consider that what qualifies as a 'museum, gallery, art exhibition or zoo' within 8.74(i) and (ii) above has to be judged by reference to the normal everyday meaning of the words and taking into account evidence such as the nature of the exhibits and whether, for example, an art gallery belongs to a representative body for art galleries.

Donations in lieu of admission

8.78 Alternatively, clubs and associations may decide not to charge an admission fee but ask attendees to make a donation. Whilst true donations are outside the scope of VAT, to be accepted as a donation for VAT purposes, it must be clear to the donor that admission can be gained whether or not a payment is given and the size of the payment is entirely up to him. Where a person has to pay to get in, or perhaps more importantly is made to think that he has to do so, the payment is a taxable one. One relevant case in this context is *C&E Commrs v Tron Theatre, CS [1994] STC 177* (see Chapter 7—*Charities*, at paragraph 7.8, for details).

Discos, dances and social events

8.79 Unless a particular event qualifies for exemption as a 'one-off' (see paragraph 8.68 above), VAT must be accounted for on the gross taxable supplies made, for example, admission and catering, and not on the net amount after expenses, for example the band, floor shows and other staff costs, have been paid.

Provision of hospitality

8.80 The provision of hospitality for a charge to members and non-members is standard-rated. However, where refreshments are provided free of charge, VAT incurred on related expenditure cannot normally be reclaimed as input tax. Having said this, a club may be able to reclaim the tax incurred in providing free refreshments to its own membership, staff and certain other people.

8.81 Where an association provides meals and hotel accommodation to its members without charge, this is standard-rated. However, where the hospitality is provided directly in connection with the aims of a non-profit-making organisation, at the annual conference for example, and the subscription payment covers such expenses, then this income must be apportioned accordingly. In other words, the cost of the accommodation should be identified separately from the other benefits of membership of the organisation concerned. In such circumstances, the hospitality is not business entertainment and input tax incurred can therefore be deducted, subject to the normal rules. The business entertaining provisions do, however, apply to free hospitality to non-members and input tax cannot be deducted. See *Tolley's VAT 1998/99, para 9.5* for further details.

Sponsorship

8.82 The granting of sponsorship rights is another good way for clubs and associations to raise funds. Customs & Excise take the view that where there is a written or oral agreement or understanding that a sponsor will receive some form of benefit (e.g. advertising, free or reduced price ticket, hospitality, etc.) from the recipient, the club or association involved makes a supply for VAT purposes. As such, the sponsorship received will be taxable at the standard rate. VAT must be accounted for on money received from the sponsor and payments made by the sponsor to third parties in respect of expenses and prizes.

8.83 Where the sponsorship relates directly to a fund-raising event which qualifies for exemption under the provisions of *VATA 1994, 9 Sch, Group 12, Item 2*, the payment from the sponsor can also be treated as exempt.

Donations in general

8.84 The above exemption aside, sponsorship is often an area where some confusion arises as often a 'sponsor' will consider that he is merely making a donation. A donation is only outside the scope of VAT if it is given entirely voluntarily and on the basis that the donor will receive nothing in return for his donation other than perhaps a mere acknowledgement of his donation, in a club's programme or annual report for example. However, a taxable supply will not be created by the simple acknowledgement of support such as giving

8.85 *VAT Business by Business*

a flag or sticker or putting the donor's name on the back of a seat in a theatre (see also paragraph 8.146 below).

Bingo

8.85 Some clubs may hold bingo nights which can often prove to be a good way of raising funds. For VAT purposes, a distinction is drawn between prize and cash bingo, as follows.

8.86 Charges made for participation in games of prize bingo (often referred to as 'session charges', which are fees for a game of bingo levied in addition to, and usually separate from, either the stakes which are risked in the game or any admission charge) are exempt.

8.87 The session and participating charges for cash bingo are also exempt *unless* the game of cash bingo is promoted on premises which are licensed or registered under the *Gaming Act 1968, Part 2* or *Betting, Gaming & Lotteries & Amusements (Northern Ireland) Order 1985, Chapter III*. If so licensed or registered, session and participation charges are standard-rated. This will normally apply only to licensed bingo clubs in particular.

VAT recovery

General

8.88 If a club or association is registered for VAT in respect of its business activities, then it can usually reclaim as input tax any VAT which is charged to it, provided that it holds the necessary evidence. This is usually a valid tax invoice although other documents are also acceptable. See *Tolley's VAT 1998/99, para 57.7* for further details.

Non-deductible input tax

8.89 Whilst this will depend on the precise circumstances in which the input tax is incurred, there are certain items which are not recoverable in any circumstances and these include:

- purchase of motor cars which are not used solely for business purposes;

- business entertainment expenses; and

- an invoice showing VAT which is issued by a person who is neither registered nor required to be registered at that time.

Clubs and Associations **8.94**

Cars

8.90 In general terms, VAT incurred on the purchase of motor cars which are not used solely for business purposes cannot be reclaimed. Any element of private use, which includes home to office travel, precludes any VAT recovery at all. No pro-rating is available. If, however, a club or association leases a car, then 50% of the VAT incurred on the leasing charges can be reclaimed. Further details on the VAT issues relating to the ownership of motor cars and other vehicles can be found in *Tolley's VAT 1998/99*, *chapter 45*.

Business entertainment

8.91 The provision of hospitality for a charge to members and non-members is standard-rated. VAT incurred in providing such services can therefore be reclaimed as input tax.

8.92 VAT incurred in providing free refreshments cannot normally be reclaimed as input tax. However, a club may be able to reclaim the tax incurred in providing free refreshments to its own membership, staff and certain other people. In the case of *Celtic Football & Athletic Club Ltd v C&E Commrs, CS [1983] STC 470*, it was held that 'entertainment' should be construed as meaning hospitality free to the recipient. The Celtic club were obliged, under the rules of the competition in which they were participating, to meet certain expenses of the visiting teams. The hotel accommodation and other facilities enjoyed at Celtic's expense was not free to them, since they were required to meet Celtic's hotel expenses for the other match in the round. There was, therefore, no provision of 'business entertainment' within what is now *VAT (Input Tax) Order 1992 (SI 1992 No 3222), Article 5*.

8.93 All other input tax incurred is potentially recoverable, although for this to be the case, the input tax must relate to taxable business activities. There must be a clear connection between the expenditure in question and the business.

Non-business activities

8.94 Any VAT incurred for the purpose of non-business activities is not input tax and cannot be deducted. (Where non-business income is received, any VAT paid on purchases cannot be deducted.) For example, if a club or association has subscriptions which are wholly or partly outside the scope of VAT, then not all its activities are business activities for VAT purposes. If the subscriptions are wholly outside the scope of tax, the servicing of the membership is a non-business activity for VAT purposes. This includes the arrangement of the Annual General Meeting or preparation of the annual report. Any club or association, whether or not its provision of membership benefits is a business activity, may have non-business activities.

8.95 VAT Business by Business

8.95 As described at paragraph 8.8 above, non-business activities are those which are not predominantly concerned with the making of supplies for a consideration. They may include free admission to premises for non-members, spreading political beliefs or lobbying for a cause, or providing free literature to non-members.

8.96 If a club or association has both business and non-business activities, then the tax which it incurs must be apportioned.

8.97 The question of the type of apportionment to be made was tested in the case of *Whitechapel Art Gallery v C&E Commrs, QB [1986] STC 156*, in which the High Court upheld the tribunal decision that the Gallery could not reclaim all the input tax it incurred as a result of it receiving income which was not generated by its business activities. The tribunal found that in apportioning input tax incurred, the following procedure may be adopted: 'having reclaimed all the VAT charged on purchases which are entirely for business purposes and not reclaimed any VAT charged on purchases which are entirely for non-business purposes, an apportionment must be made. Normally Customs & Excise would insist on an income-based method of apportionment. For example, a business which receives £10,000 worth of business income out of a total of £50,000 worth of income would be able to reclaim one-fifth of the input tax it incurred in the year.'

8.98 The income-based method of apportionment was however criticised by the Tribunal chairman in the above case, on the grounds that grants and donations received should not be included in the calculation. Customs & Excise do not however consider themselves bound by this ruling in other cases and they made this clear in their News Release No 1148 issued on 28 October 1986.

8.99 Despite this, if the above procedure is not suitable, any formula can be used subject to prior agreement with the Customs & Excise local VAT office. Provided that the chosen method is 'fair and reasonable', this should not present too many problems. It should be noted that whilst there is no legal requirement to fulfil such criteria, this is the view of Customs & Excise and therefore, in practice, it will be extremely difficult to use a formula which Customs & Excise do not consider passes this test.

Partial exemption

8.100 Where a club or association makes supplies which are exempt from VAT, this may also affect the input tax reclaimable. The same principles as those set out above apply to any input tax incurred in relation to exempt income. In general terms, such input tax is not recoverable. It is necessary to carry out a calculation to determine the amount of input tax which can be recovered.

Clubs and Associations **8.107**

8.101 The basis of a partial exemption calculation includes direct attribution of input tax. This means that input tax which directly relates to taxable income should be identified and recovered in full. Input tax which has been incurred which relates exclusively to exempt income should be identified and is not recoverable, subject to the partial exemption de minimis limits.

8.102 It is then necessary to carry out some sort of apportionment and again this will often be based on the value of income received.

8.103 Other methods are available for use by clubs and associations provided that they can be demonstrated to give a 'fair and reasonable' result. In principle, there is no difference between a 'non-business' calculation and a partial exemption calculation.

8.104 There are de minimis limits below which input tax can be treated as fully recoverable. Having carried out an apportionment calculation, it is necessary to add the exempt element of the input tax incurred on overheads to exempt input tax which is directly attributable to exempt income. Provided that the result does not exceed more than £625 per month on average (£7,500 per year) and does not exceed more than one half (50%) of all input tax incurred, all such input tax in that period is treated as attributable to taxable supplies and is therefore recoverable in full (subject to the normal rules governing tax invoices, for details of which see *Tolley's VAT 1998/99, para 57.7*).

Accounting and records

General

8.105 There are no special points in relation to accounting and records which affect clubs and associations in particular. However, if a club or association is registered for VAT, then it must follow the general rules applying to all VAT-registered entities and maintain certain records. Specifically, Customs & Excise require that the following records are kept: business and accounting records, a VAT account, copies of all VAT invoices issued, and original VAT invoices received. A brief outline of the above items is set out below. Further details of records and accounts can be found in *Tolley's VAT 1998/99, chapter 57*.

8.106 Clubs and associations must also retain copies of all credit notes, debit notes and other documents which evidence an increase or decrease in payments received and copies of all such documents that are issued. Additionally, Customs & Excise stipulate that other records must be kept and these are considered below.

8.107 Business records include orders and delivery notes, relevant business correspondence, appointment and job books, purchase and sales

8.108 VAT Business by Business

books, cash books and other account books, records of daily takings such as till rolls, annual accounts, including trading and profit and loss accounts and bank statements and paying-in slips.

8.108 Where clubs and associations charge a subscription fee which is subject to VAT, it is recommended that VAT invoices are issued, particularly where the subscription amount exceeds £100, although this is only a requirement where the recipient is also VAT-registered. Copies of invoices issued should be retained for six years—see paragraph 8.111 below for further details.

8.109 All records must be kept up to date and in sufficient detail to allow a visiting Customs & Excise officer to reconcile them easily to the figures on the VAT returns declared by the club or association. Records should be readily available on request and ideally a club should keep such records at its club house, as this will almost certainly be its principal place of business.

8.110 If a club is not registered or required to be registered for VAT, on the grounds perhaps that its taxable turnover is below the current VAT registration limit of £50,000 per annum, then it is outside the scope of VAT and is not therefore required to keep any records for VAT purposes.

Preservation of records

8.111 Every VAT-registered club and association must keep and preserve the above records for six years unless Customs & Excise allow a lesser period. If this causes storage problems or involves undue expense, the club's local VAT office should be consulted. The local office may be able to advise whether some records can be retained for a shorter period.

8.112 Records can be preserved in their full and original form, or can also be retained on microfilm and microfiche or on computer, with Customs & Excise's prior consent.

Records of output tax

8.113 Records must be kept of all supplies made in the course of business, including subscription income demanded. Where full VAT invoices are issued and filed so as to be readily available, the record required by Customs & Excise is a summary enabling separate totals to be produced for each VAT accounting period of the amount of VAT chargeable, the VAT-exclusive value of standard-rated and zero-rated supplies and the value of any exempt supplies made. A club which has a bar and catering facilities will often sell direct to its members and less detailed VAT invoices, such as those produced by most modern tills, can be issued. Copies of all till rolls should be retained. See *Tolley's VAT 1998/99, para 57.5* for further details.

Record of input tax

8.114 Records must be kept of all taxable supplies received in the course of business, in such a way that the details of each transaction and evidence of the VAT charged are entered fully or can easily be found. Unless Customs & Excise allow otherwise, the following must be held to support a claim to input tax.

Suppliers' invoices

8.115 A full VAT invoice must be retained to support input tax recovery. See *Tolley's VAT 1998/99, para 57.7* for further details.

Documentary evidence

8.116 As with output tax and the invoices issued by a club, VAT invoices on which input tax is recovered must be retained for six years, or a shorter period if Customs & Excise will allow, in order to support recovery at an inspection of the records by a visiting VAT officer. See *Tolley's VAT 1998/99, para 57.3* for further details.

Annual accounting

8.117 There is a scheme available to smaller VAT-registered businesses under which the administrative burden is alleviated by submitting a VAT return once a year. See *Tolley's VAT 1998/99, paras 63.9-63.14* for details.

Practical points

Voluntary registration

8.118 Clubs and associations which receive business income but do not exceed the registration threshold of £50,000 per annum should consider whether registering for VAT on a voluntary basis would be beneficial. Provided that the club has the resources to be able to cope with the extra administrative burden which VAT registration undoubtedly brings, there may be particular advantages to registering voluntarily for VAT, the main one being input tax recovery. In certain circumstances, the recovery of input tax may be more important than the requirement to account for output tax on some or all of the income received by a club or association.

8.119 This will certainly be the case where:

- a club receives income which is zero-rated for VAT purposes, for example, part of its subscription income relates to the provision of a magazine, book or other publication;

8.120   *VAT Business by Business*

- part of its income is exempt from VAT and the input tax which it incurs is below the partial exemption de minimis limits (see paragraph 8.104 above for further details); and/or

- the club is about to undertake significant expenditure and will incur more input tax than the output tax liability on its income for a significant period.

8.120   Where a major capital project is undertaken, the construction of a new clubhouse is an obvious example, cash flow will clearly be an important issue. This can be improved by registering for VAT and submitting VAT returns on a monthly basis. Conversely, where cash flow is not a significant issue and, perhaps the extra administration burden of VAT registration is, then annual VAT returns can be submitted (see *Tolley's VAT 1998/99, para 63.9* for further details).

Payments to 'umbrella' organisations

8.121   Quite often payments will be made by clubs and associations to their governing bodies. Customs & Excise guidance in their public notice (C&E Leaflet 701/45/94) states at para 22 that:

'...where affiliation to a governing body is restricted to groups of individuals such as members' clubs, this will not preclude the governing body from exempting the supply of playing services to clubs, provided that the affiliation fee is calculated on a basis which can be related to an individual'.

8.122   However, Customs & Excise also consider that, where governing bodies provide services such as priority purchase rights for international matches or tournament admission tickets, these will continue to be standard-rated.

Netting-off and barter arrangements

8.123   It is quite common for clubs and associations to be involved in transactions where there is an element of 'netting-off' or barter. In the author's experience, clubs will often receive payments from other parties, national associations and governing bodies, where there is a reciprocal element involved in the payment.

8.124   Care must be taken with such transactions, as Customs & Excise will expect to see that VAT is accounted for on the full value of the supply or supplies being made.

8.125   An example of where netting-off could occur is where a club or association receives a service from one of its own members, for example when the member is himself registered for VAT and has done some repair work to the clubhouse which ordinarily is subject to VAT. Rather than pay for the service directly, it may be administratively convenient to subtract the value of the work done from the subscription payment which may shortly be due from the member.

8.126 As the member is registered for VAT in his own right, then such an arrangement has implications for both parties, if the club accounts for VAT on the full value of the subscription income received. It would not be correct for the club to account for VAT simply on the net amount, the balancing payment, received from the member. The club must ensure that it accounts for VAT on the full value of its supply to the member. In turn, the member should ensure that he too accounts for VAT on the full value of the supply made, even though he may not receive payment directly. Quite often in such circumstances, an exchange of tax invoices may be all that is required.

8.127 Another common occurrence is where a club may allow one of its regular suppliers to use its facilities at favourable rates. If such arrangements involve any element of netting-off or barter, then care must be taken to ensure that the VAT involved is accounted for correctly. There is an important distinction to be drawn between giving discounts and reciprocal, barter type, arrangements. The question which a club or association should ask itself is whether it is doing anything in return for something else.

8.128 It is also worth remembering that consideration for a supply need not necessarily be in money. Non-monetary consideration, for example the provision of a supplier's goods or services in return for the use of a club's facilities, must be valued when determining the amount of VAT which the club must account for. Non-monetary consideration is also often to be found in relation to sponsorship arrangements and again care must exercised when considering the VAT implications of such arrangements. In cases of doubt, it is recommended that professional advice is sought.

Sports exemption

8.129 Paragraph 8.35 above detailed the introduction of the exemption for certain types of supply under what is now *VATA 1994, 9 Sch, Group 10*. This was intended to implement *Article 13A1(m)* of the *EC Sixth Directive*, which the UK should have implemented by 1 January 1990. The exemption was not however introduced until 1 April 1994. Accordingly, under EC law, the requirement for such clubs to account for output tax was unlawful with effect from 1 January 1990.

8.130 This allowed sports clubs which had accounted for output tax on their membership subscriptions to submit repayment claims covering the period from 1 January 1990 to 31 March 1994, as invited by a Customs & Excise News Release dated 10 March 1994. Customs & Excise announced that they would make net repayment of the amount of wrongly-paid output tax reduced by the amount of input tax for which credit had been allowed.

8.131 *VAT Business by Business*

Clubs which have not made such a claim cannot now go back and submit a claim, due to the three-year limit which Customs & Excise have now imposed.

8.131 On a related matter, it is also not possible for clubs to submit claims for wrongly-paid output tax without reducing the amount of input tax for which credit had previously been allowed. The issues involved in making such a claim are complex, involving the question of the right of an individual to rely on the direct effect of European law, and were explored in the VAT tribunal case of *Sunningdale Golf Club (14899)*. It was held that the club 'would be unjustly enriched if repaid an amount which has already been credited to or received by them as input tax'.

Apportionment of subscription income

8.132 As has been seen at paragraph 8.38 above, it may not always be necessary for a club or association to account for VAT on the full amount of the subscription income received. Even when subscriptions are liable to VAT, where some of the membership benefits supplied are identifiable supplies of zero-rated or exempt goods and services, subscriptions may be apportioned so that the part which relates to such supplies is relieved from VAT. Joining fees as well as life membership fees can also be treated in this way, unless special additional benefits are received by such members which are not available to ordinary members.

8.133 It should be noted that subscriptions can only be apportioned because a club or association *makes* supplies to its members which are either zero-rated or exempt. Subscriptions cannot be apportioned on the basis of a club or association *receiving* such supplies from a third party. For example, a sports club cannot zero-rate part of its members' subscriptions just because this income is used to pay for zero-rated goods and services. It is only possible to apply an apportionment in respect of identifiable supplies of zero-rated or exempt goods and services which clubs make to their membership.

8.134 The most common example of an apportionment is for the provision of zero-rated magazines or books supplied to members.

8.135 There are no specific rules for making an apportionment. Some general guidance can be found at Appendix E of Customs & Excise Notice 700 (the 'VAT Guide'). See also *Tolley's VAT 1998/99, para 47.3* for further details. It is generally accepted that a club can apportion total subscription income to reflect the relative cost of providing the various supplies to its members. A club can base its calculations on its annual accounts. Two things are important in this respect. Firstly, Customs & Excise will expect the club to apply the method used consistently. It should also be able to demonstrate to Customs & Excise that the method is 'fair and reasonable'. To this end, copies of all working papers relating to any apportionment calculation should be retained so that they can be inspected by visiting VAT officers.

8.136 In the author's opinion, Customs & Excise are not particularly good at publicising the fact that other methods of apportionment are available. Such methods are indeed available and the use of these, provided that they meet the fair and reasonable criteria, may be more beneficial to clubs than using a costs-based apportionment.

Partial exemption

8.137 The chosen method for the apportionment of non-attributable (or 'overhead') input tax should be carefully examined to ensure that the most favourable method is being used. There are any number of alternatives to Customs & Excise's standard outputs method. Again, any method of apportionment is permitted provided that it meets the 'fair and reasonable' criteria. Some of the more common alternative methods include looking at the number of transactions and comparing the taxable 'count' to the total number of transactions entered into. Floor space is another common example, whereby the space used to make taxable supplies is compared to the total space occupied by a particular body. Another is 'head count', where the number of staff involved in the making of taxable supplies is compared to the total number of staff.

8.138 Further details of the operation of these special partial exemption methods can be found in *Tolley's VAT 1998/99, para 49.7*.

Business/non-business apportionment

8.139 The same principles apply to the apportionment of input tax in relation to non-business activities or income. A method of apportionment based on the relative values of income received can disadvantage a club or association and can even be distortive (where large grants or donations are received). It is therefore worth exploring alternative methods which, provided they are considered to be fair and reasonable, will give a better rate of recovery. Many clubs are now also receiving grants in the form of National Lottery funding for special projects. In the author's view, such amounts should not form part of the apportionment calculation, as to do so is akin to including bank loans and other forms of commercial funding, which are clearly not relevant to the apportionment of input tax.

General VAT planning

8.140 Whilst care must always be exercised in the area of VAT planning and more aggressive, albeit legal, VAT avoidance, it is quite within the rights of any club or association to organise its affairs in the most tax- and VAT-efficient manner available under the law.

8.141 To this end, rather than examine alternative methods of apportionment for both partial exemption and business/non-business calculations, clubs

8.142 VAT Business by Business

and associations may wish to consider how to gain maximum advantage from the use of the standard income (or 'outputs') based method. There are several ways in which the amount of taxable income received by a club or association can be increased, thereby increasing the rate of recovery of overhead input tax. Some of these are set out below. It is safe to say that, provided that a club or association remained within the limits of what is 'fair and reasonable', Customs & Excise would not consider such measures to be aggressive VAT avoidance, although Customs appear to be adopting a tougher line in this area.

Option to tax

8.142 Paragraphs 8.51 and 8.52 above make brief reference to the so-called 'block bookings exemption' which applies to the letting or hiring of a pitch or court, etc. provided that certain specified conditions are met.

8.143 Whilst in some ways treating this type of income as exempt is beneficial to clubs and associations, it may be advantageous to treat this income as taxable and improve input tax recovery as mentioned above. This would be particularly important to clubs which are about to incur significant amounts of expenditure.

8.144 To treat all the income received from the hire of pitches, etc. as taxable, a club or association can elect to waive exemption (or 'opt to tax') so that the above exemption will not apply and any income received will be taxable at the standard rate (*VATA 1994, 10 Sch 2(1)*). As stated above, the purpose of the option is to allow the recovery of input tax which would otherwise be lost under the partial exemption rules.

8.145 Clubs and associations should, however, bear in mind that opting could mean higher charges to those participating in the particular sport. Furthermore, once they have made the option for a particular site or property, they must charge VAT on all future supplies made in relation to that property which would otherwise be exempt. It is not possible, for example, to exercise the option in order to tax the hiring of courts, etc. but not tax a subsequent sale of the property or site. Further details on the option to tax can be found in *Tolley's VAT 1998/99, paras 42.20 to 42.25*.

Sponsorship income

8.146 Paragraph 8.78 above deals with the VAT liability of income received from sponsors and donors and the question of what constitutes taxable income as opposed to income which is outside the scope of VAT (i.e. donations). The crucial issue is whether a sponsor/donor receives benefits (e.g. advertising) in return for his support. Customs & Excise are prepared to accept that simple acknowledgements such as a 'thank you' in a programme, etc. can be ignored.

Clubs and Associations **8.151**

8.147 It may, however, be beneficial for the club to offer more in the way of an acknowledgement, for example to display the sponsor's logo and provide some advertising. In this way, the sponsorship received will be taxable at the standard rate. Whilst it would be necessary to charge VAT in addition to the amount received from a sponsor, provided that he can reclaim the VAT charged to him as input tax he should not be too resistant to being charged VAT. Sponsors will of course need to be issued with a VAT invoice in order to be able to recover the VAT charged. This again would be advantageous to the club or association involved as it would increase the amount of its taxable income and therefore improve input tax recovery as mentioned above.

Land and property transactions

8.148 Clubs and associations will often be faced with dealing with the VAT implications of land and property transactions, most commonly in connection with their occupation of their clubhouse, site or land. They may own the freehold or have been granted a lease by their landlord. The area of land and property is extremely complex and clubs and associations are advised to seek professional help in circumstances where property issues arise.

8.149 The recent VAT tribunal case of *Abbotsley Golf & Squash Club Ltd (15042)* has highlighted some of the problems which may arise. In this case, a club was granted what it considered to be a licence to occupy land. As the landlord had not opted to tax, the fee payable under the agreement was exempt from VAT. Customs & Excise, however, considered that the agreement constituted the grant of a licence on which VAT was due, applying their test that a licence to occupy only exists where exclusive use of the site or premises has been granted. Under the agreement, the club were not entitled to exclusive use. The tribunal allowed the club's appeal, holding on the particular facts that the licence qualified for exemption.

8.150 However, in their Business Brief 25/97, dated 7 November 1997, Customs & Excise stated that whilst, on the facts of the case, they were prepared to accept the decision, they disagreed with the tribunal's reasoning. Customs & Excise maintain that the correct test is based on exclusivity of use (although they have nevertheless announced that there will be a review of this whole area).

VAT planning arrangement

8.151 The difference for VAT purposes between a lease and a licence could be used to the advantage of some clubs. The introduction of the sports exemption in 1994 has led to various ideas being mooted for reducing the amount of irrecoverable VAT suffered by clubs. It is possible to use a variation of the type of supply made in the above case to mitigate irrecoverable VAT. Whilst such arrangements may be done for straightfor-

8.152 *VAT Business by Business*

ward 'commercial' reasons, there is no doubting that Customs & Excise would look closely to ensure that any such supplies were not entered into solely for the purposes of VAT avoidance.

8.152 In view of the current uncertainty of the position, any clubs examining this type of arrangement would be well advised to await the outcome of the review following the *Abbotsley* case or otherwise expect a strong legal challenge from Customs & Excise, particularly where the ultimate motive of the arrangement is tax avoidance, in the eyes of Customs & Excise at least.

8.153 Another practical rather than VAT-related issue with such arrangements is that, irrespective of the above decision, there may be some problems to address in terms of the members of a club not having exclusive use of their own premises.

Sports club—whether a 'non-profit-making body'

8.154 Another method which has been used to mitigate VAT costs associated with the sports exemption involves the establishment of a 'non-profit-making' members' club in a corporate structure which ultimately allows for some return on any investment made by the company or individual involved. Again, whilst such arrangements may be entered into for straightforward 'commercial' reasons, there is no doubting that Customs & Excise would look closely to ensure that any such changes were not manufactured solely for the purposes of VAT avoidance. The *Value Added Tax (Sport, Sports Competitions & Physical Education) Order 1998 (SI 1998 No 586)* was laid before the House of Commons on 17 March 1998 to introduce a definition of a 'non-profit-making body'. On 9 April, in response to representations about the drafting of the Order, the Financial Secretary announced that it would not be applied, since it would have caught a number of genuine non-profit-making clubs. Customs stated in their News Release 6/98 that they would consult interested parties before laying a replacement Order before Parliament.

8.155 Whilst the case itself was not directly concerned with a VAT avoidance arrangement, the issues involved in such structures were explored in the VAT tribunal case of *Chobham Golf Club (14867)*, discussed at paragraphs 8.19 and 8.20 above.

8.156 In this case, Customs & Excise issued a ruling that a limited company which operated a golf club was not within the definition of a 'non-profit-making body', so that its supplies did not qualify for exemption under *VATA 1994, 9 Sch, Group 10, Item 3*. The club appealed, contending that, although it had been founded as a proprietary club, the holding company which had originally owned it had sold it and it was now managed as a members' club. The tribunal reviewed the evidence in detail and allowed the appeal.

8.157 The facts that the club paid significant sums in rent to the company which owned its course, and paid management fees to a management company, did not necessarily take it outside the definition of a 'non-profit-making body', since 'income is not profit'. On the evidence, the tribunal was satisfied that any surplus which remained after paying the club's overheads (which included rent and management fees) would be 'used in the improvement of the club's facilities'. Accordingly, the club was within the definition of a 'non-profit-making body', and its supplies to its members qualified for exemption under *VATA 1994, 9 Sch, Group 10, Item 3*.

8.158 It is possible that clubs may therefore wish to explore such arrangements, although it should be noted that such arrangements are at the more aggressive end of the VAT avoidance spectrum. Clubs should monitor the position outlined in paragraph 8.154 above to ensure that they do not fall foul of the new provisions, whatever form they may take. Furthermore, as noted at paragraph 8.20 above, Customs have announced that they have appealed to the High Court against this decision. Nevertheless, such arrangements may still be within the legislation and it is quite within the rights of any club or association to organise their affairs in the most tax- and VAT-efficient manner available to them.

Chapter 9

Construction Industry

Introduction

9.1 Most businesses in the industry seem to look to do three things when VAT is concerned:

(a) Charge the right amount of VAT;

(b) Make sure that they claim back all they are entitled to; and

(c) Keep the cost of administration of the tax to the minimum.

However, achieving these ends is far from simple for the average contractor. Whilst 'if in doubt, charge VAT' may well be a route to avoiding problems with Customs & Excise, it may also limit the amount and value of contracts won, especially where the customer is unable to reclaim the VAT involved.

Overlay this with the industry's own particular accounting procedures, including the use of Authenticated Tax Receipts, self-billing, retentions and liquidated damages, and it is not surprising that errors in VAT accounting can result.

From a more positive point, the special tax point rules which apply to contracts in the construction industry can also be used not only by building contractors, but also by other contractors within the construction industry including plumbers, heating engineers, electricians, carpenters, kitchen fitters, landscapers, plant hirers (where the plant is provided with an operator), scaffolders and fencing contractors. The use of these rules not only provides some protection against poor payers but also provides the potential for improving cash flow. Hence this chapter has a wider relevance than solely for the average building contractor.

Liability

9.2 If one starts with the principle that everything the contractor does is standard-rated unless there is a specific exception, it is a reasonable premise.

9.3   *VAT Business by Business*

Zero-rating

9.3   In order to charge the right amount of tax, the contractor needs to know what can be zero-rated and, more importantly, what evidence Customs & Excise will wish to see to support the zero-rating.

Zero-rating is available for the following:

(a) construction services supplied in the course of construction of new dwellings, and the materials supplied with the zero-rated services;

(b) construction services supplied in the course of construction of new 'relevant residential' accommodation and the materials supplied with the zero-rated services;

(c) construction services supplied in the course of construction of new 'relevant charitable' accommodation and the materials supplied with the zero-rated services;

(d) the 'approved alteration' of a protected (most commonly thought of as 'listed') dwelling, relevant residential or relevant charitable building;

(e) certain home improvements, and alterations to buildings run by charities, to provide facilities for the disabled;

(f) construction services provided in the course of the conversion of commercial or industrial premises into residential accommodation where the customer is a Registered Housing Association; and

(g) certain specific civil engineering services.

In the course of construction

9.4   This is an important condition which must be fulfilled in order to obtain zero-rating. In brief, it means services supplied whilst the building is being constructed, but does not extend to services supplied after the building has been completed. For example, the installation of windows prior to occupation of the new dwelling would be zero-rated, but replacement windows or, say, a conservatory added after completion would be standard-rated.

However, where the contract provides for a retention payable, say, six months after completion of the construction services, the retention payment falls to be zero-rated provided that the original services also fall to be zero-rated (*Notice 708, paragraph 14.1*).

In the *University of Hull (180)* the tribunal held that 'a building remains in the course of construction until the main structure is completed, the windows glazed and all essential services and fittings, such as plumbing and electricity, have been installed therein. Thereafter the building ceases to be in the course of construction...and the phase of fitting out and furnishing is ready to begin.' This provides useful guidance as to when the 'course of construction' ceases, as does the case of *C&E Commrs v St Mary's Roman Catholic High School, QB [1996] STC 1091*. In this case, work began on a new secondary school in 1979, the school opened to some pupils in 1981, and the buildings were finally completed in 1983. However, the school playground was not completed until 1994. Customs & Excise ruled that the construction of the playground was standard-rated. The Court upheld Customs' ruling, holding that the work was standard-rated, as related services could only qualify for zero-rating if there was 'a temporal connection between the construction of the building and the provision of other services'. On the evidence, the interval between the completion of the building work on the school and the construction of the playground was far too long to establish the necessary temporal link. These cases indicate that a contractor should take care when considering whether to zero-rate construction services on a phased contract.

What is meant by 'New'?

9.5 The legislation assists by determining what is not a new building:

(a) the conversion, reconstruction or alteration of an existing building;

(b) any enlargement of, or extension to an existing building except to the extent that the enlargement or extension creates an additional dwelling or dwellings;

(c) the construction of an annexe to an existing building.

In the case of an annexe, there is an exception, being an annexe intended for use solely for a relevant charitable purpose and:

(a) capable of functioning independently from the existing building; and

(b) the only access or where there is more than one means of access, the main access to:

    (i) the annexe is not via the existing building; and

    (ii) the existing building is not via the annexe.

(*VATA 1994, 8 Sch, Group 5, Notes 16 and 17*).

The legislation also provides guidance on when a building ceases to be an 'existing building':

(a) where it is demolished completely to ground level; or

(b) the part remaining above ground level consists of no more than a single facade or where a corner site, a double facade, the retention of which is a condition or requirement of statutory planning consent or similar permission.

9.5 VAT Business by Business

[VATA 1994, 8 Sch, Group 5, Note 18].

Customs & Excise provide further guidance in Notice 708 with the following examples:

(a) the construction of a dwelling or qualifying building (being for relevant residential or relevant charitable purposes—see paragraphs 9.9 and 9.16 below) making use of the foundations of an existing building, where the whole of the former building has been demolished to ground level (for this purpose 'ground level' may include the 'slab' of the ground floor of the former building);

(b) the construction of a dwelling or qualifying building making use of the remains of a pre-existing building where, before construction starts, this is no more than the foundations and a single facade, or double facade on a corner site, but only where the facade has been retained to comply with statutory planning consent;

(c) the building on to an existing house of another house to form two semi-detached houses without internal access to the existing building, and where planning permission, etc. does not prevent its separate use, letting or disposal (note that most small additional living accommodation either built onto an existing house or constructed adjacent to an existing house—commonly known as 'granny annexes'—will fail the internal access or disposal test and their construction will therefore be standard-rated);

(d) the building of a new house within an existing terrace of houses on the site of a house that has been totally demolished ('infilling'), or totally demolished except for the front facade, where that facade has been retained because of the conditions of the planning consent; and

(e) the construction of a new, self-contained flat which enlarges an existing building.

Nevertheless, there have been many cases determining whether a building is 'new' and following the decision in *Marchday Holdings Ltd, CA 1996, [1997] STC 272*, Customs & Excise used Business Brief 20/97 to further clarify their position. The *Marchday* case dealt with the demolition of a light industrial building, leaving considerable portions of the concrete framework and floors of the existing building, and construction of modern office accommodation using those remaining attributes of the original building (something which would no longer give rise to zero-rating). However, the importance of this case is that the Court of Appeal decided that the original building had ceased to exist, based on the view that the remaining attributes could not as a matter of common sense be described as an existing building, and that the works carried out could not therefore be sensibly or realistically described as works to an existing building. Customs & Excise state that the case applies only to supplies made before clarification of the relevant legislation, as quoted above, which was effective from 1 March 1995.

Construction Industry **9.6**

In *Wimpey Group Services Ltd v C&E Commrs, CA [1988] STC 625*, the question of buildings being demolished and a new building constructed on the same site was considered. Customs & Excise considered that the supply was one of reconstruction, upon which zero-rating would not be appropriate. The Court of Appeal held that the work was not within the definition of 'reconstruction' because it was 'not a replication or construction anew of what was there before'.

In *Trident Housing Association Ltd (10642)* a company which owned a two-storey car park obtained planning permission to build 24 flats on top of the car park. Customs ruled that the work was standard-rated, but the Tribunal allowed the company's appeal, holding that it was 'totally inappropriate' to regard the block of flats as an enlargement of the car park. The works fell to be treated as being in the course of construction and zero-rated.

New dwellings

9.6   Construction services supplied in the course of construction of a new self-contained dwelling or dwellings (detached, semi-detached and terraced houses; bungalows and new blocks of flats) are zero-rated (*VATA 1994, 8 Sch, Group 5, Item 2(a)*).

In the case of dwellings, the legislation refers to a 'new dwelling or a number of dwellings' and also provides some 'tests' to help in the decision-making process (*VATA 1994, 8 Sch, Group 5, Note 2*). The tests are as follows:

(a)   the dwelling consists of self-contained living accommodation;

(b)   there is no provision for direct internal access from the dwelling to any other dwelling or part of a dwelling;

(c)   the separate use, letting or disposal of the dwelling is not prohibited by the terms of any covenant, statutory planning consent or similar provision; and

(d)   statutory planning consent has been granted in respect of that dwelling and its construction or conversion has been carried out in accordance with that consent.

(*VATA 1994, 8 Sch, Group 5, Note 3(2); VAT (Construction of Buildings) Order 1995 (SI 1995 No 280)*).

Zero-rating applies to *all* construction services provided in the course of construction of a new dwelling. Hence the services of bricklayers, plumbers, electrical contractors, plant operators (where labour is provided with the plant) and other trades traditionally connected with the construction of new dwellings can be zero-rated. This includes the services of sub-contractors.

Zero-rating does *not* extend to professional services, such as those of an architect, surveyor or any person acting as a consultant or in a supervisory

9.7 VAT Business by Business

capacity. Professional services remain standard-rated unless combined with a supply of construction services—a common example being a 'design and build' contract—when the professional services are treated as an indivisible part of the zero-rated supply of construction services (*C&E Notice 708, para 10.1*).

New dwellings—evidence required to support the zero-rating

9.7 A contractor is not required to obtain a certificate in order to zero-rate the supplies in the course of constructing a new dwelling. However, when Customs & Excise make their periodic inspection of a contractor's records, they will expect to find sufficient commercial evidence to support the zero-rating. This might include plans or instructions from, or correspondence with, architects and developers.

Relevant residential purposes

9.8 Construction services supplied in the course of construction of a building intended for use solely for a relevant residential purpose are zero-rated (*VATA 1994, 8 Sch, Group 5, Item 2(a)*). See also paragraphs 9.6 above for the services concerned *excluding those of sub-contractors*, and 9.20 below for materials.

What is a 'relevant residential purpose'?

9.9 Accommodation used for a 'relevant residential purpose' is used as one of the following:

(a) a children's home;

(b) a home providing residential accommodation with personal care for persons in need of personal care by reason of old age, disablement, past or present dependence on alcohol or drugs or past or present mental disorder;

(c) a hospice;

(d) residential accommodation for students or school children;

(e) residential accommodation for members of the armed forces;

(f) a monastery, nunnery or similar establishment;

(g) an institution which is the sole or main residence of at least 90 per cent of its residents.

(*VATA 1994, 8 Sch, Group 5, Note 4.*)

Hospitals, prisons, etc. and hotels, inns or similar establishments are not regarded as being used for relevant residential purposes.

Construction Industry 9.11

There have been few cases as to whether or not a building is used for a relevant residential purpose. In the case of *University of Bath (14235)*, buildings designed and used as student accommodation were also used for vacation lettings for non-educational purposes. As such, the Tribunal held that the buildings were not 'intended for use solely for a relevant residential or relevant charitable purpose'. However, in a more recent case, *Urdd Gobaith Cymru (14881)*, whilst Customs & Excise argued that the words 'solely for residential purposes' meant 'residence' or 'usual place of abode or dwelling', and therefore precluded short-term accommodation for students (the appellant runs courses in the Welsh language with students staying no longer than one week at a time), the Tribunal took the view that the adjective 'residential' did not imply permanence of occupation and allowed the appeal.

In the course of construction—relevant residential

9.10 The general rules for relevant residential buildings follow those set out in paragraph 9.4 above. However, this type of development will often contain features which will not be found within a housing development. In addition, it is not unusual for such a development to progress in 'phases'.

Where a number of buildings are constructed at the same time on the same site and are intended to be used together as a unit solely for a relevant residential purpose, each of those buildings is treated as intended for use solely for a relevant residential purpose and construction will not be completed until the development is completed (*VATA 1994, 8 Sch, Group 5, Note 5*).

In practice, this will, for example, allow zero-rating for construction services in respect of a laundry block within a new residential development for the elderly, provided that it is built at the same time as the rest of the development. Customs & Excise will allow exceptions in circumstances where the construction is made in accordance with the original planning permission, but the works are phased over a limited period. [*VAT Information Sheet 10/95, 11 April 1995*].

Relevant residential—evidence required to support the zero-rating

9.11 Any supply of construction services relating to a building or part of it to be used solely for a relevant residential purpose may be zero-rated only if the supply of the services is made to the person who intends to use the building or part for the relevant purpose and, before it is made, this person gives the supplier a certificate in the form specified by Customs & Excise and to be found in Appendix A to Customs & Excise Notice 708. (*VATA 1994, 8 Sch, Group 5, Note 12*).

This can lead to a trap for contractors working for developers. In these circumstances, if the developer is selling the developed building to a nursing

9.12 VAT Business by Business

home, for example, zero-rating will not extend to the services of the contractor.

Incorrect certificates

9.12 It is the responsibility of the person who issues a certificate to make sure it is correct. If the certificate is incorrect, the person giving it is liable to a penalty under *VATA 1994, s 62(1)* equal to the amount of VAT which would have otherwise been charged (*VATA 1994, s 62(2)*).

If the giver of the certificate can satisfy Customs & Excise, or the VAT and Duties Tribunal on appeal, that there is a reasonable excuse for his having given an incorrect certificate, the liability to the penalty will be removed (*VATA 1994, s 62(3)*).

Whilst Customs & Excise expect the contractor to take every reasonable step to ensure that the supply is properly zero-rated, if the customer provides an incorrect or false certificate, Customs & Excise have stated that they will not seek to recover the VAT due from the contractor. (*C&E Notice 708, paras 3.1, 3.3; C&E Notice 48, ESC 2.11*).

Mixed use buildings

9.13 Where a contractor's services are partly in respect of a building intended to be used for a relevant residential purpose and partly for another purpose, the contractor is required to apportion the charge between the element which falls to be zero-rated and the element which falls to be standard-rated (*VATA 1994, 8 Sch, Group 5, Note 11*).

There is no prescribed method of apportioning the elements, although the certificate required from the customer (see paragraph 9.11 above) should clearly show which part of the building qualifies for relief (*VAT Notice 708, paragraph 8.9*). Hence, for example, the contractor could apportion using:

(a) cost information provided, for example, by a quantity surveyor; or

(b) the relative space of the standard-rated and zero-rated areas of the building; or

(c) another basis.

As previously stated, Customs & Excise's view is that there is no prescribed method. The attitude of Customs & Excise is that they will seek a fair and reasonable apportionment. However, there is no legislation which dictates this policy. If the parties to the contract are not connected (under *section 839 of ICTA 1988*), it would seem that the contractor can make his own commercial judgment as to the amount to be charged for each element.

However, it is clear, for example, that a contractor on a £10,000 mixed works job, choosing to charge £1 for standard-rated services and £9,999 for zero-rated services, would face very close scrutiny from Customs & Excise, including potentially a request to justify the apportionment. Customs' own internal guidance indicates that, where each 'supply' has its own consideration, then there is no scope for apportionment. It is only in cases where there is a single consideration which requires apportionment that Customs & Excise will seek to ensure that the apportionment is fair and reasonable (*Customs & Excise Manuals Part 12, Chapter 2, paragraph 3.4*). However, in *Centurions (9015)*, the issue of attributing charges (in this case, warranties sold with second-hand cars) was considered and the tribunal found that the arrangements were a 'sham', allowing Customs & Excise to assess tax due based on apportionment of the profits in the same ratio as the cost of the two supplies. Customs also place reliance on the decision of the High Court in *Tynewydd Labour Working Men's Club and Institute Ltd, QB [1979] STC 570*. Whilst this case dealt with admission charges to a club where the charge was for both exempt admission charges to bingo sessions and taxable entertainment and/or admission, the court decided that where there was more than one supply, any profit element in the charge had to be allocated to all of the supplies involved. However, in the cases of *HB and DD Geddes (3378)*, which was a further case dealing with warranties and second-hand cars, and *Thorn EMI Plc, [1993] VATTR 94 (9782)*, which dealt with the hire of televisions and an insurance policy for repairs, the tribunal found in favour of the taxpayers' own commercial agreements with their customers.

For further comment on apportionment, and examples, see paragraph 47.3 of *Tolley's VAT 1998/99*.

Sub-contractors

9.14 As stated at paragraph 9.8 above, sub-contractors can only zero-rate their services in connection with the construction of new dwellings. They cannot zero-rate their services in connection with the construction of new relevant residential buildings.

Relevant charitable building

9.15 Construction services supplied in the course of construction (see paragraph 9.6 above) of a building intended to be used solely for a relevant charitable purpose are zero-rated. See paragraph 9.6 for the type of services covered. However, it is very important to note that, in common with services supplied in the course of construction of a relevant residential building, zero-rating does not extend to the services of sub-contractors (see paragraph 9.14 above). (*VATA 1994, 8 Sch, Group 5, Item 2(a)*).

9.16 VAT Business by Business

What is 'a building intended for use solely for a relevant charitable purpose'?

9.16 A building intended for use solely for a relevant charitable purpose means a building:

(a) to be used by a charity other than in the course or furtherance of a business; or

(b) to be used as a village hall or similarly in providing social or recreational facilities for a local community.

A building to be used by a charity as, for example, a church would qualify under this relief.

In *St Dunstan's Educational Foundation (14901)* the appellant was a registered charity which owned various properties in the London area. The object of the charity was the provision of school facilities and it provided its land and buildings free of charge to another charity, a college, in pursuance of this objective. In 1995, the appellant commenced building a new sports hall on its property, for use by the college. The college would have free use of the hall and hire it out at certain times to outsiders for a charge. The appellant sought zero-rating of the construction work. Customs refused permission for zero-rating on the grounds that the use of the hall was to be by the college, which was in business, rather than by the appellant, which was not. The appellant contended, however, that the provision of the hall to the college was itself use of the building for non-business purposes. The appellant also argued that the building was to be used by the college, a charity, similarly to a village hall. The Tribunal agreed with Customs that 'use' means functional use and that the functional use was business. However, the Tribunal followed *Jubilee Hall Recreation Centre Ltd, QB [1997] STC 414* in giving the concept of a village hall a wide meaning. The sports hall, whilst not a village hall, was used similarly to a village hall and zero-rating was, therefore appropriate.

However, in *Leighton Park School (9392)*, zero-rating was refused to a charitable company limited by guarantee in respect of construction services relating to a new classroom block, the tribunal agreeing with Customs & Excise that the classroom was intended for use in the course of providing education for a consideration.

Zero-rating only applies where the building is new, effectively restricting zero-rating to first construction. However, a new self-contained annexe to be used for a relevant charitable purpose is also treated as a new building provided:

(a) it is capable of functioning independently from the existing building; and

(b) the only access or, where there is more than one means of access, the main access to:

(i) the annexe is not via the existing building; and

(ii) the existing building is not via the annexe.

(*VATA 1994, 8 Sch, Group 5, Notes 16 and 17*).

Business use

9.17   See paragraph 7.41 of Chapter 7 for the meaning of 'business use' in relation to a charity. See also paragraph 7.51 of Chapter 7 in respect of minor or incidental business use.

Relevant charitable purpose—evidence required to support zero-rating

9.18   Any supply of construction services, relating to a building or part of it to be used solely for a relevant charitable purpose, may be zero-rated only if the supply of the services is made to the person who intends to use the building or part for the relevant purpose and, before it is made, this person gives the supplier a certificate in the form specified by Customs & Excise and to be found in Appendix A to C&E Notice 708. (*VATA 1994, 8 Sch, Group 5, Note 12*).

See also paragraph 9.14 above in respect of contractors working for developers and paragraph 9.12 above in respect of incorrect certificates.

Mixed use

9.19   Where the contractor's services are partly in respect of a building intended to be used for a relevant charitable purpose and partly for another purpose, the contractor is required to apportion the charge between the element which falls to be zero-rated and the element which falls to be standard-rated. Further details can be found at paragraph 9.13 above.

Building materials

9.20   Zero-rating extends to the building materials used by the contractor in the course of supplying the zero-rated services (*VATA 1994, 8 Sch, Group 5, Item 4*). Hence, bricks supplied by the contractor would also become zero-rated, but only when supplied with the construction services. The supply only of building materials still falls to be standard-rated.

'Building materials', in relation to any description of building, means goods of a description ordinarily incorporated by builders in a building of that description, or its site, but does *not* include:

(a)   finished or prefabricated furniture, other than furniture designed to be fitted in kitchens;

9.20 VAT Business by Business

(b) materials for the construction of fitted furniture, other than kitchen furniture;

(c) electrical or gas appliances, *unless* the appliance is an appliance which is:

designed to heat space or water (or both) or to provide ventilation, air cooling, air purification, or dust extraction; or

intended for use in a building designed as a number of dwellings and is a door entry system, a waste disposal unit or a machine for compacting waste; or

a burglar alarm, a fire alarm, or fire safety equipment or designed solely for the purpose of enabling aid to be summoned in an emergency; or

a lift or hoist;

(d) carpets or carpeting material.

(*VATA 1994, 8 Sch, Group 5, Note 22*).

In all cases, it is important to note that where building materials are excluded from zero-rating, the service of fitting the materials still remains zero-rated. Hence contractors may wish to separate their charge for construction services, so that zero-rating can be applied to that element. Customs & Excise have stated that they will accept a fair and reasonable apportionment (C&E Business Brief 12/97). In *Rayner & Keeler Ltd v C&E Commrs, QB [1994] STC 724*, a case dealing with claims for input tax incurred before the effective date of registration, the High Court considered whether the services of fitting out shops were multiple supplies or single supplies. It was decided that the construction services were multiple supplies, which provides comfort for the separation of the goods and service elements as described in this paragraph. However, it is not clear what Customs & Excise mean by a 'fair and reasonable apportionment'. Whilst there are legal provisions for the valuation of supplies made between connected parties (*VATA 1994, 6 Sch 1*), where the contractor and the employer are not connected persons (in accordance with *section 839* of the *Income and Corporation Taxes Act 1988*), there does not appear to be any legislative provision to support the views of Customs & Excise. It would seem, however, that the amount to be charged for the respective elements is more a matter of commercial judgment within the contractual arrangements between the contract and the employer. Nevertheless, it seems likely that a contractor taking such a view may well be challenged by Customs & Excise should the valuations appear to be less than fair and reasonable. See further comment on apportionment in paragraph 9.11 above, and in paragraph 47.3 of *Tolley's VAT 1998/99*.

There have been a number of cases dealing with 'fitted furniture' and, specifically, whether the furniture supplied in the course of zero-rated construction services can itself fall to be treated as zero-rated (see *C&E Commrs v McLean Homes Midland Ltd, QB [1993] STC 335* and *Edmond*

Homes Ltd (11567)). The result is that the position is reasonably complex and, potentially, could lead to either overstatement or understatement of VAT on work performed by contractors. In their Business Brief 12/97, Customs & Excise have restated their policy following the tribunal decision in *SH Wade (13164)*, which provided further comment on when a supply of fitted furniture takes place. Hence:

(a) Free-standing items of furniture are to be standard-rated on the basis that they are not items incorporated into buildings. Customs include beds, chairs, bookcases, sideboards, dining tables, cupboards (with the exception of those listed below), dressing tables, bedside cabinets, chests of drawers, and linen chests;

(b) items which are not 'furniture' can be zero-rated when supplied with zero-rated construction services. Customs include:

   (i) cupboards such as airing or under-stair storage cupboards or other similar basic storage facilities which are formed by becoming part of the fabric of the building;

   (ii) baths, WCs, wash hand basins, etc.;

   (iii) items which provide storage capacity as an incidental result of their primary function, such as shelves formed as a result of constructing simple box work over pipes;

(c) in the case of bedroom wardrobes, Customs accept 'simple bedroom wardrobes' installed on their own as not being furniture and, therefore, falling to be zero-rated. To help determine what is a simple bedroom wardrobe, Customs suggest:

'It would enclose a space bordered by the walls, ceiling and floor. Units whose design includes, for example, an element to bridge over a bed or create a dressing table, are regarded as furniture. The side and back would be formed by using three walls of the room or two walls and a stub wall. For these purposes, the wardrobe could be fitted across the whole of the end of a room. The installation of a cupboard in the corner of a room where one side is a closing end panel is regarded as furniture. On opening the wardrobe you should see the walls of the building. These would normally be either bare or painted plaster. Wardrobes which contain internal panelling, typically as part of a modular or carcass system, are regarded as furniture. The wardrobe should feature no more than a single shelf running the full length of the wardrobe, a rail for hanging clothes and a closing door or doors. Wardrobes with internal divisions, drawers, shoe racks or other features are regarded as furniture.' (C&E Business Brief 12/97).

(d) in the case of vanity units, where wash hand basins installed in bathrooms and cloakrooms are supported by basin units rather than pedestals, the basin unit is not regarded as furniture. Customs indicate

9.21 *VAT Business by Business*

that the unit will typically be a box-like structure entirely below the line of the top of the basin and contain a shelf and a covering door or doors—the only storage space being directly beneath the basin itself. More elaborate vanity units, typically with other storage space constructed on either or both sides of the basin are treated by Customs as furniture and, therefore, standard-rated; and

(e) bathroom cabinets are treated as furniture and standard-rated.

Approved alterations

9.21 The supply of services in the course of an approved alteration of a protected building, which is used as a dwelling or number of dwellings or is intended for a relevant residential or relevant charitable purpose, is zero-rated (*VATA 1994, 8 Sch, Group 6, Item 2*).

Zero-rating extends to materials incorporated into the building.

The services of an architect, surveyor or any person acting as consultant or in a supervisory capacity is excluded from zero-rating.

What is a 'protected building'?

9.22 A 'protected building' is a building which is designed to remain as or become a dwelling or a number of dwellings, or is intended for use solely for a relevant residential or relevant charitable purpose after the reconstruction or alteration and which, in either case, is:

(a) a listed building, within the meaning of:

   (i) the *Planning (Listed Buildings and Conservation Areas) Act 1990*; or

   (ii) the *Planning (Scotland) (Listed Buildings and Conservation Areas) Act 1997*; or

   (iii) the *Planning (Northern Ireland) Order 1991*; or

(b) a scheduled monument, within the meaning of:

   (i) the *Ancient Monuments and Archaeological Areas Act 1979*; or

   (ii) the *Historic Monuments Act (Northern Ireland) 1971*.

(*VATA 1994, 8 Sch, Group 6, Note 1*).

What is an 'approved alteration'?

9.23 'Approved alteration' means works, other than any works of repair or maintenance, or any incidental alteration to the fabric of the building which results from the carrying out of repairs, or maintenance work:

(a) in the case of a protected building which is an ecclesiastical building to which *section 60* of the *Planning (Listed Buildings and Conservation Areas) Act 1990* applies, any works of alteration; and

(b) in the case of a protected building which is a scheduled monument within the meaning of the *Historic Monuments Act (Northern Ireland) 1971* and in respect of which a protection order, within the meaning of that Act, is in force, works of alteration for which consent has been given under *section 10* of that Act; and

(c) in any other case, works of alteration which may not, or but for the existence of a Crown interest or Duchy interest could not, be carried out unless authorised under, or under any provision of:

   (i) *Part I* of the *Planning (Listed Buildings and Conservation Areas) Act 1990*;

   (ii) *Part IV* of the *Planning (Scotland) (Listed Buildings and Conservation Areas) Act 1997*;

   (iii) *Part V* of the *Planning (Northern Ireland) Order 1991*;

   (iv) *Part I* of the *Ancient Monuments and Archaeological Areas Act 1979*, and for which, except in the case of a Crown interest or Duchy interest, consent has been obtained under any provisions of that Part.

[*VATA 1994, 8 Sch, Group 6*].

Hence, for the contractor to be able to zero-rate the supply of his services, the work has to be:

(a) an 'approved alteration' within the terms of the relevant legislation; and

(b) treated as an alteration for VAT purposes.

This is easier said than done, and in many instances there is little choice but to gain the advance agreement of the local VAT office as to which works are to be treated as alterations and which as repair or maintenance. However, if Customs & Excise do not agree, and the employer is not willing to undertake the contract with VAT added, the contractor would then need to consider making an appeal to the independent VAT and Duties Tribunal.

9.24 VAT Business by Business

Alteration for VAT purposes

9.24 As a rule of thumb, if the works 'improve' the building, they will be zero-rated. For example, if a window is replaced and at the same time the size of the aperture is changed, it will be treated as an alteration, whereas replacing a window frame with one of identical design would be treated as a repair.

The application of the legislation relies on determining whether or not works are alterations. In this respect the leading case is *Customs & Excise Commissioners v Viva Gas Appliances, HL [1983] STC 819; [1983] 1 WLR 1445*. This case dealt with the supply and installation of gas fires to existing houses. The work necessitated the breaking out of a fireclay firebrick, the fixing of the fires in front of the opening created and, in some cases, running the gas supply from the meter to the newly installed fire. The work was considered sufficient to be treated as an alteration and fulfil the zero-rating criteria for alterations then in force.

In *CN Evans (4415)* the owner of a protected building obtained consent for replacement of the roof, which was in slate. Customs & Excise took the view that the work was repair and maintenance, and therefore standard-rated. The tribunal allowed the owner's appeal, holding that the works were 'works of alteration', rather than 'repair and maintenance' and therefore qualified for zero-rating. However, in *Meanwell Construction Co Ltd (10726)*, a construction company obtained listed building consent to replace the roof of a protected building, and did not account for VAT on the work. Customs & Excise assessed for the VAT and the company appealed, contending that the work was an 'approved alteration'. In this case the tribunal held that the work constituted repair and maintenance and dismissed the appeal.

In *Dodson Bros. (Thatchers) Ltd, [1995] VATTR 514 (13734)* the company rethatched the roofs of two listed buildings. Customs & Excise issued an assessment charging tax, but the appellant satisfied the tribunal that the works were approved alterations in that reeds were used, rather than straw, which gave the roof a different appearance, and also satisfied the tribunal that neither of the roofs had been in need of repair, so that the work went beyond 'repair and maintenance'.

There have been several other cases where the taxpayer has successfully claimed that works should be treated as approved alterations, further details of which can be found in *Tolley's VAT Cases 1998*, involving:

(a) replacement of guttering in order to improve drainage of a church roof (*All Saints Church (Tilsworth) Parochial Church Council, [1993] VATTR 315 (10490)*);

(b) insertion of additional floor timbers (*Davenport Brickwork Ltd (10692)*);

(c) alterations to an outbuilding to form a gamesroom, where this was treated as part of the owner's private residence (*N Forman Hardy, [1994] VATTR 302 (12776)*); and

(d) the construction of an indoor swimming pool connected to an existing listed building (a farmhouse) by a covered walkway (*C&E Commrs v M Arbib, QB [1995] STC 490*).

Additional cases involving partial success for the taxpayer included:

(e) within a roof replacement, changing the height of the ridges and the pitches of the roof slopes, along with increasing the height of roof valleys (*CN Foley (13496)*);

(f) reroofing that portion of a roof which was not in need of repair and maintenance (*NF Rhodes (14533)*);

(g) installation of new lighting in church (excluding the repair and maintenance element) (*Holy Trinity Church (Heath Town Wolverhampton) Parochial Church Council (13652)*);

(h) installation of a new drainage system on a 21 acre estate, where the works went far beyond mere repair or maintenance (*Walshingham College (Yorkshire Properties) Ltd, [1995] VATDR 141 (13223)*);

(i) erection of railings on a churchyard wall around a churchyard (*RG Powell (t/a Anwick Agricultural Engineers) (14520)*); and

(j) construction of a greenhouse utilising two walls of the protected building (*CW Mann (14004)*).

What services are covered?

9.25   See paragraph 9.6 above for the scope of the services qualifying for zero-rating and paragraph 9.20 above in respect of materials supplied with zero-rated construction services.

Approved alterations—evidence required to support zero-rating

9.26   In the case of construction services supplied in connection with relevant residential or relevant charitable buildings, certificates are required from the employer (see paragraph 9.11 above). Certificates are not required in respect of works carried out on dwellings or groups of dwellings.

However, the contractor would be wise to obtain and safely retain evidence, which Customs & Excise may ask to see, such as:

(a) confirmation that the building is protected;

9.27 VAT Business by Business

(b) a copy of the listed building consent, or equivalent—it is important to note that for the works to be zero-rated, Customs & Excise expects that the consent will not only be required but also obtained;

(c) copies of plans;

(d) any relevant correspondence; and

(e) where an apportionment has been made, details of the method used.

Mixed use

9.27 Where part of the services fall to be zero-rated and part fall to be treated as standard-rated, the contractor may make an apportionment to determine the extent to which zero-rating can be applied. See also paragraph 9.13 above.

Conversions of a non-residential building

9.28 Zero-rating is applied to the supply of construction services to a registered housing association in the course of conversion of a non-residential building or a non-residential part of a building into:

(a) a building or part of a building designed as a dwelling or number of dwellings; or

(b) a building or part of a building intended for use solely for a relevant residential purpose.

(*VATA 1994, 8 Sch, Group 5, Item 3*).

Zero-rating applies to all construction services provided by a main contractor in the course of conversion of a non-residential building. The services of sub-contractors are zero-rated only in the case of conversions to dwellings.

Zero-rating also extends to the materials used by the contractor. The supply only of building materials still falls to be standard-rated.

Zero-rating does not extend to:

(a) professional services, such as those of an architect, surveyor or any person acting as a consultant or in a supervisory capacity. Professional services remain standard-rated unless combined with a supply of construction services—a common example being a 'design and build' contract—when the professional services are treated as an indivisible part of the zero-rated supply of construction services.

(b) certain builders' fixtures.

Where there is a mixture of zero-rated and standard-rated services, the contractor is required to apportion the supplies, although no method of apportionment is specified.

(*VATA 1994, 8 Sch, Group 5, Note 11*).

What is a 'registered housing association'?

9.29 A 'registered housing association' means a registered housing association within the meaning of the *Housing Association Act 1985* or *Part II* of the *Housing (Northern Ireland) Order 1992*.

What is a 'non-residential' building?

9.30 'Non-residential' in relation to a building or part of a building means:

(a) neither designed nor adapted for use as a dwelling or number of dwellings nor for a relevant residential purpose; or

(b) if so designed or adapted, was constructed before, and has not been used as a dwelling or number of dwellings or for a relevant residential purpose, since 1 April 1973.

(*VATA 1994, 8 Sch, Group 5, Notes 7 to 9*).

Conversions—evidence required to support the zero-rating

9.31 The contractor is not required to obtain a certificate in order to zero-rate the supplies in relation to conversions of non-residential buildings into dwellings. For relevant residential buildings, the contractor is required to hold a certificate (see paragraph 9.11 above).

Civil engineering services

9.32 Zero-rating applies to the following civil engineering services:

(a) supplies in the course of constructing any civil engineering work necessary for the development of a permanent caravan park (*VATA 1994, 8 Sch, Group 5, Item 2(b)*); and

(b) any supplies in the course of construction of a dwelling or a number of dwellings or a relevant residential building or a relevant charitable building.

Civil engineering services supplied in connection with (b) above qualify for zero-rating provided that they are carried out contemporaneously or consecutively in relation to the new building and have a substantial

9.33 VAT Business by Business

connection with it. Zero-rating applies to the edge of the development although, in a case where a mains connection point lies outside the perimeter of the development, zero-rating can be extended to the work required to make connection with the nearest existing supply. (*C&E Notice 708, para 11.7*).

Records

9.33 The record-keeping requirements for a contractor are the same as those for any other VAT-registered business. However, there are also accounting arrangements, in addition to the requirements for certificates set out in preceding paragraphs, which are particular to the construction industry and these contain specific requirements. These issues are dealt with in the following paragraphs.

Input tax recovery

9.34 As previously stated, provided that a taxable supply is made, there is an entitlement to deduct input tax on related expenditure, with specific exceptions such as business entertaining expenses and the VAT on the purchase of a new car (see *Tolley's VAT 1998/9, chapter 35*).

For all contractors, there is a right to deduct tax because all of their supplies are taxable. The issue, therefore, is when the tax can be deducted and against what documentation.

Posting of purchase invoices

9.35 Most contractors will seek to account for VAT on purchases by entering them into their records when the invoice is received. Some contractors, however, in an attempt to simplify their bookkeeping, will only enter their purchase invoices when they are paid. For these contractors, maximising their VAT cash flow is a case of working their way through their unpaid invoices file and claiming the VAT shown on those invoices. However, they also need to remember to reverse the claim when they calculate VAT recoverable on their next VAT return.

Cash accounting scheme

9.36 It is possible that smaller contractors may choose to use the Cash Accounting Scheme. Under this scheme, tax on invoices issued is only accounted for when the customer pays, but tax on invoices received can only be recovered when the supplier is paid. However, the scheme may not be attractive for many contractors, especially when they are using applications for payment or similar arrangements (see paragraph 9.38 below). Where it might be attractive is for the smaller jobbing builder working for the public or, more likely, small companies, who will only pay against a full tax invoice, and take a very long time to pay. These contractors also tend to be in a position where they have to pay their suppliers on a cash on delivery basis. Please see also Chapter 24—Small Businesses, paragraphs 24.8 to 24.15).

Tax points

9.37 This aspect of the administration of the tax can create problems as well as providing opportunities to manage VAT cash flow.

Special tax point rules apply for supplies of construction services. The tax point is the date which determines upon which VAT return output tax is accountable, and input tax can be claimed (with the exception of those using the cash accounting scheme, for which see paragraph 9.36 above). If the contract provides for stage payments, and this can include the situation where the contract solely provides for a retention, the tax point occurs at the earlier of the date of issue of the tax invoice or receipt of payment. However, with effect from 1 January 1998, a further tax point was introduced whereby VAT becomes due eighteen months after the services have been performed. There is no definition of 'performed' in this respect. However, in the context of other supplies of services, 'performed' is generally taken to mean the date when all work except invoicing has taken place.

(Value Added Tax Regulations 1995 (SI 1995 No 2518), reg 93).

There are also special tax point rules for retentions. Where the contract calls for a retention, the tax is due when the invoice is issued, if the retained amount is not excluded from the sum shown as due, or at the earlier of receipt of payment or the issue of an invoice for the retention or, failing that, with effect from 1 January 1998, within eighteen months of the work being performed. Accordingly, it is wise for the contractor to ensure that a tax invoice is not issued for the retention initially, and not before the retention is released by the customer. For practical purposes, however, many contractors will find that their customer will only release the retention against the issue of a tax invoice or equivalent document.

(Value Added Tax Regulations 1995 (SI 1995 No 2518), reg 89).

One thing is apparent from the VAT tax point rules for contractors—there is no great need of either the cash accounting scheme or VAT bad debt relief if the rules are applied judiciously.

Applications for payment

9.38 It is common practice in the industry for contractors to seek payment against an application for payment or similar device. The developer or main contractor will then confirm what works are to be paid for, commonly against an architect's certificate. At that stage contractors can consider the use of self-billing (9.39 below), authenticated tax receipts (9.40 below) or tax invoices (9.41 below).

9.39 VAT Business by Business

Problems can arise where sub-contractors claim payment against applications for payment. Contractors have been known to make VAT claims too early against unpaid applications, giving rise to assessments from Customs & Excise when their records are inspected. The contractor is allowed to claim VAT against the payment to the sub-contractor, at the time the payment is received by the sub-contractor, but will also be required to satisfy Customs & Excise that his VAT return was correct by obtaining and keeping the invoice or authenticated receipt subsequently issued by the sub-contractor.

This has given rise to disputes between contractors and Customs & Excise in cases where cheques in payment have been issued at the end of the contractor's VAT period, but the cheque has not been received and/or banked by the sub-contractor until a number of days later. Contractors may consider it to be wise to consider whether the procedures for the timing of the issue of invoices and the banking of cheques in settlement should be clearly set out within the agreement between the parties.

Self-billing

9.39 The customer will raise the contractor's invoice and forward a copy of the invoice to the contractor. The self-billed invoice will be treated as the VAT invoice required to be provided by the supplier (*Value Added Tax Regulations 1995 (SI 1995 No 2518), reg 13(3)*). Use of the system is subject to the express approval of Customs & Excise. The contractor and customer must also both agree to the process. The procedure is potentially onerous for the customer—it is possible for Customs & Excise to collect VAT understated on the self-billed invoice from the customer. The self-billed invoice must be the only document purporting to be a tax invoice to be issued between the parties. Failure to comply with this condition can lead to a VAT assessment and penalties. Worse though, certainly for the customer, is the risk that approval to use self-billing will be withdrawn. Companies using self-billing do so for a variety of reasons, but in the main, those reasons lead to a reduction of costs for the recipient of the supply. There is no requirement in VAT law for the customer to pay the contractor on the same day that the self-billed document is issued, which differs from the position with authenticated tax receipts. However, it is not uncommon for Customs & Excise to require the agreement of the parties to such a condition when approval for self-billing is sought.

Authenticated tax receipts

9.40 Under this procedure, the customer will prepare the receipt which is issued with payment. Upon receipt of the payment, the contractor will authenticate the receipt and return it to the customer to use as evidence for reclaiming the VAT shown thereon. The authenticated receipt must bear all of the details which are contained on a 'normal' tax invoice (*Value Added Tax Regulations 1995 (SI 1995 No 2518), reg 13(4)*). Both the contractor and the customer must agree to use the system, although no prior approval is required from Customs & Excise. However, Customs & Excise encourage customers to report suppliers who fail to provide authenticated receipts and have powers to impose penalties on the contractor. It is also a requirement that, where authenticated receipts are used, no other tax invoice or self-billed invoice is issued. It is not uncommon for contractors to overlook this requirement, resulting at the minimum in additional administrative cost in putting things right, but also, potentially, leaving them with a VAT assessment for the duplicated tax shown on the invoice and authenticated receipt and, possibly, a penalty.

Tax invoices

9.41 The contractor can issue a tax invoice under the normal rules. This is seen by many as disadvantageous—if the customer does not pay, or disputes part of the bill, the VAT shown on the invoice is still due to be paid to Customs & Excise. See *Tolley's VAT 1998/99, chapter 40* for the details required to be shown on a tax invoice.

Agreed price variations

9.42 Disputes as to the value of supplies between contractors and their customers are not uncommon. Where the dispute is resolved through an agreed price variation, and an invoice has been issued, the contractor may issue a credit note for the sums involved. However, it should be noted that it is not permitted for a credit note to be issued simply because a customer refuses to pay. The VAT in those circumstances must be accounted for under the normal tax point rules and VAT bad debt relief claimed as appropriate.

However, contractors who prefer to issue an application for payment, rather than a tax invoice, will be left at an advantage in these circumstances as, if no tax invoice has been issued and payment has not been received, no tax is due to be paid to Customs & Excise (see also paragraph 9.38 above).

Liquidated damages

9.43 Liquidated damages are not the consideration for a supply and are outside the scope of VAT. Accordingly the amount of VAT originally charged on the contractor's services cannot be altered in respect of the liquidated damages. Conversely, the customer is not required to alter the amount of VAT which he has reclaimed.

Non-VAT-registered customers

9.44 Contractors with customers who are not VAT-registered may wish to remember that they are not required to issue tax invoices to those customers. Contractors will also be aware that customers, and in particular

9.44 *VAT Business by Business*

domestic customers, will not make payment unless they are in receipt of an invoice. In order to manage the VAT efficiently, contractors may wish to use an invoice which is not a tax invoice—for example a pro forma invoice or an invoice which does not bear their VAT registration number. In such circumstances, whereas the customer will hold an invoice against which they will be willing to make payment, if payment is withheld, tax will only become due when payment is made.

Chapter 10

Doctors and Dentists

Introduction

10.1 Most of the VAT issues which affect doctors will also affect dental practitioners, and it is clear that, for the majority of doctors and dentists in the UK, there are further complications due to their involvement with the National Health Service ('NHS').

10.2 At first glance, the treatment, for VAT purposes, of supplies made by a practitioner, whether it be a doctor or a dentist, within the health care industry may seem relatively straightforward. For doctors and dentists, however, the presumption that all supplies will fall to be treated as exempt from VAT under *VATA 1994, 9 Sch, Group 7* is somewhat misplaced. Indeed, care should be taken to ensure that doctors and dentists apply the correct VAT liability to their services.

10.3 The correct VAT liability of supplies by doctors and dentists is partly determined by reference to who the supplier is and not solely to what is being supplied. Part of this chapter, therefore, will deal with the different legal entities within the two professions and the consequential VAT treatment of their business activities.

10.4 Prior to changes affecting the long-standing arrangement between the medical profession and Customs & Excise (C&E), the VAT treatment of a General Practitioner's ('GP') services was deemed to be the provision of 'non-business' health care provided as part of the NHS. As they were not considered to be in business, Customs & Excise treated GPs' income, derived from their medical supplies, as outside the scope of VAT and thus prohibited the recovery of any related input tax.

10.5 Following representations made by the medical profession, however, Customs & Excise, in Press Release 44/93 on 19 March 1993, announced a change in their view of the VAT liability of GPs activities. The Press Release advised that, from 19 March 1993, GPs were to be treated as independent contractors supplying their medical services to the NHS. Customs & Excise acknowledged that such supplies by GPs were made in the course of their businesses, and revised the VAT treatment of such income from 'outside the scope' to exempt. In some circumstances, and subject to the partial exemption rules, this change allowed GPs to recover VAT incurred prior to

10.6 *VAT Business by Business*

19 March 1993 which had previously been denied. See also C&E Business Brief 8/96.

VAT liability

10.6 The EC legislation relating to the VAT liability of supplies made by doctors and dentists is embodied in *Article 13A(1)(c)* of the *EC Sixth Directive (77/388)*. This provides exemption from VAT for 'the provision of medical care in the exercise of the medical or paramedical professions as defined by the member states concerned'.

10.7 The UK legislation gives effect to this provision, in respect of supplies by doctors in *Item 1(a)* and *(c)*, and dentists in *Item 2* (see paragraphs 10.23 to 10.26 below), of *VATA 1994, 9 Sch, Group 7*.

Supplies by doctors

10.8 *Item 1(a)* and *(c)* sets out the qualified medical personnel whose services fall within the exemption, namely those persons whose names appear on the following registers:

Item 1(a): '...the register of medical practitioners or the register of medical practitioners with limited registration...'

Item 1(c): '...any register kept under the *Professions Supplementary to Medicine Act 1960*...'

10.9 Only those professions that are listed in the above mentioned provisions will be entitled to exemption. In *JR Barkworth v C&E Commrs, QB [1988] STC 77*, the High Court held that supplies of services by an osteopath were not listed in *9 Sch, Group 7*, and therefore could not be treated as exempt. In *C Pittam (13268)*, the tribunal held that services supplied by chiropractors were also not covered by the exemption provisions and were therefore liable for VAT at the standard rate.

10.10 A supply of medical services by a person who is not registered under *Item 1(a)* or *(c)* may still be eligible for exemption if the services are carried out by or directly supervised by a person who is enrolled in either of the registers (*VATA 1995, 9 Sch, Group 7, Note 2*). The services of the unregistered person must be of a type that would be provided by the registered medical practitioner in the course of his profession, in order to qualify for the exemption. For instance, a nurse working for a doctor who specialises in mental illnesses cannot exempt the supply of acupuncture (see the VAT tribunal decisions in *Dr AR Evans, [1976] VATTR 175 (285)* and *Easyway Productions Limited (14938)*).

Doctors and Dentists 10.13

10.11 Customs & Excise consider the following factors to indicate that a person is 'directly supervised' by a registered person:

(a) The supervisor (it need not be the same individual; a number of professionals working within a practice can supervise different unqualified staff as required), must:

    (i) be an appropriately registered person;

    (ii) see the client at the outset of treatment and at the outset of any new treatment required thereafter;

    (iii) be readily available for the whole of the time that the unqualified staff are working, and be able to take appropriate action in an emergency;

    (iv) decide the treatment to be provided by the unqualified staff; and

    (v) be able to demonstrate that he monitors the services of the unqualified staff.

(b) Supervision cannot take place via a third party—i.e. the supervisor must always be in a direct relationship with the unqualified staff (see *Elder Home Care Ltd (11185)*).

(c) The qualified supervisor must be present at appropriate times during the process and he or she must be responsible, contractually, for supervising the unqualified staff. Customs will not accept that direct supervision exists where a supervisor is introduced primarily to gain VAT exemption and in practice carries out little or no supervision.

(d) The services performed by the unqualified staff must be of a nature that requires supervision. Customs will not accept exemption for services performed by unqualified staff for which no supervision is required and will not accept that services which are not broadly of a medical or caring nature can gain exemption simply by the use of a qualified individual in a supervisory or managerial role.

(e) The ratio of registered professional to unqualified staff must be such that it enables the requirement above to be fulfilled. (C&E News Release 23/96, 11 April 1996).

10.12 Within the scope of the exemption is the supply of services of an urgent medical nature, as set out in *section 18(3)* of the *Medical Act 1983*, if supplied by a person who is not medically registered in the visiting EC practitioners list at the time he performs the services, but who is entitled to be registered in accordance with *section 18(3)* (*VATA 1994, 9 Sch, Group 7, Note 4*).

10.13 The supply of medical goods by a doctor can qualify for exemption if the goods are a minor or inseparable part of the overall service of medical care. For example, the bandages and dressings and the materials needed to

10.14 *VAT Business by Business*

inject drugs can be treated as part of the service of medical care and thus qualify to be exempt from VAT. The case of *C&E Commrs v British United Provident Association ('BUPA')*, *QB [1995] STC 628* clarified this position by determining that any prostheses (for example, hip joint replacements, heart pacemakers and heart valve replacements) were in fact part of an exempt composite supply of medical care that did not fall to be zero-rated under the provisions of *VATA 1994, 8 Sch, Group 12* (Drugs, Medicines, Aids for the Handicapped, etc).

Pharmacy services

10.14 The *Value Added Tax (Supply of Pharmaceutical Goods) Order 1995 (SI 1995 No 652)* added a new *Item 1A* to the existing *VATA 1994, 8 Sch, Group 12*. The new item zero-rated:

'...The supply of any goods in accordance with a requirement or authorisation under

(a) *regulation 20* of the *NHS (Pharmaceutical Services) Regulations 1992*

(b) *regulation 34* of the *NHS (General Medical Services) (Scotland) Regulations 1995*; or

(c) *regulation 41* of the *Health and Personal Social Services (General Medical and Pharmaceutical Services) Regulations (Northern Ireland) 1973*,

by a person registered in the register of medical practitioners or the register of medical practitioners with limited registration ...'

10.15 Following the changes in the VAT status of GPs in March 1993, there was increased concern among NHS dispensing doctors about the anomalous VAT treatment of the drugs which they dispensed. With effect from 1 April 1995, Customs & Excise recognised that the supply of drugs or prostheses by an NHS authorised GP, or a GP providing NHS pharmacy services (i.e. dispensing doctors) could be zero-rated. The change in treatment extended the existing zero-rating provisions to apply to supplies of prescribed drugs dispensed by medical practitioners (*VATA 1994, 8 Sch, Group 12, Item 1A, Notes 1 & 5*).

NHS dispensing doctors

10.16 If GPs serve patients who are unable to visit a retail pharmacy because of distance or some other inadequacy, they can be authorised or required by the NHS to provide NHS pharmacy services to those patients. As a consequence of the above change, these supplies of 'take-away' drugs by

Doctors and Dentists **10.22**

dispensing doctors became liable to zero-rated VAT. For some dispensing doctors, these taxable supplies put them over the VAT registration threshold.

10.17 It should be noted, however, that the exemption that applied to the professional services of doctors was not affected by these changes. In order to restrict zero-rating to the supply of prescribed drugs, Customs & Excise policy is that NHS dispensing doctors should treat any charges they make for their dispensing services when supplying prescribed drugs as a non-business NHS activity which is outside the scope of the tax. In addition, the actual statutory prescription fee is not affected by the 1 April 1995 changes and continued to be outside the scope of VAT.

10.18 The effect of the 1 April 1995 change is that dispensing GPs can register for VAT and reclaim the VAT on their purchases of drugs and a proportion of overhead VAT incurred in relation to the NHS pharmacy services. Alternatively, if their zero-rated supplies exceed the VAT registration threshold, and they decide that it may be administratively inconvenient to register for VAT, they can apply to be granted exemption from VAT registration.

10.19 The vast majority of ordinary GPs, however, were not affected by the changes and their professional charges as medical practitioners remain exempt from VAT.

Doctors and medico-legal services

10.20 Following a legal challenge to Customs & Excise, it has been agreed that services which are predominantly legal, as opposed to medical, are liable to VAT at the standard rate, as opposed to being exempt.

10.21 Taxable medico-legal services are those where the doctor plays an integral role in the legal work required by a third party, such as insurers or solicitors. The legal work would include:

(i) arbitration, mediation and conciliation services;

(ii) investigating the credibility of medical claims made against insurers;

(iii) consideration of medical reports in order to resolve disputes following personal injury.

10.22 The above ruling applied retrospectively back to 20 January 1997. Therefore, from that date, many doctors may be entitled or required to be registered for VAT and may recover any related input tax (subject to the normal rules). Services provided by a doctor in the course of his normal doctor/patient relationship, and services which are predominantly medical and not legal (for example medical reports for employers and life assurance policies) will continue to be exempt from VAT. (C&E Business Brief 26/96, 19 December 1996).

10.23 VAT Business by Business

Supplies by dentists

10.23 Like many industries, representatives from the dentistry profession have gathered under the umbrella of their association, in this case the British Dental Association ('BDA'), to meet with officials of Customs & Excise to produce an Information Sheet (see VAT Information Sheet 5/96, May 1996) which clarifies the VAT treatment of supplies made by dentists.

10.24 The legal provisions for determining the liability of supplies by dentists can be found within *VATA 1994, 9 Sch, Group 7, Item 2*, which exempts from VAT:

'...the supply of any service or dental prostheses by—

(a) a person registered in the dentists' register;

(b) a person enrolled in any roll of dental auxiliaries having effect under *section 45* of the *Dentists Act 1984*; or

(c) a dental technician...'

10.25 By virtue of this legislation, therefore, no VAT is charged on the supply by a dentist on his supply of dental services or dental goods such as false teeth. This exemption can also be interpreted to extend to cover any services supplied by a dentist in his professional capacity. For example, a dentist can exempt his service of providing professional advice on dental matters. This is a somewhat loose definition and is clearly open to debate. For instance, is it possible for a dentist to exempt his services of lecturing on dental matters to a medical school? On consideration of the reasoning behind the exemption schedule for health care, it seems likely that the exemption, in terms of professional advice, only relates to conventional advice in relation to the diagnosis of an individual patient. Consequently, an educational lecture by a registered dentist would fall outside the scope of the health care exemption and VAT should be charged on the supply of dental lecturing.

10.26 The supply of services and dental prostheses by a dental technician (for a definition of 'dental technician', see *JA Bennett (865)*) or auxiliary are also covered by *VATA 1994, 9 Sch, Group 7*, and this exemption will apply irrespective of whether the supply is made to a patient or to another dentist. The separate supply of the services of a dental hygienist is also exempt, providing that the person performing the service is enrolled as a dental auxiliary under *section 45* of the *Dentists Act 1984*. Exemption will also apply to a supply of goods if the goods are used as an inseparable part of the course of treatment. For example, a dentist may exempt supplies of mouthwashes and teeth-braces. However, the exemption does not include the sale of other related 'oral hygiene' products held out as separate sales, such as toothpaste and toothbrushes.

Accounting records

VAT registration

10.27 As the majority of services provided by GPs and dentists are exempt from VAT, many doctors are not required to register for VAT. Providing that the level of any taxable supplies does not exceed the present VAT registration threshold of £50,000, there is no legal requirement for a doctor's business to register for VAT. However, subject to the partial exemption status of the business, it may be beneficial for the business to register voluntarily if it is making some taxable supplies. This is because the business may be able to at least recover a certain percentage of the VAT incurred on expenditure.

10.28 If a doctor or dentist registers for VAT he will, of course, be subject to the normal rules and regulations (see *Drs Dunn, Bryant, Lee & Franklin (14788)*).

Records

10.29 If a doctor or dentist is registered for VAT, his business records should be no different to those of any other VAT-registered entity. Records will normally consist of sales and purchase ledgers as the main source of the doctor's book-keeping. As with all VAT-registered businesses it is a mandatory requirement to keep a separate VAT account, which is used to keep an ongoing record of the business's VAT liability. Once a partial exemption method is in place, these records will serve to provide the figures for the quarterly partial exemption calculation, resulting in a quantification of recoverable input tax.

10.30 Most VAT-registered businesses complete VAT returns on a three-monthly basis. However, for businesses which are in a situation where VAT is consistently repaid by Customs & Excise, there may be a cash flow advantage in considering an application to make monthly VAT returns.

10.31 If a VAT-registered GP makes a combination of taxable and exempt supplies, he will normally use an approved partial exemption method to calculate how much input tax he will be able to reclaim. With the majority of doctors making primarily exempt supplies, the majority of the VAT which they incur on purchases will be irrecoverable.

10.32 If a VAT-registered dentist makes a combination of taxable and exempt supplies, the business will be deemed to be a 'partly exempt' business. As such, the full recovery of the VAT incurred on purchases (input tax) may well be prohibited. Under these circumstances, the business will normally use an approved partial exemption method to calculate how much input tax it will be able to reclaim. With the majority of dentists making primarily exempt supplies, most of the VAT they incur on purchases will be irrecoverable. However, some dental practices, in order to obtain a proportion

10.33 *VAT Business by Business*

of input VAT suffered on their overheads, voluntarily registered for VAT and then held out for sale products which were taxable at the standard rate, such as toothbrushes. After Customs accepted their partial exemption methods, small medical and dental practices found that they could recover a proportion of VAT incurred on overheads, which would previously only ever have been treated as a VAT cost. Customs soon caught up with this planning arrangement and consequently revised the de minimis limits on the levels of exempt and total input tax, making it more difficult for businesses to treat all input tax as attributable to taxable supplies and thus recoverable in full.

Practical points

10.33 To the outsider, a general medical or dental practice may appear to be a single practice and a single legal entity. However, the actual working structure may be very different. This section explores the various arrangements which affect the VAT liability of the supplies made.

Expense-sharing agreements

10.34 These types of arrangements can take many forms. Usually they will take the form of independent GPs or dentists agreeing to share the costs of operating common premises, support staff, equipment etc. Importantly, it remains the case that the doctors or dentists will act independently of each other and no legal partnership arrangement will exist.

10.35 Typically, the parties agree to bear a certain share of the most common expenses of the practice, for example insurance premiums, heating and lighting expenses, etc. In some situations, one party will then pay the whole cost of the supply of, for example, heating and then re-charge the amount to the other affected parties, the charge being in proportion to each doctor's or dentist's agreed share.

10.36 Under this scenario, there are supplies from one doctor or dentist to another. If the amounts paid form the consideration for the supplies of facilities, then the supplies will be exempt from VAT under *VATA 1994, 9 Sch, Group 7, Item 1*. Where taxable goods are supplied, (for example, the sale of medical/dental equipment from one doctor or dentist to another), VAT will be due on the sale price (see *AW Roberts (353)*).

10.37 If, however, an agreement provides for common ownership of the equipment, any payment from one of the parties, in respect of its share in the goods, is not consideration for a supply and VAT will not be due. On the other hand, if a doctor or dentist initially buys equipment and the second party takes exclusive ownership on payment of the agreed sum, that sum will constitute consideration for the supply of goods and will be liable for VAT at the standard rate.

10.38 Commercially, an expense-sharing agreement may take place if a doctor attempts to 'buy-in' to an established practice. If an established GP or dentist owns the lease of the premises, the assets and the goodwill of the business, he may well sell a 50% stake in these assets to a second practitioner. Thereafter, the two doctors or dentists may operate on an expense-sharing basis as two separate businesses. The sale of part of the original business to the second practitioner should not be liable to VAT as it should qualify to be the transfer of part of a business as a 'going concern'.

Partnerships

10.39 For VAT purposes, partnerships are treated as a single business. If the partnership is VAT-registered, any taxable supply by one or more of the partners is seen as a supply by the single business. Supplies of goods or services between partners are disregarded for VAT purposes.

Employer/employee relationships

10.40 In some situations a doctor or dentist will enlist the services of another doctor. The new recruit is referred to as the 'assistant'. Under a typical contract of employment, the employer makes goods or services available to the assistant, solely for the benefit of the assistant's employment. For VAT purposes there is no supply.

Associate agreements

10.41 It is common for one doctor or dentist, or a number of doctors in partnership, to own the whole medical practice. The practice owner (often termed the 'principal') may then make all the facilities available to the other GPs or dentists (or the 'associates'). Each associate is self-employed and is, in fact, a separate 'business' for VAT purposes. Indeed, most associates have their own patients and supply their services either to private patients or the NHS as independent practitioners. The associate is not, as many mistakenly believe, acting as an agent or sub-contractor for the principal.

10.42 Under this arrangement, there will be supplies of goods and services by the practice-owner to the associate GP or dentist. Such supplies may consist of the use of a fully equipped surgery, the supply of materials and consumables necessary in the provision of treatment, laboratory services, accountancy services and the use of chair-side/reception staff. The practice owner may also provide guidance to the associates on specific medical or dental services. In return, the associate will pay the practice owner for the use of the services offered. The income which the practice owner receives is known as 'retainer fees'.

10.43 Over the years, the VAT liability of the supplies of facilities by the practice owner to the associate, in return for the 'retainer fee', has been

10.44 *VAT Business by Business*

somewhat problematic. Following protracted discussions with Customs & Excise, it has been agreed that:

'Supplies of services such as staff, facilities and prostheses by one dentist to another, for the purpose of enabling the recipient practitioner to carry out his business within the practice, can be regarded as exempt from VAT under *VATA 1994, 9 Sch, Group 7, Item 2*.' (see VAT Information Sheet 5/96, para 8).

10.44 Despite this lenient treatment, some major limitations within the 'associate agreement' arrangements remain. These are:

(i) supplies of non-medical or non-dental prostheses which are held out for sale by one doctor or dentist to another are standard-rated. Supplies of mouthwashes and other products used within the dental profession which are used by the associate but owned by the practice-owner should be included within the exempt supply of facilities. The sale to an associate of dental equipment, such as seats or lighting, is also treated as a taxable supply at the standard rate.

(ii) Supplies of other products used within the profession, which are used by the associate but owned by the practice-owner, should be included within the exempt supply of facilities.

(iii) The sale to an associate of dental equipment, such as seats or lighting, is also treated as a taxable supply at the standard rate.

(iv) Exemption only applies to supplies which allow the associate to carry out medical or dental services. For example, the supply of reception staff will not be included in any exemption from VAT.

(v) Supplies performed by a doctor or dentist who has ceased to practise are not covered by the exemption. (However, supplies by a practice-owner who does not work in his own practice are covered by the exemption as long as he works in a practice elsewhere (see VAT Information Sheet 5/96).

Chapter 11

Education

Introduction

11.1 The VAT implications for institutions in the education sector have historically been complex, and matters have been complicated by changes in VAT legislation and by the limited resources that the institutions have available to them. Although, to a large extent, the institutions and their staff are becoming better acquainted with VAT on a day to day basis, the 'simple' tax can create unforeseen difficulties for the uninitiated.

11.2 When VAT was introduced in the UK in 1973, relatively few educational institutions qualified to be registered for the tax. This was primarily because many establishments were, at that time, under the control of other bodies. Typically, such establishments were polytechnic institutions and what have become further education colleges (formerly technical colleges) which were all under the control of local authorities. Similarly, many schools came under the jurisdiction of their local authorities. In the early days of the regime, therefore, those that did register were provided with certain concessionary measures which made accounting for VAT more straightforward than for the 'normal' kind of business. For a variety of reasons, which will be covered in this chapter, many institutions have only relatively recently become fully embroiled in the VAT system.

Business activities

11.3 The meaning of 'business' for VAT purposes has been considered in depth in Chapter 7— Charities. Many educational institutions, as charities themselves, are affected by whether their activities are business or non-business. They receive income from a variety of sources including central government grants, fees received from students, Research Councils, donations and general trading activities to name but a few. In general, the business and non-business implications for the various types of establishment are covered in their separate categories later in this chapter.

11.4 *VAT Business by Business*

Liability

11.4 In European VAT legislation, the provision of education is exempted from VAT by virtue of *Article 13A(i)* of the *EC Sixth Directive*. It is interesting to note that European Community legislation makes no provision for the exemption of research. *Article 13A(i)* of the *EC Sixth Directive* is enacted in UK VAT law by *VATA 1994, 9 Sch, Group 6*. This provides that the following are exempt supplies for VAT purposes:

- the provision, by an 'eligible body' (see paragraph 11.12 below for the definition of an eligible body), of education, research and vocational training (where research is provided *by* an eligible body, it must also be provided *to* an eligible body to qualify as exempt from VAT) (*VATA 1994, 9 Sch, Group 6, Item 1*);

- the provision of private tuition, provided that it is in a subject ordinarily taught in a school or university and is provided by an individual teacher acting independently of an employer (*VATA 1994, 9 Sch, Group 6, Item 2*);

- the provision of examination services by or to an eligible body or to a person receiving education (or vocational training) which is exempt by virtue of *VATA 1994, 9 Sch, Group 6, Item 1* or is provided otherwise than in the course or furtherance of a business; and

- the supply of any goods and/or services (other than examination services) which are closely related to the principal supply (i.e. a supply within *VATA 1994, 9 Sch, Group 6, Item 1*), providing

    - the supply is made by or to the eligible body making the principal supply,

    - the goods and/or services are for the direct use of the pupil, student or trainee receiving the principal supply; and

    - where the supply is made to the eligible body making the principal supply, it is made by another eligible body.

These provisions do not apply to goods or services supplied to pupils by commercial providers of English as a foreign language, which remain taxable (see paragraph 11.52 below).

Definition of education

11.5 'Education' is not specifically defined in UK VAT legislation. Before the substantive changes to the relevant UK VAT legislation on 1 August 1994, it was commonly accepted that education could be defined as 'tuition in a subject taught as part of the national curriculum or taught to degree level at universities and other higher education colleges'. With the widening of the VAT exemption on 1 August 1994, there came a widening of the accepted definition of education. It is now regarded by Customs & Excise as being 'a course, class or lesson of instruction or study in any subject, whether or not that subject is normally taught in schools, colleges or universities and regardless of where and when it takes place'. Education 'includes lectures, educational seminars, conferences and symposia, together with holiday, sporting and recreational courses. It also includes the provision of distance teaching and associated materials, if the student is subject to assessment by the teaching institution' (*Customs & Excise Notice 701/30 (October 1997), paragraph 3.11*).

Definition of research

11.6 As with education, 'research' is similarly undefined in VAT legislation. Customs & Excise accept that research is 'original investigation undertaken to gain knowledge and understanding'. As such, there is a very thin dividing line between research and consultancy, and this is an area which often provides educational institutions with difficulty. The tribunal case of *Joseph Rowntree Foundation (12913)* considered the definition of research. In this case, a charity operated a fund to financially assist families which provided care for handicapped children. The data relating to the fund's activities was retained on computers at a university in the fund's locality and the university charged the fund for costs directly associated with the operation of the computers in relation to the fund's activities. In practice, this purely involved a recharge of a proportion of salaries of the university's staff which operated the computers. The recharge was treated as exempt by the university. Customs & Excise thought differently and issued an assessment for an underdeclaration of VAT, suggesting that the supply made by the university was subject to VAT at the standard rate. The charity appealed, contending that the supplies were the provision of research and, therefore, exempt in accordance with *VATA 1994, 9 Sch, Group 6, Item 1(b)*. The tribunal upheld the appeal, finding that the computerised data was a 'valuable research source' of statistical data, so that the supplies made by the university were of research and were, therefore, exempt. Whilst this definition might not appear in strict accordance with the accepted definition of research, the tribunal has, in this case, provided guidance as to what kinds of activities it considers might fall to be treated as research.

Definition of vocational training

11.7 'Vocational training', which is defined by legislation, means training, retraining or, from 1 January 1995, the provision of work experience for any trade, profession or employment or any voluntary work connected with education, health, safety, welfare or the carrying out of activities of a charitable nature. It includes many differing methods of training intended to prepare the delegates for employment, including conferences, lectures,

11.8 *VAT Business by Business*

seminars, courses and workshops. It does not, however, include services such as counselling, business advice and consultancy. The provision of vocational training is exempt to the extent that the consideration payable is ultimately a charge to funds provided pursuant to arrangements made under *Employment and Training Act 1973, s 2*; *Employment and Training Act (Northern Ireland) 1950, s 1A* or *Enterprises and New Towns (Scotland) Act 1990, s 2*. Included within the exemption is the supply of goods and services essential to the vocational training directly to the trainee by the person providing the training. This provides for the exemption to extend to providers of vocational training under government-funded training schemes which are not eligible bodies (*VATA 1994, 9 Sch, Group 6, Item 5, Notes 3, 5*).

Definition of private tuition

11.8 The VAT tribunal considered the definition of 'private tuition' in the case of *Mrs A E Wright (10408)*. Here, an experienced teacher of English in the United Kingdom became a consultant in the field of a process which originated in the United States, concerning assisting people with learning difficulties caused by sciotopic sensitivity syndrome. The pupils' conditions were remedied by using glasses with coloured lenses. Mrs Wright's new activities caused her turnover to exceed the then VAT registration threshold and she registered for VAT on the grounds that the activities generated income which were subject at the standard rate. Mrs Wright subsequently reconsidered her position and formed the opinion that the supplies should be treated as exempt under what is now *VATA 1994, 9 Sch, Group 6*. Customs & Excise ruled that the income generated by the activities was standard-rated, and Mrs Wright appealed. The VAT tribunal dismissed her appeal, deciding that the supplies she made could not be described as 'tuition in subjects which are usually taught in the course of education provided by a school or university', and were not, therefore, exempt under *VATA 1994, 9 Sch, Group 6*.

11.9 In another case concerning the VAT liability of educational activities, *Mrs V Ellicott (11472)*, a qualified teacher taught private pupils in accordance with a programme conceived by a private company. As part of the agreement, Mrs Ellicott would pay the private company 50% of the fees she received from her pupils. She did not account for VAT on the fees. Customs & Excise assessed on the grounds that the supplies were, in fact, standard-rated. Mrs Ellicott appealed to the VAT tribunal, contending that the activities were services of private tuition and exempt under *VATA 1994, 9 Sch, Group 6*. The VAT tribunal upheld Mrs Ellicott's appeal, holding that, despite her obligations under the contractual relationship with the private company, she was providing private tuition and was 'acting independently of any employer or organisation'. The tribunal went on to say that 'So far as there is an element of dependence (with the private company)...it is not the sort that excludes (the appellant's) supplies from the scope of 6 Schedule Group 6' (the legislative reference at the time). Therefore, the activities were exempt as contended.

'Closely related' supplies

11.10 Prior to the 1994 changes in VAT legislation specifically affecting the education sector, supplies which are now exempt because they are 'closely related' to the provision of education, research and vocational training (the 'principal supplies'), were exempt because they were 'incidental' to the provision of education, etc. Although it was commonly felt at the time of the changes that the effect of the change in terminology for such supplies would limit the extent of the exemption, in practice, the implications for providers of education and other services within *VATA 1994, 9 Sch, Group 6, Item 1* have been governed by the provisions set out in the preceding paragraphs. Under current legislation, the term 'closely related' is limited to the provision of goods and services which are necessary for students to enable them to undergo their education. Such supplies predominately include accommodation and catering. However, Customs & Excise also accept that other supplies, such as transport and classroom sales of certain goods required by students for their course of study, can also be exempt. Indeed, there have been instances where Customs & Excise have agreed that supplies of standard-rated goods such as confectionery, crisps and soft drinks supplied to students as part of a meal in a student refectory may also qualify for exemption. Supplies which do *not* qualify for the exemption include:

- sales of goods from tuck shops, student shops, campus shops and student bars;

- sales of goods which are specifically required by the pupils or students for regular use in classes;

- sales of confectionery, crisps and ice cream from vending machines;

- accommodation and catering to staff and other non-students;

- separately charged laundry and other personal services;

- sales of school uniforms and sports clothing;

- admission charges to plays, concerts, dances, sports activities, exhibitions, museums, zoos, etc;

- administration and management charges;

- commission for allowing third-party organisations to sell goods at an educational establishment;

- land and property transactions.

11.11 *VAT Business by Business*

Eligible bodies

11.11 The concept of 'eligible bodies' was introduced with the changes to VAT legislation in the UK on 1 August 1994. Prior to that date, the VAT liability of supplies typically made by educational establishments was very much dependent on whether the supplier qualified as a school, university or 'eligible institution', the nature of the courses, and whether or not they were profitable. With effect from 1 August 1994, the widening of the exemption meant that the VAT treatment became reliant on whether or not the supplier (or recipient) qualified as an eligible body.

11.12 The definition of 'eligible body' can be found in *VATA 1994, 9 Sch, Group 6, Note 1*. An eligible body can be any one of the following:

(a) A school within the meaning of *Education Acts 1944 to 1993, Education (Scotland) Act 1980, Education and Libraries (Northern Ireland) Order 1986 (SI 1986 No 594)* or *Education Reform (Northern Ireland) Order 1989 (SI 1989 No 2406)*, which is

 (i) provisionally or finally registered (or deemed to be registered) as a school within the meaning of that legislation in a register of independent schools;

 (ii) a school in respect of which grants are made by the Secretary of State to the proprietor or managers;

 (iii) a maintained school within the meaning of *Education Act 1993* or *Education and Libraries (Northern Ireland) Order 1986*;

 (iv) a public school within the meaning of *Education (Scotland) Act 1980, s 135(1)*;

 (v) a grant-maintained school within the meaning of *Education Act 1993, s 22*;

 (vi) a self-governing school within the meaning of *Self-Governing Schools (Scotland) Act 1989*;

 (vii) a grant-maintained special school within the meaning of *Education Act 1993, s 182(3)*; or

 (viii) a grant-maintained integrated school within the meaning of *Education Reform (Northern Ireland) Order 1989, Article 65*.

Schools not covered by (i)–(viii) above may be covered by the eligible body criteria in (e) below.

(b) A UK university, and any college, institution, school or hall of such a university. *Excluded* are subsidiary companies that universities set up to pursue commercial business interests and UK campuses of foreign universities (but see (e) below).

(c) An institution

Education 11.13

(i) falling within *Further and Higher Education Act 1992, s 91(3)(a)* or *(b)* or *91(5)(b)* or *(c)*;

(ii) which is a designated institution as defined in *Further and Higher Education (Scotland) Act 1992, s 44(2)*;

(iii) managed by a board of management as defined in *Further and Higher Education (Scotland) Act 1992, s 36(1)*; or

(iv) to which grants are paid by the Department of Education for Northern Ireland under *Education and Libraries (Northern Ireland) Order 1986, Article 66(2)*.

This includes all further education colleges or organisations defined or designated as such under the various Education Acts (including the Workers' Educational Association (WEA)), together with higher educational institutions defined in the Education Acts but not covered by (b) above.

(d) A government department or local authority (or a body which acts for public purposes and not for its own profit and performs functions similar to those of a government department or local authority). Included are executive agencies and Health Authorities.

(e) A body which

(i) is precluded from distributing and does not distribute any profit it makes; and

(ii) applies any profits made from exempt supplies of education, research or vocational training to the continuance or improvement of such supplies.

Most such bodies will be charities, professional bodies or companies limited by guarantee. However, provided that they satisfy the conditions in (i) and (ii) above, ad hoc groups organising specific conferences or training events are eligible. The UK campuses of foreign universities are also eligible bodies, but non-profit-making organisations that belong overseas do not qualify as eligible.

(f) From 1 January 1995 (but applied from 1 August 1994 by extra-statutory concession), a body not falling within (a)–(e) above which provides the teaching of English as a foreign language.

The Concordat

11.13 To assist establishments making supplies of education, research and vocational training with their VAT accounting procedures, the Committee of Vice Chancellors and Principals of the universities of the United Kingdom ('CVCP') reached agreement with Customs & Excise in 1973 in relation to VAT accounting for establishments in the sector. As a result, the CVCP

11.14 VAT Business by Business

produced guidelines to assist VAT-registered entities in the sector. Better known as the 'Concordat', the guidelines not only provided information as to how to deal with VAT issues on a day to day basis but also set out concessionary arrangements agreed with Customs & Excise in relation to the recovery of VAT on costs and expenses.

11.14 From a VAT liability perspective, the Concordat provided guidance as to the correct VAT treatment of the kinds of activities often prevalent in institutions in the education sector, including the liability of education, research and vocational training which have already been considered in this chapter. The guidance extended to the VAT treatment of supplies of goods and services closely related to supplies of education, research and vocational training (or, under the terminology of the legislation prior to the 1994 changes, incidental to the provision of education, etc). It also set out the types of supplies which are covered by concessionary arrangements, for example the 'majority use' concession for supplies of catering made in student refectories. The application of this particular concession is covered later in this chapter at paragraph 11.27.

11.15 When the former polytechnics and further education colleges became independent from local authority control in 1989 and 1993 respectively, Customs & Excise agreed that the use of the Concordat could be extended to these types of institutions. However, as educational establishments have increasingly become aware of their obligations so far as VAT is concerned and are accordingly seeking to minimise their exposure to VAT, the Concordat began to be seen by Customs & Excise as being too simplistic for the VAT accounting needs of the sector.

11.16 The use of the Concordat by educational institutions was, therefore, withdrawn by Customs & Excise with effect from 1 September 1997. The withdrawal meant that institutions in the higher and further education sectors could no longer rely on the definitions, VAT recovery procedures and, generally, the concessions, including the majority use concessions, previously permitted by the Concordat. The only concession which was allowed to remain after the withdrawal concerned the zero-rating relief for construction of new student accommodation, which is discussed further at paragraph 11.80 below.

Universities and other higher education providers

11.17 When the current VAT legislation appropriate to the education sector was introduced on 1 August 1994, the changes were such that the scope for the exemption of services provided by certain bodies was extended. The widening of the exemption affected all institutions providing education-related services in different ways.

11.18 The university system of education has existed in the United Kingdom for hundreds of years. When VAT was introduced in the UK on 1

Education **11.21**

April 1973, the number of institutions which became subject to the VAT regime was much smaller than it is today (it was for these institutions that the Concordat was originally introduced). It was not until 1 April 1989 that a new type of university became part of the VAT network. Until that time, what became known as the 'new' universities (which had formerly been polytechnics), were under the control of their respective local authorities.

Income

11.19 The principal sources of income for universities and other providers of higher education are grant income from central government funding and fees for the provision of education to students. Until now, the grant income from central government has not usually been seen to be consideration for supplies and has been treated, therefore, as being outside the scope of VAT. Fee income from the provision of education or similar services, which may be received from the students, their employers or their local authorities, is consideration for a supply of services and exempt from VAT. The VAT treatment by universities in respect of these services was not, therefore, affected by the changes in 1994.

Research

11.20 Perhaps the most important development resulting from the 1994 changes affects research. Research is a common activity of universities, other higher education establishments and specialist research institutions (which often qualify to be treated as eligible bodies for VAT purposes by virtue of their charitable status) and is often a primary source of income. Where an institution receives a grant from a third party commissioning it to carry out a research project (and the research is original investigation undertaken to gain knowledge and understanding), the VAT treatment is firstly dependent on the contractual arrangements between the parties and whether the associated funding is consideration for a supply, in which case it is necessary to examine the conditions under which the grant income is provided:

(a) If the contractual arrangements are such that the results of the research are made freely available to the general public, the funding will not be consideration for a supply of services, regardless of whether the person commissioning the research is an eligible body. The grant income is, therefore, outside the scope of VAT.

(b) Conversely, if the intellectual property rights in the results of the research must, in the first instance, be provided to the person commissioning the research, the income will be consideration for a supply of research and will, therefore, be within the scope of the tax.

11.21 If there is a supply, it is then necessary to consider whether the person to whom the supply is made qualifies to be treated as an eligible body. If the research is provided to another eligible body, the supply will be

11.22 VAT Business by Business

exempt. If it is not, it will be standard-rated. If, of course, the research is not original investigation, it will automatically be standard-rated, whether or not the recipient is an eligible body.

11.22 There are special rules which apply to research undertaken on behalf of certain international organisations, although, in order to determine the correct VAT treatment, it is once again necessary to determine at the outset whether the international organisation is actually the recipient of the services and, thus, whether the funding is consideration for a supply of research to the international organisation. If the results of the research are made available to the general public and are not for the private consumption of the international organisation, the funding can be seen to be a grant and, therefore, outside the scope of VAT.

11.23 However, in accordance with *Article 15(10)* of the *EC Sixth Directive*, a person *supplying services to* an international organisation recognised as such by its host EC Member State, which receives the services for its private consumption, is able to zero-rate those services. Conceivably, the principal international organisation which regularly commissions research projects with universities, higher education and other research institutions for its own consumption is the EC Commission (these contracts are commonly known as Fourth RTD Framework contracts), although there are a number of other international organisations which also commission research projects (including the World Bank, NATO, etc.). In practice, the ability to zero-rate such contracts will enable the supplier to recover VAT on costs directly associated with the project, in addition to increasing the taxable turnover and potentially reducing overhead VAT costs (see *Tolley's VAT 1998/99, paragraph 49.6*).

Consultancy

11.24 Consultancy services are commonly provided by universities and higher education institutions. Whereas research is defined as being original investigation undertaken to gain knowledge and understanding, consultancy can possibly be defined as being any kind of activity which does not fall within the definition of research. The provision of consultancy services is standard-rated.

Vocational training

11.25 Some universities and higher education establishments provide vocational training. As has been seen at paragraph 11.4 above, such services are exempt from VAT. The VAT treatment of such services did not change with the revised legislation, although prior to 1 August 1994, the legislation merely exempted supplies of training, retraining for any trade, profession or employment. With effect from 1 January 1995, the definition of vocational training includes the provision of work experience for any trade, profession or employment or any voluntary work connected with education, health, safety, welfare or the carrying out of activities of a charitable nature. Such services are exempt.

Closely-related supplies

11.26 Invariably, universities and other higher education institutions make supplies to their students which are closely related to the provision of education, research and vocational training. Perhaps the most common closely-related supplies are catering and accommodation.

Catering

11.27 Many campuses will have student refectories which are solely used by students. Clearly, these supplies to students are exempt because the services are provided for the direct use of the students receiving the exempt principal supply (of education, etc). Occasionally, non-students may use the catering facilities. Following the withdrawal of the Concordat where, under the majority use concession, supplies made from these facilities were exempt if the majority of users were students, institutions are now required to account for VAT at the standard rate on all supplies of catering made to non-students. In practice, this means that institutions should either differentiate between users at point of sale or use an alternative basis (such as electronic 'credit cards') to calculate the VAT due to Customs & Excise. In certain circumstances, Customs & Excise will accept an apportionment exercise to calculate the VAT due in accordance with the status of the users, but any such apportionment should be substantiated by real usage details over an acceptable period of time.

11.28 If, of course, the users of the catering facilities are visitors during vacations, differentiation at point of sale or any alternative basis for the calculation of the VAT due will not be applicable (unless, for example, the institution has large numbers of post-graduate students) and the supplies will automatically be standard-rated. Supplies of catering made through staff dining rooms are not for the direct use of students and are not, therefore, closely related to the provision of education. Such supplies are also automatically standard-rated. Other standard-rated supplies of catering commonly made by educational establishments include the provision of facilities for weddings, banquets etc. Supplies made from vending machines are not closely related to the provision of education, etc. and are also automatically standard-rated.

Accommodation

11.29 Most universities and some higher education institutions offer accommodation facilities to students. As with catering, provided the accommodation is for the direct use of the student receiving the exempt principal supply, its provision will also be exempt. When supplies of

11.30 VAT Business by Business

accommodation are made by an institution to students from another educational establishment, the supply of accommodation will be made by one eligible body to another eligible body which makes the principal supply. Thus, the provision of the accommodation will be an exempt supply as being closely related to the provision of education and for the direct use of the students receiving the principal supply. Term-time lettings to non-students, if made, will not qualify for the exemption. Similarly, vacation lettings will not usually be closely related to the provision of education and will, therefore, be standard-rated. Accommodation facilities may also be offered to members of the professorial staff or non-academic staff. The provision of such facilities does not fall within the exemption and these supplies will, therefore, be standard-rated.

Sales of goods

11.30 Sales of goods to students which are required as an integral part of the course will be seen to be closely related to the provision of the principal supply if they are made as 'classroom' sales, as opposed to sales from retail outlets. For example, a student on a chemistry course might require special eye protectors with which to observe chemical experiments. If the student buys them from the university as part of the course, the supply will be exempt from VAT. If, however, a student on an art course buys drawing equipment from the student shop, the supply will be standard-rated.

Conferences, etc.

11.31 In recent years, particularly in view of cuts in funding, universities and other higher education institutions have become increasingly involved in trading activities in an attempt to generate additional income. Universities often allow third parties to use their facilities to be used for conferences and seminars. In such instances, the establishment will allow third parties to use facilities such as teaching accommodation, lecture rooms (with facilities such as overhead projectors and other electrical equipment), catering and sports facilities. The grant of an interest in land (including the right to occupy a commercial building or part of a commercial building) is usually exempt from VAT with the election to waive exemption (or 'option to tax') being available (see *Tolley's VAT 1998/99, paragraph 42.2*). However, the income generated from letting where additional facilities form part of the supply, as is usually the case for conferences, will be consideration for standard-rated supplies. Occasionally, an educational institution will run non-term time conferences itself. If these are educational in nature, it may be possible to treat the supplies as being exempt. Thus, the provision of accommodation and catering will be seen to be closely related to the provision (in this case) of education and also exempt.

11.32 An establishment might also allow third parties to use its student accommodation for their own purposes. If the third party merely requires the use of a room (without facilities), the supply will be exempt, although the

Education **11.34**

supplier does have the opportunity to elect to waive exemption. The effect of the election would be to convert an exempt supply into a standard-rated one. Establishments should take care when electing to waive exemption and should consider all the associated implications. If, however, facilities are provided as part of the supply, for example furnished accommodation, etc., the supply will be one of facilities and, therefore, standard-rated.

Sporting activities

11.33 Generally, the provision of facilities for playing any sport, or participating in any recreational activity, is standard-rated. However, exemption is available in specific circumstances (*VATA 1994, 9 Sch, Group 1, Note 16*). When an establishment grants a third party the right to use the facilities for a period exceeding 24 hours, or if there is a series of lettings to the same person over a period of time, the supply is exempt. In the case of a series of lets, the granting of sports or recreational facilities should be to a school, club, association or an organisation representing affiliated clubs or constituent organisations where:

- each period is in respect of the same activity carried on at the same place (a different pitch, court or lane at the same sports ground or premises would be seen to be the same place);

- the interval between each period is not less than one day and not more than fourteen days;

- consideration is payable by reference to the whole series and is evidenced by written agreement (a formal agreement, an exchange of letters or an invoice issued in advance of the series requiring payment for the whole of the series would be acceptable as evidence); and

- the grantee has exclusive use of the facilities.

Car parking

11.34 Universities and other higher education institutions occasionally become involved in the provision of car parking facilities. The grant of a right to park a vehicle is standard-rated if the charges made for the facility are purely in relation to car parking. If a car parking facility is provided which is covered by the grant of an interest in land, for example where a landlord lets a commercial building to a tenant and includes in the lease a right to use a number of car parking spaces which are incidental to the main use of the building, the supply will be exempt, providing that the election to waive exemption has not been exercised. If the election to waive exemption has been exercised, the supply will automatically be standard-rated. If the lease relates to land or buildings (other than garages) and the lease contract makes no mention of parking facilities, the supply will similarly be exempt.

11.35 VAT Business by Business

Advertising

11.35 In order to generate additional income, universities and similar institutions often provide advertising space in an in-house publication such as a newsletter or prospectus. The supply of advertising space is standard-rated.

Further education colleges

11.36 As the former polytechnics became independent from local authority control on 1 April 1989, so did further education colleges on 1 April 1993. Further education colleges were often known as technical colleges during the days when they were part of their local authority, and the activities in which they were involved were classed as non-business activities of the authority.

11.37 Prior to the 1994 changes to VAT legislation affecting the education sector in general, for a further education college to determine the VAT liability of its supplies it was necessary to consider whether the services provided by the college were, in fact, education. If the services were provided by a body other than the college itself, for example a trading company, then it additionally became necessary to consider whether a profit was being made in relation to the activities. This provided a number of problems for further education colleges.

11.38 Since 1 August 1994, the situation has become much more straightforward for further education colleges. The effective widening of the exemption for educational services which affected many educational institutions has brought colleges into line with universities and higher education institutions, and the courses which they provide are likely to fall within the exemption.

11.39 Like universities and other higher education institutions, further education colleges receive centrally funded grant income. This, along with fees received for the education of students, forms by far the largest proportion of most further education colleges' income. There is one primary difference between the treatment of universities' income and further education colleges' income. The education of students under the age of 19 years is a statutory requirement in the United Kingdom. This means that the education of the under-19s is a non-business activity of further education colleges. The principal effect of this is the restriction of VAT incurred on costs and expenses which relate to the non-business activities. Input tax recovery is discussed later in this chapter.

11.40 It is not common for colleges to provide research to other bodies, as they do not usually have the facilities to enable them to do so. If, of course, they did provide research, then to qualify for the exemption, the same criteria would apply to the colleges as it does to universities and higher education colleges. That is to say, both the college and the recipient of the services would be required to be eligible bodies.

Education **11.46**

11.41 Most further education colleges provide services which are closely related to the provision of education (or exempt research or vocational training). In accordance with *VATA 1994, 9 Sch, Group 6, Item 4*, such services are also exempt from VAT. For further education colleges, this will primarily involve catering and classroom sales (see paragraphs 11.27 to 11.30 above).

11.42 Further education colleges usually have less grant income, less fee income and fewer other income-generating activities than universities, etc. Nevertheless, VAT usually plays an important part in the day to day accounting of the typical further education college. It should be noted that further education colleges were able to use the 'Concordat' in the same way as universities and other higher education colleges to assist with their VAT accounting prior to its withdrawal on 1 September 1997.

11.43 Further education colleges are not usually registrable by virtue of their trading activities, although not all of their taxable income is generated this way. Often, further education colleges will provide courses in subjects such as hairdressing and catering. Where this occurs, it is common for the students to provide services for a fee to the general public as part of their tuition. This is taxable income for the college. Similarly, a college might open its training restaurant to the general public in order to provide the students with practical training. Any income generated from this type of activity would also be standard-rated.

11.44 Further education colleges, like universities, also generate taxable income from activities such as consultancy services, sales of goods produced from educational activities, retail sales, vending machine sales and car parking. They are unlikely to generate income through bar sales because the majority of students will be less than 18 years old in their time at the college.

11.45 However, some colleges choose to channel certain educational or training activities through trading companies where the recipients of the services are fully taxable businesses for VAT purposes and can recover all the VAT they are charged. As before, if these trading companies are included in VAT groups with their respective colleges, then it may serve to improve the VAT group's partial exemption recovery position.

11.46 With the advent of the *Further and Higher Education Act 1992*, further education colleges became responsible, in certain circumstances, for the provision of adult education. These responsibilities were transferred from local authorities. Prior to 1994, certain adult education courses may not have fulfilled the criteria necessary for exemption, thus requiring a college to account for VAT at the standard rate on appropriate supplies. However, with the widening of the exemption in 1994, the provision of adult education by further education colleges now usually qualifies to be treated as exempt.

Education provided by local authorities

11.47 A local authority is an eligible body for VAT purposes. Therefore, the provision of education or vocational training which is charged for at or above cost is a VAT-exempt business activity of the local authority. Education or vocational training provided by a local authority which is free of charge or is subsidised is a non-business activity. Thus, the provision of education by primary and secondary schools operated by a local authority, which is free of charge or is subsidised by the local authority, is a non-business activity of the local authority.

11.48 As mentioned at paragraph 11.46 above, the *Further and Higher Education Act 1992* transferred certain responsibilities for the provision of adult education from local authorities to further education colleges. The Act, however, does not preclude a local authority from providing adult education. If the local authority is statutorily obliged to provide adult education, it is a non-business activity of the local authority. Conversely, if it is not statutorily obliged to provide the adult education, it is (if it is provided for a consideration) a business activity of the local authority, which means that the supply will be exempt for VAT purposes.

Independent schools

11.49 Schools which are independent of local authority control are eligible bodies. They must register for VAT if the value of their standard-rated activities exceeds the VAT registration threshold. They can also voluntarily register for VAT which provides them with the benefit of being able to recover VAT incurred on costs and expenses, although this benefit should be considered against the potential administrative cost of maintaining a VAT registration. Commonly, the value of the taxable activities of an independent school does not exceed the registration threshold.

11.50 An independent school's activities generally include the provision of education and, hence, supplies which are closely related to the provision of education by an eligible body are exempt from VAT. The standard-rated activities include the provision of vacation lettings, third party catering, tuck shop sales (which may also be zero-rated), school clothes (which may also be zero-rated depending on the age of the pupil) and sports equipment, etc.

Charities

11.51 The VAT implications for charities in general are covered in Chapter 7 of this publication. In relation to education, however, charities qualify as eligible bodies because they are precluded from distributing, and do not distribute, any profits they make, and apply any profits made from the provision of education, research and vocational training to the continuance or improvement of such supplies. Typically, activities which will be exempt when provided by charities are education services, training services and research provided to other eligible bodies.

Providers of teaching in English as a foreign language (EFL)

11.52 Before the 1994 changes in VAT legislation, the definition of 'education' in the VAT legislation excluded 'courses in EFL which are provided for payment which exceeds the full cost of providing the courses'. Thus, where courses in EFL were provided by a commercial entity which made a profit in respect of those supplies, it was necessary for that entity to treat the supplies as standard-rated.

11.53 However, UK legislation was not in accordance with European VAT legislation in this respect as there was (and still is) a requirement for all public sector education to be exempt. Therefore, to retain some tax equity, the *Value Added Tax (Education) (No 2) Order (SI 1994 No 2969)* came into force on 1 August 1994 and extended exemption to certain commercial providers of EFL. Because there are many activities marketed under the heading of EFL, it was decided to restrict the exemption to those providers accredited under the British Council Recognition Scheme.

11.54 The laying of the Order precipitated a number of representations from the sector to the effect that the limiting of the exemption resulted in a distortion in the EFL market. The representations were considered and accepted, as a result of which the Order was extended to apply equally to EFL providers who are not accredited under the British Council Recognition Scheme. Therefore, the provision of courses in EFL is exempt, regardless of the status of the provider and whether a profit is made in relation to the supply.

Examination and inspectorate services

11.55 The provision of 'examination services' by or to an 'eligible body', or to a person receiving education or vocational training which is exempt, or provided otherwise than in the course or furtherance of a business, is an exempt supply. In this instance, 'examination services' includes the setting and marking of examinations, the setting of educational or training standards, and the making of assessments and other services provided with a view to ensuring educational and training standards are maintained (*VATA 1994, 9 Sch, Group 6, Item 3, Note 4*).

11.56 School inspections generally fall within the exemption here. Any supplies made direct to a school or to a local authority are exempt, although supplies made under contract to the Office for Standards in Education may continue to be standard-rated (*Customs & Excise Notice 701/30 (October 1997), paragraph 5.3*).

11.57 *VAT Business by Business*

Youth clubs

11.57 The provision of facilities by a youth club or an association of youth clubs to its members is exempt (*VATA 1994, 9 Sch, Group 6, Item 6(a)*). Similarly, the provision of facilities by an association of youth clubs to members of a youth club which is a member of that association is also exempt (*VATA 1994, 9 Sch, Group 6, Item 6(b)*).

11.58 For these purposes, a youth club is a club established to promote the social, physical, educational or spiritual development of its members where those members are mainly under 21 years old (i.e. at least 51% of the members must be 20 years old or younger). In addition, the club should be a body which is precluded from distributing any profits it makes, and any profits made from supplies it makes are used for the continuance or improvement of such supplies. Youth clubs of organisations such as sports clubs and cultural societies are not seen to be youth clubs unless they are separately constituted (*Customs & Excise Notice 701/35 (July 1995), paragraph 2*).

11.59 The exemption applies to the provision of any facilities which the members receive in return for their subscriptions or, if the facilities are directly related to the club's normal activities, for an additional payment. The exemption does not extend to activities which do not constitute normal supplies by a youth club to its members (for example sales of food and drink, purely recreational holidays, etc). Neither does it extend to supplies which are not made to members.

11.60 There have been a number of tribunal cases which have considered the VAT status of youth clubs and whether their activities qualify for the exemption. In *World Association of Girl Guides and Girl Scouts [1984] VATTR 28 (1611)*, Customs & Excise issued a ruling that the Association's supplies were exempt in accordance with what is now *VATA 1994, 9 Sch, Group 6, Item 6*. This meant that the Association could not recover input tax, as it had been doing, in respect of payments which it received from its affiliated organisations. The Association appealed to the VAT tribunal, which upheld the appeal on the grounds that the Association was not an association of youth clubs in its own capacity, even though its constituent members were associations of youth clubs. The supplies were, therefore standard-rated and not exempt, and the input tax was accordingly recoverable.

11.61 In *Hastings & Rother YMCA (2329)*, Customs & Excise ruled that the association's supplies were standard-rated on the basis that it did not constitute a youth club. The tribunal found that the association was an organisation which provided recreational, educational, social or cultural activities for members who were mainly under 21 years of age. Accordingly, the association was a youth club and its supplies were exempt.

Education **11.65**

11.62 The case of *National Council of YMCAs Inc, [1990] VATTR 68 (5160)* hinged on whether supplies made by a youth club to non-members qualified to be treated as exempt from VAT in the same way that supplies to members were exempt. Customs & Excise contended that the provision of facilities to non-members was standard-rated. The tribunal upheld the Council's appeal, concluding that the provider of the facilities was a youth club and the supplies of facilities it made were exempt, regardless of whether the recipient of the supply was a member.

11.63 In the case of *International Gymnastic School Ltd (6550)*, Customs & Excise ruled that a gymnastic club was not a youth club in accordance with what is now *VATA 1994, 9 Sch, Group 6, Item 6*. The tribunal dismissed the School's appeal on the grounds that it was not a charity and that it provided income for the directors rather than being a non-profit-making entity.

Input tax recovery

VAT recovery in the higher education sector

11.64 Universities, like other partly exempt organisations, are entitled to recover input tax, or a proportion of it, incurred on the costs of goods and services which are used wholly or in part to generate taxable supplies. The methods by which partly exempt organisations are able to calculate the recoverable proportion of their input VAT are set out in Customs & Excise Notice 706 (see also *Tolley's VAT 1998/99, chapter 49*). This Notice sets out the standard partial exemption method, which takes account of input VAT exclusively attributable to specific supplies and apportions non-attributable input VAT by reference to the value of taxable and exempt income. In the early days of VAT, the use of such a partial exemption method was not generally effective for educational establishments, principally because they did not have the administrative resources to carry out the complex related VAT calculations.

11.65 Accordingly, special arrangements were agreed between Customs & Excise and the Committee of Vice Chancellors and Principals (and published in the Concordat) whereby each taxable activity could be dealt with separately. The concept of these arrangements, which became known as 'tunnelling', was such that input tax incurred on costs of goods and services could be offset against output VAT in relation to each taxable activity, providing that each taxable activity was accounted for separately. These arrangements became standard procedures for many educational institutions, allowing them to recover at least an element of the input VAT they had incurred in relation to specific taxable projects. Of course, the tunnelling arrangements, which were considered to be a special partial exemption method, did not take any account of non-attributable input tax. Hence, input tax incurred in relation to overhead costs and expenses was treated as a cost to the establishment concerned when it used the arrangements. As a result, many institutions decided not to use the arrangements and, as will be seen in

11.66 *VAT Business by Business*

paragraph 11.67 below, changed to using other partial exemption methods instead.

Removal of the Concordat

11.66 The use of the Concordat by institutions in the education sector was withdrawn with effect from 1 September 1997. Thus, institutions in all areas of the education sector, which did not voluntarily cease to use the methods set out in the Concordat to calculate recoverable input VAT, became compulsorily required to do so with effect from 1 September 1997. As the calculation of recoverable input VAT using the mechanisms set out in the Concordat was considered to be the use of a special partial exemption method, institutions which had not already implemented an alternative VAT recovery method found that they would not be able to recover any input VAT at all unless they implemented a method for the future.

Alternative partial exemption methods

11.67 As mentioned at paragraph 11.65 above, institutions have gradually become more educated in VAT accounting matters. Largely as a result of a case which was brought to the VAT tribunal by the *University of Edinburgh (6569)*, institutions considered reviewing their VAT recovery positions, usually with the assistance of their professional advisors, particularly with reference to recovery of input tax on overheads. In this specific case, the University used the tunnelling arrangements and recovered VAT attributable only to taxable activities. However, the University argued that, in addition to the VAT directly attributable to taxable supplies through the tunnelling arrangements, it should be permitted to recover an element of the VAT it incurred in relation to the activities of its computer department, activities which were both exempt and taxable for VAT purposes. Moreover, it argued that it should be able to recover an element of the non-attributable input tax retrospectively. The Tribunal Chairman agreed and said that the University should be entitled to recover a proportion of the VAT in question on the basis that it was input tax that it was permitted to recover both retrospectively and for the future.

11.68 The outcome of this tribunal case precipitated a raft of retrospective claims for previously unrecovered overhead input tax by institutions in the sector. Significantly, this led to increased awareness of VAT accounting matters to the extent that institutions had to consider the benefits of maintaining a VAT accounting structure that would provide recovery of a proportion of the VAT recovered in relation to overheads on an on-going basis.

11.69 Most institutions favoured the standard partial exemption method (see *Tolley's VAT 1998/99, paragraph 49.6*), both for administrative simplicity and for effectiveness, given that Customs & Excise permitted the exclusion of centrally funded grant income from the calculations. Using the standard method, the recoverable element of the total overhead input VAT was calculated by reference to taxable income expressed as a percentage of total income (excluding the centrally funded grant income). Thus, an institution's recoverable input VAT was calculated as being the total of input tax exclusively attributable to taxable supplies, plus the recoverable element of the overhead VAT through application of the partial exemption recovery percentage.

11.70 Whilst Customs & Excise have, in the past, allowed higher education institutions to use partial exemption methods based on the standard method but with the exclusion of centrally funded grant income from the calculations, they are currently reviewing their policy on this issue. They are now suggesting that, as centrally funded grant income predominantly subsidises exempt educational activities, the income should not be excluded from the calculations, but should be included within the total income figure. Generally, this would have the impact of significantly reducing the level of overhead input tax recovery for higher education institutions. A pre-requisite of a partial exemption method is that it is 'fair and reasonable' (*VATA 1994, s 26(3)*). Submissions have been made to Customs & Excise, by bodies representing the sector, to the effect that the inclusion of the grant income in the total income figure only would not, generally, be fair and reasonable because the grant income could, conceivably, be used to subsidise some of the taxable activities of an institution. Customs & Excise are currently considering the representations.

VAT recovery in the further education sector

11.71 When further education colleges became independent from local authority control in 1993, many of them also decided to implement full partial exemption methods rather than the calculation of recoverable input VAT by reference to the Concordat, the use of which had been extended to the further education sector. The partial exemption methods implemented by further education colleges were the same, in concept, as those used by higher education institutions (see paragraph 11.69 above).

11.72 However, the VAT recovery calculations for further education colleges were given an added degree of complexity. Typically, a further education college has non-business activities through the education of pupils under the age of 19 years. VAT incurred which is attributable, either directly or indirectly, to non-business activities is not input tax and, therefore, is not recoverable in any part by the college concerned. Thus, it became necessary for an FE college wishing to calculate recoverable input tax using a partial exemption method to make a business/non-business apportionment of the total VAT incurred prior to carrying out the partial exemption calculations. Often the business/non-business apportionment has been made using full time weighted student numbers aged over and under the age of 19 years respectively.

11.73 *VAT Business by Business*

11.73 The actual partial exemption calculations have typically been carried out using the standard recovery method, excluding centrally funded grant income from the Further Education Funding Council. The inclusion of the grant income in the calculations would undoubtedly be distortive because a proportion would relate to the education of the under-19s, and the recovery calculations would have already been adjusted for this factor through the business/non-business apportionment.

VAT recovery for schools

11.74 Special VAT recovery rules apply to local authorities, which are allowed repayment of VAT incurred in relation to their non-business activities. Education provided by local authorities is a non-business activity and VAT incurred in relation to schools run by a local authority is, therefore, recoverable by the authority in question.

11.75 The education provided by independent fee-paying schools is considered to be a business activity, because the schools charge fees for the education. Independent schools are eligible bodies for the purposes of VAT legislation and, therefore, the provision of education is exempt, as are closely-related supplies such as accommodation and catering. Independent schools often make taxable supplies, the value of which sometimes exceeds the VAT registration threshold, rendering them partly exempt for VAT purposes. In the past, VAT-registered schools have been permitted to use the Concordat for VAT recovery, although some have calculated recoverable input tax using a more complicated partial exemption method, such as the standard method. The withdrawal of the Concordat has meant that independent schools which calculated recoverable input tax using the guidelines have been required to revert to orthodox VAT recovery procedures.

11.76 As the education provided by grant-maintained and other similar schools, such as voluntary aided schools and (in Scotland) self-governing schools, is funded by government grants and not by making a charge, it is a non-business activity for VAT purposes. Thus, such institutions are not registrable for VAT and cannot recover the VAT incurred on costs. However, if, as is common, the schools are charities, they are able to take advantage of certain VAT reliefs, such as the relief available for the construction of new buildings intended for non-business use by a charity (see Chapter 7—Charities).

Practical points

Customs & Excise

11.77 The VAT accounting position of institutions in the education sector in general has significantly changed in recent years. Whereas special accounting considerations were given to institutions in the early days of VAT, there has recently been a major change in attitude to the sector by Customs & Excise, as the ability of the institutions to carry out complex VAT calculations and to enter into VAT planning arrangements has increased. It would appear that Customs & Excise now see education as a sector which has, in the past, been allowed to recover too much VAT incurred in relation to costs and expenses and, as a result, they are increasingly focusing on the sector in terms of VAT control. As has already been discussed, Customs & Excise have taken a particularly aggressive stance in relation to VAT recovery by educational institutions, particularly the inclusion of centrally-funded grant income in the apportionment calculations (see paragraphs 11.69 and 11.70 above). The representations made by representative bodies acting on behalf of institutions in the sector are, at the time of writing, under consideration. The ultimate response by Customs & Excise will be of significant importance to the sector.

Property planning

11.78 Customs & Excise have also instigated changes to VAT legislation which have decreased the ability of institutions in the education sector to enter into planning arrangements designed to mitigate VAT costs associated with, inter alia, property construction. Whilst many of the planning mechanisms were available for partially exempt businesses in general, institutions in the education sector, having received cuts in central funding, particularly saw property planning arrangements as a way of reducing their costs, thereby mitigating the effects of the cuts in funding. When anti-avoidance legislation was introduced from 1994 onwards, institutions in the education sector were particularly affected to the extent that the opportunities for planning are now limited. However, a number of property planning arrangements remain possible although the introduction of general anti-avoidance measures, which has been mooted by Customs & Excise, remains a distinct possibility.

Student accommodation

11.79 Whilst the concessions previously allowed by the Concordat ceased to be valid with the withdrawal of the guidelines with effect from 1 September 1997, Customs & Excise did permit concessionary treatment to remain in relation to the construction of new student accommodation (which, for VAT purposes, is considered to be a 'relevant residential' building).

11.80 The VAT legislation states that the first grant of a major interest in a building to be used *solely* for 'relevant residential' purposes is zero-rated. In practice, this would mean that educational institutions would only be able to secure zero-rating, and thus full VAT recovery on associated costs, if they used the relevant building solely for student accommodation. However, institutions are increasingly using student accommodation as a source of additional income by letting the accommodation facilities during student

11.81 *VAT Business by Business*

vacations, meaning that the accommodation in question would not be used solely for relevant residential purposes. The Concordat previously allowed, by concession, educational institutions to consider that student accommodation would be used solely for relevant residential purposes, notwithstanding the vacation lettings. By concession, this treatment has been preserved by Customs & Excise despite the withdrawal of the Concordat.

Self-supply rules

11.81 Institutions in the education sector generally print their own stationery. Special VAT rules apply for partially exempt businesses which produce their own stationery and, therefore, generally extend to educational institutions (the workings of the special rules are set out in *Tolley's VAT 1998/99, chapter 62*). On the assumption that an institution which produces its own stationery is partially exempt, the self-supply rules would not apply if the value of the stationery which would fall to be treated as self-supplied did not give the institution in question a liability to be VAT-registered if they were the only supplies it made. These rules would also not apply if Customs & Excise could be satisfied that the amount of VAT that would fall to be accounted for (less corresponding input tax) is negligible.

Catering concession

11.82 A concession exists for institutions which use third-party caterers to provide their catering facilities under agency arrangements. Under such arrangements, a caterer will typically incur costs for consumables which are subsequently recharged to the institution concerned. The caterer will also charge the institution for its staff costs, along with a management fee. Normally, a supply of staff would attract VAT, as would a management fee. However, in these circumstances, the recharge of staff costs can, by concession, be ignored for VAT purposes. This is on the basis that, if the institution provided the catering services from its in-house resources, it would not incur a VAT charge on the employment costs. As the caterer acts as agent for the institution, the staff costs are treated as though they are disbursements for the caterer.

Trading companies and VAT grouping

11.83 An educational institution will often use a trading company through which to channel its trading activities. Under current VAT legislation, it is possible to group companies to form, for VAT purposes, a single body under a VAT group registration (although Customs & Excise have recently announced their intentions to review the VAT grouping processes through a consultation document which is to be issued during 1998). Thus, it becomes possible to group together an institution, as a body corporate, and its subsidiary companies to form a VAT group, providing that certain control requirements are fulfilled (see *Tolley's VAT 1998/99, chapter 31*).

11.84 The benefits of VAT grouping are such that transactions which take place between members of a VAT group can be disregarded for VAT purposes. However, additional benefits can be achieved for VAT groups which are partially exempt.

11.85 A trading company will not be an eligible body. To create taxable supplies, certain activities may be channelled through a trading company, including some educational activities, if the recipient of the supplies is able to recover the VAT which it is charged. By structuring its activities effectively, a VAT group may be able to increase its taxable activities and, therefore, increase the level of its recoverable overhead VAT if it uses a partial exemption method based on income.

Chapter 12

Employment Businesses

Introduction

12.1 Employment businesses (often referred to as employment agencies) can either act as principal or agent when providing temporary workers to clients. This is a matter of fact and law and will depend upon the contractual arrangements established between the employment business, the client and temporary worker. However, the contractual position should also be reflected in the administrative structure and day to day mode of operation of the business.

12.2 There has been much debate in the past about whether such businesses should act as principal or agent for VAT purposes. This debate has centred around many highly publicised VAT tribunal cases, such as *Allied Medicare Nursing Services Ltd (5485)*, *BUPA Nursing Services Ltd (10010)* and *Reed Personnel Services Ltd, QB [1995] STC 588* to name a few. Customs & Excise's initial view tended to be, and indeed continues to be, that the employment business has acted as principal, although their success rate has varied. The impact of such decisions has been to highlight the VAT issue, sometimes at the neglect of the legal and other commercial aspects, not least the employment issues.

Principal contracts

12.3 Under a principal contract, the employment business will charge the client for the supply of the temporary workers' services. The contract will outline the terms for the engagement with the client as principal. Temporary workers should be notified that, contractually, they will be engaged to work for a client. Temporary workers will either be employees of the employment business or self employed staff under a contract for services with the agency. The employment business has a contract of service (employer/employee relationship) with the worker or the worker is self employed, in which case he/she will be under a contract for services with the employment business who will in turn supply the services of that individual to the client. The legal and commercial relationship is therefore (i) between the employment business and the client and (ii) between the temporary worker and the employment business. That is, there is no direct relationship between the client and the temporary worker.

12.4 VAT Business by Business

12.4 When acting as principal, an employment business is providing the services of the temporary worker to its client and, where the services provided are subject to VAT, VAT is due on the full value of the total charge to the client, including the amounts paid to temporaries, i.e. salary, and the amounts of Income Tax (PAYE) and NIC paid to third parties.

Agency contracts

12.5 For a full definition of an agent, see *Tolley's VAT 1998/99, para 4.1*. In brief, an agent is someone who acts on behalf of his principal in arranging a supply of goods or services between the principal and his customer. The agent provides his services to the principal in return for a fee. It must be clear from the contracts in place, either written or oral, that the agent is not trading on his own account but is representing the principal.

12.6 Under an agency contract, the employment business is entitled to a fee for introducing a suitable temporary worker to the client. The temporary will thereafter provide his or her services directly to the client. The only service the employment business is providing is the procurement of the temporary worker. There may also be an agreement in place between the employment business and the temporary worker which outlines the basis on which the employment business is acting. Under such an arrangement, the temporary worker is not employed by the employment business.

12.7 An agent will normally not be expected to bear any risks and in this context, where introducing temporary workers, the employment business should not accept any ongoing responsibility for such workers during the assignment. Temporary workers on an assignment should report to a specified employee of the client, will be subject to the client's disciplinary and grievance procedures etc. and should not be under the control of the employment business in any respect. Any risk presented by the temporary worker, or any unsatisfactory performance, will normally be rectified by the client. However, some clients may seek protection from the employment business in the form of indemnities in the event of certain actions or omissions of the temporary worker (see paragraph 12.43 below).

12.8 When acting as agent, the employment business is introducing the temporary worker to the client and the temporary then provides his/her services direct to the client. Any agreement between the employment business and the temporary worker will not oblige the worker to provide services to the client.

12.9 As such, the agency will charge an introductory fee to the client, which will be liable to VAT at the standard rate. Under this arrangement, the client will accept responsibility for paying the temporary worker's salary, expenses and any PAYE, NIC thereon. However, the employment business will normally agree to pay the temporary salaries on behalf of the client and make payments to the statutory authorities as required (see paragraphs 12.35

Employment Businesses **12.14**

and 12.36 below). Under this arrangement, the employment business is effectively providing a payroll service to its client. The fee for this service is included in the introductory/agency fee charged to the client. The client will reimburse the temporary worker's salary, PAYE and NIC to the agency. Such reimbursements will be outside the scope of VAT. This position will be reflected in the invoicing by the employment business.

12.10 If the temporary worker is self-employed and registered for VAT, he/she will be required to charge VAT to the client and the agency will not be able to treat the salaries/PAYE and NIC element charged to the client as disbursements. Instead, VAT will be due on the full value of the charge to the client. Such a situation is usually found in the computer industry.

VAT liability

12.11 For VAT purposes, the difference between acting as principal and acting as agent will be the amount of VAT that will be charged to the employment business's clients. For a fully taxable client, the VAT charged by the employment business will not represent a real cost but will instead be a cashflow cost. Therefore, this issue is more pertinent to exempt or partly exempt businesses such as banks, public sector bodies and charities etc., which cannot recover all of the VAT charged and therefore can benefit from reduced VAT costs. The benefit for these clients is that under an agency arrangement, they will only bear VAT on the agency's introduction fee and costs of operating the payroll (see paragraph 12.22 below) but not on the wages paid to the worker or the PAYE/NIC elements paid to third parties. The benefit to partly exempt clients will be less than that for wholly exempt clients. However, this VAT saving can lead to other tax and employment issues for the client which can in some cases negate the potential VAT savings, e.g. increased employer liability under employment law (see paragraph 12.31 below).

12.12 In the VAT tribunal case of *British Nursing Co-operation Ltd (8816)* trading as British Nursing Association (BNA), BNA had for a number of years acted as agent and accounted for VAT on the margin only and also recovered its input tax in full.

12.13 Customs & Excise ruled that BNA was in fact acting as principal and was making exempt supplies of nursing services which would result in a significant restriction in input tax. The nurses were deemed to be either employees of BNA or self-employed and providing their services to BNA who in turn provided these services to clients.

12.14 The contracts stated that BNA acted as agent for the nurses and carers when introducing them to clients and the case was decided and won by BNA on the basis of the content of the contracts. This is in contrast to the *Reed* case (see paragraph 12.16 below), where the contracts were unclear but

12.15 *VAT Business by Business*

the actions and understanding of the parties pointed conclusively to an agency arrangement.

Nursing agencies

12.15 Employment businesses providing nursing and auxiliary services will have the added complication that the supply of nursing services can either be taxable or exempt from VAT. If such agencies are acting as principal, the services of nursing staff to the client will be exempt from VAT. The provision of auxiliaries and carers may also be exempt if such staff are 'directly supervised' by qualified staff. 'Supervised' does not require physical supervision, but includes situations where the supervision is carried out at a distance. (See *Tolley's VAT 1998/99, paragraph 32.8* for a full definition of 'direct supervision'.) If the services of unsupervised non-qualified staff, e.g. carers, are being provided, such services will be liable to VAT at the standard rate.

When acting as agent, the nursing agency will be procuring the services of the nurse on behalf of the client. The fee for introducing such staff will be standard-rated. The payment to the nurses will be disbursements made on behalf of the client and will be exempt from VAT where such staff are providing exempt services as described above.

12.16 In the VAT tribunal case of *Reed Personnel Services Ltd, QB [1995] STC 588* (trading as Reed Nursing), Reed provided temporary nurses (self-employed) to the NHS, private hospitals and institutions. Reed maintained that it was not supplying nursing services as principal but was, in fact, introducing nurses to its clients and the nurses were providing their services directly to the clients. In effect, therefore, Reed maintained that it was acting as an agent. The issue in question was whether Reed's services were exempt under *VATA 1994, 9 Sch, Group 7* (principal) or whether its services were taxable at the standard rate as the supply of introductory services (agent).

12.17 Most of the nurses in question also worked in the NHS and were on Reed's books in respect of work in their own hospitals, as is common industry practice. The contracts between the parties did not expressly state that Reed was acting as agent, however, Reed maintained that this was implied by the content of the contracts and actions of the parties involved.

12.18 The crucial factor in this case was what had been agreed between the parties, both orally and factually as demonstrated by the evidence presented to the tribunal. The marketing brochures suggested that Reed was introducing nurses to clients, and also the 'conditions of work for the temporary' stated that Reed would find and offer work where available to those nurses on its register. The reference to 'wages' although unusual in a self-employed situation, did not preclude a contract for services from existing, and merely indicated that the nurses would look to Reed in the first instance for their remuneration.

12.19 Although the contracts did not state that Reed was acting as agent, it was implied under the terms recognised by all parties. The tribunal therefore ruled that Reed Nursing was acting as agent, and the High Court upheld this decision.

Time of supply

12.20 The supply of introductory services or services of the temporary worker by the employment business is usually a continuous supply of services (*Value Added Tax Regulations 1995, regulation 90*), that is, a tax point occurs on the earlier of the issue of a tax invoice or receipt of payment (see *Tolley's VAT 1998/99, paragraph 64.26*)). In normal circumstances, clients of the employment business will be invoiced on a weekly basis, having confirmed receipt of the services of the temporary worker by signing a timesheet/work record, and the charges (although in respect of continuous supplies of services), are based on an hourly rate as published in the employment business' terms of business.

Value of supply

12.21 The value of the supply will depend upon whether the employment business is acting as agent or principal, as described above. Where the business is acting as principal, the value of the supply for VAT purposes will be the full amount received from the client, i.e. the temporary worker's salary, PAYE, NIC and the introductory fee commonly referred to as the 'margin'. Where the business is acting as agent, the value of the supply by the employment business will be the margin only, the other elements being disbursements.

12.22 Depending upon the contractual position between the employment business and the client, there will be two methods of invoicing clients as follows:

Example 1—acting as principal

(i) Value of charge to client £1,000.00

(ii) Salaries paid to temporary worker including PAYE and NIC deductions paid to third parties £800.00

(iii) Margin £200.00

(iv) VAT at 17.5% on full charge at (i) above £175.00

12.23 *VAT Business by Business*

Example 2—acting as agent

(i) Value of introductory charge
to client £200.00

(ii) Disbursements paid on behalf of
client including PAYE and NIC
paid to third parties £800.00

(iii) VAT at 17.5% on charge at
(i) above £35.00

However, the invoicing in itself will not determine whether an employment business is acting as principal or agent.

VAT recovery

12.23 Employment businesses are in general fully taxable entities and so are able to recover in full the VAT incurred, subject to the normal conditions. However, if they are acting as principals in providing exempt nursing services, as described at paragraph 12.15 above, they will be making exempt supplies under *VATA 1994, 9 Sch, Group 7, Item 1*. This will lead to the employment business being subject to the partial exemption rules (see *Tolley's VAT 1998/99, chapter 49*) and will lead to a restriction of VAT incurred by the employment business (subject to de minimis limits). Employment businesses acting as agent in providing nursing staff will be fully taxable.

Accounting and records

12.24 There are no special VAT accounting requirements in relation to employment businesses. (See *Tolley's VAT 1998/99, para 57.1* for the normal VAT accounting requirements.) However, the day to day accounting records of the business will play an important part in determining how Customs & Excise will view the status of the business, i.e. whether it is acting as agent or principal. Although the contracts between the parties will normally be the most important documents when determining the correct VAT treatment, the other internal records and documents will be a factor taken into consideration by Customs & Excise in the event of any dispute regarding the VAT treatment of an employment business's supplies. Where acting as both principal and agent, the business's records and accounting systems should clearly differentiate between the two modes of operation.

12.25 The accounting records which are particularly important are the temporary application forms, timesheets, client assignment, booking records and staff procedure manuals. Other documents which could also be relevant are the corporate brochures and invoices where wording may advertise or indicate the mode of operation. References to 'employees', 'staff', 'wages', etc. may influence Customs & Excise when determining the status of the business and should be avoided for agency arrangements. This could mean that separate documents are required and in such circumstances, care should be taken to ensure that branch staff do not use inappropriate documents.

Practical points

12.26 Where an employment business is acting both as principal and agent, the contracts in each case should be fundamentally different, although it may be possible to have a dual purpose contract for both arrangements. Such contracts are likely to have increased risks in relation to the VAT treatment. Also the day to day practices should reflect the different contractual relationship.

12.27 All parties should be aware in advance of the commencement of the assignment of the contractual position for the agency arrangements to work successfully. The terminology in the contracts will not in itself be a deciding factor. This can lead to practical difficulties where temporary workers are regularly notified of assignments by telephone, for example, and do not receive the timesheet/contract until after the assignment has commenced. This could indicate that the temporary worker is not aware of the two different kinds of assignment.

12.28 Most employment agencies which have acted as principal appear to have been reluctant to change their status to agent, primarily as it involves having to reveal profit margins (see paragraph 12.22 above) but most of the larger employment businesses dealing with the financial sector have been unable to avoid doing so, due to market pressure.

12.29 Customs & Excise have been somewhat reluctant in the past to accept that employment businesses can act as agent, as demonstrated by the many protracted tribunal cases on the issue. They remain unconvinced and may initially attempt to argue against such a position where it appears that the contracts have merely been altered to achieve a reduced VAT charge and there is no change in the day to day practices of the business, or in the contractual relationship between the parties. An agency situation will therefore have to demonstrate that it has substance over form.

12.30 In the VAT tribunal case of *Allied Medicare Nursing Services (5485)*, Allied had acted as a principal until 1988 and sought to change its status at that time to 'agent' and only accounted for VAT on the margin. The tribunal found that the nursing staff were in fact employees of Allied and that Allied continued to act as principal in every way other than name. The case centred on the fact that Allied had control over the nurses and could replace or discipline such nurses in the same way as an employer could deal with an employee. The tribunal found the relationship to be one of master/servant,

12.31 VAT Business by Business

and Allied were deemed to be the employer and ultimately to be providing the services of the temporary staff as principal.

Employment law

12.31 The question of whether temporaries are employees or self-employed has been an area of ambiguity for many years and has not been resolved or assisted by the changing VAT treatment. In fact, it could be said that VAT has further complicated the matter. Under an agency arrangement, temporary workers are normally deemed to be self-employed. They cannot be employees of the employment business, but whether they can be employees of the client will depend upon the extent to which the temporary worker is subject to the control of the client. Many temporary workers prefer to be employees to enjoy protected employment rights, e.g. paid holidays, statutory sick pay, maternity leave, etc. and may be willing to take the issue to tribunal.

12.32 Generally, VAT tribunals and industrial tribunals will have different criteria in relation to the meaning of employer/employee when looking at the status of an employment business. For example, industrial tribunals are more likely to find in favour of employees. In the case of *McMeechan v Employment Secretary, CA 1996, [1997] IRLR 353*, a temporary worker of an employment agency was held to be an employee of the agency despite the fact that the contract stated that the worker would provide his services to the agency on a self-employed basis. The important factors which decided the outcome of this case were:

- the agency had control over the allocation of assignments and whether temporaries were suitable for a particular assignment.

- the worker could be dismissed and had a right to appeal under the agency's grievance procedure.

- the agency had control over weekly pay etc.

All of these rights and legislations overruled the label of 'self-employed' as set out in the contract.

12.33 In reality, an employment business is always at risk that the temporary worker will claim to be an 'employee' of the agency. Temporary workers have always been in a position to claim that they are employees of either the employment business or the client and not self-employed and, as a result, are entitled to similar terms and conditions to actual employees. (See the *McMeechan* case as detailed at 12.32 above.) When the employment business is acting as agent, the temporary is providing his services direct to the client and as such, there is a potential increased risk to the client that the temporary will successfully claim to be an employee of the client. It is of course possible that such a worker is not employed at all, however, the status of such workers is often uncertain.

12.34 Another significant industrial tribunal case on this point was the *'Metal Box'* case (*Pertemps Group plc v Nixon*, Employment Appeal Tribunal 1 July 1993 unreported), where it was held by the tribunal that an agency worker who had worked at one client for a ten year period was an employee of the client, and not the agency, for the purposes of claiming a redundancy payment. (This case was not followed, and was implicitly disapproved, in the subsequent *McMeechan* case.) The factors to be taken into consideration when determining whether there is an employer relationship or whether the person is self-employed are as follows: the degree of control, financial risk or loss, ownership of equipment, integration, method of payment, holiday pay and sick pay, mutuality of obligating and the terms used by the parties to the contract.

Pay As You Earn (PAYE) and National Insurance Contributions (NIC)

12.35 Although most temporary workers are deemed to be self-employed, there is a provision in employment law which ensures that PAYE is collected by an employment agency and paid to the relevant statutory authority. *Section 134* of the *Income and Corporation Taxes Act 1988 (ICTA 1988)* taxes, under Schedule E, the remuneration of a worker supplied by or through an agency rendering services to a client where the worker is subject to supervision by the client as to the way in which he carries out his duties.

12.36 Where an employment business acts as agent for VAT purposes, the temporary worker cannot be the employee of the employment business and potentially can become the employee of the client. As such, the employment business is legally not responsible for paying the temporary worker's wages but in practice is still responsible for collecting PAYE under *ICTA 1988, s 134*. The responsibility to pay the temporary worker is passed to the client because the temporary worker effectively comes under the control and management of the client and is no longer the responsibility of the employment business. In practice, however, the employment business will still pay the temporary worker and deduct PAYE and NIC on behalf of the client, and as such will effectively operate a payroll bureau for the client. The role of this bureau will purely be to administer the payment of earnings, PAYE and NIC and does not alter the self-employed status of the temporary worker. Strictly speaking, the employment business should therefore operate a separate payroll for each client and make payments of PAYE and NIC to each client's Collector of Taxes. However, in practice, the Collector of Taxes may, for administrative simplicity, continue to accept payment of PAYE and NIC under the existing principal arrangement for the employment business. This would appear to be a concession given by the Revenue and clearance should be obtained in advance.

12.37 Similarly, under the *Categorisation of Earners Regulations (SI 1978 No 1689)* an agency worker is deemed to be an 'employed earner' where 'earnings are paid by or through the [agency]'. As such, this provision catches

12.38   VAT Business by Business

the payment of wages under a payroll bureau arrangement. The same NIC regulations define the employment business as the secondary contributor (Employer's NIC) and as such the burden for accounting for Employer's NIC is placed on the employment business whether it is acting as principal or as agent providing a payroll service.

12.38   The result of this legislation is that PAYE and National Insurance Contributions are due from payments made to workers as if they were emoluments. The agency is responsible for collecting and remitting such statutory payments as required. This would be the position where an employment business supplies temporaries as principal.

Dual status

12.39   It is possible for an employment business to have dual status for VAT purposes, that is, to act as principal for certain clients and as agent for others. This can, however, in practice lead to operational difficulties and may further complicate the contractual position. This arrangement could lead to a situation where a temporary worker was assigned to a client on an agency basis and to another client on a principal basis and will have payroll implications (see paragraph 12.35 above).

Training

12.40   An employment business must always be able to provide a pool of first-class staff, whether it is acting as agent or principal for VAT purposes. When acting as principal, an employment business has the choice of employing its staff with a view to retaining quality staff from which it can provide suitably trained staff. However, clients will expect such businesses to continue to provide suitably qualified people even when acting as an agent. It should be possible for an employment business to continue to provide training when acting as an agent. The provision of such training will, however, require careful structuring to avoid jeopardising the agency status of an employment business. As mentioned above, employment businesses which act as agent should not exert any continuing control or direction of the workers whom they introduce to clients. The provision of training to clients or temporaries for a charge would be a standard-rated supply by the employment business as principal. However, where the employment business does not charge clients or temporaries for such training, the cost of this training is arguably an overhead cost of the employment business and a necessary part of introducing suitably enhanced and qualified temporaries.

Holiday and sick pay

12.41   Under an agency arrangement, holiday pay and sick pay would normally be the responsibility of the client and therefore payable at the discretion of the client.

Indemnities

12.42 If clients wish to enter into a contract with an employment business on an agency basis, they may seek to reduce any potential risk of being deemed to be the employer of such temporary workers by seeking indemnities or guarantees from the employment business. Such indemnities will generally be so wide that they will expose the employment business to potentially significant liabilities. From a VAT viewpoint, under an agency arrangement, the employment business should not accept any ongoing responsibility or liability for temporary workers introduced to clients. Customs & Excise are likely to view such indemnities as weakening the argument that a business is acting as agent, although in the competitive market in which employment businesses exist, such indemnities may be necessary in order to retain existing clients or indeed to sign up new clients. Such a decision would be a commercial one and may often override the VAT risk.

12.43 Some clients may also seek indemnities to cover the situation where the employment business, having acted as agent, is subsequently found to be acting as principal. The indemnity would cover the increased VAT charge to the client if partly exempt, who would be unable to reclaim part or all of such VAT. The VAT liability of such indemnities would depend upon the contractual agreement. However, such payments to the client are likely to be seen as compensation (i.e. liquidated damages) and as such outside the scope of VAT.

Commercial aspects

12.44 An opportunity exists to reduce the VAT costs to certain clients which are not fully taxable businesses. The ability to offer reduced VAT costs is undoubtedly a valuable sales and marketing tool and, in the current marketplace, it is fast becoming a necessity to retain existing clients in the face of competitors offering this opportunity and also to encourage new clients to sign up. However, if the employment business is to act as agent, it should be borne in mind that some clients may be reluctant to enter into an agency relationship on the basis that their perception is that there is an increased risk of the temporary workers being deemed to be their employees under such arrangements.

12.45 The disadvantages in acting as agent are firstly that the employment business is required to disclose its commission to its clients. This can have the effect of putting additional pressure on the business to keep its margin to a competitive minimum. Secondly, where a dual status is required, the business is required to operate two modes of operation, one for principal and one for agent. In implementation terms, this could lead to errors by branch staff and could lead to an attack by Customs & Excise on the basis that there is in fact no actual difference between principal and agency arrangements.

12.46 *VAT Business by Business*

12.46 There is also the cost of restructuring to consider. It is normally necessary to draft new contracts and to amend internal procedures and documentation. There is always the risk of attack from Customs & Excise and even where advance clearance is obtained, a close inspection of accounting records and day to day procedures can occur at future VAT inspections.

Conclusion

12.47 The issue of capacity of an employment business (i.e. whether it is acting as principal or agent) will be determined by the conduct and representations made by the employment business to the client and to the worker. In short, it will be dependent upon the facts and circumstances and reality will be more important than the wording contained in such contracts.

12.48 In order for an employment business to act as agent for VAT purposes, the following issues should be considered:

(i) substance over form

(ii) clear contracts

(iii) clearance from Customs & Excise

(iv) the client must accept responsibility for the worker under employment law and PAYE regulations.

Chapter 13

Farming and agriculture

Introduction

Background

13.1 Farming is one of the largest and most widespread industries in the UK. However, over recent years the sector has been in decline, relying to a considerable degree on subsidy and price support. The European Union ('EU') Common Agricultural Policy has had a major impact on the way the industry operates. Its purpose is to create stability for the agricultural sector but, in reality, it has had the reverse effect.

The situation has led to significant changes in the way land is farmed and managed and also in the range of activities carried out by farmers, growers and landowners. As far as VAT is concerned, farming activities and sales of agricultural products have traditionally generated income which is predominantly zero-rated. Having registered for VAT, farm businesses are usually in a VAT repayment position due to the high proportion of zero-rated income. It is usual for farmers and growers to submit VAT returns on a monthly basis to obtain a cashflow benefit from the repayment situation. However, many farmers and landlords have been obliged to increase the range of their activities, both agricultural and non-agricultural, to compensate for loss of profitability as regards the main farming income.

Due to this general trend towards diversification, farmers and landowners are exposed to a much wider range of VAT issues nowadays than they are likely to have been historically. The proportion that standard-rated income bears to total income is gradually increasing for many agricultural businesses so that, firstly, the chance of committing VAT errors increases. Secondly, more and more farmers and growers may find that the monthly VAT repayment position is edging towards monthly VAT payments. Given that the administrative demands will also increase as a result of diversification, the rendering of VAT returns on a quarterly basis may be a more suitable option.

The way in which agricultural land is farmed and managed has also been subject to change, with increasing diversity of arrangements for occupying farmland. The exploitation and letting of land for purposes other than farming has also increased. At the same time, the VAT rules governing land-related transactions have grown in complexity, despite moves by Customs & Excise

13.2 VAT Business by Business

towards simplification. Consequently, farmers and landowners are dealing with more and more complex VAT problems and are increasingly susceptible to making VAT accounting mistakes.

Contract farming and share farming

13.2 Contract farming and share farming arrangements are now widely practised within the farming sector. Both are essentially means of dividing the rising costs of farming. In the past, share farming arrangements were popular with landowners because they did not have to enter into a tenancy agreement with the contractor, thus avoiding the problem of security of tenure that existed at that time. By dint of changes to the agricultural land law, which took effect from 1 September 1995, farmers now have much greater flexibility in terms of the length of tenure that they wish to grant. Consequently, share farming arrangements have lost a vital aspect of their appeal. Contract farming is now the more popular option, as regards splitting and sharing farming costs. The VAT implications of both types of arrangement are considered below.

Contract farming

13.3 A standard contract farming arrangement is structured such that a farmer uses a contractor to farm certain land on his behalf and in accordance with his instructions. The contractor might be another local farmer or a regional or national farming company. Direct inputs and machinery are generally provided by the contractor, together with the labour. Contract farming arrangements resemble those of share farming in that the agreement must avoid the granting of a tenancy or creating a partnership between the two individuals, as both of these will give rise to very different VAT, as well as other tax, implications.

As with share farming agreements, the landowner and the contractor are treated as separate businesses for VAT accounting purposes. The income arising from the venture is earned by the farmer and he should account for VAT on sales of produce, if applicable, under his own VAT registration number. The contractor accounts for VAT on the management fee that he receives from the landowner. Conversely, VAT incurred on the fee by the farmer forms part of his recoverable VAT on purchases. A commission may also be paid by the farmer to the contractor as an incentive; again, this will be subject to VAT at the standard rate. VAT on expenditure incurred by the contractor in carrying out the husbandry services is recoverable under his own VAT registration. Costs which, under the terms of the agreement, are to be borne by the farmer should be recharged by the contractor to the farmer at the appropriate VAT rate.

Share farming

13.4 The calculation of the share of profits can be complex but, under a typical share-farming agreement, a landowner provides the land and the cost of materials, i.e. seeds, fertilisers, sprays, etc., whilst the other party provides the requisite labour, machinery and equipment. All income deriving from the venture is then shared between the two parties on an agreed proportional basis. A share-farming contract is specifically structured so that the landowner does not grant a right over the shared land to the other party. As long as the landowner and contractor are careful to ensure that the agreement cannot be construed as one of a partnership, each party accounts for its own activities under its own VAT registration.

Thus, each party accounts for VAT, if applicable, on his portion of the income and reclaims VAT on his costs associated with the venture. If Customs were to take the view that a partnership arrangement had been created, the parties would be required to register for VAT as a partnership with joint liability for each other's debts.

Landfill tax

13.5 Landfill tax, a new, indirect form of taxation, was first made public in the 1994 Budget. In essence, it taxes disposals of most types of waste to landfill. The detailed provisions are contained in *FA 1996*. The new tax became effective from 1 October 1996 and may impact on farmers and landowners to the extent that they accept disposals of waste on their land. If this is the case, a farmer must register with Customs for landfill tax.

Different rates of tax apply according the nature of the waste:

- inactive / inert waste is taxed at a lower rate of £2 per tonne;

- all other eligible waste is taxed at a rate of £7 per tonne.

A number of disposals are exempt from landfill tax, one of which is particularly relevant to rural landowners; materials arising naturally from mining or quarrying activities are exempt provided that these have not been subject to separate processes and their chemical characteristics are intact.

Landfill tax is unlikely to have a direct effect on many farmers. However, it will affect a larger number of landowners indirectly, where they lease land to operators of landfill sites. The VAT treatment of this type of letting is exempt unless the landowner has opted to tax the land in question. Landowners seeking further guidance on the operation of landfill tax should refer to the information notes published by Customs and available from their local Business Advice Centre.

13.6 VAT Business by Business

VAT liability

Principal activities

Zero-rated income

13.6 The principal activities of farmers engaged in livestock, arable, dairy or mixed farming will give rise to zero-rated income. Most supplies of food or animal feed by farmers will fall within one of the following reliefs:

(1) Food of a kind used for human consumption.

(2) Animal feeding stuffs.

(3) Seeds or other means of propagation of plants.

(4) Live animals of a kind generally used as, or yielding or producing, food for human consumption.

Notes

(1) 'food' includes drink.

(2) 'animal' includes bird, fish, crustacean and mollusc.

[*VATA 1994, 8 Sch, Group 1*].

Thus, the large majority of agricultural produce is zero-rated. Inevitably, there are exceptions to the basic rule. One of the main exceptions for farmers and growers to note is that the sale of pet food is standard-rated. [*VATA 1994, 8 Sch, Group 1, Excepted Item 6*].

Another important factor which affects whether a product may be zero-rated is the way in which it is *held out for sale*. Care should be exercised in the way in which food for working dogs is held out for sale; meat and other food for guard dogs or greyhounds is zero-rated but Customs may challenge this treatment if the product is held out for sale in the same way as pet food. Sales of hay and straw for animal feed, for example, will be zero-rated but if these products are held out for sale as bedding straw or as pet food the supply becomes standard-rated. Similarly, sales of peat will ordinarily be zero-rated but, if held out for sale as fuel, the supply is subject to VAT at the lower rate. The use to which the product is ultimately put is immaterial. The VAT treatment will be dependent on the way in which the seller holds out the product for sale. For these purposes, regard will be had to the packaging, labelling, advertising and promotional signs and literature and instructional literature (if any) relating to the product.

Apart from basic supplies of agricultural and farming produce, the other main source of zero-rated income, pertinent to farmers and landowners, may be from any supplies of produce and livestock to customers outside the UK.

Farming and agriculture **13.8**

Farmers involved in property development such as the construction and sale of a newly constructed dwelling, or of a building converted to a dwelling, or of a substantially reconstructed protected building [*VATA 1994, 8 Sch, Group 5* and *VATA 1994, 8 Sch, Group 6*] will also derive zero-rated income from such activities. For further detail see paragraphs 13.20 *et seq.* below. A summary of the various kinds of zero-rated supplies generally made by farmers is provided, for ease of reference, in the Appendix to this chapter.

Exempt income

13.7 The legislation covering exemption of supplies of land [*VATA 1994, 9 Sch, Group 1*] is likely to affect many agricultural landowners in so far as they are engaged in the sale or letting of agricultural land and properties. Zero-rated and exempt transactions are similar in that VAT is not chargeable on either of these types of income. However, there is a fundamental difference between the two categories. VAT incurred on costs which are referable to zero-rated activities is reclaimable, but VAT incurred on expenditure related to the earning of exempt income is irrecoverable. The legislation relating to both the zero-rating and the exemption of land and property supplies is not straightforward and such transactions often require careful consideration of the precise nature of the transaction to identify the correct VAT coding. Insurance premiums payable by farmers and landowners are commonly coded incorrectly for VAT; these will generally be exempt. A list of the main sources of exempt income likely to be earned within the agricultural sector is set out in the Appendix to this chapter.

Standard-rated income

13.8 Agricultural supplies not falling within the legislation for either zero-rating or exemption will fall to be standard-rated. The main sources of standard-rated income associated with the farming sector are the sale of horticultural flowers and plants, sales of wool and charges for the provision of farm contracting services such as combine harvesting, threshing, sowing and planting. As mentioned above, exceptions to the main items falling within the zero-rated category will attract VAT and this applies to canned, packaged or prepared pet food including wild bird food and biscuits and meal for cats and dogs. Standard-rating would not apply, however, to loose food which is not specifically held out for sale as pet food. (See the case of *B Beresford (9673)*). Biscuits and meal for cats and dogs are standard-rated, regardless of whether they are packaged or prepared. The other notable exception relevant to farmers and growers is the sale of alcoholic beverages; these are always standard-rated. The range of other kinds of standard-rated goods and services provided by farmers and agricultural landowners is diverse. Examples of the most common types of standard-rated farming income are given in the Appendix to this chapter.

13.9 VAT Business by Business

Outside the scope of VAT

13.9 The fourth category of VAT coding, which will impact on farmers and landowners as much in relation to their purchases as to their sales, is supplies which fall outside the scope of the VAT law. On the income side, the most common form of outside the scope receipts will comprise government-funded grants and subsidies. As far as expenses are concerned, it is not uncommon for certain types of expenditure which are outside the scope of VAT, such as gun licences and MOT certificates for example, to be inadvertently miscoded as VATable expenses, leading to overclaims of VAT. A list of supplies which fall outside the scope of VAT pertaining to farmers and rural landowners is included in the Appendix to this chapter.

Ancillary activities

13.10 Pressure on agricultural margins has given many farm businesses difficulty in maintaining a satisfactory level of profitability. As a result, the farming sector has had to look increasingly to diversification, both on an agricultural and on a non-agricultural basis. Diversified activities enable farmers and landowners to supplement traditional farming income and to maximise the income earning capacity of their land and buildings.

It is important that farmers pay due consideration to the VAT treatment of any supplementary activities in which they engage. The VAT rules relating to these diverse activities will be less familiar to them and in certain circumstances, particularly as regards non-agricultural use of land and buildings, the VAT position may be quite intricate.

Holiday accommodation

13.11 Nowadays, a large proportion of farmers and landowners supplement their main income by offering holiday accommodation in some form or another. The provision of bed and breakfast accommodation to holiday-makers, visitors and other travellers is subject to VAT at the standard rate [*VATA 1994, 9 Sch, Group 1, Item 1(d)*]. If a charge is made solely for sleeping accommodation, the supply will still be standard-rated. This will cover charges for temporary accommodation in hostels and basic bunk accommodation. Similarly, standard-rating will apply to income received in respect of furnished holiday lets, including holiday flats and cottages, chalets and even beach huts, following the case of *Poole Borough Council, [1992] VATTR 88 (7180)*. [*VATA 1994, 9 Sch, Group 1, Item 1(e)*]. Any deposit received in relation to a supply of holiday accommodation is treated as a part payment. VAT is due upon receipt of such a payment.

It is not uncommon for cottages used as holiday accommodation during the season to be let off-season by rural landowners on a short term tenancy basis. Where this is the case, the let may be treated as one of residential accommodation so that rental charges would be exempt from VAT. However,

Farming and agriculture **13.15**

Customs may challenge the recovery of VAT incurred on maintenance costs where properties are the subject of taxable holiday lets and winter rentals producing exempt income. The VAT treatment of holiday accommodation, including time share schemes, is dealt with in greater detail in Chapter 15 below.

Caravan and camping facilities

13.12 In areas popular with holidaymakers, land with minimal agricultural potential may be used by farmers to provide caravan and camping facilities. Charges for holiday accommodation in permanently sited caravans are standard-rated, as are charges for caravan pitches and associated facilities such as fuel and power and washing facilities [*VATA 1994, 9 Sch, Group 1, Item 1(f)*]. Equally, income for the provision of tent pitches or camping facilities is subject to VAT at the standard rate. Charges for related facilities carry the same VAT liability. Charges for pitches for residential caravans which are used as a permanent residence are exempt.

Parking facilities

13.13 Agricultural landowners may allocate plots of land to provide either permanent car parking facilities for nearby attractions or to provide additional parking facilities for ad hoc events such as shows or sporting events. VAT is due on all such car parking charges at the standard rate [*VATA 1994, 9 Sch, Group 1, Item 1(h)*]. Land which is usually used as a car park is sometimes let for other purposes such as a venue for a daily market, a fete, or, increasingly, for car boot sales. In these circumstances, the supply of the land to the organiser of the event will be exempt.

Other land uses

13.14 The grant of a licence by a farmer or landowner to a contractor over a specified area of land, for the purpose of providing tipping facilities or for the extraction of mineral deposits for example, is exempt from VAT, subject to the election to waive exemption (also known as the 'option to tax'). If a farmer allocates land to the provision of tipping facilities for the general public, tipping charges will give rise to standard-rated income.

Farm shops and direct sales

13.15 Farm shops and direct sales of farm produce to the public are one of the most common methods adopted by farmers to supplement the core farming income. The majority of agricultural produce sold in farm shops or direct to the public, either at the farm or on a pick-your-own basis, is likely to be zero-rated supplies of food. Not all supplies of food are eligible for zero-rating, and VAT will be due on any farm shop takings in respect of sales of confectionery, soft drinks, alcoholic drinks, crisps, nuts, savoury snacks,

13.16 VAT Business by Business

chocolate biscuits, ice creams, ice lollies and similar frozen products [*VATA 1994, 8 Sch, Group 1, Items 1–5*]. Standard-rated takings from sales of these products will need to be separately identified from the zero-rated takings at point of sale and VAT accounted for accordingly. It may be appropriate to use one of the VAT retail schemes to calculate the VAT due on farm shop retail sales. A summary of the VAT retail schemes available and their operation is provided in Chapter 23 below.

Sales of any non-food products within farm shops are likely to be standard-rated. The following supplies are typically standard-rated; flowers, shrubs, plants, bulbs, flower seedlings, pet food supplies, bedding straw, turf, topsoil, manure, pre-germinated grass seed, ornamental fish and timber. However, not all non-food products will be standard-rated. Sales of logs and firewood, as well as peat and charcoal held out for sale as domestic fuel, are subject to VAT at the reduced rate of 5%. Further guidance on the VAT treatment of products typically supplied by farmers direct to the public is provided in the Appendix to this chapter.

Crafts and craft fairs

13.16 Rural crafts and associated sales constitute another type of ancillary business that has grown in popularity in recent years. Typical craft sales such as pottery, woodwork, metalwork and wickerwork will be standard-rated.

As far as craft fairs are concerned, whilst sales of craft products will generally be standard-rated, the supply of the actual site can give rise to VAT liability problems. In general terms, the supply of the craft fair site by the farmer is seen as the granting of a licence to occupy land and is exempt from VAT, subject to the option to tax. However, if the event is organised in such a way that individual stall holders are granted non-exclusive use of part of a site by a farmer, with or without use of facilities, charges to stall-holders will be standard-rated. In cases of doubt, the VAT liability treatment will normally hinge on whether or not exclusive occupation rights are granted by the landowner. If they are, exemption will apply (unless the option to tax is in force). If they are not, charges will be subject to VAT at the standard rate.

Farm tours

13.17 The provision of farm tours is an attraction which proliferates nowadays, providing a useful source of subsidiary income. Farm trips and tours for educational and recreational purposes are particularly popular with schools and families where farms are situated within access of urban areas. Admission charges are standard-rated, as are any additional charges made for tractor rides, animal rides and supplies of catering. Bags of animal feed, provided for an additional charge, are zero-rated. If a single charge is levied for admission to the farm which includes a supply of animal feed, the whole amount charged will be subject to VAT.

Ancillary farming services

13.18 The range of ancillary services provided by farmers to complement the main husbandry income is continually diversifying. Income from the provision of ancillary services will generally be standard-rated, be it in respect of traditional agricultural contracting services such as cultivating and harvesting, or in respect of evolving services such as food and timber processing, purification or seed cleaning services.

Both machinery hire and the carrying out of repairs to agricultural equipment generate standard-rated income. If machinery is hired out free of charge, no VAT is due. The exclusive hiring of plant and machinery which is fixed to the land, such as a grain dryer, will be subject to the rules governing supplies of land. Lease charges will thus be exempt, subject to the option to tax. Short-term hire of the grain drying facilities will be a standard-rated supply. In some circumstances animals may be hired, for insemination services for example, by one farming enterprise from another. The VAT treatment of animal hire follows the liability of the animal(s) on loan. Thus, the hire of a stallion is a standard-rated supply but the hire of a herd of cows is zero-rated.

Horse breeding and racing

13.19 Horse breeding activities generate two principal types of income; the loan of a horse for breeding purposes and the sale of horses. Both types of activity are standard-rated.

As far as racing activities are concerned, a special VAT registration scheme exists for racehorse owners. Customs are currently reviewing the operation of this scheme and any changes to it are likely to be implemented during 1997. VAT issues affecting the bloodstock industry are dealt with in greater depth in Chapter 5 above.

Agricultural land and property

13.20 The rules governing the VAT treatment of property transactions have been subject to considerable change and amendment during the last seven years. Some of the legislative changes have resulted in simplification, while others have been introduced to counteract VAT avoidance. Despite the simplifications, the VAT rules in this area can still be most complex. This can lead to unsuspected difficulties for the unwary. Landowners about to engage in any land or property transaction will need to pay careful attention to the VAT consequences. Failure to do so could result in a substantial VAT cost, in the form of irrecoverable VAT or a large VAT error attracting a penalty and additional interest charges. In circumstances such as these, it is prudent to seek expert advice before the transaction takes place.

13.21 VAT Business by Business

The VAT treatment of issues specific to agricultural landowners is examined below. Further guidance on the way in which VAT impacts upon property owners and developers in general is set out in Chapter 21 below.

Option to tax agricultural holdings

13.21 An important change to the legislation governing the option to tax agricultural holdings was introduced with effect from 1 March 1995. Before then, the option to tax could not be applied to specified parcels of land because the option applied to all adjoining land in the same ownership. This rule proved impractical and very few landowners took advantage of it. From 1 March 1995 it became possible to opt to tax specific pieces of agricultural land. As a result, the option to tax agricultural holdings has become more attractive to farmers and other rural landowners. Written notification of the option must be made to Customs, together with a plan or map delineating the opted area. As a final point, it should be noted it is Customs' policy not to permit landowners to opt over minor lets such as individual pylons or wayleaves.

A further concession introduced by Customs at the same time allows for a three month 'cooling-off' period within which the option can be revoked. However, this is only on condition that no VAT has been charged or claimed in that three month period, which limits the scope of the concession considerably. Otherwise, an option is binding for a period of 20 years.

The main benefit of opting to tax agricultural holdings is that it enables VAT incurred on associated costs to be recovered. An agricultural landlord or estate owner who opts to tax tenanted farm land is thus entitled to recover VAT incurred by him on any day to day repairs or improvements carried out in respect of that land. Consequently, his overall VAT costs will decrease.

Furthermore, by opting to tax let farms and any other leases of agricultural land or commercial buildings, it may be possible to avoid the burden of partial exemption. Opting to tax will however mean increased administrative demands; VAT charges on rents and sales will need to be invoiced and accounted for, and recoverable VAT on purchases referable to opted holdings will also need to be recorded and reclaimed.

As regards one-off disposals of land and buildings, the question of whether to exercise the option to tax must be considered with particular care. One way in which a number of landowners have sought to maximise output from land with minimal farming potential is to develop the land, typically to provide sporting or recreational facilities such as a golf course. If the development is carried out by the landowner himself, no VAT recovery difficulties will arise as long as the recreational activity gives rise to taxable income. More usually, however, the landowner will let the land to a developer. If the land is let unopted, VAT incurred on the planning costs and other professional fees

Farming and agriculture **13.24**

associated with the disposal of the land will be irrecoverable. By opting to tax, this VAT cost, which can often be quite substantial, can be eliminated.

However, the long-term benefits may be less clear-cut. Future marketability of the holding may be diminished in the event that the land is to be re-let or disposed of outright at some point in the future. Some tenants will be unable to recover the vast majority of the VAT they incur on their expenditure, health and charitable organisations or providers of education for example, and may be unwilling to buy or lease land or property that is opted. On balance, however, the likelihood is that most future prospective tenants of agricultural holdings will engage in fully taxable activities so that any VAT they incur on rental charges or on acquisition will be reclaimable.

Gifts of land

13.22 The option to tax may have unforeseen consequences as regards gifts of land or other transfers of property without consideration. The gifting of land from one member of a family to another, or into a separate trust, commonly occurs either following the retirement of the head of the estate or in conjunction with inheritance tax planning. Whatever the reason for the gift, where the gifted farmland or buildings have been opted by the donor, a VAT liability will be triggered [*VATA 1994, 4 Sch 5(1)*]. If the land or buildings are transferred outright, VAT is due from the donor on their current market value [*VATA 1994, 6 Sch 6(2)*]. If the recipient of the gifted land uses it for taxable farming purposes, the VAT charged on the gift will be recoverable. The donor should not raise a VAT invoice in respect of a gift transaction, which is subject to the option to tax, as it is a supply for no consideration. In these circumstances, Customs will permit the VAT due to be accounted for by means of a VAT certificate instead. In this way, the recipient of the gift is able to reclaim the VAT incurred on the gifted land, provided the land is to be used for business purposes. The document should state 'Tax certificate. No payment is necessary for these goods. Output tax has been accounted for on the supply'. (Customs' Press Notice 889, 1 March 1984).

Transfer of a going concern

13.23 Agricultural land and property may be transferred as part of a business from one party to another. As long as certain conditions are fulfilled, the transfer would not be a taxable transaction and no VAT would be due.

Conversions

13.24 Prior to 22 July 1994, the disposal of a disused farm building which had been converted into a dwelling was an exempt supply. Consequently, the VAT incurred by the farmer on the costs of conversion was suffered as a cost. The conversion of barns, cowsheds, stables and other redundant farm buildings, which, in broader terms, is encouraged amongst landowners as a

13.25 VAT Business by Business

means of maximising output from their capital assets, was thus discouraged from a VAT viewpoint.

Changes to the VAT rules governing non-residential conversions were implemented with effect from 1 March 1995 (but were available from 22 July 1994 by extra-statutory concession). Thus, the granting of a major interest in a commercial farm building converted into a dwelling is now a zero-rated supply. A major interest in a property equates to the sale of the freehold of the property or the grant of a lease for a term exceeding 21 years. This has certainly made barn conversions a more attractive proposition for rural landowners. However, zero-rating will only be applicable where there are no restrictions put upon the use of the dwelling as a main residence throughout the year. Otherwise, the sale will be exempt from VAT. If a disused farm building is converted into a dwelling and then let, the VAT incurred by the farmer on the conversion costs will normally be an irrecoverable VAT cost, unless the partial exemption de minimis rules apply. Alternatively, an attractive option might be for a neglected farm building to be converted and supplied as a furnished holiday let. In this way, VAT incurred on the conversion costs as well as any associated fees would be fully recoverable.

The current trend towards conversion of redundant farm buildings also extends to conversions for non-residential use such as office accommodation or workshops. Recoverability of the VAT on associated expenditure will be dependent upon whether or not the owner has opted to tax the converted building. The easing of the rules governing the scope of the option, as regards agricultural land and buildings, has provided landowners with greater flexibility when dealing with non-residential conversions and now places them on a more competitive footing with other commercial property developers.

Protected buildings

13.25 Special rules apply to protected buildings, or listed buildings as they are more commonly termed, but only in so far as the listed building is used for residential or charitable non-business purposes. Listed buildings used for commercial purposes are subject to the normal VAT rules governing land and property transactions. A listed building is one which is covered by the *Planning (Listed Building and Conservation Areas) Act 1990* if it is situated in England or Wales, or by the *Planning (Listed Building and Conservation Areas)(Scotland) Act 1997* if located in Scotland, or by the *Planning (Northern Ireland) Order 1991* if located in Northern Ireland.

Where a separate building is reconstructed to create a garage, simultaneous to the reconstruction of the main house, the garage will also have the same status as the protected building to which it belongs.

Farming and agriculture **13.27**

Approved alterations

13.26 The main way in which the VAT treatment of listed buildings (used as dwellings) differs from other buildings is that any approved alterations carried out to such a building are zero-rated [*VATA 1994, 8 Sch, Group 6, Item 2; SI 1995 No 283*]. Alterations are approved if they are required to, and have received, listed building consent. Professional fees incurred in relation to approved alterations, architects and surveyors fees for example, do not qualify for zero-rating. However, building materials used by a builder to carry out approved alterations are also eligible for zero-rating [*VATA 1994, 8 Sch, Group 6, Item 3*]. Building materials are defined as 'goods of a description ordinarily incorporated by builders in a building of that description (or its site)' [*VATA 1994, 8 Sch, Group 5, Item 4, Note 22*].

Approved alterations are also defined in the legislation to specifically exclude any works of repair or maintenance or any incidental alteration resulting from repair or maintenance work [*VATA 1994, 8 Sch, Group 6, Note 6*]. Despite this definition in the VAT law, the distinction between what constitutes an approved alteration as opposed to a work of repair, or maintenance, has been rather a grey area. This distinction has been the subject of innumerable VAT tribunal cases but, as some of the decisions given by the chairmen have been contradictory, a lack of clarity has remained. As a general rule, approved alteration work should result in a visible degree of transformation to the structural fabric of the building. Customs have recently published further guidance on this matter in VAT Notice 708: Property and Construction. With effect from March 1995, Customs now require alterations to be substantial and not to be an incidental result of repair work. If the alteration is incidental to the repairs, it will not qualify for zero-rating. In cases of doubt, it would be prudent to seek professional advice.

Reconstructions

13.27 The second special feature as regards protected buildings (i.e. residential / charitable listed buildings) relates to reconstruction works. The substantial reconstruction of a protected building is zero-rated [*VATA 1994, 8 Sch, Group 6, Item 1*]. It should be noted that zero-rating applies to the freehold sale of the reconstructed building or the first premium or rent payment payable under a long lease. Subsequent payments are exempt from VAT. A protected building is deemed to be substantially reconstructed where either of the following conditions are fulfilled:

(a) A minimum of 60% of the cost of the reconstruction works relates to zero-rated approved alterations and/or building materials, or;

(b) the finished building incorporates no more of the original building (i.e. just prior to reconstruction begins) than the external walls and any other external feature of architectural or historic interest. [*VATA 1994, 8 Sch Group 6, Note 4*].

13.28 VAT Business by Business

The zero-rating of substantial reconstructions of protected buildings used to be a valuable means of obtaining favourable VAT treatment. Since 1 March 1995, when zero-rating became available for conversions of non-residential buildings to create dwellings, the importance and usefulness of this item has decreased.

Sporting rights

13.28 The VAT consequences of providing fishing or gaming rights hinges on whether or not there is also an associated supply of land. The legislation governing sporting rights has twice been amended [*VATA 1994, 9 Sch, Group 1, Item 1(c); Note 8*]. The resulting rules are consequently somewhat convoluted. The main points to highlight are as follows:

(a) The supply of fishing or gaming rights without land is standard-rated;

(b) The supply of fishing or gaming rights with freehold land is exempt unless the land is subject to the option to tax;

(c) The supply of sporting rights in conjunction with a lease is standard-rated if the land is subject to the option to tax;

(d) Where fishing or gaming rights are supplied together with an unopted lease and the value of those rights exceeds 10% of the whole supply, an apportionment must be made between the standard-rated sporting rights and the exempt lease;

(e) The provision of sporting rights in conjunction with a lease is exempt if the land is not subject to the option to tax and the value attributable to the sporting rights is less than 10% of the total rental value.

Shooting activities

13.29 Shooting rights supplied by way of business give rise to standard-rated income, regardless of the status of the customer. Standard-rating applies to the freehold sale of the shooting rights as well as to the letting of land by a landowner over which he has the rights to shoot.

It is important, as far as shooting activities are concerned, to distinguish between activities which are purely business and those that are marginal, otherwise an unexpected VAT cost could arise. Where an estate owner or farmer organises shooting in hand for recreational purposes, contributions received from participants towards the cost of running the shoot will not give rise to a VAT liability. Similarly, contributions by members of a syndicate, set up so that costs can be pooled and shared, will be outside the scope of VAT, provided the shoots are basically for enjoyment and without a business motive. Clearly, where shooting syndicates and shooting in hand is pursued for recreational purposes, it will not be possible to recover any VAT incurred on guns, cartridges and other expenses associated with the running of the shoot.

In the notable case of *C& E Commrs v Lord Fisher, QB [1981] STC 238*, it was held that pheasant shoots organised by the appellant did not amount to the carrying on of a business, despite the fact that detailed accounts were maintained, as part of the estate records, and that the shoots were organised in a very professional manner. However, in the case of *JO Williams (14240)* a shooting syndicate was held to be part of a farmer's business activities. Whilst it is acceptable to keep detailed records of shoot incomings and expenses, it is vital to exclude these transactions from the profit and loss account of the main estate or farm business.

To determine whether or not a shoot is carried out privately, Customs will want to ensure that the following criteria are adhered to:

(a) Participants consist of friends and family only;

(b) The shoot is not advertised or publicised in any way;

(c) The shoot accounts should run at an annual loss at least equivalent to the yearly contribution of one of the participants;

(d) The loss must be funded by the farmer or landowner personally, rather than by the farm business.

Shooting activities that are carried out for recreational purposes but also with a profit motive are standard-rated. VAT incurred on related expenditure can be offset against the VAT charged on shoot fees and recovered in full.

Grazing rights and animal keep

13.30 The VAT treatment of grazing rights is a supply of grasskeep as opposed to a supply of land. The granting of grazing rights in respect of a specific area of land is therefore zero-rated, as a supply of animal feed. Zero-rating is still applicable where a small amount of care is provided by a farmer on behalf of the animals' owner but this should not amount to any more than a daily check on them. If grazing rights are supplied together with care of the animals, the whole supply will be seen as a supply of animal keep and standard-rated. Customs consider 'care' to include turning the animals out to graze, feeding, mucking out, spreading straw, exercising and taking responsibility for the animals welfare on behalf of the owner.

Customs will examine grazing arrangements carefully to ensure that they fulfil the necessary criteria. In the case of *JA King, [1980] VATTR 60 (933)*, a farmer owned two fields in which he grazed his own animals as well as those of others on an ad hoc basis. No element of animal care was provided. It was held that the services were not eligible for exemption as they did not amount to a licence to occupy land. Nor could the supply be seen as one of zero-rated grazing rights, as the animals were not allocated a specific plot of grazing land. Consequently, the supply was held to be standard-rated. Customs may also challenge the VAT treatment of grazing agreements between farmers, where the owner of the livestock does not live within easy access of where

13.31 VAT Business by Business

the animals graze. In these circumstances, they will consider the service to be one of agistment and subject to VAT at the standard rate.

Livery services

13.31 The supply of animal accommodation such as stables and stalls, including a basic amount of bedding, is exempt from VAT, with the option to tax available. As with grazing rights, this VAT treatment is dependent upon exclusivity of use of the allotted area. Where animal feed and/or grazing provisions are also supplied in return for payment, and these can be identified and quantified, a separate zero-rated charge can be made. Similarly, bedding which does not form an inherent part of the stabling arrangement should be charged at the standard rate. Again, however, where any care of the animals is also provided, the whole supply of stabling, feeding and care is treated as standard-rated.

If the animals' owner does not have exclusive use of the stable or part of it, the accommodation charges will be standard-rated. The provision of animal feed or grasskeep by the owner under these circumstances cannot be separately itemised and the whole supply is subject to VAT at the standard rate.

Milk quota

13.32 Milk quotas are akin to grazing rights in that they are normally attached to land. As a result, there are a number of different ways in which milk quota transactions can be structured. Historically, milk quota could not be transferred without being attached to a supply of land. The regulations governing transfers of milk quota have been amended so that it is now possible, in certain circumstances, to supply milk quota without land, subject to approval from the Intervention Board. This type of structure is particularly prevalent amongst retiring farmers as it enables them to derive a form of pension income from the quota without the need to dispose of their interest in the underlying land.

Given that there is a variety of different ways in which milk quota transactions can be structured, the VAT treatment is not always straightforward. A summary of the more usual types of milk quota transactions is set out below:

(a) A sale of land together with milk quota under a single agreement is exempt, subject to the option to tax. The supply is exempt (but subject to the option to tax) irrespective of whether the values of the land and quota are separately quantified and invoiced.

(b) A lease of land together with milk quota under a single agreement is exempt, subject to the option to tax. The supply is exempt (but subject

Farming and agriculture **13.34**

to the option to tax) regardless of whether the land and milk quota values are separately identified and shown on the invoice.

(c) A sale of milk quota without land is standard-rated.

(d) Leasing of milk quota without a supply of land is standard-rated.

(e) Sale of milk quota together with the provision of grazing rights is treated as two separate supplies. The supply of the grazing is zero-rated and the supply of the milk quota is standard-rated.

(f) Statutory compensation where milk quota is stopped or suspended temporarily is treated as outside the scope of VAT.

(g) A landlord's statutory compensation to a tenant following the serving of a notice to quit, in respect of the tenant's interest in milk quota, is also outside the scope of VAT.

(h) Non-statutory compensation relating to a tenant's surrender of his interest in land, where milk quota is also attached to that land, is exempt unless the option to tax has been invoked by the tenant. If this is the case, it is standard-rated. The VAT treatment remains the same regardless of whether the milk quota is separately identified and quantified.

Care needs to be exercised with regard to tax points and timing when dealing with a supply of quota that requires Intervention Board approval. This type of transaction is normally handled by an intermediary stakeholder who collects payment on behalf of the vendor. It should be noted that the purchaser is not entitled to recover VAT incurred on the milk quota purchase, despite having handed over funds to the agent, until approval has been granted by the Intervention Board.

The trading of sheep quota, i.e. ewe premium quota, differs from that of milk quota in that the sheep quota is not treated as if it is attached to land. Consequently, both the sale and leasing of sheep quota are standard-rated.

Landlords and tenants

13.33 In general terms, supplies of land and property by landlords to tenants are exempt from VAT but with the option to tax. The VAT consequences of a number of transactions, relevant to agricultural landowners and their tenants, are worthy of particular scrutiny.

Surrenders

13.34 The legislation relating to agricultural tenancies was subject to major change in 1995. Prior to 1 September 1995, when the *Agricultural Tenancies Act* took effect, agricultural tenancy law was quite distinct from general land law. Under the old legislation, agricultural tenancies were protected. A tenant had lifetime security of tenure and a rental agreement

13.35 VAT Business by Business

could not normally be severed by a landlord unless the tenant had failed to fulfil his obligations under the tenancy agreement. From 1 September 1995, however, agricultural tenancy law became analogous to standard commercial land law. An agricultural landlord is now able to grant a tenancy for a specified duration and the incidence of tenants surrendering their interest in land is also more prevalent.

The VAT liability of lease surrenders was also subject to change in 1995. Following the case of *Lubbock Fine & Co, CJEC 1993, [1994] STC 101*, Customs conceded that a surrender payment by a landlord to his tenant, by way of business, is exempt from VAT. If the tenant has opted to tax the land or property to which the surrender applies, the surrender is standard-rated. Prior to the decision in *Lubbock Fine & Co*, the surrender of a lease by a tenant, in the course of business, was compulsorily standard-rated.

A surrender is exempt, subject to the option to tax being in place, if it is made in the course or furtherance of business. On occasion non-business property, such as a farmhouse for example, may be included in the surrender of a holding. Surrender payments in respect of non-business accommodation fall outside the scope of VAT. Thus, where a surrender payment is received by a tenant and it relates to opted land which includes a private farmhouse, VAT need only be accounted for on the consideration referable to the business assets.

Statutory compensation

13.35 Statutory compensation paid to a tenant, where the tenancy is terminated by an agricultural landlord following a notice to quit under the *Agricultural Holdings Act 1986*, is outside the scope of VAT. Statutory compensation received by a tenant upon termination of his agricultural lease in accordance with the *Agricultural Tenancies Act 1995* is also outside the scope of VAT. Occasionally, discretionary payments are made to the tenant in addition to statutory compensation; these will be treated for VAT purposes in the same way as a surrender of the tenancy. If a tenancy is to be terminated and statutory compensation does not apply, any payment received by the tenant will be exempt, unless the option to tax is in place, even if it is valued by reference to a statutory amount.

Dilapidation payments

13.36 Customs do not normally regard payments made by a tenant to a rural landlord, in respect of making good dilapidations, as a supply in the course of business in the situation where the tenancy is ended in accordance with the *Landlord and Tenant Act 1954* or the *Agricultural Holdings Act 1986*. Consequently, dilapidation payments received by an agricultural landlord on termination of a lease are outside the scope of VAT. If the landlord passes the dilapidation payment on to the subsequent tenant, there is again no supply for VAT purposes. Likewise, in some instances, payment is made by a landlord to his tenant, when a lease is terminated under the terms of the agricultural holdings legislation, to compensate the tenant for improvements which should have been carried out. This type of payment is also outside the scope of VAT.

Reverse surrenders

13.37 Sometimes it is the farming tenant who requires a lease to be terminated before its term has expired. In these circumstances, the tenant pays the agricultural landlord a reverse surrender which, with effect from 1 March 1995, is exempt from VAT. If the landlord has opted to tax the holding in question, the payment is standard-rated.

Restrictive covenants

13.38 Restrictive covenants are commonly placed on land to prevent development of that land. Payment received by landowners for the lifting of such a restriction is exempt from VAT, unless the option to tax is in force. Similarly, any payments received by an agricultural landlord for allowing a variation to the terms of a lease agreement are exempt, subject to the option to tax.

Inducements

13.39 Payment from a landowner to a prospective tenant, to induce him to take on an agricultural lease, is subject to VAT at the standard rate. Equally, payment by the tenant to a prospective sub-lessee or assignee is also subject to VAT at the standard rate. In situations where a landlord pays his tenant to carry out improvements or repairs to the property, in lieu of paying an inducement, the payment is standard-rated as it represents a supply of taxable services by the tenant to the landlord.

VAT Recovery

13.40 Farming is a taxable activity. With the exception of one or two items which are not VAT deductible, a fully taxable farming business is able to reclaim in full the VAT incurred on its expenditure. Basic farming purchases such as seeds, livestock and forage costs are zero-rated so that VAT recovery will not apply. Most of the other farming expenses will fall within the standard-rated category; pesticides, fertilisers, contractors' fees, machinery, tools, motor fuels and commercial vehicles.

VAT recovery issues of particular relevance to farming businesses generally revolve around whether expenditure relates to business activities and the extent to which it is recoverable. Estate owners and landowners, on the other

13.41 VAT Business by Business

hand, are more likely to be faced with VAT recovery problems relating to exempt income in the form of agricultural land lettings and sales.

Partial exemption

De minimis limit

13.41 VAT incurred on costs referable to exempt income is not reclaimable. For example, a farmer who leases agricultural holdings on an exempt basis (i.e. without opting to tax) is not able to recover VAT incurred on the day to day costs and fees directly related to the exempt letting activities. This irrecoverable VAT is known as exempt input VAT.

There is, however, a de minimis limit for exempt input VAT which, provided it is not exceeded, will enable the majority of farmers and rural landowners to treat VAT on all their costs, including that associated with exempt income, as fully recoverable. The current de minimis limit is set at £625 per month, that is £7,500 on an annual basis. This is equivalent to expenditure of approximately £3,500 per month or £42,800 per annum. In addition, exempt input VAT must not constitute more than half of the total VAT on costs of the business, either on a monthly or annual basis.

For farming businesses that receive exempt income from unopted agricultural lettings, but with negligible costs of upkeep, or for landowners who make the occasional exempt disposal of unopted land or property, the de minimis limit may sometimes be exceeded on a monthly or quarterly basis. In these circumstances, the exempt input VAT may not be reclaimed for that particular VAT period. Viewed on an annual basis, however, if no further exempt input VAT has arisen, the exempt input VAT, initially disallowed, may well fall below the annual de minimis limit and will therefore be recoverable. Timing of the carrying out of repair and maintenance works to exempt holdings can be crucial if the de minimis limit is not to be exceeded.

Estates and let farms

13.42 The partial exemption de minimis limit is unlikely to apply to larger agricultural estates which may receive predominantly exempt income from let farms, domestic tenancies and a miscellany of other exempt lets. VAT suffered on all costs directly relating to exempt income, such as VAT incurred on the renovation costs of a let farm cottage for example, cannot be reclaimed. VAT incurred on expenditure which is referable to a mixture of taxable and exempt income, for instance VAT on the administrative costs of running an estate, will require apportionment. The standard method of carrying out an apportionment is by reference to the value that exempt income bears to total income. If this method is used, the value of ad hoc disposals of land and property, opted or unopted, should be excluded from the apportionment calculation as it will lead to a distortive result.

Other methods of apportionment are permitted by Customs, provided that approval is sought and it can be demonstrated that they are fair and reasonable. It may therefore be worthwhile exploring alternative ways of calculating the exempt to taxable ratio. Numbers of exempt and taxable properties might be used, or, for example, different apportionment methods can be applied to particular sectors of the estate to keep the total amount of VAT to be restricted by the business to a minimum.

Election to waive exemption ('Option to tax')

13.43 The election to waive exemption (often referred to as the 'option to tax') can be a useful tool in partial exemption planning, particularly now that it is possible to opt to tax individual parcels of land without tainting surrounding land in the same ownership. The majority of agricultural tenants will be engaged in activities that are fully taxable and the imposition of VAT on rents will not be problematic for them. If the option is exercised selectively, it may be possible for an estate whose exempt input VAT wavers close to the annual de minimis limit to keep within that limit and retain its fully taxable status. Likewise, by opting to tax specific farm buildings, a significant increase in the overall proportion of VAT recoverable under an estate's partial exemption method can be achieved.

Repairs to farmhouses

13.44 VAT recovery in relation to farmhouses can cause difficulties because they are used for a mixture of private and business purposes. Up until 1994, the proportion of VAT that could be treated as relating to business use and recovered, as regards farmhouse repairs, or conversions of redundant farm buildings for use as farmhouses, was negotiable. In quite a number of instances, the matter had to be decided by a VAT tribunal. These rulings formed the basis of an agreement between Customs and the National Farmers' Union in October 1994. The agreement allows farming businesses to recover 70% of the VAT they incur on repairs and improvements and general redecorations e.g. replacement windows, roof repairs, etc.

Use of this recovery percentage is subject to a number of stipulations:

(a) The agreed percentage can only be applied by sole proprietors and farming partnerships. It does not apply to farming companies;

(b) The farmhouse must be part of a full-time farming operation;

(c) The farmer must live in the farmhouse throughout the year;

(d) Eligible expenses must be of a general nature; repairs, replacements, maintenance, renovations, refurbishments and improvements (alteration works and fitting-out costs are excluded);

(e) The 70% must be a realistic representation of the business use of the expenditure.

13.45 *VAT Business by Business*

The practical effects of the agreement are that VAT on works carried out in isolation to an area of private accommodation, such as a bedroom for example, is unlikely to be recoverable. If that work forms part of the general redecoration of the whole farmhouse, however, a 70% recovery of all the VAT incurred on the redecorations can be secured. Customs will also permit VAT incurred on costs associated with the conversion of a disused farm building into a working farmhouse to be treated as 70% recoverable.

Alterations, extensions and enlargements will not qualify for 70% recovery, particularly if usage of the newly created space is predominantly private. For works of this kind, percentage recovery must be separately agreed with Customs. While case law indicates that they are unlikely to approve more than a 30% recovery, particular circumstances may justify a higher recovery.

Retrospective claims

13.45 Farmers who have not claimed any VAT, or who have only claimed a small proportion of VAT incurred on eligible farmhouse expenditure, may be able to make a retrospective reclaim, subject to the three-year cap on repayment claims effective from 18 July 1996. If no VAT has been recovered to date, the 70:30 (business: non-business) ratio may be adopted. Farmers who have recovered only a small proportion of the relevant VAT, under the instruction of their local VAT officer, may make a VAT adjustment to bring themselves into line with the 70% recoverable allowance. Some farmers will have calculated their own recovery percentage; if this is the case, no retrospective adjustment can be made because Customs take the view that the claim will have been made on a fair and reasonable basis.

Farming companies

13.46 The agreement between Customs and the NFU does not include farming companies because they are governed by rules in the main VAT legislation which take precedence [*VATA 1994, s 24(3)*]. This legislation gives farming directors less scope for VAT recovery than sole farmers and farming partnerships because it prevents them, or anyone connected with them, from recovering any VAT incurred on accommodation for domestic use. If a part of the farmhouse is used specifically for the purposes of the farming business, an apportionment must be agreed with Customs and be made to reflect the amount of business use. A calculation based on square footage is the normal method of calculation favoured by Customs for this type of apportionment. Other methods of apportionment can be negotiated provided that it can be demonstrated that they produce a reasonable result.

Work on tenanted properties

13.47 The VAT position with regard to recovery of VAT on the cost of repairs or improvements to tenanted property turns on which party has responsibility for carrying out those works under the terms of the agricultural tenancy agreement. Customs tend to scrutinise the VAT situation carefully and may disallow amounts of VAT which have been reclaimed by the incorrect entity. An agricultural landlord with responsibility for carrying out repairs can therefore recover VAT incurred on works to any opted properties. VAT on repair and maintenance works to tenanted domestic properties will not be recoverable.

Under a tenant-repairing lease, the tenant will be able to reclaim VAT on repair works to the extent that the property is used for taxable, commercial purposes. If the property is his dwelling and no business use applies, VAT on repair works will be irrecoverable. Contributions towards improvements made by landlords to tenants, or vice versa, under the *Agricultural Holdings Act 1986* upon termination of a tenancy agreement, are outside the scope of VAT.

In the situation where a tenant carries out work for his landlord that, under the terms of the tenancy agreement, is the responsibility of the landlord, the tenant is deemed to make a supply of services to the landlord on which he must account for VAT. However, where repair or renovation work is carried out by a tenant, which neither the tenant nor the landlord are required to do under the terms of the lease, any voluntary contribution made by the landlord to the tenant does not constitute a taxable supply and no VAT is due on the amount.

Tied accommodation

13.48 Where farm cottages or other tied properties are provided to farm or estate workers in return for services rendered, Customs do not treat this as a supply for VAT purposes. Expenditure relating to tied accommodation is treated as used for the farm business and is fully recoverable, as long as the farm has a fully taxable status.

It is not uncommon for retired employees to continue to reside in tied accommodation on a gratuitous basis. VAT incurred on repairs to cottages occupied by retired employees can be reclaimed provided that the intention is that the property will be used by a future employee, once it falls vacant again. If a specific rental charge is made to the retired occupant, any VAT incurred on repair and maintenance work will be referable to an exempt transaction and will be rendered wholly irrecoverable.

Assured shorthold tenancies

13.49 In order to maximise the opportunity for obtaining vacant possession of farm cottages, agricultural landlords have negotiated a greater number of assured shorthold lettings with their staff. Under the terms of this type of tenancy agreement, a rental charge is made to the tenant. The receipt of exempt rental income by a farm business or estate would normally render

13.50   VAT Business by Business

VAT on associated costs irrecoverable. However, where a rent is charged but the agricultural or estate worker's pay is grossed up accordingly, Customs accept that the rental payment is merely notional. Consequently, VAT on costs referable to employee's accommodation can be recovered. In circumstances where an agricultural worker occupies a tied property under an assured shorthold tenancy and a rental charge is made by the business but not reimbursed, Customs view VAT on works carried out to the property as relating to an exempt supply and, thus, irrecoverable.

Private use

13.50   VAT incurred on private expenditure is not reclaimable. Thus, VAT incurred on goods and services purchased by the business but not put to business use is not recoverable. VAT on expenses which are used for a mixture of business and non-business activities must be apportioned [*VATA 1994, s 24(5)*]. Fuel, power and telephone bills for farmhouses or other agricultural properties which are used for both business and private purposes will require the VAT to be apportioned. VAT on veterinary fees for both livestock and pets will also need to be split proportionally. A method of apportionment is not specified; Customs apply the 'fair and reasonable' test in these circumstances. VAT on domestic goods such as household furniture and kitchen appliances is normally irrecoverable. Some one-off expenses such as the fitting of a security system or new fitted carpets will arguably have an element of business use and the VAT should therefore be apportioned accordingly.

Edible produce from the farm which is consumed by members of the farm or estate does not create a VAT problem as the goods in question are zero-rated.

Business entertainment

13.51   VAT on the cost of providing business entertainment such as meals or accommodation to anyone who is not an employee of a farm or estate is specifically excluded from recovery [*SI 1992 No 3222, article 5(1)*] together with costs of any incidental entertainment provided to employees. Directors of farming companies and casual agricultural workers are treated the same as full-time employees. Entertainment functions held for employees by a farmer or estate owner is regarded as staff entertainment and is not specifically excluded from recovery by the legislation, but Customs may argue for restriction of the VAT incurred, depending on the scale of the entertainment and the presence of guests.

Motor vehicles

13.52   VAT on the purchase of a motor car, whether outright, via hire purchase, or by lease purchase, is not normally reclaimable by farmers even if the car is bought for business purposes. Changes were made to the rules concerning VAT and motor cars with effect from 1 August 1995. Under the new rules, it is possible for VAT to be reclaimed on cars acquired by the business which are not available for private use. In practice, this is unlikely to be of relevance to most farmers as their motor vehicles are generally used for both business and domestic purposes. The new provisions also affect cars leased for business purposes. VAT incurred by farmers on car lease rentals can be recovered at a rate of 50%, where the car has an element of private use, large or small. VAT on lease rentals for cars used by farmers which are not available for any private use can be reclaimed in full. VAT on car servicing and repair costs is reclaimable in full, even if the car is used for both business and private purposes, provided the expenditure is borne by the business. VAT on the purchase of farm vehicles and machinery is fully recoverable, as is the VAT incurred on repairs and maintenance works, as long as the farm or agricultural business has fully taxable status.

Motor fuel

13.53 VAT on motor fuel for farm vehicles, including vans, and other agricultural machinery is fully recoverable. VAT on motor fuel for cars which are used privately is subject to special rules [*VATA 1994, s 56*]. By virtue of these rules, VAT is accounted for on the private use of petrol by means of an output VAT charge, i.e. a scale charge. At the same time, VAT incurred on all petrol, purchased for both business and private use, can be recovered in full. The amount of scale charge payable is dependent on the engine size of the vehicle. Details of the scale charge amounts and alternative methods of restricting VAT on private petrol purchases can be found in *Tolley's VAT 1998/99, paragraphs 45.16 and 45.17.*

It is possible to avoid the scale charge method of accounting for VAT, if car mileage is low for example, by not reclaiming VAT on any business-funded motor fuel purchases, either for business or for private motoring. See Customs Notice 48, ESC 2.1. This is unlikely to be a viable option for farmers as VAT on all fuel purchases, including petrol for vans, trucks and other business vehicles, would not be recoverable.

Definition of a motor car

13.54 The question of whether or not a vehicle is a motor car, so that associated VAT is irrecoverable, is of particular significance to the agricultural sector. The definition of what constitutes a motor vehicle is very much open to interpretation; consequently a great number of rulings given by local VAT offices have been the subject of appeals to an independent VAT tribunal.

In the legislation, a motor car is defined as 'any motor vehicle of a kind normally used on public roads which has three or more wheels and either—

13.55 VAT Business by Business

(a) is constructed or adapted solely or mainly for the carriage of passengers; or

(b) has to the rear of the driver's seat roofed accommodation which is fitted with side windows or which is constructed or adapted for the fitting of side windows; but does not include:

   (i) vehicles capable of accommodating only one person or suitable for carrying twelve or more persons;

   (ii) vehicles constructed for a special purpose other than the carriage of persons and having no other accommodation for carrying persons than such is incidental to that purpose;'

[*VAT (Cars) Order 1992 (SI 1992 No 3122)*].

Particular attention should be paid where vehicles which have not been constructed as motor cars, e.g. pick-up vehicles, have been permanently adapted in any way. If, for example, rear side windows have been fitted or additional seating added, the vehicle is likely to fall within the VAT definition of a motor car and a VAT self-supply charge will then be triggered, effectively disallowing recovery of the VAT on the initial purchase.

Commercial vehicles that are adapted in such a way that they could be regarded as having been converted into a motor car have a greater chance of retaining commercial vehicle status if the conversion is of a temporary or easily removable nature, as demonstrated by the case of *KM Batty (2199)*. Conversely, modifications carried out to a motor car to convert it into a commercial vehicle, as in the case of *Intercraft UK Romania (13707)*, should be of a permanent nature if the vehicle is to fall outside the VAT definition of a motor car. In short, it is the physical attributes of the vehicle that Customs tend to focus upon when dealing with the issue of what constitutes a motor car, irrespective of whether the conversion is motivated by a business need.

Grants and subsidies

13.55 A range of government grants and subsidy schemes is available to farmers and landowners providing support for agricultural and forestry activities as well as assisting with the conservation and development of the rural environment. Many of these grants are outside the scope of VAT.

A number of EU CAP government grant schemes, notably the Set-Aside scheme, involve the giving up of production rights by farmers in return for the funding. The VAT treatment of these grants has been under review by Customs for some time; Customs' policy, in the meantime, is to treat grants of this type as if they are outside the scope of VAT. Other grant schemes which are treated in this way include the Woodland Grant Schemes, the Farm Woodland Premium Scheme, the Environmentally Sensitive Area Scheme and Section 15 Management Agreements. Price support mechanisms such as arable area payments, sheep annual premiums, suckler cow premiums and similar payments are also treated as if they are outside the scope of VAT. It is not possible to provide a comprehensive list of all the grant schemes which are treated in this way, as schemes are continually created or deleted by the relevant authorities.

It is worth noting that the European Court's decision in the case of *Mohr v Finanzamt Bad Segeberg, CJEC [1996] STC 238*, where it was ruled that grant income received by a German dairy farmer to compensate him for discontinuing his milk production was outside the scope of VAT, endorses the UK position, i.e. there is no supply for VAT purposes.

Similarly, government-funded BSE payments to farmers in respect of the culling of cows are outside the scope of VAT. This is because they constitute basic compensation payments, rather than reimbursement in respect of the giving up of certain farming rights.

Receipt of such funding can thus be ignored by farmers and landowners, and VAT incurred on expenditure can be recovered in full, assuming that the business is otherwise fully taxable. It is understood that Customs are also prepared to allow farming businesses which are funded wholly by income from subsidies, such as set-aside payments, to fully recover VAT incurred on their costs.

Accounting and records

Flat-rate farmers' scheme

13.56 A special accounting scheme is available to farmers and agricultural producers as an alternative to VAT registration. The scheme was introduced in the UK on 1 January 1993 and it is fair to say that the uptake has been low. There are currently around 800 certified flat-rate farmers in the UK.

Accounting

13.57 Members of the scheme do not charge VAT on their sales, neither do they reclaim VAT on their purchases. Consequently, flat-rate farmers do not submit VAT returns, and farmers will need to deregister if they wish to join the flat-rate scheme.

The scheme operates by means of charging what is termed a flat-rate addition (FRA) to the selling price of the farmer's goods. The FRA is 4% and can be charged on all produce and services, supplied by a farmer, which fall within the scheme. This includes produce which is zero-rated for VAT purposes. A flat-rate farmer keeps the FRA; it is not paid over to Customs. In effect, the FRA compensates the flat-rate farmer for the inability to recover VAT on his purchases. The FRA is only charged to VAT-registered customers. It is not

13.58 *VAT Business by Business*

charged on sales to the general public, nor is it charged on sales to other flat-rate farmers.

Eligibility

13.58 Any farmer or agricultural producer who engages in 'designated farming activities' (as set out in the Schedule to the *VAT (Flat-rate Scheme for Farmers) (Designated Activities) Order 1992 (SI 1992 No 3220)*) is eligible to join the scheme. Broadly, this covers farmers involved in crop production, stock farming, forestry, fisheries, processing services and agricultural services. Processing services must be carried out with the farmer's own machinery and by his own employees. Agricultural services covers a wide range of services; Customs require a farmer providing agricultural services to also engage in at least one of the main designated production activities. Further information about eligible activities is to be found in VAT Leaflet 700/46/93—Agricultural flat-rate scheme.

Application to join the flat-rate scheme should be made to the local VAT office by completing and submitting a VAT Form 98. Customs will then issue a certificate to the farmer. This is the flat-rate scheme equivalent of a VAT registration certificate.

A farmer will be certified by Customs as long as the following stipulations are fulfilled:

(a) The farmer must engage in designated activities.

(b) The farmer must not have been convicted for a VAT offence, accepted an offer to compound proceedings in connection with a VAT offence, or received a penalty for VAT evasion involving dishonest conduct in the three years prior to making an application.

(c) The farmer's income from non-agricultural activities must be less than the VAT registration limit. If this is not the case, deregistration will not be possible.

(d) The farmer must be able to demonstrate to Customs that he will not gain more than £3000 by flat-rate certification—i.e. the annual value of flat-rate additions must not exceed the value of the farmer's annual VAT on purchases by more than £3000 (*SI 1995 No 2518, reg. 204*).

(e) The application must be made on VAT Form 98.

Records

13.59 Normal accounting records should be maintained by a flat-rate farmer, as well as a copy of all FRA invoices issued. The FRA amounts charged can be recovered by VAT-registered customers as if they were normal VAT on purchases.

Non-agricultural activities

13.60 A flat-rate farmer can earn income from non-agricultural activities, such as holiday lettings for example, as long as income from such activities does not exceed the VAT registration limit. Ancillary income can thus be earned by a flat-rate farmer on a VAT-free basis. Once ancillary income exceeds the VAT registration threshold, the flat-rate farmer must cancel his certification and register for VAT. Alternatively, the non-farming activity could be operated as a separate business, perhaps by a farm partnership or a limited company, and registered for VAT independently.

Conclusion

13.61 In limited circumstances, the flat-rate scheme may be beneficial. Producers whose goods are standard-rated, nursery owners and viticulturists for instance, may stand to gain from the flat-rate scheme, as they would not have to charge VAT on sales to the public. The fact that the flat-rate scheme is less administratively onerous than VAT registration may also appeal to some farmers. Agricultural producers who would like further details about the scheme should refer to Customs VAT Leaflet 700/46/93—Agricultural flat-rate scheme.

Accounting records

13.62 For VAT accounting purposes, farmers and agricultural landowners must preserve all of their normal, day-to-day accounting records. Specifically, they are required to keep a record of all their standard-rated, zero-rated and exempt income as well as their standard-rated and zero-rated purchases. Details and documentation relating to any gifts of goods or property, goods allocated to private use and any self-supply transactions must also be kept.

Customs also require farmers and estate owners to maintain a VAT account with monthly or quarterly totals, depending on whether the farmer renders monthly or quarterly VAT periods, of VAT charged on sales and VAT incurred on purchases. All business and accounting records which provide back-up to the VAT account must be kept for six years.

Sales

13.63 Copy sales invoices in respect of all standard-rated supplies must be retained to support entries on the VAT account. The retention of sales invoices in respect of zero-rated goods and services is not mandatory but is advisable to ensure completeness of records.

Sales of produce to the general public can be recorded in one of two ways. They can either be recorded by keeping a record of the daily gross takings from the till rolls or by keeping a record in a note book. Alternatively, a

13.64 VAT Business by Business

record of VAT due on sales to the public can be kept by operating one of the special VAT retail schemes offered by Customs. A retail scheme will be particularly suitable for producers selling both standard-rated and zero-rated goods to the public, as it enables the values of the two rates of goods to be separately identified. Details of the various VAT retail schemes are available in Customs' Notice 727—Retail schemes.

Sales direct to the public do not need to be invoiced, but if a receipt is required this can be in a simpler form than a normal tax invoice, provided that the sale value is less than £100. A till receipt can show a total VAT-inclusive amount payable; proper VAT invoices must separately identify the amount of VAT chargeable. Both till receipts and proper VAT invoices must show zero-rated and standard-rated supplies totalled separately. Exempt income may be separately totalled on a normal VAT invoice but may not be included on a simpler-style invoice. Amounts subject to VAT included in gross takings from sales to the public must be added to the VAT charged on sales invoices in respect of standard-rated sales to arrive at the total VAT due on sales for the period.

Sales of agricultural produce via the appropriate marketing board or livestock market are generally accounted for using self-billing procedures. Thus, a VAT invoice is raised by the marketing body for supplies of standard-rated products, such as wool sales, on the farmer's behalf. For the purposes of VAT accounting, a farmer should treat this self-billed invoice in the same way as a normal VAT invoice.

Purchases

13.64 Original VAT invoices need to be held by a farm business or estate to support the recovery of VAT on purchases. Proforma invoices are not acceptable and replacement or duplicate purchase invoices are generally only allowed by Customs if they are clearly marked as such by the supplier. VAT on purchases can be reclaimed by farms and rural enterprises upon receipt of a VAT invoice. Where invoices have been received but not paid, a VAT cashflow advantage can be obtained.

Minor expenses in the form of car park charges, coin-operated machines and calls from public or private telephones do not need to be supported by a receipt or VAT invoice, provided that the VAT-inclusive cost is £25 or less.

Self-billed documents, commonly received from agricultural markets and agricultural marketing bodies generally show not only the farmer's sales, and VAT due on those sales if they are standard-rated, but also a commission charge or auctioneer's fee for services provided to the farmer in relation to the transaction. VAT chargeable on the agency fee forms part of a farmer's VAT on purchases. A self-billed document is therefore used by farmers to account for VAT on both sales and purchases. Because two transactions are

Farming and agriculture **13.67**

recorded on one invoice, values can be incorrectly transposed to the VAT accounting records with relative ease.

The way in which purchase invoices are filed is a matter of preference. Alphabetical, chronological or any other method of filing will be acceptable to Customs as long as corresponding purchase invoices can be readily traced from day-book entries, etc. Sales invoices should be filed to mirror the numerical sequence in which they are issued.

Accounting systems

13.65 Many, but not all, accounting records maintained by farming and other agricultural businesses are computerised nowadays. The type of accounting system operated by a farm business or estate will depend on the size and scale of the business. Small businesses may find that manual or computerised day books plus supporting invoices are satisfactory. Larger businesses will need to adopt an accounting system that is suitable for both VAT and other tax purposes and also for general management purposes. Farming companies will be subject to statutory accounting requirements, so the VAT system adopted should be complementary.

Single entry book-keeping

13.66 As mentioned above, day-book listings of sales and purchases by month or by quarter, together with supporting invoices, may provide an adequate VAT accounting system for some small to medium sized farming operations. For manual accounts, ordinary business day-books can be used or, alternatively, the NFU produces its own NFU Invoice Record Book for VAT which is suitable.

Single entry cash book accounting is popular among farmers. Again, the NFU produces a Business Records Book for single entry cash accounting which incorporates VAT accounting requirements as well. Since normal VAT accounting operates on an invoice basis and cash analysis operates on a cash received and paid basis, tax point errors can arise when accounting for VAT on sales. Modifications may need to be made to the cash received analysis to ensure that VAT on any sales which have been invoiced but not paid is included in the correct VAT accounting period.

Double entry book-keeping

13.67 Most of the computerised farm accounting packages are based on a double entry system. VAT is analysed out within the sales and purchase day-books and then posted to a VAT account in the nominal ledger. Cash expenses and cash received from direct sales which are to a cash book account will also require the VAT amounts to be separated out. The VAT is then posted to the VAT account in the nominal ledger. A number of farm

13.68 *VAT Business by Business*

accounting packages operate on a cash accounting basis. If this is the case, the special cash accounting scheme for VAT could be considered, as detailed in paragraph 13.70 below. Otherwise, tax point errors, particularly as regards VAT on sales, can easily arise.

Correction of errors

13.68 There are two ways in which VAT errors can be rectified depending on the size of the mistake. If an error, or the combined net value of a number of errors, is £2,000 or less, the VAT account for the current VAT period should be adjusted accordingly. The combined net value equals the total amounts payable to Customs less the total amounts reclaimable from them. Default interest will not be charged for errors adjusted in this way.

An error, or the combined net value of a number of errors, which does exceed £2,000 must be disclosed to Customs. Disclosure can be made either on VAT Form 692 or by letter to the local VAT office. Where errors are disclosed by letter, Customs will need to know to which VAT period each error relates, the value of the error(s) and whether each error is referable to VAT on sales or VAT on purchases. Default interest will apply to errors with a combined total over £2000, so it is prudent to include payment with the disclosure to keep the amount of interest payable to a minimum. A copy of the disclosure document should be kept with the current VAT account summary for purposes of completeness.

Three-year cap

13.69 With effect from 18 July 1996, a three-year time limit was introduced on claims for refunds of amounts overpaid as VAT. See *Tolley's VAT 1998/99, paragraphs 51.7 and 51.8*. The VAT tribunal upheld the legality of the three-year time limit in the case of *Marks & Spencer plc (15476)*.

Cash accounting

13.70 The cash accounting scheme is open to any agricultural business with a VAT-exclusive turnover of £350,000 or less. VAT is accounted for on the basis of cash received and payments made. The scheme does have the advantage of providing automatic bad debt relief, but this will not be particularly relevant to farmers where the vast majority of their income is zero-rated. In addition, the scheme is unlikely to be attractive to farming enterprises which are regularly in a net VAT repayment position. It may be of benefit to businesses whose products are predominantly standard-rated, such as cider makers and flower growers.

Annual accounting scheme

13.71 A scheme whereby VAT is accounted for by means of compiling and submitting one annual VAT return, but by making several interim payments, may appeal to some agricultural producers who are keen to reduce their paperwork. In particular, the scheme could benefit rural businesses whose income is principally standard-rated; wholesale nurseries, garden centres and vineyards, for instance. The scheme is unlikely to benefit farmers and producers whose monthly or quarterly VAT returns normally result in VAT repayments.

As with the cash accounting scheme, a taxable turnover limit applies. This is currently set at £300,000, excluding VAT. Under the scheme, quarterly or monthly payments, depending on the turnover of the business, are made to Customs during the VAT year. At the end of the year, an annual VAT return is completed and submitted, together with any balance outstanding. Retail businesses operating the annual accounting have the administrative advantage of only having to carry out their normal retail scheme calculation once a year.

EU transactions

Sales

13.72 Goods and produce supplied to business customers in other member states are zero-rated provided that the customer's EU VAT registration number is shown on the sales invoice. Goods supplied to non-business customers in the EU are standard-rated unless the goods themselves are zero-rated. This may well be the case for many farming supplies to private customers within the EU.

Valid documentation showing that the goods have been physically transported from the UK should be held, and must be retained to support zero-rating of goods which are standard-rated within the UK. The value of all zero-rated goods supplied to the EU must be included in both box 6 and box 8 of the VAT return.

Unless a farmer's turnover is low and his EU sales are also minimal, an additional form called an EC sales list (VAT Form 101) will have to be completed on a quarterly basis. If a farmer renders monthly VAT returns, Customs will normally permit EC sales lists to be submitted on a monthly basis as well, if this is more convenient for the farmer. Information required on an EC sales list is used by Customs for control purposes and includes the VAT registration number of each EU customer and the value of goods sold to each customer in the period. All EU sales must be recorded, regardless of how small their value. The only concession is that low value EU transactions may be recorded on an annual, as opposed to a quarterly, basis.

13.73 VAT Business by Business

Purchases

13.73 Special VAT accounting rules apply to agricultural machinery, equipment and any other goods which are standard-rated within the UK, when acquired by a UK farm business from another EU member state. VAT is imputed on the value of the item and accounted for in box 2 of the VAT return as VAT payable. At the same time, VAT on the value of the same item is recovered in box 4 of the VAT return, subject to the normal VAT recovery rules. Thus, VAT on acquisitions from the EU will only be a cost to a farmer, if his business is partially exempt. The invoice value of the acquisition must be included in boxes 7 and 9 of the VAT return. Documentation relating to goods purchased from an EU supplier should be retained as part of the businesses' VAT records to comply with Customs' requirements. Further details about the completion of EC sales lists and accounting for goods acquired in the EU is available in the Customs VAT Notice 725—The Single Market (1994 with Updates Nos. 1 and 2).

Intrastat

13.74 Further statistical returns must be produced by a farmer if his level of trade with the EU exceeds a certain threshold. At the time of writing, the threshold stands at £225,000, and applies to both supplies to the EU ('dispatches') and purchases from the EU ('acquisitions'). Farmers will have to complete Intrastat declarations for dispatches to the EU even if they are supplying goods which are zero-rated. Separate declaration forms are completed for dispatches and acquisitions. Full details pertaining to the completion of Intrastat declarations is provided in Customs Notice 60—Intrastat.

Practical points

Part exchange

13.75 Part exchange, for instance of a tractor, gives rise to two separate transactions; the purchase of a new tractor and the disposal of an old tractor. The second part of the transaction is commonly overlooked by farm businesses and estates. VAT is due on the VAT-inclusive value accorded to the traded-in tractor. This VAT treatment is also applicable to services provided by one farmer to another in return for other goods or services. Thus, if combining services are provided in exchange for hedging services, VAT should be accounted for on the value of both of the services provided by the two farmers. For VAT purposes, the two transactions cannot be netted off.

Businesses which sell reconditioned agricultural machinery and equipment often do so in exchange for inoperable machines. In these circumstances, the transaction is treated as one of reconditioning services, even where the value of the broken item is taken into account when arriving at a value for the reconditioned machine.

Returnable containers

13.76 Charges raised with respect to returnable containers are subject to VAT at the standard rate. VAT must be accounted for depending on the terms under which the containers are supplied. Possible arrangements are as follows:

(a) If containers are supplied as part of a product's normal packaging and not separately charged for, no VAT is due on the supply of the containers.

(b) A tax point occurs when a separate charge is made for refundable containers regardless of whether it will be refunded to the customer upon return of those containers. If and when the containers are returned, the original VAT charge can be cancelled by issuing a credit note. Alternatively, a VAT reduction can be made to a customer's invoice for a subsequent supply.

(c) VAT is due when charges are raised for containers which customers have failed to return.

(d) Garden centres and nurseries which use a retail scheme for VAT accounting purposes should include separate charges for a supply of containers in their daily gross takings. Once the containers are returned, the daily gross takings can be reduced accordingly.

Legal entities

13.77 Agricultural estates are usually operated by a sole trader or a family partnership or, in some cases, by a limited company. It is not uncommon, however, for larger estates to be divided into a number of different legal ownerships, trusts being a popular vehicle for family ownership of land and property. A number of points arise in this context.

Ancillary businesses

13.78 Ancillary businesses, such as bed and breakfast activities, can gain a benefit from separate VAT registration from the existing farm business, if the income earned from the ancillary business is below the VAT registration threshold. Customs are empowered, however, to direct that disaggregated activities should be treated as a single business unit [*VATA 1994, 1 Sch 2(1)-(5), as amended by FA 1997, s 31*]. It is therefore important to ensure that the ancillary business is operated wholly independently from the main business. Particular regard should be paid to:

(a) premises and equipment;

13.79 *VAT Business by Business*

(b) records and accounts;

(c) sales and purchase invoices;

(d) legal responsibility;

(e) bank accounts;

(f) employees' wages;

(g) income tax issues.

Invoices

13.79 Invoicing problems arise where estates comprise a number of legal ownerships. Employees may not always be aware which entity has responsibility for which particular types of activity. Customs are very alert to VAT reclaims by incorrect entities and will almost certainly disallow them. Management charges between different entities can also lead to VAT omissions, tax point errors and additional VAT costs.

Co-ownership

13.80 Farmland that is jointly owned, or let, by family members or tenants-in-common for instance, must be treated for VAT purposes as if it were owned by a single legal entity. If the land is opted and VAT registration is applicable, the co-owners are required by Customs to register for VAT as a partnership even if, legally, they are not. Normally the beneficiary, or beneficiaries, of land that is held under trust is treated for VAT purposes as the owner of the land [*VATA 1994, 10 Sch 8*]. Thus, it is the beneficiaries who must register for VAT if the taxable income from the holding exceeds the VAT registration limit. In other circumstances, it is the trustees rather than the beneficiaries to whom the benefit of the proceeds from the property accrues. If this is the case, and VAT registration is applicable, it is the trustees who will need to do so. The legislation governing co-owned land is currently subject to review and changes may be introduced in the future.

Co-operatives

13.81 Some farmers use a purchasing group or co-operative as a cost-effective means of acquiring goods. There are two ways in which the VAT accounting can be structured. One is that the co-operative is registered for VAT individually, so that it recharges members for their proportion of the purchases, plus VAT if appropriate, and recovers VAT on the group's own purchases. Alternatively, one member of the co-operative can act as a representative, within his own VAT registration, by reclaiming VAT on the bulk purchases and recharging other members for their share and accounting for VAT, if appropriate.

Farming and agriculture **13.App**

Common errors

13.82 VAT error often arises within the farming sector in relation to items which are outside the scope of VAT. Types of transactions which are outside the scope of VAT and commonly miscoded include:

(a) insurance claims;

(b) dividend income;

(c) monetary gifts;

(d) business rates;

(e) grants and subsidies;

(f) vehicle and gun licences;

(g) MOT certificates;

(h) other taxes—income tax, stamp duty, inheritance tax etc;

(i) wages, PAYE and NIC.

All of these items are outside the scope of VAT and should be excluded from box 6 (value of total sales) and box 7 (value of total purchases) of the VAT return.

Appendix

Standard-rated agricultural income

Agistment feeding
Alternative (non-food) crops
Animal horns, furs, skins, hoofs and hair (i.e. non-feeding purpose)
Animal keep including care
Animal products used for pharmaceutical purposes
Artists' charcoal
Bait
Bedding materials
Blood for fertiliser
Boat mooring rights
Canary and millet and sunflower seed
Castor oil seed residue
Christmas trees
Cider and perry
Coarse fish
Colourings
Contracting services
Dogs
Farmhouse teas and catering activities
Farmyard tours

13.App *VAT Business by Business*

Fertilisers including animal derivatives
Fishing rights
Flavourings
Flax
Flowers
Gallop fees
Gaming rights
Greaves held out for sale as pet food
Grit (soluble or insoluble) for poultry or game
Hire of horses/ponies/donkeys
Horse breeding
Horses
Horticultural peat
Inducements
Livery services
Machinery hire
Machinery sales (cf. Part exchange)
Manure
Mowing services
Mushroom growing kits in plastic or reusable container—packaging is standard-rated
Nutritional supplements for livestock
Ornamental poultry and fish
Packaging materials—sacks, bags, punnets etc.
Pesticides and sprays
Pet food
Pets
Plants, seeds and fruit used for non-edible purposes
Pot plants
Pre-germinated grain seed
Probiotics
Product processing services
Quota leasing—milk, potatoes, sheep, cows
Quota sales—milk, potatoes, sheep, cows
Racing pigeons
Returnable containers
Root stock (excluding cucumber and tomato)
Seeds, tubers, bulbs, corms, crowns, rhizomes, cuttings of flowers
Semen
Shooting rights
Shrubs and alpines
Sports facilities*
Storage facility services
Thatching reeds
Timber
Timber rights
Tipping charges—general
Topsoil
Tractor rides

Trees
Turf
Urea—non-animal feed
Wool sales
(*—Sports facilities are exempt if they are hired to certain qualifying organisations for more than 24 hours or hired on a regular basis, with a minimum of 10 bookings.)

Lower-rate agricultural supplies

Charcoal sold as domestic fuel
Firelighters
Firewood and logs, chips, scrap and damaged wood sold as domestic fuel
Fuel and power for domestic use
Peat sold as domestic fuel

Zero-rated agricultural supplies

Animal feeding stuffs
Exports of agricultural produce
Food for human consumption
Grazing rights
Hatching eggs
Live animals
Mowing rights
Mushroom growing kits in cardboard container
Newspapers and journals
Ostriches and ostrich eggs
Sale of a building converted to a dwelling
Sale of a new dwelling
Seeds and plants for propagation of food for human consumption

Exempt agricultural supplies

Advertising hoardings
Commercial rentals
Land rentals
Mineral rights
Restrictive covenants
Reverse surrenders
Sales of land
Storage—specific sites only
Surrenders
(Note: An exempt interest in or grant of a right over land is generally subject to the 'option to tax'.)

Outside the scope of VAT—Agricultural transactions

BSE compensation payments
Dilapidation payments
Dividends

13.App VAT Business by Business

Grants and subsidies (see paragraph 13.55)
Insurance claims
Monetary gifts
Statutory compensation

Chapter 14

Hospitals and Nursing Homes

Introduction

14.1 The origin of the favourable VAT treatment accorded to hospitals and nursing homes is to be found in the *EC Sixth Directive*. The Sixth Directive requires Member States to grant wide-ranging exemptions from VAT to supplies made by certain institutions in connection with the provision of health care and welfare, which it designates 'activities in the public interest':

- hospital and medical care and closely related activities undertaken by bodies governed by public law or, under social conditions comparable to those applicable to bodies governed by public law, by hospitals, centres for medical treatment or diagnosis and other duly recognised establishments of a similar nature (*EC Sixth Directive, Article 13A1(b)*);

- the supply of services and of goods closely linked to welfare and social security work, including those supplied by old people's homes, by bodies governed by public law, or by other organisations recognised as charitable by the Member State concerned (*EC Sixth Directive, Article 13A1(g)*).

Since the applicability of the exemption is restricted by a requirement to consider the status of the supplier, certain activities which might otherwise have been regarded as provision of health care or welfare, such as those carried on by unregistered nursing homes without charitable status, must fall outside its scope. There is no right of input tax recovery in connection with the making of exempt supplies.

Member States are also allowed discretion to apply a 'reduced rate' of VAT to supplies of certain other goods and services commonly used by hospitals and nursing homes, such as pharmaceutical products and aids for disabled persons (*EC Sixth Directive, Annex H*). At the present time, the UK applies the zero rate to such supplies. In contrast to the VAT exemption provisions, it is normally the status of the recipient of the supply that determines eligibility for zero-rating. There is a full right of input tax recovery in connection with the making of zero-rated supplies. Where a supply satisfies the criteria for

14.2 *VAT Business by Business*

both exemption and zero-rating, it should be regarded as zero-rated (*VATA 1994, s 30(1)*).

Certain activities of providers of health care and welfare must or may be treated as 'non-business', and therefore fall outside the scope of VAT. There is not normally a right of VAT recovery in such cases, although there are special rules allowing public authorities to reclaim VAT suffered on their non-business activities in certain circumstances.

Supplies which do not fall within one of the above categories are standard-rated, and VAT must be accounted for in the normal way.

Liability of supplies

Provision of care or medical or surgical treatment

14.2 The provision of care or medical or surgical treatment and, in connection with it, the supply of any goods, in a hospital or other approved institution is exempt from VAT (*VATA 1994, 9 Sch, Group 7, Item 4*). Approved institutions for these purposes include the following:

- NHS hospitals;

- private hospitals;

- nursing homes or mental nursing homes registered under the *Registered Homes Act 1984* or the *Nursing Homes Registration (Scotland) Act 1938* or approved under the *Abortion Act 1967*, or exempted from registration under the 1984 Act as Christian Science homes, or private mental hospitals registered under *section 12* of the *Mental Health (Scotland) Act 1984*;

- residential homes registered under the *Registered Homes Act 1984* for elderly or disabled people or for people with past or present dependence on alcohol or drugs or past or present mental disorder.

The provision of care, treatment and medical goods to patients by NHS hospitals is normally regarded as a non-business activity. The special status of NHS trusts for VAT purposes is discussed at paragraph 14.6 below.

The importance of the status of the supplier in determining entitlement to the exemption was underlined by a case recently heard before the VAT and Duties Tribunal (*Kaul (t/a Alpha Care Services) (14028)*). The tribunal ruled that the exemption may not apply to activities carried on by individuals or 'natural persons', notwithstanding the approved status of these persons under the relevant UK legislation. This is because the corresponding provisions in the Sixth Directive exempt only the activities of bodies corporate or 'legal persons' (*EC Sixth Directive, Article 13A1(b)*—see also the CJEC decision in *Bulthuis-Griffioen v Inspecteur der Omzetbelasting, [1995] STC 954*).

Customs have stated that they will not implement the decision, as to do so would create unacceptable distortion of competition in the sector and give rise to considerable difficulties in both administering the tax and monitoring the scope of the exemption (see Business Brief 1/97). However, it remains to be seen whether the European Commission will commence infraction proceedings against the UK to bring Customs' policy into line with the interpretation of the Sixth Directive favoured by the European Court of Justice.

Accommodation

14.3 The exemption covers accommodation (including the provision of accommodation for mothers of very young children—see *Nuffield Nursing Home Trust, [1989] VATTR 62 (3327)*), catering for patients or residents (*Viewpoint Housing Association Ltd (13148)*), medical and nursing care, and drugs and appliances supplied in connection with that care. The exemption excludes the provision of catering for staff and visitors (*Dr AJ Cameron, [1973] VATTR 177(41)*) and telephone services (*Poole General Hospital League of Friends (10621)*). The supply may be made by, or directly to, the approved institution, or by another body such as a charity or a nurses agency (VAT Leaflet 701/31/92). Contractors providing ancillary services to hospitals may exempt the supply of services which involve personal contact with patients (*Crothall & Co Ltd, [1973] VATTR 20(6)*).

Blood, organs and tissue

14.4 The supply or importation of human blood, organs and tissue for therapeutic purposes or medical research is always exempt (*VATA 1994, 9 Sch, Group 7, Items 6–8*).

Home care services

14.5 There is an increasing demand, particularly among the elderly and sufferers from chronic illnesses, for medical care and treatment of a kind traditionally provided in hospitals and nursing homes to be performed in the patient's own home. However, unless such 'homecare' services are either wholly performed or 'directly supervised' by certain registered practitioners (*VATA 1994, 9 Sch, Group 7, Item 1*), they will fall outside the exemption. Customs recognise that this position is anomalous and have adopted a more relaxed interpretation of what constitutes 'direct supervision' in the case of commercial agencies using unqualified staff to provide homecare services to elderly or disabled persons. News Releases 48/95 and 23/96, containing detailed guidelines on what constitutes 'direct supervision' in the homecare sector, are available from relevant professional representative bodies and local VAT offices.

14.6 VAT Business by Business

Status of NHS trusts

14.6 National Health Service trusts are public authorities and are, as such, accorded special status by the Sixth Directive:

'States, regional and local government authorities and other bodies governed by public law shall not be considered taxable persons in respect of the activities and transactions in which they engage as public authorities, even where they collect dues, fees, contributions or payments in connection with these activities or transactions' (*EC Sixth Directive, Article 4(5)*).

Thus the statutory provision of care, treatment and medical goods to patients by the NHS is regarded as a non-business activity falling outside the scope of VAT.

The *Sixth Directive* further provides that some non-business activities of public authorities should be deemed to be business activities in certain circumstances:

'However, when they [public authorities] engage in such [non-business] activities or transactions, they shall be considered taxable persons in respect of those activities or transactions where treatment as non-taxable persons would lead to significant distortions of competition [i.e. with the private sector]' (*EC Sixth Directive, Article 4(5)*). See *Ufficio Distrettuale delle Imposte Dirette di Fiorenzuola d'Arda v Comune di Carpaneto Piacentino* and *Ufficio Provinciale Imposta sul Valore Aggiunto di Piacenza v Comune di Rivergaro and Others, CJEC 1989, [1991] STC 205,* and *Comune di Carpaneto Piacentino and Others v Ufficio Provinciale Imposta sul Valore Aggiunto di Piacenza, CJEC [1990] 3 CMLR 153.*

This provision is enacted in the UK by *VATA 1994, s 41(2)*, which confers a power on the Treasury to make directions in respect of which certain non-business activities of public authorities are to be deemed to be business activities. Where Treasury Directions specify that an activity is to be treated as a supply made in the course or furtherance of a business, the normal rules in relation to VAT liability apply, and output tax must be accounted for where appropriate.

The provision of private health care by NHS hospitals is a VAT-exempt business activity, subject to the rules outlined in paragraph 14.2 above. Input tax suffered in relation to business activities may be recovered to the extent permitted by the NHS trust's approved partial exemption method.

In common with other public authorities, NHS trusts may apply for the refund of VAT suffered in relation to certain 'contracted-out' services used for the purposes of their non-business activities (*VATA 1994, s 41(3)*). The contracted-out services rules were introduced to eliminate the additional VAT cost involved in placing service contracts with external suppliers in the private sector. The special status of NHS trusts cannot extend to independent third parties to whom their activities or functions have been delegated; see *EC v Kingdom of the Netherlands, CJEC Case C-235/85*, and *Ayuntamiento de Sevilla v Recaudadores de Tributos de las Zonas Primera y Segunda, CJEC [1993] STC 659*. The list of contracted-out services in respect of which NHS trusts may make refund claims is to be found in the Treasury Directions published annually in the *London Gazette*.

Claims for the refund of VAT suffered on contracted-out services are subject to the following conditions:

- the claim is made in respect of approved supplies of *services* (VAT suffered in respect of supplies of goods incidental to a main supply of approved services may be refunded under the contracted-out services rules: the Treasury Directions published on April 26 1996 contained a new provision permitting the refund of VAT suffered on the supply of accommodation leased for more than 21 years (a supply of goods), where this was part of a supply of approved services);

- the services were not used for the purpose of any actual or deemed business activity (although, in practice, Customs may allow apportionment where business use is incidental);

- the services must be of the kind traditionally performed 'in-house';

- Customs' requirements, both in respect of the timing, form and manner of the claim, and the keeping, preservation and production of records, are complied with.

Dispensing of drugs

14.7 The dispensing of drugs by a registered pharmacist on the prescription of a doctor may be zero-rated under *VATA 1994, 8 Sch, Group 7, Item 1*, and input tax suffered on the purchase of the drugs is therefore recoverable. However, Customs have always insisted that supplies of drugs to patients or residents by private hospitals and nursing homes should be regarded as incidental to a main supply of exempt medical treatment or care.

In January 1997 the Court of Appeal ruled on the question of the extent to which the supply of certain goods (i.e. drugs and prostheses) made in connection with the provision of care etc., which would otherwise qualify for zero-rating, must fall within the scope of the health care exemption (*Wellington Private Hospital Ltd v C&E Commrs, CA [1997] STC 445*). Millett LJ held that Customs could treat as separate supplies what the contracting parties had treated as a single supply, but they could not join together what the contracting parties had treated as separate supplies. Although Customs were refused leave to appeal to the House of Lords, secondary legislation has now been introduced to remove zero-rating for drugs and prostheses supplied to hospital in-patients and private nursing home residents with effect from 1 January 1998 (*VATA 1994, 8 Sch, Group*

14.8 *VAT Business by Business*

12, Note 5A, introduced by *VAT (Drugs, Medicines and Aids for the Handicapped) Order 1997 (SI 1997 No 2744)).* Institutions affected by the *Wellington Private Hospital* ruling should ensure that retrospective claims for directly and indirectly attributable input tax suffered prior to 1 January 1998 are made as soon as possible, as such claims will be subject to the three-year time limit introduced by the *Finance Act 1997.*

As the dispensing of drugs to NHS hospital patients forms part of the statutory provision of health care, it is considered to be a non-business activity in relation to which there is no right of VAT recovery. Customs have indicated that drugs supplied and dispensed by an independent pharmacist on the prescription of a doctor to a named hospital outpatient or inpatient may be zero-rated, but as drugs dispensed to NHS patients are generally dispensed by an in-house pharmacist from ward stock, there would seem to be little scope to mitigate irrecoverable VAT.

The dispensing of drugs to private patients by the NHS is a business activity. Provided the relevant conditions are satisfied, the supply may be zero-rated and input tax suffered in relation to the purchase of the drugs may be recovered.

Welfare

14.8 The supply, otherwise than for profit, by a charity or public body of welfare services and goods in connection therewith is exempt from VAT (*VATA 1994, 9 Sch, Group 7, Item 9*). 'Welfare' in this context includes services directly connected with the provision of care or treatment designed to promote the physical or mental welfare of elderly, sick, distressed or disabled persons. 'Care' should be taken to mean continuing personal contact, i.e. looking after, helping or supervising people (*VAT Notice 701/1/95*). 'Public bodies' include local authorities and NHS trusts. Broadly, the term 'otherwise than for profit' means that any surpluses generated by qualifying activities must not be capable of distribution or of virement to non-qualifying activities; it does not mean that the activity itself must be run at a loss (Customs & Excise News Release 30/89).

There are, however, some important exclusions from the welfare VAT exemption as defined above. The statutory provision of welfare by NHS trusts is a non-business activity, and VAT suffered in relation to certain contracted-out services used for these purposes may be refunded under the rules outlined at paragraph 14.6 above.

The provision by a local authority of residential accommodation under the *National Assistance Act 1948*, the *Health Service Act 1977* or the *Mental Health (Scotland) Act 1984* to that local authority's own clients is a non-business activity. Unlike NHS trusts, local authorities may obtain refunds for all VAT suffered by them in carrying on their non-business activities (*VATA 1994, s 33*). See also Chapter 19—Local Authorities.

Hospitals and Nursing Homes **14.10**

By concession, Customs allow supplies of welfare services by charities provided at significantly below cost to be treated as a non-business activity. The concession may only apply where there is a consistent policy of subsidising such services by at least 15%. The concession may not be applied selectively, but must apply to all activities satisfying the necessary criteria.

Supplies of aids for the 'handicapped'

14.9 The supply to hospitals and nursing homes with charitable status of certain goods and services designated as aids for the 'handicapped' may be eligible for zero-rating (*VATA 1994, 8 Sch, Group 12, Items 2–20*). In the context of the legislation, 'handicapped' means 'chronically sick or disabled'. In *Help the Aged, QB [1997] STC 406*, it was held that this term may be taken to include persons whose health is so impaired on account of old age that they require the use of a wheelchair or walking aid. (Other aspects of the decision in this case have been overtaken by the enactment of *VATA 1994, 8 Sch, Group 15, Notes 4A, 4B*, introduced by *FA 1997, s 34*.)

Goods catering for special needs

14.10 A supply to a hospital or nursing home with charitable status for making certain categories of goods available to handicapped patients or residents by sale or otherwise, and the service of letting those goods on hire, may be zero-rated (*VATA 1994, 8 Sch, Group 12, Item 2*). These goods include the following:

– medical or surgical appliances designed solely for the relief of a severe abnormality or injury;

– certain adjustable beds, sanitary appliances, lifts or hoists designed for the use of handicapped persons;

– motor vehicles designed or substantially and permanently adapted for the carriage of a person in a wheelchair or on a stretcher and no more than five other persons;

– any other equipment or appliances designed solely for use of handicapped persons (but not normally hearing aids, dentures, spectacles or contact lenses).

The supply of spare parts and accessories designed solely for use in conjunction with any of the above goods, or the supply of services necessarily performed in their repair, maintenance or installation, may also be zero-rated.

The supply of goods or services in connection with the adaptation of goods to suit the condition of handicapped persons may be zero-rated where the goods are supplied to a charity which will make the goods available to a handicapped person (*VATA 1994, 8 Sch, Group 12, Item 4*).

14.11 *VAT Business by Business*

The wide-ranging nature of these reliefs has inevitably given rise to disputes over their interpretation. Customs have become concerned at what they regard as the exploitation of the reliefs to obtain zero-rating for goods well outside their original intended scope. Their response has been an increasingly strict interpretation of the legislation, particularly the provision covering 'any other' equipment and appliances designed solely for the use of handicapped persons (*VATA 1994, 8 Sch, Group 12, Item 2(g)*). This approach is evidenced by their recent change in policy towards incontinence products.

With effect from 1 August 1996, Customs no longer accept that NHS or non-charitable nursing homes can make zero-rated supplies of incontinence products to their patients and residents, maintaining that such supplies constitute non-business activities provided free of charge in the former case, and an indissociable part of an overall provision of exempt health care in the latter (Business Brief 16/96). Input tax recovery is denied in both cases. However, health care providers have been able to frustrate this policy to some extent by entering into an agency arrangement with main suppliers of incontinence products whereby they continue to take delivery of the goods, but without actually taking legal title which passes directly to the handicapped patient or resident. The main supplier is therefore able to zero-rate the supply of the goods as the supply is no longer to the health care provider, but to a handicapped person for their 'domestic or personal use'. (*VATA 1994, 8 Sch, Group 12* also allows zero-rating where qualifying goods or services are provided to handicapped persons for their domestic or personal use.) The general validity of such arrangements has been upheld by the VAT and Duties Tribunal in the case of *Mölnlycke Ltd (14641)*. Customs were partially successful in challenging such arrangements where the mental condition of the inpatient or resident was such that their consent to the contract was a sham. Interestingly, Customs do not believe that this decision has wider application to other medical goods, but this remains to be seen. (See Business Brief 5/97.)

Facilitation of access

14.11 Zero-rating may also apply to certain building adaptations carried out by hospitals and nursing homes with charitable status to facilitate or improve access by handicapped persons to their buildings or facilities. The services of architects and surveyors fall outside the scope of this relief. (See *Strachan (2155)* and *Hewitt Overall Associates (9374)*.)

The supply to a charity of goods and services in connection with the construction of ramps and the widening of doorways or passageways for the purpose of facilitating access by handicapped persons to any building may be zero-rated (*VATA 1994, 8 Sch, Group 12, Items 9, 13*). However, other reliefs in relation to supplies to charities are more restrictive and tend to be interpreted strictly.

Hospitals and Nursing Homes **14.12**

Charities providing a permanent or temporary residence or day centre for handicapped persons may obtain zero-rating for the installation of a lift where this is necessary to facilitate the movement of handicapped persons between floors in such a building (*VATA 1994, 8 Sch, Group 12, Items 17, 18*).

Charities may obtain zero-rating for the provision, extension or adaptation of bathroom, washroom or lavatory facilities, where these are provided for the use of handicapped persons in a residential home or in a building, or part of a building, used principally by a charity for charitable purposes, and the work was necessary by reason of the condition of the handicapped persons (*VATA 1994, 8 Sch, Group 12, Items 11–13*).

Supplies to charities and other eligible bodies

14.12 The supply of relevant goods for donation to a nominated eligible body, or direct to any eligible body, where the goods are purchased with funds provided by a charity or from voluntary contributions, may be zero-rated (*VATA 1994, 8 Sch, Group 15, Items 4, 5*).

'Relevant goods' for these purposes include the following:

- medical or scientific equipment for use in medical or veterinary research, training, diagnosis or treatment;
- ambulances;
- goods included in *VATA 1994, 8 Sch, Group 12, Item 2* (see paragraph 14.10 above);
- certain motor vehicles designed or substantially and permanently adapted for the safe carriage of a handicapped person in a wheelchair;
- certain motor vehicles for use by an eligible body providing care for blind, deaf, mentally handicapped or terminally sick persons mainly to transport such persons.

(*VATA 1994, 8 Sch, Group 15, Note 3*). See VAT Notice 701/6/97 for more detailed guidance.

Where relevant goods are to be used partly for a qualifying and partly for a non-qualifying purpose, Customs will allow zero-rating only if the goods are 'mainly' for the qualifying use. See VAT Notice 701/6/97.

'Eligible bodies' include health authorities, NHS trusts, hospitals and research institutions whose activities are not carried on for profit, and charitable institutions providing care or medical or surgical treatment for handicapped persons (*VATA 1994, 8 Sch, Group 15, Note 4*). A charity will not be regarded as providing care or medical or surgical treatment to handicapped persons unless it provides that care or treatment in a day centre, the primary purpose of which is not social or recreational, and unless the

14.12 VAT Business by Business

majority of persons who receive care or treatment are handicapped persons (*VATA 1994, 8 Sch, Group 15, Notes 4A, 4B*). Charities providing medical care to persons in their own homes may obtain zero-rating only in respect of medical equipment (*VATA 1994, 8 Sch, Group 15, Note 5B*).

By concession, Customs are prepared to allow the zero-rating of adapted minibuses and other relevant goods to charities which exclusively serve the needs of handicapped persons, where these organisations would not otherwise qualify as eligible bodies. See News Release 9/97 and Business Brief 13/97.

The question of what constitutes an eligible body for the purposes of these provisions was considered by the High Court in *Help the Aged, QB [1997] STC 406*. The tribunal rejected Customs' argument that a charity must have as its principal object and activity the provision of care to handicapped persons, holding that a charity which included the provision of care to handicapped persons among its objects and provided some such care may also qualify as an eligible body. The High Court upheld this decision.

See now, however, *VATA 1994, 8 Sch, Group 15, Notes 4A, 4B*, introduced by *FA 1997, s 34* with effect from 26 November 1996. The new provisions were intended to restrict the scope of the zero-rating provisions to 'charities providing personal care or treatment predominantly for the handicapped...in an institutional or a domiciliary setting'.

Despite their apparently restrictive nature, these provisions afford an important and valuable relief. They also give rise to planning opportunities. For example, supplies of incontinence products to eligible bodies without charitable status fall outside other zero-rating provisions (*VATA 1994, 8 Sch, Group 12, Item 2*); but provided they are purchased with funds provided by a charity or from voluntary contributions, such products may still be zero-rated under the 'relevant goods' rules. It should be noted, however, that there are anti-avoidance provisions disapplying zero-rating where the donee of the relevant goods is not a charity and has contributed to the funds for the purchase of the goods (*VATA 1994, 8 Sch, Group 15, Note 6*), or where the body to whom the goods are supplied is not a charity and has contributed to the funds for the purchase of the goods (*VATA 1994, 8 Sch, Group 15, Note 7*). See also the *VAT (Drugs, Medicines and Aids for the Handicapped) Order 1997 (SI 1997 No 2744)*, which came into force on 1 January 1998, amending and adding new Notes to *VATA 1994, 8 Sch, Group 12, Items 1, 1A, 2*.

The supply to a charity, providing care or medical or surgical treatment for human beings or animals, or engaging in medical or veterinary research, of a medicinal product where the supply is solely for use by the charity in such care, treatment or research may be zero-rated (*VATA 1994, 8 Sch, Group 15, Item 9*). Zero-rating also extends to the supply to a charity of a substance directly used for synthesis or testing in the course of medical or veterinary research (*VATA 1994, 8 Sch, Group 15, Item 10*).

Zero-rating certificates

14.13 Before a supplier may zero-rate any supply, a certificate must first by obtained from the handicapped person, charity or eligible body to whom the supply is to be made, making a declaration of entitlement to the relief. Suppliers should retain such certificates as evidence that they were entitled to apply the zero rate. There is no set form for such certificates, but there is a reasonable requirement that they should follow the layouts suggested by Customs. For aids for disabled persons see VAT Notice 701/7/94; for charity-funded equipment for medical uses see the supplement to VAT Notice 701/6/97. Where a customer makes an incorrect declaration of entitlement to zero-rating, Customs will not seek to recover the VAT due from the supplier, provided they are satisfied that all reasonable steps were taken to check the validity of the declaration (Extra-statutory concession 2.11; see VAT Notice 48).

Chapter 15

Hotels and Holiday Accommodation

Introduction

15.1 The majority of supplies made in the holiday industry are subject to VAT at the standard rate. There are, however, some important exceptions. As a result, partial exemption issues may affect traders in this industry and should therefore be considered. Also relevant may be the rules affecting tour operators.

Liability

Hotels, inns, boarding houses and similar establishments

15.2 The provision of sleeping accommodation in an hotel, inn, boarding house or 'similar establishment' is subject to VAT at the standard rate (*VATA 1994, 9 Sch, Group 1, Item 1(d)*). This includes the provision of ancillary accommodation such as living rooms, and accommodation provided for the purpose of a supply of catering.

For the VAT liability relating to long-term stays, see paragraph 15.8 below.

'Similar establishment' includes premises which are used by or are held out as suitable for the use by travellers or visitors, which provides furnished sleeping accommodation. This includes 'bed and breakfast', private residential clubs, hostels and motels. (*VATA 1994, 9 Sch, Group 1, Note 9*).

A hotel, inn, boarding house or similar establishment would usually provide either meals or facilities for the preparation of food. However, it is not necessary for either of these to be provided for the establishment to be regarded as a hotel, etc. (C&E Leaflet 709/3/93, Para 2).

Service charges

15.3 Service charges which are left to the discretion of the guest are outside the scope of VAT. Mandatory service charges are treated as additional consideration for the supply and therefore follow the liability of

15.4 VAT Business by Business

that supply. For example, a mandatory service charge added to the cost of a restaurant meal will be standard-rated.

Booking fees, deposits and cancellation charges

Booking fees

15.4 Booking fees charged by an agent who arranges a supply on behalf of someone else are the consideration for a taxable supply and VAT is due at the time that the charge is made. A booking fee charged by the hotel, etc. is treated as a deposit.

Deposits

15.5 A deposit taken at the time of a booking is treated as advance payment for the supply, and VAT is therefore due at the time when the payment is received. However, if a prospective guest then cancels a booking and in doing so forfeits the deposit, the VAT which was declared when the deposit was received can be reclaimed from Customs & Excise. (C&E Leaflet 709/3/93, para 7).

Cancellation charges

15.6 If a cancellation charge is levied on someone who cancels a booking, no VAT is due on that charge as it is considered to be a payment of a compensatory nature; as there has been no supply of services, the payment is outside the scope of VAT.

If a guarantee or insurance is arranged or provided, against customers cancelling bookings, any charge for this is standard-rated. However, where:

(i) the person providing the insurance is permitted to carry on an insurance business under *Insurance Companies Act 1982, s 2*; or

(ii) he arranges, as agent, for insurance to be provided by a permitted insurer and, under the policy, it is the individual customer's risk which is insured;

then the charge which is made for that insurance becomes exempt. Any commission charged by the agent will also be exempt. See Chapter 17—Insurance.

A charge for 'non-arrivals', for example against a confirmed booking, is treated as standard-rated (*C&E Commrs v Bass plc, QB 1992, [1993] STC 42*).

Disbursements

15.7 If a guest receives goods or services from a third person, but for convenience the cost of the supply is paid by the hotel, with the exact sum recovered later from the guest, then no VAT is due when this recovery takes place. These costs are treated as disbursements for VAT purposes and are therefore outside the scope of VAT.

Reduced value rules—stays of over four weeks

15.8 For the first four weeks of any stay in an hotel, VAT is due on the full amount payable in the normal way. Where accommodation is provided to an individual for a continuous period exceeding four weeks, VAT is due on a reduced value from the 29th day of the stay. This does not apply to block bookings by tour operators, airlines, etc., where accommodation is used for a succession of short-term occupants.

Under the reduced value rules, VAT is due from the 29th day on the value attributable to meals, drinks, service charges and facilities other than the right to occupy the accommodation. Facilities include the cleaning of rooms, the provision of television and radio, coffee and tea making facilities etc. The value of the facilities must not be less than 20% of the total amount due for the accommodation and other facilities together (*VATA 1994, 6 Sch 9*).

Where the actual value of the facilities is more than 20% of the total charge, that value should be used when calculating the reduced value rules (C&E Leaflet 709/3/93, para 5(a)).

Normally, the reduced value rules cannot be used unless the guest stays for a continuous period of more than four weeks. For example, regular stays of three weeks out of four are subject to VAT on the full value. Similarly, if a guest stays for six weeks, is away for a week and then returns for another stay exceeding 28 days, each stay is treated separately and the reduced value basis can only apply for the 29th day onward of each stay. There are three exceptions to this rule:

(a) a long term resident who leaves for the occasional weekend or holiday;

(b) a student who leaves during the vacation but returns to the same accommodation for the next term; and

(c) where a retaining fee is paid.

For any of these three exceptions, a period of absence will not end a stay, which may then be treated as continuous and VAT only charged in full on the first four weeks of the overall stay. It is not necessary for the guest to return to the same room for his stay, in order for it to be treated as continuous.

15.9 VAT Business by Business

Retaining fees

15.9 A retaining fee paid during an absence in the first four weeks of a stay is subject to VAT at the standard rate. Where a fee is paid after the first four weeks, it may treated as part of the reduced value rule. If the fee is no more than the amount of the charge which is treated as being for accommodation, under the reduced value rule, no VAT is due on the retaining fee. Where it exceeds this level, the fee should be apportioned between accommodation and facilities (see paragraph 15.30 below).

Rooms supplied for the purpose of catering

15.10 Where catering is supplied by the hotel, guest house, etc., it is standard-rated (*VATA 1994, 9 Sch, Group 1, Item 1(d)*) regardless of the length of the supply. However, where the room is hired without the catering, or the catering is supplied by a person other than the hotel etc., the supply of the room is normally exempt (subject to the option to tax). If the hotel grants a concession for another person to operate a kitchen, bar, restaurant or kiosk within the hotel, which involves the preparation or service of food or drink, the supply by the hotel to the concessionaire would also normally be exempt, as it is the provision of a room, not the supply of catering. As an exempt supply, there will be issues arising on the recovery of related costs. (For details of the partial exemption provisions, see *Tolley's VAT 1998/99, chapter 49*.)

Where a supply is made to a customer, both for the use of conference rooms and for catering, e.g. where a conference is held at a hotel and the hotel also provides refreshment, there will be a mixed liability supply (unless the hotel has opted to tax the property). VAT should be charged only on the taxable element of the supply.

Any supply of additional items, such as car parking and the use of equipment, e.g. overhead projectors, and any items which are charged for separately, e.g. telephone calls, are standard-rated (C&E Leaflet 709/3/93, para 4).

Supplies to staff

15.11 If staff are provided with food and drink, or accommodation, and it is provided free of charge, or the contract of employment allows for a deduction from the gross wages, there is no VAT due (*RW & MJ Goodfellow, [1986] VATTR 119 (2107)*). However, if the staff are charged, and payment is made either in cash or by deduction from their wages (and the supplies are not provided for in the contract of employment), then the payments are deemed to include VAT at the appropriate rate. The value of the supply to the staff is deemed to be equal to the consideration paid, not by reference to the normal charges made by the hotel, etc. (*VATA 1994, 6 Sch 10(2)*).

Holiday accommodation

15.12 The supply of holiday accommodation is standard-rated, regardless of the length of stay or how the charges are described (*VATA 1994, 9 Sch, Group 1, Item 1(e)*). The exceptions to this are set out in paragraph 15.15 below.

Holiday accommodation is defined in *VATA 1994, 9 Sch, Group 1, Note 13* as:

> 'any accommodation in a building, hut (including a beach hut or chalet), caravan, houseboat or tent which is advertised or held out as holiday accommodation or as suitable for holiday or leisure use, but excludes any accommodation within paragraph (d)'
>
> (para (d) covers the supply within an hotel, inn, boarding house etc.)

Examples of 'advertised or held out as' are described in C&E Leaflet 709/3/93, paragraph 10 as being:

(a) where the property is advertised in one of the following ways:

- advertised or allowed to be advertised for holiday or leisure use;
- advertised in a specialist publication involving tourism, holidays or leisure activities; or
- advertised by a body which promotes such activities.

(b) where the terms and conditions of the property indicate that it is for holiday or leisure use; or

(c) where the supply is during the holiday season only.

These tests were applied in the case of *RW & B Sheppard, [1977] VATTR 272 (481)*, which involved the supply of short lettings of furnished flats which were treated as holiday accommodation.

The supply of residential accommodation which happens to be located on a holiday site is not necessarily regarded as the supply of holiday accommodation, unless there are other factors which determine its use (C&E Leaflet 709/3/93, para 10).

Property which has been held out as holiday accommodation, but which is then let for some other purpose, is not regarded as the provision of holiday accommodation and the VAT liability is determined by the other purpose the property is then put to. There must, however, be no connection between any advertisement for holiday accommodation and the subsequent use that is then made of the property (*Cooper & Chapman (Builders) Limited v C&E Commrs, QB 1992, [1993] STC 1*).

15.13 VAT Business by Business

Liability of a grant of a right in holiday accommodation

15.13 The grant of any right to call for or to be granted an interest or right in the property, which would have been standard-rated under the provision above, is also standard-rated. Included are equitable rights, a right under an option or right of pre-emption and, in relation to Scotland, a personal right (*VATA 1994, 9 Sch, Group 1, Item 1(n)*). It is not clear, however, whether the liability of the right is determined on the basis of the underlying supply at the time the right is granted or when the right can be exercised.

Restrictions on permanent use

15.14 The supply of a fee simple or a tenancy, lease or licence in a property designed as a dwelling which is new, and cannot be occupied throughout the year, or cannot be used as a principal private residence because of a covenant, planning restriction or similar constraint, is taxable. VAT must be accounted for on the initial charge and on any periodic charges such as ground rent, service charges or other charges. (C&E Leaflet 709/3/93, para 11). A 'new building' is one that is supplied within three years from the date on which a certificate of practical completion was issued, or it was first fully occupied, whichever is the earlier.

Any payment for the freehold sale or premium payment for a lease of a property which is no longer new will be exempt from VAT, but subsequent charges, including rent and service charges, will be taxable where the permanent use is restricted.

Exclusions from the standard-rated supply of holiday accommodation

15.15 The sale or lease of a flat or house which can be used as a person's principal private residence, but which cannot be occupied throughout the year due to a time-related restriction on occupancy, is exempt, but only where the development on which it is situated is not a holiday development and it is not advertised or held out as such. The exemption in this case then extends to any periodic charges such as a service charge and rent (*Mrs B A Ashworth, [1994] VATTR 275 (12924)*).

Provision of sites for holiday accommodation

15.16 The provision of a site for holiday accommodation under a tenancy, lease or licence is taxable even if the person to whom the supply is made is responsible for erecting the accommodation. However, the sale of the freehold interest in a site is exempt, unless an option to tax has been made over the site.

Off-season letting

15.17 Where holiday accommodation is supplied off-season, at lower rates, it can be treated as an exempt supply of residential accommodation if the following conditions apply:

(a) it is let to a person for residential, not holiday accommodation; and

(b) the let is for more than four weeks; and

(c) the holiday trade is clearly seasonal.

Where this is the case, the whole of the let, including the first four weeks, is seen to be an exempt supply (C&E Leaflet 709/3/93, para 13). The holiday season is considered to span at least the period between Easter and the end of September, but an area such as London is not regarded as having any seasonal holiday trade.

Time-share and multi-ownership schemes

15.18 A supply of holiday accommodation in a house, flat, chalet etc. under a time-share or multi-ownership scheme is standard-rated if the initial supply is of new accommodation and exempt if it is no longer new (see paragraph 15.14 above for the definition of 'new'). Any additional maintenance and periodic charges are standard-rated in all cases. These liability rules apply however the supply is effected, e.g. by lease or licence, through membership of a time-share club, or through shares in a company set up for that purpose (C&E Leaflet 709/3/93, para 14).

The supply of time-share certificates which allow the holder to occupy a property for a period each year were held to be taxable as holiday accommodation in *American Real Estate (Scotland) Ltd [1980] VATTR 80 (947)*, being held to be excluded from exemption by *VATA 1994, 9 Sch, Group 1, Item 1(e)*.

The time-share of a yacht was held to be taxable in *Oathplan Ltd, [1982] VATTR 195 (1299)*.

The construction of holiday accommodation

15.19 A builder can zero-rate the supply of services in the course of construction of a dwelling even though it will be used to supply holiday accommodation. The word 'dwelling' takes on its normal everyday meaning (C&E Leaflet 709/3/93, para 19).

15.20 VAT Business by Business

Caravans

15.20 Holiday accommodation provided in any type of caravan already sited on a pitch is standard-rated. The hire of a caravan for holiday purposes, or any other use, where it is:

(a) suitable for use as a trailer drawn by a motor vehicle having an unladen weight of less than 2,030 kilos; or

(b) a caravan unit designed to be mounted and carried on, and demounted from, a motor vehicle

is standard-rated (*VATA 1994, 8 Sch, Group 9, Item 3; 9 Sch, Group 1, Item 1(e)*) (C&E Leaflet 709/3/93, para 15).

Where a caravan exceeds these limits and is either more than 7 metres long or more than 2.3 metres wide, then the supply is zero-rated (*VATA 1994, 8 Sch, Group 9, Item 1*) (C&E Leaflet 701/20/96, para 1).

The hire of a caravan already sited on a pitch designated by a local authority as for permanent residential use, and having been let as such, is exempt.

Caravan pitches

15.21 The provision of 'seasonal pitches' for caravans, and the grant of facilities at caravan parks to persons for whom such pitches are provided, are standard-rated. A 'seasonal pitch' is a pitch which is provided for a period of less than a year, or which is provided for a period during which the person to whom it is provided is prevented by the terms of any covenant, statutory planning consent or similar permission from occupying it by living in a caravan throughout the period (*VATA 1994, 9 Sch Group 1, Item 1(f) and Note 14*). Following the tribunal decision in *Ashworth, [1994] VATTR 275 (12924)*, Customs accept that, where the pitch is provided for a period of a year or more, a pitch will only be regarded as seasonal if it is on a site or part of a site which is advertised or held out for holiday use (C&E Leaflet 701/20/89, para 4).

The supply of other pitches, for example at permanent residential caravan parks, is exempt.

Additional charges

15.22 A proportion of the rates charged to the owner of a caravan park is normally attributable to the individually owned caravans on the site. If a proportion of this charge is passed on to the individual caravan owners, it is outside the scope of VAT and no VAT should be charged on it.

The official apportionment provided in the valuation list or on the rates demand should be used to determine the amount of the charge which can be passed on. The remainder of the rates charged to the owner, i.e. the element for the communal buildings and general facilities at the park, in addition to the caravans owned by the park owner, are treated as general overheads of the business. If any element of these charges are passed on to the individual caravan owners, they are regarded as part of the pitch fee.

Service charges

15.23 Charges made to individual caravan owners for the general upkeep and maintenance of the caravan park as a whole, e.g. for grass cutting, are part of the overall consideration for the supply of the pitch and will therefore be taxable.

Car parking

15.24 The supply of parking facilities is taxable, as part of the supply of a pitch for holiday accommodation (C&E Leaflet 701/20/89, para 8).

Insurance

15.25 The supply of insurance by a permitted insurer, to cover the general liability of the park owner, is exempt. If the cost is recovered from the caravan users, the recharge follows the liability of the pitch and is therefore subject to VAT. Where the park owner is asked to arrange insurance on behalf of a caravan user, the charge by the park owner for arranging the insurance will be exempt from VAT, provided that the caravan owner is the recipient of the supply of insurance made by the insurer (C&E Leaflet 701/20/89, para 9). See Chapter 17—Insurance.

Supply of a caravan

15.26 The supply of a caravan, for example by selling it, by leasing it under a long-term lease (in excess of one year) where the lessee can remove the caravan to a park of their choice, or by diverting it from business use to personal use, is zero-rated if the caravan is either:

- more than 7 metres long; or

- more than 2.3 metres wide,

excluding towing bars and other attaching apparatus. Supplies of other caravans are standard-rated.

Zero-rating will also extend to the internal goods which a builder would ordinarily incorporate into a new house, for example, sink, shower, fixed

15.27 VAT Business by Business

partitions and water heaters. Removable contents supplied with the caravan are standard-rated. See 15.32 below for the accounting procedures.

Camping

15.27 The provision of holiday accommodation in a tent, and the provision of pitches for tents or of camping facilities, is standard-rated (*VATA 1994, 9 Sch, Group 1, Items (e) and (g)*). Any associated facilities are also standard-rated.

VAT recovery

Input tax recovery

15.28 VAT can be recovered where it relates to the onward taxable supply made by the trader. Where both exempt and taxable supplies are made, the trader should consider whether it is required to operate a partial exemption method. In all cases, the VAT incurred should be directly attributed, as far as possible, to the onward supply.

Hotel disbursements

15.29 As disbursements, the hotel should not recover any VAT charged on the cost of the goods or services purchased on behalf of its guests, and should recharge the gross amount, without identifying the VAT element. An example of this is where an hotel purchases theatre tickets or pays for taxi fees on behalf of its guests.

Accounting and records

Calculating the reduced value hotel accommodation exceeding four weeks

15.30 For the purposes of the examples below, the proportion for the meals is taken to be 40% of the total charge.

(a) Where charges are expressed as tax exclusive:

Total weekly charge	£100.00
Of which:	
– proportion relating to meals	(£40.00)
– proportion relating to accommodation and facilities	£60.00
Value of facilities (not less than 20% of accommodation)	£12.00

Hotels and Holiday Accommodation **15.30**

VAT is due on the value relating to the meals and the facilities:

£40.00 + £12.00 = £52.00 × 17.5% = £9.10 VAT.

(b) Where charges are expressed as tax inclusive, the VAT element is the same as (a) but the calculation is as follows:

Total weekly charge	£117.50
Of which:	
– proportion relating to meals	(£47.00)
– proportion relating to accommodation and facilities	£70.50
Value of facilities (not less than 20% of accommodation)	£14.10

VAT is due on the value relating to the meals and the facilities:

£47.00 + £14.10 = £61.10 × 7/47 = £9.10 VAT.

(c) Where charges are expressed as tax inclusive but the charges are not reduced to take account of the lower element of tax:

Total weekly charge	£117.50
Of which:	
– proportion relating to meals	£47.00
– proportion relating to accommodation and facilities	£70.50

VAT due on the value relating to the meals and the facilities is calculated as follows:

Fraction to apply to the accommodation and facilities element:

$$\frac{17.5 \times \text{facilities element}\%}{100 + (17.5 \times \text{facilities element}\%)}$$

(e.g., where facilities element is 20%, the fraction is 7/207)

The VAT element is calculated as £70.50 × 7/207 = £2.38, plus VAT on the meals element, £47.00 × 7/47 = £7.00. Total VAT due is therefore £9.38.

Although VAT is due only on the reduced amount of the charges for the supplies (i.e. not on the payment for accommodation), the full tax-exclusive amount must be included in box 6 of the VAT return. This is because the accommodation element of the total charge continues to be the consideration for a standard-rated supply, even though the value of the consideration for the purposes of calculating VAT due becomes nil after the first 28 days (C&E Leaflet 709/3/93, Annex B).

15.31 *VAT Business by Business*

Registration threshold

15.31 When calculating the value of taxable turnover for purposes of the VAT registration threshold, the value of accommodation under the reduced value rules becomes nil and should not be included for this purpose.

Calculating VAT on the removable contents of caravans

15.32 Customs identify two methods of dealing with VAT on the removable contents of used caravans. The chosen method must be applied consistently, rather than alternating between the methods. The methods are set out in Annex C to Customs' Leaflet 701/20.

(a) *The standard apportionment of values*

This apportionment has been agreed with the National Caravan Council Ltd and the British Holiday and Home Parks Association Ltd. The value of the standard-rated removable contents is taken as being 10% of the overall tax exclusive selling price.

(b) *The actual value method*

This requires calculations to be carried out to assess the actual value of each of the standard-rated removable contents, and must be supported by adequate documentary evidence to support each valuation.

Chapter 16

Housing Associations

Introduction

16.1 Housing associations account for 25% of all new dwellings; partly funded by public money through the Housing Corporation, and partly through private money. This statement demonstrates the significance of the sector within the general economy of the country and the political scene.

Housing associations are normally corporate bodies incorporated under the *Industrial & Provident Societies Act 1965*, with or without charitable status. Those with charitable status tend to supply housing needs to the elderly, such as sheltered housing, whereas those without charitable status tend to cover the wider social housing sector. Housing associations are regulated by the Housing Corporation and have their own accounting standards.

Housing associations are unable to distribute profits to members and as such are 'non-profit-making' bodies applying their surpluses to maintain and expand their existing housing stock. Nevertheless, they are competitive but their ethos is to help other associations.

Following the stepped abolition of grants under *Housing Act 1988 s 54*, there is likely to be a move towards more housing associations seeking charitable status or having a charitable body under their umbrella. *Section 54* gave the Housing Corporation discretionary powers to make a grant payment towards the corporation tax liability of the non-charitable housing associations.

The Housing Corporation is a conduit for implementation of Government policy and recent examples are the encouragement of shared ownership by the allocation of grants specifically set aside for this purpose. Another recent innovation is the introduction of *registered social landlords* under the *Housing Act 1996*, which not only includes housing associations but also potentially a number of other 'not for profit' housing agencies, and housing companies which could gain advantage in registering with the Housing Corporation and gaining access to public funds.

There is very little VAT legislation actually directed at housing associations and the purpose of this chapter is to bring together the plethora of VAT legislation which could be applied to the activities of housing associations.

16.2 *VAT Business by Business*

Terminology

16.2 Within the world of housing associations the terminology used can be confusing and needs to be understood in order to establish the nature of the supply and, thus, the VAT treatment and to give meaningful advice. The following are common terms:

Amalgamations

Associations formed under the *Industrial & Provident Societies Act 1965* may amalgamate to form a new entity. Properties are transferred into the new entity by special resolution thus avoiding the need and expense of any form of conveyance.

Community leasehold

This is now superseded by *shared ownership*. The difference under community leasehold is that the occupier is unable to increase his equity share in the property and thus buys and sells a set percentage stake in the property.

Consortium arrangements

Occasionally, associations join together to undertake large scale developments which would also include joint arrangements procuring finance, services and goods at more favourable prices than could be obtained by a single association. In such circumstances it is normal to have a lead association which would secure contracts, etc. and the other associations would make contributions for their share of the costs.

Co-ownership association

An association registered as an *Industrial & Provident Society* under which membership is restricted to tenants or prospective tenants of the association and precludes the granting of tenancies to non-members. On ceasing to be a member, and thereby a tenant, the person leaving would become entitled to a sum calculated by reference to the value of the accommodation.

DIY shared ownership (DIYSO)

A scheme where a person, or body, identifies an existing property suitable for social letting and then encourages an association to purchase the property and sell it back on a shared ownership basis. The property would be managed by the association.

Housing co-operative

A co-operative association in which the members comprise the tenants or potential tenants. Unlike a *Co-ownership association*, tenants can include non-members.

Housing Trust

Normally created as an *Industrial & Provident Society*, a housing trust is a non-profit-making body which is required to devote all funds to the provision of social housing or to charitable purposes under *Housing Act 1985, s 6*.

Large Scale Voluntary Transfers (LSVT)

A mechanism for 'privatising' local authority housing stock whereby an association is formed to receive the housing stock of local authorities. The transfer is regulated by the Department of Environment and a transfer must first be approved through a ballot of existing tenants. The price paid by the association for the properties transferred is based on the existing rental values of the property portfolio.

Leasehold Schemes for the Elderly (LSE)

Under this scheme housing is offered on the basis of a lease to the occupier. In many cases the price would be reduced by a Housing Association Grant (HAG) from the Housing Corporation.

Nomination rights

An arrangement whereby a specific proportion of homes to be constructed by an association are set aside for people suggested by a particular body, usually a local authority, as part of gaining planning consent.

Right to buy

A right available to tenants of non-charitable associations under *Housing Act 1985* whereby the tenant is able to acquire the property, at a discount, after a minimum of two years' occupation.

Shared ownership

This is the sharing of the equity in a property between the occupier and an association, typically 50% in the first instance with the right to the occupier to increase their equity stake until full ownership is achieved.

Staircasing

A term used in *Shared ownership*, to describe the purchase by the occupier of additional tranches of the equity in the property.

16.3 VAT Business by Business

Tenants' Incentive Schemes (TIS)

A cash payment scheme enabling tenants of participating associations to purchase a property on the understanding that the vacated home would be used to house a homeless family.

Transfer of engagements

This is a mechanism enabling the transfer of assets and liabilities of an association that is an *Industrial & Provident Society* to another association. No conveyance nor assignment is necessary and no stamp duty is payable. The transferring association loses its separate existence on the transfer.

Types of Tenancy agreements

Assured tenancy arrangements were introduced by the *Housing Act 1988* and the *Housing (Scotland) Act 1988* and are now the normal tenancy terms for new lettings. Under the Act, a housing association is expected to charge a rent affordable by those on low incomes and the tenant is assured of certain standards of service under contractual rights.

Secured tenancy arrangements existed prior to the Housing Acts of 1988 and remain unaffected by the change in legislation. Secured tenants enjoy security of tenure in respect of existing and renewed tenancies and are charged a fair rent which is determined by the local Rent Officer.

Liability

Core activity

16.3 The core activity of a housing association is the provision of affordable accommodation which would be in the form of letting *dwellings* or property used for a *relevant residential purpose*. It is unlikely that a housing association would become involved in property used for relevant charitable purposes because rental charges would create a business activity and thus put it outside the scope of any charitable relief (*VATA 1994, 8 Sch, Group 5, Note 6*).

Where a major interest has been granted in the form of a lease in excess of 21 years, the first rental payment under the lease will be zero-rated provided that the freehold has not been sold previously; subsequent rental payments under the lease will be exempt. However, the *Housing Corporation* rules prevent the granting of a major interest except, for example, under *shared ownership* and *right to buy* schemes.

A definition of a *dwelling* was introduced into the legislation on 1 March 1995; prior to that date a common-sense approach prevailed although this inevitably led to disputes. A dwelling is now defined as consisting of self-contained living accommodation with no direct internal access to any other dwelling. Additionally, the separate use or disposal of a dwelling must not be prohibited by the terms of any covenant, statutory planning consent or similar provision. Furthermore, the dwelling must have been constructed or converted within the terms of a statutory planning consent. (*VATA 1994, 8 Sch, Group 5, Note 2*).

Within the context of a housing association activity, *relevant residential* would include a home providing residential accommodation with personal care for persons in need of such care by reason of old age or disability (including people suffering from drug or alcohol dependency or mental disorder), or any other living accommodation which is the sole or main residence for at least 90% of the residents. However, the sole or main residence test was successfully challenged in the *Urdd Gobaith Cymru (14881)* case where it was held that, for residential accommodation to qualify for zero-rating, a minimum length of stay was not relevant. The tribunal held that, in ordinary English, 'residential accommodation' merely signifies lodging, sleeping or overnight accommodation and did not suggest the need for any fixed or minimum period of stay. Also included within the definition of 'relevant residential' are armed forces' living accommodation, such as barrack blocks and unaccompanied officers' quarters; married quarters are treated as dwellings.

With effect from 1 March 1995, where a number of buildings are constructed at the same time and on the same site, and are intended to be used together as a unit solely for a *relevant residential purpose*, then each of those buildings is to be treated as intended for use solely for a relevant residential purpose. (*VATA 1994, 8 Sch, Group 5, Notes 4 and 5*). An example would include a separate laundry block constructed at the same time as other buildings. A building constructed at a later date as an addition to an existing establishment would not be treated as a relevant residential building unless it qualifies in its own right.

It should be noted, however, that Customs do not consider sheltered housing as being for relevant residential use where each unit constitutes a separate dwelling, e.g. in a court where the individual units are in the form of self-contained flats. This is particularly relevant to a housing association with charitable status when considering relief available under *VATA 1994, 8 Sch, Group 12*—see paragraph 16.26 below. The writer considers that perhaps the law has not maintained pace with current trends inasmuch that the provision of sheltered housing in courts is more desirable to tenants than accommodation in a home.

The *rental income* received by a housing association will normally be exempt. The two common types of tenancies are *assured* and *secured* tenancies. Rent paid by way of housing benefits by the Department of Social Security will be treated as an exempt supply.

16.4 VAT Business by Business

Where accommodation supplied by a housing association is in the form of that supplied by a hotel, inn or boarding house, e.g. a temporary hostel for the homeless, and the accommodation provided is very similar to that provided in the hotel sector, bed and breakfast, then the rental income would be treated as a standard-rated supply; such establishments are excluded from the definition of a relevant residential building. (*VATA 1994, 8 Sch, Group 5, Note 4*).

It is not uncommon for housing associations to own commercial premises, usually in the form of shop units at the base of a block of flats or maisonettes. Such units are normally let under a lease agreement and the rent will represent an exempt supply unless an 'option to tax' (election to waive exemption under *VATA 1994, 10 Sch*) has been made whereupon the rents will be subject to standard-rated tax.

Rent on stand-alone garages let to tenants will normally follow the terms of the tenancy agreement and will be exempt from tax. However, where the garage is not let as part of a tenancy agreement for a dwelling or a relevant residential building, then the rent receivable is subject to tax as a standard-rated supply. (*VATA 1994, 9 Sch, Group 1, Item 1(h)*). In *C&E Commissioners v Trinity Factoring Services Limited, CS [1994] STC 504*, the court held that the lease of a lock-up garage was standard-rated even though the garage was used for the storage of goods.

Service charges to tenants

16.4 *Customs & Excise Business Brief 3/94* outlines an extra-statutory concession that came into effect on 1 April 1994 for certain service charges paid in respect of dwellings.

From 1 April 1994 various mandatory service charges paid by the tenants of residential property have followed the main supply and as such are exempt from VAT. These charges include:

- the upkeep of common areas (e.g. paths, landscape general areas, general corridors and stairwells), and

- the provision of a warden, caretaker or people connected with the day to day running of the dwelling or block of flats, and

- the general maintenance of the exterior of the block of flats or individual dwellings (e.g. painting and window cleaning).

It is interesting to note that under the *Landlord and Tenant Act 1987, s 42*, the landlord, in this case the housing association, has to hold such funds in trust and any interest earned on the funds is automatically applied to the trustees of the trust. The tenant is not entitled to any refund on vacating the property and on termination of all of the tenancies any balance in the trust fund belongs to

Housing Associations **16.4**

the housing association. Hence the interest income arising from investing the moneys held in the fund would belong to the housing association but would be excluded from any partial exemption calculation. This is seen as incidental to the main business activity.

Prior to 1 April 1994 service charges, as outlined above, were exempt when paid under the terms of the lease to the lessor or ground landlord. However, where they were paid for by freehold owners of domestic property, and by anyone for services not supplied under the direction of the lessor or ground landlord, they were taxable as standard-rated because they could not be regarded as consideration for any supply of land. This led to an anomaly for the tenants because the liability of the service charge did not depend on the services provided but on the tenure of the residence and the status of the supplier. The concession removed this anomaly, but on domestic accommodation only.

Optional services, often referred to as domestic services supplied to the tenant, such as carpet and upholstery cleaning, remain taxable as standard-rated in their own right.

In respect of commercial premises, lease agreements would normally state that the housing association will provide, and the tenant shall pay, for the upkeep of the commercial unit. The lease may provide for an inclusive rental, or it may require the tenant to make a contribution for the upkeep of the unit. Such contribution may be referred to as 'additional rent', 'maintenance', or 'service charge'. Provided that the service is to be considered as part of the supply of the property, and:

- is of a nature which is connected with the external fabric or the common parts of the building or estate as opposed to the demised areas of the property of the individual occupants; and

- it is paid for by all of the occupants through a common service charge; then,

the service charge assumes the same VAT liability as on the rents payable under the lease, the concession mentioned above does not apply.

With regard to insurance or rates, if the housing association is the policy holder, or rateable person, any payments which the housing association receives is part payment of the main supply, i.e. it assumes the same VAT liability as the rents payable under the lease. Should the tenant be the policy holder, or rateable person, and the housing association makes payments on behalf of the tenant, then these should be treated as disbursements.

16.5 VAT Business by Business

Other services to tenants

16.5 Other services provided to tenants would include the provision of fuel and power, community facilities, and, particularly in sheltered accommodation, the provision of meals, care and laundry services.

Fuel and power. Any separate charge for the unmetered supplies of gas and electricity to the tenants is treated as part of the consideration for the supply of the residential accommodation and will assume the same VAT liability as the rents payable by the tenant: an exempt supply. However, where the tenants have a secondary meter, including coin operated meters, or receive an identifiable supply of gas and electricity for which a separate charge is made, then the charge for the supply by the landlord represents a separate supply of fuel and power subject to the lower-rated VAT, currently 5%.

Community facilities. The supply of community facilities (e.g. a communal lounge) without a separate charge or a specific extra charge being made, will follow the liability of the main supply; exempt.

Sheltered accommodation may offer a mix of supplies dependent upon the status and general well being of the tenant. In general there are two types of supply; in-care and out-of-care.

In-care services will normally include the provision of meals, possibly in a community dining room, the provision of general care, and the provision of a laundry service. The provision of fuel and power has been dealt with above. It is the normal practice of a housing association to charge a set rental embracing all of the services without identifying the separate parts and as such the charge made represents a supply of accommodation; an exempt supply. In the unlikely circumstances that the charge made identifies the separate constituent parts, the appropriate rate of VAT should be applied to each part, e.g. the provision of a laundry service would be taxable as standard-rated. However, it should be noted that the supply of catering to the elderly in sheltered accommodation was held to be ancillary to the provision of care and was, therefore, exempt. (See *Viewpoint Housing Association Ltd (13148)*).

Out-of-care services would normally exclude day to day care services, and the provision of meals. The VAT treatment would follow the same lines as for in-care services.

Disposals of property

16.6 Property sales by housing associations are restricted by reason of the *Housing Act 1985*; the legislation is monitored by the Housing Corporation. The two main areas are *right to buy* sales and *shared ownership*.

Right to buy

16.7   Under the *Housing Act 1985* local authority tenants have the right to buy their homes and this right continues should the local authority transfer its housing stock to a housing association by a *Large Scale Voluntary Transfer (LSVT)*. This right does not extend to new tenants appointed by the housing association after the date of transfer from the local authority.

The housing association is not regarded as the person constructing the property; this status remains with the local authority, and hence the sales made are regarded as an exempt supply.

As part of the transfer arrangement from the local authority to the housing association a percentage of the proceeds received by the housing association under the *LSVT* agreement may be payable to the local authority; this payment would be outside the scope of VAT. The background behind such payments hinges on the transfer value of the properties. The price paid for the properties by the housing association would be based on the rental value at the time of the transfer; needless to say, this would be considerably less than open market value with vacant possession. Under the right to buy rules, the price paid by the tenant is based on open market value but discounted according to the length of tenancy. Thus, the housing association could receive a considerable windfall surplus and the local authority might wish to participate in this windfall to the benefit of local council tax payers and other services supplied.

Some housing association rules will permit the tenant to have the option to buy the house after a specific period has elapsed. In the case of *C&E Commissioners v Link Housing Association Ltd, CS [1992] STC 718*, the tribunal held that the term *person constructing* means a *person who has constructed* so that a person constructing always makes a zero-rated supply when it grants a major interest; this view was upheld in the Scottish Court of Session. Customs have taken the view that the decision applies only to input tax on disposal costs.

Shared ownership

16.8   This has gained popularity over the years and specific grants have been made available by the Housing Corporation to encourage such schemes. Shared ownership can be achieved through a new build policy by the housing association or by making existing housing stock available. The new build tends to be more favoured because it is more acceptable to the prospective purchaser.

Under this arrangement the housing association will sell part ownership in a dwelling (normally 50%) and the purchaser can increase his equity in the property (*staircasing*) by acquiring additional tranches until achieving outright ownership. The individual will pay rent to the housing association

16.9 VAT Business by Business

for the equity percentage held by the housing association. As the equity percentage held by the housing association reduces then there will be a corresponding reduction in rent. There is no time limit for individuals to increase their equity stake but annual rent reviews (commonly the higher of 5% or the rate of inflation) are likely to sway the issue.

Since 1 March 1995, it is only the first grant of a major interest that can qualify for zero-rated treatment (*VATA 1994, 8 Sch, Group 5, Item 1*). Thus where the housing association is the person regarded as constructing the dwelling, full input tax recovery will be available, including disposal costs. Additional payments made by the occupier to increase their share of the equity will be treated as exempt supplies.

The annual rental income received on the equity retained in the property will be treated as an exempt supply and if the association remains responsible for any repairs then input tax relief on such expenditure will be denied.

BES Assured Tenancy Arrangements

16.9 A number of housing associations participated in *BES Assured Tenancy Arrangement* schemes. Under this arrangement the BES company attracted outside investors, who gained a direct tax advantage, and entered into contracts with bodies such as housing associations to acquire dwellings on behalf of the BES company (in some cases the housing association bought the properties and granted a major interest to the BES company by way of long leases, normally 99 years) and then managed the properties. Separate contracts would have been entered into for the various services supplied by the housing association to the BES company.

The BES moneys raised were put into a bank account held in escrow upon which the housing association could draw funds to purchase the dwellings. These dwellings were either sold or leased to the BES company at a marked-up price or premium. For a new build by the housing association the disposal would be a zero-rated supply, whereas the purchase and onward disposal of an existing dwelling would be an exempt supply.

The housing association then managed the properties, including meeting maintenance costs, for which a charge was made to the BES company. Such charges represented a standard-rated supply.

Under direct tax rules, the BES company had to continue for 5 years and there would normally have been a put and call option on each property with the managing agent at a predetermined price, thus guaranteeing the external investors a fixed return. At the time that these arrangements were prevalent, housing associations saw the arrangement as being a relatively cheap form of finance to increase their housing stock without seeking any grant from the Housing Corporation. For direct tax reasons the housing association would, normally, acquire the shares in the BES company, which would then become a wholly-owned subsidiary company of the association. The acquisition of the shares would constitute an exempt supply, resulting in a possible restriction of input tax on costs associated with the acquisition of shares.

In the event that the properties remain in the newly-acquired subsidiary company, then it would be advisable to consider group VAT registration so as to avoid irrecoverable input tax in the subsidiary company on charges made by the housing association. Whilst group registration may have an adverse impact on the partial exemption recovery of the housing association, nevertheless, there should be an overall saving.

Services supplied to other organisations

16.10 Despite their competitiveness a number of housing associations do provide services to other housing associations, local authorities, and similar bodies.

Services provided could be the management of housing stock, including finding tenants, rent collections and completing repairs and maintenance, and providing building design and legal services. All of these are standard-rated supplies creating irrecoverable VAT in the recipient housing association; although local authorities may be able to claim full input tax relief under *VATA 1994, s 33*.

Where such services are supplied to a housing association under common control, then the charges may be made without VAT by forming a VAT group. A VAT grouping is less obvious than with companies with share capital, where control is usually by means of share ownership. A company formed under the *Industrial & Provident Societies Act 1965* would not have shareholders but its members offer a guarantee of liability, albeit a nominal sum. Thus control would be exercised through members and two housing associations being under the majority control of similar members might be able to be a member of a VAT group. Similarly, if the articles of association of a housing association permitted the members of another association to have the controlling vote then too there would be grounds to form a VAT group. To consider whether or not a VAT group election is permissible, it is necessary to look closely at the constitution of the relevant associations. The full implications of forming a VAT group are considered in *Tolley's VAT 1998/99, chapter 31*.

Design and build contracts

16.11 Where a housing association is providing building design and planning services to other bodies, then it may be advantageous to the recipient body to enter into a '*design and build*' contract on new builds so that the recipient does not suffer input tax restrictions on the professional costs. Under such a contract, the design, workmanship, and materials are supplied under a lump sum contract without any separate identification of the

16.12 VAT Business by Business

design element. The VAT liability of the design element would follow that of the building work, i.e. zero-rated where dwellings or property to be used solely for a relevant residential purpose are being constructed. Whilst this arrangement creates a VAT saving, it is necessary to consider the overall commercial implications.

Management contracts

16.12 An alternative form of contract is a *'management contract'*. Under such a contract, the developing housing association advises its client throughout from site acquisition to completion of the development. The management contractor's fee is based on the likely total costs of the project, but it does not undertake any of the building works itself. The management contractor directly employs contractors to complete the work as agent of the client. The management contractor's fee and the cost of development are paid to the management contractor by the client and this amount represents the consideration of the contract. The VAT liability follows that of the nature of the contract, i.e. where dwellings or property to be used solely for relevant residential purposes are constructed then zero-rating will apply. As with the design and build contracts, commercial considerations must be taken into account.

Management contracts should not be confused with contract management which is a supply of services in planning, managing and co-ordinating the project where the orders for building works are placed by the client. The contract manager charges a fee for his work and this fee is standard-rated.

Large Scale Voluntary Transfers

16.13 Under a *Large Scale Voluntary Transfer*, an approved transfer from a local authority to an established housing association, or to a new association established for that purpose, agreements will vary. There might be a full or partial transfer with the housing association taking full ownership of the property. An alternative arrangement might be where the local authority retains ownership but commissions a housing association to manage and renovate the properties, possibly leading to an eventual transfer of ownership. In these circumstances the supplies made, management and renovation, will be taxable as standard-rated supplies.

Consortium agreements

16.14 Large developments can be undertaken by several housing associations working together, *consortium agreements*. Normally, a lead association will be responsible for instructing third party contractors to carry out a development. The other housing associations will make contributions to the lead association for their share of the costs. Where the lead contractor alone employs the contractors, then the contributions made by other members

Housing Associations **16.16**

are liable to VAT. On the other hand, where the contractors are employed jointly by all of the consortium members, then payments to the lead contractor are deemed to be recharges outside the scope of VAT.

Provision of care

16.15 There has been a tendency for some housing associations with charitable status to extend their activities into the provision of care; this action being supported by the Government initiative *Care in the Community*. Care services supplied direct to an individual will be an exempt supply. Where a care service contract is to another organisation, i.e. the provider housing association is acting as an agent for, say, a local authority, then the supply will be standard-rated except where the supply is made by a charity *otherwise than for profit* (*VATA 1994, 9 Sch, Group 7, Item 9*). If a surplus is made on care services and this surplus is applied to fund future care services, then the supply will be regarded as made other than for profit and be an exempt supply. However, should the surplus be used for another activity, e.g. housing or general activities of the supplier, then the care services are not supplied other than for profit and the supply becomes a standard-rated supply.

Emergency alarm systems

16.16 Emergency alarm systems are another growing feature associated with housing associations. The supply to a disabled person for his personal use, or to a charity for making available to a disabled person, by sale or otherwise, for domestic personal use, of an alarm system designed to be capable of operation by a disabled person, and to enable him to alert directly a specified person control centre, is a zero-rated supply. (*VATA 1994, 8 Sch, Group 12, Note 19*).

In order to gain zero-rated treatment, it is necessary for the customer to supply an eligibility declaration to effect that he, the customer, is disabled. This begs two questions.

Firstly, the definition of disabled. *Customs & Excise Notice 701/7/94* states that an able-bodied person does not qualify. The law in fact refers to a person being 'handicapped' which is defined as 'chronically sick or disabled' (*VATA 1994, 8 Sch, Group 12, Note 3*). 'Disabled' is not defined within the law and reference to The New Shorter English Oxford Dictionary, a practice increasingly adopted by VAT and Duties Tribunal chairmen, defines disabled as *possessing a disability*. Disability is defined as *lack of ability (to do something)* and continues *a physical or mental condition that limits a person's activities or senses*. The writer is of the opinion that an elderly person by reason of age is limited in his activity, whether able-bodied or not, but Customs refuse to accept this argument although it is acceptable for direct tax purposes.

16.17 *VAT Business by Business*

The second point concerns the status of the housing association. If the housing association has charitable status then it can supply the necessary declaration on behalf of the end user and need not make a separate charge to the individual. On the other hand, if the housing association does not have charitable status then it must obtain the declaration from the individual to pass onto the supplier. Furthermore, assuming that the housing association meets the costs of supply, it will have to make a charge, albeit nominal, to the individual for the use of the system in order to gain zero-rated treatment and recover any associated input tax.

The zero-rated treatment also applies to the supply made by the control centre provided that the control centre:

- makes a supply of services to a disabled person, and
- obtains an eligibility certification from the customer, and
- holds information on the disabled person to assist in the event of illness, injury or similar emergency.

(*VATA 1994, 8 Sch, Group 12, Item 20 and Note 9*).

Nomination rights

16.17 Some housing associations have encountered difficulties where land is given, or sold at a reduced price, by a local authority in return for a nomination rights agreement where a proportion of homes to be constructed by the association are set aside for people nominated by the local authority.

In some cases Customs have directed that the grant of such rights is taxable, the consideration being the discount on the price of land. In an attempt to remove inconsistencies an agreement was reached between Customs and the National Federation of Housing Associations which was published in a briefing note in November 1995 and summarised in *Customs & Excise VAT Notice 708, para 4.4*.

The VAT treatment depends upon the drafting of the relevant contracts but the essence of the agreement is:

(a) where nomination rights are not specified in the contract, then there will be no supply for VAT purposes;

(b) similarly, where the reduction in the price of land is not consideration for the grant of nomination rights, then Customs will not treat the grant of nomination rights as a separate supply;

(c) if the contract includes a clear link between the grant of nomination rights and the receipt by the association of consideration, monetary or non-monetary (e.g. in the form of a discount), then Customs will take the view that a separate taxable supply has been made in respect of the nomination rights.

A blanket ruling cannot be given to meet all situations, and rulings in individual cases will depend on the drafting of the relevant contracts.

Housing associations are sometimes required to grant a local authority nomination rights as a precursor to receiving grants from the Housing Corporation. This is not regarded as a taxable supply unless consideration passes between a third party and the housing association for the grant of nomination rights to that third party.

Guest accommodation

16.18 Accommodation for visiting guests, particularly to those that have travelled long distances to visit a sick relative, is a common feature in sheltered housing, even though a separate room may not be set aside solely for this purpose. Some associations may apply a fixed charge for this service which is taxable as standard-rated. Some associations, particularly with charitable status, may not make a charge but would accept an unsolicited donation towards running costs; such a donation would be outside the scope of VAT.

Whilst an argument could be put forward that the supply of such accommodation is exempt by reason of being within the scope of welfare of the person being visited (see *Nuffield Nursing Home Trust (3227)*), this has been rejected by Customs. In the *Nuffield* case the tribunal held that the provision of food and accommodation for the mother of a child patient was an exempt supply because it was a necessary ingredient of the supply of care by the hospital for the child.

Sometimes a housing association may make available, say, its common lounge for use of others for a payment. Should the hire charge include facilities, such as the provision of refreshments or equipment, then the charge will be subject to standard-rated VAT. If no facilities are provided, the supply will be exempt as being one of an interest in land.

Other standard-rated supplies

16.19 These would include:

- money collected from telephone call boxes;
- staff payments towards the cost of meals in a canteen;
- car park charges other than to tenants under a tenancy agreement;
- hire of any equipment;

16.20 *VAT Business by Business*

- sale of an asset used for business purposes;

- laundry work not included in service charges to tenants;

- insurance commission where no advice nor help with claims are given.

Outside the scope supplies

16.20 These would include:

- grants received from the Housing Corporation towards capital schemes and the like;

- contributions from tenants towards TV licences;

- costs recovered from the issue of a summons for recovery of rent arrears.

Where a local authority transfers its housing stock under a *Large Scale Voluntary Transfer (LSVT)* (see paragraph 16.13 above), a statutory right exists under *General Rate Act 1967, s 56* whereby the local authority determines what percentage of rates is to be paid by the housing association which agrees to take responsibility for the rate debt on behalf of the tenant. The housing association would seek to collect the rate debt in full and pass the agreed percentage to the local authority. This 'commission' is considered to be outside the scope of VAT because the local authority has assigned its debt and has the right to take legal action against the housing association for the recovery of the amount agreed per the transfer contract.

Recovery of input tax

16.21 Housing associations in general face a severe restriction in the recovery of input tax because their core activity represents an exempt supply. Some associations take the view that it is not worthwhile, in terms of recovery of input tax to costs and effort, to even consider a partial exemption method. However, depending upon the nature of supplies ancillary to renting dwellings, partial exemption can generate extra cash. This section looks at the various recoveries which can be achieved and also considers possible partial exemption methods.

New buildings

16.22 Supplies made by a building contractor in the course of construction of a new dwelling or building to be used solely for a relevant residential purpose are zero-rated for VAT purposes. The definition of a dwelling and a relevant residential building is covered in paragraph 16.3 above.

Zero-rating only applies to services which are supplied as part of the construction or civil engineering work relevant to the beginning or ending of the construction work and are carried out prior to the first occupation. Such work would include:

- demolition work carried out as an integral part of the construction contract (see paragraph 16.25 below);
- site clearance;
- earth moving;
- necessary civil engineering work within the contract;
- foundation work;
- bricklaying, plastering, carpentry, roofing and plumbing services;
- mechanical and electrical services;
- plant hire provided with an operator;
- scaffolding-erection and dismantling;
- 'builders' clean'—internal and external;
- first-time decoration;
- remedial and repair work carried out during the course of construction;
- site restoration, which would include clearance, levelling and drainage of land, laying top soil and grass, pathways.

Standard-rated supplies would include:

- site investigation before building contracts are entered into;
- temporary fencing around the site;
- site security;
- catering;
- cleaning of site office, etc.;
- temporary lighting;
- transport and haulage to and from the site;

16.22 VAT Business by Business

- plant hire without an operator;

- professional services of architects, engineers, surveyors, consultants and other persons supplying supervisory services;

- construction management services;

- landscaping including the planting of trees and flowers.

A new garage built at the same time as a new dwelling and intended for use together will also attract zero-rated treatment. Should the garage be constructed afterwards, then the supply will be standard-rated. Similarly, all buildings constructed at the same time on a site to be used solely for a relevant residential purpose will qualify for zero-rating; additions made at a later date will be standard-rated unless the addition qualifies in its own right.

The building contractor should automatically zero-rate supplies in the course of construction of a new dwelling, whereas for a building to be used solely for a relevant residential purpose the housing association must supply a certificate: a copy of the required certificate can be found in *Customs & Excise VAT Notice 708, Annex A*.

Housing associations that have their own architects and legal departments will not suffer any input tax on legal and design fees. Those associations without such in-house facilities which must therefore seek such services from a third party, should consider a *'design and build'* (see paragraph 16.11 above) arrangement so as not to suffer the irrecoverable loss of input tax on professional fees. An alternative arrangement might be a *management contract*—see paragraph 16.12 above.

Whilst the same VAT result is obtained, i.e. zero-rating, it is important to distinguish between the two types of work: a dwelling or a building to be used for a relevant residential purpose, because the onus of certification rests with the housing association which could find itself in conflict with Customs. This is particularly true in respect of sheltered housing projects. Where the sheltered housing project consists of individual flats with their own facilities, then they are regarded as dwellings and do not require a certificate. On the other hand, a building not consisting of separate dwellings may be regarded as a residential home. The significance of a property to be used solely for a relevant residential purpose by a housing association with charitable status is demonstrated in paragraph 16.26 below.

Where only part of a new building is to be used as a dwelling or intended to be used solely for a relevant residential building, then that portion can be zero-rated; the remainder would be treated as standard-rated. This apportionment would apply also to civil engineering works (roads, mains services, etc.).

Apart from construction costs, with effect from 1 March 1995 the supply of building materials attract zero-rated treatment. Examples of items qualifying for zero-rated treatment when installed in a new dwelling or a building to be used solely for a relevant residential purpose are:

- window frames and glazing;
- doors;
- certain built-in wardrobes;
- letter boxes;
- fireplace and surrounds;
- guttering;
- power points (but not light bulbs or tubes);
- outside lights where they are standard fittings (but not light bulbs or tubes);
- immersion heaters, boilers, hot and cold water tanks;
- radiators;
- built-in heating appliances;
- fire and burglar alarms and smoke detectors;
- air-conditioning equipment;
- ventilation equipment;
- dust extractors;
- lifts and hoists;
- work surfaces or fitted cupboards in kitchens and utility rooms;
- kitchen sinks;
- baths, basins and bidets;
- lavatory bowls and cisterns;
- shower units but excluding curtains;
- fixed towel rails, toilet roll holders, soap dishes, etc.;

16.23 *VAT Business by Business*

- communal TV aerials;
- warden call systems.

(*VATA 1994, 8 Sch, Group 5, Item 4 and Notes 22 and 23; SI 1995 No 280*).

Prior to 1 March 1995 similar provisions applied except that the legislation referred to *materials, builders' hardware, sanitary ware or other articles of a kind ordinarily installed by builders as fixtures*.

A detailed explanation of *Construction Services* can be found in Chapter 9 of this book.

Land

16.23 The grant of any interest or right over land is normally an exempt supply but there are exceptions which include:

- the supply of a major interest in:

    (a) a new dwelling or a building which is to be used solely for a relevant residential purpose, or a building for relevant charitable use (i.e. non-business use) by the person constructing it,

    (b) a dwelling converted from a non-residential building by the person constructing it, or

    (c) a substantially reconstructed protected building which qualifies for zero-rating by the person converting it.

- any supply which would otherwise be exempt but in respect of which an 'option to tax' (election to waive exemption—*VATA 1994, 10 Sch 2*) has been exercised.

Where a major interest in land and buildings has been supplied as above, then zero-rated treatment would apply and thus the housing association would not suffer any input tax.

Where the option to tax has been made, then the supply will be standard-rated. However, an option to tax cannot apply where the grant is made to a housing association and the association has given to the grantor a certificate stating that the land is to be used (after any necessary demolition work) for the construction of a building or buildings which are to be used as a dwelling or a number of dwellings, or solely for a relevant residential purpose—*VATA 1994, 10 Sch 2(3)(a)*. The relevant certificate can be found in *Customs & Excise Notice 708/5, Appendix B*.

An exception to this rule is where the purchaser, i.e. the housing association, expects to make a zero-rated grant of a dwelling after conversion and will be able to reclaim any tax incurred. The purchaser may then agree with the vendor that tax may be charged on the sale.

Whilst seen as a relieving provision for housing associations this can, nevertheless, create problems because the vendor will be unable to claim input tax on costs incurred associated with the land. This could lead to re-negotiating the price, which is a commercial decision, but it should be remembered that any increase in the price of the land may increase the vendor's direct tax liability.

It has been known for vendors not to proceed with a sale where a certificate has been issued. Whilst adding initial costs to the project, a subsidiary company of the housing association could acquire the land and complete the development. On completion the subsidiary company could then sell the completed project to the housing association which would be a zero-rated supply with the subsidiary company gaining full recovery of input tax associated with the project. Before entering into such an arrangement it is advisable to consider the commercial and direct tax implications.

Converting non-residential buildings

16.24 From 1 March 1995 a housing association registered with the Housing Corporation can obtain zero-rated treatment on supplies of construction services and related goods when converting a non-residential building into a dwelling or number of dwellings or for relevant residential use. The housing association must issue a certificate to the builder; the required certificate can be found in Customs & Excise Notice 708/5, Appendix B. Such relief was available by concession, in respect of dwellings only, from 22 July 1994.

Before a housing association gives a certificate it should ensure that:

- it is registered with either the Housing Corporation in England, Scottish Homes, Housing for Wales or the Department of Environment in Northern Ireland; and

- the building being converted was not designed for residential use; and

- if so designed, was constructed before 1 April 1973 and has not been used for residential purposes since that date; and

- after conversion the building will be a dwelling(s) or used solely for relevant residential purposes.

By concession, the above relief may apply to charities not registered with either the Housing Corporation in England, Scottish Homes, Housing for Wales, or the Department of Environment in Northern Ireland, and which by

16.25 VAT Business by Business

reason of their articles of association are prevented from selling property belonging to the charity. It is advisable for a housing association falling within this category to gain clearance that the concession applies before issuing a certificate to the builder.

Demolition

16.25 Demolition costs are zero-rated where the work falls within a single contract for construction and the demolition work is part of the contract. Partial demolition of a building is standard-rated whether or not the demolished part is to be replaced. The requirement of being within a construction contract can create problems in circumstances where, for example, the site has been acquired but full planning permission has yet to be granted. For environmental or safety reasons, there may be a need to demolish some or all of the existing buildings, and if this work is not completed as part of a construction contract then it will be treated as standard-rated, thus adding to the costs of the project.

Charitable reliefs

16.26 There is no general relief from VAT for charities because of their charitable status. The law does, however, seek to provide reliefs which are aimed to benefit charities; although often with building projects a charity will find that it does not meet the narrow requirements of the law and may, unwittingly, incur penalties.

The first important test for general relief is whether the activity of a housing association is a 'business' or a 'non-business' activity. As housing associations collect rent for the occupation of their properties, then they will be construed as conducting a 'business' and immediately the reliefs available become restricted.

A second test is whether or not the property is 'relevant residential' or a 'dwelling', bearing in mind the definitions as mentioned at paragraph 16.3 above. If the property is a 'dwelling' then there is further restriction of reliefs available.

The main zero-rated reliefs are contained in *VATA 1994, 8 Sch, Group 12* and, for charitable housing associations, include the following:

the supply to a handicapped person for domestic or personal use, or to a charity for making available to handicapped persons *by sale or otherwise*, for domestic or their personal use, of:

- medical or surgical appliances designed solely for the relief of a severe abnormality or severe injury;

- electrically or mechanically adjustable beds designed for invalids;

- commode chairs, commode stools, devices incorporating a bidet jet and warm air drier and devices for sitting over or arising from a sanitary appliance;

- chair lifts or stair lifts for use in connection with invalid chairs or designed for use by invalids;

- adapting goods to suit a handicapped person;

- supply of an emergency alarm system (see paragraph 16.16 above).

The reader will observe that if the above are supplied to the charitable housing association for onward supply to the handicapped person, then they must be made by the association by way of *sale or otherwise*. *Otherwise* is not defined and there is no formal definition issued by Customs. Thus, to be sure of obtaining zero-rating, it would be necessary to make a separate supply for a consideration. The consideration could be in the form of additional rent, but this would need to be shown separately. Alternatively, a one-off payment could be sought which could be a nominal amount. An alternative route might be for the supply to be made direct to the handicapped person with the charitable housing association, or an associated charity, making a donation to the individual to cover the cost of the appliance, including the installation costs.

The following can be supplied either direct to the handicapped person or via the housing association without *payment or otherwise*:

- constructing ramps or widening doorways or passages for the purpose of facilitating entry or movement within a handicapped person's private residence or within any building if the supply is made to a charitable housing association;

- the installation of a lift within a handicapped person's private residence, or where a charitable housing association provides a permanent or temporary residence or day centre facilities for handicapped persons, the installation of a lift for the purpose of facilitating the movement of handicapped persons within that building.

On the first point of constructing ramps and widening doorways and passages, there appears to be an inconsistency within Customs in allowing relief. This arises where, for example, gates or pathways are widened to accommodate wheelchairs. Relief has been denied on the basis that the grounds are not *within the private residence*. Similarly lift installations within buildings used, or partly used, as a day centre give rise to inconsistencies in treatment.

16.27 *VAT Business by Business*

Further zero-rating relief applies on the supply to a handicapped person of the provision, extension, or adaptation of a bathroom, washroom or lavatory in his private residence where such work is necessary by reason of that person's condition. It should be remembered that old age alone does not constitute a handicap—see paragraph 16.16 above.

Zero-rating relief is also available on the supply to a charitable housing association of a service of providing, extending, or adapting a washroom or lavatory for use by handicapped persons in a *residential home* where the work is necessary because of the condition of the handicapped persons. The relief does not apply where the work is carried out in a *dwelling*—for the definition of which see paragraph 16.3 above.

Expenditure on protected buildings

16.27 Expenditure on approved alterations to a protected building qualifies for zero-rated treatment. The conditions to be met are:

(a) *protected building* means a building which is a dwelling, or number of dwellings, or intended for use solely as a relevant residential building or a relevant charitable purpose after the reconstruction or alteration; and

(b) the building is a listed building within the meaning of the *Planning (Listed Building and Conservation Areas) Act 1990*; or *Town and Country Planning (Scotland) Act 1972*; or *Planning (Northern Ireland) Order 1991*; and

(c) the work has listed building consent; and

(d) the work is not repair or maintenance or an alteration incidental to repair and maintenance; and

(e) a certificate is supplied to the builder in accordance with *Customs & Excise Notice 708*.

In ascertaining whether or not the work constitutes an alteration, thus qualifying for zero-rated relief, Customs will rely heavily on the planning consent order and the nature of the work as described in that order. Thus, an early stage planning point is to ensure that the work is described accurately when seeking permission to undertake the work.

Further details can be found in Chapter 9—Construction Industry.

Partial exemption

16.28 Supplies made by housing associations are in the main exempt from VAT and this will mean that there will be a restriction on input tax relief on VAT on expenditure incurred in the running of the associations. Basically, it will only be possible to claim input tax relief on goods or services to be used in making taxable supplies. Detailed partial exemption explanations can be found in *Tolley's VAT 1998/99, chapter 49*. This section will consider in broad terms the application of partial exemption to housing associations.

A few examples of methods which could be adopted by housing associations are:

- Looking at the number of units managed by the housing association including those which the association manages on behalf of other bodies. Where the association manages units on behalf of another body, the related management charge represents a taxable supply and thus the total income belonging to the association on this arrangement would be taxable. Other taxable units might include commercial premises, e.g. shops, or garages let to non-tenants of the association. When including garages, Customs may seek to apply a weighting factor as it is arguable that garages take up less administration. An example could be that two garages are the equivalent of a single residential unit.

- Taking into account the headcount within the association by considering those people who generate taxable supplies as against exempt supplies. There will invariably be people who generate both taxable and exempt supplies, e.g. a direct labour force which spends time on own units and does work for other bodies, and in these circumstances it should be possible to apportion their time according to the nature of their work.

- Identifying branches or cost centres, particularly those which have above average taxable supplies. It might be possible to ring fence these cost centres and apply a special method to each. In these circumstances it might be advisable to charge each centre with an allocation of central overheads that bear VAT, e.g. telephone costs, stationery etc., so as to improve the level of recoverability.

- Under the standard method, the residual VAT is apportioned by reference to the level of taxable income over total income. An alternative may be to apply the same principle but based on levels of expenditure.

The above are a few of the options available but a special method must be approved by Customs before being operated.

Practical points

Professional fees on new building

16.29 When commissioning new building work, consider the use of a design and build contract (see paragraph 16.11 above) or a management contract (see paragraph 16.12 above) to avoid the loss of input tax on professional fees. If, for commercial reasons, this is not feasible, any objections might be overcome by entering into such a contract with a wholly-owned subsidiary company.

Relevant residential

16.30 When constructing a complex to be used for residential purposes only, try to ensure that all buildings are covered by a single planning consent to achieve zero-rated treatment on the construction costs of all buildings (see paragraph 16.3 above).

Capital expenditure

16.31 Recovery of input tax on capital expenditure, e.g. computer or telephone network, is limited to the partial exemption recovery rate. A cash-flow saving could be achieved by leasing the equipment. Alternatively, the equipment could be purchased by a wholly-owned subsidiary company, which is separately registered for VAT, and then leased to the housing association. Using a wholly-owned subsidiary company would ensure that all profits are retained under the same umbrella. Direct tax issues would need to be considered. Should the housing association have charitable status, or have an associated charity, then the subsidiary company could covenant its profits to the charity, thus reducing its direct taxation liability.

Parallel charities

16.32 If the housing association does not have charitable status, then it may be advisable to consider forming a separate charitable company which could be under common ownership. The charity could be funded by gift-aiding some or all of the taxable profits of the housing association, thus reducing direct tax liabilities. The funds could then be used, for example, to facilitate compliance issues on emergency alarm systems (see paragraph 16.16 above) and to take advantage of charitable reliefs (see paragraph 16.26 above) so as to secure zero-rated treatment and reduce the level of irrecoverable input tax.

A housing association with charitable status may also find that a parallel charity could be used to secure charitable reliefs where these appear difficult to achieve, e.g. adaptations of bathrooms in dwellings.

Joint contracts of employment

16.33 Wage costs recharged between companies outside a VAT group are taxable as standard-rated. Whilst this should enhance input tax recovery in the providing association, the recipient organisation may face restriction of input tax relief. Where employees regularly undertake work for more than one organisation, the VAT charge on wage recharges can be avoided by that employee having a joint contract of employment with both organisations. The main employer would remain the paymaster and the second employer would make a contribution towards the wage cost; this contribution would be regarded as a disbursement which would be outside the scope of VAT.

Charity advertising

16.34 A housing association with charitable status should take advantage of zero-rating on advertising which is for fund-raising or making known the objectives of the charity. It is necessary to give the supplier a completed declaration. Further details are contained in *Customs & Excise Notice 701/1/95, paragraph 16, Annex H*.

Consortium agreements

16.35 When entering into a consortium agreement (see paragraph 16.14 above), try to ensure that contractors are employed jointly by all consortium members, thus avoiding a standard-rated charge which would arise where one member enters into such contracts.

Demolition works

16.36 Wherever possible, ensure that there is a single contract for demolition and new construction work, so that the total work undertaken is treated as a zero-rated supply (see paragraph 16.25 above).

Accounting records

16.37 To maximise and facilitate recovery under a partial exemption method, ensure that accounting records can readily identify input tax suffered.

Chapter 17

Insurance

Introduction

17.1 This chapter examines the VAT issues affecting businesses in the insurance sector. It covers the activities both of insurers and insurance intermediaries. The VAT position of these businesses is often complex, in terms both of the liability of particular supplies and of the recovery of related input tax. VAT is often a considerable burden to insurance businesses due to the amount of irrecoverable VAT incurred on expenditure and as a result of the necessary compliance involved in meeting the various VAT accounting requirements.

17.2 In addition to their main business of providing insurance cover, insurers will also receive significant investment income, both from financial instruments and property. Again, the VAT rules pertaining to these types of investments can be complex. Insurance intermediaries also sometimes receive investment income but to a much lesser extent. This chapter does not explain the various rules for the different types of investments, as they are outlined in detail in Chapter 3—Banking and Securities and Chapter 21—Property Development.

17.3 As will be seen from the subsequent paragraphs, supplies made by businesses in the insurance sector are predominantly exempt from VAT. The complexity in the sector arises mainly from businesses trying to ensure that they maximise their recovery of VAT costs. Some supplies will be taxable, giving the right to VAT recovery. Also, businesses may recover VAT on exempt insurance supplies made to non-EU counterparties. Therefore, in addition to determining the correct VAT liability of their supplies, insurance businesses will often expend considerable resources in determining an appropriate partial exemption method for securing recovery of their VAT costs.

17.4 With effect from 1 October 1994, insurers have been required to account for Insurance Premium Tax ('IPT') on much of their premium income. More recently the scope of this tax has been extended, in certain limited circumstances, to the activities of insurance intermediaries. Although there are occasions when VAT and IPT interact, such matters are not covered in this chapter as they are more relevant to a discussion on IPT rather than to the VAT issues affecting insurers.

17.5 *VAT Business by Business*

Liability

17.5 The following paragraphs provide details of the VAT liability of services supplied by insurers or insurance intermediaries. Supplies of insurance and insurance-related services are exempt from VAT under *VATA 1994, 9 Sch, Group 2*. The conditions attaching to the exemption are both detailed and complex, particularly in relation to insurance intermediary services. For information, the text of the exemption is shown at Appendix A to this chapter.

17.6 In addition to the basic exemption given for insurance and insurance related services, there are other legal provisions which need to be considered to determine the place of supply and recovery of VAT expenditure relating to these services. These are the *Value Added Tax (Place of Supply of Services) Order 1992 (SI 1992 No 3121)* and the *Value Added Tax (Input Tax) (Specified Supplies) Order 1992 (SI 1992 No 3123)*.

Supplies made by insurers and reinsurers

17.7 The VAT exemption for the provision of insurance or reinsurance is found under *VATA 1994, 9 Sch, Group 2, Items 1 and 2*. However, exemption is only available where the insurance or reinsurance has been provided by a 'permitted' insurer. In this chapter, the term 'permitted insurer' is used generically to denote an insurance business whose services qualify for exemption as the provision of insurance in accordance with the terms of the VAT legislation.

17.8 For these purposes, and in accordance with the legislation, the following are treated as 'permitted' insurers by Customs & Excise ('Customs'):

- any insurance business which a person is authorised to carry on under *Insurance Companies Act 1992 ('ICA 1982'), section 3 or 4*;

- any business in respect of which a person is exempted under *ICA 1982, s 2* to be so authorised;

- an insurer who belongs outside the UK providing insurance against any of the risks described in *ICA 1982, Schedules 1 and 2*; and

- certain types of businesses which do not require authorisation under *ICA 1982*, namely:

    – a member of Lloyd's;

    – a Friendly Society;

- a trade union or employer's association where the insurance business is linked to the provision for its members of provident benefits or strike benefits; and

- an insurance company only providing benefits in kind insurance.

17.9 In addition to the above, VAT exemption for insurance provided by the Export Credits Guarantee Department is given specifically under *VATA 1994, 9 Sch, Group 2, Item 3*.

17.10 Where a non-permitted insurer supplies insurance in the UK, this service is taxable at the standard rate. However, one exception to this is financial guarantees or sureties, where it is possible that exemption could be available under *VATA 1994, 9 Sch, Group 5* (see Chapter 3—Banking and Securities). In practice it is unlikely that non-insurers charging for 'insurance' will be supplying insurance as such. Often the insurance element will merely be part of another supply. A typical example of this is in the case of 'collision damage waivers' charged by vehicle hire companies. Even though a separate charge may be made, this charge is normally no more than an increase in the vehicle hire charge to take into account the vehicle hire company's own insurance cover.

Place of supply

17.11 The VAT liability of insurance services is determined by the place of supply of the services in question. As outlined above, there is an underlying VAT exemption for insurance services supplied by a permitted insurer in the UK. However, in order to determine the place of supply of those services, it is necessary to consider the provisions of the *Value Added Tax (Place of Supply of Services) Order 1992 (SI 1992 No 3121)*. In addition, the extent to which input tax may be recovered on these supplies is determined in accordance with the provisions of the *Value Added Tax (Input Tax) (Specified Supplies) Order 1992 (SI 1992 No 3123)*.

17.12 Under these provisions, the VAT liability of international supplies of insurance and the position regarding the recovery of related input tax is as follows:

- exempt from VAT with no input tax recovery if the insured is a private individual in another EU Member State;

- outside the scope of VAT with no input tax recovery if the insured is in business and belongs in the EU;

- outside the scope of VAT with full input tax recovery if the insured belongs outside the EU.

17.13 Insurance which is directly linked to the export of goods (including that provided by the Export Credits Guarantee Department) follows the rules

17.14 *VAT Business by Business*

outlined above. However, additionally, if the insurance provided is in respect of an export of specific goods by the recipient of the insurance, from a place inside the EU to a place outside the EU, the insurer has the right to recover input tax related to the supply of insurance, even if the recipient belongs in the UK or elsewhere in the EU. In this instance, the insurance supplied must be directly linked to the goods being exported and cover the risks of the person who owns the goods or is responsible for their export.

Marine, Aviation and Transport ('MAT') insurance

17.14 MAT insurance covers the risks relating to hull and cargo and those identifiable with journeys involving the carriage of passengers or goods. The supply of MAT insurance follows the same rules as in paragraph 17.12 above. However, prior to the enactment of the *VAT (Place of Supply of Services) Order 1992*, it was the practice of underwriters of MAT insurance to use the following codes for VAT purposes:

- X (for exempt) if the journey being insured was wholly within the EU;

- Z (for zero-rated) if the journey was to or from a place outside the EU or wholly outside the EU;

- M (50% exempt, 50% zero-rated) if the journey could not be identified as either X or Z.

17.15 Under these rules, insurers recovered all VAT costs relating to policies coded Z (including 50% of policies coded M). By concession, as a transitional measure, Customs allowed MAT insurers to follow these guidelines up to 5 July 1993. After that date, MAT insurers were required to follow the provisions of the *VAT (Place of Supply of Services) Order 1992*. The change in the rules whereby the liability of risks for MAT insurance is now governed by the place of belonging of the insured has, in many instances, resulted in a substantial reduction in the amount of VAT recovered by insurers in this respect. Under new guidelines agreed with Customs, the same coding is used but is now applied as follows:

- X (no right to deduct input tax) if the insurance is provided to a person belonging within the EU, and it is not directly linked to the export of goods to a place outside the EU;

- Z (right to deduct input tax) if the insurance is provided to a person belonging outside the EU or it is linked directly to the export of goods to a place outside the EU.

17.16 In order to use the above codes, it is necessary to determine the place of belonging of the insured. The address of the insured as shown on the broker's slip (or equivalent documentation) is taken as the place of belonging of the insured. This applies where the insured has more than one address unless it is clear that this is merely an administrative address for payment purposes, etc.

17.17 It is often the case that, for certain MAT insurance risks, there are multiple insured persons who are party to the risk. In these instances, where possible, the insurer should identify the principal insured and use his address as the place of belonging for coding the risk. Where there is no principal insured (or it is not possible to determine the principal insured), and the identities of all of the insured persons are known, the following guidelines apply:

- X if all insured persons belong inside the EC;

- Z if all insured persons belong outside the EC; and

- M if the insured persons belong both inside and outside the EC.

17.18 As under the old guidelines, the use of the M code means that 50% of any attributable input tax may be treated as recoverable and 50% as irrecoverable. If the place of belonging of the insured persons cannot be determined, then the following rules apply to determine the place of supply:

- the country of origin of the business;

- the address of the originating broker/cover holder; and

- any additional information on the slip.

17.19 These new guidelines, which are effective from 5 July 1993, are published by Customs as part of a trade agreement.

Value of insurance services

17.20 Generally, the value of a supply of insurance is the gross premium received in respect of the risk which has been insured. The gross premium is the amount received by the insurer before deductions, where appropriate, for brokerage, claims, reinsurance premiums and local taxes.

17.21 For direct MAT business, however, it is often difficult to establish the gross premium received. Therefore, Customs accept that, where actual figures are not available, insurers may add, as a 'rule of thumb', 5% to the net premium to determine the gross equivalent.

17.22 For reinsurance business, the value of the supply for VAT purposes is taken as the gross premium, after the deduction of:

17.23 VAT Business by Business

(i) the reinsurance commission agreed between the reinsurer and the insurer to cover the costs of the insurer in obtaining the business in the first place; and

(ii) the profit commission which may be payable by the reinsurer to the insurer if the business is profitable.

Supplies made by insurance intermediaries

17.23 VAT exemption is also available to intermediaries who provide certain insurance-related services. This provision is found under *VATA 1994, 9 Sch, Group 2, Item 4*. In this context, intermediaries include brokers, agents and persons such as solicitors, accountants, estate agents and those who arrange for insurance to be provided with other goods and services.

17.24 The VAT position of insurance intermediaries was clarified as a result of changes to the main legislation which became effective from 19 March 1997. Previously, in order to qualify for VAT exemption, intermediaries had to be seen to be 'making arrangements' for the provision of insurance. This resulted in considerable confusion and difficulty in determining what constituted the making of arrangements. In particular, it was seen that the UK legislation did not reflect the exemption given by underlying European law.

17.25 The change to the legislation was, in part, prompted by the success of a number of VAT appeals. The most notable of these were *Barclays Bank plc, [1993] VATTR 466 (6469), Countrywide Insurance Marketing Ltd, [1993] VATTR 277 (11443)* and *Curtis Edington Say Ltd (11699)*. In all of these cases, Customs took the view that VAT exemption was not appropriate as the services provided by the appellants were not directly related to the provision of insurance. However, the appellants were able to argue successfully that they were providing VAT-exempt insurance-related services in accordance with the provisions of the *EC Sixth Directive, Article 13B(a)*.

17.26 Under the revised legislation, the exemption of services provided by insurance intermediaries now depends on whether a relevant insurance related service has been supplied and whether that service has been provided in an intermediary capacity. The detailed notes to the legislation in this area provide guidance and set out the conditions which must be met for VAT exemption.

Insurance-related services

17.27 Insurance-related services are defined in the legislation as:

- bringing together, with a view to the insurance or reinsurance of risks, of persons who are or may be seeking and persons providing insurance or reinsurance;

- work preparatory to the conclusion of a contract of insurance or reinsurance;

- assistance in the administration and performance of such contracts, including claims handling; and

- the collection of premiums.

17.28 There are three main exceptions to the exemption for insurance related services. These are:

- market research, product design, advertising, promotional or similar services;

- valuation or inspection services; and

- the services of loss adjusters and claim assessors.

17.29 However, if one of the above exceptions is provided as a minor part of a supply of otherwise exempt insurance-related services, Customs often accept that there is an overall single composite supply.

Intermediary capacity

17.30 As outlined above, in addition to providing relevant insurance-related services, an insurance intermediary must be seen to be acting in an intermediary capacity in order for those services to qualify for VAT exemption. The legislation is not particularly helpful on this issue but Customs have produced some guidance in Notice No 700/36/97—Insurance.

17.31 An insurance intermediary is regarded as somebody who acts somewhere in the chain of supply between a permitted insurer and an insured person or potential insured person. The first point to note is that if the services provided by the insurer do not qualify for VAT exemption, the related services provided by the intermediary will also not qualify. Also, intermediary status in respect of one supply does not mean that a person is an intermediary in respect of another. Finally, a supply of insurance-related services made by somebody acting in an intermediary capacity is exempt, even if a contract is not concluded, provided that all the other relevant conditions are met.

17.32 Introductory services are also within the scope of the exemption for insurance-related services when performed by an intermediary. However, often it can be difficult to establish whether the intermediary is providing relevant insurance-related services or excepted services. In particular, intermediaries often provide both introductory and advertising services on behalf of an insurer. In these circumstances, Customs accept that there is a

17.33 VAT Business by Business

single composite exempt supply of insurance-related introductory services where:

- the intermediary is paid in accordance with the successful conclusion of each insurance contract; and

- the intermediary is targeting its own customer base; and

- the product of the insurer is endorsed by the intermediary.

Claims handling

17.33 The exemption for intermediary services also applies for claims handling services. Claims handling is not specifically defined in the VAT legislation but rather is a generic term used for various different services which may be provided following the making of a claim by the insured. Typically, such services may include any one or more of the following:

- checking that documents are correctly completed;

- ensuring that the claim falls within the terms of the policy;

- processing the claim;

- ensuring that insurers are advised of their exposure;

- agreeing the validity and/or quantum of the claim; and

- arranging settlement to be made.

17.34 Often, claims handling involves certain services which are taxable, e.g. advice, administration or investigation. Where these services form a minor part of an overall claims handling service, Customs accept that this is a single composite exempt supply of claims handling.

17.35 As outlined above, the services of loss adjusters and claims assessors are specifically excluded from the exemption for insurance intermediary services. However, Customs accept that where loss adjusters or similar experts are appointed by insurers to settle claims and have full binding written delegated authority to do so when they commence work, they are regarded as insurance intermediaries for the purposes of the VAT exemption. In such cases, even where the loss adjuster or other expert provides both claims handling and assessment services, Customs accept that there is a single exempt supply of claims handling.

17.36 The terms of the written delegated authority from the insurer are important in determining whether the services of the loss adjuster or other expert qualifies for VAT exemption. Often, written delegated authority may be given by the insurer allowing the loss adjuster to settle claims up to a fixed monetary limit or in respect of specific types of claim. In these instances, where a loss adjuster provides services which are not within the terms of the written delegated authority, the services in question will be taxable.

Non-permitted insurance

17.37 Where an intermediary receives commission, etc. in respect of 'insurance' provided by a non-permitted insurer, this will not qualify for exemption. In this instance, the services of the intermediary will be taxable. The service will be regarded as a Schedule 5 service (see Appendix B) and the VAT liability will be determined in accordance with the *Value Added Tax (Place of Supply of Services) Order 1992*.

Place of supply

17.38 As with the provision of insurance itself, the VAT liability of insurance intermediary services is governed by the provisions of the *Value Added Tax (Place of Supply of Services) Order*. Similarly, the extent to which input tax may be recovered is determined by the *Value Added Tax (Input Tax) (Specified Supplies Order 1992)*.

17.39 There has long been some confusion over the question of to whom does an insurance intermediary provide its services, i.e. to the insurer or the insured. Indeed, it is often possible to view an insurance intermediary as supplying its services to both the insurer and the insured. Customs take the view that insurance intermediary services should be assumed to be supplied to the insured. Therefore, the place of belonging of the insured must be established in order to determine the VAT liability of insurance intermediary services. It should be noted that there will be circumstances where it could be argued strongly that services have been supplied to insurers, e.g. underwriting agents. Consequently, each transaction must be considered on its own merits.

International services: non-MAT

17.40 For insurance intermediary services supplied in respect of the provision of non-MAT insurance, the position is as follows:

- exempt from VAT with no input tax recovery if the underlying insurance is provided to a private individual in another EU Member State;
- outside the scope of VAT with no input tax recovery if the underlying insurance is provided to a business belonging in another EU Member State;
- outside the scope of UK VAT with the full input tax recovery if the

17.41 *VAT Business by Business*

underlying insurance is provided to a person belonging outside the EU.

17.41 For insurance intermediary services provided in respect of insurance related directly to the export of goods, the position is:

- exempt from VAT with no input tax recovery where goods have been exported to another EU Member State and the underlying insurance is provided to a UK person or a private individual in another EU Member State;

- exempt from VAT with full input tax recovery where goods have been exported to a non-EU country and the underlying insurance is provided to a UK person or a private individual in another EU Member State;

- outside the scope of UK VAT with no input tax recovery where goods have been exported to another EU Member State and the underlying insurance is provided to a business belonging in another EU Member State;

- outside the scope of UK VAT with full input tax recovery where

    (i) goods have been exported to a non-EU country and the underlying insurance is provided either to a business in another EU Member State or a person belonging outside the EU; or

    (ii) goods have been exported to another EU Member State but the underlying insurance has been provided to a person belonging outside the EU.

International services: MAT

17.42 The place of supply for insurance intermediary services in relation to MAT insurance follows the guidelines set out by Customs for the provision of MAT insurance itself. These are explained earlier in this chapter at paragraphs 17.14 to 17.19 above.

Value of insurance intermediary services

17.43 The value of a supply of insurance-related services by an insurance intermediary is generally the gross commission received. If alternative methods of remuneration are applied, e.g. a flat-rate fee or recharge of costs incurred, the value for VAT purposes is again the gross amount received. With regard to commission, no deduction should be made for any commission allowable in turn to other intermediaries when determining the value of the supply for VAT purposes.

Miscellaneous points affecting certain supplies

Lloyd's arrangements

17.44 Special arrangements have been agreed by Customs regarding the VAT treatment of supplies made by members of Lloyd's. A brief outline of these arrangements is detailed below. The arrangements in respect of the recovery of input tax by these bodies and their partial exemption position is set out in the section in this chapter on 'Input Tax Recovery' at paragraphs 17.67 *et seq.* below.

17.45 The rules regarding the VAT treatment of supplies made by members of Lloyd's are basically the same as those which are applied to other insurers. However, special arrangements are required to take into account the particular way in which the Lloyd's insurance market operates.

17.46 Underwriting on the Lloyd's market is, in effect, carried on by the individual names operating and trading on their own account. However, in practice, the underwriting is done by the various syndicates to whom the individual names belong. Often individual names will belong to more than one syndicate. These syndicates are not partnerships as such but merely reflect the way that underwriting at Lloyd's is administered. As it would be highly impractical for names to be registered for VAT individually, their registration is effectively achieved through their managing agents.

17.47 Managing agents are required to include the details of premiums received from the syndicates they manage in their own VAT returns. The large majority of the syndicates' premium income is processed through the Lloyd's Policy Signing Office ('LPSO'), which is responsible for the coding of the risks insured by each syndicate. Each quarter, the LPSO will advise managing agents of the split of premium income for each syndicate under management between risks which are exempt or outside the scope of VAT with no input tax recovery (coded X) and risks which are outside the scope of VAT with the right to input tax recovery (coded Z).

17.48 The management fees, salaries or profit commissions of managing agents are split between that part coded X for VAT purposes and that part coded Z on the same basis as the split for all of the syndicates under their management.

17.49 However, unlike other insurance businesses, managing agents do not have to account for outputs arising from financial investments. This concession has come about because Customs accept that the majority of investment is carried out abroad and does not give rise to significant related input tax.

17.50 *VAT Business by Business*

17.50 Individual names are normally required to appoint a members' agent who is responsible for placing them on appropriate syndicates. Members' agents are deemed to be insurance intermediaries providing insurance-related services which are exempt from VAT. However, as members' agents have no responsibility for managing syndicates, it is not possible for them to determine the VAT liability of their supplies (i.e. the apportionment between X and Z codes). Therefore, the taxation department of Lloyd's provides members' agents with a standard percentage each VAT quarter which reflects the business of the Lloyd's market as a whole.

Protection and indemnity ('P&I') insurance

17.51 Protection and indemnity insurance essentially covers shipowners for risks relating to their ships and cargoes. The underwriting of this insurance is generally carried out by P&I Clubs which are non-profit-making mutual associations of shipowners. P&I Clubs are deemed to be making supplies of insurance and the liability of their supplies follows the guidelines detailed earlier in this chapter for insurers and reinsurers. P&I Clubs must register for VAT if the value of their taxable supplies (including imported services) exceeds the VAT registration threshold.

17.52 The businesses of P&I Clubs are organised and run by P&I Club managers. These managers are required to be registered for VAT separately from the club or clubs which they manage. Where P&I Club managers are empowered to accept risks on behalf of the club(s) they manage, they are regarded as providing insurance-related intermediary services. The liability of their supplies follows that of the P&I Club.

17.53 Where a P&I Club manager has no establishment in the UK, he will invariably appoint an agent to act as his representative in the UK. P&I Club agents are deemed to supply management services to the P&I Club manager. Customs generally accept that these management services fall under *VATA 1994, 9 Sch, Group 5*. This means that the P&I Club agent's supplies will invariably be outside the scope of VAT with the right to input tax recovery.

Friendly Societies

17.54 The provision of insurance by a Friendly Society is exempt from VAT under *VATA 1994, 9 Sch, Group 2, Item 1*. Friendly Societies are membership organisations and the subscriptions paid by members will cover them against distress in accident/sickness, old age and widowhood. Where the subscription also covers other goods and services, normally only that part of the subscription which relates to the provision of insurance will be exempt. Accordingly, Friendly Societies may have to apportion subscriptions received between the respective taxable and exempt elements. However, it is possible that the goods and services themselves could qualify for exemption in their own right. In particular, certain supplies relating to health and welfare are exempt from VAT under *VATA 1994, 9 Sch, Group 7*.

Broker-managed funds

17.55 These are managed funds provided under contracts between a life company which operates the fund, the policyholder and a broker who arranges the policy. Often, the broker, in addition to arranging the policy, will provide investment advice to the life assurance company regarding the funds invested by the policyholder. In addition to any commission received from the life assurance company, the broker may also receive fees for providing investment advisory services.

17.56 The commission received by the broker is consideration for insurance-related intermediary services and is exempt from VAT. However, any additional fees received for the provision of investment advisory services are taxable. This treatment of fees received by brokers in respect of broker-managed fees has applied since 1 November 1993 (see Business Brief 27/93, dated 2 September 1993). Prior to that date, Customs regarded all fees and commissions received by the broker as exempt from VAT. The change brought the position of brokers in line with that of other third party investment managers.

Engineering insurance

17.57 Engineering insurance is concerned with the insurance of plant, machinery and other structures on land. Often, such policies will include a provision, or a contract, for the inspection of the property insured. In these circumstances, under a trade agreement, Customs used to allow, in specified circumstances, insurers to treat their inspection services as part of a single composite supply of insurance. This agreement was withdrawn with effect from 1 April 1997, and insurers are now regarded as making separate supplies of insurance and inspection services. Inspection services are taxable and fall to be taxed where the property in question is located.

Run-off services

17.58 An insurance or reinsurance business which ceases to underwrite certain types of insurance but still has a liability to deal with claims under contracts already underwritten is said to be in 'run-off' for those areas of business. In such circumstances, the insurer will often appoint a third party to administer the run-off of those insurance contracts. Typically, the third party will provide claims services of managing the business in run-off, settling and handling of, and dealing with, adjustments to premiums. These services are deemed to form a composite supply of effecting insurance contracts and claims handling and qualify for VAT exemption as insurance-related services provided by an insurance intermediary. However, if separate administrative services are supplied, e.g. supplies of staff, management of invested premiums, etc., these will not qualify for exemption from VAT but are taxable at the standard rate.

17.59 VAT Business by Business

Salvage

17.59 Insurers sometimes settle claims by accepting that damaged property should be treated as a total loss rather than repaired. In these circumstances, the insurer will acquire the damaged property and, often, subsequently dispose of the goods, etc., to a third party. The disposal generally represents a taxable supply and VAT will be due on the entire proceeds realised.

17.60 However, where the goods in question are works of art, antiques and collector's items or second-hand goods, then, subject to certain conditions, the disposal is outside the scope of VAT. The position for such disposals is contained at *Article 4* of the *Value Added Tax (Special Provisions) Order 1995 (SI 1995 No 1268)*. Under this provision, VAT need not be accounted for provided that:

- the goods are sold in the same condition as when acquired by the insurer; and

- the policyholder would not have been required to charge VAT had he been selling the item himself (e.g. acquisition from a private individual or from a dealer operating one of the schemes for second-hand goods. If the conditions are not met, the insurer must charge VAT on the disposal of goods. However, it should be noted that certain large boats and aircraft will qualify for zero-rating (*VATA 1994, 8 Sch, Group 8*). Also, if goods are salvaged and sold outside the UK, they will be outside the scope of VAT.

Warranties/Insurance supplied with other goods and services

17.61 It is common practice for manufacturers or retailers of 'white goods' (e.g. washing machines, refrigerators, televisions and videos) to provide a warranty as part of their sales package. Where this warranty merely represents the retailer's or manufacturer's obligation to provide repair services or offer a replacement if the goods prove faulty, Customs take the view that there is no separate supply of insurance. In other words, any consideration received for the warranty is regarded as part of the overall consideration of a single composite supply of goods.

17.62 The position regarding insurance warranties supplied with white goods was considered in the case of *Thorn EMI plc; Granada plc, [1993] VATTR 94 (9782)*. In this case, two groups of companies let television sets on hire. In both instances, the television sets were let on hire by one subsidiary company, and another subsidiary provided insurance. 70% of the total consideration was allocated to the rental subsidiary, the other 30% being allocated to the insurance subsidiary. The groups did not account for VAT on the amounts allocated to the insurance subsidiaries, treating them as exempt from VAT. Customs issued assessments charging output tax on the full amounts of the payments, on the basis that there was a single composite supply which did not qualify for exemption. The tribunal allowed the groups' appeals, holding that there were two separate supplies in each case.

17.63 Often, manufacturers or retailers offer 'extended warranties' to provide cover over a longer period. Typically, this would involve a separate contract between the manufacturer or retailer and the customer. In these circumstances, Customs take the view that there have been two supplies, the sale of the goods and the provision of the warranty. However, the provision of the warranty will not be an exempt supply as the manufacturer or retailer is not a permitted insurer. (It is also arguable whether such a warranty supplied is, in fact, insurance).

17.64 Where the extended warranty is an insurance policy supplied by a permitted insurer, any charges made by the manufacturer or retailer may be treated as insurance intermediary services or disbursements depending on the circumstances. Where the charges are consideration for insurance intermediary services, the supply will be exempt subject to the conditions and disclosure requirements outlined below.

17.65 The supplier may treat his services as an exempt supply of insurance-related services by an insurance intermediary provided that the following conditions are met:

- the insurance must be supplied by a permitted insurer whose insurance services qualify for exemption from VAT;

- it is the customer's risk and not the supplier's risk which is being insured, i.e. the individual customer's risk is covered in the policy. It is not necessary for the customer to be specifically named. Where both the supplier of the goods and services and the customers are the insured persons, it is acceptable for the policy to refer to the supplier company and their customers; and

- where the supplier is selling goods or services which are liable to VAT, the amount of the premium, and any fee charged over and above that premium, are identified in writing on a document issued to the customer at or before the time when the insurance transaction is entered into.

The legislation provides for Customs to set out in a notice the form of the document in which the matters outlined above should be disclosed. Further details on this are outlined in the section 'Accounting and Records' at paragraph 17.81 *et seq.* below, and at Appendix C.

Valuation

17.66 Valuation services for insurance purposes will normally be a separate taxable supply. However, sometimes it is possible that such services

17.67 *VAT Business by Business*

are subsumed into a single exempt composite supply of insurance. The case of *Lancaster Insurance Services Ltd (5455)* considered this issue. This case concerned the valuation of cars by an insurance broker which arranged for the provision of insurance in respect of the cars in question. The broker charged clients a fee of £8 for determining the agreed value. Customs contended that these fees were taxable but the tribunal ruled that they were exempt as an integral part of the provision of particular insurance policies.

Input tax recovery

Partial exemption

17.67 As with financial services businesses, insurance providers and intermediaries are generally unable to recover all of their VAT on expenditure. Such businesses may only recover VAT that relates to certain types of activities. In addition to irrecoverable VAT costs, the partly exempt status of insurance businesses often results in a significant compliance burden. This arises from the need for these businesses to consider and obtain agreement from Customs for a suitable partial exemption method for the recovery of VAT costs where appropriate.

17.68 A detailed summary of the partial exemption regulations in general can be found in Chapter 3—Banking and Securities. The purpose of this section is to explain and outline aspects of input tax recovery and partial exemption particular to the insurance sector.

Sectorisation

17.69 It will rarely be appropriate (or accepted by Customs) for insurance businesses to use the standard partial exemption method. Normally, Customs will require insurance businesses to use a special method based on sectorisation. In other words, different aspects of an insurer's business will be treated as separate activities for VAT purposes. Input tax will be allocated, in accordance with an agreed method, to the various sectors.

17.70 With regard to sectorisation, Customs invariably insist that investments from dealings in securities should be treated as a separate activity. Due to the very large values of many securities disposals, it would have a distortive impact on any values-based partial exemption method if such disposals were included with insurance premium income. With this exception, it is often possible for insurance businesses to mix their other activities in such a way as to secure a favourable input tax recovery using a sectorised partial exemption method.

Input tax incurred on claims

17.71 The actual payment or settlement of a claim by an insurer to the insured is not consideration for any supply for VAT purposes. Consequently,

Insurance **17.76**

the payment of claims *per se* will not give rise to any input tax costs for the insurer.

17.72 Services such as repairs and legal services and the supply of replacement goods pertaining to a claim are regarded as supplied to the policy holder rather than the insurer. Also, where, under a subrogated claim, an insurer exercises his right to pursue or defend a claim in the name of the policyholder, services are generally regarded as supplied to the policyholder. Where policyholders are registered for VAT and the claim in question relates to their business, they may deduct the related input tax incurred subject to the normal rules.

17.73 There are, however, circumstances where insurers obtain claims-related services for their own purposes, for example, legal services relating to a dispute with a policyholder. The services of loss adjusters and similar experts in relation to a claim are regarded as being supplied to the insurer. However, loss assessors, who are normally appointed by the policyholder and act in the interest of the policyholder, are regarded as supplying their services to the policyholder and, therefore, any related input tax is not recoverable by the insurer.

17.74 Also, where insurers have goods supplied to them to be transferred to a policyholder in settlement of a claim, they may treat the VAT incurred as their input tax. However, in this instance, they must account for output tax on the cost price of the goods when they are transferred to the policyholder. Alternatively, the insurer may choose not to claim input tax deduction on such goods and, therefore, has no requirement to account for output tax on their transfer.

17.75 The position taken by Customs with regard to the input tax recovery of claims-related costs incurred by insurers changed following the dismissal by the High Court of Customs' appeal in the case of *Deutsche Ruck UK Reinsurance Co Ltd, QB [1995] STC 495*. As a result of the failure of their appeal in this case, Customs announced that, with effect from 1 May 1995, VAT incurred on claims costs by insurers should be regarded as directly attributable to the original supply of insurance. Therefore, if the original supply gave a right to input tax deduction, the VAT on related claims costs is recoverable in full. Conversely, if the original supply did not give rise to any input tax deduction, VAT incurred on claims costs is not recoverable.

17.76 Previously, Customs regarded claims costs as general overheads of insurance businesses. This meant that the VAT thereon was treated as non-attributable input tax and apportioned for the purposes of VAT recovery in accordance with the insurer's agreed partial exemption method. The ruling which gave rise to the revised treatment of VAT incurred on claims costs

17.77 *VAT Business by Business*

allowed many insurance businesses to make a retrospective claim for input tax not recovered. In allowing such claims, Customs normally insist that the revised policy is applied consistently to take into account direct attribution both to those policies that have a right to input tax deduction and to those which do not.

Lloyd's method

17.77 As explained at paragraphs 17.44 to 17.50 above, special arrangements apply to the underwriting of insurance at Lloyd's and the recovery of related input tax. In particular, managing agents take on the responsibility of accounting for all of the outputs and inputs of the syndicates under their management. The coding of the policies underwritten by the syndicates, and thus the calculation of the recovery percentage of related input tax, is carried out by the LPSO.

17.78 One exception to the position outlined above relates to the treatment of motor insurance. With effect from 1 April 1987, this has been required to be dealt with separately. Where appropriate, for the syndicates under their management, managing agents will regard motor insurance as a separate activity from the other insurance business coded by the LPSO. Any related input tax should be irrecoverable as motor insurance will invariably be exempt from VAT because it is supplied to UK insured persons.

17.79 Under the agreed Lloyd's special method, managing agents apportion their own income in respect of insurance-related supplies on the basis of the liability of the insurance of all of the syndicates under their management. In other words, managing agents amalgamate the values of the exempt and 'zero-rated' premiums reported by the LPSO for their syndicates and the exempt motor insurance premiums. To this, managing agents add any other non-insurance-related taxable or exempt supplies which they make. The ratio of the value of the 'zero-rated' insurance supplies and other taxable supplies to the total value of all supplies made by the managing agent will determine the extent of the recovery of the managing agent's own input tax.

17.80 A further special arrangement has been agreed with regard to corporate names. Essentially, these involve all corporate members applying a fixed recovery percentage advised by Lloyd's each quarter. This is based on the VAT liability of all of the premiums processed through the LPSO in the previous quarter.

Accounting and records

17.81 The basic requirements for VAT accounting, and the records which must be kept by all VAT-registered businesses, are set out in Chapter 57 of *Tolley's VAT 1998/99*. There are, however, a number of additional matters which need to be considered by insurance businesses in this respect.

Tax points

17.82 As a general rule, it will have been noted from the preceding paragraphs that VAT is not due on supplies of insurance and insurance-related supplies. Nevertheless, it is still often important to determine the time of supply of such services, in particular for partial exemption calculations carried out by these businesses.

17.83 As outlined in Chapter 64 of *Tolley's VAT 1998/99*, the basic tax point for supplies of services is treated as the time when the services are performed. For insurance businesses, this is taken to occur on completion of the insurance cover, i.e. when the insurance contract is finalised and signed.

17.84 The actual tax point for insurance services generally occurs when the underwriter accepts a portion of the risk by signing the broker's slip. However, often the underwriter will not always know the value of the supply until he receives notification from the broker on the 'closing' slip which lists the share of the risk taken by each underwriter and the premium receivable. Therefore, Customs allow insurers to apply to use an accommodation tax point where the time of supply is taken as the date of the closing slip.

17.85 The time of supply of services provided by intermediaries follows the normal rules. The actual tax point for brokers occurs when a debit note is issued to the insured to collect the premium, or the date on which payment is received, whichever happens first.

Reverse charge

17.86 A major concern for insurance businesses is the identification and the subsequent VAT accounting of services received from overseas which are subject to the reverse charge. Essentially, the reverse charge applies to the services listed in *VATA 1994, 5 Sch* (see Appendix B). However, it does not apply to services which would be exempt or zero-rated if supplied in the UK.

17.87 Under the reverse charge procedure, insurance businesses have to account for VAT on services from overseas as if they had supplied the service themselves. This VAT is also treated as the input tax of the insurance business. As insurance businesses are, almost without exception, partially exempt, the reverse charge procedure results in irrecoverable VAT costs.

17.88 With regard to overseas services received by Lloyd's managing agents on behalf of the syndicates under their management, Customs have agreed that Mendez & Mount and Citibank Trustee fees are not subject to VAT under the reverse charge procedure. However, Customs have ruled that LeBoeuf Lamb Leiby & Macrae fees are subject to VAT.

17.89 The amount paid by an insurance business to an overseas supplier of services will, of course, exclude UK VAT. The value of the transaction on

17.90 *VAT Business by Business*

which UK VAT must be accounted by the insurance business is the total amount paid, including any taxes levied abroad, converted into sterling. The value of reverse charge services must also be excluded from partial exemption calculations based on values.

Disclosure requirements

17.90 Insurance intermediaries, who sell insurance with other taxable goods and services, are required to disclose the premium (inclusive of any commission they receive for arranging the insurance) in order to exempt their services in this respect. In addition, if the intermediary charges a fee above and beyond the amount of premium for arranging the insurance, this too must be disclosed for them to exempt their services of arrangement. Customs have identified that the disclosure requirements can cause practical difficulties where the sale has been made by telephone or electronically. Therefore, Customs have provided guidelines and detailed the records which must be kept in order for exemption to apply in these circumstances. These guidelines are contained in Customs' Notice 701/36—Insurance and are shown at Appendix C.

Practical issues

Industry agreements

17.91 Customs have entered into a number of industry agreements with the various insurance trade bodies, mainly regarding the treatment of insurance services in certain circumstances and with regard to partial exemption methods. The current agreements are as follows:

Partial exemption: Agreement with the ABI. The agreement details an accepted partial exemption method for the recovery of input tax incurred in the UK in connection with supplies made outside the European Union ('EU') by branches of insurance businesses.

Claims-related input tax and associated imported services: Agreement with certain insurance trade associations. This agreement sets down the procedure for the recovery of claims-related input tax and associated imported services where claims costs are co-ordinated by trade associations. Claims expenses and related input tax and associated imported services VAT are re-allocated by the trade associations to individual members on the basis of the percentage of the risk underwritten by each.

Coding supplies of marine, aviation and transport insurance services: Agreement with the ABI, Lloyd's of London, the Institute of London Underwriters and the British Insurance and Investment Association. The agreement provides guidelines for the coding of policies to determine the VAT liability of supplies of marine, aviation and transport insurance services.

Insurance **17.94**

The guidelines take into account the place of supply rules effective for marine, aviation and transport insurance services from 5 July 1993, i.e. input tax recovery must be based on the place of belonging of the insured person rather than on where the journey takes place.

VAT notices

17.92 Customs have published various public notices which are useful to insurance businesses. These include:

Notice No 700/57/95   Administrative agreements entered into with various trade bodies

Notice No 701/36/97   Insurance

Notice No 701/44/94   Securities

Notice No 706   Partial Exemption

Notice No 741   Place of supply of services

Notice No 742   Land and Property

Overseas businesses

17.93 Similarly to financial services businesses, overseas insurers setting up in the UK will often form a representative office which does not actually trade in the UK. A summary of the points relevant to the VAT registration of representative offices and their recovery of input tax is given in Chapter 3—Banking and Securities. The same points apply equally to insurance businesses.

17.94 Overseas insurers who are not established in the UK, either through carrying on business or through a representative office, can often incur UK VAT costs, e.g. the services of a loss adjuster in respect of assessing a claim related to a property in the UK. It is sometimes possible for the overseas insurers to recover such input VAT under the provisions of the *EC Eighth Directive* (other EU insurers) and the *EC Thirteenth Directive* (non-EU insurers). The provisions allow overseas insurers to reclaim input tax incurred in the UK subject to certain conditions, e.g. that the input tax in question is not non-deductible input tax. For overseas insurers, Customs will sometimes refuse claims if the country where the insurer belongs does not provide reciprocal arrangements.

Appendix A

Item no

(1) The provision of insurance or reinsurance by a person who provides it in the course of:

    (a) any insurance business which he is authorised under *section 3* or *4* of the *Insurance Companies Act 1982* to carry on, or

    (b) any business in respect of which he is exempted under *section 2* of that *Act* from the requirement to be so authorised.

(2) The provision by an insurer or reinsurer who belongs outside the United Kingdom of:

    (a) insurance against any of the risks or other things described in *Schedules 1* and *2* to the *Insurance Companies Act 1982*, or

    (b) reinsurance relating to any of those risks or other things.

(3) The provision of insurance or reinsurance by the Export Credits Guarantee Department.

(4) The provision by an insurance broker or insurance agent of any of the services of an insurance intermediary in a case in which those services:

    (a) are related (whether or not a contract of insurance or reinsurance is finally concluded) to any such provision of insurance or reinsurance as falls, or would fall, within item 1, 2 or 3; and

    (b) are provided by that broker or agent in the course of his acting in an intermediary capacity.

Notes:

(1) For the purposes of item 4 services are services of an insurance intermediary if they fall within any of the following paragraphs:

    (a) the bringing together, with a view to the insurance or reinsurance of risks, of

        (i) persons who are or may be seeking insurance or reinsurance, and

        (ii) persons who provide insurance or reinsurance;

    (b) the carrying out of work preparatory to the conclusion of contracts of insurance or reinsurance;

(c) the provision of assistance in the administration and performance of such contracts, including the handling of claims;

(d) the collection of premiums.

(2) For the purposes of item 4 an insurance broker or insurance agent is acting 'in an intermediary capacity' wherever he is acting as an intermediary, or one of the intermediaries, between:

(a) a person who provides any insurance or reinsurance the provision of which falls within item 1, 2 or 3, and

(b) a person who is or may be seeking insurance or reinsurance or is an insured person.

(3) Where:

(a) a person ('the supplier') makes a supply of goods or services to another ('the customer'),

(b) the supply of the goods or services is a taxable supply and is not a zero-rated supply,

(c) a transaction under which insurance is to be or may be arranged for the customer is entered into in connection with the supply of the goods or services,

(d) a supply of services which are related (whether or not a contract of insurance is finally concluded) to the provision of insurance in pursuance of that transaction is made by:

(i) the person by whom the supply of the goods or services is made, or

(ii) a person who is connected with that person and, in connection with the provision of that insurance, deals directly with the customer,

and

(e) the related services do not consist in the handling of claims under the contract for that insurance, those related services do not fall within item 4 unless the relevant requirements are fulfilled.

(4) For the purposes of Note (3) the relevant requirements are:

(a) that a document containing the statements specified in Note (5) is prepared;

(b) that the matters that must be stated in the document have been disclosed to the customer at or before the time when the transaction mentioned in Note (3)(c) is entered into; and

17.App A *VAT Business by Business*

(c) that there is compliance with all such requirements (if any) as to:

(i) the preparation and form of the document,

(ii) the manner of disclosing to the customer the matters that must be stated in the document, and

(iii) the delivery of a copy of the document to the customer, as may be set out in a notice that has been published by the Commissioners and has not been withdrawn.

(5) The statements referred to in Note (4) are:

(a) a statement setting out the amount of the premium under any contract of insurance that is to be or may be entered into in pursuance of the transaction in question; and

(b) a statement setting out every amount that the customer is, is to be or has been required to pay, otherwise than by way of such a premium, in connection with that transaction or anything that is to be, may be or has been done in pursuance of that transaction.

(6) For the purposes of Note (3) any question whether a person is connected with another shall be determined in accordance with section 839 of the Taxes Act.

(7) Item 4 does not include:

(a) the supply of any market research, product design, advertising, promotional or similar services; or

(b) the collection, collation and provision of information for use in connection with market research, product design, advertising, promotional or similar activities.

(8) Item 4 does not include the supply of any valuation or inspection services.

(9) Item 4 does not include the supply of any services by loss adjusters, average adjusters, motor assessors, surveyors or other experts except where:

(a) the services consist in the handling of a claim under a contract of insurance or reinsurance;

(b) the person handling the claim is authorised when doing so to act on behalf of the insurer or reinsurer; and

(c) that person's authority so to act includes written authority to determine whether to accept or reject the claim and, where accepting it in whole or in part, to settle the amount to be paid on the claim.

(10) Item 4 does not include the supply of any services which:

    (a) are supplied in pursuance of a contract of insurance or reinsurance or of any arrangements made in connection with such a contract; and

    (b) are so supplied either:

        (i) instead of the payment of the whole or any part of any indemnity for which the contract provides, or

        (ii) for the purpose, in any other manner, of satisfying any claim under that contract, whether in whole or in part.

Appendix B

VATA 1994, 5 Sch

Relevant 'reverse charge' services

(1) Transfers and assignments of copyright, patents licences, trademarks and similar rights.

(2) Advertising services.

(3) Services of consultants, engineers, consultancy bureaux, lawyers, accountants and other similar services; data processing and provision of information (but excluding from this head any services relating to land).

(4) Acceptance of any obligation to refrain from pursuing or exercising, in whole or part, any business activity or any such rights as are referred to in paragraph 1 above.

(5) Banking, financial and insurance services (including reinsurance, but not including the provision of safe deposit facilities).

(6) The supply of staff.

(7) The letting or hire of goods other than means of transport.

(8) The services rendered by one person to another in procuring for the other any of the services mentioned in paragraphs 1 to 7 above.

Appendix C

Insurance sold with other goods and services:

Records to be kept in certain situations (telesales, internet, etc.)

In order to treat a supply of arranging insurance as exempt, an intermediary is required to disclose the premium as well as any fee charged over and above

17.App C *VAT Business by Business*

that premium. This disclosure is to be made in writing to the customer at, or before, the time when the insurance transaction is entered into.

This disclosure condition may create a problem for businesses which effect transactions which take place over the telephone, or by some other form of electronic communication where the customer and the salesperson are not physically in the same place at the same time.

To ensure that the disclosure requirement does not disadvantage these businesses too much, but equally, to ensure compliance with the disclosure conditions set out in the law and reproduced at paragraph 3.7 of Customs Notice 701/36—Insurance, Customs have introduced a further record keeping requirement.

Under paragraph 6(1) of Schedule 11 to the VAT Act 1994, the Commissioners are permitted to set out in regulations those records a taxable person is required to keep. Regulation 31(1) of the VAT Regulations 1995 sets out the records which a taxable person is required to keep for the purposes of accounting for VAT. Regulation 31(2) provides that the Commissioners may supplement, by means of a notice, the list of records a taxable person is required to keep.

Any person who is selling insurance with taxable goods and services, by means of electronic communication, must fulfil the following three criteria for their insurance related services to fall within the exemption:

- the trader must make full disclosure of the premium at the time of the transaction. For example, if the trader is selling holidays over the telephone then they must orally inform the customer of the amount of the premium and any fee charged over and above the premium in relation to the insurance;

- the document which the trader is required to prepare and issue to the customer must contain the statements set out in Legal Note 5 to Group 2, Schedule 9, VAT Act 1994 as amended by the Finance Act 1997; and

- the trader must have in place a system whereby the sales staff must annotate a document (even if this only involves ticking a box) at the time they make the oral disclosure to customers to indicate that they have done so. Traders must retain a copy of these records as they would their normal VAT records.

Chapter 18

Leasing and hire-purchase

Introduction

18.1 It is important to note at the outset that, although this chapter will deal almost exclusively with the VAT consequences that must be taken into consideration when advising lessors and lessees with regard to leasing or hire-purchase transactions, these VAT consequences cannot be looked at in isolation. At the foundation of the leasing industry is a complex tax base, on which the profitability of any transaction can be wholly dependent on the correct corporate tax or indirect tax treatment being applied from the outset of the deal. 'Hidden' or unforeseen tax costs at the end of the leasing transaction will obviously not be welcome, and for the indirect tax specialist or advisor there are a number of complex areas to consider.

18.2 Putting aside direct taxes, the leasing industry is involved in some of the most complex areas of VAT for any practitioner or advisor. This is made more so because of an industry shift towards specialising in particular areas, i.e. motor cars, domestic appliances, veterinary equipment and the like. This brings with it the need for specialist advice within each sub-sector of the leasing industry.

Scope of this chapter

18.3 This chapter, on the VAT aspects of leasing and hire-purchase will be confined to motor vehicles, transport and equipment leasing. Leasing transactions involving land and buildings are covered in Chapter 21— Property Development.

18.4 The chapter will look separately at the VAT issues affecting both the lessor and lessee and will examine the VAT treatment of finance leases, equipment leases and hire purchase agreements.

Terminology used

18.5 For the purposes of this chapter the term 'Hire-Purchase' will include finance leases, conditional sale and credit sale agreements, and will be used where there is a lease which substantially transfers all the risks and rewards arising from the ownership of an asset to the lessee, as is the case

18.6 *VAT Business by Business*

with hire purchase. The term 'Operating Lease' is used to denote a transaction whereby the risk and the reward remains with the lessor.

Liability

18.6 When looking at the basic VAT treatment of hire-purchases and operating leases, it is necessary to first address the following issues:

- the nature of the supply (i.e. is it one of goods or services),
- the time of supply (tax point),
- the liability of the supply,
- the value of the supply,
- the place of supply (where the lessor and lessee belong in different countries).

Each of these areas is covered in more detail below.

Nature of supply as it affects the lessor

18.7 For the lessor, it is essential to consider whether, under the terms of the agreement, the supply is one of goods or services. The relevant UK VAT legislation to determine the nature of a supply is contained in *VATA 1994, 4 Sch 1*. Specifically, *4 Sch 1* determines whether a lessor is making a supply of a hire-purchase or an operating lease. *VATA 1994, 4 Sch 1(2)* states:

'if the possession of goods is transferred—

(a) under an agreement for the sale of the goods, or

(b) under arrangements which expressly contemplate that the property will pass at some time in the future (determined by, or ascertainable from, the agreements but in any case not later than when the goods are fully paid for), it is then, in either case, a supply of goods.'

18.8 Under a hire-purchase agreement, the lessor's documentation will either provide for the implicit transfer of legal ownership of the asset to the lessee or allow an option for the lessee to purchase the asset, usually when the final payment is made under the agreement. As a hire-purchase agreement expressly contemplates that title will pass from the lessor to the lessee, such agreements are supplies of goods for VAT purposes.

18.9 In their Notice No 700, Customs & Excise provide some brief guidance on the nature of supplies made under hire-purchase, conditional sale and credit sale agreements. See *Tolley's VAT 1998/99, para 27.19*. All the examples given demonstrate that, at the outset of the agreement, there is a supply of goods where it is expected that title will pass. However, in practice, where there is any doubt that the agreement expressly contemplates that title will pass, then specific advice should be sought from a VAT practitioner.

18.10 It is important to note that although Customs & Excise take the view that the supply of assets under a hire-purchase agreement constitutes a supply of goods for VAT purposes, the finance element which is separately disclosed on the agreement will be supply of exempt financial services. The consequences of this are explained at paragraph 18.24 below.

18.11 It follows that, where it is not expected that there will be a transfer of legal title to the asset, then, in contrast to hire-purchase, the supply by the lessor will be a supply of services only. The fact that a lessee may often be involved in the disposal of the lessor's asset at the end of the lease term should not impact on the fact that the supplies by the lessor are those of services. It is common practice, particularly for leases of motor cars, that lessees act as the lessor's agent in selling the goods at the end of the lease term. It is therefore necessary to look at the agreement and not at who is selling the goods, to determine whether there is a supply of goods or services.

Nature of supply as it affects the lessee

18.12 It is important for the lessee to understand whether the supply under a lease agreement is one of goods or services since a number of VAT issues arise from this, key considerations being when and how much VAT the lessee may reclaim input tax and on what value the lessee may reclaim input tax. The implications of these issues are discussed in more detail below.

Time of supply

Issues affecting the lessor

18.13 Where an agreement is for a supply of goods, the normal VAT rules in *VATA 1994, s 6* will apply. Therefore, it is most likely that under a hire-purchase agreement the tax point will be the date that the lessor issues a tax invoice or receives payment in respect of the supply, whichever occurs first. It is usual practice that, when leasing documentation is set up for a hire-purchase agreement, the requirements of a tax invoice are incorporated in the documentation. However, if goods are made available to the customer in advance of documentation being issued, then subject to the 14-day rule, the tax point reverts to the date when the goods are sent to the customer or are made available to the customer. Where appropriate, an application can be made to extend the 14-day limit.

18.14 Under a hire-purchase agreement it is normal business practice for lessors to demand a payment at least equivalent to the output tax which the

18.15 VAT Business by Business

lessor is obliged to pay over to Customs & Excise with the first instalment payment.

18.15 With regard to deposits taken by lessors, it is important to note that the normal tax point rules apply and, therefore, output tax should be accounted for by the lessor on the value of the deposit taken in the VAT accounting period in which the deposit payment is received. This may be particularly important to lessors who are involved in leasing high value goods which have a long lead time on delivery.

18.16 As stated at paragraph 18.9 above, separate supplies will be recognised for hire-purchase agreements, where the finance element of the rentals is separately disclosed to the lessee. The supply of the finance is treated as being made over the life of the agreement. The effect of this is that exempt supplies will be made in each subsequent VAT accounting period in which a payment is made, resulting in an ongoing restriction of overhead input tax over the life of the hire-purchase agreement.

18.17 Special tax point rules exist in respect of operating leases. Here the supplies are treated as continuous supplies of services. As it is usual practice for lessors to issue a scheduled invoice setting out the dates on which successive payments of services are due, the provisions of *VAT Regulations 1995 (SI 1995 No 2518), reg 90(2)* will apply. Where the lessor issues a scheduled invoice, it may only set out supplies to be made for a period of up to one year. Furthermore, in addition to the normal requirements of a VAT invoice, the invoice must also show:

(a) the dates on which payments under the agreements are to become due in the period;

(b) the amount payable (excluding VAT) on each such date; and

(c) the rate of VAT in force at the time of issue of the VAT invoice and the amount of VAT chargeable in accordance with that rate on each payment.

18.18 In this instance services are to be treated as separately and successively supplied each time that a payment becomes due or is received, whichever is the earlier. Where a lessor does not issue a scheduled invoice, then the normal tax point rules for continuous supplies of services, as detailed in *VAT Regulations 1995 (SI 1995 No 2518), reg 90(1)* will apply, i.e. a tax point will be created each time a tax invoice is issued or a payment is received, whichever is the earlier.

Issues affecting the lessee

18.19 Under hire-purchase agreements it is important for lessees to ensure that the documentation qualifies as a proper tax invoice which allows the lessor to recover the full amount of VAT paid at the outset of the agreement subject to the lessor's general VAT recovery position. Where high value goods are being supplied to a lessee, the claim for input tax in a single VAT accounting period may well generate an enquiry by Customs and it may be advisable in such circumstances to notify Customs, at the time the relevant VAT return is submitted, that an unusually large repayment is expected. Such action may avoid unnecessary delays in receiving repayments from Customs.

18.20 Under operating leases, lessees should pay particular attention to receipts of scheduled invoices from lessors. The lessee must not reclaim any VAT shown on the scheduled VAT invoice as input tax until the date on which the payment is due or until payment has been received by the supplier, whichever happens first. When advising lessees in receipt of scheduled invoices, it is important to pay particular attention to the time of supply in order to ensure that the lessee is recovering input tax at the right time.

VAT liability of supplies—Lessor

18.21 Under a hire-purchase agreement, the VAT liability of the supply of the goods will follow the normal VAT liability. For example, under a hire-purchase agreement for the supply of office furniture, the supply of the goods will be subject to VAT at the standard rate, but a hire-purchase transaction involving a large commercial aircraft will be zero-rated.

18.22 Coupled with the supply of the goods, be it standard-rated or zero-rated, there is a separate supply of finance, which, subject to certain conditions being met, is treated as an exempt supply where the finance is provided to a lessee in the UK or a private individual belonging in the EU. The conditions which must be met for exemption to apply are set out in *VATA 1994, 9 Sch, Group 5, Item 3*. Under this provision, in order to obtain exemption, there is a requirement to disclose the finance charge to the recipient of the supply of the goods.

18.23 Whether a finance charge was separately disclosed was considered in the case of *Freight Transport Leasing Ltd, [1991] VATTR 142 (5578)*. Here a finance company provided finance for the purchase of vehicles under lease purchase agreements but it did not separately identify the finance charge, instead quoting customers the purchase price and the number and the amount of instalments. It did not account for VAT on the amount which represented the finance charge, treating this as an exempt supply. Customs issued an assessment but the tribunal allowed the company's appeal on the basis that the amount of the finance charge could be ascertained by a simple calculation.

18.24 For operating leases, the VAT liability of the lease payments will follow the liability of the goods themselves. For example, the letting on hire of a qualifying aircraft is zero-rated. Although there is certainly a finance element built into an operating lease agreement, there is no facility to exempt the supply of the finance. Therefore, if VAT is chargeable on the operating lease, it is chargeable on the full value of the consideration received for the standard-rated supply.

VAT documentation—Lessor

18.25 For the lessor there are a number of issues to consider in relation to the documentation in any single hire-purchase. Initially, there is a purchase of equipment by the lessor, and this requires proper documentation to be held in order that input tax can be reclaimed. Secondly, there is the supply of the goods to the lessee and, where the lessee is a taxable person, the lessor must ensure that a proper VAT invoice is issued to enable the lessee to recover input tax on the transaction. There is no legal obligation for lessors to provide non-taxable persons (i.e. private individuals) with proper tax invoices. It should also be noted that, under a hire-purchase agreement, there is no ongoing documentation required since VAT has already been accounted for at the outset and the only remaining supplies will be exempt finance charges.

18.26 For supplies under operating leases, the lessor must ensure that proper documentation is in place which will enable the lessor to reclaim input tax on the purchase of the equipment. Secondly, the lessor must ensure that, where the lessee is a taxable person, proper documentation is issued to the lessee so as to avoid any ambiguity on the part of the lessee as to its right to reclaim input tax. Lastly, the lessor will have a requirement to sell the equipment at the end of the lease term, and proper VAT documentation must be issued to ensure that VAT is accounted for properly on the sale of the equipment. The disposal of equipment is covered in more detail at paragraphs 18.48 to 18.51 below.

Effect of VAT on lessors

18.27 In addition to the considerations outlined above with regard to liability issues, and the ability to reclaim input tax, the lessor may also care to consider the commercial consequences. This has been clearly demonstrated by companies involved in leasing motor cars since 1 August 1995, where lessors have made significant efforts to separate the constituent supplies of maintenance, insurance etc., so as to minimise the amount of irrecoverable VAT in the hands of the lessees.

VAT Recovery

Lessors and Input Tax Recovery

18.28 One of the key issues affecting lessors who carry out both hire-purchase and operating lease transactions is the effect which exempt supplies have on the lessor's ability to reclaim overhead input tax.

Leasing and hire-purchase **18.32**

18.29 The amount of allowable input tax which a lessor is entitled to claim at the end of any period is so much input tax on supplies, acquisitions and importation in the period as can be directly attributed to taxable supplies (this will include sales of goods under hire-purchase and equipment leases), supplies made outside the UK which would be taxable if made in the UK, and supplies of services made to a person who belongs outside the member states (see *Tolley's VAT 1998/99, chapter 49*). The lessor who makes exempt supplies must therefore have procedures in place to monitor VAT which it incurs on the purchase of goods, and should be able to identify as far as possible input tax which relates to its taxable supplies in respect of these goods.

18.30 It is also important to note that leasing companies will generally fall under the heading of 'finance houses', or will be carrying on a 'business similar to...a finance house', and therefore cannot take advantage of the provisions set out in *VAT Regulations 1995 (SI 1995 No 2518), reg 105(1)*. Similarly, hire-purchase transactions are specifically excluded from supplies that may be disregarded for the purposes of *regulation 105*. Therefore, input tax which is attributable to any deposit of money, services of making arrangements for the provision of insurance or reinsurance, services of arranging mortgages or hire purchase, credit sale or conditional sale transactions, the assignment of any debts due to the assignor in respect of supplies of goods or services made by him, and the granting of certain lease or tenancies, cannot be disregarded when determining the amount of input tax which the leasing company can reclaim. However, where an operating lease has been granted by a business which is not a finance house or similar business, then it may be possible to take advantage of *regulation 105*.

Partial exemption methods

18.31 The normal partial exemption rules apply to leasing companies as they do to any other partly exempt business. However, in respect of leasing and hire purchase companies there is an industry-agreed method which is regarded by Customs & Excise as producing a fair and reasonable attribution of overhead input tax. The method which was agreed with the Finance Houses Association in September 1994 and is set out at Appendix 1 to this chapter. In essence, this method allows all overhead VAT relating to operating leases to be recovered in full; 15% of all overhead VAT relating to hire-purchase agreements may also be recovered in full, with no recovery of overhead VAT relating to exempt loans.

18.32 The industry-agreed method is widely used, as the required records, e.g. outstanding balances relating to each type of business undertaken (hire-purchase, leasing loans etc.) are retained for other accounting purposes and thus there should be little difficulty for leasing companies to adopt the industry method. However in some circumstances the use of the agreed industry method may not necessarily produce a 'fair and reasonable' result and advisors should be aware that the industry-agreed method is not

18.33 *VAT Business by Business*

mandatory. It is therefore open to all leaving companies to agree a bespoke partial exemption method with Customs, provided that it can be demonstrated that the bespoke method rather than the industry method produces a fair and reasonable result.

Other effects of partial exemption

18.33 As with any partly exempt business, leasing companies must take account of the VAT implications of imported services (and the corresponding VAT costs associated with the reverse charge). See *Tolley's VAT 1998/99, para 39.4*. For details of the Capital Goods Scheme, see *Tolley's VAT 1998/99, paras 10.1 to 10.12*. Hire-purchase and leasing companies which are purchasing new computer systems or upgrading existing systems should take account of the Capital Goods Scheme and adjust input tax recovery over a five-year period in respect of any computer equipment which is used for making both taxable and exempt supplies and has a value in excess of £50,000 (excluding VAT). Similarly, if a hire-purchase or leasing company is substantially re-developing (re-creating additional floor-space in excess of 10% of the existing floor-space) or refurbishing a building which it currently occupies, or is relocating to a different building, adjustments under the Capital Goods Scheme must be made over a ten-year period if the value of the standard-rate supplies received is in excess of £250,000. This will result in ongoing administrative and VAT costs.

18.34 VAT charged by a lessor to a lessee will generally be treated in the normal way, but there are some exceptions. For example, if a lessee buys a car, which is not to be used wholly for business purposes, under a hire-purchase agreement, the lessee will not be entitled to reclaim the VAT included. It is this point which led in part to a distortion in the leasing industry in respect of motor cars whereby wholly exempt or partly exempt lessees would prefer to acquire motor vehicles under hire purchase arrangements because VAT on the finance element of the charges by the lessor would be exempt and would not create further irrecoverable VAT costs. The interaction of irrecoverable VAT on the part of the lessee and the fact that, prior to 1 August 1995, lessors were unable to reclaim VAT on the purchase of cars which they were to lease under operating leases led to effective double taxation on behalf of the customer since the irrecoverable VAT on the purchase by the lessor was structured into the lease payments. However, since 1 August 1995, the VAT anomaly has been corrected and hire purchase and leasing of motor cars is now on a more level footing. This will be covered in more detail in paragraphs 18.57 to 18.61 below.

18.35 As stated at paragraph 18.9 above, for hire-purchase and conditional sale agreements, there is a single supply of goods and the normal tax point is the earlier of the date of removal of the goods; the date of issue of the agreement (assuming that the agreement is in the form of a VAT invoice); and the date of the issue of a separate VAT invoice. However, lessors should

Leasing and hire-purchase **18.39**

note that the signing of an agreement, or its date, does not constitute a tax point.

The effect of a change in VAT rate

18.36 Where there is a change in the VAT rate, the tax point which will be whichever tax point results in the lower rate of VAT being charged (see Customs & Excise Notice 700, Appendix C, Paragraph 11). If there is a change of rate after an agreement is signed but before the goods are supplied, then, unless the contract provides otherwise, the consideration for the supply will be increased or decreased by an amount equal to the change (*VATA 1994, s 89(1)*).

18.37 Leasing companies which supply equipment under operating leases must also be aware of the consequences when there is a change of rate of VAT. As detailed at paragraph 18.17 above, the lessor may have issued a scheduled invoice covering a period of up to one year, showing the VAT due at the rate applying at each tax point. Any VAT invoice issued up to one year ahead, giving the amounts and dates when payments are due, is invalid in respect of payments due after the change of rate (*SI 1995 No 2518, reg 90(3)*). A lessor must issue a new invoice, as the lessee cannot use the original invoice to support a claim for input tax after the change in rate.

18.38 Where a continuous supply of services spans a change in VAT rate, VAT may be accounted for at the old rate on that part of the supply made prior to the change even though the normal tax point would occur after the change. Conversely, VAT may be accounted for at the new rate on that part of the supply made after the change even though the normal tax point occurred before the change. In each case, VAT should be accounted for on the basis of the value of services performed (see *Tolley's VAT 1998/99, para 56.9*).

Practical points

Lease termination payments

18.39 A lessee may be required under the terms of its leasing contract to make a payment to the lessor to secure agreement to the early termination of an equipment lease. How this is treated for VAT purposes depends on the circumstances and, in particular, the legal nature of the payment. Although termination payments from the lessee to the lessor have traditionally treated as being liable to VAT if the underlying goods are liable to VAT, this has been clouded by recent VAT tribunal cases. The essence of the cases is that the payments made by the lessee are not consideration in the hands of the lessor for any supply of goods or services made by the lessor to the lessee and are therefore treated as outside the scope of VAT, particularly where a lease termination payment is a compensation payment made by the lessee to the

18.40 VAT Business by Business

lessor because there has been a breach of contract. This is supported by the cases of *Holiday Inns (UK) Ltd, [1993] VATTR 321(10609), Financial & General Print Ltd (13795)* and *Lloyds Bank plc (14181)*. In *Holiday Inns (UK) Ltd*, it was decided that a compensation payment received by that company, with regard to the early termination of a management contact by the recipient of its management services, constituted liquidated damages for the loss of future income. Accordingly, the compensation payment was outside the scope of VAT as it was not received in respect of any taxable services. This case established an important principle which was subsequently reinforced in a leasing case involving *Financial & General Print Ltd*. In this case the company entered into a hire-purchase lease but subsequently went into receivership and the lease was terminated. The lessors claimed compensation and Financial & General Print Ltd reclaimed input tax on the compensation payment. It was held that the termination of the lease was not a supply of services by the lessor to Financial & General Print Ltd. Consequently, the compensation payment was outside the scope of VAT. The case of *Lloyds Bank plc* raised a number of arguments about whether lease termination payments in respect of property transactions should be regarded as supplies of services. It was held that there had not been a unilateral act by the lessee which brought about a breach of contract. The payment for the termination of the lease was not compensatory in nature and therefore VAT was chargeable. Accordingly, in situations where a termination payment becomes payable in respect of leases being terminated, it is important to identify the nature of the payment and in particular whether it is compensatory in nature.

18.40 It should be noted that the decision in *Holiday Inns (UK) Ltd* was not followed in the 1997 case of *Croydon Hotel & Leisure Co Ltd (14920)*, where the tribunal held (in relation to an appeal by the company which made the compensation payment) that the payment in question did constitute consideration for a supply of services. (However, the tribunal in *Croydon Hotel & Leisure Co Ltd* did not refer to the decision in *Financial & General Print Ltd*, so that its decision may be considered to be of doubtful authority. The conflicting decisions have the effect that this area of VAT law remains unclear.)

18.41 An important aspect of lease termination is the fact that the lessor will take possession of its equipment and in most cases will arrange to sell the equipment. Lessors should be aware that VAT will be due on the sale of the asset (assuming that input tax was claimed on the original equipment).

18.42 As demonstrated in the case of *Financial & General Print Ltd*, the VAT treatment of lease termination payment is particularly important for lessees who may be unable to reclaim the VAT which the lessor charges in respect of the termination of the lease. In such cases lessees should seek to argue that the payments they make are not consideration for supplies made by the lessor, thus avoiding the imposition of VAT which the lessee would not be able to recover. If it is agreed between the parties that VAT will be

Leasing and hire-purchase **18.47**

charged on a lease termination, then a proper tax invoice must be issued by the lessor to the lessee if the lessee is a taxable person.

Part-exchange transactions

18.43 Part-exchange transactions typically arise where a lessee wants to upgrade a piece of equipment, and wants the new equipment to be financed. In such occasions it is quite usual for the equipment which is being 'traded-in' to still be subject to a finance lease or operating lease, and these transactions can present particular administrative difficulties for leasing companies, lessees and equipment suppliers.

18.44 Particular care must be taken to ensure that each supply made under a part-exchange transaction, where the goods are subject to a hire-purchase agreement, is properly accounted for and that there is no set-off of the value of the part-exchanged goods by the equipment supplier. The supplies of the old and new equipment must be treated as separate supplies for VAT purposes.

18.45 Where a lessee wishes to upgrade equipment which is subject to an operating lease, the lessor must take account of the fact that, if there is a part exchange, the goods which are being traded in belong to the lessor, who must ensure that VAT on the old equipment and new equipment is properly accounted for, i.e. that a credit note is issued to cancel any outstanding VAT due with regard to the old equipment, and that a new invoice and schedule of payments is issued in respect of the new equipment. VAT on the equipment will then be paid over to Customs by the lessor. It is also usual in the leasing industry for the lessee to act as the lessor's agent in disposing of the equipment, and lessors should have procedures to ensure that the lessees are properly aware that VAT may have to be accounted for on the disposal of the equipment, when agreeing the part-exchange price on behalf of the lessor. If VAT is not taken into account when agreeing the part-exchange value, this can affect the profitability of the whole lease deal.

Documentation fees

18.46 It is very common for lessors to charge documentation fees to lessees when setting up new finance lease agreements. Provided that the value of the documentation fee does not exceed £10 and that the fee is disclosed to the lessee, the documentation charge may be treated as an exempt supply (see *VATA 1994, 9 Sch, Group 5, Item 6*).

18.47 It is important to note that the exemption does not apply to documentation fees charged in connection with operating leases.

Disposals of leased assets/Rebates of rentals

18.48 Lessors are involved with the disposal of equipment in a number of circumstances. Equipment under a finance lease may be repossessed and sold but, in most cases, equipment disposals arise where an operating lease runs its full term and there is no further use of the equipment by the lessor.

18.49 It is usually a condition of most operating leases that the lessee will arrange to dispose of the equipment on behalf of the lessor at the end of the lease term. Although the lessee is treated as the lessor's agent in respect of that disposal, lessors must ensure that output tax is properly accounted for on the disposal of the equipment and procedures should be in place to ensure that the correct VAT accounting is followed. Although typically there will be no transfer of money between the lessee and the lessor in respect of the equipment disposal, there are two separate supplies for VAT purposes taking place. The first is the disposal of the equipment which the lessor must account for and secondly, there is a credit to the lessee for arranging the disposal of the equipment (normally referred to as a rebate of rentals or sales commission).

18.50 Under normal circumstances the lessee would be expected to raise a VAT invoice to the lessor for the sales commission or the lessor would raise a VAT credit note for the rebate of rentals. However, in practice, there is an agreement between Customs and the Finance and Leasing Association that:

- no VAT need be adjusted in the VAT accounts of the lessee or lessor, provided that no VAT is shown on any documentation between the two parties;

- no adjustment is made by the lessor to correct VAT already charged on supplies of the rentals, and any documentation clearly shows that the document is not a credit note for VAT purposes.

18.51 Where equipment has been leased to a lessee who is not registered for VAT or is partly exempt and may not have been able to reclaim all the VAT previously charged by the lessor, the lessee is likely to or should insist on a VAT credit note being issued by the lessor. In this instance, the lessor will be able to reduce its output tax by the amount of VAT shown on the credit note, but the lessee is only obliged to adjust its previous input tax recovery to the extent that the original VAT charge was restricted.

Repossession of goods

18.52 Where goods are supplied under a hire-purchase agreement, output tax will have been accounted for on the 'sale' at the outset of the agreement even though payment for the goods is made over a period of time and title will not have passed to the lessee. Because title in the goods has not passed to the lessee when the goods are repossessed by the lessor, the lessee cannot be treated as making a supply of the goods back to the lessor. The lessor is unable to issue a credit note to the lessee in respect of the outstanding capital repayments (*Mannesmann Demag Hamilton Ltd, [1983] VATTR 156 (1437)*). As a consequence, Extra-Statutory Concession 8 was introduced to enable the lessor to receive relief in respect of the VAT already accounted for at the outset of the agreement.

18.53 Extra-Statutory Concession 8 allows lessors to obtain relief from VAT paid at the outset of finance lease agreements provided the following conditions are met.

For agreements with VAT-registered customers:

(a) The customer must expressly agree to the reduction in the original valuation.

(b) The goods have been repossessed or returned under the terms of the agreement. If the goods cannot be repossessed (e.g. because they have been lost), this condition cannot be met.

(c) There are unpaid instalments due from the customer for which the owner is making no claim and for which he has issued a credit note to the customer to cover the full amount.

(d) The owner keeps a record of the credit which has been allowed.

(e) The resale of the goods would be a taxable supply.

(f) The owner has satisfactory evidence from the customer that he has accepted the credit note.

For agreements with non-registered customers:

(i) The goods have been repossessed or returned under the terms of the agreement. If the goods cannot be repossessed (e.g. because they have been lost), this condition cannot be met.

(ii) There are unpaid instalments due from the customer for which no claim is being made.

(iii) The resale of the goods would be a taxable supply.

(iv) The owner keeps documentary evidence to show the nature of the adjustment and the reason for it.

The amount of the credit note should be calculated as the total price shown on the original agreement, less any payment received for the supply, less any amounts being claimed from the customer or any one else for the goods, less any credit charges which have been treated as exempt supplies. The VAT credit is then calculated by applying the VAT fraction to the residual value (i.e. the total price less the deductions detailed above).

18.54 VAT Business by Business

Sale of repossessed goods

18.54 An important point to note when advising on the disposal of repossessed goods which are subject to a hire-purchase or similar agreement, and may contain a retention of title clause until the final payment has been received, is that although the goods may legally belong to the lessor, for VAT purposes, they are treated as still belonging to the lessee. This is on the basis that a supply has taken place for VAT purposes upon delivery of the goods, with a charge to tax arising at this point. Any subsequent repossession does not negate this supply. This principle was confirmed in the court decision in *Re Liverpool Commercial Vehicles, Ch D [1984] BCLC 587*. Customs' practice was subsequently confirmed in their Press Notice 931 issued on 3 August 1984. Accordingly, the lessor is selling the goods on behalf of the lessee and the lessor should follow the procedures set out by Customs (i.e. where the lessee is registered for VAT, the lessor must account for output tax using Form VAT 833).

In most cases, the sale of repossessed goods will be taxable at the standard rate. However, special rules apply for disposals of certain goods. Disposals of the following assets are treated as outside the scope of VAT and special conditions apply to the disposals of:

(a) used motor cars, by a person who repossessed them under the terms of a finance agreement (*SI 1992 No 3122, Article 4*);

(b) boats and aircraft repossessed by a mortgagee under the terms of a marine or aircraft mortgage; or

(c) works of art, antiques and collectors' items, and second-hand goods other than motor cars, by a person repossessing them under the terms of a finance agreement or by an insurer settling a claim under an insurance policy. (*SI 1995 No 1268, Article 4*).

In each instance, the goods must be in the same condition as when they were repossessed.

Transfers of agreements

18.55 Where a lessor sells all or part of its lease portfolio to a bank or other financial institution, the assignment of the goods and the right to collect future rentals is treated as a transfer of a business as a going concern for VAT purposes (*VAT (Special Provisions) Order 1995 (SI 1995 No 1268), Article 5(4)*). Consequently, VAT will not be charged on the sale (see *Baltic Leasing Ltd, [1986] VATTR 98 (2088)*).

18.56 Assuming that the contracts allow, where a lessee transfers his rights and obligations under a hire-purchase agreement to another person, the transfer is treated as a taxable supply of goods and VAT should be accounted for on the consideration payable.

Specific leasing activities

Cars

Effect of changes from 1 August 1995

18.57 The changes which Customs introduced on 1 August 1995 focused a great deal of attention on the car leasing industry, which in turn had to react quickly to quite radical changes in the VAT legislation affecting cars. Prior to 1 August 1995, leasing companies which entered into operating leases involving cars were unable to reclaim input VAT on the purchase of the cars and therefore had to structure the VAT cost into the lease calculation. Customers who were not in a position to reclaim all or part of the VAT charged on the lease rentals were therefore suffering a double tax charge (an issue which the cases involving *Royscot Leasing Ltd, Allied Lyons plc* and *TC Harrison Group Ltd, CJEC Case C-305/97* sought to address). Hence it was more cost-effective from a VAT perspective for such customers to buy cars outright or to opt for hire-purchase arrangements.

18.58 The legislation introduced on 1 August 1995 placed finance and operating leases for cars on the same footing by allowing leasing companies to reclaim VAT on the purchase of cars used under operating lease agreements. The requirement to restrict VAT for non-business or exempt purposes was transferred to the lessees, so that if the lessee did not use the car exclusively for business purposes, only 50% of the VAT charged on the lease rental could be claimed (with a further restriction of the remaining 50% for wholly or partly exempt lessees).

18.59 The effect of the change in legislation was to produce a two-tier VAT leasing system; one for car leases entered into prior to 1 August 1995 and the other involving 'qualifying' cars (i.e. those cars upon which VAT has been reclaimed by the lessor on the original purchase). The old VAT accounting system will continue until all leases under the pre-1 August 1995 arrangements expire.

18.60 As a result of the new VAT legislation and particularly the restriction on the lessee's entitlement to reclaim VAT on the lease rental charges, leasing companies reacted to the requirements of their customers to split out the constituent parts of the lease so that the 50% restriction applied only to the value associated with the provision of the car and not to ancillary services such as maintenance, etc. Customs & Excise have accepted this (see the agreement between Customs and the British Vehicle Rental and Leasing Association as set out in C&E Notice 700/57/95) and it is now an accepted way of minimising irrecoverable VAT for lessees.

18.61 Assuming that the appeals in the cases of *Royscot Leasing Ltd and others* (see paragraph 18.57 above) are not successful, leasing companies will continue to operate VAT accounting procedures under both the old and new

18.62 VAT Business by Business

arrangements, possibly having to provide the same customer with different-style VAT invoices to reflect the split of old and 'qualifying' cars in the fleet.

Disposal of qualifying motor cars

18.62 It is important to note that, where 'qualifying cars' are disposed of at the end of an operating lease, output tax must be accounted for by the lessor on the disposal proceeds. This is a significant change for leasing companies and their lessees (who will in most cases act as the lessor's agent in disposing of the cars). Leasing companies should make sure that adequate procedures are in place to capture all the information needed to account for the right amount of output tax in the correct VAT period on disposals of qualifying cars.

Pre-1 August 1995 claims for input tax recovery

18.63 Leasing companies which have not lodged an appeal with the VAT and Duties Tribunal in respect of unclaimed input tax on the purchase of cars used in operating lease agreements prior to 1 August 1995 should consider the possible advantages and disadvantages. The cases involving *Royscot Leasing Ltd, Allied Lyons plc* and *TC Harrison Group Ltd* have clearly raised the profile of the arguments involved and in view of the restriction of VAT claims to three years, lessors should give urgent consideration to making a claim.

Captive leasing companies

18.64 Following the 1 August 1995 changes, for companies which purchased cars outright, there are clear benefits in setting up captive leasing companies to procure the cars and lease them on to the user company. The benefits of such an arrangement are to allow input tax recovery in full in the captive leasing company (thereby generating a cashflow saving) and to allow the user company to reclaim 50% of the VAT charged by the captive on the lease rentals. In this circumstance, the interaction of VAT and corporation tax is important, particularly where the cars involved are of a value greater than £12,000 (i.e. the leases by the captive would be in respect of 'expensive' cars). Although the VAT savings alone might at first sight appear to make the arrangement worthwhile, the impact of the direct tax restrictions for 'expensive cars' is significant, so that the VAT savings are eroded. Accurate calculations of the overall net savings must therefore be made to determine the overall savings which might be possible. In addition, there is a requirement for the leases between the captive and the user company to be calculated on a commercial basis, i.e. the charges must be equivalent to those which an unconnected leasing company might charge.

Cross-border leasing

Considerations for the UK lessor

18.65 The rules for cross-border leasing are complicated, as the VAT treatment in other EU Member States is not always consistent with that applied in the UK. Consequently, UK lessors involved in leasing to lessees in other EU countries may find themselves involved in dealing with two different VAT regimes. In essence this differentiation arises from the conceptual distinction between finance leases and operating leases applied in each Member State. Some tax authorities in the EU, for example, will always treat leases as supplies of services, whereas in other EU countries, including the UK, there is a differentiation between supplies of goods and services.

18.66 Having determined the VAT treatment in each Member State, it is necessary for the lessor (and its advisors) to consider whether the supply is one of goods and/or services and to determine the place of supply. Although each EU Member State will apply its own local VAT legislation, the overriding European law as to whether a supply is of goods or services is in *Article 5(1)* and *5(4)(b)* and *Article 6(1)* of the *EC Sixth Directive*. The place of supply rules are detailed in *Articles 8* and *9* of the *EC Sixth Directive*.

18.67 *Article 5(1)* states that supplies of goods shall mean the transfer of the right to dispose of tangible property as owner. *Article 5(4)(b)* states that the actual handing over of goods, pursuant to a contract for the hire of goods for a certain period or for the sale of goods on deferred terms, which provides that in the normal course of events ownership shall pass at the latest on completion of the final instalment, shall also be considered a supply. *Article 6(1)* states that a supply of services shall mean any transaction which does not constitute a supply of goods within the meaning of *Article 5*.

18.68 If the supply is one of the goods, then the place of supply will be the place where the goods are at the time when despatch or transport to the lessee begins. Where the goods are being exported from the UK to a lessee which is registered for VAT in its own country, then UK VAT may be avoided if the lessee provides the lessor with its local VAT registration number. Otherwise UK VAT will be chargeable. If the goods are purchased and sold locally by the lessor in the lessee's own country, this will be outside the scope of UK VAT. However, it may be necessary for the lessor to determine the local VAT consequences of such transactions, particularly in respect of motor cars, as it may be possible to avoid both UK and local VAT if the lessee's Member State treats all leasing as supplies of services.

18.69 If a lessor based in the UK sources equipment to be used in another EU Member State locally from a supplier in that other EU Member State, the UK lessor will be charged local VAT on the purchase of the equipment. The lessor must then reclaim this VAT under the provisions of the *EC Eighth Directive*, and cash flow costs can arise as a result of delays in repayments under this procedure. Again, for corporation tax purposes, there are

18.70 *VAT Business by Business*

restrictions in capital allowances claimable by the lessor in respect of equipment which is subject to cross-border lease. There may also be additional overseas VAT costs where the equipment must be maintained or repaired and local contractors are hired to carry out this work. It is likely that VAT will be charged on these supplies of services, which will again need to be reclaimed by the lessor under the *EC Eighth Directive*.

18.70 If the lessee belongs in a non-EU country and the goods are exported from the UK, then the supply will not be subject to UK VAT provided that the lessor retains proof of export. Again, consideration must also be given to any local tax consequences arising from such transactions, particularly in countries which operate VAT regimes. Similarly, if the lessor purchases and supplies the goods locally, then consideration must be given to any local tax consequences arising from such transactions.

18.71 If however the cross-border leasing transaction, or part of it, is one of services, then it is necessary to consider the place of supply of leasing services. This is set out in *Article 9* of the *EC Sixth Directive*, the principle of which is that the supply should only be taxed in one EC Member State. *Article 9(1)* deals with the place of supply of means of transport. This area has been the source of some debate in the courts and has been clarified in the recent European Court of Justice decision in *ARO Lease BV v Inspecteur der Belastingdienst Grote Ondernemingen, CJEC [1997] STC 1272*.

18.72 It should also be noted that within the European legislation there is a general anti-avoidance clause contained in *Article 9(3)(b)* of the *EC Sixth Directive*. This provision allows Member States to override the basic rules in *Article 9(2)(e)* and to treat services as being provided in the lessor's own country (e.g. the UK) if the lessee uses and enjoys the goods in the lessor's own country.

18.73 A similar provision (*Article 9(3)(a)*) also exists to shift the place of supply from the lessee's own country in the EU to a lessor's country outside the EU if the effective use and enjoyment takes place outside the EU.

18.74 The purpose of *Article 9(3)* is to ensure that there is no double taxation of leasing services, or indeed any avoidance of taxation between EC Member States. Although *Article 9(3)* has not been implemented within the UK VAT legislation, it is important to be aware of its existence, particularly given the present trend of anti-avoidance legislation. It is also important to note that *Article 9(3)* cannot move place of supply of a leasing service from one EC Member State to another but is in fact designed to ensure that the supply under a lease agreement is taxed somewhere in the EU, if the effective use and enjoyment of the leased assets takes place in the EU.

18.75 Further problems can arise as a result of cross-border leasing transactions in connection with the VAT treatment of the disposal of the equipment at the end of the lease term. In the UK, disposals of capital equipment are excluded from the VAT registration threshold when determining whether a business is required to register in the UK, and therefore it is unlikely that non-UK lessors would have a liability to register for VAT as a result of disposing of goods in the UK at the end of an operating lease. This however, is not the case in other EU Member States and the VAT treatment of the disposal of the assets is a key consideration which must be taken into account when entering into cross-border leasing. Consequently, UK lessors must be aware that at the end of an operating lease, the disposal of the underlying goods may have local VAT consequences.

Considerations for the UK lessee

18.76 The rules governing whether a supply is of goods or services and the place of supply, as detailed at paragraph 18.7 above, will also apply to UK lessees.

18.77 Although a UK lessee may be leasing goods from abroad, the consequences are broadly the same as if the goods were being leased from the UK, except on certain occasions where the lessee may incur local VAT charged in another EU Member State rather than UK VAT. In particular, where motor cars are being leased, then although it is possible to attempt an Eighth Directive reclaim in respect of any local VAT incurred from the lessor's local tax authorities, most EU Member States impose a degree of restriction on the amount of VAT that is recoverable.

18.78 If a UK lessee is leasing goods other than means of transport under an operating lease, the UK lessee will have to impute reverse-charge VAT and account for this on its UK VAT return. This reverse-charge VAT is recoverable by the UK lessee to the extent that the underlying goods are used to make taxable supplies. If the UK lessee is not registered for VAT in the UK, then the value of the lease-rentals will count towards the value of taxable supplies made by the lessee for the purposes of determining whether it is registrable for VAT in the UK. If liability to register can be avoided, the UK lessee must also demonstrate to an EU lessor that the assets are used for business purposes, otherwise there is the danger of incurring local VAT chargeable in the EU lessor's own Member State.

18.79 If the goods are being leased under a hire-purchase agreement or finance lease, then unless they are being used in pursuance of an exempt supply for a non-business purpose, a UK VAT-registered lessee must account for acquisition VAT if the goods are acquired from another Member State. Furthermore, if the lessee is not currently registered for VAT, the value of the acquisition may create a liability to register if it exceeds the registration limits. If acquisition VAT is due, this must be accounted for on the lessee's UK VAT return. However, it may be possible for the lessee to recover this as input tax, subject to the normal rules governing VAT recovery. Similarly, if the assets are being imported from a non-EU country and the lessee is responsible for importation, import VAT may be due. This input VAT is again potentially recoverable subject to the normal rules.

18.80 VAT Business by Business

18.80 In practice, however, as the goods are more likely to be sourced in the UK, any responsibility for VAT accounting should fall with the lessor. Whether the goods are sourced in the UK or otherwise, it should be possible for a UK lessee to avoid reverse-charge VAT on the finance element of a hire-purchase on the basis that this would be ordinarily exempt in the UK.

Arrears of rentals/Bad debts

18.81 Lessors should have procedures to identify when payments under any contracts fall into arrears. There are a number of VAT aspects to consider in respect of arrears of rentals. These will vary depending on whether the lease contract is rescheduled (i.e. the lessee agrees to make payments) or the lease is subsequently terminated because the lessee is unable to make any further payments under the contract.

18.82 For the lessor, there are two points to consider in respect of bad debt relief claims. Firstly, the effect of bad debt relief on hire purchase transactions and secondly, the effect of bad debt relief on operating leases where there are continuous supplies of services.

18.83 In respect of hire purchase agreements before 1 May 1997, it was difficult for the lessor to claim any VAT bad debt relief in respect of goods which are supplied to the lessee. This is because finance agreements usually include a reservation of title clause (a *Romalpa* clause). Accordingly, unless the lessor wrote to the lessee notifying it that all rights and interests in the property were transferred to the lessee (which was unlikely to be commercially acceptable), the conditions of *VATA 1994, s 36(1)(b)* could not have been met as the debt had not been written off, and a bad debt relief claim could not have been made. This sub-paragraph has now been repealed, allowing bad debt relief claims to be made for VAT purposes in accordance with the normal rules even if a *Romalpa* or retention of title clause exists to protect the lessor for other commercial purposes.

18.84 In respect of operating leases, bad debt relief claims are common and it is important for lessors to ensure that claims are made properly and timeously. (See *Tolley's VAT 1998/99, chapter 7* for details of how to make bad debt relief claims).

18.85 One particular aspect of bad debt relief claims involving leasing companies is the dividing line between arrears and termination. Bad debt relief can be claimed by the lessor for any unpaid rentals prior to termination. The six month period for determining when the supply was made will be the date shown on the scheduled invoice, i.e. the due date. Once early termination of the lease has occurred, it is not possible for the lessor to claim bad debt relief in respect of lease rental payments due after the termination date on the basis that supplies under the lease cease upon termination. Here, the lease termination payment provisions will apply. If, however, the lessee fails to make a payment in respect of the lease termination and all the conditions for the lessor to claim bad debt relief are in place, i.e. VAT is properly chargeable on the termination payment and has been accounted for by the lessor, then the lessor would be eligible for bad debt relief in respect of the VAT on the lease termination payment if this has been written-off by the lessor for VAT purposes and six months have elapsed since this payment was due.

Appendix 1

Industry-agreed partial exemption method

Agreement with the Finance Houses Association Limited about finance houses and partial exemption (September 1984)

Outstanding balances

(1) We are prepared to accept that outstanding balances may be used in any pro-rata calculation for each tax period; details of the outstanding balances to be used are to be agreed with the local VAT office.

Deductions of Input Tax for each tax period are, of course, only provisional, and at the end of each tax year the annual adjustment must be made on the basis of receipts for the tax year. For this purpose, the receipts are to be calculated in the following way:

– Outstanding balance at the start of the year plus the value of new business written during the tax year minus the outstanding balance at the end of the tax year;

– Calculations on this basis will be subject to review at any time.

General principles

(2) Discussions and exchanges have been in general terms and have not dealt specifically with the variety of supplies made by members. In fact, for purposes of simplification, we have referred to the most common type of supply, and we think it might be helpful to set out how the deductibility of input tax is determined. The fundamental principle is that input tax related to taxable supplies is recoverable, but that related to exempt and other supplies is not. Input tax on goods bought and sold in the same state and on goods which are the subject of a taxable lease is normally recoverable in full, but the input tax on goods or plant bought in connection with an exempt supply is not. Input tax related to taxable leasing is deductible, but the input tax incurred in connection with exempt leasing, exempt loans and hire purchase credit is not. How these principles are to be applied in practice is illustrated below.

Hire purchase receipts related to goods

(3) We have agreed, subject to review, that 15% of the input tax related to hire purchase credit can be regarded as being properly attributable to the sale of the goods in respect of which the credit is granted. Where any member makes a variety of supplies, the amount of input tax which

can be regarded as related to hire purchase credit is to be identified in each tax period as follows:

$$\frac{\text{Total input tax less any tax directly attributable to goods or plant}}{\text{Total outstanding balances}}$$

Hire purchase only

(4) Where only hire purchase supplies are made, the deductible input tax is as follows:

(a) All the input tax incurred on goods bought and sold in the same state, plus;

(b) 15% of the remaining input tax.

Hire purchase and taxable leasing supplies

(5) Where only hire purchase and taxable leasing supplies are made, the deductible input tax is as follows:

(a) All the input tax incurred on goods bought and sold in the same state; and

(b) 15% of the input tax related to hire purchase credit (see above); and

(c) The residue of the total input tax after that dealt with under (a), plus the whole of the input tax related to hire purchase credit have been deducted.

Hire purchase, taxable and exempt leasing and exempt loans

(6) Where the supplies made consist of hire purchase, taxable and exempt leasing and exempt loans, the deductibility of input tax is as follows:

(a) None of the input tax on goods or plant bought in connection with an exempt leasing supply is deductible;

(b) All the input tax on goods bought for sale in the same state, or to be disposed of in the same state as the subject of a taxable leasing supply, is deductible;

(c) 15% of the input tax related to hire purchase (see above) is deductible;

18.App 1   *VAT Business by Business*

(d) After the input tax calculated under (a) and (b) above has been determined and deducted from the total tax together with all the input tax relating to hire purchase, a further percentage may be deducted according to the following formula:

$$\frac{\text{Outstanding balance for taxable leasing supplies}}{\text{Outstanding balances for exempt loans, exempt leases and taxable leases}} \times 100$$

Acceptable method

(7) The activities of members is so varied, it is not practical to give examples which will apply to all situations. Nevertheless, the examples set out above, together with the general principles, provide a guide to the sort of method of calculating deductible input tax which will be regarded as acceptable to this department.

Annual adjustments

(8) At the end of each tax year, the amount of input tax which a member is entitled to deduct is to be recalculated on the basis of the figures for the tax year. The deductible input tax is to be identified in precisely the same way as for each tax period, except that receipts for the tax year calculated as in the opening paragraph are to be used instead of outstanding balances in all calculations including that which is used to identify the input tax related to hire purchase credit. Any difference between the amount of input tax deducted for the tax periods in the year and the amount deductible on the basis of the figures for the tax year is to be regarded as an over or under declaration of VAT and an entry is to be made in the VAT account for the first tax period after the end of the tax year.

Chapter 19

Local Authorities

Introduction

Special position of local authorities

19.1 Local authorities and certain other public bodies undertake activities in the 'public interest' for the public good. As such these bodies would be unable to recover VAT incurred in the performance of these functions.

The European legislation, governing the common system of application of VAT throughout the EC, permitted local government authorities and other bodies governed by public law generally to be outside the scope of VAT in respect of their public functions (*EC Sixth Directive, Article 4(5)*).

Additionally, when VAT was introduced in 1973, the Government introduced a special refund mechanism to ensure that the new tax did not become an addition to, or a burden, on the local authority rates (now replaced by the council tax).

Refund mechanism

19.2 *VATA 1994, s 33* describes the terms of this refund mechanism and lists the local authorities and public bodies to which it applies. It does not apply to all public bodies. (This chapter principally applies to local authorities proper but reference to 'local authorities' should also be taken to include all those bodies listed in *s 33*, as amended by various Treasury Orders. A full list is provided as an Appendix to this chapter).

The refund mechanism applies only to those statutory or non-business functions of local authorities. In respect of the business activities of local authorities, whether taxable or exempt, the normal rules apply although there is an additional partial exemption limit of 5% of input tax relating to exempt supplies, above which authorities must restrict their VAT recovery.

The three year cap on repayment by Customs & Excise of overpaid VAT will not apply to VAT refunded under *VATA 1994, s 33*.

19.3 VAT Business by Business

Definition—what is a local authority?

19.3 The definition of a local authority for the purpose of VAT is contained in *VATA 1994, s 96(4)* which states:

'In this Act *"local authority"* means the council of a country, district, London borough, parish or group of parishes (or, in Wales, community or group of communities), the Common Council of the City of London, the Council of the Isles of Scilly, and any joint committee or joint board established by two or more of the foregoing and, in relation to Scotland, a regional, islands or district council within the meaning of the Local Government (Scotland) Act 1973, any combination or any joint committee or joint board established by two or more of the foregoing and any joint board to which section 226 of that Act applies'.

The refund mechanism is available to any local authority, whether or not it is registered.

Unregistered authorities—obtaining a refund

19.4 Unregistered local authorities have to apply in writing for a refund. The period covered by a claim must be at least one calendar month ending on the last day of such a month. The claim must be made in an agreed format, preferably on a form VAT 126. Customs & Excise require that if the claim is for less than £100, the period of the claim must be for at least 12 months.

Customs guidance

19.5 Customs have produced their own guidance on VAT and local authorities, which is contained in two Public Notices: No. 749, dealing with general matters and No. 749A, which gives their interpretation of the VAT liability of various supplies.

Vires—is s 33 legal?

19.6 It is arguable whether EC law provides the vires for the UK government to enact *s 33* and it is understood that some of the EC partners are unhappy about the position. It is clear that Customs considers that refunds of VAT under the terms of *s 33* are not repayments of input tax but the payment of a subsidy calculated by reference to the VAT incurred. This is an interesting argument that no doubt seeks to remove the threat of infraction proceedings in the European Court of Justice ('CJEC') but does raise the question of the vires of assessing for overclaimed VAT.

Registration

Obligation to register

19.7 Any local authority which makes any taxable supplies (that is business supplies liable to VAT), even if at the zero rate, is obliged to register for VAT (*VATA 1994, s 42*).

'Section 102 committees'—shared registration

19.8 Separate registration will usually also be required for any separately constituted board or joint committee, even if there are close links with a local authority. However, if such joint committees or boards satisfy the conditions of *Local Government Act 1972, s 102(1) (as amended by Local Government and Housing Act 1989)* to be considered as 'local authority committees', they will fall within the terms of *s 33*.

In that circumstance, and if the local authority members wish, written application may be made to Customs to account for VAT through the registration of the parent (or a member) authority.

Other bodies

19.9 Committees or bodies that fall within the terms of *Local Government Act 1972, s 102(4)*, for example advisory committees, do not qualify for *s 33* status. Neither do other legally separate bodies such as Enterprise Agencies and Housing Trusts. In these circumstances separate registration will be required when the taxable supplies exceed the VAT registration threshold. Voluntary registration can also be sought.

Practical steps

19.10 A local authority (or committee, etc.) may apply for deregistration from VAT if it considers that it no longer is entitled or needs to be registered. In practice, this is likely to affect small community, parish or town councils, joint committees etc. which have ceased to make taxable supplies.

Section 33 status should always be considered when local authorities set up joint committees. As a general rule such bodies would benefit from retaining *s 33* status and their constitutional arrangements should be drafted accordingly. Where such bodies make only exempt supplies, but incur VAT on costs, it would be better that they were not separately registered for VAT and included within the VAT registration of the parent or member authority.

19.11 *VAT Business by Business*

Liability

Ability to recover all input tax

19.11 The VAT liability of local authority supplies is complex, with some supplies being made that are taxable at the standard and zero rates (and possibly also the reduced rate), some being exempt and some being outside the scope of VAT.

Ordinarily, this would provide considerable problems in the attribution of VAT on expenditure, with the potential for significant error were it not for *s 33* status and the 5% de minimis rule. This has ensured that to date, nearly all local authorities are 'fully taxable' for VAT and recover all VAT incurred.

The changes from 1 April 1997, under which local authorities are required to apportion all VAT on expenditure between their various supplies, may lead to some authorities exceeding the 5% de minimis level. See paragraph 19.24 below.

Goods and services generally

19.12 Goods supplied by local authorities by way of business are always liable to VAT at the appropriate rate, no matter to whom they are supplied.

The liability of the supply of services depends upon the circumstances of the supply. Customs have determined the following criteria:

• Services which are supplied as a statutory obligation and which are not in competition with the private sector.	non-business
• Services which are not supplied as a statutory obligation and which are not in competition with the private sector	non-business
—but by agreement of both parties.	taxable
• The supply of services which are in competition with supplies made by the private sector on a significant scale.	taxable
• The supply of services which also includes a supply of goods which are not an integral part of the supply of the service itself.	taxable

Although Customs have published a list of local authority supplies and their VAT liabilities, it is not exhaustive and is in any case only their interpretation of the relevant liability. This list may be found in Notice 749A. Many of the supplies made by local authorities will change depending upon the circumstances. For example, catering supplied in a school canteen to pupils would be non-business, but catering to teachers separately or supplied in a staff canteen would be taxable at the standard rate. Supplies of educational services and materials made to an authority's own schools would be non-business, but to grant-maintained schools they would be a business supply and potentially liable to VAT.

Correct coding

19.13 The issue for Chief Financial Officers is to ensure that there are adequate codes to reflect the varying liabilities and that staff have sufficient VAT awareness to code the income correctly.

Problem areas

Supplies between local authorities

19.14 At one time supplies of both goods and services between local authorities made under the terms of the *Local Authorities (Goods & Services) Act 1970, s 1(1) ('Goods & Services Act')* were considered to be non-business supplies and outside the scope of VAT. However this was changed as a result of the decision of the ECJ in *Comune di Carpaneto Piacentino and others v Ufficio Provinciale Imposta Sul Valore Aggiunto di Piacenza, CJEC [1991] STC 205*.

Now goods supplied by one local authority to another are considered to be business supplies and are liable to VAT.

Services supplied by one local authority to another under the terms of the *Goods & Services Act* must first satisfy the criteria listed in paragraph 19.12 above for them to be considered outside the scope of VAT, otherwise they are liable to VAT at the appropriate rate.

If the supply of such services includes the supply of materials, which are clearly part of or closely related to the service itself, such items may be considered to be part of the supply of the service. Other goods supplied as part of a single price contract for both goods and services will be liable to VAT at the appropriate rate.

Supplies of goods or services made under the *Goods & Services Act* to any body not included in the terms of *s 33* (see the Appendix to this chapter) are considered to be business supplies and liable to VAT under the normal rules.

19.15 *VAT Business by Business*

Land and property

19.15 This is a complicated area of VAT liability in any case and chapters 8 and 22 deal with this in detail. See also *Tolley's VAT 1998/99, chapter 42*.

The situation in local authorities can be further complicated by the often complex nature of their supplies, for example Town Centre redevelopments where land and buildings may be acquired by private treaty or compulsory purchase and supplies made by means of gift, planning gain agreements (or section 52 agreements), peppercorn rental etc.

As error can lead to significant VAT costs, authorities should ensure that VAT is considered at the earliest stage of any transaction.

Tour operators margin scheme (TOMS)

19.16 TOMS (see chapter 26 below) is a very complicated area of VAT liability into which many local authorities have strayed unwittingly, for example, with regard to school trips. It is essential that the requirements of TOMS are understood by all those who will be organising trips or holidays and VAT properly brought to account.

As a general rule visits/trips/holidays arranged for pupils by a local authority and which are provided to the pupil either free of charge or at a substantially subsidised rate can be considered to be non-business.

See *Tolley's VAT 1998/99, chapter 66* for more detailed information.

Local government review

19.17 Local Government Review or Local Government Re-organisation ('LGR') poses particular problems for those authorities affected. There are four principal areas of concern.

Transfer of assets

19.18 All assets transferred to a new authority (or to the new separate Fire Authorities and National Park Authorities) will be contained in the official transfer document. Customs have advised that, as this is a statutory obligation, the transfer is a non-business supply and outside the scope of VAT.

Residuary bodies currently in existence have not, so far, been accorded *s 33* status and this looks to be the pattern for subsequent rounds of LGR.

Nevertheless, surplus assets, etc. transferred to the residuary body will be non-business and outside the scope of VAT.

The new separate Fire Authorities and National Park Authorities have been given *s 33* status but will need to register for VAT.

Registration

19.19 VAT incurred by shadow authorities can be recovered by the existing councils either pro rata or by one 'representative'.

However, Customs will allow a shadow authority to register for VAT in its own right, prior to Vesting Day, if the authority considers it appropriate. Once registered, the shadow authority cannot de-register and all VAT recovery must then be made through that VAT registration.

Debts and errors

19.20 After Vesting Day, the usual practice would be for the successor authority to 'close the books' of its predecessor.

Bad debt relief can be recovered by the successor authority through its own VAT registration, subject to the normal rules (see *Tolley's VAT 1998/99, chapter 7*). An authority that adopts this practice must equally ensure that repayment of the relief is made in respect of monies subsequently received against such debts.

Experience of LGR to date suggests that, in settling the debts, etc. of the previous authorities, Customs will allow VAT input and output tax to be accounted for through the new authority's own VAT registration.

It will not always be possible to determine whether VAT is due or whether overclaims or underdeclarations have been made. The new authorities are separate legal entities and any authority that wishes to adopt this practice should only do so on the express understanding that it is *not* accepting responsibility for such VAT and should confirm this with Customs in writing.

As a matter of general principle it is not open to Customs to seek to recover VAT incurred by another legal entity. As any VAT assessment raised would have to be in the name of the previous authority, this would give Customs practical problems in serving and processing the assessment, as the assessed entity would no longer exist and would not, in any event, have any cash or assets.

Nevertheless it would be prudent to avoid such an eventuality and new authorities are recommended to follow Customs' own prescribed procedures for accounting for VAT due from or to deregistered entities. This is known as

19.21 *VAT Business by Business*

the 'VAT 427 procedure' and the relevant forms can be obtained from Customs.

Options to tax

19.21 In the first round of LGR it was felt that the legislation intended that elections to waive exemptions (commonly known as 'options to tax') would carry through into the succeeding authorities, but it was understood that Customs were reviewing the position.

They have apparently done so and now accept that options exercised by preceding authorities become invalid on Vesting Day. They have required renotification of such options within 30 days of the new authority coming into existence, although in most cases this period has been extended.

The effect of this is that a new authority can decide whether it wishes to re-opt. Clearly, where there are significant ongoing VAT costs attributed to the building, etc. then continuing with the option would be sensible, given the changes to the partial exemption rules commencing on 1 April 1997.

For more information on the general application of options to tax, see *Tolley's VAT 1998/99, paras 42.20 to 42.25*.

Awareness

19.22 LGR also poses problems in the integration of Finance departments, functions and cultures. Chief Finance Officers should therefore ensure that there is a designated officer responsible for VAT and encouraging awareness of its implications. Most importantly, Chief Finance Officers should be aware of the new authority's partial exemption position from the first day of operation. Failure to keep below the 5% de minimis limit could be costly.

VAT recovery

19.23 There are several conditions which need to be fulfilled before VAT may be recovered—these are considered below with particular reference to local authorities.

Taxable, exempt and non-business supplies—implications for VAT recovery

19.24 The first issue which has to be resolved in deciding whether VAT is recoverable, as with all other types of business, is the nature of the supply to which the VAT relates. However, there are several special rules which apply only to local authorities and other bodies named in *VATA 1994, s 33*.

For local authorities, any VAT which relates solely to the making of non-business supplies, or to an activity which does not result in the making of any supply, is recoverable in full. VAT which relates solely to an exempt supply may be recovered (up to 31 March 1997) as long as the total amount of such VAT does not exceed 5% of the total input VAT of the authority. After 1 April 1997, VAT which relates only partly to exempt supplies will also have to be apportioned and be included in the 5% calculation. Further details on the principles and methods of partial exemption are at paragraph 19.36 below.

Comments below on other issues concerning the recoverability of input VAT assume that the VAT concerned is allowable according to the partial exemption position of the authority, either because it relates wholly to exempt or taxable income or because the authority's exempt input tax does not exceed the 5% limit.

Tax invoices—need for the supply to be made to the authority

19.25 In order for VAT to be recoverable, it is important to establish that it relates to a supply which has been made to the registered person, in this case the local authority. This can be a difficult area for local authorities, particularly where supplies are made to organisations which are closely allied to the authority itself. It is important to ensure that such supplies are identified and that steps are taken to ensure that invoices are correctly addressed and the authority only recovers VAT which it has incurred itself.

However, where a local authority buys goods or services which it then makes available without charge to organisations such as voluntary bodies, then the local authority is considered to be making a non-business supply of the goods or services concerned, and the VAT incurred is therefore recoverable under *VATA 1994, s 33*.

Requirements of a tax invoice—practical problems/agreements with Customs

19.26 Local authorities are very diverse organisations, with many people, often in remote locations, involved in making purchases and obtaining invoices which the authority will use to claim VAT. The requirements for VAT invoices for purchases above and below £100 are set out in *Tolley's VAT 1998/99, para 40.3 et seq*. In some cases authorities have been able to obtain concessions or special agreements from Customs about the details needing to be shown on VAT invoices, especially for small purchases. However, if there has been no such agreement with Customs, authorities need to ensure that all invoices on which VAT is recovered meet the legal requirements.

VAT Business by Business

Business entertaining—special rules for local authorities

19.27 The normal VAT rule is that VAT cannot be recovered on the purchase of hospitality or accommodation which is used to provide entertainment other than for employees of a business. However there are special rules in the case of local authorities which allow VAT to be recovered under *VATA 1994, s 33* if it relates to the non-business activities of the authority. Any VAT incurred which relates to business activity will be disallowed under the normal rules.

Self-billing

19.28 Many local authorities use self-billing arrangements, particularly for supplies in the construction industry. The requirements for using such arrangements are set out in *Tolley's VAT 1998/99, para 40.2*, but there are particular issues of which authorities should be aware.

VAT is only recoverable on self-billed invoices in the VAT period in which the payment is received by the contractor. It is therefore important to ensure that VAT on payments made at the very end of the VAT return period is not reclaimed before payment has been received.

Estimation

19.29 Due to the accounting processes of most local authorities and the sheer number of invoices involved it is often not possible for many authorities to have entered all the relevant invoices and so claim all the input tax to which they are entitled in any one period.

VAT Regulations 1995 (SI 1995 No 2518), reg 29(3) allows any registered person to apply for the permission of Customs to estimate the amount of VAT due in any period. This has to be adjusted in the next period but this VAT return can also be estimated.

Normally, estimation can only be approved on a period by period basis and for the VAT return as a whole. However, for local authorities Customs will consider a *general* application for *input* tax only. By using this procedure local authorities will ensure that they are recovering the maximum amount of VAT as soon as possible in the correct period. The first use of estimation will also produce a one-off cash flow benefit.

Authorities may also apply to estimate output tax if they consider this to be advantageous.

Relocation expenses

19.30 The usual rules apply to the recovery of VAT on employees' relocation expenses. VAT may be recovered provided that the cost is borne by the authority, and if the cost is only partly borne, then only that proportion of the VAT may be recovered. After 1 April 1997, it will be necessary to ascertain whether an employee is partly involved in exempt activities, and if so, the VAT incurred may need to be apportioned to determine the part which relates to taxable or non-business activities of the authority and which may therefore be recovered.

Insurance-related payments

19.31 Where authorities pay the VAT on costs which are covered by an insurance claim, the VAT may be recovered provided that a tax invoice is obtained which is addressed to the authority, and the VAT incurred relates to taxable or non-business supplies. Again, additional care will be needed after 1 April 1997 to ensure that any VAT attributable to taxable supplies is identified.

Imports and acquisitions

19.32 VAT may be incurred by local authorities on imports of goods into the UK, or on goods which have been acquired from other member states of the EU. The normal rules described in *Tolley's VAT 1998/99, paras 23.8 and 34.11* should be followed regarding recovery of such VAT.

Agency payments

19.33 Many authorities become involved in arrangements where they make payments or receive income as the agent of another party. Especially in the light of the case of *Metropolitan Borough of Wirral, QB [1995] STC 597*, it is very important to ensure that the rules regarding the recovery of VAT are followed. It is particularly important that the timing rules are followed and that the correct evidence is held for VAT recovery.

Local authority pension funds

19.34 Some local authorities are responsible for the administration of pension funds for the benefit of their own employees, those of other authorities in the same area and of other bodies. The VAT on expenses which they incur in the administration of such a fund is recoverable, either under *VATA 1994, s 33* where they relate to the authority's own employees or those of other authorities to which a non-business charge or no charge is made, or by attribution to standard-rated supplies where a taxable supply of administration services is made to another body.

19.35 VAT Business by Business

However, VAT incurred on expenditure which relates to the investment activity of the fund can only be recovered either to the extent that it relates either to the making of taxable supplies (for example rental income received from an opted property) or to income which is outside the scope of VAT with the right to VAT recovery (for example income from share investments located outside the European Union). VAT which relates to the making of exempt supplies will only be recoverable if the total exempt VAT incurred by the authority as a whole (including the pension fund) is less than 5% of the total VAT incurred by the authority.

Identification and attribution of exempt input tax

19.35 The High Court judgment in the case of *London Borough of Haringey, QB [1995] STC 830* has led Customs to change their interpretation of the way in which local authorities should treat VAT which they incur in the course of exempt activities. In the edition of Public Notice 749 which was published in April 1995 they require local authorities to begin to monitor the amount of exempt VAT they incurred on a regular basis, but this still only applied to VAT attributable only to exempt supplies, not to any VAT which had a mixed use, such as the telephone bill received by the Treasurer's department. However, Customs subsequently announced that, with effect from 1 April 1997, all exempt VAT incurred by an authority would count towards the 5% limit. This introduces a new requirement to apportion VAT which has a mixed use, but the main problem for many authorities will be to identify such VAT in the first instance.

Partial exemption methods

19.36 In their Business Brief 20/96 and subsequent information paper, Customs & Excise proposed a special partial exemption method which could be used by authorities who notified Customs of their intention to do so before 1 April 1997. This method involves using the authority's committee structure to identify exempt or partly exempt income and relate associated costs. There is then an additional requirement to attribute input VAT incurred on recharged overhead expenditure using a formula yet to be finalised by Customs.

Once an authority has established by the use of the local authorities method that exempt input VAT has exceeded the 5% limit, then it is possible for any other partial exemption method to be used to quantify the amount of VAT which is recoverable.

Transitional rules

19.37 The transitional partial exemption rules introduced by Customs & Excise to cover the period up to 1 April 1997 require authorities to monitor their partial exemption position at least on an annual basis. There are also special rules for large capital projects (defined by Customs as those with a value of over £1 million), requiring special permission from Customs on the attribution of the related input VAT. This permission is not required for capital projects which had received full Council approval before 1 September 1995. Customs have also announced that the new rules will not apply to projects with a value below £1 million which were included in an authority's capital programme before 1 April 1995. The period of transitional relief will expire on 31 March 2000.

Accounting records

Coding of income and expenditure

19.38 In order that the VAT liability of income and the deductibility of input VAT can be monitored, it is important that accounting systems and coding structures are designed to identify whether VAT on expenditure relates wholly to taxable, exempt or non-business activities or is not directly attributable to any one activity. This will require detailed knowledge of the VAT liability of all activities on the part of those staff who are responsible for the coding of invoices and other expenditure.

Computer systems—approval by Customs & Excise

19.39 All computer systems which are used in the preparation of VAT returns are required to be approved by Customs. The introduction of a new system should therefore be notified to the local VAT office, preferably in advance of its implementation.

Devolved accounting

19.40 There is an increasing trend in local authorities for the devolution of accounting functions into operational areas. This can lead to a large number of people being responsible for making decisions which affect the VAT liabilities declared by the authority, many of whom will be geographically removed from those staff responsible for VAT compliance in the authority. In order to reduce the risks caused by this, authorities need to have adequate controls in place to validate VAT coding decisions, etc. and also a framework for educating staff who account for VAT and keeping them up to date with VAT changes.

Volume of transactions

19.41 The high volume of low value transactions which are a characteristic of local authorities' activities has the effect of accentuating minor issues. It is essential that clear guidance on the VAT policies and procedures of the authority are made available to all staff who are involved in VAT, and this should be supported by training wherever possible.

Error adjustments

19.42 Errors on past VAT returns are required to be separately disclosed to Customs when they exceed certain limits (see *Tolley's VAT 1998/99, para 57.11*). In view of the large number of people within a local authority who are likely to be involved in accounting for VAT, it is especially important that errors relating to past periods can be identified in order to monitor compliance with these limits. This can be done, for example by restricting access to the VAT account so that the past period adjustments can only be made by a limited number of staff. It should also be possible to identify these adjustments whenever a VAT return is completed.

Practical points

Agreements with Customs & Excise

19.43 Historically, authorities have often reached individual agreements with Customs & Excise over the VAT treatment of problematical areas. It is very important to ensure that such agreements are regularly reviewed to ensure that they remain appropriate, and also that such agreements are clearly stated in writing by Customs & Excise. It is also important to be aware that an agreement which has been agreed by Customs in the particular circumstances of one authority will not apply to any other authority.

Changes in activities

19.44 Authorities are often required by legislation to dispose of various activities or to run them through an organisation with which it has an arms length relationship (such as a Direct Service or Direct Labour Organisation). It is important in these circumstances to determine whether an activity is leaving the authority itself, or whether, although at arm's length, it is still legally part of the local authority for VAT purposes. If the activity is leaving the control of the authority completely, the VAT liability of the supply of the assets of the activity needs to be considered. In certain cases, the disposal may be treated as the transfer of a business as a going concern, or as a non-business activity, or as a supply having its own VAT liability—usually either standard-rated or exempt. It is also important to identify and consider the VAT liability of any supplies which the authority will make to, or receive from, the new body.

Appendix

Bodies to which s 33 applies:

- a local authority;

- a river purification board established under section 135 of the Local Government (Scotland) Act 1973, and a water development board within the meaning of section 109 of the Water (Scotland) Act 1980;

- an internal drainage board;

- a passenger transport authority or executive within the meaning of Part II of the Transport Act 1968;

- a port health authority within the meaning of the Public Health (Control of Disease) Act 1984, and a port local authority and joint port local authority constituted under Part X of the Public Health (Scotland) Act 1897;

- a police authority and the Receiver for the Metropolitan Police District;

- a development corporation within the meaning of the New Towns Act 1981 or the New Towns (Scotland) Act 1968, a new town commission within the meaning of the New Towns Act (Northern Ireland) 1965 and the Commission for the New Towns;

- a general lighthouse authority within the meaning of Part XI of the Merchant Shipping Act 1894;

- the British Broadcasting Corporation;

- a nominated news provider, as defined by section 31(3) of the Broadcasting Act 1990; and

- any body specified for the purposes of this section by an order made by the Treasury

  which are:

  - Anglian Water Authority

  - Authorities established under Local Government Act 1985, s 10

  - Charter Trustees constituted by Local Government Act 1972, s 246(4) or (5)

19.App *VAT Business by Business*

- Commission for Local Administration in England
- Commission for Local Administration in Wales
- Commission for Local Authority Accounts in Scotland
- Commission for Local Administration in Scotland
- Environment Agency
- Fire authority constituted by a combination scheme made under Fire Services Act 1947, s 6
- Inner London Education Authority
- Inner London Interim Education Authority
- London Fire and Civil Defence Authority
- London Residuary Body
- Magistrates' courts committee established under Justices of the Peace Act 1979, s 19
- Metropolitan county Fire and Civil Defence Authority
- Metropolitan county Passenger Transport Authority
- Metropolitan county Police Authority
- Metropolitan county Residuary Body
- National Park authority within the meaning of Environment Act 1995, s 63
- National Rivers Authority
- North West Water Authority
- Northumbria Interim Police Authority
- Northumbrian Water Authority
- Probation committee constituted by Powers of Criminal Courts Act 1973, s 47(1) and Sch 3, para 2
- Severn-Trent Water Authority
- South West Water Authority

Local Authorities **19.App**

- Southern Water Authority

- Thames Water Authority

- Waste regulation and disposal bodies established under Local Government Act 1985, s 10

- Welsh National Water Authority

- Wessex Water Authority

- Yorkshire Water Authority

Chapter 20

Motor Dealers

Introduction

20.1 A car dealer is defined for VAT purposes as 'a taxable person who carries on a business which consists of or includes the sale of motor cars' *(VAT (Cars) Order 1992 (SI 1992 No 3122), article 2)*. In practice the term encompasses a diverse industry profile which ranges from major plcs and franchised dealerships to the Arthur Daley 'one man band' corner site operation. Any legislation relating to cars therefore needs to be both flexible and robust.

Sales of motor cars represent a substantial part of economic gross domestic product with the total revenue collected by way of VAT, Corporation Tax and Income Tax being a major source of income for the Treasury. Cars are also an extremely emotive subject. It is not surprising therefore that detailed attention is paid to this industry sector by Customs & Excise.

Liability

20.2 On 1 August 1995 major changes were made to the recovery of VAT incurred on the acquisition of motor cars. The changes extend VAT recovery to taxable persons acquiring cars 'wholly for a business purpose'. In the future this means that car dealers will have to maintain separate systems for new cars, second-hand cars on which input tax has been restricted, and second-hand cars on which it has been recovered.

All new motor cars are liable to VAT at the standard rate when supplied in the UK. For the definition of a motor car for VAT purposes, see paragraph 20.18 below. VAT is due on the full value of the consideration. This can cause difficulties when used cars are taken in part-exchange (see paragraph 20.17 below).

The VAT liability of second-hand cars depends on whether they are 'qualifying' or 'non-qualifying' cars.

20.3 VAT Business by Business

Qualifying cars

20.3 A qualifying car is a car that has never been supplied, acquired from another Member State, or imported in circumstances in which the VAT on that supply, acquisition or importation was wholly excluded from credit as input tax. In effect this means that the seller, and hence each previous owner, of a qualifying car was able to recover input tax.

Transitional provisions enabled car dealers to elect that cars which were in stock on 1 August 1995, but were not registered until after that date, were to be treated as qualifying cars. The election could either be on a car by car basis or for a block of vehicles.

Since the seller of a qualifying car has recovered all his input tax in relation to the vehicle, output tax is charged on the full value of the consideration.

Non-qualifying cars

20.4 Any cars which do not meet the strict criteria of 'qualifying cars' are described as non-qualifying cars. This will include most cars registered before 1 August 1995, and any cars registered after 1 August 1995 that are not used 'wholly for business purposes'. Business purpose is very strictly defined (see paragraph 20.14 below).

It will be appreciated that qualifying cars become non-qualifying as soon as they are acquired by someone who is not registered for VAT or are used by a VAT-registered business other than for business purposes. Once cars have become non-qualifying, there is no mechanism for them to become qualifying cars.

When non-qualifying vehicles are sold, VAT is only chargeable on the profit margin; accordingly, if they are not sold at a profit, no VAT has to be accounted for. For the purposes of the Second-hand Car Margin Scheme (see paragraph 20.16 below), a distinction is drawn between car dealers and other persons who may occasionally sell cars. Car dealers must comply fully with all the requirements, including the record-keeping requirements, of the Scheme if they wish to adopt this treatment. Other persons who occasionally sell motor cars do not need to comply fully with the record-keeping requirements as long as the other conditions are met (VAT Notice 718, paragraph 5).

Second-hand cars

20.5 For cars to be treated as second-hand, and thus eligible for margin scheme treatment, it is essential that they are used vehicles. This means that they have to have been driven on the road for business purposes or pleasure or have been used in the dealer's business before being sold (e.g. demonstration cars). Cars which are registered but unused, and cars whose only mileage is the delivery mileage to the dealer, cannot qualify as second-hand cars. This can cause problems for dealers in premium or nearly-new vehicles (see paragraph 20.21 below).

Transactions outside the scope of VAT

20.6 The following transactions are outside the scope of VAT:

(a) *Repossessed cars*—the disposal of a non-qualifying used car by a person who repossessed it under the terms of a finance agreement. The vehicle must be in the same condition as it was when it was repossessed.

(b) *Insurance disposals*—the disposal of a non-qualifying used car by an insurer who has taken it in settlement of a claim under a policy of insurance. The car must be disposed of in the same condition as it was when taken in settlement.

(c) *Business gifts*—the disposal of a car for no consideration provided that no input tax has ever been claimed on the car. Cars used as prizes for promotional purposes therefore have two alternative treatments:

   (i) claim input tax and account for output tax as a business gift; or

   (ii) do not claim input tax in which case the disposal is outside the scope of VAT.

(d) *Inter-group leasing*—where a taxable person has purchased or is leasing a motor car and either wholly or partially restricts his input tax, any subsequent letting of the car on hire is outside the scope of VAT. This applies where either there is no consideration for the second letting, or where the consideration is 'less than that which would be payable in money if it were a commercial transaction conducted at arm's length'. Therefore if a corporate group were to lease a car and restrict its input tax on the rentals to 50% of the VAT paid, any subsequent intra-group supply would be outside the scope of VAT.

(e) *Private use charges*—where a taxable person has purchased or is leasing a motor car and either wholly or partially restricts his input tax, any subsequent supply whereby he makes the car available (otherwise than by a letting on hire) to a person for private use is outside the scope of VAT. This means that since 1 August 1995, most private use charges to employees have been outside the scope of VAT.

Road fund licences

20.7 The provision by a motor dealer of a vehicle with a valid road fund licence ('RFL') is treated for VAT purposes as a single supply. If the vehicle is sold under the second-hand margin scheme, the selling price entered into the stock book will include the value of the RFL. If the vehicle being sold is

20.8 VAT Business by Business

either a new or a qualifying vehicle, VAT is added to the full cost of the vehicle including the RFL.

It is possible to offer a vehicle for sale without a valid RFL, with the supplier later obtaining the RFL on behalf of the customer. In these circumstances the value of the licence should be separately identified on the documentation and the amount excluded from the selling price of the vehicle.

If a RFL is surrendered, any refund received is outside the scope of VAT. If a car is purchased and the RFL subsequently refunded, the price of the car should not be adjusted to take account of the refund.

Delivery and pre-delivery inspection ('PDI') charges

20.8 Customs & Excise regard delivery and PDI charges as part of the value of the supply of the car and not as a separate service. This means that if the customer is unable to recover the VAT incurred on the car, he is also unable to recover the VAT incurred on the delivery charge.

This position was recently challenged in the case of *British Telecommunications plc*. On the facts of this case, the tribunal held that the delivery and PDI charges could constitute a separate supply and that the input tax incurred on these supplies was not subject to the general blocking order. The Court of Appeal has upheld this decision (*CA [1998] STC 544*).

Car dealers are largely unaffected by this decision, as in general they can recover any VAT incurred on cars purchased for resale.

Accessories

20.9 Where a motor dealer fits accessories to a car before delivery, they are regarded as part of the supply of the car, and where the customer is unable to recover VAT on the car, input tax recovery is also blocked on the accessories. This applies even where the dealer separately itemises them on the invoice or raises a separate invoice.

Accessories that are fitted after delivery are subject to the normal rules. However, it is unlikely that many will have a business use to qualify for input tax deduction.

Extended warranties

20.10 The inclusion of extended warranties and mechanical breakdown insurance ('MBI') as part of the bargain complicates the record-keeping.

Where a warranty or MBI is included in with the selling price of the vehicle, neither the sales invoice nor the stock book should show a separate charge.

If a charge is made for an extended warranty or MBI, the VAT treatment will depend on the provider of the warranty and whose risk is covered. If the warranty is provided by the dealer or someone who is not a permitted insurer (see below), any charge will be standard-rated.

If the warranty is provided by someone who is permitted to carry on insurance business by the Department of Trade and Industry (a 'permitted insurer'), the charge will be exempt if it is clear that the contract is between the insurer and the customer and the policy is restricted to the customer's risk. If the policy is between the motor dealer and the insurer, and it is the dealer's risk that is being covered, the charge to the customer will be standard-rated.

Care should be taken to ensure that the supply of the car and the warranty (or MBI) are in fact separate supplies. Only where:

(i) the charge is exempt under the above provisions,

(ii) the warranty (or MBI) is advertised for a separate price, and

(iii) the warranty (or MBI) is a genuine option for the customer,

can the price charged for the warranty (or MBI) be treated as exempt.

If the dealer advertises the car and the warranty (or MBI) at a single price, or the customer is obliged to purchase the warranty (or MBI), there is a single supply and Customs & Excise state that the dealer has to apportion the purchase price. VAT Notice 718 contains suggested apportionment methods.

If the motor dealer sells extended warranties or MBI schemes, it is advised to keep copies of advertised prices, etc. to substantiate the bargains entered into and the amounts involved. Exempt warranties (or MBI) should be separately itemised on the invoices.

International supplies of new means of transport

20.11 Most franchised Motor Dealers are prohibited by their franchisor from selling outside their territory or from sourcing their vehicles from another country. However, some dealers in specialist marques and second-hand dealers may be involved in international supplies.

Movements of motor cars into the EU are treated for VAT purposes as any other movement of goods and VAT, car tax and duty are payable on importation. Exports can be zero-rated providing the appropriate documentation providing appropriate proof of export is retained. For full details of the VAT treatment of imports and exports, see *Tolley's VAT 1998/99, chapters 25 and 34*.

20.12 *VAT Business by Business*

Movements of cars within the EU are the subject of special rules to determine the place of supply. The basic rules, which state that goods are taxable where they are situated before the supply takes place, could lead to a significant distortion of the market where diverse VAT rates apply. Therefore special place of supply rules apply to new means of transport, the definition of which includes motor cars.

The place of supply rules applying to new means of transport determine that cars are supplied where they are physically located at the point of delivery. This is achieved by exempting intra-Community supplies from VAT in the country of origin and making the acquisition of cars taxable in the country where they are supplied.

Therefore a German distributor delivering cars to a private individual in the UK would not charge German VAT (MWST) but would be obliged to register in the UK and charge UK VAT.

Self-supply

20.12 The *VAT (Cars) Order 1992, Article 5,* contains a number of situations where a supply of a motor car is deemed to occur. These are:

(a) where a car is produced otherwise than by conversion (e.g. constructed from motor vehicle parts or kits);

(b) where a car is produced by the conversion of another vehicle (whether a motor car or not);

(c) where a car is supplied to a taxable person; or

(d) where a car is acquired from another Member State or imported by a taxable person.

A charge will not arise where the car is subsequently supplied by the taxable person or is used by him exclusively for the purposes of his business (i.e. it is a qualifying car) or it is put to one of the uses detailed at paragraph 20.13 below.

A charge will only arise under (b) to (d) above if the tax on the supply, acquisition or import is not wholly excluded from credit. This is to prevent double taxation.

Where a deemed supply arises the taxable person must treat the supply as a taxable supply made to him (i.e. recover any input tax that is not blocked) and by him (i.e. account for output tax). In the majority of cases where the self-supply is required, recovery of input tax is blocked. Therefore, the application of this rule usually results in a VAT charge.

A practical application of these rules occurs where a car which has been purchased for a qualifying purpose is subsequently put to a non-qualifying use, e.g. where a car is taken from stock to be a demonstration vehicle, or where a 'car' is produced by conversion from a van or pickup truck.

For vehicles that are taken from stock, the value of the supply is deemed to be the current cost price of a replacement vehicle at the time of adoption. If accessories have been fitted to the vehicle before adoption the consideration should also include the current VAT exclusive purchase price of the accessories at the time of adoption.

VAT recovery

20.13 Ever since the introduction of VAT, the UK has maintained a general block on the recovery of input tax on cars. At present the block is contained in the *VAT (Input Tax) Order 1992 (SI 1992 No 3222)*. This acts by excluding the tax charged on the supply of a motor car from credit under *VATA 1994, s 25*. A number of exemptions to the general exclusion have been enacted since the introduction of the Order.

The principal relief that has related to motor dealers since the introduction of VAT was for cars which were unused and supplied to a taxable person for the purpose of being sold. This enabled motor dealers to recover the input tax on vehicles bought for resale.

With effect from 31 July 1992, input tax could be recovered on cars which were supplied, acquired or imported primarily for the purpose of:

(a) being provided for hire with the services of a driver for the purposes of carrying passengers;

(b) being provided for self-drive hire; or

(c) being used as a vehicle in which instruction in the driving of a motor car is to be given.

With effect from 1 January 1994, input tax could also be recovered on cars which were supplied, acquired or imported for the purpose of being let on hire for one of the purposes in (a) to (c) above.

Since 1 August 1995, VAT recovery has been available to any taxable person who purchases a car to be used wholly for business purposes. Purchasing for resale qualifies as a business purpose so that, for motor dealers, the recovery of input tax is largely unaffected by the changes in the legislation.

Demonstration and courtesy cars

20.14 The 'wholly for business purposes' test is applied by Customs & Excise very strictly. It is not sufficient to be able to demonstrate that a car or cars are only used for business purposes; the cars must genuinely be unavailable for private purposes if they are to be qualifying cars. This presents a problem for motor dealers in respect of demonstration and courtesy cars. VAT Information Sheet 12/95 presents Customs & Excise's interpretation of 'wholly business purposes'. It states that the test to be applied is that the cars:

- are not available for private use,
- are not allocated to a single individual, and
- are never kept overnight at home.

Most demonstration cars are allocated to salesmen and are taken home by them. These cars therefore do not meet the 'wholly for business purpose' test and should not be treated as qualifying cars. Where cars are purchased by motor dealers for stock but are subsequently adopted to be demonstration cars, VAT has to be accounted for on the self-supply (see paragraph 20.12 above).

Courtesy cars are frequently provided to customers whilst their car is being serviced or repaired. Arrangements for courtesy cars differ greatly between dealerships with some maintaining a stock of dedicated vehicles whilst others transfer vehicles from their hire fleets. The provision of cars to customers for their private use is part of the business of the dealership and would not therefore disqualify the cars involved.

The ultimate disposal of these vehicles will usually be under the Margin Scheme for second-hand cars (see paragraph 20.16 below).

Accounting and records

New cars and other qualifying cars

20.15 There are no special accounting or invoicing requirements that apply to the sale of qualifying motor cars. However if a motor dealer sells a qualifying car to another VAT-registered trader he must, on request, issue a VAT invoice. Likewise, a motor dealer purchasing a motor car from another dealer, from any VAT-registered business, or at an auction, needs to ascertain the VAT status of the vehicle and, if it is a qualifying vehicle, needs to obtain a tax invoice in order to recover input tax on the vehicle.

Before 1 August 1995 a concession existed that exempted self-drive hire companies from the requirement to issue a tax invoice if selling a vehicle to a motor dealer. This was because the motor dealer would not have been able to recover the VAT, and if the dealer wanted to use the margin scheme a non-tax invoice would be required. Since motor dealers will now normally be qualifying users entitled to input tax deduction, this concession ceased from 1 August 1995.

Second-hand car scheme

20.16 Full details of the second-hand car margin scheme can be found in VAT Notice 718 which has legal force in respect of the records and accounting requirements for motor vehicles.

Briefly, the scheme enables a person selling a used motor vehicle on which his input tax has been restricted to account for VAT only on the margin between his purchase cost and selling price. If the margin is nil or negative, i.e. the vehicle has been sold at a loss, no VAT is due.

Motor dealers are expected to meet fully all of the record-keeping requirements of the scheme. If they do not, VAT must be accounted for on the full selling price, without any subsequent allowance for input tax on the vehicles sold.

Exceptionally, where a motor dealer cannot meet all the record-keeping and accounting requirements of the scheme, Customs & Excise may as a concession allow special treatment on application to the dealer's local VAT office (LVO). Depending on the records that are available, where the mark-up achieved on the sale does not exceed 100% the LVO may allow the dealer to account for VAT on either the purchase price of the vehicle or half the selling price. However, since this treatment is dependant on Customs & Excise extending concessionary treatment, motor dealers are advised to comply with the requirements of the scheme.

Full details of the second-hand margin scheme can be found in *Tolley's VAT 1998/99, paras 45.22 and 61.1 to 61.35.*

Practical points

Part-exchange transactions

20.17 When a motor dealer accepts a vehicle in part-exchange for one he is selling, two transactions are treated as taking place: a sale and a purchase. The consideration for the sale must include the amount allowed for the vehicle taken in part-exchange as well as any amount received in cash.

For example, where a vehicle advertised for £2,500 is sold for £2,000 cash plus a £500 allowance on a part-exchanged vehicle, the sales invoice and stock book will both show a selling price of £2,500 for the vehicle sold and the purchase invoice and the stock book will both show a cost of £500 for the vehicle purchased. In practice it is common for invoices used for part-exchanges to be a single document, with separate sections containing the purchase and sales details.

20.17 VAT Business by Business

Both the sales and purchase invoices must contain signed declarations that the goods have been sold at the stated price and that 'Input tax deduction has not been and will not be claimed by me in respect of the goods sold on this invoice'. The purpose of the signed declarations on the invoices is to prevent post-sales adjustment of the margin.

The price agreed between the parties is the price that must be used to calculate the margin. In *James A Laidlaw (Edinburgh) Ltd; James A Laidlaw (Dunfermline) Ltd (1376)* the two companies offered 'minimum' trade-in values of £1,500 with no reservation about the true value of the vehicles that were traded in. The offer prices of the vehicles sold was inflated to take into account any resulting loss. On sale the customer was given an invoice for the new car and a credit note for the traded-in car. However credit notes were subsequently issued to adjust the value of the invoices to the actual value of the traded-in cars which treated the differences as a 'special trade-in offer'. The traded-in car was entered in the stock book at its adjusted value whilst the 'special trade-in offer' was treated as a discount and deducted from the sale price of the car sold thus reducing its margin under the margin scheme. The tribunal upheld assessments issued by Customs & Excise on the basis that the sale price was the amount agreed with and invoiced to the customer. A similar decision was reached in the more recent case of *North Anderson Cars Ltd (15415)*.

Where part-exchange negotiations are being conducted, the dealer often has to choose between offering a discount on the car being sold or enhancing the trade-in value of the part-exchanged car. His overall VAT liability will be affected by this decision.

To illustrate this, suppose that a motor dealer advertises a car for sale for £14,000. The cost of the car for margin scheme purposes was £10,000. To sell the vehicle, the dealer accepts a car in part-exchange plus £6,000 cash. The part-exchanged vehicle has a true value of £6,000 at auction but the dealer is prepared to inflate this to £8,000.

The VAT liability under the margin scheme will be:

	£
Selling price	14,000
Purchase price	(10,000)
Margin	4,000
VAT on margin—£4,000 × 7/47ths	595

If the part-exchanged car is sold at auction for its true value of £6,000 or less, no VAT liability arises on that vehicle.

However if, instead of inflating the trade-in value of the part-exchanged vehicle, the motor dealer had offered a £2,000 discount, his VAT liability would be reduced:

	£
Selling price	12,000
Purchase price	(10,000)
Margin	2,000
VAT on margin—£2,000 × 7/47ths	298

Again, if the traded-in vehicle is sold for its trade value of £6,000 or less, no VAT liability arises on that vehicle.

As the VAT is accounted for out of the motor dealer's margin, the 'saving' of £297 represents additional profit.

Clearly, in an arm's length situation, it is up to the dealer and the customer to strike a bargain at whatever value they determine. Therefore there is nothing wrong with the bargain being struck in the latter way. However the invoices must reflect the agreed values with the appropriate declarations being signed. If the records were to be adjusted after the values have been agreed with the customer, it would probably be regarded by Customs & Excise as a serious offence.

A recent case has confirmed that increased consideration for a part-exchanged vehicle cannot be regarded as a 'discount' on the sale of a new vehicle. See *Howletts (Autocare) Ltd (14467)*.

Definition of a motor car

20.18 The definition of a motor car is important for the application of the input tax 'blocking' order and for the purposes of the self-supply charge (see paragraph 20.12 above). Before 1 January 1995, it was also important for deciding whether a vehicle could be dealt with under the second-hand car margin scheme. As would be expected, there have been many cases in this often-disputed area.

It should be noted that, from 1 January 1995, the margin scheme was extended to cover all second-hand goods. However, the definition of a motor car remains important for input tax and self-supply purposes.

A motor car is defined as any motor vehicle of a kind normally used on public roads which has three or more wheels and is either:

20.19 *VAT Business by Business*

(i) constructed or adapted solely or mainly for the carriage of passengers, or

(ii) has to the rear of the driver's seat roofed accommodation which is fitted with side windows or which is constructed or adapted for the fitting of side windows.

Certain vehicles which would otherwise qualify are excluded from this definition, namely:

(i) vehicles capable of accommodating only one person or suitable for carrying twelve or more persons;

(ii) vehicles of not less than three tonnes unladen weight;

(iii) caravans, ambulances and prison vans;

(iv) vehicles of a type approved by the Assistant Commissioner of Police of the Metropolis conforming to the conditions laid down by him for the purposes of the *London Cab Order 1934*; or

(v) vehicles constructed for a special purpose other than the carriage of persons and having no other accommodation for carrying persons than such as is incidental to that purpose.

Included in the definition of a 'motor car' are Land Rovers fitted with hard tops, estate cars licensed as commercial vehicles, and pickup trucks with covered seating accommodation to the rear of the driver. Even though a vehicle is registered as a heavy goods vehicle, this does not prevent it being regarded as a motor car for VAT purposes (*C&E Commrs v Jeynes t/a Midland International (Hire) Caterers, QB 1983, [1984] STC 30*). For cases concerning vehicles held to be motor cars, see *Tolley's VAT Cases 1998, paras 9.27 to 9.58*.

Vehicles which have been held not to be 'motor cars' include Toyota Landcruisers adapted as recovery vehicles, Land Rovers fitted with folding seats and Peugeot vans with side windows. For cases concerning vehicles held not to be motor cars, see *Tolley's VAT Cases 1998, paras 9.59 to 9.72*.

Sale or return transactions

20.19 Most franchised motor dealers will receive cars on a sale or return basis under which cars are delivered to the dealers but are not invoiced until a sale has been agreed.

Under these circumstances, the tax point is triggered not when the cars are delivered but when the dealer 'adopts' the cars, or if sooner, twelve months after delivery. Adoption by the dealer occurs when it either notifies the manufacturer or indicates by its actions that the car has been adopted (i.e. it finds a buyer for the car or takes it for its own use as a demonstration or courtesy vehicle).

VAT group registrations

20.20 In large multi-site dealerships it is not uncommon for vehicles to be transferred between sites, some of which trade as separate legal entities. Where stock books are maintained locally, it is possible that a margin is recognised on which VAT is paid whereas by looking at the group as a whole a smaller liability or no VAT liability at all, would arise. One possible solution to resolve this is VAT grouping. In a VAT group all transactions between VAT group members are disregarded for VAT purposes. Only transactions outside the group are accounted for.

For example, let us assume that SmartCar and SecondCar are both trading subsidiaries of the same Parent plc. SmartCar sells new cars whilst SecondCar is a used car dealership. SmartCar, on selling a new vehicle, takes a used car in part-exchange. It allows the customer a value of £4,000. Since it only sells new vehicles, the car is transferred to SecondCar at its trade value of £3,000. Since it has accepted a loss on the car, no VAT is accounted for. SecondCar holds the car in stock for some time before selling it for £4,250. It accounts for VAT on its margin of £1,250, resulting in a VAT liability of £186. If, however, both companies were in the same VAT group, the actual margin for VAT purposes would be only £250 and the resulting VAT liability would be only £37, a saving of almost £150.

However, practical problems often arise when considering VAT grouping for motor dealers. Use of the second-hand margin scheme requires that the purchasing company reveals to the selling company the price paid for the vehicles. This is often politically difficult. In addition, problems concerning the location of the stock book, centralisation of records and submission of VAT returns can make the operation of a motor dealership as a VAT group very difficult.

'Premium and nearly new' and 'personal import' cars

20.21 'Premium and nearly new' cars are vehicles whose market value is greater than the manufacturer's list price because of their scarcity value. Manufacturers often go to some length to ensure that their cars are only sold by franchised dealers. Franchised dealers are not usually permitted by the terms of their franchise to sell new cars to other motor dealers. Therefore, to sell 'new' vehicles, non-franchised dealers must obtain supplies from other sources. Often these are imports from other countries such as Ireland. Alternatively, agents can be appointed to purchase cars from the franchised dealer network. However, problems are encountered when these cars are re-sold, as they cannot be sold under the second-hand car margin scheme. In addition, the invoice will be addressed to the agent, not to the motor dealer, so that input tax could not be reclaimed. This could lead to double taxation. Similar problems arise when cars are imported by a private individual who then immediately sells them to a registered dealer.

20.21 VAT Business by Business

Following consultation with the Motor Agents Association, Customs & Excise stated that if an employee, director or agent of a non-franchised dealer acquires a car on his behalf, output tax will be due on the full selling price of the car when re-sold. However, VAT charged by the franchised dealer on the original sale can be counted as input tax by the non-franchised dealer provided that he holds the original VAT invoice. Likewise, in the case of 'personal imports', the dealer may count the VAT paid at importation as input tax provided that he holds evidence of the VAT paid. It is also accepted that, as long as there is no direct association between the dealer and the person from whom he obtains the motor car, the car is eligible for the second-hand car margin scheme. The full text of the concession is contained in HM Customs & Excise Press Notice 748, 25 June 1982 but was withdrawn with effect from 1 April 1998: see Business Brief 4/98.

Chapter 21

Property Development

Introduction

21.1 This chapter deals with the issues facing businesses which develop, trade in and exploit for income, what in European VAT terms is usually referred to as 'immovable property'. More commonly in the UK, it will be known as simply 'property', or alternatively, 'land and buildings'. This chapter does not address the liability of the construction of property, except where a reference is required to make sense of an otherwise illogical and apparently contradictory VAT liability. For a detailed explanation of how VAT affects the construction industry, see Chapter 9 of this book.

21.2 What is land? The term is used to mean that which includes buildings, walls, trees, plants and other structures and natural objects in, under or over the land, as long as they remain attached to the land.

21.3 What is a building? This is a question which vexes Customs, lawyers, advisers and businesses alike. No single all-encompassing definition has ever been formulated which satisfies all the requirements of those who are concerned with the taxation through VAT of land and buildings. To avoid what would in all probability be a major if futile argument, the path of least resistance has been chosen, and unless it is clear from the text that some alternate definition has been adopted, in this chapter the term is given its ordinary dictionary definition of a stationary structure with walls and a roof.

21.4 There are many pitfalls which await the unwary businessman in this trade sector. Some of these undoubtedly stem from the basic requirements of VAT, and these will confront most businesses at some point in time. However, others stem from the fact that English land law has been evolving since the time of William the Conqueror and therefore has a rich, but often all too convoluted, heritage and evolution, whereas VAT in the UK has been with us for just 25 years.

21.5 In many cases, the basic concepts of land law and VAT law are at best uneasy bedfellows, and at worst are well-nigh wholly incompatible. There is no other commodity which is so widely used and enjoyed which, depending on the circumstances prevalent at the time it is used or traded, can be either zero-rated, standard-rated, exempt, or outside the scope of VAT altogether.

21.6 VAT Business by Business

21.6 Property transactions can indeed be all of these, but fortunately, not all at the same time. However the transition from one liability to another is occasionally so well hidden as to be completely overlooked, an act of omission which can have expensive consequences for buyer and seller alike.

21.7 Whatever certainty exists on the matter of the liability of a transaction which may be present for most other commodities or services for virtually every other sector of the business community, is eroded for land and property developers by the presence of the 'option to tax' (see paragraphs 21.32 et seq. below).

21.8 Property developments can broadly be split into two main categories, commercial and residential.

21.9 Commercial developments can be exempt, liable to VAT at the standard rate because of the option to tax, or liable to VAT at the standard rate in their own right. Commercial developments cannot normally be zero-rated, but on occasions may often appear to be so by virtue of being used for a qualifying purpose. Qualifying purposes are limited to developments that either have some similarity to domestic residential accommodation (such as military barracks, monasteries and nunneries, halls of residence and the like for students or school pupils) or are used for certain non-business purposes by charities.

21.10 Domestic accommodation can be exempt from VAT or zero-rated. For the purposes of this chapter, projects such as extensions to domestic accommodation, which are always standard-rated (but see Chapter 9 above for zero-rating for certain alterations to protected or 'listed' buildings) are ignored.

21.11 Builders of new houses make a zero-rated supply when they sell the freehold, or grant a lease of over 21 years, of a brand new house. In addition, with effect from 1 March 1995, certain property which was commercial and which is converted into domestic accommodation can also be zero-rated. This ensures that builders can recover their input tax, and thus VAT does not fall as a burden on domestic accommodation. The sale of second-hand domestic accommodation is exempt from VAT, relieving the private individual from having to register for VAT to sell a house or flat, and again, ensuring that VAT does not fall as a burden on domestic accommodation.

21.12 To summarise, the basic rule for property transactions is that disposals and grants of interests in land are exempt. This means that no VAT is charged to the purchaser or tenant but input tax is generally not recoverable by the vendor or landlord. There is an option in the non-residential sector to treat exempt transactions as taxable (option to tax) and zero-rating is available in respect of certain qualifying buildings (residential and charitable use). Conversion and construction of buildings and civil engineering work are standard-rated except for zero-rating of certain work on residential and charitable buildings.

VAT liability

Exemption

21.13 As exemption is very much the norm for transactions in land and property, it is appropriate to look at precisely what is exempt from VAT. There is one complete group within the exemption schedule to VATA 1994 which is devoted entirely to land and buildings: *VATA 1994, 9 Sch, Group 1*.

21.14 From *VATA 1994, 9 Sch, Group 1*, we can derive a basic principle that the grant of any interest in or right over land or licence to occupy land is exempt unless it is:

(i) excluded from exemption (and therefore standard-rated) under *VATA 1994, 9 Sch, Group 1, Item 1 paras (a) to (n)* or

(ii) zero-rated under either *VATA 1994, 8 Sch, Group 5* or *Group 6* or

(iii) standard-rated if the supplier has opted to tax the land in question (*VATA 1994, 10 Sch, para 2*).

21.15 The default position is therefore that where the grant of any interest in property is made, it is exempt, unless it can be made to fall outside *VATA 1994, 9 Sch, Group 1*.

21.16 This seemingly simple statement conceals a vast tranche of uncertainty, as it is not always clear that a supply is in fact an interest, right, or licence, in or over land. The area in which difficulty is most frequently encountered is in connection with licences to occupy land. Often, these licences are not written licences, and this will make it very difficult to establish their terms. As a simple rule of thumb, the supply of a licence to occupy land will be an exempt supply (with the option to tax) only if the terms of the agreement allow for the land to be occupied, rather than used. An agreement which allows the customer the enjoyment of the facilities which the land may have to offer is standard-rated. Examples of such standard-rated licences which are often encountered are:

(a) the right to enter onto a piece of land to view the scenery;

(b) admission to a theatre, cinema and the like;

(c) the making available of an undesignated storage space in a warehouse.

21.17 There have been a number of cases considered by the VAT tribunals and the courts, where the issue to be decided was whether the supplier granted an exempt licence to occupy land, or was what the customer or tenant received a standard-rated right to enjoy facilities. An example of the former was *British Airways Authority (No. 1), CA 1976, [1977] STC 36*, where it was held that the operator of shops at Heathrow Airport received an exempt licence to occupy the shops. A recent example of the latter, where it was held

21.18 *VAT Business by Business*

that a right over land was not granted, was *Wolverhampton & Dudley Breweries plc, [1990] VATTR 131 (5351)*, in which it was held that the payment made for the right to place a coin-operated gaming machine in a public house was not a right over land, but a supply of the right to enjoy the facilities that the land had to offer. More recently, this principle was confirmed in *Sinclair Collis Ltd (14950)*.

21.18 A glance at *VATA 1994, 9 Sch, Group 1, Item 1 paras (a)–(n)* will reveal all of the statutorily listed mandatory exclusions from exemption, which are therefore standard-rated, unless relief can be found within the zero-rating schedule, *VATA 1994, 8 Sch*.

21.19 The most obvious and frequently met examples of grants (of rights and interests in immovable property) which are specifically excluded from exemption are:

- new commercial buildings;
- the right to take game or fish;
- accommodation in hotels and similar establishments;
- holiday accommodation;
- seasonal pitches for caravans;
- camping facilities;
- car parking facilities;
- storage facilities including moorings;
- boxes or seats at sporting events;
- places of entertainment;
- facilities for playing sports.

21.20 But even within these headings there are exceptions. For example, mooring fees for a residential houseboat are seen by Customs as being on all fours with rent payable for domestic accommodation on dry land, and are therefore mandatorily exempt.

21.21 Not so much an exception, but more of a pitfall which can often be overlooked, is the 'new' building. The key word here is 'new' because the freehold disposal of a new building is excluded from exemption under *VATA 1994, 9 Sch, Group 1 item 1, para (a)(ii)*. When is a building 'new'? Customs say that a building is 'new' for VAT purposes for three years from the date it is completed. This means that any sale of the fee simple (freehold) within that three-year period will be liable to VAT at the standard rate. A building can be sold many times within a three-year period, and still, for VAT purposes, remain 'new' and therefore liable to VAT at the standard rate.

21.22 The date of completion of the building may also often be less than clear. Customs take the view that, for VAT purposes, a building will be completed on the earlier of two alternative events. These are, either the date that the certificate of practical completion is issued, or the date the building is first fully occupied. Documentary evidence should be retained to ensure that there are no disputes with Customs about whether a building is new. If a building is occupied to any significant degree before the certificate of practical completion is issued, disputes with Customs may arise over whether full occupancy is attained before the certificate is issued. However, common sense would dictate that full occupancy is a term of science, rather than one of art, and will therefore be achieved only when all parts of the building are occupied.

Rights in and over land

21.23 At the very heart of exemption for land and buildings is the word 'any'. VAT law says, very clearly, 'the grant of *any* interest in or right over land or of *any* licence to occupy land'. But to make any sense at all, the interest can only be interpreted from the perspective of land law, all 900-odd years of it. Without this approach, absolutely anything at all which had any connection with land would come within the scope of the exemption. Unfortunately, it is seemingly all too often the case that Customs policies are formulated independently of the land law perspectives.

21.24 As an example of a case where VAT liability hinges on the land law perspective, consider a situation where a landlord negotiates a loan (the identity of the lender is irrelevant) in order to buy land and develop property for letting, and he agrees to repay the loan by passing 50% of the income stream (or proceeds of sale) from a particular property. Is the lender granted a right over the land? Customs have been considering this very point, and for the moment have concluded that it is not. In the author's view, Customs have undoubtedly come to the correct decision, as in this case for the lender, we have a financial transaction, not a property transaction.

21.25 To qualify for exemption as an interest in land and property, the 'interest' must therefore be thought of in land law terms in order to make any sense, and in order to achieve consistency of practice. However, again there are traps for the unwary, as a lender of money in such cases may require that he be given an interest in the land itself, in which case, despite all the best efforts of the landlord, the supply of an interest in land within *VATA 1994, 9 Sch, Group 1* will have been granted.

21.26 As any student of law will know, legal textbooks devote whole chapters to determining what constitutes rights over and interests in land,

21.27 VAT Business by Business

with repeated references to the various land law statutes and to an immense catalogue of case law on the subject, and it serves no good purpose to explore such matters further in this book.

Zero-rated transactions in land and property

21.27 Zero-rated supplies of land and property are dealt with in some depth in Chapter 9 above, but it is appropriate to consider them briefly in this chapter.

21.28 A transaction in land and/or property can only be zero-rated in certain quite rigidly defined circumstances. The legislation found in *VATA 1994, 8 Sch, Groups 5 & 6*, allows the first grant of a major interest to be zero-rated, when it is made by a person who:

(a) has constructed or is in the process of constructing a dwelling or other building which is intended solely for 'relevant residential use' or for use by a charity for 'relevant charitable use'; or

(b) has converted or is in the process of converting a commercial building or part of a commercial building, into a dwelling or other building intended for relevant residential use; or

(c) has substantially reconstructed a protected building (listed building) which remains a dwelling.

21.29 It is important to recognise the significance of the fact that what is zero-rated is 'only' the first grant of a major interest. Perhaps the best illustration of this is to consider a housebuilder who zero-rates the freehold sale of a new house. It is quite common for housebuilders to accept houses in part-exchange, and such a business may find itself taking in part-exchange a house which it had originally built some years previously. The subsequent sale of the second-hand house is not a zero-rated supply (which would allow the builder to recover all the VAT on his expenses), but is an exempt supply. It is exempt because although it is clearly the grant of an interest in land, it does not fall to be zero-rated under *VATA 1994, 8 Sch*. Although the vendor is the person who constructed the house, the vendor is not making the first grant of a major interest in the property.

21.30 Certain long leases will be treated as major interests in land for VAT purposes, if they are for a period of 21 years or more. In such a case, the 'first grant' for VAT purposes will be either the first rent reserved by the lease or, if applicable, the premium payment. On the face of it, this seems very satisfactory, and in the landlord's favour. If he is the person who has constructed or converted the property he will be able to recover the VAT incurred on the construction/conversion costs, and also on legal and other professional costs relating to that property. However, all subsequent rental payments will constitute exempt supplies for VAT, and thus the tax incurred on on-going costs of repairs and maintenance and any legal and professional fees will not be recoverable by him, as they will have been incurred in the making of exempt supplies.

21.31 The advantage of zero-rating, as discussed earlier, is that it does provide what is effectively a complete relief from VAT. When supplies are zero-rated, there is no overall VAT cost to either the supplier or the consumer.

The 'option to tax'—standard-rating by choice

21.32 Uniquely in UK VAT law, this provision allows the supplier, vendor or landlord (the terms will vary in practice only where semantics dictate the use of one over another, but they amount to the same thing—the supplier of the commodity which is the subject of the transaction) to exercise a degree of choice. Thus the supply of a piece of land or a building may well carry with it an exempt VAT status by default, but will be transformed into a supply which will bear VAT at the standard rate by virtue of the supplier having made the decision—'I wish to add VAT to the charge I will levy on my customer'.

21.33 One might ask why it is that anyone with a choice would wish to charge his customers VAT? Zero-rating provides complete relief from the burden of VAT, but exemption imposes a burden of hidden 'sticking' tax on businesses making exempt supplies, and on their customers. The next best thing to zero-rating is, strangely enough, standard-rating, as a business making standard-rated supplies is able to recover the VAT incurred on the making of those supplies.

21.34 The answer to why anyone would wish to opt to tax is of course to be able to recover as input tax the VAT incurred on the expenditure relating to the supply. Standard-rating of a supply of property by virtue of the landlord having 'opted to tax' will result in the tenant being charged VAT. If the tenant is registered for VAT, and makes use of the property for making taxable supplies in the course and furtherance of his business, then he can recover the tax charged to him as his own input tax. The tax will then wash through, as both UK and EC legislation envisages, and there is no 'sticking' tax. However, if the tenant is not able to recover the VAT incurred, then it will in turn add to his overhead costs; it may therefore be the case that the option to tax, advantageous to the landlord's VAT recovery position, may affect the marketability of the property such that a buyer or tenant might be difficult to find.

21.35 The option to tax was brought into UK VAT law in 1989 shortly after the UK finally lost the legal battle to retain what had until then been a widespread application of the zero rate to supplies of land and property. The UK lost its case to defend the wide usage of zero rates when the European Court of Justice (CJEC) ruled that zero-rating could only apply where it was of direct benefit to the final consumer.

21.36 *VAT Business by Business*

21.36 Thus, having lost the battle to retain the application of zero-rating to a wide tranche of supplies of land and property, the UK had no option but to apply the liability which is enshrined within EC VAT law, and that is that most supplies of land and property are exempt.

21.37 Exemption, whilst apparently relieving the consumer from the burden of VAT, also removes from the vendor the privilege and benefit of recovering VAT on expenditure. Exemption therefore usually results in 'sticking' or non-recoverable VAT accruing to the vendor, who quite naturally will seek to pass on this overhead cost to his customer when he is calculating his selling price. Exemption is therefore not the panacea that the uninformed observer may believe it to be, and it will never be the case that exemption, in VAT terms, indicates that either the vendor or the customer is totally relieved of the burden of VAT.

21.38 As discussed above, the option to tax permits an unusual result in that a supply of land and property, which clearly falls within the exemption under *VATA 1994, 9 Sch, Group 1*, can at the 'whim' of the vendor or landlord be taken out of exemption and placed firmly (and, until recently, irrevocably) within the scope of VAT at the standard rate.

21.39 The option to tax, or to give it its more correct legal terminology, the 'election to waive exemption' is permissive (under both UK and EC Law). This means that a vendor cannot be forced to opt to tax, but has the right to decide the VAT liability for himself. Clearly, significant tax burdens can flow from such a decision, but at least there is some freedom of choice.

21.40 It is a truism to say that there are exceptions to every rule, and the option to tax is no exception. In some cases, vendors or landlords have no freedom of choice; there are some supplies over which they cannot opt to tax. (Technically, the correct position is that the option to tax can be made on any property, but in some cases, it is disapplied and will have no effect.)

21.41 The VAT liability of the following supplies of land or property are not affected by the option to tax:

(a) the sale or letting of a building or part of a building intended for use as a dwelling, or for use solely for relevant residential purposes (*VATA 1994, 10 Sch, para 2(2)(a)*);

(b) the sale or letting of a building or part of a building intended for use solely for relevant charitable purposes (*VATA 1994, 10 Sch, para 2(2)(b)*);

(c) the sale or letting of a pitch for a residential caravan (*VATA 1994, 10 Sch, para 2(2)(c)*);

(d) the sale or letting of facilities for the mooring of a residential houseboat, where the residents are not prevented from occupying the houseboat throughout the year by any restrictive covenant or other restriction *(VATA 1994, 10 Sch, para 2(2)(d))*;

(e) the sale or letting of a property to a registered housing association (now termed 'Registered Social Housing Landlords') which has provided a certificate to the vendor or landlord that it will, after any necessary demolition, construct a building or buildings for use as domestic residential accommodation or solely for relevant residential purposes *(VATA 1994, 10 Sch, para 2(3)(a))*;

(f) the sale or letting of a property to an individual who will, after any necessary demolition, construct a dwelling for his or her own occupation (the so called 'DIY Housebuilders') *(VATA 1994, 10 Sch, para 2(3)(b))*;

(g) the sale or letting of property between two persons, legal or real, who are connected persons under the terms of *ICTA 1988, s 839* where either or both persons are not fully taxable in the VAT period in which the grant is made. (This category was introduced from 30 November 1994 as an anti-avoidance measure, to counter what was perceived as a significant tax avoidance mechanism. It was enacted as *VATA 1994, 10 Sch, para 2(3A)*, which was repealed on 26 November 1996 following the 1996 Budget.);

(h) the sale or letting of property between two persons, legal or real, where the property is an asset falling within the terms of the Capital Goods Scheme, when the property is occupied by either the person who granted the interest, or a person connected with him under the terms of *ICTA 1988, s 839*, or a person who directly or indirectly provided finance for the creation or acquisition of the property, or a person connected with someone who has directly or indirectly provided finance for the creation or acquisition of the property under the terms of *ICTA 1988, s 839* and, when the occupier used the property wholly or mainly to make supplies which do not carry the right to recover input tax *(VATA 1994, 10 Sch, paras 2(3AA) and 3A(1) to 3A(14))*.

21.42 This last category of restriction, introduced as a result of the 1996 Budget, is exceptionally complex even for VAT land and property legislation, and contains many new terms and conditions, the ultimate effect and application of which are yet to be tested and determined by Customs, or indeed by the VAT Tribunals and the courts. However, it is clear that Customs intend that 'directly or indirectly provided finance' should have very wide application, which may possibly include any premium payable but thankfully does not encompass ordinary rent payments. As to 'wholly or mainly', 'wholly' is clear enough, but Customs' view of 'mainly' is 80% or more. Clearly a strong counter-argument can be made that, in the absence of a specific definition in the legislation, 'mainly' must be given its ordinary meaning, and that would be anything exceeding 50%. But for the time being, Customs' policy is that 'mainly' for this purpose is 80% or more.

21.43 VAT Business by Business

21.43 It is interesting to note that a landlord may opt to tax, and have that option take effect, only to be then disapplied if one of the above circumstances prevail. The two commonest occurrences are probably where a brewery opts to tax, when it rents out a public house, and where a landowner sells or leases land to a housing association.

21.44 In the former example, as many public houses were at one time dwellings which have been converted into public houses, it is not uncommon for brewery chains to dispose of surplus pub properties to persons who intend to convert them back into houses. Provided that the purchaser makes his intentions clear to the vendor (see the decision of the VAT tribunal in the case of *J Watters (13337)* for further details as to what evidence a purchaser is required to provide to the vendor), the brewery must disapply the option to the sale of that property. In this case, the brewery will make an exempt sale (as per the exclusion at paragraph 21.41(a) above) and will not be able to recover any VAT incurred on the expenses of the sale, such as legal and other professional fees. The benefit of the disapplication of the option to tax accrues entirely to the purchaser who will therefore not have to pay VAT on the purchase price, although the brewery will undoubtedly increase its selling price by the amount of non-recoverable VAT it incurs.

21.45 In the latter case, a landowner may incur large amounts of VAT in making the land fit for re-sale, only to find that the VAT so incurred is no longer recoverable as input tax, because his customer is a housing association which has provided him with the certificate referred to in paragraph 21.41(e) above. The landowners sale will now be exempt, and the expenses of preparing and selling the land will now be attributable to an exempt supply, and irrecoverable.

21.46 This disapplication was intended to ensure that housing associations, which are for the most part unable to recover any VAT they incur, are not burdened with large amounts of VAT on the purchase of land and buildings. However, this admirable intention often works against housing associations, as it is not uncommon for some landowners, because of the resulting 'clawback' of input tax by Customs & Excise, to refuse to sell land to a housing association which intends to issue a certificate. Some landowners may still be willing to sell to housing associations, but will inflate the selling price of the land by the amount of VAT which they have to repay to Customs, because the supply of the land now becomes exempt.

How the option to tax is made

21.47 All options to tax have to be notified in writing to Customs within 30 days of the decision to opt having been made. There is no set format to the notification, but the following information should be provided:

(a) the VAT registration number of the person 'opting';

(b) the name and address of the person 'opting';

(c) the date of the option;

(d) the property or properties covered by the option, including the full postal address, postcode(s) where appropriate, and building name, if any. (In the case of bare or agricultural land, it is very desirable and highly recommended that Customs be supplied with a map or other plan which highlights or otherwise clearly delineates the area over which the option is being made.)

21.48 It is possible to notify a 'global option' to Customs, but developers may often find that their local VAT office is reluctant to accept a notification in such terms. A global option is one where the person opting will declare that they are opting to tax on their supplies of all properties currently owned, or perhaps on all properties currently owned and which will be owned in the future. Whilst this may seem to be the easy answer to the problem of having to notifying Customs in writing each time the option to tax is made, it has its drawbacks in that it removes the element of choice. A further difficulty often arises in that a global option is seldom accompanied by a detailed list of the properties currently owned, and it is clearly impossible to provide such a list if the global option is intended to cover all properties acquired in the future. Opting on a global basis is a course of action which is generally not recommended.

21.49 Once the option to tax has been made, it must be notified to Customs within 30 days (*VATA 1994, 10 Sch, para 3(6)*). If a business forgets to notify Customs of the option, but then goes ahead and acts in all ways as if the notification had been made—for instance, by charging VAT on the rents—then Customs are likely to agree that the option has been made, and accept a late notification. This point has been considered by the VAT tribunals who have accepted that the option has effect in cases where Customs were not notified within the correct timescale, but the landlords nevertheless proceeded as if this had been done (see *Fencing Supplies Ltd, [1993] VATTR 302 (10451)*).

21.50 A late notification is of course completely different to a retrospective option. It may often become clear to a business (or its advisers) that it would have been beneficial if the option to tax had been exercised at some time in the past. There is no provision in law for an option to be back-dated (made retrospective). The option can only be made on a current, or prospective basis (see *Newcourt Property Fund (5825)*).

21.51 The decision to opt is a real event, made at a finite point in time. An example often used for the purposes of illustration is where a landlord (or perhaps in the case of a corporate landlord, the Director of Estates) says to himself, 'I will opt to tax my property at No. 1 High Street, as I wish to recover the VAT I will incur on refurbishing that property'. At the precise moment in time when the landlord has made that decision, the option to tax has been made, and must be notified to Customs within 30 days. From that illustration, it can be seen that whilst a late notification to Customs of the

21.52 *VAT Business by Business*

option to tax having been made is perfectly possible, there can be no such thing as retrospective or back-dated options to tax.

Permission to opt

21.52 In some circumstances, even though the decision to opt has been made and notified to Customs, it is not effective unless and until such times as Customs give their permission (*VATA 1994, 10 Sch, para 3(9)*). Fortunately, the circumstances where Customs' permission is required are straightforward, although in many cases obtaining that permission can be fraught with difficulties.

21.53 As an example, take the case of the landlord of No. 1 High Street. The landlord is already VAT-registered, as a maker of taxable supplies (perhaps he manufactures widgets, or maybe he has other properties on which he has opted to tax his supplies). If he has already been renting out No. 1, the landlord has been making exempt supplies, and he has not charged his tenant VAT on the rent. Where a property has already been used in the making of exempt supplies, Customs' permission is required before an option can take effect. The reason for this is that Customs assume that the landlord will have incurred non-recoverable input tax in making those exempt supplies. As the landlords' supplies will (if permission is given) henceforth become taxable supplies, he will (it is further assumed) now wish to recover some of that previously non-recoverable input tax on the grounds that his future supplies are taxable.

21.54 In addition to notifying Customs of the option, the person making the option should also provide proposals for determining how the input tax previously incurred should be attributed between the exempt supplies (made prior to the option taking effect) and the taxable supplies (made after the option has taken effect). See *VATA 1994, 10 Sch, para 3(9)*. If Customs are satisfied that the proposed attribution is fair and reasonable, they will give their permission to opt to tax on the date stated. If the landlord then accepts Customs' permission and proceeds with the option, he can then recover the amount of VAT which Customs have agreed is attributable to his future taxable supplies of the property. This may be illustrated by the following example.

21.55 As a landlord, you grant a 15-year lease on No. 1 High Street, on 1 January 1992. You have not opted to tax, and hence you make exempt supplies. In order to attract a good tenant at a reasonable rent, you have refurbished the property, and incurred VAT of £150,000 on the refurbishment costs. None of this VAT is recoverable, as you have not opted to tax. On 1 January 1997, you decide to opt to tax—but you need Customs permission as you have used the property to make exempt supplies. How do you go about agreeing an attribution? You write to Customs, advising them of your wish to opt to tax No. 1 High Street but you also state that as you have previously made exempt supplies using this property, you require their permission. You

Property Development **21.59**

advise Customs that you incurred £150,000 input tax on refurbishing the property, which you did not recover. You point out that on your desired date for the option, your tenant has 10 years remaining, of a 15 year lease. Therefore, one-third of the VAT on the refurbishment costs should be attributed to the period of the exempt supply, and two-thirds of the VAT on refurbishment costs should be attributed to the period of the standard-rated supply. You are therefore proposing that you will now recover £100,000 of the original VAT.

21.56 Customs agree that this is a fair and reasonable attribution, and give their permission. You then confirm that you opt to tax on 1 January 1997, and as agreed, you proceed to recover £100,000 as input tax. Although this is a very simplistic example, Customs have accepted this methodology.

21.57 If Customs do not accept your proposals, they are not under an obligation to suggest an alternative method, although it is not at all unusual for them to do so. In the case of *C&E Commrs v Trustees for R & R Pension Fund, QB [1996] STC 889*, the trustees wished to opt to tax on a property which had previously been used in the making of exempt supplies. The trustees and the local VAT Office could not agree on an attribution and Customs therefore withheld their permission to opt to tax.

21.58 The matter was referred to Customs Headquarters, who ruled that the VAT in dispute had to be adjusted under the terms of the Capital Goods Scheme regulations. This decision, which would have provided a significantly less favourable VAT recovery than that which had been proposed by the local VAT Office, was not acceptable to the trustees, who appealed to the VAT tribunal. Although the tribunal found against Customs, the High Court overturned the tribunal decision, finding that the Capital Goods Scheme did apply.

21.59 There are a few very limited circumstances when properties have been used in the making of exempt supplies where it is not necessary to seek Customs' prior permission to opt to tax. These may conveniently be thought of as cases where permission to opt has already been given. Automatic permission does not, however, relieve the landlord or property owner from the obligation to notify Customs that the option has been made. The few exceptions which constitute 'automatic permission' are listed in Customs Land & Property Notice (Notice 742, paragraph 8.6) and, at the time of writing, these are:

(a) where the (opted) property is a mixed use development and the only exempt supplies (sales, leasing or lettings) have been in relation to the dwellings; or

(b) it is proposed that there will be no input tax recovery on expenditure made prior to the effective date of the option, AND

(c) the only income received from the property has been by way of rent, AND

21.60 *VAT Business by Business*

(d) the only input tax to be recovered after the option takes effect is on day to day overheads; or

(e) it is proposed that input tax incurred prior to the option will be recovered, but this input tax relates solely to tax charged by the tenant upon the surrender of a lease, AND

(f) the building, or relevant part, has since been unoccupied, AND

(g) there will be no further exempt supplies of the property; or

(h) the exempt supplies have been incidental to the main use of the property (e.g. the siting of an advertising hoarding within the curtilage of a building).

The extent of the option to tax

21.60 The most obvious drawback to the option to tax, for the landlord or property owner, is that the option, where applicable, can only be exercised on a whole building. As there is no definition of what is a single or a whole building, for the purposes of opting to tax, this may cause some concern. The important thing to remember is that if a landlord exercises the option to tax on a building, then it has the effect of taxing the landlord's entire interest in that building.

21.61 If No. 1 High Street is a tower block, and a landlord only owns floors 1 to 10, then he might be forgiven for thinking that his option only applies to those floors. In a way, he would be right, as he is certainly not in a position to make supplies of any other floor. But, if he has opted on his interest in No. 1 High Street (albeit that his interest is limited to floors 1–10) and he then acquires floors 11–20, the option he has already made will automatically apply to those floors too. If he eventually ends up with the entire building, then his original option automatically extends to the entire building. A landlord or property owner cannot choose to opt only on one floor, or part of that floor. When a landlord opts to tax, he opts to tax his entire interest in a property.

21.62 What may often catch the innocent landlord is a decision to opt to tax No. 1 High Street, when he also owns the adjacent building. He may think it is a separate building, but it may not be a separate building in the eyes of Customs. It will, of course, often be very obvious if two or more 'structures' are in reality a single building, or if two or more properties with separate postal addresses are in reality one single building. But if two or more buildings are not otherwise linked or connected, then they are deemed to be a single building for the purposes of opting to tax if they are:

(a) linked internally, or by a covered walkway; or

(b) a complex consisting of a number of units grouped around a fully enclosed concourse (*VATA 1994, 10 Sch, para 3(3)*).

21.63 The option to tax, when made on a building, 'infects' the whole building and all the land within its curtilage. Customs accept that if an opted building is demolished down to ground level (or indeed, below ground level if desired) then the option is extinguished. Thus, any new building subsequently constructed will not be infected by the previous option. This may catch the unwary, as a new option is required.

21.64 But what if the option is made and notified on a piece of bare land, on which a building is then constructed? Customs say in their Land & Property Notice that buildings subsequently constructed on that land are not affected by the original option on the land. The rationale for this view is not difficult to understand; presumptions are often dangerous, but one might presume that Customs have said to themselves, 'when the option was made and notified, the land was bare, and what was in the taxpayer's mind at the time was to opt to tax on that which existed at that time, i.e. the land'.

21.65 But a respectable case for a contrary argument exists, which is to hold that, once the option to tax has been made (and notified) on a piece of land, it will infect everything on that land, both at the time the option was made, and at any time in the future until such times as the option is extinguished. Be that as it may, Customs' view is clearly stated in the Notice, and the taxpayer is entitled to take appropriate comfort from it even though that part of the Notice does not have the force of law. However, it should always be remembered that, under this policy, if a building is subsequently constructed, a separate option to tax must be made and notified to Customs if the landlord wishes to charge VAT on the rents and recover his input tax.

Revocation of the option to tax

21.66 The option to tax was, until 1 March 1995, irrevocable. It is appropriate to take a few moments to consider just what this meant in practice. If the landlord of No. 1 High Street opted to tax, and then sold the freehold at some later time, he was not rid of the option. If he acquired any interest in that property at some future time, his original option still applied and he was bound by it. The same applied if the landlord was in a VAT group. The option binds every member of the VAT group (*VATA 1994, 10 Sch, para 3(3)*) and a member leaving the VAT group and acquiring an interest in the property years later would still be bound by the option. The option to tax had an infinite duration.

21.67 As a result of legislation introduced after the 1995 Budget, the option can now be extinguished (*VATA 1994, 10 Sch, paras 3 & 4*). A taxpayer may now apply to Customs for written permission to have the option revoked. However, there are conditions, and these are basically twofold. The revocation can only take effect 20 years or more after the option is first made, or within three months from the date it was made (provided that no output tax has been charged and no input tax recovered as a result of the option having been made).

21.68 *VAT Business by Business*

21.68 Customs are believed to have chosen the 20-year duration period to ensure that revocation is not used for tax avoidance purposes. Under the 20-year limit, they will not receive any applications for revocation until the year 2009, since the option to tax was only introduced in 1989. Customs intend that the three-month period shall have effect as a 'cooling-off period' to allow those who opt to tax in haste to have at least some leisure to consider whether they wish to repent of their actions, and provided they have not actually acted upon the option, to ask for it to be revoked.

VAT recovery

Input tax on new dwellings

21.69 Although the first grant of a major interest in a new domestic residential dwelling is zero-rated, housebuilders are not able to recover all the VAT they incur on building a new dwelling. As an anti-avoidance measure, intended to ensure that the final consumer does not acquire certain domestic fixtures and fittings free of VAT, housebuilders are not able to recover VAT on some items which are sometimes supplied as part of a new house. In the main, these non-recoverable fixtures and fittings are some fitted furniture, some electrical appliances and carpets. The rationale for this is that VAT can be recovered only on items 'ordinarily' installed by builders, in new houses. (See Chapter 9 above for a more detailed explanation.)

Capital goods scheme (CGS)

21.70 The Capital Goods Scheme was introduced by Customs to deal with the very real problem of input tax incurred on an asset which was used to make a mixture of taxable and exempt supplies. It was intended to ensure that businesses could not acquire large capital assets, recover the input tax on the grounds that they made taxable supplies, and then change the use of those assets to making exempt supplies whilst retaining all of the VAT originally incurred. This was the old 'first supply' rule where, if the first supply was a taxable supply, the input tax was recoverable, and subsequent exempt supplies had no effect on the input tax recovery.

21.71 In property terms, the CGS only applies if a business acquires certain interests in property, the value of which is not less than £250,000. As a result of changes introduced by the *Value Added Tax (Amendment)(No.3) Regulations 1997 (SI 1997 No 1614), paras 10–13*, with effect from 3 July 1997, payments exceeding £250,000 for civil engineering works and refurbishment or fitting-out costs also trigger the CGS. From that same date, these new regulations also apply to rent paid, payable or invoiced more than 12 months in advance, when the amount exceeds £250,000. (The CGS also applies to items of computer equipment where the value is not less than £50,000). Broadly speaking, the CGS covers a period of 10 years from the time the asset is acquired, and if in any one of those years the property is put to an exempt use, then 10% of the original input tax has to be repaid to Customs. For a more detailed explanation of how the Capital Goods Scheme works, including a full explanation of all the changes introduced by the *Value Added Tax (Amendment)(No.3) Regulations 1997 (SI 1997 No 1614), paras 10–13*, please refer to *Tolley's VAT 1998/99, chapter 10*.

21.72 Thus, if our mainstay, No. 1 High Street, was acquired for £10 million plus £1,750,000 VAT, we would recover that VAT if we used the property in our taxable business. But if a few months later, we decide that there is more of a return on our investment to be made in renting out the property, under the old rules we could keep the input tax even if we granted our newly acquired tenant an exempt lease in the property. Under the Capital Goods Scheme, in the above circumstances, although we can still recover all of our VAT in the first year, each subsequent year we have to review the use to which the building is put. In later years, if the building is put to a wholly exempt use, then we are required to repay to Customs 10% of the input tax we incurred.

21.73 The above explanation is a great over-simplification, as the adjustment percentage can be less than 10% to allow for mixed use. However, it serves to illustrate the general principles involved.

Accounting records

21.74 For the most part, the accounting records required to cope with the application of VAT to land and property transactions are no different to those required for any other kind of business.

21.75 There are, however, some exceptions. It is always necessary to retain all correspondence and records relating to the making, and notifying, of the option to tax. Disputes can often arise with Customs over which properties were opted, and when, but in addition, as the option can be revoked 20 years after it takes effect, it will presumably be necessary in the future to be able to demonstrate to Customs the date from which the option is no longer in force.

21.76 When the Capital Goods Scheme (CGS) is triggered, adjustments to input tax recovery may be required for the following 10 years, and clearly sufficient records must be retained to allow businesses to carry out the annual adjustment calculation—or to justify that no annual adjustment is necessary.

21.77 Finally, an often overlooked point is that, when a property is acquired by means of a Transfer of a Going Concern (TOGC), if it was subject to the CGS in the hands of the vendor, then the purchaser inherits the remaining CGS annual adjustment liabilities. When a property is acquired under a TOGC, then the purchaser should make the necessary arrangements to have the appropriate accounting records relating to that property transferred to him, to ensure that he properly discharges his inherited liabilities under the CGS.

21.78 *VAT Business by Business*

Practical points

The transfer of a business as a going concern ('TOGC')

21.78 When a business, or part of a business is sold as a going concern, it is not liable to VAT. The legal vires for this is to be found, in UK law, in a Statutory Instrument, the *VAT (Special Provisions) Order 1995 (SI 1995 No 1268), para 5(1)–5(3)*. A TOGC is neither a supply of goods nor a supply of services for VAT purposes. It is, in effect, not a supply within the scope of the tax. Although it may sometimes seem that the TOGC provisions act as a relieving measure, they were originally introduced as an anti-avoidance measure, as Customs were worried that the vendor of a business might default on paying output tax to the Exchequer, whereas the purchaser would still be entitled to recover his input tax. The question of whether a TOGC has, or has not taken place, is in itself a separate topic, and one on which there is much case law. It is only dealt with in this chapter insofar as it has relevance to property. For further information, please refer to *Tolley's VAT 1998/99, para 8.10*, and *Tolley's VAT Cases 1998, chapter 57.*

21.79 TOGC for the property developer is inextricably linked to the option to tax. Returning to No. 1 High Street, let us suppose that it is an office block with a number of tenants in residence. The landlord has opted to tax, and now wishes to dispose of the entire interest in the property. If it was to be sold as a straightforward sale of goods or services, as the option is already in place, the landlord would have to charge VAT on the entire selling price, which may amount to a very significant sum.

21.80 If the transfer of the interest in the property would otherwise qualify to be treated as a TOGC (i.e. it is tenanted, and the purchaser intends to carry on with the business of property lettings), then in order to qualify for a TOGC the purchaser must opt to tax (and notify Customs of that option under the terms of the *VAT (Special Provisions) Order (SI 1995 No 1268), para 5(2)*, before the sale actually takes place. In some cases, if the purchaser is not yet registered for VAT, the option to tax may have to accompany an application for registration.

21.81 If the purchaser neglects to opt to tax, then the sale cannot be treated as a TOGC, and VAT becomes chargeable on the entire selling price. If the vendor has omitted to allow for the possibility of VAT in addition to the selling price, he might find himself having to account to Customs for the output tax, from within the amount already received for the sale. This would reduce the proceeds of the sale by 7/47ths, which would be costly indeed.

21.82 Unfortunately, the dire consequences of a TOGC may also affect a purchaser. It is not unknown for Customs to take the view that a property disposal which was treated as an ordinary sale within the scope of VAT, is, after all, a TOGC. But how would this affect the purchaser? Well, the purchaser will no doubt have recovered, as input tax, the VAT he was charged. But under TOGC rules, there has been no transaction which is within the scope of the tax and the purchaser, in law, has no entitlement to recover any input tax. Input tax recovered, albeit in good faith, will then be disallowed, and the purchaser could be faced with what might be a significant VAT assessment.

21.83 In theory, whether the disposal or transfer of an interest in a property is a TOGC should be a matter of fact, a matter of science rather than art. However, the fact that there is a catalogue of case law on the subject and that Customs have issued assessments on both vendors and purchasers who have managed to fall foul of TOGC rules, indicates that this is yet another area of the tax which is built, if not on shifting sands, then certainly on foundations which are to say the least, shaky. Where there is a desire to have a transaction treated as a TOGC, or even if there is a possibility that it could be a TOGC, it is advisable to seek professional advice, and even advance clearance from the local VAT Office on whether a particular deal will be given TOGC status.

Covenants

21.84 Restrictive covenants are conditions placed on land to control or limit the use of the land, or any buildings thereon. Tenants and others with interests in land will often want restrictive covenants to be altered, or lifted altogether. In their Land & Property Public Notice, Customs state that their policy is that the charge made by the landlord, or ultimate freeholder as the case may be will be exempt, but with the option to tax. If the person receiving the payment has exercised the option to tax, the charge for lifting the restrictive covenant will be standard-rated.

21.85 The right to enforce a restrictive covenant may be retained by a person who has disposed of all other interests in that property. Given that this person no longer possesses an interest in the property, what is the liability of his supply of lifting the restrictive covenant? The answer is that whatever liability attached to that person's last supply of the property also attaches to the lifting of the covenant. Thus, if there was a freehold disposal which was exempt (but with the option to tax available), the charge for the lifting of the covenant will also be exempt (but with the option to tax available).

Variations to leases

21.86 Variations, as with other supplies of land and property, are generally exempt with the option to tax. Where there is no charge made for a variation, Customs may accept that no supply has taken place, which opens an interesting point. Developers wishing to have lease terms varied may not wish to trigger a new and separate supply for VAT purposes, but on the face of it they have little choice. However, Customs currently take the view that where the variation has not resulted in a significant change to the nature of

21.87 VAT Business by Business

the lease, for VAT purposes the variation can be ignored, and for VAT purposes, it will be as if the 'old' lease remains in place. This eminently practical and pragmatic approach, whilst welcomed, cannot be taken for granted, and, once again, professional advice should be sought.

Statutory payments

21.87 Statutory payments, for example under the *Landlord and Tenant Act 1954* or the *Agricultural Tenancies Act 1995*, are outside the scope of VAT. But if the landlord and tenant agree that the tenant will receive payments over and above those provided for by statute, then the additional payments will be exempt, with the option to tax. In such cases, it is the tenant who makes the supply, and therefore the option to tax rests with the tenant. Examples of 'outside the scope payments' often encountered in practice are payments for residual milk quotas and payments for manurial values.

Compulsory purchase

21.88 A compulsory purchase will arise in cases where a local or central government body issues a notice to the owner of a piece of land, requiring that the land be sold to the body issuing the notice. Although this is clearly a sale under a statutory compulsion, it is nevertheless a business activity for the vendor. The VAT liability is not affected by the fact that the sale is 'forced', and the liability will be that which would apply, if the sale was being made on an entirely voluntary basis—i.e. usually exempt with the option to tax.

Dilapidations

21.89 Dilapidation payments, where the terms of a lease permit the landlord to recover from the tenant the cost of restoring the property to its original condition, at or near the end of a lease, are considered to be compensation, and are also outside the scope of VAT.

Inducements

21.90 An inducement is a sum payable by a landlord to a tenant, to induce the tenant into accepting a lease. Customs currently take the view that inducement payments are payments for a supply which takes place before an interest in land is granted. By this logic, as there has been no supply of the land, the inducement cannot bear the same liability as the supply of the land. An inducement is therefore standard-rated, as it is a payment for agreeing to enter into a transaction.

21.91 Once again, it is easy to see how Customs have arrived at this decision, but it is also easy to see how it could be held that the inducement should also be regarded as a transaction in land or property. The inducement can have no separate existence if the transaction in the property is not completed. In the decision given in the case of *Lubbock Fine & Co v C&E Commrs, CJEC 1993, [1994] STC 101; [1994] 3 All ER 705*, the European Court of Justice recognised that transactions affecting rights and interests in property should bear the same liability as the grant of the interest in the property. (This point has recently been considered by the VAT tribunal in the case of *Cantor Fitzgerald International (15070)*, in which it was confirmed that the liability of a variation to a contractual relationship should bear the same liability as the original contractual relationship.) As an inducement clearly has an effect on a supply of land, it could be argued that the inducement should bear the same liability as the supply of the land itself. This is another area which Customs are thought to have under review. However for the time being, the liability of an inducement is standard-rated.

21.92 A slightly different type of inducement takes place where a landlord agrees to allow the tenant to finish off or fit out a property to his own requirements, and to meet the tenants' costs in doing so. Once again, Customs take the view that there is a supply by the tenant—albeit in this case it will be a supply of construction services, and/or alteration, and/or fitting out works. These supplies, if made to the landlord by an independent contractor would be standard-rated for VAT, and so they will be similarly liable, if made by the tenant.

21.93 Here too, it could be argued that this is a transaction affecting the letting and leasing of the property between landlord and tenant, but the argument is less sustainable, and it seems unlikely that Customs will alter their view that landlords' contributions to tenants fitting out costs are always standard-rated.

Surrenders

21.94 A tenant may surrender his interest in a property back to the landlord. Depending on the state of the property market, the landlord may pay the tenant a sum in return for surrendering his interest. This is an ordinary, straightforward, surrender and it seems clear beyond any reasonable doubt that the tenant has supplied his interest in the land, albeit back to the original landlord. The supply is therefore an exempt supply (*VATA 1994, 9 Sch, Group 1, Note (1)*) with the option to tax. Once again, the option to tax rests with the tenant, as it is he who makes the supply of his interest in the land or building. If the tenant has opted to tax, output tax will be due on the payment he receives.

Reverse surrenders

21.95 When the property market is depressed, tenants will often seek to rid themselves of onerous leases, by surrendering their remaining interest back to the landlord. In a depressed market, the landlord will usually refuse to accept such a surrender unless the tenant pays him to do so. This is a 'reverse' surrender because, although the surrender still passes to the landlord, the payment also passes to the landlord.

21.96 When both supply and payment pass in the same direction, this will give rise to the question of accounting for VAT. It is normally the person receiving the payment who accounts for output tax, but in the case of reverse surrenders, the person receiving the payment is also the person receiving the supply.

21.97 This conundrum has been considered by both Customs and the VAT tribunals. Initially, Customs took the view that, following *Lubbock Fine*, reverse surrenders were not interests in land, but were payments to a landlord for releasing the tenant from a future onerous obligation—and hence always standard-rated.

21.98 Two VAT tribunal cases dealt with the question of whose option should apply to a reverse surrender. In the case of *Marbourne Ltd (12670)*, the tribunal decided that the option to tax a reverse surrender lay with the tenant. This would have led to the bizarre result of an option made by the tenant forcing the landlord to account for tax to Customs.

21.99 In a different ruling, given in the case of *Central Capital Corporation Ltd (13319)*, the VAT tribunal held that the option lay with the person who received the payment which, for a reverse surrender, is the landlord. As a result, Customs changed their earlier policy and now accept that a reverse surrender is in fact an interest in land, hence exempt with the option to tax. See C&E Business Brief 17/94, 12 September 1994 and Business Brief 18/95, 6 September 1995. The legal provisions are contained in *VATA 1994, 9 Sch, Group 1, Notes (1) and (1A)*.

Co-ownership

21.100 In strict legal terms, where land or buildings are owned by more than one person, they are held in trust. This is a complex legal situation which, fortunately, need not be explored further in what is intended to be a general broad-ranging consideration of VAT.

21.101 Somewhat simpler, and easier to understand, is the concept that co-owners may make taxable supplies of the property they own. But if co-owners have a single legal existence, which they do, the question of registration for VAT when taxable supplies are made is less simple to resolve. Current VAT legislation has no provision in force allowing registration of co-owners as such. Customs therefore register co-owners as if they were a partnership. As property developers may wish to avoid entering into 'real' partnerships, it is important to remember that this type of registration is not a true partnership, either in form or substance. It is often, and probably more correctly, referred to as a quasi-partnership, and it is understood that within

Customs headquarters, this is the term used to differentiate between 'real' partnerships and VAT registration for co-owners of land.

21.102 If co-owners have a liability to register, Customs' 'quasi-partnership' arrangements allow them to do so, and also to opt to tax, and recover VAT incurred. In an attempt to provide for a more specific and legally correct mechanism for the registration of co-owners of property, legislation introduced in the 1995 Budget found its way into *VATA 1994* as *section 51A*. This legislation would allow co-owners to register as a single new entity, the 'property-owner'. However, this legislation is dormant, as it has not yet been brought into force. Customs continue to register co-owners of property as a quasi-partnership.

Beneficial interests and trustees

21.103 One of the complexities of land law is that property may be held in trust for others. Thus the legal title to a piece of land may be held by a trustee or trustees, but the benefit of the income arising from the land can pass to a third party. For VAT purposes, it will be the case more often than not, that Customs will regard the beneficiary, rather than the trustees, as being the person who is deemed to be selling, leasing or letting the property. The legal interest held by the trustees is therefore separated from the beneficial interest, which is held by the person(s) receiving the benefit of the income accruing from the property.

21.104 Where the benefit accrues directly to someone other than the owner of the legal title, then it will be the owner of the beneficial interest whom Customs will hold accountable for any VAT liability, and who will bear the obligation to register for VAT. But of course, it will then be the beneficiaries who have the ability to opt to tax, and to recover any input tax (*VATA 1994, 10 Sch 8*).

21.105 When the benefit accrues to the trustees—that is to say, the trustees have absolute and complete discretion (within the limits of trust law) over how the income is distributed and to whom, current VAT legislation has no provision in force allowing registration of trustees as such. Accordingly, Customs register the trustees for VAT as a single taxable person if taxable supplies are made.

21.106 Strictly speaking, of course, the benefit can never accrue directly to trustees, as they would then be placed in breach of trust. For the purposes of deciding who has the obligation to register for VAT, when taxable supplies are made it is, however, convenient to think in terms of the trustees having the beneficial interest where they possess the discretion to distribute revenue accruing from land.

Service charges

21.107 Leases between landlords and tenants will commonly lay down that the landlord shall provide, at the tenants' expense, for the upkeep of the building as a whole. The lease will either provide that the rental payment shall include a charge for this service, or that the tenants shall suffer an additional charge, over and above the basic rental. These charges are service charges, and may sometimes be referred to as 'maintenance charges' or 'additional rent'.

21.108 If the service charge satisfies certain conditions, then (even if it is separately invoiced) it will be deemed to be part of the basic overall supply of the property, and carry the same VAT liability. The conditions are:

(a)   it is a charge connected with the external fabric of the building, or the common parts of the building (as opposed to the individual demised areas occupied by individual tenants); and

(b)   it is paid for by all tenants through a common service charge.

21.109 A charge which relates to a tenant's own demised area, for example painting a reception area which a tenant has constructed within his own exclusively rented floor space, will not be a service charge bearing the same liability as the rent. It will be a separate charge for painting services, and hence standard-rated for VAT. However, a charge for painting the foyer and reception area of a multi-tenanted building which is raised by the landlord and shared by all tenants, albeit perhaps on a pro-rata basis depending on such variables as usage, floor space occupancy etc., is likely to be classed as a service charge, and will bear the same VAT liability as the rent.

21.110 Thus, for commercial buildings, service charges will be either exempt or standard-rated, but will always bear the same liability as the rent.

21.111 Service charges for domestic accommodation follow the same broad lines of logic, but with an important exception. Where domestic accommodation is held on a leasehold basis, there is a supply of an interest in land from the landlord to the tenant. The service charge (again, as with commercial property, provided that it is a true service charge relating to the fabric of the building, or the common parts) will bear the same liability as the supply of the accommodation, which is always exempt. Individual charges for demised parts will, again as is the case for commercial property, be standard-rated. However, where property is held freehold, it is not unusual for freeholders to have to pay service charges relating to common parts. But here, of course, there can be no supply of any interest in land, as the property is already held freehold. The service charge would therefore have to be automatically standard-rated, but for the fact that under the terms of an Extra-Statutory Concession (ESC 2.22, 'Exemption for all domestic service charges'—see C&E Notice No 48, September 1997) the service provider can choose to exempt his supply.

21.112 It is important to remember that this Extra-Statutory Concession is permissive, not mandatory, and the service provider can, if he wishes, continue to charge VAT. If exemption is chosen, the service provider may suffer a restriction on his input tax recovery, and he can be expected to take any irrecoverable VAT into account in setting the level of charges which will be levied on the freeholders. As has been discussed earlier, exemption does not bring with it a complete relief from VAT and, in the end, the freeholders will find that the service providers' VAT costs are passed on to them, even though the invoices they receive do not show a separate charge to VAT.

Supplies of fuel and power within a service charge

21.113 There is one apparent anomaly within the VAT liability of service charge which is worth a separate mention. It applies only to commercial property, and arises if a landlord makes a charge for unmetered fuel and power. In such cases, for VAT purposes, there is no separate supply of what would otherwise be standard-rated fuel and power. If the supply is genuinely unmetered (i.e. the charge is not based directly or indirectly on the tenant's actual consumption), then there is a single supply of (fuelled and powered) accommodation, which will be exempt with the option to tax.

Chapter 22

Public Houses

Introduction

22.1 There are four types of public house, which can be categorised by the degree of interest which the publican holds in the property, with each having different implications for VAT registration and accounting purposes.

Managed houses

22.2 These are public houses owned by the brewery. The manager, an employee of the brewery, is employed by them to run the operation. The retail sales of beers, wines, spirits, etc. will be supplied under the brewery's VAT registration, and it is they who will account for VAT on the sales.

The brewery can franchise the catering side of the operation to the manager. Thus the catering services provided become a private enterprise of the manager, and as such, these activities are considered separately for VAT registration purposes. The normal registration and liability rules will apply if the registration limits are exceeded.

A public house does not have to be owned by a brewery to be a managed house. The term can apply equally to circumstances where the owner of the premises is not a brewery but runs the business through a manager. The owner is then the person liable to be registered for VAT and to account for output tax on sales (subject to the comments above regarding catering).

Tenanted houses

22.3 These are public houses (tied houses) where the tenant rents the property from the brewery which owns the premises. Under normal arrangements the tenant is required by the terms of the contract to buy all his 'wet' purchases (beers, spirits, etc.), and sometimes also crisps and tobacco, etc., from the brewery.

The tenant is a separate legal entity responsible for accounting for VAT if the turnover of all of his business activities exceeds the VAT registration threshold. Therefore, it is possible that whilst the turnover of the public house does not exceed the registration limit on its own, when considered with other

22.4 VAT Business by Business

business activities of the tenant, the combined turnover may exceed the registration limit and the tenant must register and account for VAT accordingly.

The brewery, as landlord, is able to exercise the 'option to tax' in respect of the properties it owns. Where the option is invoked, VAT would be accounted for on any rents charged by the brewery. It should be noted that the option to tax cannot normally apply to domestic accommodation (e.g. the tenant's apartments); however, this may not be the case with residential accommodation within a public house, and the tribunal decision in *AJ White (15388)* should be considered.

Leased houses

22.4 This arrangement is very similar to tenanted houses, except that there will generally be no requirement to purchase stock from the brewery which owns the premises. Apart from this, the differences between the two situations relate to how the agreements between the parties operate to compensate the brewery for the possible reduction in income from reduced stock sales under a leased house, as opposed to a tenanted house, arrangement, and the additional risks for the publican, who will usually be responsible for any repairs and maintenance to the property.

Free houses

22.5 These are public houses where the publican owns the freehold or leasehold of the property independent of a brewery. Therefore, there is no restriction on the sourcing of the 'wet' purchases.

The VAT position is similar to that for a tenanted or leased house, in that the publican in his business capacity is responsible for all aspects of VAT accounting in respect of the activity.

Liability of supplies

General principles

22.6 Normally all sales from public houses are at the standard rate (i.e. alcoholic and soft beverages, snacks and confectionery) and VAT would be calculated and accounted for under a VAT retail scheme. The usual scheme operated prior to 1 August 1997 was Scheme A; this merely required the publican to account for the VAT element of cash takings on the basis that these were all tax-inclusive. However, from 1 August 1997 the retail schemes existing at that time were withdrawn and a new set of retail schemes was introduced. Scheme A (and Scheme F) were replaced by the 'point of sale scheme' ('TPOSS') which operates on similar principles. TPOSS is now the retail scheme generally used in public houses.

Public Houses **22.9**

It is usual for a public house to receive income from ancillary supplies in addition to those mentioned above. Some of the other supplies which may be made, and upon which VAT must be accounted for, are as follows.

Catering

22.7 Most public houses now supply meals, snacks and, in many cases, full restaurant facilities. If the catering is an activity of the registered trader, VAT must be accounted for on the takings from those supplies. Where there are some zero-rated sales, for example, a public house making sales of cold takeaway sandwiches to local office workers which are eaten away from the premises, these sales fall within, and should be accounted for under, TPOSS.

Where it is not possible to calculate the level of zero-rated catering sales using TPOSS (e.g. because the tills used do not distinguish between the VAT liabilities of the different types of sales and the business operation is too hectic to record the liability of any particular sale), Customs have issued details of a concession (Public Notice 727, Appendix C) which enables zero-rated sales to be estimated on the basis of a sample taken during the period. Where this concession is used, the publican must be able to prove that the sample is representative.

Accommodation and functions

22.8 The provision of overnight accommodation by a public house is always standard-rated. Whilst in some instances the landlord's wife may run the bed and breakfast facility as a separate business below the registration limit, serious consideration must be given to whether this position can be challenged by Customs under the disaggregation provisions (see paragraph 22.15 below). In normal circumstances the provision of overnight accommodation will be part of the main business activity and VAT must be accounted for accordingly.

The hire of a room, where the primary supply is that of the room, is exempt from VAT, unless the option to tax has been made in respect of the premises (see *Tolley's VAT 1998/99, paragraph 42.20*). Where the room hire is ancillary to a supply of catering or other facilities, e.g. for a wedding or other function, the hire will be a taxable supply of facilities.

Gaming and amusement machines

22.9 The majority of public houses have some type of coin-operated gaming or amusement machine on the premises, whether it be a one-armed bandit, video game or bar billiards table. These machines are not usually owned by the publican but hired from a specialist firm. The takings, i.e. the net balance after the deduction of amounts returned as winnings and restoration of the float, are liable to VAT at the standard rate. Whether it is

22.10 VAT Business by Business

the hirer or the publican who has to account for the VAT on the takings will depend on who exercises day-to-day control over the machine and who is entitled to the takings. For gaming machines, this will be the person named on the permit issued under *Part III* of the *Gaming Act*. For amusement machines, it will vary according to the circumstances. Where an amusement machine is hired and operated by the publican, it is the publican's responsibility to account for VAT on the takings. Any charge by the owner of the machine is a hire charge, and VAT thereon will be recoverable by the publican as input tax.

The situation is more complex where the amusement machine is owned and operated by a third party. In these circumstances the third party will collect the takings and account for the VAT on them, and the publican will be given a percentage share of the income. The tribunal has held that such payments are consideration for a standard-rated supply of facilities by the publican to the hirer (see *Wolverhampton & Dudley Breweries plc, [1990] VATTR 131 (5351)* and *Sinclair Collis Ltd (14950)*). However, Customs have appealed against the *Sinclair Collis* decision and contend that the supply is of a right to occupy land and is therefore exempt (or taxable if the publican has elected to waive exemption). The position could be put beyond doubt where the contractual arrangements are clear as to the services provided, for example by the publican being paid a commission.

Vending machines

22.10 In many public houses the sale of cigarettes and other goods is through wall-mounted vending machines. The supplier of the machines normally fills them, removes the money and is responsible for the gross takings. The publican is paid a commission based on the volume of goods sold. When considering the VAT liability of the commission received the comments above in respect of gaming machines and bar games should be taken into account.

Sales of cigarettes, etc. over the counter are generally from the publican's own stock and VAT should be accounted for in the normal manner.

Payphones

22.11 Most public houses will have a payphone. The takings from these will be taxable, with the input tax on the associated bill being recoverable. In the instance where the payphone is supplied by an external operator who collects the income, only the value of any commission received will be subject to VAT (again see the comments at paragraph 22.9 above in relation to gaming machines).

VAT recovery

22.12 Public houses are, in the main, fully taxable businesses and, therefore, are able to recover in full the VAT they incur on business purchases, subject to the normal rules. However, if they make exempt supplies, e.g. of room hire, it is conceivable, although in the normal course of events unlikely, that they could be partly exempt in a given period. See *Tolley's VAT 1998/99, chapter 49*).

Accounting and record-keeping

Purchases

22.13 The use of a retail scheme does not simplify the record-keeping requirements in respect of purchases, which will follow the normal record-keeping requirements (see *Tolley's VAT 1998/99, paragraph 57.7*).

Sales

22.14 Whilst a publican must maintain normal VAT records in respect of sales to other VAT-registered businesses (see *Tolley's VAT 1998/99, chapter 40*), virtually all of the supplies will be to the public and will fall within the VAT retail scheme. TPOSS only requires a business to keep records of daily gross takings for total goods sold at each applicable VAT rate. The scheme does not specify how this should be done. Nevertheless, a publican should be aware that if records such as till rolls and stock records are maintained, even if not for the purposes of VAT accounting, they are considered to form part of the records of the business, and as such, Customs have the right to examine them upon request.

Customs' experience of the licensed trade has indicated that, due to the high volume of transactions and cash sales, and the limited documentation, there is potential for the publican to manipulate his takings figures for the purpose of underdeclaring output tax. Therefore, the trade is an area which requires close attention and this is borne out by the number of VAT tribunal cases that have been heard.

When visiting a public house Customs will normally undertake to verify the declared takings by marking-up the value of the goods purchased to arrive at an expected sales figure, based on their experience of the trade and comparability with other public houses. It is, therefore, important for the publican to maintain correct and accurate VAT accounting records. To this end, it is possible to buy an accounting ledger specifically designed for the licensed trade.

22.15 VAT Business by Business

The maintenance of records will give confidence to anyone reviewing the income of the business and will assist the publican in answering any of Customs' enquiries and refuting any allegations that might be made.

Separate records should be maintained in respect of those areas which are most likely to generate discrepancies between Customs' credibility checks and actual sales. Details of the areas at issue are outlined in paragraph 22.16 *et seq.* below.

Practical points

Business splitting

22.15 It is common practice within the licensed trade to separate the business into retail sales of wet goods on the one hand, and catering supplies (dry goods) on the other. A common example is for the publican to run the wet sales and his wife to run the catering business, the receipts of which might be below the registration limit. If it is argued that two separate entities are operating the different aspects of the business, the operations must be run so as to avoid Customs alleging that the arrangements are artificial and that in fact there is only one business. If Customs' allegations were successful, it would result in the catering activities being combined with the husband's business for VAT accounting purposes.

Historically, it was possible to maintain that two entities were operating separate businesses from the same premises if the records of the two businesses were kept separately and any interaction between the operations was treated commercially. However, in March 1997, Customs introduced new legislation (*VATA 1994, 1 Sch 1A*) stipulating that the criteria for considering such arrangements to be artificial were based upon how closely the parties were bound to one another by financial, economic and organisational links. Therefore, it is now more difficult to defend such arrangements where there are strong organisational links, such as shared staff, equipment, etc.

Where such arrangements are in place, it is necessary to ensure that the following criteria are met in order to refute any suggestion by Customs that the activities are inseparable:

- a separate bank account should be operated for each business and should be in the name of the person carrying on the business;

- any wages and national insurance contributions paid in respect of staff that are employed in the particular business should be borne by the person carrying on that business;

- for income tax purposes each business should be assessed separately;

- the person carrying on each business should be responsible for all the trading activities;

- the normal day-to-day records should be separately maintained and annual accounts drawn up in the name of each business;

- purchase and any sales invoices should be made out in the name of the person who is operating the business;

- premises and equipment used by the businesses, where possible, should be kept separately. If this is not practical, then the registered person (the publican) should supply any goods or services such as catering equipment or hire of rooms to the non-registered connected person (e.g. the caterer), at a charge based on the open market value and, if appropriate, add VAT accordingly.

Wastage

22.16 The issue of wastage and VAT is not normally one which concerns a publican until such time as Customs challenge the credibility of the sales figures. Therefore, it is wise to be aware of possible causes of wastage, especially prior to commenting to Customs in respect of any discrepancies that have been identified.

Wastage occurs in public houses for a variety of reasons which can be categorised as follows.

Storage of beer

22.17 A small amount of beer which cannot be drawn off is left in the cask, and will not usually be sold. The 'bottoms', as they are referred to, are accepted as wastage and an allowance is generally made.

Kegs are designed to deliver the full barrel, and therefore, generally, no allowance is given for anything remaining in the container. However, as this beer is dispensed under gas pressure, too much gas will result in too big a head on the beer which can cause losses.

Tanks are cleaned when empty, although there may in fact be up to three gallons remaining in the bottom. As the beer is generally in sound condition, it is unlikely that it will be thrown away. Nevertheless, the allowance for wastage should be similar to the allowance given for 'bottoms', but it will be up to the publican to substantiate his own case.

22.18 VAT Business by Business

Pipe cleaning

22.18 Beer drawn through the pipes after they are cleaned may be contaminated by the detergents and water used, and therefore some of it must be drawn off and thrown away. The amount of beer lost during pipe cleaning depends on the length and bore of the pipes. It is up to the publican to ensure that he gets an adequate allowance if the question of pipe cleaning is significant.

Drawing off

22.19 It is normal for a publican to draw off a pint or so from each pump before commencing each day/session of business, as the beer may be flat. The drawn-off beer may be returned to its casks or used in mixer drinks; however, a publican may, through custom or necessity, require it to be thrown away, and if this is the case, an allowance must be given.

Spillage

22.20 This is the beer which collects in the drip trays at the dispense points. If the publican is using the brim measure type of glass, it is possible that an overspill can occur. If oversize glasses are being used which have a Crown stamp mark, it should be possible to serve a full-pint or half-pint without any spillage. There is generally very little wastage on the changing over from one cask to another or in the tapping of a new cask.

Breakages

22.21 Wastage will also occur from time to time through the breakage of bottled beers, wines and spirits and customer rejections.

Total losses

22.22 The report of the Price Commission in 1977 *Beer Prices and Margins* (Price Commission Report No. 31), allowed a rate of 3% to cover all forms of wastage of draught beer. If there is a high proportion of traditional ale, then this percentage can increase to 4%. Wastage through breakages was not expected to exceed 1%.

Off-sales

22.23 Off-sales will not normally generate the same level of profit as bar sales. Therefore, for any significant volume of off-sales, it is recommended that a record be maintained to support the reduced margins applicable.

Prices and price reductions

22.24 Breweries recommend the selling price of their products for public bar sales. The majority of tenants adopt these prices, which are required to be displayed within the public house, in the public bars, and they will usually be noted by Customs on their visits. Where there is increased competition, selling prices may be reduced by a few pence to entice the customer, and records of the charges can often be useful in contesting suggestions that takings should be higher than they actually are. Equally, details of 'Happy Hour' promotions and prices should be recorded.

Pilferage by employees

22.25 If a publican contends that he has dismissed employees because of theft, thereby claiming that his stock has been reduced and not sold, Customs will normally enquire about the action taken to substantiate this claim, for example, asking for confirmation in the form of insurance claims made and paid or evidence of the involvement of the police.

If, however, it is cash that has been stolen, Customs will take the view that this has occurred after a taxable supply has been made and that VAT should be accounted for on any shortage. This view was upheld by the VAT tribunal in *G Benton, [1975] VATTR 138 (185)*.

Own consumption

22.26 Where a publican supplies himself from his own bar with goods, such as beers, wines and spirits, for personal use, this supply is taxable on the cost. VAT must be accounted for on these supplies, the value of which can be taken as cost.

Free food and drinks

Employees

22.27 Where a publican supplies free food and drink to his employees for no consideration, the value of the supplies is taken as nil and there is no requirement to account for output tax. Input tax is still recoverable.

Customers, draymen, darts teams, etc. and outside bodies

22.28 Publicans may on occasions provide food and drink free of charge to persons other than employees for consumption either on the premises or outside.

Where, for example, bottles are supplied to a local charity free of charge (and with nothing being supplied in return), provided that the supply is not part of

22.29 *VAT Business by Business*

a succession of gifts to the same body and the cost to the publican does not exceed £15, no output tax has to be accounted for. Input tax is still recoverable. If these conditions are not met, output tax will have to be accounted for on the cost of the supply.

Where cigarettes, drinks, etc. are supplied to draymen or, for example, to darts, dominoes or pool teams for immediate consumption, this is regarded as business entertainment and the publican cannot recover the input tax on the purchase. As it will usually not be possible to identify such goods, Customs allow output tax to be accounted for on the supply of the goods at cost (i.e. equivalent to the input tax which would have been restricted).

Conclusion

22.29 As stated at paragraph 22.14 above, the potential ease with which a publican can suppress takings, particularly by acquiring purchases other than from his normal suppliers (e.g. wholesale warehouses, or shuttle trips to France), means that the licensed trade continues to be seen by Customs as an area of high risk. This is borne out by the significant number of cases that Customs have taken to tribunal after concluding that VAT has been under-declared following a visit. It is therefore in a publican's interest to ensure that he has correctly recorded takings and is in a position to provide accurate figures which can be reconciled to the VAT paid and are supported by purchases. If this information is not available, Customs can be expected to query whether the takings declared are accurate and to issue an estimated assessment.

Chapter 23

Retailers and Retail Schemes

Introduction

23.1 The great majority of businesses which deal direct with the public are not required to issue detailed invoices for their sales nor, because they deal very largely for cash, do they need to keep their sales records in the same detail or format as manufacturing or wholesaling businesses would expect to do. They therefore do not have the same discipline of issuing VAT invoices that other businesses have and consequently would find difficulty in determining sales and output tax by conventional means.

The Commissioners therefore have authority to allow 'retailers' to operate special arrangements known as retail schemes for determining the amount of output tax which they have to account for on their retail sales. It should be noted that, under the relevant regulations, parts of *Notice 727—Retail Schemes* and the supporting notices dealing with individual schemes have legal force.

In determining who can use a retail scheme, a 'retailer' is someone, not necessarily a shopkeeper, who deals primarily with the final consumer. Thus the use of a retail scheme is open to businesses such as mail order houses and those supplying services primarily to the general public, such as places of entertainment, hotels and restaurants. In Customs' view, however, a retail scheme should only be used where the retailer cannot be expected to account for VAT in the normal way, which, whilst it does not require the issue of tax invoices to unregistered customers, does require that a retailer can identify the tax-exclusive value, and the VAT value, of each individual supply. Customs also take the view that retail supplies are generally of low value and are made to a large number of customers in small quantities. This may preclude a furniture retailer, for example, from using a retail scheme.

A retail scheme may be used for a distinct retail part of a larger business which accounts for the remainder of its VAT liability in the usual way. However, sales to other VAT-registered businesses must be excluded from a retail scheme. The only exception to this is occasional cash sales, for example a DIY shop selling materials to a VAT-registered builder.

23.2 VAT Business by Business

VAT Liability

23.2 The retail schemes are methods of arriving at the value of taxable retail supplies ('gross takings') and of apportioning these takings between rates of VAT, which are currently the standard rate (17.5%), the reduced rate (5%) and the zero rate (0%). Once the VAT-inclusive sales have been apportioned between rates, the relevant VAT fraction is applied to calculate the VAT amount due to Customs & Excise.

Standard Schemes and Bespoke Schemes

23.3 Customs & Excise have introduced three classes of standard schemes for retailers to use. They are:

(i) the Point of Sale scheme—this scheme requires retailers to identify the VAT liability of goods or services at the time the sales are made.

(ii) the Apportionment schemes—these schemes apportion sales on the basis of an apportionment of purchases between the different rates, but may require the use of anticipated retail selling prices; and

(iii) the Direct Calculation schemes — these use anticipated selling prices of the 'minority rate' sales deducted from total sales to give a presumed value for sales at the most common VAT rate.

A retailer can choose any of the published schemes for which he or she is eligible. However, Customs & Excise may refuse the use of a retail scheme if the retailer can reasonably be expected to account for VAT in the normal way (e.g. retailers who can identify the value of, and VAT payable on, each supply; or if the chosen scheme does not produce a fair and reasonable result; or for the protection of the revenue.

Adaptations to the schemes

23.4 Special arrangements apply to florists, retail caterers selling take-away food, and retail pharmacists and other businesses which buy goods at one rate of VAT and sell them at another.

Bespoke Retail Schemes

23.5 The standard schemes are not available to retailers with a VAT-exclusive turnover in excess of £10 million per annum. Once the value of a retailer's sales in the last 12 months exceeds this amount, it is required to negotiate a 'bespoke' retail scheme agreement with its local VAT office. A bespoke scheme may still be based on one of the published schemes described above, but it will be tailored to suit the individual business.

Daily gross takings ('DGT')

23.6 A trader who opts to use a retail scheme must keep a record of his daily gross takings. This will usually be a till roll or similar record, adjusted for certain relevant events. Before March 1997 there were two methods used to determine 'gross takings', the 'standard' method and the 'optional' method. Since the withdrawal of the standard method from 1 March 1997, however, only the method which was previously termed the 'optional' method can be used.

Definition of gross takings from 1 March 1997

23.7 Gross takings are based on payments made for cash sales plus the value of the credit sales made at the time of supply. Thus, when payments for credit sales are received, they should be excluded from the gross takings. Payments for credit sales which are made prior to the adoption of a scheme should be ignored and excluded from the scheme calculations.

An obvious disadvantage from 1 March 1997 is that, where supplies on credit give rise to a bad debt, output tax will already have been accounted for at the time of the supply but credit will not be given until the debt is at least six months old.

Additions, subtractions and adjustments

23.8 There are a number of factors which can affect the amount of gross takings that have to be recorded. The following should be particularly borne in mind—

(i) *Cash discounts.* The figure to be recorded is the full amount payable at the time of supply after any discount which is taken up by the customer at the time of the supply.

(ii) *Credit cards, trading cheques and similar transactions.* These are treated as cash, the value of the supply being included in the gross takings.

(iii) *Credit transactions.* The full value of any supplies on credit must be added to DGT. A separate charge for the credit facilities is exempt if disclosed to the customer and should be excluded from DGT. When instalment payments are subsequently received, they should also be excluded from DGT.

Additional rules may apply, however, depending on the way the credit sales are financed:

(a) *Supplies involving a finance company.* If you arrange credit for your customer through a finance company, Customs' view is that

23.8 VAT Business by Business

in most cases you should include the full amount paid by the customer in your DGT at the time you make the supply. However, in some circumstances VAT may only be due on the amount you receive from the finance company. Customs & Excise Business Brief 15/96 explains the circumstances in which this treatment may be appropriate.

    (b) *Self-financed credit supplies.* If you make a separate charge for credit (additional to the cash price) and you disclose it to the customer, this is exempt from VAT and should be excluded from your DGT.

(iv) *Delivery charges.* The most common examples of delivered goods are milk and newspapers. If the contract with the customer is for the supply of 'delivered goods' and no separate charge is made for such deliveries, there is only a single supply, the liability of which follows the liability of the goods supplied. A separate delivery charge to cover delivery, postage, etc. is a separate supply of delivery services and must be excluded from DGT, and VAT accounted for as appropriate.

(v) *Deposits.* A refundable deposit (e.g. to cover the safe return of goods) can be excluded from DGT. However, if the deposit is accepted as being an initial payment for goods, or to secure the purchase of goods, then it must be included in the gross takings as a part payment. This applies, for example, to hamper sales and Christmas clubs.

(vi) *Disbursements.* Payments made by customers in respect of disbursements (e.g. as agents) must be excluded from the gross takings.

(vii) *Dishonoured or unsigned cheques.* A reduction to DGT may be made for dishonoured cheques, credit cards and similar transactions. This also applies to counterfeit currency and foreign currency for which no credit is given by the bank.

(viii) *Electronic payments.* These are treated as cash and included in gross takings.

(ix) *Exempt supplies.* Payment for exempt supplies (e.g. rent received) should be excluded from the scheme calculations. Also, certain retail supplies will be exempt (or outside the scope of VAT) and sales of these items must be excluded from gross takings. Examples are lottery tickets, stamps and phonecards.

(x) *Goods on sale or return.* A record should be kept of goods supplied on a 'sale or return' basis. The goods remain part of the supplier's stock until they are adopted. Once adopted, the amount payable should be included in gross takings.

(xi) *Own use and consumption.* If the retailer decides to take into his private use goods which he has initially obtained for retailing, this constitutes a taxable supply of goods. It is necessary to include in the gross takings the actual cost price of the goods that have been appropriated. The

Retailers and Retail Schemes 23.8

landlord of a public house and the proprietor of a corner-shop, grocery or greengrocery is often in this position.

(xii) *Part-exchange*. The important point to bear in mind here is that where goods or services are supplied on a part-exchange basis, the transaction must not be netted off. The gross takings figure must include the full selling price of the article sold. A separate record must be kept of the part-exchange transactions, showing the amounts included in the gross takings. If the goods taken in part-exchange are from another registered supplier or retailer, then the related VAT can be deducted as input tax as long as a proper VAT invoice is obtained. In many cases, the item taken in part-exchange is from a non-registered supplier (e.g. a member of the public) and there will be no input VAT to be reclaimed. It is important to note that when these part-exchange goods are resold, the fact that they have been purchased from a non-registered supplier does not affect the situation that the retailer's selling price has to be inclusive of VAT and brought into the scheme calculations in the normal way. It may however be possible to use one of the special schemes for second-hand goods, under which VAT may only be due on the margin made on resale.

(xiii) *Payments in kind*. If a debt is settled by means of a payment in kind, the normal selling price, including VAT, of the supplies made must still be included in the gross takings.

(xiv) *Refunds*. Where refunds are made to customers because goods are faulty, unsuitable or have been inadvertently overcharged, then the amount of such refunds may be subtracted from the daily gross takings. Care must be taken, however, when goodwill or similar payments are made, as these cannot be deducted from DGT.

(xv) *Repossessed goods*. Where goods have been supplied on hire-purchase and are subsequently repossessed, gross takings may be reduced by the amount of the outstanding payments for the goods. The onward supply of repossessed goods is treated in the same way as the supply of any other goods, VAT being accounted for via the gross takings, unless sold under a second-hand scheme, where the second-hand scheme rules will come into operation.

(xvi) *Retail export schemes and exports*. Goods that are exported directly may be zero-rated provided that the proper documentary evidence is obtained. Retailers are also allowed to zero-rate certain goods that are sold to overseas visitors by using the retail export scheme. Retailers must account for VAT through gross takings when the goods are sold but they may adjust the output tax at the end of the VAT period by allowing for the exports. This will entail totalling up the amounts shown on the officially certified forms returned during that period.

23.8 VAT Business by Business

(xvii) *Returnable containers*. The full retail selling price of goods, including the charge for the returnable container (e.g. a lemonade bottle), must be included in the gross takings. Amounts refunded to customers in exchange for these returned empty containers may be deducted when working out the gross takings.

(xviii) *Sale of debts*. There is no adjustment required to DGT as the correct output tax is accounted for when the sale is made. Receipts in respect of the sale of debts must be dealt with outside the retail scheme.

(xix) *Sale of discount vouchers (or discount cards)*. If a retailer sells such a voucher or card entitling the holder to discounts on purchases from that retailer, the payment received must be included in DGT. If a retailer sells vouchers or cards which give discounts with *several traders*, this is a separate standard-rated supply of services and must be dealt with outside the retail scheme.

(xx) *Theft*. VAT has to be accounted for on any monies stolen, as the supply has been made and payment has been received. Where stock is stolen, there is no supply and therefore no requirement to account for output tax. Independent evidence of the theft (e.g. an insurance claim or report to the police) may be required.

(xxi) *Tokens*. Where book tokens, record tokens, gift tokens, etc. are sold for their face value, the amount received should be omitted from the gross takings. When goods are supplied in return for such tokens, the face value of the tokens accepted should be included in the calculation of gross takings. Where tokens are sold at a price greater than their face value, the additional charge is always subject to VAT and this amount should be dealt with outside the retail scheme. Where tokens are sold at a discount, and therefore at less than face value, then the amount received can be omitted from the gross takings. When these tokens are redeemed, only the discounted amount is included in gross takings, as long as the discounted tokens can be separately identified from other face value tokens.

(xxii) *Voids*. DGT may be reduced by the value of void transactions (i.e. where an incorrect transaction has been voided at the time of the error).

(xxiii) *Vouchers*. Discount vouchers, such as '50% off' or '£1 off', which are accepted as part payment towards a supply, should be excluded from gross takings at the time the supply is made. Any payment subsequently received from another source, such as the manufacturer, should be included in gross takings in the period in which it is received. If a retailer makes a handling charge to a manufacturer for handling its coupons, this is an exempt supply and the payment received should be excluded from gross takings. Vouchers which have no specified value but which can be redeemed for whole items are subject to different rules, as follows:

- No VAT is due on vouchers which are issued to customers making specific purchases and which are then used to obtain 'reward goods'. Nor is any VAT due on the supply of the reward gift. The sum paid by the customer for its original purchase is deemed to be consideration both for the main goods and the 'reward goods'.

- Where vouchers of this sort are freely given away by a retailer, no VAT is due on their free issue. When they are redeemed for goods, no VAT is due on the supply if the VAT-exclusive cost of the goods is less than £15. If the cost is greater than £15, then VAT is due on the cost value of those goods.

Goods linked in a promotion

23.9 These include promotions where two different articles are sold for a single price in a combined offer, for example a washing machine with some washing powder; or where a number of articles are sold in a multi-buy offer, for example 'buy two and get a third free'. If both articles are liable at the same rate of tax, there are no additional rules to follow under the point of sale scheme unless any contribution is received from a manufacturer or joint sponsor, in which case this contribution should be included in gross takings at the time of receipt. If the articles are liable at different rates of tax (for example, a jar of coffee with a packet of chocolate biscuits), the selling price must be apportioned in accordance with the usual guidelines (see Appendix E of Notice No 700—*The VAT Guide*).

In the case of goods linked by the manufacturer, the articles may be treated in accordance with the information shown on the supplier's invoice. For example, if the invoice shows separate prices and amounts of tax, the retailer may apportion the selling price on the same basis. As a concession, where the minor article

- is not charged to the customer at a separate price; *and*

- costs the retailer no more than 20% of the total cost of the combined supply (excluding VAT); *and*

- costs the retailer no more than £1 (excluding VAT) if included with goods intended for retail sale; or £5 (excluding VAT) otherwise,

the retailer may, as a concession, account for VAT on the minor article at the same rate as the main article, i.e. no apportionment is necessary.

23.10 *VAT Business by Business*

If an apportionment of the selling price is necessary, the retailer must separate the amount allocated to the zero-rated article from the standard-rated takings before calculating the VAT payable.

There are no additional rules for multi-buys, unless any contribution is received from a manufacturer or joint sponsor. If this contribution represents partial payment for the goods supplied to the retail customer, it should be included in gross takings at the time of receipt. In addition, if the retailer is using a retail scheme that involves estimated selling prices, these prices must be adjusted to reflect the full consideration received for the supply.

If the manufacturer or joint sponsor makes any payment, for example towards advertising, the retailer has made a separate supply of services and this must be dealt with outside the retail scheme.

Change in rate of VAT

23.10 VAT is due on a supply at the rate in force at the time of the supply. Consequently, the tax should be determined by identifying the timing of the sales using the basic rules for determining the time of supply. If the change of rate falls half way through a tax period, a retailer will have to make two calculations, one under the old VAT rate and one under the new rate. This will reflect supplies made before and after the rate change. These amounts should then be added together to give the tax liability for the period.

Choosing a retail scheme

General principles

23.11 The Commissioners have the power to refuse permission to use a scheme (e.g. if they consider it will not reflect the proper liability) but the retailer does have the right to appeal to a VAT tribunal against such refusal. Once a retailer has started to use a scheme, he or she will not normally be allowed to change it except at the end of any complete year of operating it. A scheme must be used for 12 months, unless the retailer becomes ineligible to use it, or Customs allow or require an earlier change. The turnover limits for the schemes apply to the total tax-exclusive turnover from retail supplies. This means, for example, that if a company's total turnover is £20 million, but only £1 million of this is in respect of retail sales, the company may still be eligible for all the schemes.

It is imperative from a tax planning point of view to choose the correct retail scheme from the outset. The choice of scheme can affect a retailer's VAT payments, cashflow and the record-keeping requirements; the wrong choice can prove expensive. A retailer can operate different retail schemes in different parts of its business. This is particularly relevant for large retailers with different trading activities, for example, a supermarket with a retail pharmacy department may choose to separate its food sales from its pharmacy sales and apply different methods of apportioning sales to these distinctly different parts of its business. However, there are restrictions as to how different schemes can be combined. A Point of Sale scheme can be combined with either a Direct Calculation scheme or an Apportionment scheme, but different versions of the Apportionment or Direct Calculation schemes cannot be used together. Furthermore, the Apportionment scheme cannot be used with the Direct Calculation scheme. The methodology of the standard schemes is briefly outlined at paragraphs 23.12 to 23.18 below.

The Point of Sale scheme

23.12 To use this scheme, a retailer must be able to identify the correct VAT liability for a sale at the time it is made, and keep records to verify the value of sales made at each rate of VAT. This can be done, for example, by having separate tills for sales at different rates, or by using tills which can separate sales into departments and use different departments for each different rate. These methods are often reliant on the staff operating them, who must ensure that sales are rung up in the appropriate till or department. Alternatively, it can also be done by using a till system, such as an Electronic Point of Sale (EPOS) system, which is capable of recording sales at item level and VAT coding each item sold using information held in the barcode. However, there is still margin for error even with the most sophisticated EPOS systems, as information held on the bar codes themselves may be incorrect, or information may be lost if the system fails for any reason.

Once a retailer establishes the value of sales at each different rate, it then applies the VAT fraction to calculate the VAT due. A retailer who makes supplies at only one rate of VAT must use this scheme.

The Apportionment schemes

23.13 There are two apportionment schemes which can be used by retail businesses which make supplies at more than one rate of tax.

Apportionment Scheme 1

23.14 This is a simpler scheme designed for smaller businesses with a tax-exclusive turnover not exceeding £1 million. The value of purchases for resale made in the period must be calculated and separated into purchases at different rates of VAT. The proportions of these purchase values are applied to the takings for the period. For example, if 50 per cent of the value of goods purchased for retail sale are standard-rated, then 50 per cent of takings are treated as standard-rated. Output tax is then calculated by applying the relevant VAT fraction (or fractions if more than one positive rate is used) to the apportioned takings figures. Once a year a similar calculation must be performed, based on purchases for the year and takings for the year. The

23.15 VAT Business by Business

VAT thus calculated is compared with the VAT already paid and any over or under payment is corrected on the VAT return.

The scheme is relatively simple, but it assumes that the mark-up is the same for goods at all different rates of VAT. If on average, a business achieves a higher mark-up for zero-rated goods than lower-rated or standard-rated goods, this scheme will not reflect that, and the proportion of sales which are positive-rated will be overstated. This means that more VAT will be due under this scheme than would perhaps be due using a different method.

This scheme cannot be used for supplies of services, or for supplies of goods which a business has made or grown itself, or for supplies of catering.

Apportionment Scheme 2

23.15 This version of the scheme is slightly more complex, and takes into account the different mark-ups applied to different goods by using as it does the resale value of goods rather than the purchase value. Using this scheme, the business calculates the expected selling prices (ESPs) of standard-rated and lower-rated goods received in the period for retail sale. Then the ratio of these goods to the expected selling prices of *all* goods received for retail sale is calculated, and this ratio is applied to the takings for the period.

For example, if 60 per cent of the ESPs of goods purchased for retail sale are standard-rated and 40 per cent are zero-rated, then 60 per cent of takings are treated as standard-rated and 40 per cent as zero-rated. Output tax is then calculated by applying the relevant VAT fraction to these takings figures.

There is no annual adjustment, but for improved accuracy opening stock is included in the calculation in the first period in which the scheme is used, and the ESPs are based on purchases over a rolling 12-month period in order to take account of seasonal trading patterns.

As with Apportionment Scheme 1, this scheme cannot be used for supplies of services or catering. Also, if goods purchased at one rate of VAT are to be sold at another rate, e.g. goods sold on prescription, certain adjustments will be required to ensure that VAT is not overpaid or underpaid. Details of these adjustments can be found at paragraphs 23.30 and 23.31 below. The scheme is available to businesses with an annual tax-exclusive retail turnover of less than £10 million.

The Direct Calculation schemes

23.16 There are two direct calculation schemes.

Direct Calculation Scheme 1

23.17 The first direct calculation scheme is available to businesses with a tax-exclusive turnover not exceeding £1 million and works by calculating the expected selling price of goods for retail sale at one or more rates of VAT so that the proportion of takings on which VAT is due can be calculated. Expected selling prices must be calculated in respect of the 'minority goods'. These are the goods at the rate (or rates) of tax which form the lower proportion of the retail supplies being made.

For example, if a business makes 60 per cent standard-rated sales and 40 per cent zero-rated sales, the minority goods are the zero-rated goods. The ESPs for the zero-rated goods purchased, made or grown for resale in the period are calculated and this value is deducted from the takings for the period. This gives the figure for standard-rated supplies, to which the VAT fraction is applied to arrive at the output tax liability.

If a retailer's minority supplies are zero-rated, it cannot use the scheme for zero-rated services; if a retailer's minority supplies are standard-rated, it may not use the scheme for standard-rated services, The scheme may also not be used for supplies of catering.

This scheme can be relatively simple if a retailer has only a small proportion of supplies at one rate. But the scheme can produce inaccuracies if expected selling prices are not calculated accurately. Additionally, it can be complex to work if a retailer sells goods at three rates of tax, although it may be possible to account for a small number of goods at a third rate outside the scheme.

Direct Calculation Scheme 2

23.18 This scheme works in exactly the same way as the first scheme, but requires an annual stock adjustment. It is available to businesses with an annual tax exclusive retail turnover not exceeding £10 million. In order to use this scheme, a business must know the ESPs of the minority goods in stock when it starts to use the scheme.

Customs & Excise provide full details of the stock adjustment and other matters in the Public Notices which explain the different schemes.

Bespoke Retail Schemes

23.19 If the tax-exclusive retail turnover of a business exceeds £10 million, there is no entitlement to use a published retail scheme. If turnover exceeds that limit, the retailer must either:

- account normally. This does not require the issue of a tax invoice to unregistered customers. It does however, require the retailer to

23.19 VAT Business by Business

       identify for each supply the tax-exclusive value and the VAT, and be able to produce periodic totals of those amounts; or

- agree a bespoke scheme. Customs recognise the difficulties some large retailers could have in accounting normally and will only withhold agreement for the reasons in *VAT Regulations 1995 (SI 1995 No 2518), regulation 68* (these criteria are specified below) or where they consider it necessary to do so for the protection of the revenue.

A retailer which is ineligible for any of the standard schemes by virtue of its turnover must be very careful when agreeing its bespoke scheme, as these are binding agreements which must be signed by an officer of Customs & Excise as well as by an authorised signatory of the registered business. Retrospective change will not normally be allowed unless it is discovered that there is a fundamental flaw in what has been agreed. Otherwise, the agreement will remain in force for the agreed period (usually two years) unless there is a significant change in the business structure or trading patterns. If such changes happen, Customs & Excise must be notified in writing.

A bespoke scheme will usually be based on a published scheme, but it can be based on any method which produces a fair and reasonable result, reflects commercial reality and does not require unnecessarily complicated accounting. Also, it must be possible for Customs to audit the method of accounting. It may include a mixture of different schemes, but Customs are unlikely to agree bespoke schemes which are based on, or include schemes with a threshold cap of £1 million. A bespoke scheme will be agreed in writing and include:

- the start date and review date of the agreement, the start date being no later than the date at which the business became ineligible to use a published scheme;

- details of which supplies will be accounted for within a bespoke scheme, and which will not form part of the scheme and will therefore be accounted for normally;

- details of how gross takings and expected selling prices will be quantified; and

- the names, status and signature of an officer of Customs & Excise, and an authorised signatory of the registered person/business/company.

The bespoke agreement will be based on full disclosure and in the context of a retailer's current business structure and trading patterns. Should there be any changes in this structure, or any changes in trading patterns, to such an extent that the agreed method ceases to produce a fair and reasonable result, Customs should be informed in writing immediately.

The key advantage of a negotiated agreement is the mutual certainty it provides. Any changes will normally be made by mutual consent, although Customs may withdraw their agreement and may refuse use of a scheme for the reasons provided for in *Regulation 68*, namely that:

- it does not produce a fair and reasonable result;

- it is necessary for the protection of the revenue; and

- the retailer could reasonably be expected to account normally.

Ceasing to use a Scheme

23.20 Specific adjustments may be required when a retailer ceases to use a particular retail scheme. These are set out at paragraphs 23.21 to 23.25 below. Customs may require additional adjustments when unusual patterns of trade prevent a scheme from producing a fair and reasonable result. Apart from these special rules, a retailer should also remember that only goods sold by retail can be included in the retail scheme. If a retailer ceases to use a scheme because part or all of the business is transferred as a going concern, the value of stock transferred will have to be excluded from the retail scheme. Additionally, if a retailer ceases to trade, VAT may become due on the value of stocks and assets held (see *Notice No 700/11— Cancelling your registration*).

Point of Sale Scheme

23.21 No adjustment is required on ceasing to use this scheme, either for all or part of a VAT registration.

Apportionment Scheme 1

23.22 The retailer must perform a closing adjustment, as for the annual adjustment, even if the retailer leaves before the anniversary of starting to use the scheme.

Apportionment Scheme 2

23.23 Normally no adjustment is necessary. However, if a trader is ceasing to use this scheme in part of its business but is continuing to use it in other parts of the business, it is necessary to ensure that the 'rolling calculation' reflects the expected selling prices of stock now excluded from the apportionment calculation.

Direct Calculation Scheme 1

23.24 Normally no adjustment is necessary.

Direct Calculation Scheme 2

23.25 The trader must make a closing adjustment, as for the annual adjustment, even if he or she leaves before the first anniversary of starting to use the scheme. The adjustment must include the tax periods since the adjustment and must take account of any disposals made during the year which were not by way of retail sale. This is done by excluding from the figures used in the calculation the value of any goods which were previously part of the scheme calculation but have not been sold by way of retail.

Specific retail businesses

Cinemas and theatres

23.26 A Point of Sale scheme would normally be operated for the admission charges, but as sales via the kiosk and at intermission times normally require separate records to be kept, it is possible to account for VAT using a different scheme for these sales. Nevertheless there is likely to be only a very small number of zero-rated sales from this source.

Garages and filling stations

23.27 If a garage supplying petrol can satisfy Customs & Excise that it can effectively record daily gross takings for supplies by means of meter readings, then approval may be given for this; it should be obtained in writing.

For discount given for cash sales in particular circumstances (e.g. quantity discounts), the discounted quantities sold must be recorded and the gross takings adjusted. It is also permissible to adjust the gross takings where a motorist drives off without paying.

Catering and take-away food suppliers

23.28 The Apportionment and Direct Calculation schemes assume that goods bought at one rate of VAT will be sold at the same rate. However, food bought at the zero rate often becomes standard-rated when supplied in the course of catering. Therefore, a caterer must normally use the Point of Sale scheme to establish its VAT liability.

Retailers and Retail Schemes **23.29**

An alternative to the Point of Sale scheme which may be used by small businesses with a tax-exclusive retail turnover not exceeding £1 million is explained below.

(1) Establish the gross takings for the accounting period.

(2) Calculate the percentage of total supplies of catering made at the standard rate. The method of calculation must be able to satisfy a visiting VAT officer that the catering adaptation gives a fair and reasonable result in any period. Whichever way a trader chooses to make the calculation, he or she must always:

- base the calculation on a sample of the actual sales for a representative period. The representative period will depend on the nature of the business, but the trader must be able to satisfy a visiting officer that it takes account of hourly, daily and seasonal fluctuations;

- retain details of the sample, including the dates and times at which it took place; and

- carry out a new calculation in each tax period. The trader must not use a calculation that has been established by a previous owner of the business.

(3) Apply the percentage at step 2 to the gross takings at step 1.

(4) Multiply the total at step 3 by the VAT fraction (7/47 for VAT at 17.5%). This is the output tax on supplies of catering for this period.

The catering adaptation is published under *VAT Regulations (SI 1995 No 2518), reg 67.*

Pharmacists

23.29 The supply of goods dispensed by a registered chemist on the prescription of a medical practitioner is zero-rated under *VATA 1994, 8 Sch, Group 12.* Special arrangements have been agreed for pharmacists who dispense and supply goods on prescription, as these may be bought at the standard rate but supplied at the zero rate. An adjustment may need to be made to the gross takings otherwise too much tax could be accounted for. A number of items supplied on prescription, such as gluten-free bread, are zero-rated at purchase so a further adjustment may also be necessary.

Retailers using a Point of Sale scheme will be accounting for VAT at the correct rate, as the rate of tax is identified at the time the supply is made. No adjustment is therefore necessary.

Other retail schemes require the adjustments explained below to reduce the output tax which the scheme would otherwise produce.

23.30 VAT Business by Business

Direct Calculation Schemes

23.30 Whether the trader is using the first or the second Direct Calculation scheme, the following adjustment must be made:

(1) Calculate gross takings, including the total amount from the prescription charges and NHS cheque (less the value of any exempt supplies such as rota payments).

(2) Work out the output tax as explained in the Direct Calculation scheme Notice.

(3) Add up the payments received in the period for all *Group 12* goods—even if they were not supplied in the period. Remember that the NHS cheque may include payments for supplies not zero-rated under *Group 12*, but exempt or standard-rated. Such amounts must not be included in this total.

(4) Estimate the value of goods included in step 3 that were zero-rated when received (see paragraph 23.32 below).

(5) Subtract the total at step 4 from the total at step 3.

(6) To work out the VAT which will have been included in step 2 from *Group 12* goods, multiply the total at step 5 by the VAT fraction (7/47 for VAT at 17.5 per cent).

(7) The output tax is the total at step 2 minus the notional output tax at step 6.

Apportionment Schemes

23.31 If a trader is using an Apportionment Scheme, the following adjustment must be made to the scheme calculation:

(1) Calculate gross takings including the total amount from prescription charges and NHS cheque (less the value of any exempt supplies such as rota payments).

(2) Work out the output tax as explained in the Apportionment Schemes Notice.

(3) Add up the payments received in the period for all *Group 12* goods—even if they were not supplied in the period. Remember that the NHS cheque may include payments for supplies not zero-rated under *Group 12*, but exempt or standard-rated. Such amounts must not be included in this total.

(4) Estimate the value of goods included in step 3 that were zero-rated when received (see paragraph 23.32 below).

(5) Subtract the total at step 4 from the total at step 3.

(6) To work out the VAT which will have been included in step 2 from *Group 12* goods, multiply the total at step 5 by the VAT fraction (7/47 for VAT at 17.5%).

(7) The output tax is the output tax from step 2 minus the notional output tax at step 6.

Estimating the percentage of zero-rated supplies

23.32 A trader must be able to satisfy a visiting VAT officer that the estimation of zero-rated supplies gives a fair and reasonable valuation in any period. Whichever way the estimation is made, the trader must always:

- base the estimation on a sample of the actual purchases for a representative period. The representative period will depend on the nature of the business but must take account of seasonal fluctuations, etc;

- retain details of the sample;

- carry out a new estimation in each tax period. A trader must not use an estimation that has been established by a previous owner of the business.

Retail florists

23.33 There are special arrangements made for retail florists who are members of the Interflora, Teleflorist and Flowergram organisations. The adjustments to be made will depend on the scheme adopted, and whether or not the trader is the member receiving payment direct from the customer (the sending member) or the member delivering the flowers and receiving payment from the organisation (the executing member).

Point of Sale Scheme

23.34 For the sending member, no adjustment is necessary. The trader should simply include the payments received in gross takings when the order is taken, and can ignore the documentation received from the agency.

The executing member must not include payments received from the agency in gross takings, and must account for any tax due outside the retail scheme.

Apportionment Schemes

23.35 The sending member must identify the value of the supplies made from the agency documentation, must not include the payments for these supplies in gross takings under the retail scheme calculation, and must account for any tax due outside the retail scheme.

The executing member must account for any tax due outside the retail scheme on the basis of the agency documentation, and must not include the agency payments in gross takings. If using Apportionment Scheme 1, the member must exclude the value of the flowers from the purchase records. If using Apportionment Scheme 2, the member must adjust the expected selling prices for the value of flowers sent as executing member and accounted for outside the retail scheme.

Direct Calculation Schemes

23.36 The sending member must identify the value of the supplies made from the agency documentation, must not include the payments for these supplies in gross takings under the retail scheme calculation, and must account for any tax due outside the retail scheme.

The executing member must account for any tax due outside the retail scheme on the basis of the agency documentation, must not include the agency payments in gross takings, and must adjust the expected selling prices for the value of flowers sent as executing member and accounted for outside the retail scheme.

Sub-post offices

23.37 The supply of services by sub-postmasters to the Post Office is regarded for VAT purposes as not made in the course of a business, and is therefore outside the scope of VAT.

Where a sub-post office operates together with a normal retail shop outlet and under the same management, takings from the post office should be completely separated from the takings from the retail section of the business. It is only the retail part of the business which is covered by a retail scheme.

Vending and amusement machine operators

23.38 The normal tax point is the date on which money is removed from the machine. Output tax is due in the period in which the removal takes place. It is therefore necessary to record the dates and the amounts of monies removed.

VAT Recovery

23.39 The rules for VAT recovery are the same for retailers as for any other business. VAT can be claimed on purchases and expenses in the normal way, subject to any partial exemption method in place. A retailer can ignore sales of postage stamps when considering its partial exemption position, but it cannot ignore exempt commission received in respect of, e.g. lottery ticket sales. For details of partial exemption, see *Tolley's VAT 1998/99, chapter 49*.

Accounting Records

23.40 When choosing a retail scheme, amongst the considerations a retailer must look at is the ability to maintain an adequate system of records to enable him to satisfy the conditions of that scheme. The minimum record-keeping requirements of a retailer are as discussed below.

Daily gross takings record

23.41 Normally when a retailer receives cash he records it in one of the following ways:

(1) a cash register with a till roll showing the gross total of cash received. It may also give an analysis or a breakdown of the type of goods sold;

(2) a cash register which is capable of giving only a summary total; or

(3) a cash tin or drawer with no reconcilable add list to compare with the total cash put into that drawer.

Whichever method is used, it is imperative that the retailer records his or her gross takings figure on a daily basis.

Purchase invoices

23.42 VAT invoices from suppliers should be entered into a purchase day book or similar record to enable the retailer to reclaim any VAT charge thereon as input tax.

Many retailers use cash and carry wholesalers to obtain stock. Cash and carry invoices are often only in the form of a till receipt using code numbers to identify the goods. It will in these cases be necessary for the retailer to obtain and retain with his records a copy of the product code list supplied by the wholesalers to support the actual claim for input tax.

For apportionment-based and direct calculation schemes, it will also be important to ensure the separation of standard-rated and zero-rated purchases of goods for resale, of purchases of capital equipment, e.g. cash registers, vans and shop fittings, and of overheads, e.g. stationery, petrol, telephone accounts, etc.

23.43 *VAT Business by Business*

VAT account

23.43 A VAT summary or VAT account must be maintained separately for each VAT accounting period, with an adequate 'trail' back to the other records.

Computer records

23.44 Any business which is planning to computerise its records will need to contact the local VAT office to ensure that the records meet with the Commissioners' requirements.

Practical Points

Provision of VAT invoices by retailers

23.45 Although a retailer is not generally expected to issue VAT invoices for sales he makes, he must do so if asked by a customer (e.g. one who is registered for VAT and for whom the purchase is a business expense). Any such invoice must meet the relevant regulations and it is important therefore that a retailer is aware of, and responsive to, the formal requirements in this area.

Shops within shops

23.46 Large department stores often lease part of their internal capacity to other specialist retailers and may use their own staff to sell the other retailer's goods.

It is the responsibility of the specialist retailer to account for the VAT on any sales made by him. The department store will often be paid a commission and must issue a VAT invoice for it to the lessee. The department store must also ensure that any receipts and charges are not included in its own retail scheme calculations.

The charge made by the department store, however this may be calculated, is generally consideration for the supply of the right to use the designated area, floor space, stores, etc. Prima facie, it is for the exempt supply of an interest in land, subject to the store's election to waive exemption.

Disposal of a business

23.47 Where a retailer disposes of either the whole or a separate part of his business as a going concern, provided that the buyer is registered for VAT (or will be required to be registered when he acquires the business), the transaction is outside the scope of VAT. However, if the vendor has elected to waive exemption in respect of any property being transferred, then the purchaser must make a similar election and must notify the election to the Commissioners before the sale is completed, if he is to prevent VAT being charged on the property in question.

It is particularly important to exclude VAT on the value of any stock transferred, as this is not reclaimable by the purchaser. It may also be necessary to adjust retail scheme calculations (see paragraphs 23.20 to 23.25 above).

Deregistration

23.48 Where a retailer ceases to make taxable supplies, either through having transferred the business or through having ceased to trade, then he or she will need to deregister. He or she may also wish to consider doing so if total turnover falls below the deregistration limits. VAT must be paid on any business asset, including stock in hand, at the date of deregistration as if it had been supplied at that time. It must be remembered that the VAT records must be retained for a period of six years even though deregistration has taken place. It may also be necessary to adjust retail scheme calculations (see paragraphs 23.20 to 23.25 above).

Cash accounting and annual accounting

23.49 It is open to traders with an annual taxable turnover (tax-exclusive) of £350,000 or less to opt for accounting for VAT on a cash basis, and for traders with an annual taxable turnover (tax-exclusive) of £300,000 or less to opt for accounting for VAT on an annual basis. A retailer who is already operating a special scheme suitable to his or her needs should consider carefully whether either of these choices offers any material advantage.

Chapter 24

Small Businesses

Introduction

24.1 A number of measures exist to relieve small businesses of all or part of the compliance burden associated with VAT. In the main, the measures are aimed at reducing the actual compliance burden of those functions associated with record keeping although, as will be seen, the measures can result in an actual saving in VAT paid. The measures are as follows.

VAT registration limits: These are intended to relieve a business from the burden of having to keep some of the records required for VAT, but may also result in an actual saving in VAT payable.

Cash accounting scheme: This allows a business to account for VAT when the consideration for a supply of goods or services is received, but also requires the business to defer claims for VAT paid (other than on hire and lease purchase agreements) until the time payment is actually made.

Annual accounting scheme: This relieves a business from having to make quarterly or monthly returns but requires VAT payments on account except in the case of very small businesses.

Partial exemption reliefs: These are intended to relieve a business from having to deal with the restriction of input tax recovery where minimal exempt supplies are made.

The formalities of the various measures are set out in greater detail in *Tolley's VAT 1998/99, chapter 59* (Registration), *paragraphs 63.2-63.8* (Cash accounting), *paragraphs 63.9-63.14* (Annual accounting) and *paragraph 49.4* (Partial exemption de minimis limits). The purpose of this chapter is to highlight the factors that need to be taken into account in deciding whether any of these measures apply.

24.2 VAT Business by Business

VAT registration limits

Liability to register

24.2 A person is required to register for VAT if the value of his taxable supplies exceeds the turnover limits contained in *VATA 1994, 1 Sch 1*, currently £50,000. Although the limits are expressed in terms of an absolute limit, in practice the actual amount relieved from VAT will vary from business to business according to the incidence of the person's taxable supplies. This gives some small businesses a limited opportunity to plan to remain unregistered for a slightly longer period than may have been the case had they not carried out any planning.

Example:

B is a building contractor, who carries out repairs and minor alterations to residential properties. None of the work qualifies for zero-rating. He enters into a contract to do work over three months for a fixed sum of £95,000 including VAT if applicable. If, as a result of entering into the contract, B is able to foresee that his taxable supplies in the next 30 days will exceed the current turnover limit of £50,000, he must notify Customs & Excise, and will be registered for VAT from the beginning of the period of thirty days in which that liability arises. The tax point for building services is the receipt of payment or the issue of a document acting as a tax invoice, whichever is earlier. Therefore, assuming the contract is his only source of income, B could remain unregistered for three months if he can arrange that the payments under the contract are received as follows -

July 1	Payment	£45,000	No liability to notify - turnover less than £50,000
Aug 1	Payment	£35,000	
Sept 1	Payment	£15,000	

Under *VATA 1994, 1 Sch 1(1)(a)*, B becomes liable to be registered at the end of August (as the value of his taxable supplies in the period of one year ending has exceeded £50,000). Under *VATA 1994, 1 Sch 5(1)*, he must notify the Commissioners within 30 days of the end of the relevant month—i.e. in the above example, by 30 September. However, under *VATA 1994, 1 Sch 5(2)* he will only be registered from the end of the month following the relevant month—i.e. from 30 September. (Additionally, under *VATA 1994, 1 Sch 3*, if he can show that his turnover in the twelve months following 1 August will not exceed the turnover limits, he can escape registration altogether.)

One problem which small businesses frequently overlook is the fact that it is the person that is registered for VAT and not the business. The effect of this is that the turnover that has to be counted towards the registration limits is the aggregate turnover of all businesses owned by the taxable person. A partnership is treated as a separate person from one of its partners and it used to be possible to avoid registration by varying the ownership of different businesses in which a person has an interest, e.g. a person could be the sole proprietor of a shop and a partner with his wife in another type of business. The business relationships must be real if they are to be regarded as separate businesses for VAT purposes. Customs & Excise have powers to counter the separation of businesses in order to avoid registration using what are known as the 'disaggregation' provisions (*VATA 1994, 1 Sch 2*). The relevant legislation was amended by *FA 1997* with effect from 19 March 1997. The amended legislation now provides that a direction is valid if the avoidance of VAT is an effect of the separation of the business. The previous requirement for the Commissioners to be satisfied that the avoidance of VAT liability was a 'main reason' for the way in which the business is organised has now been abolished. It is therefore important to ensure that if businesses are held in different ownership, it is possible to demonstrate that they are separately run and have not been artificially split for the purpose of VAT avoidance. See *Tolley's VAT 1998/99, paragraphs 8.5 to 8.9*.

Monitoring turnover

24.3 A person who is not registered for VAT, but makes taxable supplies, must monitor the level of those taxable supplies to determine whether and when he becomes liable to be registered for VAT. In order to do so, he will have to determine the value of his taxable supplies and the date when those supplies fall to be included in his turnover. These values then have to be aggregated and the total for each period of twelve months compared with the annual turnover limit.

Taxable supplies arising from the sale of capital assets, other than certain interests in fixed property, are excluded from turnover for the purposes of determining whether the limits have been reached.

Anyone who makes taxable supplies needs a basic understanding of the VAT tax point rules governing the time of supply. For a full discussion of these rules, see *Tolley's VAT 1998/99, paragraphs 64.16 to 64.34*.

The normal rule is that the time of supply is the earlier of the date of issue of a tax invoice or the date payment received. An exception to this rule arises in the case of continuous supplies of services. Customs & Excise used to take the view that, since only a taxable person can issue a tax invoice, the tax point of continuous supplies where a person was not registered was the date a payment was received. This meant that if payment for a supply made before the date of registration was only received after registration, the tax point was the date of the payment. Accordingly, supplies made before registration could become liable to VAT. However, this view was rejected by the Court of Appeal in the case of *BJ Rice & Associates, CA [1996] STC 581*. A consequence of this decision would appear to be that the value of an invoice issued for a supply made prior to registration must be taken into account in

24.4 VAT Business by Business

the period the invoice was issued in calculating a person's turnover for registration purposes.

Choosing to remain unregistered

24.4 A person whose input tax will exceed any output tax liability, e.g. because he makes zero-rated supplies, may be exempted from registration notwithstanding that he has exceeded the turnover limits (*VATA 1994, 1 Sch 14*).

The choice of whether or not to remain unregistered in these circumstances, or to take steps such as those illustrated in the example at paragraph 24.2 above to remain unregistered for as long as possible, depends on a number of factors, the most important of which is usually whether or not the recipients of the taxpayer's services are likely to be registered and able to recover any VAT charged. However, other non-tax issues may be important, e.g. not being VAT-registered announces to the world that the business's turnover is less than the limits, and this is sometimes a reason why a business will register notwithstanding the additional cost.

Effect on input tax recovery

24.5 A person who chooses to remain unregistered needs to bear in mind that he will not be entitled to recover any VAT incurred while he is not registered unless the input tax relates to supplies he makes after registration and, in the case of goods, are still on hand at the date of registration or, in the case of services, was incurred not more than six months prior to registration (*VAT Regulations 1995 (SI 1995 No 2518), reg 111*). Although the VAT is treated as input tax, it is not input tax. The main implication of this distinction is that any tax which is so treated and which relates to an exempt supply is not treated as input tax falling within the de minimis rules (see paragraphs 24.21 to 24.23 below).

It is now provided that input tax can only be recovered if it is claimed within three years of the period in which it was incurred and could have been claimed in a VAT return (*VAT Regulations 1995 (SI 1995 No 2518), reg 29(1A)*). This would appear to prevent VAT incurred on goods more than three years prior to registration being recoverable.

Conversely, VAT incurred after registration will not be deductible if the supplies to which it relates were made prior to the date of registration. See *Schemepanel Trading Ltd, QB [1996] STC 871*.

Example:

S starts up a business selling holiday courses (not exempt) for children. He takes deposits of £45,000 in his first month and a further £15,000 in the second month. He is subsequently registered and collects a further £47,000 after registration. He incurs VAT of £7,000 on expenditure in relation to the above income. Assuming the £47,000 to be inclusive of VAT, S must account for VAT of £7,000. Although the whole of his supplies would have been taxable if he had been registered, the VAT referable to the £60,000 (i.e. £45,000 + £15,000) is not recoverable. He can therefore only recover VAT as follows -

$$\frac{\text{(Value of taxable supplies) £40,000}}{\text{(Value of all supplies) £100,000}} \times \text{(input tax) £7,000} = £2,800$$

Voluntary registration

24.6 A person who is not required to be registered for VAT may nevertheless find it an advantage to be registered for VAT in order to recover any VAT incurred.

The most common situation where this is the case is where a business only sells to customers who are registered for VAT and able to recover any VAT charged. Where a person has a mixture of customers, some of whom are able to recover their VAT and others who are not, the position is more complex. It is also possible that even where most of a business's customers are unable to recover their VAT, the existence of substantial start-up costs, coupled with a likelihood that the business will soon exceed the turnover limits in any event, may make voluntary registration a viable option. While, in theory, it may be possible to backdate a voluntary registration, there are circumstances in which backdating may be refused, leaving the person with a VAT cost (see paragraph 24.7 below).

Backdating registration

24.7 It frequently happens that a person who is not required to register for VAT discovers that it would have been advantageous for him to register voluntarily from an earlier date. Whether the person is entitled to require Customs & Excise to backdate any registration where he was not required to be registered is doubtful and will probably depend on the particular circumstances. Customs & Excise will generally investigate why an applicant did not apply for voluntary registration before agreeing to backdate a registration. While, under EC VAT law, a person who carries out an economic activity is entitled to be registered, Member States are allowed to grant exemption from registration. Therefore, someone who decides to take advantage of exemption from registration, e.g. because he makes only zero-rated supplies, may find that he will not be allowed to backdate a registration.

The position may be different where the person fails to apply for voluntary registration because of an oversight or a misunderstanding of his entitlement to register. It follows that a person should consider carefully whether or not he should register, as mistakes may not be capable of being rectified later. Customs & Excise have a policy of not permitting voluntary registrations to be backdated for more than three years—see Business Brief 8/97, issued on 25 March 1997.

24.8 VAT Business by Business

Cash accounting

Introduction

24.8 The cash accounting scheme enables a person who is registered for VAT to account for his VAT liability on the basis of the cash that he receives for the supplies of goods and services he makes, rather than on the basis of the normal time of supply. However, a person using the scheme must also defer the recovery of any VAT incurred (subject to one exception set out below) until the time when he pays for the supply on which the VAT was incurred. See *Tolley's VAT 1998/99, paragraphs 63.2 to 63.8*. The 1997 Finance Act introduced changes aimed at curbing avoidance arising from businesses which used the scheme invoicing goods and services in advance to provide a cash-flow advantage to customers.

Benefits of using the scheme

24.9 The scheme will only benefit businesses which supply goods or services on credit. However, the scheme has the effect of giving automatic bad debt relief without the need to wait six months to claim. Previously, retailers were able to take advantage of a method of accounting for VAT which allowed them to account for VAT on their takings as they were received while still recovering the VAT they paid as it was incurred. This has now been withdrawn. Small retailers may now find it advantageous to use the cash accounting scheme.

Potential disadvantages

24.10 Among the businesses which will not benefit from the use of the scheme are:

- Those whose main supplies of goods or services are made on a continuous basis and are able to account for VAT on a cash basis (provided that they can defer the issue of any tax invoice until the date when cash is received);

- Barristers and advocates, who, by virtue of *VAT Regulations 1995 (SI 1995 No 2518), reg 92*, are able to account for VAT on a cash received basis provided that they do not issue a tax invoice until payment is made (see Chapter 4 above).

Before using the scheme, a business should also consider when any input tax is likely to be incurred. A business that is in a development phase or in a process of building up stocks may find that the output tax deferred may be exceeded by any input tax incurred. It is important to note that the comparison that has to be made is the deferral of input tax against the deferral of output tax at the time of the decision to use cash accounting. In some cases, it may be appropriate to delay the decision to use the cash accounting scheme until input tax on major purchases has been recovered. Other considerations (e.g. seasonal factors) may also affect the decision.

The cash accounting scheme requires a business to keep a record of payments made or received in respect of taxable supplies. Where existing records can be used for this purpose, no problems arise but, in other cases, this may entail the creation of additional records. Where part payments are made either by the taxable person for supplies received or by customers for supplies made to them, the payments have to be apportioned to the invoices to which they relate. While there are no specific rules as to how any apportionment must be made, the apportionment must be reasonable. The process of apportionment may make it more difficult from an accounting viewpoint to operate the scheme than to account for VAT on an invoice basis. This is an issue that needs to be considered before deciding to use the scheme.

Eligibility to use the scheme

24.11 A taxable person who wishes to use the scheme can do so from the beginning of a VAT accounting period, without the need for permission, provided that he meets the requirements, which are:

- He must have reason to believe that the value of his taxable supplies in the twelve months commencing on the first day on which the scheme is to be used will not exceed the registration limit, currently £350,000.

- He must not be excluded from using the scheme for any of the reasons set out in paragraph 24.12 below.

For fuller details of the formalities, see *Tolley's VAT 1998/99, paragraph 63.3*.

Exclusions from use of the scheme

24.12 A taxable person is not permitted to use the scheme if he is in arrears with payment of his VAT liability, unless he has made arrangements with Customs & Excise for the discharge of any amount due in instalments. A taxable person is also not permitted to use the scheme if he has been convicted of any offence in relation to VAT, accepted an offer to compound any such offence or been assessed to a penalty for conduct involving dishonesty (see *Tolley's VAT 1998/99, paragraph 63.7*). However, he does not cease to be eligible solely because of his becoming liable to a default surcharge or misdeclaration penalty.

Customs & Excise are empowered to withdraw entitlement to use the scheme where they consider it necessary for the protection of the revenue.

24.13 VAT Business by Business

Operating the scheme

24.13 Although the scheme can only be operated in relation to a business as a whole, there are a number of exceptions to the requirement that VAT on supplies must be accounted for on a payments basis.

The scheme must not be used to account for VAT in relation to imports, exports and acquisitions of goods.

Input tax relating to the following supplies received by a taxable person operating the scheme can be claimed in full at the normal time provided that the recipient is in possession of the appropriate evidence:

- goods purchased under a hire purchase agreement or a conditional sale agreement or a credit sale agreement;

- goods acquired under a lease purchase agreement or other supplies where a tax invoice has been issued for the full amount but payment is to be deferred for more than twelve months.

The scheme may also not be used in respect of a supply in respect of which a VAT invoice has been issued but payment is not due for a period of more than six months after the invoice date or where the invoice is issued in advance of performance of the obligation to make a supply.

Date payment is received

24.14 Customs & Excise have set out guidance in relation to when payment is to be taken as having been received or made in respect of any supplies of goods (for details, see *Tolley's VAT 1998/99, paragraph 63.6*). It should also be noted that payment is effected when a person validly offsets an amount of money due to him against an amount of money owed by him to his debtor.

Similarly, where a person allows a customer to trade-in other goods against a supply made, there will be payment to the extent of the trade-in.

Leaving the scheme

24.15 A taxable person does not have to leave the scheme unless the value of his taxable supplies in the prescribed accounting period just ended has exceeded £437,500 and the value of his taxable supplies in the next year are likely to exceed the current turnover limit of £350,000. A taxable person can now voluntarily withdraw from the scheme at the end of any prescribed accounting period. (Before 3 July 1997, a person had to use the scheme for two years unless he was required to leave it because he had exceeded the limits.)

One issue of concern will be what happens when he leaves the scheme.

Accounting for VAT on a cash basis will mean that the payment of VAT is deferred but not avoided. On leaving the scheme, the taxpayer must account for all the VAT on the supplies made while still in the scheme and which have not been brought to account. However, Customs & Excise may waive this requirement and allow VAT to be accounted for at the time it would have been accounted for had the person not left or been required to leave the scheme. At the same time, however, he will have to account for VAT on current supplies in the normal way. Therefore, until all old debts have been collected and the VAT paid, the business will be paying more VAT than would otherwise have been the case and this factor will have to be taken into account in planning the cash flows of the business.

Annual accounting

Introduction

24.16 The annual accounting scheme relieves a taxable person from the requirement of having to make quarterly VAT returns. Instead, a single VAT return can be submitted after the end of the person's financial year end. In addition to benefiting from having to make only one return, the time limit for making that return is extended to two months unless the period for which the return is lodged does not exceed four months. For full details, see *Tolley's VAT 1998/99, paragraphs 63.9 to 63.14.*

Except for certain very small businesses, whose taxable turnover does not exceed £100,000 and whose net VAT liability is less than £2,000, a person using the scheme must make payments on account of his annual VAT liability during the year. The payments have to be made by electronic means. The requirement to make payments on account can result in a small cash flow advantage but it is also possible for the payments on account to result in adverse VAT cash flows. In deciding whether to use the scheme, a taxpayer therefore needs to consider carefully the advantages and disadvantages of using the scheme.

Conditions for admission to the scheme

24.17 A person who wishes to use the scheme must meet the following conditions:

- He must have reasonable grounds for believing that his taxable turnover, excluding the sale of capital assets, in the next twelve months will not exceed £300,000;

- He must have been registered as a taxable person for at least twelve months;

24.18 VAT Business by Business

- He must not have ceased to use the scheme in the twelve months preceding the application for any of the following reasons:

    - His turnover has exceeded the limit for leaving the scheme (currently £375,000);
    - He has been removed from the scheme by Customs & Excise;
    - He has ceased business;
    - He has voluntarily withdrawn from the scheme.

It is not possible for a VAT group to join the scheme.

The scheme conditions

24.18 A taxable person who is admitted to the scheme must comply with the following conditions:

- He must make any interim payments on account by electronic means by the due dates. A person whose taxable turnover exceeds £100,000 must make nine payments equal to one tenth of his previous year's net VAT liability at the end of each month commencing from the fourth month. A person whose taxable turnover is less than £100,000 but whose net VAT liability is greater than £2,000 must make three quarterly payments of 20% of his annual previous year's net VAT liability at the end of the fourth, seventh and tenth months of his VAT accounting year;

- He must render a VAT return together with a payment equal to his VAT liability less any interim payments by the end of the second month following the end of his VAT accounting year.

There are special transitional provisions relating to a person whose VAT accounting period following admission to the scheme is less than a year.

For fuller details of the conditions of the scheme, see *Tolley's VAT 1998/99, paragraphs 63.9 to 63.14.*

Deciding whether to use the scheme

24.19 The cash flow impact of the scheme is, in most cases, relatively small and therefore the prime consideration is likely to be whether the administrative benefits justify use of the scheme. A person may, for example, decide not to use the scheme because it is easier to do four small VAT returns rather than a single VAT return more than a year after some of the transactions took place.

As far as cash flow is concerned, the following factors are indicative of possible VAT cash flow savings through the use of the scheme:

- taxable turnover tends to be concentrated in earlier rather than later months of the VAT year;
- input tax tends to be incurred later rather than earlier in the VAT year;
- taxable turnover in the current year is likely to exceed taxable turnover in the previous year.

The scheme is designed so that, in general terms, a business whose net VAT liability remains static and is spread more or less equally over the year will benefit very marginally.

Leaving the scheme

24.20 A person must leave the scheme if his taxable supplies in any year, including any transitional period, exceeds the limits. Customs & Excise can expel a person from the scheme. For details of the conditions under which Customs & Excise can exercise this power, see *Tolley's VAT 1998/99, paragraph 63.14*. A person who leaves the scheme will not be allowed to rejoin it for one year after leaving it.

Partial exemption 'de minimis' limits

Introduction

24.21 Although the partial exemption 'de minimis' limits (for details of which, see *Tolley's VAT 1998/99, paragraph 49.4*) were originally intended as a measure to relieve businesses from having to carry out any partial exemption calculations, the nature of the limits means that a calculation almost invariably does have to be done and the only benefit of the limits is a saving of a small amount of exempt input tax which would otherwise not be recoverable.

Nevertheless a significant amount of planning has centred on the use of the limits by small businesses, particularly in relation to so-called 'toothbrush schemes' designed to allow almost wholly exempt small businesses to recover their VAT (see paragraph 24.23 below). The introduction of the 50% test has restricted but not removed the planning opportunity. Attempts to use the de minimis limits in conjunction with the registration limits in order to maximise input tax recovery while reducing output tax liability have largely failed.

24.22 *VAT Business by Business*

VAT incurred before registration

24.22 A number of cases have come before the tribunal where an appellant has attempted to claim VAT incurred prior to registration that is referable to exempt supplies under the de minimis limits. The tribunals have consistently held that VAT which is deemed to be input tax under *VAT Regulations 1995 (SI 1995 No 2518), reg 111* is not in fact input tax. Since the regulations only allow exempt input tax to be recovered under the limits, the tribunals have upheld Customs & Excise decisions not to allow deduction of the tax. The solution where only input tax is involved is to ask for registration to be backdated. However, this only works where the input tax that will become recoverable under the de minimis limits in those circumstances will exceed any output tax that would fall to be charged by virtue of backdating the registration. Since, in many cases, the attempted use of the de minimis limits has been coupled with planning aimed at keeping certain supplies out of the tax charge, this has not been an option in some such arrangements. (For a discussion of backdating registration, see paragraph 24.7 above.)

'Toothbrush' schemes

24.23 'Toothbrush' schemes were designed to allow dentists and other businesses which were almost wholly exempt to use the de minimis limits to recover VAT referable to their exempt supplies. In essence, the schemes worked provided that a person did not incur more VAT on exempt supplies than the limits (£7,200 per annum until 2 December 1994 and £7,500 thereafter). In practice, this meant, before 2 December 1994, that provided expenditure subject to VAT did not exceed approximately £48,000 per annum (inclusive of VAT), all the VAT could be recovered.

From 2 December 1994, the limits were changed so that, in addition to meeting new higher limits, the input tax referable to exempt supplies could not exceed 50% of all input tax. The effect of the change was to require substantial taxable business in addition to any exempt business before the exempt input tax could be recovered.

Although the changes have severely limited this type of planning, it remains possible for some substantially exempt businesses to recover input tax under these provisions through careful planning. A number of methods can be used to increase input tax referable to taxable supplies in any year (e.g. through purchase of assets) or to reduce input tax referable to exempt supplies (e.g. by hiring rather than buying assets). Some other activities, such as the provision of staff meals and the application of goods to private use, result in an increase in the total input tax without any increase in the amount of input tax referable to exempt supplies and could therefore be useful in bringing a business within the limits.

In practice, however, it would be unusual for a substantially exempt business to be able to use the de minimis limits for any continuing period to avoid a disallowance of input tax.

Chapter 25

Solicitors

Introduction

25.1 The VAT treatment of services provided by solicitors may at first seem relatively simple. It is easy to assume that the services are taxable and, therefore, that all VAT incurred on expenses can be fully recovered. However, this is not necessarily the case. This chapter looks at the nature and variety of services provided by solicitors, some of which may be exempt, the corresponding VAT treatment, and the impact on the solicitor's ability to recover VAT incurred on expenses.

Liability of a solicitor's supply

25.2 Generally speaking, most legal services provided by solicitors are taxable at the standard rate. This will be the case for litigation services, advisory work and corporate work, whether the services are supplied to a business or a private individual in the UK. However, where a client belongs overseas, the VAT treatment of certain services can vary depending on whether the recipient belongs outside the EC and, if he belongs in another Member State, whether the services are received for business or personal purposes.

Place of supply

25.3 Establishing the place of supply is crucial to determine whether or not UK VAT is chargeable on the solicitor's services. This is particularly the case for certain services supplied to persons outside the UK, and some services relating to land.

25.4 The general rule for determining the place of supply of services is where the supplier belongs. The relevant UK legislation is found at *VATA 1994, ss 7(10)(11), 9* and *VAT (Place of Supply of Services) Order 1992 (SI 1992 No 3121), Article 16*. Consequently for UK solicitors the place of supply will be the UK and hence UK VAT will be due. However, there are exceptions to this rule for services supplied to persons abroad, or services relating to land.

25.5 VAT Business by Business

25.5 In particular, services within the scope of *VATA 1994, 5 Sch 1–8*, which is based on *EC Sixth Directive, Article 9(2)(e)*, are deemed to be supplied where the recipient belongs provided that this is in another Member State of the EC and that he receives the services for business purposes, or that the recipient belongs outside the EC (and Isle of Man). Examples of services likely to be provided by solicitors which are within Schedule 5 are litigation, consultancy and tax advisory services. For example, if a solicitor advises a person belonging in Canada, the services are deemed to be supplied in the customer's country by virtue of *SI 1992 No 3121, Article 16*. As a result the services are outside the scope of UK VAT and there is no requirement to charge UK VAT. However, VAT incurred in relation to these can still be reclaimed in full. In addition, the figures can still be treated as taxable for partial exemption purposes, and if appropriate, included in any partial exemption calculations as taxable income.

25.6 If a client is in business in another Member State, the place of supply is the recipient's country, but the client accounts for local VAT on the services received through his VAT registration.

25.7 However, where a person receives services in another Member State in a personal capacity, he is not able to account for VAT on the services received and the place of supply is not covered by *SI 1992 No 3121, Article 16*. Hence the place of supply reverts to the normal rules, i.e. where the supplier belongs, and if this is the UK, the solicitor must charge UK VAT.

25.8 Obviously difficulties can arise in relation to services provided to a person in the EC since it is necessary to demonstrate that the recipient receives the services for business purposes before the supply can be treated as outside the scope of UK VAT. Unfortunately, this is not always easy, although Customs & Excise have indicated that they will accept a business letterhead as proof that this is the case. Nonetheless, the best evidence of the status of the recipient will be his VAT registration number, so it is worth obtaining this where possible. There is no legal requirement for the recipient's VAT registration number to be shown on the solicitor's invoice, although there is no harm in doing so.

Services relating to land

25.9 There are special rules for determining the place of supply of services relating to land. Essentially, this is determined depending on where the land is situated. The relevant UK legislation is found at *VAT (Place of Supply of Services) Order 1992 (SI 1992 No 3121), Article 5*. Thus, if the land is situated in the UK, the place of supply is the UK and the services are subject to VAT, regardless of where the recipient belongs. Similarly if the land is situated outside the UK, the place of supply is outside the scope of UK VAT and no UK VAT charge arises. Of course, this may create a liability for a solicitor to become VAT-registered in the country where the land is situated and thus where the services are supplied.

25.10 Services must be directly related to the land (which includes buildings, plant and machinery). For example, services of conveyancing, surveying, valuation or dealing with planning permission for a property relate directly to land and are, therefore, supplied where the land is situated. However, the legal administration of a deceased person's estate, which may include property, does not relate directly to the land and the place of supply is determined under the normal place of supply rules. For example, the services of administering a deceased person's estate for an executor in the US, even if it includes property in the UK, are outside the scope of UK VAT. One word of warning is that if the services are supplied to an administrator or executor in another Member State, it is important to establish whether the recipient receives the services for business or private purposes as this will affect the place of supply and UK VAT may be chargeable.

Commission

25.11 A solicitor may offer insurance to clients involved in property transactions and receive a commission. Where the commission is received in consideration for making arrangements for the provision of insurance, this will be exempt from VAT under *VATA 1994, 9 Sch. Group 2*. However, where the solicitor merely introduces the client to an insurance broker or insurance company, any commission received is not necessarily exempt from VAT, but may be standard-rated. Furthermore, if the solicitor merely provides general advice in relation to a supply of insurance, the commission received is likely to be standard-rated.

25.12 Where the commission is shared with an insurance broker, the VAT liability follows that above.

25.13 A growing number of solicitors now have agencies with the major banks and building societies and can arrange for mortgages to be provided to their clients in the course of purchasing a house. Similar to the insurance commission, the commission received by the solicitor will be exempt or standard-rated depending on the extent of the solicitor's involvement. In order to qualify for exemption, the intermediary solicitor must be actively involved in arranging a specific supply of a loan to the client. This would include assistance with the completion of, and checking, the relevant forms as well as submitting the forms to the lender. If the solicitor merely introduces the client to a broker or lender, the services do not qualify for exemption and VAT must be accounted for on the amounts received, on a VAT-inclusive basis if VAT is not identified as a separate charge.

25.14 Further instances when a solicitor might receive exempt income include commission received where a solicitor instructs a stockbroker to sell shares for representatives of an estate. The commission received by the solicitor is likely to be for introductory services rather than broking services which will usually be undertaken by the stockbroker. However, the service

25.15 VAT Business by Business

of introducing a client to a person effecting a transaction in securities is exempt from VAT under *VATA 1994, 9 Sch, Group 5, Item 7, Note 5*.

25.15 The solicitor's clients will generally be in the UK, which means that the services will be exempt. This is also true if the client is a private individual in another Member State and does not receive the solicitor's services for business purposes. However, where any of the services are exempt and are provided to a person in business in another Member State, the place of supply is outside the scope of UK VAT, but there is no input VAT credit. However, under *VATA 1994, s 26(2)(c)* and *VAT (Place of Supply of Services) Order 1992 (SI 1992 No 3121), Article 16*, the supply is outside the scope of UK VAT with recovery of related VAT if the recipient belongs outside the EC.

Disbursements

25.16 This is another area where problems arise, mainly in relation to valuing supplies for the purposes of calculating the VAT due. Before invoicing a client, the solicitor must calculate the value of the supply on which VAT is due, excluding any payments which are to be treated as disbursements. However, not all expenses incurred by the solicitor can be treated as disbursements.

25.17 It is standard practice that a solicitor will incur costs in the course of providing his services to the client, but it is important to bear in mind that costs incidental to a supply, which are incurred by the supplier in the course of making his own supply to his client, are not disbursements and must be included in the value of the supply before VAT is calculated. This is the case even where the expense which has been incurred did not carry a VAT charge, i.e. it was exempt from VAT or zero-rated.

25.18 Where amounts are paid to a third party as agent of a client, the payments can be treated as disbursements and are excluded from the value when calculating VAT. The relevant EC legislation is found at *EC Sixth Directive, Article 11A(3)(c)*. There is no corresponding UK legislation, but Customs' Notice No 700, paragraph 10.8, specifies the conditions which must be satisfied before a payment can be treated as a disbursement. The conditions include:

(a) the solicitor acted for his client when paying the third party;

(b) the client actually received and used the goods or services provided by the third party. (This condition usually prevents the agent's own travelling expenses, telephone bills, postage, etc., being treated as disbursements for VAT purposes);

(c) the client was responsible for paying the third party;

(d) the client authorised the agent to make the payment on his behalf;

(e) the client knew that the goods or services would be provided by a third party;

(f) the agent's outlay must be separately itemised when invoicing the client;

(g) the agent must recover only the exact amount he paid to the third party;

(h) the goods or services paid for must be clearly additional to the supplies made to the client.

25.19 It is vital to ascertain whether or not an item of expenditure is a disbursement to ensure that the correct amount of VAT is brought to account.

25.20 A solicitor often incurs certain expenses in the course of providing his services to the client. The goods or services which he purchases to enable him to provide his own service cannot be treated as disbursements since the goods or services were supplied to the solicitor in his own right and not as agent of the client. Typical examples include:

(a) postage and telephone costs;

(b) an airfare incurred by a solicitor (the flight is not enjoyed by the client, but by the solicitor in making his supply to the client—see the tribunal case noted at paragraph 25.21 below);

(c) photocopying services by a third party;

(d) investigation services used to trace missing persons;

(e) services of a barrister (see special rules below).

25.21 This means that when the solicitor recovers these costs from his client he must charge VAT. The treatment of travelling expenses incurred by a solicitor was tested in the case of *Rowe & Maw v C & E Commrs, QB [1975] STC 340*. The solicitor treated travelling costs as disbursements on which no VAT was charged. The Commissioners issued an assessment on them and the tribunal dismissed the firm's appeal. This decision was upheld by the High Court, which agreed that the airfare was expenditure incurred by the solicitor rather than the client, and as such was an integral part of his service on which VAT should be charged.

25.22 The treatment of telegraphic transfer fees has also been disputed at tribunal. In the case of *Shuttleworth & Co (12805)*, the standard charge by a bank for transferring money from a client account to another client account was held to be supplied to the solicitor rather than to the client. Consequently, the payment did not qualify to be treated as a disbursement when calculating the value of the supply for VAT purposes. Similar decisions have been reached in the cases of *BL Westbury (1168)* and *J & L Lea (2018)*.

25.23 Customs do allow some concessions in relation to certain items of expenditure, for example local authority search fees. Generally, it is

25.24 VAT Business by Business

Customs' view that search fees cannot be treated as disbursements. This is usually the case where the solicitor undertakes a personal search of official records. However, if the solicitor pays a fee for a postal search this may, by concession, be treated as a disbursement on the basis that the solicitor is merely obtaining the document as agent of the client.

Oath fees

25.24 Solicitors may exercise the powers of a Commissioner of Oaths. Fees earned from administering oaths are considered to derive from the personal qualification of the solicitor, so that the fees are received in a personal capacity. This means that for solicitors practising as a sole proprietor or as a partner in a firm of solicitors, VAT must be accounted for on the fees received (providing the practice or partnership is VAT-registered), as all activities undertaken by a sole practitioner or partner are deemed to be in the course or furtherance of business. The fees received should, therefore, be treated as inclusive of VAT.

25.25 For assistant solicitors, the VAT treatment depends on whether or not the assistant retains the fees. If the assistant is obliged to account for the fees to the practice or firm, the fees are treated as part of the firm's income and VAT should be accounted for. However, if the assistant is permitted to retain the fees, no VAT is due unless the assistant solicitor is VAT-registered on his own account (because of other taxable activities), or if the level of oath fees are such that they exceed the VAT registration threshold.

25.26 In the case of retired solicitors or solicitors who are not practising, the fees are not subject to VAT unless the solicitor providing the service is VAT-registered as a result of the level of oath fees generated, or other taxable activities.

Other activities

25.27 Of course, solicitors may engage in other activities outside the practice. As with the situation for oath fees discussed at paragraphs 25.24 to 25.26 above, the question of whether or not VAT should be charged on other services depends on the circumstances. The treatment of remuneration received outside the solicitor's firm or practice has been tested at tribunal. In the case of *Lean & Rose, [1974] VATTR 7(54)*, a partner in a firm of solicitors was employed part-time by the local council. The question arose whether or not this income was received by the firm of solicitors, and therefore liable to VAT, or by the partner in a personal capacity. The tribunal found that the firm was not liable to account for VAT on his salary since the contract was between the individual and the council and not the firm. This demonstrates that solicitors must consider any activities in which they engage to establish whether or not output VAT is due on the income received.

Recovery of VAT

25.28 Solicitors can occasionally receive income which is exempt from VAT. It is important that this is identified so that VAT is charged where appropriate, and also because it may impact on the recovery of VAT on direct and overhead expenditure. For example, exempt income can be received from rental income (where the property is not subject to an option to tax—see chapter 21—Property Development), or commissions received for arranging mortgages or insurance (see paragraphs 25.11 to 25.15 above). It is feasible that exempt income is received on a one-off basis, which would mean that no restriction of input VAT would be necessary. In addition, it is possible to receive exempt income and be treated as fully taxable, provided that the VAT on costs attributable to the exempt supplies falls within certain limits known as the *de minimis* limits (see *VAT Regulations 1995 (SI 1995 No 2518), Regulation 106*). This is an extensive subject which is covered in more detail in *Tolley's VAT 1998/99, para 49.4*.

25.29 It is important to distinguish between income which is exempt and standard-rated in order to account for VAT where appropriate, and to monitor the level of this income to ascertain whether a restriction of VAT incurred on costs is necessary.

Accounting and Records

Time of supply

25.30 The nature of the services supplied by a solicitor means that the services can be supplied over a long period of time. This may mean that payment is requested at intervals or when the services are completed. The tax point, i.e. the time at which VAT becomes payable, depends on whether there is a single supply, for example, the preparation of a contract, or a continuous supply, i.e. ongoing litigation work. A point to note is that a series of separate jobs for one person does not amount to a continuous supply purely because it continues over a period of time, but it is important to distinguish between a one-off service and continuous supplies of services because of the differing VAT tax point rules.

Single supply

25.31 The basic tax point for a single supply of services occurs when the service is completed and this is when VAT becomes payable. In practice, this is usually when all the work (except the invoicing) has been carried out. However, the basic tax point is overridden by an actual tax point. The actual tax point occurs when:

(a)   a payment is received before the basic tax point; or

25.32 VAT Business by Business

(b) a tax invoice is issued in advance of the basic tax point, or within 14 days of the service being completed.

25.32 It is agreed practice under Law Society rules that, where payment for services is accepted, the solicitor should generate a fee note within 7 days. In certain circumstances, however, it may be necessary to extend the 14-day rule, for example, when it is not possible to ascertain a fee at the time the services are completed, if third party services have not been invoiced to the solicitor. To avoid difficulties in complying with VAT legislation in this area, the Law Society has an agreement with Customs & Excise which extends the 14-day rule to three months.

25.33 As the services to the client can include settling costs, the basic tax point will not occur until the fees have been agreed with the opposing solicitor or, where the case is referred to the court for taxation, until the taxation is complete.

Continuous supplies

25.34 Where services are provided over a period of time, and payment is due periodically, there is no basic tax point. A tax point occurs every time a tax invoice is issued by the solicitor, or whenever a payment is received, whichever is earlier.

Accounting for commission

25.35 As can be seen from paragraphs 25.11 to 25.15 above, a solicitor can earn various types of commission. In practice, the solicitor may wish to pass on the benefit of the commission to the client by reducing the value of the fee by the amount of commission received. In this situation, VAT is chargeable on the reduced fee. However, if the commission is shown on the invoice as a deduction from the amount payable by the client, VAT is still due on the full fee, although the client will pay a reduced amount.

Example:

The solicitor's fee is £500, and he receives a commission of £50 from an insurance underwriter. He reduces the fee thus:

Fee	450 (net of commission)
VAT at 17.5%	78.75
	£528.75

Alternatively:

Fee	500
VAT at 17.5%	87.50

	587.50
less commission rec'd	50
Amount due	£537.50

VAT treatment of counsel's fees

25.36 Customs allow further concessionary treatment in relation to counsel's fees. Counsel may be engaged by a solicitor where his client requires such services. The services provided by counsel are standard-rated. However, the question arises to whom the services are supplied, and consequently which party is entitled to reclaim the VAT charge. It is possible for counsel to invoice the client directly, which avoids any problems with VAT recovery on his services. However, it is often the case that the invoice is sent to the solicitor. In these circumstances, the solicitor may treat the fees as an ordinary cost of his business, recovering the VAT charged and charging VAT on his own invoice to his client.

25.37 Alternatively, he may treat counsel's advice as supplied directly to his client, and his settlement of counsel's fees as a disbursement. In this case he may amend counsel's tax invoice by adding the name and address of the client and inserting 'per' before his own name and address. The fee note from counsel will then be recognised as a valid tax invoice in the hands of the client. Unfortunately, this concession is not widely known and can often lead to problems with local VAT offices.

25.38 Customs also permit this treatment to be used, exceptionally, for agency disbursements involving other kinds of suppliers, provided that the solicitor has asked the supplier to address the invoice to the client. However, where the supplier fails to address the invoice as requested, the solicitor can subsequently obtain his approval to amend the invoice by adding the name and address of the client. Nevertheless, Customs have stated that this concessionary treatment should be regarded as an exception. Their stated position is as follows:

> 'In these circumstances, the addition of a client's name and address to a tax invoice for a supply which would qualify for treatment as a disbursement for VAT purposes is intended to operate only as a long stop, i.e. a solicitor, like any other taxable person operating in a similar situation, would normally be expected to request the supplier to make out the tax invoice in the name of the client. In the case of solicitors only, it has been agreed that where, despite this, a supplier makes out the tax invoice to the solicitor, the latter, after obtaining the approval of the supplier, may pass it on after adding to it his client's name and address.'

25.39 If the solicitor considers that the services of counsel, when supplied directly to the client, are properly outside the scope of UK VAT, he may

25.40 *VAT Business by Business*

certify counsel's fee note to this effect and pay counsel the fee net of VAT. This would apply if, for example, the client belongs in another Member State and receives the supply in a business capacity, or belonged outside the EC.

25.40 Where an expense meets the conditions outlined above, and can be treated as a disbursement, it should be itemised on the solicitor's invoice and shown as payable after VAT has been calculated on the services provided. In practice, a disbursement can be passed on gross to the client which prevents the solicitor reclaiming input tax on the supply (since no goods or services have been supplied to him). Furthermore, the client may also be prevented from reclaiming input tax as he does not hold a valid tax invoice in his name.

25.41 Generally, therefore, it is only advantageous to treat a payment as a disbursement for VAT purposes if:

(a) no VAT is chargeable on the supply by the third party (i.e. the supply is exempt or zero-rated); or

(b) the client is not entitled to reclaim the VAT.

25.42 If the solicitor treats a payment as a disbursement, he must keep evidence to enable him to demonstrate that he was entitled to exclude the payment from the value of his supply to his client. He must also show that he did not reclaim input tax on the supply by the third party.

Credit notes

25.43 Occasionally the solicitor's fee is required to be reviewed by the Law Society in accordance with the *Solicitor's (Non-contentious Business) Remuneration Order 1994*. VAT is still due if a basic or actual tax point has occurred, but if the fee is subsequently reduced the solicitor can issue a credit note.

25.44 Generally speaking, credit notes can only be issued where there is a genuine reduction in the fee. Where a solicitor issues a credit note as a result of a compulsory fee reduction (i.e. the fee has been reviewed by the Law Society), or where fees are reduced by agreement with the client, the solicitor should reduce his output VAT account accordingly in the period in which the credit note is issued.

Reverse charge services

25.45 It is possible that in the course of supplying services, a solicitor may use the services of someone established abroad. It is important to recognise that there may be a requirement to account for VAT in the UK on services which are within the scope of *VATA 1994, 5 Sch*. For example, if legal services of a solicitor in France are received by the UK solicitor he must account for UK VAT on the value of the services received. The VAT charged can be reclaimed as input tax in the same VAT accounting period according to the partial exemption position of the receiving solicitor.

25.46 However, excluded from this are services from an overseas supplier relating to land either in or outside the UK, neither of which are liable to reverse charge accounting in the UK. In relation to land in the UK, it may be necessary for the person supplying the services to become VAT registered in the UK and charge UK VAT accordingly. For services in relation to land situated outside the UK, local VAT may be charged which can only be reclaimed via a claim to the authorities in the country in which the VAT was incurred.

Practical points

Third party costs

25.47 It can often be difficult to ascertain the recipient of a supply. This situation arises in particular in relation to third party costs, i.e. where someone other than the client is paying the solicitor's fees. It is worth remembering that the paying party does not necessarily receive the services, so the solicitor should still invoice his own client. Whether or not the person paying the bill is required to meet the gross or net cost will depend on the status of the person who received the services and the amount of VAT which he is entitled to claim on the solicitor's services.

25.48 Further difficulties can arise in relation to loss recovery services provided in connection with an insurance claim. Legal services are generally provided to the policy holder rather than the insurer, even if the insurance company commissions the work on behalf of the policy holder, or if the claim is subjugated to the insurance company. This can have implications for the place of supply rules, particularly where services are supplied to persons outside the UK. For example, the services of a solicitor instructed by a UK insurance company where a US person has subjugated a claim are outside the scope of UK VAT. However, an insurance company can also receive legal services for its own purposes, for example, in drafting or interpreting policies and in disputes with the policy holder. It is recommended that the identity of the recipient of the services is determined at the outset, to avoid complications at a later date.

Chapter 26

Tour Operators

Introduction

26.1 Under the normal VAT rules, a tour operator who provides package holidays in other EC Member States, using bought-in travel services, would be liable to account for VAT in each country where the traveller receives the services, and might possibly require a VAT registration in all the 15 Member States. However, to remove this difficulty, a simplification measure under *EC Sixth Directive, Article 26* provides a special scheme for tour operators which allows tour operators to account for VAT entirely within their home country. To ensure that the Member States where the services are enjoyed are not deprived of revenue, the scheme prevents the tour operator from recovering any VAT paid when buying-in the travel services, and taxes only the tour operator's gross margin. Therefore, VAT at the local rate on the cost price of the travel facilities flows to the Member State where they are enjoyed, and VAT on the gross profit margin flows to the tour operator's home country at its local rate.

26.2 *EC Sixth Directive, Article 26* was implemented in UK VAT legislation on 1 April 1988 by *VATA 1994, s 53* and the details of the special scheme are included in the *VAT (Tour Operators) Order 1987 (SI 1987 No 1806)* which will be referred to as the 'TOMS Order' in this chapter. The wording of the UK legislation gives a blanket application of the margin scheme across all types of businesses and is not restricted to tour operators which provide overseas package holidays. The UK rules apply to all supplies of travel services which are bought-in and re-supplied to a traveller without any material alteration. This means that any business could be affected, not just those who consider themselves to be tour operators. It also means that tour operators who buy-in and re-supply travel services wholly within the UK must account for VAT under the margin scheme even though they are not affected by any potential overseas VAT difficulty of the type which Article 26 seeks to remove.

26.3 It is important to distinguish between the travel services that fall to be treated under the margin scheme and the details of the scheme itself. The Tour Operators Margin Scheme, which will be referred to as the 'TOMS' in this chapter, is the set of rules in the TOMS Order (as supplemented by additional items in VAT Notice 709/5). Only those travel services that fall within the term 'designated travel service' as defined in paragraph 3 of the

26.4 VAT Business by Business

TOMS Order are subject to accounting under the TOMS. These will be referred to as 'TOMS supplies'. Travel services that are provided by a tour operator using his own resources are referred to as 'in-house' supplies and VAT is payable on the full price under the normal rules. However, in-house supplies may need to be taken account of in output VAT calculations under the TOMS if package holidays are provided that include a mixture of in-house supplies and TOMS supplies.

Liability

Definition of a TOMS supply

26.4 To qualify as a TOMS supply, goods and services must be bought-in by an EC-based tour operator acting in his own name and must be re-supplied for the benefit of a traveller without material alteration. The phrases 'tour operator', 'benefit of a traveller' and 'material alteration' are the key components of the definition and are all open to debate when deciding whether a particular supply qualifies as a TOMS supply. The definition of a TOMS supply in UK law relies wholly on these phrases and does not point to any particular types of goods and services that must be treated as travel services. In contrast, *EC Sixth Directive, Article 26* refers to the operations of travel agents (including tour operators) who deal with customers in their own name and use the supplies of other taxable persons in the provision of travel facilities. The features of the three key components of the UK definition are considered in paragraphs 26.5 to 26.11 below.

Tour Operator

26.5 The phrase 'tour operator' is not defined in *EC Sixth Directive, Article 26*, but *VATA 1994, s 53(3)* specifies that the term includes a travel agent acting as a principal and also any other person providing, for the benefit of travellers, services of any kind commonly provided by tour operators or travel agents. Consequently, Customs & Excise take the view that any business is a tour operator if it supplies any of the services that could be found in a package holiday (e.g. transport, accommodation, catering, entertainment, excursions etc). However, in the case of *Virgin Atlantic Airways Ltd, [1993] VATTR 136 (11096)*, Customs argued that the provision of bought-in limousine transport to or from the airport before and after a flight was a TOMS supply, but Virgin successfully argued that it was an air transport provider and not a tour operator. In another notable case, *TP Madgett & RM Baldwin (13009)*, the operators of a hotel that provided hotel packages which included bought-in transport, successfully argued before the tribunal that they were hoteliers and not tour operators. Customs & Excise appealed to the High Court which could not decide whether a hotelier could also be a tour operator and referred the question to the European Court of Justice (*QB 1995, [1996] STC 167*). The decision of the European Court is still awaited at the time of writing. Therefore, until the position is clarified, all businesses should be prepared to apply the TOMS to any bought-in supplies of travel facilities that are provided to travelling customers. However, if this would be disadvantageous, they should examine whether the mere provision of travel services of a kind provided by a tour operator is sufficient to make them a 'tour operator' in their individual circumstances.

26.6 Businesses, including travel agents, who are intermediaries acting on behalf of tour operators do not fall within the TOMS. It is only the tour operator who provides the travel services as principal that is required to account for VAT under the TOMS. Agency commission is subject to the normal VAT accounting rules, but the VAT treatment can depend upon how the travel services are dealt with by tour operators, as discussed in paragraphs 26.19 to 26.22 below.

'Direct benefit of a traveller'

26.7 The word 'traveller' is not defined in the TOMS Order and there is scope for debate when deciding whether, in a particular case, the customer is a traveller or the supply concerned is for the benefit of a traveller. Clearly, a supply of bought-in transport made directly to a passenger will qualify as a TOMS supply (all other conditions being satisfied) as will any other services, such as catering, that are provided during the journey. It is also assumed that when a passenger is temporarily away from his home on a package holiday, he is a 'traveller' for the whole period of absence and not just during the outward and return journeys. The position is less clear when the supplier does not arrange the passenger's transport, but provides associated travel services such as accommodation. However, in the case of *Beheersmaatschappij Van Ginkel Waddinxveen BV and Others v Inspecteur der Omzetbelasting Utrecht, CJEC 1992, [1996] STC 825*, the European Court of Justice ruled that a supply of bought-in holiday accommodation provided by a tour operator to holidaymaker falls within the special scheme notwithstanding the fact that the passenger uses his own transport for the journey. In other cases, it will be necessary to consider the individual facts to judge whether the goods and services are for the direct benefit of a traveller.

26.8 The UK definition of a TOMS supply refers to 'the benefit of a traveller' whilst *EC Sixth Directive, Article 26* is more specific and refers to 'the *direct* benefit'. Up to 31 December 1995, Customs & Excise took the view that any bought-in travel services which ultimately benefited a traveller were TOMS supplies whether or not the customer was another business rather than the actual traveller. However, as a result of the tribunal decision in the case of *Independent Coach Travel (Wholesaling) Ltd, [1993] VATTR 357 (11037)*, Customs & Excise announced that, from 1 January 1996, the customer must be the traveller, so that any supplies between businesses will not generally be TOMS supplies. In paragraph 4.2 of Notice 709/5, Customs & Excise state that, as a trade facilitation measure, businesses that supply bought-in travel services to other businesses for onward supply can elect to treat them as TOMS supplies if they wish, but only if prior permission is

26.9 VAT Business by Business

obtained from the local VAT office. With effect from 1 January 1998, the exclusion from the TOMS for business-to-business TOMS supplies was restricted to wholesale supplies for retail. If the recipient business consumes the TOMS supplies, the services fall within the TOMS. This latest announcement could receive further modification since the phrase 'for the benefit of a traveller' suggests that the recipient should be a physical person such that corporate persons in law might not be capable of being a traveller. A second trade facilitation measure is provided in paragraph 4.3 of Notice 709/5, under which permission can be sought for supplies to business customers for consumption falling within the TOMS can be treated as *not* within the scheme. This second measure is subject to a number of conditions, one of which is that VAT is paid locally in any EC Member State on any TOMS supplies that are enjoyed in that Member State.

26.9 The legal basis for this 'trade facilitation' measure appears to be wholly within UK law, which has a wider interpretation of the phrases 'tour operator' and 'direct benefit of a traveller' than that in *EC Sixth Directive, Article 26*. In the case of *Norman Allen Group Travel Ltd (14158)* the VAT tribunal was in no doubt that the wholesale supplies of travel services by this company to other businesses fell within the definition of TOMS supplies under UK law, but that the special scheme required by *EC Sixth Directive, Article 26* could not be applied to the supplies because they were not made directly to the travellers who finally enjoyed them. If UK law is brought fully into line with European law, the in-TOMS 'trade facilitation' measure may need to be withdrawn and tour operators that supply travel services to other businesses for resale may not be able to treat them as TOMS supplies when they might otherwise wish to do so.

Material alteration or further processing

26.10 Whether or not a bought-in travel service is 'materially altered or further processed' by a tour operator when it is re-supplied to a traveller is a further item for debate when deciding whether a particular supply falls to be treated as a TOMS supply. The mere bringing together of two or more components to make a package could materially alter each bought-in element to make the package an in-house supply rather than a TOMS supply. For example, if a tour operator hires a holiday chalet from the owner for a whole season, buys-in the services of local agents to service the chalet between each let and re-lets the accommodation to a number of holidaymakers for one or two weeks, the short holiday lets would be materially different from the bought-in right to occupy the chalet for the whole season. The supply of holiday accommodation would be an in-house supply and not a TOMS supply even though all the elements of the package were bought-in. Another example is the hiring of hotel accommodation, catering and visiting speakers by a conference organiser who supplies delegates with a right to attend a conference. However, conference organisers must take care, because some bought-in travel services (such as overnight accommodation for delegates and particularly for their guests) which are not part of the conference might not be materially altered when re-supplied.

26.11 Appendix I of Notice 709/5 includes a number of examples of material alteration that are recognised by Customs & Excise as disqualifying bought-in supplies from counting as TOMS supplies. For example, the re-supply of seat-only transport on aircraft charter flights can be materially altered if additional items are added to the basic air flight (see paragraph 26.41 below). Operators of camping holidays might buy-in the hire of pitches on campsites and the hire of camping equipment, but if they erect and service the tents the two bought-in supplies could be materially altered to make a single supply of in-house accommodation.

Special exclusion

26.12 *Article 3(4)* of the TOMS Order allows Customs & Excise to specify that a particular supply which would otherwise qualify as a TOMS supply can be deemed not to be a TOMS supply. The features of the TOMS supplies which Customs & Excise allow not to fall within the TOMS are quoted in paragraphs 2.3 and 4.5 of Notice 709/5. These features are:

- that the supplier concerned is not involved in buying-in any accommodation or passenger transport for re-supply as a TOMS supply;

- that the turnover expected from the TOMS supplies which are not to be treated as TOMS supplies, is not expected to exceed 1% of the total annual turnover.

Paragraph 4.5 cites an example that a hotelier who buys-in car hire services for re-supply to hotel guests would not need to apply the TOMS. However, in any case, it could be argued (see 26.5 above) that the hotelier would not be a 'tour operator', so that the bought-in car hire would not fall within the definition of a TOMS supply.

Single supply of TOMS services

26.13 Bought-in goods and services which pass the tests to qualify as TOMS supplies are further distinguished from normal supplies by being treated as a single supply of services. Therefore, a holiday package containing a number of elements would represent one TOMS supply if all the components are bought-in. However, if the elements included a mixture of bought-in supplies and in-house supplies, the bought-in components would be a single TOMS supply whilst each in-house component would be a separate stand-alone supply. The place where each of the supplies takes place and the rate of VAT that applies could then differ between the single TOMS supply and the in-house supply.

26.14 VAT Business by Business

26.14 Up to 31 December 1995, *article 10* of the TOMS Order allowed any transport element within a single TOMS supply to be zero-rated under *VATA 1994, 8 Sch, Group 8*. Similarly, any educational element which qualified under *VATA 1994, 9 Sch, Group 6* could be exempted. However, this legislation did not comply with the EC Sixth Directive since a single supply can only be subject to a single rate of VAT. Therefore, from 1 January 1996, *article 10* of the TOMS Order was repealed, so that a TOMS supply must now be treated as a single supply of services which is wholly standard-rated, irrespective of the VAT treatment of the individual components when bought-in by the tour operator. This means that the VAT content within the VAT-inclusive selling price of package holidays, which include bought-in elements, was increased from 1 January 1996.

Place of supply of TOMS services

26.15 A TOMS supply, as a single supply of services, is deemed to be made in the place where the tour operator has established his business. When this place is in a Member State of the EC, VAT will be payable on the gross margin of the TOMS supply at the rate applicable in the country concerned. Tour operators who are established outside the EC are not liable to account for any EC VAT on the margin, whether or not travel services are bought-in and made available to travellers in the EC.

26.16 If a tour operator has more than one fixed establishment, a TOMS supply is deemed to be made from the establishment that is most directly concerned with providing the travel services and VAT will be payable when this is in an EC country. When considering whether an establishment exists in the UK, it must be remembered that *VATA 1994, s 9(5)* requires that a branch or agency in the UK is treated as an establishment. In the case of *DFDS A/S*, Customs & Excise argued that TOMS supplies made by a Danish tour operator through an agent in the UK were taxable in the UK. The tribunal disagreed but the High Court, on appeal, referred a question to the European Court of Justice for a ruling on the meaning of 'fixed establishment'. The CJEC agreed with Customs & Excise and ruled that, where a tour operator established in one Member State provides services to travellers through the intermediary of a company acting as an agent in another Member State, VAT is payable on the services in the latter state if the company acting as the agent has the human and technical resources characteristic of a fixed establishment (*C &E Commrs v DFDS A/S, CJEC [1997] STC 384; [1997] AEECR 342*).

Value of supply

26.17 For all VAT purposes, the value of a TOMS supply is the margin (exclusive of VAT) by which the amount receivable from the traveller exceeds the actual cost to the tour operator of the travel services that are bought-in and re-supplied. As package holidays are normally sold at a single VAT-inclusive price, a method is required to calculate the value of the margin on the single TOMS supply contained within the selling price. The method must take account of packages which contain a TOMS supply together with in-house supplies. The value of a TOMS supply is required to be determined under the TOMS Order 'by reference to sums paid or payable to and sums paid or payable by the tour operator in respect of that service, calculated in such manner as the Commissioners of Customs & Excise shall specify'. This manner is specified in Appendices A and B of Notice 709/5 together with a simplified method in Appendix C.

Zero-rating

26.18 Although a TOMS supply made by a UK-based tour operator is a taxable supply, the margin can be zero-rated under *VATA 1994, Sch 8, Group 8, Item 12* to the extent that the supply is enjoyed outside the EC. Appendix H of Notice 709/5 gives guidance on when a journey can be regarded as wholly or partly outside the EC depending upon the kind of stops that take place within the EC. If a journey is partly inside and partly outside the EC, an apportionment must be made between the two elements. This could be based upon the amount of time spent inside and outside the EC or the number of miles travelled. Since a TOMS supply is defined as being a single supply of services, the normal VAT rules would suggest that it should be either wholly standard-rated or wholly zero-rated. Therefore, the continued acceptance by Customs & Excise that the margin on combined EC/non-EC holidays can be apportioned within the TOMS must be regarded as a concession which could be challenged by the EC Commission. Tour operators can elect to carry out a separate margin scheme calculation for holidays which are enjoyed wholly outside the EC, if permission is obtained from Customs & Excise.

Travel agents' commission

26.19 The services of arranging a zero-rated supply of transport can also be zero-rated under *VATA 1994, Sch 8, Group 8, item 10*. However, as a result of the change on 1 January 1996, by which UK TOMS supplies now have to be treated as a single supply of standard-rated services (see paragraph 26.14 above), Customs & Excise issued guidance on the VAT treatment of travel agents' commission in Business Brief 2/96. The introduction of the revised treatment was postponed to 1 May 1996 to allow travel agents and tour operators who issue self-billed invoices, to amend their accounting systems. Prior to 1 May 1996, agent's commission for arranging seat-only passenger transport was zero-rated irrespective of whether it was provided to the passenger by a transport provider using in-house resources or by a tour operator using bought-in transport. From 1 May 1996, agents' commission for arranging seat-only transport is zero-rated only when it is provided as an in-house supply. If the seat-only transport is provided by a tour operator as a bought-in TOMS supply, the transport is a standard-rated TOMS supply and hence the agent's commission is also standard-rated. Therefore, travel agents now need to know the VAT treatment that the tour operator is applying to the transport before they can determine the VAT treatment of the commission.

26.20 Agents' commission for selling package holidays, upon which the tour operator accounts for UK VAT, is standard-rated. As discussed in paragraph 26.15 above, the place of supply of TOMS services is the country where the tour operator has established his business and not where the holiday is enjoyed. Consequently, agent's commission for arranging a TOMS supply will be standard-rated if it is received from a UK-based tour operator, irrespective of where the holiday is enjoyed. Under the EC Single Market rules, an agent is deemed to supply his service in the same place that his principal makes the supply to the customer. Therefore, if a UK travel agent arranges a holiday which is a TOMS supply made by an overseas tour operator, both the holiday and the service of arranging it will be supplied outside the UK. Consequently, neither the holiday itself nor the commission will be subject to UK VAT whether or not the holiday is enjoyed in the UK. In these circumstances, the agent's commission is subject to VAT in the same EC country where the tour operator accounts for VAT on the holiday. However, travel agents do not need to register for VAT in the EC overseas countries concerned, because the overseas tour operator must charge himself local VAT on the agency fee using the reverse charge procedure. This shift of VAT accounting on commission to the overseas tour operator is conditional upon the tour operator being registered for VAT in the country concerned.

26.21 Some tour operators provide holidays which include in-house supplies of accommodation provided from their own resources. The place of supply of such accommodation is where the hotel is situated and the travel agent's service of arranging the accommodation is deemed to be supplied at the same place. Therefore, travel agents must not assume that all commission received from UK tour operators will be subject to UK VAT, because the tour operator might be accounting for VAT on the holiday services via another VAT registration abroad. In this case, the agent's commission will be outside the scope of UK VAT. Similarly, travel agents must not assume that all commission received from overseas tour operators is not subject to UK VAT. If the overseas operator makes in-house supplies in the UK, the travel services will be subject to UK VAT and so will the agent's commission.

26.22 Many tour operators self-bill the commission that they pay to travel agents and they take on the responsibility of determining the VAT treatment of the commission. Therefore, both tour operators and travel agents need to be familiar with the VAT rules relating to agent's commission. UK tour operators who self-bill commission payable to overseas travel agents, relating to holidays upon which the tour operator accounts for UK VAT, must also account for UK VAT on the commission by applying the reverse charge procedure.

VAT recovery

26.23 It is a key feature of both EC and UK law that no recovery can be made of input VAT incurred on the cost of buying-in travel services that are re-supplied as a TOMS supply. The tour operator receives an effective credit for the input tax because the output VAT that he pays is the VAT component of the tax-inclusive margin between the tax-inclusive selling price and the tax-inclusive cost. This is a helpful simplification for tour operators who provide buy-in travel services in other EC Member States because effective VAT recovery is achieved without the need to make overseas EC VAT recovery claims under the *EC Eighth Directive*.

26.24 The blocking of input tax recovery applies only to the costs of acquiring bought-in services and does not affect the overhead expenditure of the tour operator. It also does not affect input VAT incurred on the costs of making in-house supplies of travel services, which is always recoverable subject to the normal rules.

26.25 The recipient of a TOMS supply is also unable to recover input tax because the TOMS prevents VAT being shown separately on sales invoices for TOMS supplies. In any case, the TOMS annual calculation does not provide a separate margin for each individual TOMS supply and tour operators would not wish to show the amount of VAT hence revealing their profit margin. The travelling public who buy package holidays are not VAT-registered and are not affected by this feature. However, some businesses which acquire a TOMS supply could be disadvantaged. For example, a fully taxable business that organises a residential sales conference for its employees, and purchases transport and accommodation which are TOMS supplies, would not be aware of the VAT content and would not be able to recover any input tax.

26.26 Up to 31 December 1995, supplies of bought-in travel services made to other businesses counted as TOMS supplies, but *article 3(3)* of the TOMS Order allowed Customs & Excise to treat such supplies as not being TOMS supplies if the tour operator made a written request. This provision remains in the TOMS Order, but because wholesale TOMS supplies for resale are no longer within the TOMS (unless Customs & Excise allow otherwise), the provision relates only to the non-TOMS 'trade facilitation' measure (see paragraph 26.8 above).

Accounting and records

26.27 VAT must be accounted for using the TOMS when a supply is made which is a single TOMS supply or which involves a package comprising a TOMS supply and one or more in-house supplies provided for a single consideration. The purpose of the TOMS is to generate a margin for the standard-rated TOMS supplies and it results in all elements of a travel package being allocated the same average percentage profitability. However, it is only the TOMS supplies for which VAT must be accounted for on the margin. Businesses that provide both in-house supplies and TOMS supplies which have different rates of profitability may prefer to invoice them separately so that the TOMS calculations are restricted only to the TOMS supplies.

Annual accounting

26.28 The TOMS is an annual accounting method whereby a single gross margin is calculated for all the TOMS supplies made in a year. The year is the financial accounting period of the business and not the VAT year. This allows for the seasonal nature of holiday supplies and for timing differences between receipts of payments from travellers and payments to suppliers for bought-in travel supplies. It is not necessary to calculate a gross margin for each individual TOMS supply, nor to calculate the gross margin for the TOMS supplies made in an individual VAT period.

26.29 The results of the annual TOMS calculation for the previous each year are used to provide a provisional estimate of the standard-rated portion of the margin on the TOMS supplies for use in the following year. For each VAT period in the year, the estimate is applied to the turnover arising from TOMS supplies to calculate a provisional amount of output tax. These provisional output tax amounts are adjusted on the first VAT return following the end of the year when the full annual TOMS calculation is made. This procedure does not provide for provisional output tax calculations in the first year in which a tour operator commences to use the TOMS when there is no previous year to refer to. New tour operators who bought an existing business may be able to use the previous owner's prior-year calculation. Alternatively, a projection of income and expenditure could be made to predict the outturn of the TOMS calculation in the first year, or an actual margin calculated for each VAT period.

Tax points

26.30 Tour operators must choose one of two methods to determine the tax point of all their TOMS supplies. Method 1 adopts the date of departure for the journey concerned or the date of first occupation of any accommodation, whichever happens first. Method 2 adopts the tax point under Method 1 or the date of receipt of payments of a certain size, whichever happens first. Method 2 is designed for the normal travel industry practice of requiring a deposit to be paid when the package holiday is booked and the balance to be paid at a specified time in advance of departure. If only one payment is received, or a deposit of 20% or less is received followed by one final payment, the tax point is the date of the main payment (unless this is overridden by an earlier date of departure/first occupation). If the deposit is more than 20%, or there are interim payments of more than 20%, there is a tax point on the date of receipt of each payment (subject to any earlier date of departure/first occupation). As a result of these specific TOMS tax point rules, tour operators using the TOMS cannot use the cash accounting scheme which would otherwise allow all output VAT to be accounted for by reference to the date of cash receipt.

Tour Operators 26.35

Bad debt relief

26.31 If a tax point arises for a TOMS supply because a traveller is allowed to depart or take up accommodation (as the earliest event) without having paid, and the traveller then fails to pay thus creating a bad debt, the tour operator is entitled to claim bad debt relief after the waiting period of six months. However, since the output VAT calculation in each period is a provisional estimate, the relief is obtained by reducing the turnover figure in the full annual TOMS. Consequently, bad debt relief is not available until after the end of the financial year in which the supply was made.

The simplified calculation

26.32 If all the turnover of a tour operator comprises TOMS supplies, the annual margin scheme calculation is quite simple. The total tax-inclusive cost of buying-in travel services that were re-supplied with a tax point in the year is deducted from the total tax-inclusive turnover of those TOMS supplies. The difference is the tax-inclusive margin and the annual VAT payable is $\frac{17.5}{117.5}$ of the margin (for a VAT rate of 17.5%). Under the simplified calculation in Appendix C of Notice 709/5, the margin is treated as wholly standard-rated. If any of the holidays are wholly or partly enjoyed outside the EC, VAT will be paid on the associated margin even though it is eligible to be zero-rated. If this margin is small, the administrative savings may compensate for the extra VAT cost, but otherwise the full TOMS calculation must be used.

26.33 As a concession, Customs & Excise may give permission, upon application, for TOMS supplies which are wholly enjoyed outside the EC to be subject to a separate individual annual TOMS calculation. There would then be two simplified calculations in which the margin on the wholly non-EC TOMS supplies would be zero-rated and the margin on the EC TOMS supplies and mixed EC/non-EC packages would be standard-rated.

The full TOMS calculation

26.34 The full annual TOMS calculation is described in Appendix A of Notice 709/5 (February 1998 edition) and Appendix B defines the provisional taxable output ratios for the next year, derived from Appendix A.

26.35 There are 22 steps in Appendix A leading up to the calculation of the total output VAT payable for the year. The cost value in some of steps 2 to 9 could be nil depending upon the mix of in-house and TOMS supplies made in the year. From 1 January 1996, costs of bought-in transport must be included in step 2 rather than in step 3, which will include only the direct cost of TOMS supplies (with a tax point on or after this date) that are provided to travellers outside the EC. Similarly, bought-in services relating to previously exempt TOMS supplies must be included in step 2 rather than in the old

26.36 *VAT Business by Business*

step 4 and as a result, the old step 4 has been removed from Appendix A in the February 1998 edition.

26.36 There are some specific points to watch when determining the values to be included in each step:

- **Turnover in step 1.** This step comprises the annual total of the selling prices of all single TOMS supplies (with a TOMS tax point in the year) and all packages which combine a TOMS supply with one or more in-house supplies having a tax point in the year concerned. The prices must be the gross amount before deduction of any commission paid to agents, but can be net of any discounts or refunds given to the travellers. Step 1 should not include any income from in-house supplies that are provided independently of TOMS supplies.

- **Direct costs in steps 2 and 3.** Step 2 includes the direct costs of buying-in the travel services which were used to make the standard-rated TOMS supplies included in the turnover in step 1. Similarly, step 3 comprises the direct costs of making the zero-rated TOMS supplies included in the turnover in step 1. In both steps the value is inclusive of any UK or overseas input tax incurred on the costs, since this VAT is not recoverable. Indirect overheads cannot be included.

- **In-house costs in steps 4 and 7.** Step 4 includes all costs, including any direct overheads, incurred in making any standard-rated in-house supplies which were combined in a package with a TOMS supply and are included in step 1. The costs can include taxable, exempt and non-taxable items and the standard-rated costs are exclusive of the input tax which is fully recoverable. If items of expenditure relate partly to wholly in-house supplies which are not included in step 1 and partly to combined packages that are included, the cost must be apportioned to determine the amount to be included in step 4. For example, in Appendix K of Notice 709/5, Customs & Excise state that guest booking numbers must be used as the basis for apportioning the costs of supplying in-house accommodation between the TOMS and non-TOMS elements. Appendix K also requires the prior approval of Customs & Excise if any other basis of apportionment is used. To give comparability to the tax-inclusive turnover in step 1 and the tax-inclusive costs in steps 2 and 3, the total cost in step 4 must be uplifted by the UK standard rate of VAT to give a notional expense as if all the costs were standard-rated. The same principle is applied in step 7 when a positive-rated in-house supply is enjoyed by a traveller in another EC country and the tour operator is registered for VAT there. However, the uplift will be at the VAT rate applicable in the country concerned and, if in-house supplies were made in a

Tour Operators **26.36**

number of countries with different VAT rates, step 7 will require separate cost totals for each country.

- **In-house costs in steps 5 and 6.** Step 5 comprises all the costs incurred in making any zero-rated in-house supplies that were combined in a package with a TOMS supply in step 1. Step 6 comprises all the costs relating to exempt in-house supplies (generally eligible tuition in educational packages). No VAT uplift to the cost total is required in either step 5 or 6 because the uplift for step 5 is at the zero-rate and step 6 relates to exempt supplies. Apportionments of some costs may be required when they relate partly to in-house supplies which are combined as a TOMS supply in a single package. In Appendix J of Notice 709/5, Customs & Excise state that mileage performed must be used as the basis of apportioning the costs of making in-house supplies to determine the component for step 5. Appendix J also requires the prior approval from Customs before any other basis is used.

  Input tax on costs in step 5 is fully recoverable, being attributable to in-house zero-rated supplies, and hence is not included in the step 5 value. Some input tax on costs in step 6 may not be recoverable as they are attributable to an in-house exempt supply, but the amounts concerned will depend upon the partial exemption position of the tour operator. Any VAT on costs in step 6 that is irrecoverable can, of course, be included in step 6.

- **'Costs' of agency supplies in steps 8 and 9.** When agency commission is received for arranging supplies of travel services and it is readily identifiable, the commission is not included in the TOMS calculation. However, if the commission cannot be clearly linked to the arranged services, the services must be included in the TOMS calculation as if the tour operator is a principal rather than an agent. The gross amount receivable from the traveller must be included in step 1 and the net amount after commission has been deducted that is payable to the actual principal must be included as a 'cost' in step 8 for standard-rated commissions and in step 9 for other commissions.

- **Apportioning the margin in steps 12 to 19.** Having determined the overall margin between the turnover in step 1 and the total of all costs in step 10, this margin is split into amounts relating to the types of supplies that were included in the turnover (e.g. UK standard-rated and zero-rated TOMS supplies, UK standard-rated, zero-rated and exempt in-house supplies, and EC in-house supplies). The split is achieved by calculating the fraction of the overall total cost in step 10 that is represented by the individual total cost in step 2 to 9 of making each type of supply, and applying these fractions to the margin.

26.37 *VAT Business by Business*

- **Calculating output tax in steps 20 to 22.** Having determined the fraction of the overall margin which relates to UK standard-rated TOMS supplies, the VAT content of this tax-inclusive amount is extracted in step 20 by applying the VAT fraction (7/47 for the 17.5% rate). Output tax is also payable on the full value of in-house UK standard-rated supplies. The fraction of the overall margin allocated to the standard-rated in-house supplies by step 14 must be added to the cost of making the supplies (recorded in step 4) to calculate the tax-inclusive full value of the standard-rated in-house supplies. The VAT content is extracted in step 21 by applying the VAT fraction.

- **The annual adjustment.** The final total of output tax (from steps 20 to 22) that is payable for the year must be compared to the total of the actual amounts of output tax that were provisionally declared on the VAT returns submitted for the year concerned (see paragraph 26.37 below). Any difference between the final TOMS output VAT and the total of the provisional VAT output VAT must be adjusted on the VAT return for the VAT period immediately following the end of the financial year.

The provisional output ratio calculation

26.37 Appendix B of Notice 709/5 describes the method by which output tax is provisionally calculated in each period in the following year, based upon the results of the annual calculation for the previous year. The tax-inclusive value of the fraction of the margin on standard-rated TOMS supplies from step 12, plus the tax-inclusive full value of in-house standard-rated supplies (step 4 plus step 14) and the tax-inclusive value of the fraction of the margin on standard-rated agency supplies from step 18, is expressed as a percentage of the turnover in step 1. This percentage is then applied to the selling prices of TOMS supplies and combined packages having a tax point in each VAT period in the next year to provisionally estimate the tax-inclusive output value subject to VAT in each period.

Practical points

VAT registration

26.38 When first commencing to trade, new tour operators should bear in mind that the value of a TOMS supply is the margin calculated under the scheme. Therefore, when checking whether the VAT registration turnover threshold has been or is likely to be exceeded, it is the margin that must be taken into account not the gross turnover. In the first year of operation, there will not be a prior-year calculation from which a provisional TOMS margin could be adopted to estimate the value of TOMS supplies generated as trading proceeds. Consequently, new tour operators may prefer to register from the start of trading and also consult Customs & Excise to agree an estimated provisional output VAT rate to be used in the first year. The estimated provisional rate might be based upon the budgeted income and expenditure that was projected when setting the brochure prices for the holidays.

Single supply of transport services

26.39 Tour operators who provide packages that include in-house transport provided from their own resources together with other travel facilities (whether in-house or TOMS supplies) should examine whether the package represents a single supply of in-house transport. A single supply of in-house transport will be wholly zero-rated and will not fall within the TOMS even though some elements of the package might be standard-rated if supplied independently. For example, Customs & Excise accept that certain elements of an air flight (e.g. in-flight catering, transfers to/from the airport, accommodation between connecting flights) can be regarded as 'perks' which are part of the air transport. Similarly, a cruise on a ship could be a single supply of transport although passengers receive catering and sleeping accommodation during the journey. The High Court decided, in the case of *Peninsular & Oriental Steam Navigation Co Ltd, QB [1996] STC 698*, that the cruises provided by the company were single supplies of zero-rated transport although Customs & Excise continue to argue that cruises in general are mixed supplies of transport and other services including accommodation.

Avoiding the TOMS on bought-in passenger transport

26.40 From 1 January 1996, the re-supply of bought-in passenger transport is a single TOMS supply which is standard-rated, although the transport may be zero-rated when bought-in from a transport provider. However, it is possible to maintain an effective zero rate on such transport if the commercial arrangements are changed to remove one or more of the key features which otherwise characterises the bought-in transport as a TOMS supply. Customs & Excise have approved two such arrangements, known as the 'charter scheme' and the 'agency scheme' and published in VAT Information Sheets 3/96 and 4/96 respectively. A third arrangement, known as the 'transport company scheme', and published in VAT Information Sheet 2/96 (superseded by VAT Information Sheet 1/97), does not change the final supply of bought-in transport from being a standard-rated TOMS supply, but transfers most of the margin into an additional transport company where the bought-in transport escapes being treated as a TOMS supply and remains zero-rated.

The Charter Scheme

26.41 The 'charter scheme' seeks to add further items to a supply of bought-in transport so that it is materially altered before it is re-supplied to the traveller. The supply would not then count as a single standard-rated

26.42 VAT Business by Business

TOMS supply, but would count as a single zero-rated in-house supply of transport. As its name suggests, the charter scheme was designed for bought-in seats on aircraft charter flights and full details are included in VAT Information Sheet 3/96. Customs & Excise expect that, as well as adding additional items to the air transportation, such as transfer journeys at either end or in-flight catering, the tour operator must also charter the whole aircraft for a specified journey slot for a whole season. The principle could also be used by tour operators who buy-in road, rail or sea transport, although care would be needed to ensure that the bought-in transport is materially altered. For example, the addition of catering to a coach trip would require the meals to be provided on the coach whilst it was moving and preferably because no stops were available to obtain roadside catering.

The Agency Scheme

26.42 Under the 'agency scheme', the tour operator ceases to be a principal, buying and re-selling a standard-rated TOMS supply of transport, but becomes an agent of the transport provider. The transport provider then constitutes a principal in providing in-house transport direct to the customer which continues to be zero-rated. The agency commission would also be zero-rated, although Customs & Excise take the view that any further travel agents involved cannot zero-rate their commission. For this arrangement to be credible, the contractual relationship between the three parties must clearly show the agency basis with the financial risk being taken by the transport provider and the tour operator not acting in his own name. Therefore, care is required in introducing the arrangements, particularly when the tour operator is otherwise buying-in transport and accommodation for inclusion in a package, which he continues to advertise in a holiday brochure as before, but seeks to act as an agent for the transport element and a principal only for other components. VAT Information Sheet 4/96 lists the minimum features of the arrangements which Customs & Excise expect to be present for the scheme to work.

The Transport Company Scheme

26.43 This scheme works by introducing a captive transport company between the original provider of the transport and the tour operator that buys and re-supplies it as a TOMS supply. The captive intermediate transport company would buy-in and re-supply the transport, but because its sale would be to another business rather than to a traveller, the resale of the transport would not constitute a TOMS supply, but would count as a zero-rated in-house supply. Although the transport would be part of a standard-rated TOMS supply when bought-in from the transport company and re-sold by the tour operator, the captive company would be able to maximise the transfer price for the zero-rated transport. This in turn, would minimise the tour operator's taxable margin so that less output tax would be payable. When setting the transfer price, it must be remembered that the TOMS Order includes an anti-avoidance measure allowing Customs & Excise to make a

Tour Operators **26.45**

direction that the cost of buying-in services for re-sale as a TOMS supply must be included in the TOMS margin calculation at its open market value. However, Customs & Excise accept the validity of the scheme, and VAT Information Sheet 1/97 outlines their views relating to the maximisation of the transfer price for the transport.

Mathematical effects of the TOMS

26.44 The mathematical basis of the TOMS is to compute a single margin for all components of the packages that were sold during the whole year and to apportion this margin between the various components. The apportionment of the margin is performed in the TOMS calculation by applying for each component, its cost as a fraction of the total costs (see steps 12 to 19 of the TOMS calculation in paragraph 26.36 above). This apportionment method involves an assumption that the proportion of the selling price relating to each component is the same proportion that its cost represents in the total TOMS costs. This assumption is only valid if all the components have the same mark-up. When the components of the packages have differing mark-ups, the mathematical effect of the scheme is to allocate the overall average profitability to each component irrespective of its actual mark-up. If the standard-rated elements have a lower mark-up than the zero-rated or exempt elements in the turnover, overall the average profitability that is effectively applied to those standard-rated elements will be higher than the actual mark-up. The effect of the TOMS calculation will then result in VAT being paid on a higher apparent margin than that which was budgeted for in the selling price of the package. An example of this effect is seen in a coach excursion to an entertainment show provided by a coach operator which comprises a supply of in-house transport together with a bought-in entrance ticket. If the combined price is costed as including the entrance ticket price with no mark-up, together with the coach fare containing all the profit, the TOMS will produce a standard-rated margin on the entrance ticket (at the average profitability) when no margin had actually been incorporated into the selling price for the entrance element of the combined package. Coach operators in this position could consider selling separate tickets for the coach fare and the entrance ticket so that the in-house zero-rated transport can be wholly omitted from the TOMS calculation. The TOMS calculation would then include only the purchase and selling price of the entrance ticket so that the coach operator would pay VAT only on the actual margin that is applied to the cost of the entrance tickets.

Maximising TOMS costs

26.45 Since the output VAT payable on TOMS supplies relates to the margin between the income and direct costs relating to the supplies, it is important to ensure that all appropriate costs are included in the calculation to minimise the margin. For holiday packages which comprise only bought-in items that are re-supplied as a single TOMS supply, it appears at first sight that the direct costs would comprise only the amounts paid to the providers

26.46 VAT Business by Business

from whom the travel services are purchased. However, the definition of the value of a TOMS supply in the TOMS Order refers to the difference between the sums paid or payable to, and the sums paid or payable by, the tour operator in respect of the travel service. Therefore, it is open to the tour operator to identify any other cost which is incurred directly in connection with the acquisition of the services that are re-supplied as TOMS supplies. For example, if a buyer is employed to find and book accommodation, it could be argued that the employment costs are part of the direct cost of buying-in the accommodation when it is re-sold.

26.46 If the holiday packages contain a mixture of bought-in TOMS supplies and in-house supplies provided from the tour operator's own resources, the TOMS calculation must include the full costs incurred in providing the in-house component of the package (see steps 4 to 7 of the annual TOMS calculation in paragraph 26.36 above). It is important to ensure that every individual expense relating to the making of the in-house supplies is identified fully. The expenses concerned are not only the direct costs of making the in-house supplies, which can include direct items such as fuel and maintenance costs of running a coach, but also items such as depreciation on the asset value of the coach. The making of in-house supplies will also involve elements of general overhead costs and apportionments of such overheads may be needed. For example, a coach operator may have insurance policies which cover all vehicles and all buildings used in the business. Only that part of the insurance relating to the running and garaging of the coaches can be included and not that relating to other vehicles and buildings used in connection with making the TOMS supplies. Appendices J and K of Notice 709/5 give examples of the sort of costs that Customs accept as being reasonable for in-house transport and in-house accommodation. The items quoted are not exhaustive and each tour operator is entitled to include any direct cost for which a reasonable case can be made.

26.47 It must be remembered that, in the annual TOMS calculation, the final sales value of the standard-rated in-house component of the turnover is the relevant proportion of the overall margin together with the costs of making the supplies (see step 24 of the annual TOMS calculation). Therefore, failing to identify fully the costs of making a standard-rated in-house supply (e.g. accommodation) will have two opposing consequences. Firstly, the understated in-house cost value will give a higher overall margin and potentially a higher in-house component of the turnover, but secondly, the proportion of the margin which is deemed to relate to the in-house component will be smaller. This is because the overall margin is apportioned by the ratio of the in-house cost value as a fraction of the total cost value. Clearly, if the numerator of the apportionment fraction is understated, the fraction itself will be understated. These two opposing effects of (*a*) increasing the overall margin but (*b*) decreasing the proportion of it that relates to the in-house supplies can either increase or decrease the final amount of output VAT depending upon which of the two effects is the greater. This will depend upon the particular mix of in-house and bought-in components in the packages, their VAT rates, and the relative mark-ups employed by the tour operator when costing the packages.

26.48 Clearly, the most important category in which to ensure that all costs of making an in-house supply are included fully in the steps 4 to 7 of the annual TOMS calculation, is that of in-house supplies of zero-rated passenger transport. If the cost of making in-house supplies of transport is understated, the overall costs in the TOMS calculation will also be understated and hence the overall margin for all components of the packages will be increased. Furthermore, understating the overall costs in step 10 of the annual calculation will decrease the denominator of all the cost apportionment fractions used in steps 12 to 19. Since the cost of making the standard-rated TOMS supplies in the numerator of the fraction in step 12 remains the same, a decrease in the denominator will increase the fraction. Both of these two effects will act to increase the VAT payable on the bought-in TOMS elements of the packages. This is because the overall margin in the annual TOMS calculation is increased and so is the proportion of it which is deemed to relate to the standard-rated TOMS supplies. Therefore, it is critical that tour operators such as coach operators, shipping companies and airflight operators who sell holidays which comprise their own in-house transport together with bought-in accommodation, must identify fully all the costs of making their in-house supplies of transport.

Future developments of the TOMS

26.49 The feature in the TOMS calculation whereby an overall margin relating to every component of a travel package is apportioned by the cost ratios of those components is not reflected in *EC Sixth Directive, Article 26*. It is possible that future litigation in the European Court of Justice could require amendment of the TOMS to unbundle the in-house components from the TOMS supplies.

26.50 Furthermore, tour operators who provide bought-in travel supplies to other businesses for onward supply that do not now count as TOMS supplies, but who have chosen to adopt the in-TOMS 'trade facilitation' measure to continue to account for VAT under the TOMS (see paragraph 26.9 above), should review their position as it is possible that the facilitation measure will be withdrawn. Tour operators in general who find the TOMS a difficult subject can take heart from the EC Commission's proposals to introduce a common system of VAT which would remove the need for a special scheme for tour operators. Businesses would be registered only in the home country and would account for VAT at the local rate irrespective of where in the EC the supplies took place. They would also be able to recover input incurred in any EC country. However, a common system of VAT will require the harmonisation of VAT rates and therefore the TOMS is likely to be with us for some time yet.

Chapter 27

Transport and Freight

Introduction

27.1 This chapter considers a variety of various transactions which fall under the general heading of 'transport and freight'. These are:

- supply of a means of transport, such as a ship or aircraft;
- supply of passenger transport services;
- supply of freight transport services; and
- supply of services ancillary to freight transport services.

The types of transactions covered are a reflection of the diversity of activities which are included in this sector.

Liability

Zero-rating applied to certain means of transport

27.2 The supply of various means of transport in the UK is zero-rated under *VATA 1994, 8 Sch, Group 8*. However, it is important to note that the zero-rating applies only to a means of transport which fits precisely the strict definitions. Where the means of transport falls outside the definitions, standard-rating will apply. It is important, therefore, that no assumptions are made as to the VAT liability of a means of transport and that full details are obtained. To do otherwise would be to lead to costly mistakes.

The zero-rating allowed by legislation follows closely that laid down in EC law, which allows for the exemption of supplies of certain means of transport, with the right of refund of VAT relating to the supply (*EC Sixth Directive, Article 15(5)(6)*).

Ships

27.3 Zero-rating applies to qualifying ships, i.e. those which are:

27.4 VAT Business by Business

(a) of a gross tonnage of not less than 15 tons; and

(b) neither designed nor adapted for use for recreation or pleasure.

There are subtle differences between the UK legislation and the EC Sixth Directive in the definition of ships which qualify for zero-rating. See *EC Sixth Directive, Article 15(4)*. In particular, the Sixth Directive does not set out any restrictions as to the gross tonnage of the vessel, but concentrates mainly on the use to which the vessel is put, as:

(a) used for navigation on the high seas and carrying passengers for reward or used for the purpose of commercial, industrial or fishing activities; or

(b) used for rescue or assistance at sea, or for inshore fishing, with the exception, for the latter, of ships' provisions.

(Article 15(4)).

Included in the UK definition of 'ships' are light vessels, dredgers and barges. Floating docks and cranes and offshore oil or gas installations used in the underwater exploitation or exploration of oil and gas resources are included provided that they are designed to be moved from place to place. Fixed installations for the oil or gas industries are not included.

According to *VATA 1994, s 96(1)*, hovercraft are also considered to be ships. The same 'qualifying' criteria will therefore apply to hovercraft.

Aircraft

27.4 The supply of a qualifying aircraft is zero-rated. In this case, 'qualifying' means an aircraft which:

(a) is of a weight not less than 8,000 kilograms; and

(b) is neither designed nor adapted for use for recreation or pleasure.

(VATA 1994, 8 Sch, Group 8, Item 2, Note A1(b)).

Once again, the Sixth Directive provides a slightly different definition of the type of aircraft for which zero-rating is available, referring to 'aircraft used by airlines operating for reward chiefly on international routes' *(Article 15(5))*.

Ships' stores

27.5 According to *VATA 1994, s 30(6)*, zero-rating is available for supplies made directly for use on a voyage or flight whose eventual destination is outside the UK. This includes goods supplied for retail sale to ship or aircraft passengers. For full details of the specific requirements which must be followed in order to obtain zero-rating, see *Tolley's VAT 1998/99, paragraph 25.3*.

Ships and aircraft—other supplies which qualify for zero-rating

27.6 In addition to the zero-rating allowed for the supply of qualifying ships and aircraft, zero-rating is available for various supplies associated with ships and aircraft, as set out at paragraphs 27.7 to 27.16 below.

Parts and equipment

27.7 From 1 January 1996, zero-rating is available for parts and equipment normally installed or incorporated in the general structure of a ship or aircraft which itself qualifies for zero-rating. The supply of life jackets and rafts, smoke hoods and other safety equipment is included. The letting on hire of such goods may also be zero-rated. This zero-rating was allowed by concession between 1 April 1993 and 31 December 1995. Prior to 1 April 1993, zero-rating only applied to the initial complement of on-board spares and necessary furnishings for operation and safety as supplied in the craft under the purchase contract. (For a detailed list of the items included and excluded from 'parts and equipment' see *Tolley's VAT 1998/99, paragraph 68.3*.)

(VATA 1994, 8 Sch, Group 8, Item 2A, Notes 2, 2A).

Repairs and maintenance

27.8 Repairs and maintenance carried out on a qualifying ship or aircraft may be zero-rated. The supplier may also zero-rate the parts supplied as a result of his work. However, when the parts are supplied to the repairer, VAT will apply at the standard rate. The zero-rating of repairs can also be extended to repairing parts, provided either that the repair is carried out on the ship or aircraft, or the part is replaced in the same ship or aircraft once the repair has been completed.

(VATA 1994, 8 Sch, Group 8, Items 1, 2; C & E Notice 744C, paragraphs 3.1 and 3.2).

Modifications and conversions

27.9 Modification or conversion services may be zero-rated provided that the craft remains a qualifying aircraft or ship after the work has been carried out.

(VATA 1994, 8 Sch, Group 8, Items 1, 2).

27.10 VAT Business by Business

Air navigation services

27.10 Air navigation services are defined in *Civil Aviation Act 1982, s 105(1)*. They may be zero-rated when supplied for a qualifying aircraft or for a person established outside the EU who receives them for the purposes of his business. The Civil Aviation Authority is the major supplier of air navigation services and has been granted taxable status in respect of them.

(VATA 1994, 8 Sch, Group 8, Items 6A, 11(b), Notes 6A, 7).

Letting on hire

27.11 For the letting on hire of a qualifying ship or aircraft to be zero-rated in the UK, the craft must be supplied without a crew or pilot and the customer must have exclusive use of the craft in order to operate it himself. However, where a UK lessor hires a means of transport and the use and enjoyment of that means of transport takes place outside the EU during the period of hire, then the supply is outside the scope of UK VAT. Any other letting on hire of ships or aircraft is standard-rated.

(VATA 1994, 8 Sch, Group 8, Items 1, 2, Note 2; C & E Notice 744C, paragraph 2.4).

Charter services for a ship or aircraft

27.12 Charter services are excluded from zero-rating and are standard-rated when the services are performed wholly in the UK and consist entirely of any one or more of the following:

- transport of passengers;
- accommodation;
- entertainment; or
- education.

(VATA 1994, 8 Sch, Group 8, Items 1, 2, Note 1).

Handling services

27.13 Handling services provided for ships and aircraft when in a UK seaport or an airport designated for landing and departure of aircraft are zero-rated provided that the ships and aircraft are qualifying craft, and/or the person receiving the supply does so in the course or furtherance of a business and belongs outside the UK.

(VATA 1994, 8 Sch, Group 8, Items 6(a), 11(b); C & E Notice 744C, paragraph 5).

Transport and Freight **27.17**

See *Tolley's VAT 1998/99, paragraph 68.9*, for the definition of handling services for ships and aircraft.

Surveys and classification services

27.14 Surveys and classification services are zero-rated when supplied in respect of qualifying ships and aircraft, or when supplied to a person who receives the supply for the purposes of his business and who belongs outside the UK. Surveys of ships for registration purposes by the Department of Trade are outside the scope of VAT. Services of arranging for the registration of ships under the *Merchant Shipping Acts* are standard-rated.

(VATA 1994, 8 Sch, Group 8, Items 9, 11(b), Note 7).

Salvage, towage and pilotage

27.15 Salvage and towage services are zero-rated whatever the type of ship. This includes inland waterway vessels. Pilotage services are zero-rated for shipping only.

(VATA 1994, 8 Sch, Group 8, Items 7, 8).

Lifeboats and slipways

27.16 Where a 'lifeboat', or equipment for launching and recovering lifeboats, or related repair and maintenance services, are supplied to a charity providing rescue and assistance at sea, zero-rating applies. (The tonnage of the lifeboat is immaterial, so that, for example, rubber dinghies are included.)

(VATA 1994, 8 Sch, Group 8, Item 3, Notes 2-4).

New means of transport

27.17 With effect from 1 January 1993, rules have existed to allow VAT-registered persons to supply 'new means of transport' to non-VAT-registered persons in other EU Member States without charging VAT. See *VAT Regulations 1995 (SI 1995 No 2518), reg 155.*

The 'new means of transport' to which the provisions apply are defined in *VATA 1994, s 95* as a ship, aircraft or motorised land vehicle, intended for the transport of persons or goods, which meet the following criteria:

(a)   any ship exceeding 7.5 metres in length;
(b)   any aircraft the take-off weight of which exceeds 1,550Kg;
(c)   any motorised land vehicle which -

27.17 VAT Business by Business

(i) has an engine with a displacement or cylinder capacity exceeding 48cc; or

(ii) is constructed or adapted to be electrically propelled using more than 7.2 kilowatts.

The definition of a 'new' means of transport depends on time limits, and upon the distances travelled from the first entry into service. A means of transport will not be considered as new where both the relevant time and distance criteria have been exceeded.

Time limits:

- for a ship or aircraft, more than 3 months since first use;
- for a land vehicle, more than 6 months since first use.

Distance travelled:

- for a ship, more than 100 hours;
- for an aircraft, more than 40 hours;
- for a land vehicle, more than 6,000 kilometres.

A UK supplier can zero-rate a supply to a non-VAT-registered person established in another Member State, provided that the person or his representative personally takes delivery of the vehicle and removes it to the Member State of destination within two months of the supply, and provided that both the supplier and purchaser make a joint declaration on Form 411.

In the case of a VAT-registered customer in another Member State, the new means of transport must be despatched or transported to the other Member State within two months of supply and the supplier should show the purchaser's VAT registration number and two-digit country code on the invoice. (*VAT Regulations 1995 (SI 1995 No 2518), regs 22(6), 155*).

The acquisition of a 'new means of transport' by a non-registered person in the UK is taxed in the Member State of destination, i.e. the UK. Under *VATA 1994, 11 Sch 2(4)(5)*, Customs are empowered to introduce a special mechanism to collect the VAT due on the acquisition. The non-taxable person must notify Customs of the acquisition within 7 days of the later of the acquisition itself or the arrival of the 'new means of transport' in the UK. Notice 728 includes a form which should be used for this purpose. VAT due will be calculated by Customs, and a written demand for the tax will be sent. This must be paid within 30 days of the issue of the demand (*VAT Regulations 1995 (SI 1995 No 2518), reg 148*).

A VAT-registered person should account for the VAT on an acquisition of a 'new means of transport' on his VAT return for the period in which the acquisition occurs.

Passenger transport

Place of supply

27.18 The place of supply of passenger transport services is defined in the *VAT (Place of Supply of Services) Order 1992 (SI 1992 No 3121), article 6* as being the country where the transport takes place. Where land transportation of passengers takes place from one country to another country, it may be necessary for the supplier to be registered for VAT in both countries.

It is important to note that while the UK allows zero-rating for many supplies of passenger transport, this is not the case in most other Member States of the EU. Thus, where a supplier of passenger transport is obliged to register in other Member States of the EU, the supplies made in other Member States may well be subject to a positive rate of VAT.

Where a journey from one place to another in the same Member State results in a journey via another Member State, the place of supply will still be considered to be the Member State where the journey begins and ends, provided that the means of transport does not put in or land in the other Member State.

VAT (Place of Supply of Services) Order 1992 (SI 1992 No 3121), article 8 also states that any goods and services provided as part of a pleasure cruise are to be treated as a single supply with the passenger transport, and the same place of supply rules will, therefore, apply. The same rules apply for accompanying luggage or motor vehicles.

Zero-rated passenger transport

27.19 *VATA 1994, 8 Sch, Group 8, Item 4* allows zero-rating of the following types of passenger transport:

(a) in any vehicle, ship or aircraft designed or adapted to carry not less than 12 passengers;

(b) by the Post Office;

(c) on any scheduled flight;

(d) from a place within a place outside the United Kingdom or vice versa, to the extent that those services are provided in the United Kingdom.

Paragraph (d) above allows zero-rating for international passenger transport, to the extent that it takes place within the UK. As mentioned at paragraph

27.20 VAT Business by Business

27.18 above, it is important to note that the zero-rating available for passenger transport in the UK is not generally available in other Member States of the EU.

Paragraph (a) above concerning vehicles 'designed or adapted to carry 12 or more passengers' will apply, by concession, to vehicles which carry fewer passengers solely because they have been equipped with facilities for people in wheelchairs. This is set out in Extra-Statutory Concession 2.12, and applies regardless of the person to whom the supply is made.

Public transport other than the conventional planes, trains and buses or coaches will also qualify for zero-rating provided 12 or more passengers can be carried. Therefore, zero-rating can be obtained for horse-drawn buses, canal boats, park and ride schemes (subject to paragraph 27.20 below) and road trains.

Case law has provided a few peculiarities, such as the decision in the very first reported VAT appeal, *Llandudno Cabinlift Co Ltd, [1973] VATTR 1(1)*, where each individual cabin in a cabinlift was treated as a separate vehicle, so that the supply had to be standard-rated, as fewer than 12 people were carried in each cabin.

Standard-rated supplies

27.20 With effect from 31 March 1995, the following supplies of passenger transport have been standard-rated (*VATA 1994, 8 Sch, Group 8, Notes 4A, 4B*):

- transport of passengers in any vehicle to, from or within a place of entertainment, recreation or amusement; or

- transport of passengers in any vehicle to, from or within a place of cultural, scientific, historical or similar interest.

These supplies are standard-rated when they are supplied by a person who also supplies a right of admission to such facilities, or by a person connected with him under the provisions of *ICTA 1988, s 839*.

The type of services which became standard-rated as a result of this provision include the following:

- transport around a theme park. The services remain standard-rated whether they are included in the overall admission price or made for a separate charge;

- transport in a motor vehicle between a car park and an airport terminal, when provided by the operator of the car park, or a person connected to the operator under *ICTA 1988, s 839;*

- aerial flights which are held out as being for the purposes of entertainment, recreation or amusement, or flights for the experience of flying. Examples of these kind of flights include flights designed to overcome fear of flying.

It should be noted that passenger transport provided to or from the place of amusement by an operator who is entirely independent from the operator of the place of amusement, remains zero-rated.

'Santa' flights might appear to be prime candidates for standard-rating as 'entertainment'. However, if they land in another country, they retain zero-rating as being international passenger transport.

Taxis and hire cars

27.21 Passenger transport in taxis and hire cars is usually standard-rated (unless the operator's supplies are below the VAT registration threshold) as these are designed to carry fewer than 12 passengers. The standard-rating of such fares also extends to charges made for carrying luggage or for waiting. Where local authorities license taxis and set maximum fare rates, these fares are considered to be VAT-inclusive.

Tips and gratuities which are voluntarily given are outside the scope of VAT.

The hire of cars or other motor vehicles is a service which is subject to VAT at the standard rate.

Freight transport

27.22 Services consisting of the transportation of passengers or goods shall be treated as supplied in the country in which the transportation takes place, to the extent that it takes place in that country (*VAT (Place of Supply of Services) Order (SI 1992 No 3121), article 6*).

There are special rules for international freight transport and intra-Community freight transport, which are discussed further at paragraph 27.23 below.

Intra-Community transport of goods

27.23 Where a supply of services consists of the intra-Community transport of goods, it shall be treated as made in the Member State in which the transportation of the goods begins (*VAT (Place of Supply of Services) Order (SI 1992 No 3121), article 10*).

This provision became effective from 1 January 1993. UK legislation does not specifically define 'intra-Community transport of goods'. However, Customs Notice 741 gives the following definition at paragraph 6.1:

27.24 VAT Business by Business

'Intra-EC freight transport is the movement of goods from one Member State to another. This includes the transport of goods:

- which takes place entirely within one Member State when it is part of a single movement of goods from one Member State to another;

- from one Member State to another when the journey goes through a non-EC country (e.g. the transport of goods from London to Rome through Switzerland)'.

Where the recipient of a supply of services of intra-Community transport of goods makes use, for the purpose of the supply, of a VAT registration number, then the supply shall be treated as made in the Member State which issued the registration number (*VAT (Place of Supply of Services) Order (SI 1992 No 3121), article 14*). Thus, the customer will declare VAT by means of the reverse charge rather then having to submit an Eighth Directive Refund claim. The recipient of the services can only use his own VAT registration number and carry out the reverse charge if the service would otherwise be treated as taking place in a different Member State from that in which he is registered for VAT.

Ancillary transport services

27.24 Where a supply consists of ancillary transport services, it shall be treated as made where those services are physically performed (*VAT (Place of Supply of Services) Order (SI 1992 No 3121), article 9*). This became effective from 1 January 1993.

Once again, 'ancillary transport services' are not specifically defined in the legislation. However, Customs Notice 741 states at paragraph 4.6 that the following services are considered to be ancillary transport services when they relate to the transport of goods:

- loading, unloading or reloading;

- stowing;

- opening for inspection;

- cargo security services;

- preparing or amending bills of lading, airway bills and certificates of ships;

- packing necessary for transportation; and

- storage.

As explained at paragraph 27.23 above, the reverse charge will apply when the recipient of the ancillary transport services makes use of a VAT registration number in another Member State.

Services of intermediaries arranging freight transport services

27.25 The place of supply of making arrangements for the intra-Community supply of freight transport services, or services ancillary to freight transport services, follows the same rules as for those supplies.

VAT recovery

Recovery of VAT incurred on the purchase of a car

27.26 As a general rule, the recovery of VAT incurred on the purchase of a car is not possible. However, certain businesses are able to recover the VAT incurred in the following circumstances:

- the person purchasing the car intends to use it to provide it on hire with the services of a driver for the purposes of carrying passengers;

- the purchaser intends to provide it for 'self-drive hire'; or

- the purchaser is a driving school.

(*C & E Notice 700/64/96, paras 16-18; VAT Information Sheet 12/95 (1 June 1995); C & E Business Brief 15/95 (31 July 1995)*).

In addition, with effect from 1 August 1995, a car leasing business has been able to recover VAT incurred on the purchase of cars to be leased to third parties.

Accounting and records

27.27 The general rules regarding the retention of records and evidence required for the deduction in input VAT apply to businesses operating in the transport sector just as they apply to other businesses. See *Tolley's VAT 1998/ 99, chapter 57*. However, there are certain additional requirements which will be necessary due to the specialist nature of this sector.

In particular, businesses buying and selling second-hand ships, aircraft, etc., have the possibility of accounting for VAT only on their profit margin. With effect from 1 January 1995, certain restrictions formerly applicable to the use of 'margin schemes' were removed, and it is possible to use this method of accounting for VAT in respect of all types of transport.

27.28 VAT Business by Business

In order to operate the margin scheme, it is necessary to comply with certain strict accounting requirements such as the holding of a stock book, and invoices are required to show additional details. For further details of the requirements, see *Tolley's VAT 1998/99, paragraph 61.23*.

It is important to note that where a second-hand vehicle is sold under the margin scheme, it is not possible to recover VAT charged on the purchase of the vehicle.

Practical points

27.28 Businesses in the transport and freight sector have to cope with tight deadlines and are often responsible for completing customer documentation, such as export documentation. With the complexities of some of the rules relating to transport, the VAT accounting formalities with which these businesses have to comply are more complex than those faced by other sectors.

The complexity is partly due to the international nature of the sector, leading to a requirement to be familiar with legislation in other Member States, not to mention third countries. It is also due to the fact that the sector's activities cross into other areas such as tour operators, catering, leasing and cars.

Some important cases which have implications outside the sector as well as within it are worth mentioning, as they show the complexities which can be faced.

Two important cases relating to composite supplies have come from the airline industry—*British Airways plc v C&E Commrs, CA [1990] STC 643* and *Virgin Atlantic Airways Ltd v C&E Commrs, QB [1995] STC 341*. The British Airways case established that supplies of catering were incidental to the supply of air transport and should thus be zero-rated. The Virgin Atlantic case was broadly similar and allowed zero-rating of the whole supply when air transport, catering and a limousine were supplied to Virgin's 'Upper Class' passengers. For fuller reports of these cases, see *Tolley's VAT Cases 1998*. Following these cases, Customs set out the treatment of various passenger perks in Business Brief 4/96.

In the similar case of *C & E Commrs v Peninsular & Oriental Steam Navigation Co, QB [1996] STC 698*, Customs had treated a cruise as a mixed supply of passenger transport, catering, entertainment etc. However, the High Court decided that where the cruise was sold at an inclusive price incorporating all these items, the supply was a single supply of passenger transport and was, therefore, taxable at the zero rate.

Index

ACCOUNTANTS	**1**
accounting and records	1.24–1.31
continuous supplies	1.7
disbursements	1.4, 1.29
goods, supplied by	1.3
land, services relating to	1.12
liability of supplies	1.2–1.4
overseas taxes	1.14
partial exemption	1.22, 1.23
place of supply	1.9–1.14
recovery of VAT	1.17–1.23
self-billing	1.25
time of supply	1.5–1.8
valuation of supplies	1.15, 1.16

AUCTIONEERS	**2**
accounting and records	2.22–2.39
auctioneers' margin scheme	2.12–2.17
catalogues	2.45
global accounting scheme	2.18–2.21
horses	5.45–5.47
overseas persons, transactions with	2.40–2.44
second-hand goods margin scheme	2.2–2.11

BANKING AND SECURITIES	**3**
accounting and records	3.100–3.109
corporate finance	3.46–3.51
deposits	3.25–3.28
foreign currency options	3.56, 3.57
foreign exchange	3.14–3.18, 3.94, 3.95
hire purchase and leasing	3.29–3.36
industry agreements	3.112, 3.113
interest rate swaps	3.58–3.61
investment management	3.52–3.55
LIFFE	3.62–3.64
loans and overdrafts	3.25–3.28
money, dealing in	3.12, 3.13
partial exemption	3.71–3.99, 3.105
registration	3.110, 3.111
representative offices	3.116–3.119
reverse charges	3.106–3.109
safe custody services	3.45
securities for money	3.19–3.21, 3.37–3.40, 3.96
stockbroking	3.41, 3.42
underwriting	3.43, 3.44

BARRISTERS	**4**
accounting for VAT	4.14–4.16
cessation of practice	4.15
chambers expenses	4.6–4.9
death	4.15
judicial offices	4.3
legal advice, supplies of	4.2
personal expenses	4.12
record-keeping	4.16
recovery of VAT	4.5–4.13
registration	4.18
reverse charge services	4.13
travel costs	4.11

BLOODSTOCK	**5**
accounting and records	5.73–5.83
agents	5.35–5.44
auctioneers	5.45–5.47
company owners	5.9, 5.10
dealers	5.11, 5.12
flat-rate farmers	5.78–5.81, 5.103–5.107
jockeys	5.57–5.63
overseas VAT	5.69–5.71
owner-breeders	5.4–5.6, 5.15–5.34
racecourses	5.48–5.51
racing income	5.33, 5.34
recovery of VAT	5.64–5.72
registration	5.92–5.99
second-hand scheme	5.82, 5.83
stallion shares and nominations	5.19–5.22
stallion syndications	5.32
temporary importation	5.100–5.102
trainers	5.11, 5.12, 5.52–5.56

BOOKS AND PUBLICATIONS	**6**
accounting and records	6.67
advertising	6.44–6.47
authors	6.66
binders	6.41–6.43
book clubs	6.39
book tokens	6.62
books and booklets	6.9
brochures	6.10, 6.32, 6.33

VAT Business by Business

Books and Publications—*Cont'd*
children's activity packs 6.31
children's books 6.19–6.21
clubs, associations and organisations 6.36–6.38
incidental reports 6.40
leaflets 6.11–6.16, 6.32, 6.33
library books 6.68
loose-leaf works 6.41–6.43
maps, charts, etc. 6.23
music scores 6.22
newspapers, journals and periodicals 6.17, 6.18
pamphlets 6.10, 6.32, 6.33
promotional items 6.48–6.54
training and educational courses 6.29, 6.30
vouchers 6.59–6.61

Business, definition,
charities 7.4
clubs and associations 8.5–8.14
education 11.3

CHARITIES 7
administration 7.64–7.66
advertising 7.14, 7.60
affinity cards 7.17
attribution of costs 7.40–7.42
auctions 7.11
business, definition 7.4
cost-sharing 7.65
cultural services 7.35
donations 7.7–7.11, 7.37
economic activity 7.5
education 7.21–7.23, 11.51
'eligible bodies' 7.59
European Community law 7.2
exemptions 7.20–7.35
exports 7.18
fund-raising events 7.9, 7.28–7.34
grants 7.12
handicapped, aids for 7.55
importations 7.63
investment income 7.13
non-business income 7.6
partial exemption 7.43, 7.44
recovery of VAT 7.39–7.63
registration 7.64
'relevant goods' 7.57, 7.58
sponsorship 7.8
subscriptions 7.16
trading subsidiaries 7.66
transport 7.45
welfare supplies 7.15, 7.24–7.27
zero-rating 7.36–7.38, 7.47–7.61

CLUBS AND ASSOCIATIONS 8
accounting and records 8.105–8.117
admission charges 8.71–8.77
amusement machines 8.60
annual accounting 8.117
apportionment of input tax 8.139
bank interest 8.66
bar sales 8.58, 8.59
barter arrangements 8.123–8.128
bingo 8.85–8.87
business,
– definition 8.5–8.14
– entertainment 8.91–8.93
cars 8.90
catering 8.58, 8.59
discos, etc. 8.79
donations 8.78, 8.84
exemption, election to waive 8.142–8.145
fund-raising activities 8.67–8.87
gaming machines 8.61
hospitality 8.80, 8.81
joining fees 8.43
land and property transactions 8.148–8.153
levies and loans 8.44–8.46
non-profit-making bodies 8.15–8.20
overseas members 8.40, 8.41
partial exemption 8.100–8.104, 8.137, 8.138
professional bodies 8.26–8.34
records, preservation of 8.111, 8.112
recovery of VAT 8.88–8.104
registration fees 8.63, 8.64
shares and debentures 8.47, 8.48
sponsorship 8.82, 8.83, 8.146, 8.147
sports clubs 8.35–8.37, 8.129–8.131, 8.154–8.158
– court fees 8.50
– entry fees 8.49
– fixture cards 8.56
– match and training fees 8.54
– pitches, hire of 8.51–8.53
– prizes 8.55
subscription income 8.22–8.41
– apportionment 8.38, 8.39, 8.132–8.136
telephones 8.62
trade unions 8.26–8.34
voluntary registration 8.118–8.120

CONSTRUCTION INDUSTRY 9
applications for payment 9.38
approved alterations 9.21, 9.23–9.26
authenticated tax receipts 9.40
building materials 9.20
cash accounting scheme 9.36
civil engineering services 9.32
conversions 9.28, 9.31
customers, unregistered 9.44
invoices, issue of 9.41
liquidated damages 9.43
mixed use buildings 9.13, 9.19, 9.27
'new' building, definition 9.5–9.7
non-residential buildings 9.30

Index

Construction Industry—*Cont'd*
  price, agreed variations 9.42
  protected building 9.22
  purchase invoices, posting of 9.35
  records 9.33
  recovery of input tax 9.34, 9.35
  registered housing associations 9.29
  relevant charitable buildings 9.15–9.18
  relevant residential purposes 9.8–9.11
  self-billing 9.39
  sub-contractors 9.14
  'tax point' rules 9.37–9.41
  zero-rating 9.3–9.32
  – incorrect certificates 9.12

DOCTORS AND DENTISTS 10
  accounting records 10.27–10.32
  associate agreements 10.41–10.44
  employment relationships 10.40
  expense-sharing agreements 10.34–10.38
  medico-legal services 10.20–10.22
  NHS, dispensing doctors 10.16–10.19
  partnerships 10.39
  pharmacy services 10.14, 10.15

Economic activity 7.5

EDUCATION 11
  accommodation 11.29, 11.79, 11.80
  advertising 11.35
  business activities 11.3
  car parking 11.34
  catering 11.27, 11.28, 11.82
  charities 7.21–7.23, 11.51
  conferences, etc. 11.31, 11.32
  consultancy 11.24
  definition 11.5
  'eligible bodies' 11.11, 11.12
  English as foreign language 11.52–11.54
  examination and inspectorate services 11.55, 11.56
  further education colleges 11.36–11.46
  goods, sales of 11.30
  independent schools 11.49, 11.50
  local authorities 11.47, 11.48
  partial exemption 11.67–11.70
  private tuition 11.8, 11.9
  property planning 11.78
  recovery of input tax 11.64–11.76
  research 11.6, 11.20–11.23
  self-supply rules 11.81
  sporting activities 11.33
  student accommodation 11.79, 11.80
  trading companies 11.83–11.85
  universities, etc. 11.17–11.35
  vocational training 11.7, 11.25
  youth clubs 11.57–11.63

EMPLOYMENT BUSINESSES 12
  accounting and records 12.24, 12.25
  agency contracts 12.5–12.10
  dual status 12.39
  employment law 12.31–12.34
  holiday and sick pay 12.41
  indemnities 12.42, 12.43
  nursing agencies 12.15–12.19
  PAYE and NIC 12.35–12.38
  principal contracts 12.3, 12.4
  recovery of VAT 12.23
  time of supply 12.20
  training 12.40
  valuation of supply 12.21, 12.22

Exemption, election to waive,
  clubs and associations 8.142–8.145
  farming and agriculture 13.21, 13.43
  local authorities 19.21
  property development 21.32–21.68

FARMING AND AGRICULTURE 13
  accounting and records 13.56–13.74
  accounting systems 13.65–13.67
  agricultural land and property 13.20–13.27
  ancillary activities 13.10–13.19
  annual accounting 13.71
  approved alterations 13.26
  assured shorthold tenancies 13.49
  business entertainment 13.51
  caravan and camping facilities 13.12
  cash accounting 13.70
  companies 13.46
  co-operatives 13.81
  co-ownership 13.80
  correction of errors 13.68
  contract farming 13.2, 13.3
  conversions 13.24
  craft fairs 13.16
  dilapidation payments 13.36
  election to waive exemption 13.21, 13.43
  EU transactions 13.72–13.74
  exempt income 13.7
  farm shops 13.15
  farm tours 13.17
  flat-rate farmers' scheme 13.56–13.61
  gifts of land 13.22
  grants and subsidies 13.55
  grazing rights 13.30
  holiday accommodation 13.11
  horse breeding and racing 13.19
  inducements 13.39
  Intrastat 13.74
  landfill tax 13.5
  landlords and tenants 13.33–13.39
  livery services 13.31
  milk quota 13.32
  motor vehicles 13.52–13.54
  parking facilities 13.13

VAT Business by Business

Farming and Agriculture—*Cont'd*	
part-exchange	13.75
partial exemption	13.41, 13.42
protected buildings	13.25
reconstructions	13.27
recovery of VAT	13.40–13.55
repairs to farmhouses	13.44
restrictive covenants	13.38
returnable containers	13.76
reverse surrenders	13.37
share farming	13.4
shooting activities	13.29
sporting rights	13.28
standard-rated income	13.8
statutory compensation	13.35
surrenders	13.34
tenanted properties	13.47
tied accommodation	13.48
transfers of going concerns	13.23
zero-rated income	13.6

HOSPITALS AND NURSING HOMES	**14**
access, facilitation of	14.11
accommodation	14.3
blood, organs and tissue	14.4
charities, supplies to	14.12
dispensing of drugs	14.7
handicapped people, aids for	14.9
home care services	14.5
NHS trusts	14.6
provision of care	14.2
special needs, goods catering for	14.10
welfare	14.8
zero-rating certificates	14.13

HOTELS AND HOLIDAY ACCOMMODATION	**15**
accounting and records	15.30–15.32
booking fees	15.4
cancellation charges	15.6
catering, rooms supplied for	15.10
deposits	15.5
disbursements	15.7
holiday accommodation,	
– camping	15.27
– caravan pitches	15.21
– caravans	15.20–15.26
– construction of	15.19
– definition	15.12
– off-season letting	15.17
– restrictions on permanent use	15.14
– sites, provision of	15.16
– time-share and multi-ownership schemes	15.18
hotels, inns, boarding houses, etc.	15.2
recovery of VAT	15.28, 15.29
reduced value rules	15.8
retaining fees	15.9
service charges	15.3
staff, supplies to	15.11

HOUSING ASSOCIATIONS	**16**
accounting records	16.37
BES assured tenancy arrangements	16.9
capital expenditure	16.31
care, provision of	16.15
charitable reliefs	16.26
charity advertising	16.34
consortium agreements	16.14, 16.35
conversion of non-residential buildings	16.24
demolition costs	16.25, 16.36
design and build contracts	16.11
emergency alarm systems	16.16
guest accommodation	16.18
joint contracts of employment	16.33
land	16.23
large-scale voluntary transfers	16.13
management contracts	16.12
new buildings	16.22
nomination rights	16.17
parallel charities	16.32
partial exemption	16.28
professional fees	16.29
property, disposals of	16.6
protected buildings	16.27
recovery of VAT	16.21–16.28
residential purposes	16.30
right to buy	16.7
service charges	16.4
shared ownership	16.8
tenants, services to	16.5

INSURANCE	**17**
accounting and records	17.81–17.90
broker-managed funds	17.55, 17.56
claims handling	17.33–17.36
disclosure requirements	17.90
engineering insurance	17.57
friendly societies	17.54
industry agreements	17.91
input tax recovery	17.67–17.80
insurance-related services	17.27–17.29
intermediaries, supplies by	17.23–17.43
international services	17.40–17.42
Lloyd's arrangements	17.44–17.50, 17.77–17.80
marine, aviation and transport insurance	17.14–17.19
non-permitted insurance	17.37
overseas businesses	17.93, 17.94
partial exemption	17.67–17.70
place of supply	17.11–17.13, 17.38, 17.39
protection and indemnity insurance	17.51–17.53
reverse charge	17.86–17.89
run-off services	17.58
salvage	17.59, 17.60
time of supply	17.82–17.85

Index

Insurance—Cont'd
  valuation of supplies   17.20–17.22, 17.43, 17.66
  warranties   17.61–17.65

LEASING AND HIRE-PURCHASE 18
  arrears of rentals   18.81–18.85
  bad debts   18.81–18.85
  captive leasing companies   18.64
  cars   18.57–18.64
  change in rate of VAT   18.36–18.38
  cross-border leasing   18.65–18.80
  disposals of leased assets   18.48–18.51
  documentation fees   18.46, 18.47
  part-exchange transactions   18.43–18.45
  partial exemption   18.31–18.38
  rebates of rentals   18.48–18.51
  recovery of VAT   18.28–18.38
  repossession of goods   18.52, 18.53
  sale of repossessed goods   18.54
  termination payments   18.39–18.42
  time of supply   18.13–18.20
  transfers of agreements   18.55, 18.56

LOCAL AUTHORITIES 19
  accounting records   19.38–19.42
  agency payments   19.33
  attribution of input tax   19.35
  business entertainment   19.27
  changes in activities   19.44
  computer systems   19.39
  debts and errors   19.20
  definition   19.3
  devolved accounting   19.40
  error adjustments   19.42
  estimation of tax due   19.29
  exemption, election to waive   19.21
  imports and acquisitions   19.32
  insurance-related payments   19.31
  invoices   19.25, 19.26
  land and property   19.15
  local government review   19.17–19.22
  partial exemption   19.36, 19.37
  pension funds   19.34
  recovery of VAT   19.23
  refund mechanism   19.2
  registration   19.7–19.10
  relocation expenses   19.30
  self-billing   19.28
  supplies between authorities   19.14
  tour operators' margin scheme   19.16
  transfers of assets   19.18
  unregistered authorities   19.4

MOTOR DEALERS 20
  accessories   20.9
  accounting and records   20.15
  definition of 'motor car'   20.18
  demonstration and courtesy cars   20.14
  delivery charges   20.8
  extended warranties   20.10
  group registration   20.20
  new means of transport   20.11
  'non-qualifying' cars   20.4
  part-exchange transactions   20.17
  pre-delivery inspection charges   20.8
  'qualifying' cars   20.3
  recovery of VAT   20.13, 20.14
  road fund licences   20.7
  sale or return transactions   20.19
  second-hand cars   20.5, 20.16
  self-supplies   20.12

'Option to tax', *see* **Exemption, election to waive**

Partial exemption,
  accountants   1.22, 1.23
  banking and securities   3.71–3.99
  charities   7.43, 7.44
  clubs and associations   8.100–8.104, 8.137, 8.138
  education   11.67–11.70
  farming and agriculture   13.41, 13.42
  housing associations   16.28
  insurance   17.67–17.70
  leasing and hire-purchase   18.31–18.38
  local authorities   19.36, 19.37
  small businesses   24.21–24.23

PROPERTY DEVELOPMENT 21
  accounting records   21.74–21.77
  beneficial interests   21.103–21.106
  capital goods scheme   21.70–21.73
  compulsory purchase   21.88
  co-ownership   21.100–21.102
  covenants   21.84, 21.85
  dilapidations   21.89
  exemption   21.13–21.26
  – election to waive   21.32–21.68
  inducements   21.90–21.93
  new dwellings, input tax on   21.69
  recovery of VAT   21.69–21.73
  reverse surrenders   21.95–21.99
  rights in and over land   21.23–21.26
  service charges   21.107–21.113
  statutory payments   21.87
  surrenders   21.94
  transfers of going concerns   21.78–21.83
  trustees   21.103–21.106
  variations to leases   21.86
  zero-rated transactions   21.27–21.31

PUBLIC HOUSES 22
  accommodation and functions   22.8
  accounting and record-keeping   22.13, 22.14
  breakages   22.21

VAT Business by Business

Public Houses—Cont'd
business-splitting	22.15
catering	22.7
drawing off beer	22.19
free food and drinks	22.27, 22.28
free houses	22.5
gaming and amusement machines	22.9
leased houses	22.4
managed houses	22.2
off-sales	22.23
own consumption	22.26
payphones	22.11
pilferage	22.25
pipe cleaning	22.18
prices	22.24
purchases	22.13
recovery of VAT	22.12–22.14
sales	22.14
spillage	22.20
storage of beer	22.17
tenanted houses	22.3
vending machines	22.10
wastage	22.16–22.22

RETAILERS AND RETAIL SCHEMES 23
accounting records	23.40–23.44
adaptations to schemes	23.4
adjustments to takings	23.8
annual accounting	23.49
apportionment schemes	23.13–23.15, 23.22, 23.23
bespoke schemes	23.5, 23.19
cash accounting	23.49
catering and take-away food	23.28
ceasing to use a scheme	23.20–23.25
change in rate of VAT	23.10
choosing a scheme	23.11–23.19
cinemas and theatres	23.26
computer records	23.44
daily gross takings	23.6–23.10, 23.41
deregistration	23.48
direct calculation schemes	23.16–23.18, 23.24, 23.25
disposal of business	23.47
florists	23.33–23.36
garages and filling stations	23.27
invoices, provision of	23.45
linked goods	23.9
pharmacists	23.29–23.32
Point of Sale scheme	23.12, 23.21
purchase invoices	23.42
recovery of VAT	23.39
sub-post offices	23.37
vending and amusement machines	23.38

Self-billing
accountants	1.25
construction industry	9.39
local authorities	19.28

SMALL BUSINESSES 24
annual accounting	24.16–24.20
– leaving scheme	24.20
cash accounting	24.8–24.15
– eligibility for scheme	24.11
– exclusions from scheme	24.12
leaving scheme	24.15
non-registration	24.4, 24.5
partial exemption	24.21–24.23
pre-registration input tax	24.22
registration	24.2–24.7
– backdating	24.7
'toothbrush' schemes	24.23
turnover, monitoring	24.3
voluntary registration	24.6

SOLICITORS 25
accounting and records	25.30–25.46
commission	25.11–25.15
– accounting for	25.35
continuous supplies	25.34
Counsel's fees	25.36–25.42
credit notes	25.43, 25.44
disbursements	25.16–25.23
land, services relating to	25.9, 25.10
oath fees	25.24–25.26
place of supply	25.3–25.8
recovery of VAT	25.28, 25.29
reverse charge services	25.45, 25.46
third party costs	25.47, 25.48
time of supply	25.30–25.34

Sports clubs 8.35–8.37
court fees	8.50
entry fees	8.49
exemption	8.129–8.131
fixture cards	8.56
match and training fees	8.54
non-profit-making bodies, whether	8.154–8.158
pitches, hire of	8.51–8.53
prizes	8.55

TOUR OPERATORS 26
accounting and records	26.27–26.37
annual accounting	26.28, 26.29
bad debt relief	26.31
definition	26.5, 26.6
liability	26.4–26.22
margin scheme calculation,	
– full	26.34–26.36
– simplified	26.32, 26.33
margin scheme costs, maximising	26.45–26.48
material alteration or further processing	26.10, 26.11
passenger transport, bought-in	26.40–26.43

Index

Tour Operators—*Cont'd*
- agency scheme — 26.42
- charter scheme — 26.41
- transport company scheme — 26.43
- place of supply — 26.15, 26.16
- provisional output ratio calculation — 26.37
- recovery of VAT — 26.23–26.26
- registration — 26.38
- transport services, single supply — 26.39
- travel agents' commission — 26.19–26.22
- travellers, supplies for benefit of — 26.7–26.9
- valuation of supplies — 26.17
- zero-rating — 26.18

TRANSPORT AND FREIGHT — **27**
- accounting and records — 27.27
- air navigation services — 27.10
- aircraft — 27.4
- ancillary services — 27.24
- charter services — 27.12
- freight transport — 27.22–27.25
- – intra-Community — 27.23
- handling services — 27.13
- hire cars — 27.21
- intermediaries, services of — 27.25
- letting on hire — 27.11
- lifeboats and slipways — 27.16
- modifications and conversions — 27.9
- new means of transport — 27.17
- passenger transport — 27.18–27.21
- – place of supply — 27.18
- – standard-rated supplies — 27.20
- – zero-rating — 27.19
- parts and equipment — 27.7
- recovery of VAT — 27.26
- repairs and maintenance — 27.8
- salvage, towage and pilotage — 27.15
- ships — 27.3
- – stores — 27.5
- surveys and classification services — 27.14
- taxis — 27.21
- zero-rating — 27.2–27.17, 27.19

NOTES

NOTES

NOTES

NOTES

NOTES

NOTES